THE HISTORY
OF THE
LEWIS AND CLARK
EXPEDITION

BY
MERIWETHER LEWIS
AND
WILLIAM CLARK

EDITED BY
Elliott Coues

IN THREE VOLUMES
Volume III

DOVER PUBLICATIONS, INC.
NEW YORK

Published in Canada by General Publishing Company,
Ltd., 30 Lesmill Road, Don Mills, Toronto, Ontario.
Published in the United Kingdom by Constable and
Company, Ltd., 10 Orange Street, London WC2H 7EG.

This Dover edition is an unabridged republication of
the four-volume edition published by Francis P. Harper
in 1893. The fourth volume of the Harper edition
consisted of illustrations and the Index; in this Dover
edition five illustrations and the Index are appended to
Volume III, and the remaining illustrations are arranged
on large plates inserted at the end of Volumes I and II.

International Standard Book Number: 0-486-21270-X
Library of Congress Catalog Card Number: 64-15500

Manufactured in the United States of America
Dover Publications, Inc.
180 Varick Street
New York, N.Y. 10014

CONTENTS

OF

THE THIRD VOLUME.

———

HISTORY OF THE EXPEDITION.

vi   CONTENTS.

CHAPTER XXXIII.

CHAPTER XXXIV.

CHAPTER XXXV.

CHAPTER XXXVI.

CHAPTER XXXVII.

CHAPTER XXV.

BOTANY AND ZOÖLOGY.[1]

[*I. Botany.*[2]]

AMONG the vegetable productions of the country, which furnish a large proportion of the food of the Indians, are the roots of a species of thistle, the fern, the rush, the liquorice, and a small cylindric root resembling in flavor and consistency the sweet potato.

1. The thistle,[3] called by the natives shanatanque, is a plant which grows in a deep, rich, dry loam, with a considerable mixture of sand. The stem is simple, ascending, cylindric and hispid, rising to the height of three or four feet. The cauline life [leaf], which, as well as the stem of the last season, is dead, is simple, crenate, and oblong; rather more obtuse at its apex than at its insertion, which is decurrent; its position is declining; its margin is armed with prickles, and its disk is hairy. The flower is dry and mutilated, but

[1] The notices of plants and animals relate more particularly to the region where the explorers then were, and to the course of the Columbia river ; but also refer to various species found in the mountains between the Columbia and the Missouri, and on the upper portions of the latter river.

[2] The botany of this chapter begins with Clark P 89, at date of Jan. 20th, 1806.

[3] The edible thistle is *Cnicus edulis* of Gray, a large and well-known plant of the order *Compositæ*. " The root of the thistle called by the natives *chan ne tak que*," etc., Clark P 87, where the printed description follows, in substance ; also shawnatâhque, Clark I 37 ; shanatoequa, I 66 ; shannatahque, I 77 ; shawnatakwe, I 99. The name is usually printed shanataque. The statement in the text that the cauline life (leaf), etc., is *dead*, means simply that it had died down at the date of the entry, Jan. 20th. So with the " dry and mutilated " flower ; and for " pericarp " read the set of bracts forming the involucre of the head. " Sagamity " is from an Algonkin word for a preparation of Indian corn we should now call hominy, boiled to the consistency of gruel. Gayarré (Hist. Louisiana, I. p. 317) renders *sagamité*, as a favorite dish of the old French population. L. and C. probably picked up this word at St. Louis.

the pericarp seems much like that of the common thistle. The root-leaves, which still possess their verdure, and are about half-grown, are of a pale green color. The root, however, is the only part used. It is from 9 to 15 inches long, about the size of a man's thumb, perpendicular, fusiform, and with from two to four radicles. The rind is of a brown color and somewhat rough. When first taken from the earth it [the root] is white, and nearly as crisp as a carrot; in this state it is sometimes eaten without any preparation. But after it is prepared by the same process used for the pashecoquamash, which is the most usual and the best method, it becomes black and much improved in flavor. Its taste is exactly (*p. 149*) that of sugar, and it is indeed the sweetest vegetable employed by the Indians. After being baked in the kiln it is eaten either simply or with train-oil; sometimes it is pounded fine and mixed with cold water, until it is reduced to the consistence of sagamity, or Indian mush, which last method is the most agreeable to our palates.

2. Three species of ferns grow in this neighborhood, but the root of only one is eaten.[4] This is very abundant in those parts of the open lands and prairies which have a deep, loose, rich, black loam, without any sand. There it attains the height of four or five feet, and is a beautiful plant with a fine green color in summer. The stem, which is smooth, cylindric, and slightly grooved on one side, rises erectly about half its height, when it divides into two branches, or rather long foot-stalks, which put forth in pairs from one side only, near the edges of the groove, declining backward from the grooved side. These foot-stalks are themselves grooved and cylindric ; and, as they gradually taper toward the extremities, put forth others of smaller size, which are alternate, and have 40 or 50 alternate, pinnate, horizontal, sessile leaves ; the leaves are multipartite for half the length of their foot-stalk, when they assume the tongue-like form altogether; being, moreover, revolute, with the upper disk

---

[4] That species of fern whose root is eaten is *Pteris aquilina* var. *lanuginosa*, very much like the common brake of the United States.

smooth and the lower resembling cotton; the top is annual
and therefore dead at present, but it produces no flower or
fruit. The root itself is perennial, and grows horizontally,
sometimes a little diverging, or obliquely descending, frequently dividing as it proceeds, and shooting up a number
of stems. It lies about four inches under the surface of the
earth, in a cylindrical form, with few or no radicles, and
varies from the size of a goose-quill to that of a man's finger.
The bark is black, thin, brittle, rather rough, and easily separates in flakes from the part which is eaten; the center is
divided into two parts by a strong, flat, white ligament, like
a piece of thin tape, on each side of which is a white substance, resembling, af- (*p. 150*) ter the root is roasted, both
in appearance and flavor the dough of wheat. It has, however, a pungency which is disagreeable; but the natives eat
it voraciously, and it seems to be very nutritious.

3. The rush [5] is most commonly used by the Killamucks
and other Indians on the seacoast, along the sands of which
it grows in greatest abundance. From each root a single
stem rises erectly to the height of three or four feet, somewhat thicker than a large quill, hollow and jointed; about
20 or 30 long, lineal, stellate or radiate, horizontal leaves
surround the stem at each joint, about half an inch above
which its stem is sheathed like the sand-rush. When green,
it resembles that plant also in appearance, as well as in having a rough stem. It is not branching; nor does it bear, as
far as we can discover, either flower or seed. At the bottom
of this stem, which is annual, is a small, strong radicle, about
an inch long, descending perpendicularly to the root; while
just above the junction of the radicle with the stem, the latter is surrounded, in the form of a wheel, with six or nine
small radicles, descending obliquely. The root attached
to this radicle is a perennial solid bulb, about an inch long
and of the thickness of a man's thumb, of an ovate form,

---

[5] This is one of the horsetails, *Equisetum telmateia*, belonging to the sole
genus of vascular cryptogamous plants which constitute the order *Equisetaceæ*.
The original description is Clark P 91.

depressed on one or two of its sides, and covered with a thin, smooth, black rind ; the pulp is white, brittle, and easily masticated. It is commonly roasted, though sometimes eaten raw ; but in both states is rather an insipid root.

4. The liquorice [6] of this country does not differ [generically] from that common to the United States. It here delights in a deep, loose, sandy soil, and grows very large, and abundantly. It is prepared by roasting in the embers, and pounding slightly with a small stick, in order to separate the strong ligament in the center of the root, which is then thrown away ; the rest is chewed and swallowed. In this way it has an agreeable flavor, not unlike that of the sweet potato. [This is culhomo or culwhamo of p. 739.]

5. The root of the cat-tail,[7] or cooper's flag, is eaten by the In- (*p. 151*) dians.

6. There is also a species of small, dry, tuberous roots, two inches in length, and about the thickness of the finger. These are eaten raw ; they are crisp, milky, and of an agreeable flavor. [No identification.]

7. Besides the small, cylindric root mentioned above is another of the same form and appearance, which is usually boiled and eaten with train-oil. Its taste, however, is disagreeably bitter. [This is possibly *Iris tenax*.]

8. But the most valuable of all the Indian roots is the wappatoo,[8] the bulb of the common sagittafolia [*sic*], or common arrowhead. It does not grow in this neighborhood, but is in great abundance in the marshy grounds of that beautiful valley which extends from near Quicksand river for 70

---

[6] Clark P 90 : see p. 739. But this liquorice, or licorice as it is better spelled, is specifically different from that common to the U. S. It is *Glycyrrhiza lepidota*, chiefly found in the Northwest, and a true licorice. The licorice of commerce is chiefly derived from *G. glabra*. Another species, which also yields a commercial product, is *G. echinata*, the prickly licorice. All these are leguminous plants.

[7] The common cat-o'-nine-tails, *Typha latifolia*, a monocotyledonous plant of the series *Nudifloræ* of the order *Typhaceæ*.

[8] The wappatoo is the root of *Sagittaria variabilis*, correctly called the common arrowhead in the text, after Clark P 91 ; *S. sagittifolia* is the European species, and there are others, as *S. sinensis* of China. They are monocotyledonous plants of the order *Alismaceæ*. See note [10], p. 693.

miles westward, and is a principal article of trade between the inhabitants of that valley and those of the seacoast.

The shrub [9] rises to the height of four or five feet; the stem is simple and much branched. The bark is of a dark reddish-brown; of the main stem somewhat rough, while that of the bough is smooth; the leaf [?] is about one-tenth of an inch long, obtuse at the apex, acute and angular at the insertion of the pedicle [?]. The leaf is three-fourths of an inch in length and three-eighths in width, smooth, and of a paler green than evergreens generally are. The fruit is a small, dark purple berry, of a pleasant flavor. The natives eat the berry when ripe, but seldom collect such quantities as to dry for winter use.

9-14.[10] The native fruits and berries in use among the Indians are what they call the shallun; the solme; the cranberry; a berry like the black haw; the scarlet berry of the plant called sacacommis; and a purple berry, like the huckleberry.

9. The shallun [11] is an evergreen plant, abounding in this neighborhood; its leaves are the favorite food of the elk. It is a thick growth, cylindrically rising to the height of three, and sometimes five feet, and varying from the size of a goose-quill to that of a man's thumb. The stem is sim-
(*p. 152*) ple, branching, reclining, and partially fluxuose

---

[9] That is, of the shallun or salal (No. 9). This whole paragraph is out of order; being duplicated from another codex in the description of *Gaultheria shallon*, and then misplaced on the page; where, however, I leave it with this explanation.

[10] The plants (Nos. 9-14) enumerated in this paragraph are mentioned as follows, Clark P 92 : " The native fruits and berrys in use amoung the Indians of this Neighbourhood [Fort Clatsop] are a deep purple [berry] about the size of a small cherry called by them *shallun* a small pale berry called *solme*, the Vineing or low brown berry, a light brown berry rather larger and much the shape of a black Haw, and a scarlet berry about the size of a small cherry. The plant called by the Canadian engages of the N. W. *Sacacommis* Produces this [scarlet] berry . . . the deep purple berry . . . much like the whortleberry," etc.

[11] The shallun is the berry of *Gaultheria shallon*, better known as the salalberry. It is the fruit of a small shrubby plant of the same genus as the wintergreen or checkerberry, *G. procumbens*, whose aromatic edible berries are well known. There are numerous species, of most countries. They belong to the heath family, order *Ericaceæ*. See also note [17], p. 731.

SOLME—CRANBERRY—CRAB-APPLE.

[flexuous], with a bark which, on the older part, is of a reddish-brown color, while the younger branches are red where exposed to the sun and green elsewhere. The leaf is three-fourths of an inch in length and two and a half in breadth, of an oval form, the upper disk of a glossy deep green, the under of a pale green. The fruit is a deep purple berry, about the size of the common black cherry, oval, and rather bluntly pointed; the pericarp is divided into five acute angular points, and envelops a soft pulp, containing a great number of small brown seeds.

10. The solme[12] is a small, pale-red berry, the production of a plant resembling in size and shape that which produces the fruit called in the United States [false] Solomon's seal berry [*Smilacina racemosa*]. The berry is attached to the stem in the same manner. It is of a globular form, containing a soft pulp, which envelops four seeds about the size of the seed of the common small grape. It grows amongst the woodland moss, and is, to all appearance, an annual plant.

11. The cranberry[13] is of the low and viny kind, and grows in the marshes or bogs of this neighborhood; it is [not] precisely the same as the cranberry of the United States.

12. That fruit[14] which, though rather larger, resembles in shape the black haw, is a light brown berry, of a tree about the size, shape, and appearance in every respect, of that of the United States, called the wild crab-apple. The leaf is precisely the same, as is also the bark in texture and color.

[12] Solme is a name not recognized in botany, and not to be found as English in the Century Dictionary. From the description, however, the berry is readily recognized as a species of *Smilacina* common in the Northwest, apparently *S. sessilifolia*. The genus belongs to the order *Liliaceæ* and tribe *Polygonateæ*.

[13] "This must be *Vaccinium macrocarpon*, the large cranberry of the north, once reported by Hooker from the ' confluence of the Columbia with the Pacific.' Neither this nor any other cranberry has ever since been found in Oregon, so this is of considerable interest." (F. H. Knowlton, *in lit.*)

[14] This has been taken for a true haw, or rosaceous tree of the genus *Cratægus*, *C. douglasi*, growing to a small tree or tall shrub with very hard, tough wood, and small blackish fruit, still much used for food by the Indians of the Northwest. But it is, without much doubt, *Pyrus rivularis*, the common and well-known Oregon crab-apple.

The berries grow in clumps at the ends of the small branches, each supported by a separate stem, and as many as from 3 to 18 or 20 in a clump; the berry is ovate, with one of its extremities attached to a peduncle, where it is to a small degree concave. The wood of which [this tree] is excessively hard. The natives make wedges of this wood, for splitting their boards, their firewood, and for hollowing out their canoes ; the wedge, when driven into solid dry pine, receives not the slightest injury. Our party made (*p. 153*) use of it likewise for wedges and ax-handles. The fruit is exceedingly acid, and resembles in flavor the wild crab. The pericarp of the berry contains a soft, pulpy substance, divided into four [or five] cells, each containing a single seed; the outer coat of the pericarp is a thin, smooth, though firm and tough pellicle.

13. The plant called sacacommis [15] by the Canadian traders derives its name from this circumstance : that the clerks of the trading companies are generally very fond of smoking its leaves, which they carry about with them in a small bag. It grows generally in an open piny woodland country, or on its borders. We found this berry in the prairies bordering on the Rocky mountains, or in the more open woodlands. It is indiscriminately the growth of a very rich or a very poor soil, and is found in the same abundance in both. The natives on the western side of the Rocky mountains are very fond of this berry, although to us it was a very tasteless and insipid fruit. The shrub is an evergreen, and retains its verdure in the same perfection the whole season round. However inclement the climate, the root puts forth a great number of stems, which separate near the surface of the ground, each stem from the size of a small quill to that of a man's finger; these are much branched, the branches form-

---

[15] Sacacommis is the bearberry, *Arctostaphylos uva-ursi*, otherwise known, in Spanish-American parts of the United States, as manzanita, and one of the plants entering into the composition of the Indian tobacco called kinnikinnik. It is very common and of wide distribution in the West. It has already been repeatedly noticed in this work, under various Indian and other names.

ing an acute angle with the stem, and all more properly procumbent than creeping. Although it sometimes puts forth
radicles from the stems and branches, which strike obliquely
into the ground, these radicles are by no means general or
equable in their distances from each other, nor do they
appear calculated to furnish nutriment to the plant. The
bark is formed of several layers of a smooth, thin, brittle,
reddish substance, easily separated from the stem. The
leaves with respect to their position are scattered, yet
closely arranged, particularly near the extremities of the
twigs. The leaf is about three-fourths of an inch in length,
oval, pointed, and obtuse, of a deep green, slightly grooved.
The footstalk is of proportionable length; the berry is
at- (*p. 154*) tached in an irregular manner to the small
boughs among the leaves, and always supported by separate,
small, short peduncles; the insertion produces a slight con-
cavity in the berry, while its opposite side is slightly convex.
The outer coat of the pericarp is a thin, firm, tough pellicle;
the inner coat consists of a dry, mealy powder, of a yellowish-white color, enveloping from four to six large, light
brown seeds. The color of the fruit is a fine scarlet. The
natives eat these berries without any preparation. They
ripen in September, and remain on the bushes all winter
unaffected by the frost. They are sometimes gathered and
hung in the lodges in bags, where they are dried without
further trouble.

14. The deep purple berry,[16] like the huckleberry, terminates bluntly, and has a cap or cover at the end. These
berries are attached separately to the sides of the boughs by
a short stem, hanging underneath; they often grow very
near each other on the same bough; the berry separates
very easily from the stem; the leaves adhere closely. The
shrub rises to the height of six or eight feet, and sometimes
grows on high lands, but more frequently on low, marshy
grounds. The shrub is an evergreen, about ten inches in

---

[16] This seems to be *Amelanchier alnifolia*, which, though normally deciduous,
becomes semi-evergreen on the Oregon coast.

circumference; it divides into many irregular branches; seldom more than one stem springs from one root, although the shrubs associate very thickly. The bark is somewhat rough and of a reddish-brown color; the wood is very hard; the leaves are alternate and attached by a short foot-stalk to the horizontal sides of the boughs; their form is a long oval, rather more acute toward the apex than at the point of insertion; the margin is slightly serrate, its sides collapsing, thick, firm, smooth, and glossy; the under surface is of a pale or whitish green, the upper of a fine deep green. This beautiful shrub retains its verdure throughout the year, and is more peculiarly beautiful in winter. The natives sometimes eat the berries without preparation; sometimes they dry them in the sun, at others in their sweating kilns; they very (*p. 155*) frequently pound and bake them in large loaves, weighing from 10 to 15 pounds. The bread keeps very well for one season, and retains its juices better by this mode of preparation than any other. When broken, it is stirred in cold water until it acquires the consistency of soup, and then eaten.

15–24. The trees of a larger growth are very abundant; the whole neighborhood of the coast is supplied with great quantities of excellent timber. The predominating growth is the fir,[17] of which we have seen several species. There is one singular circumstance attending all the pine of this country, which is, that when consumed it yields not the slightest particle of ashes.

15. The first species[18] grows to an immense size. The trunks are very commonly 27 feet in circumference six feet above the earth's surface; they rise to the height of 230 feet, 120 of that height without a limb. We have often found them 36 feet in circumference. One of our party measured one, and found it to be 42 feet in circumference, at a point

---

[17] Clark P 102 has: "There are several species of fir in this neighbourhood [Fort Clatsop] which I shall discribe as well as my slender bottonical skill will enable me," etc.

[18] The first species is probably *Abies nobilis*, the red fir of the Pacific coast.

beyond the reach of an ordinary man. This trunk for the distance of 200 feet was destitute of limbs; the tree was perfectly sound, and at a moderate calculation its stature may be estimated at 300 feet. The timber is [sound] throughout, and rives [splits] better than any other species; the bark scales off in flakes irregularly round, and of a reddish-brown color, particularly the younger growth; the trunk is simple, branching, and not very proliferous. The leaf is acerose, one-tenth of an inch in width, three-fourths in length, firm, stiff, and acuminate. It is triangular, a little declining, thickly scattered on all sides of the bough, and springs from small triangular pedestals of soft, spongy, elastic bark at the junction of the boughs. The bud-scales continue to encircle their respective twigs for several years; Captain Lewis has counted as many as the growth of four years beyond their scales. It yields but little rosin, and we have never been able to discover the cone, although we have killed several.

(*p. 156*) 16. The second[19] is a much more common species, and constitutes at least one-half of the timber in this neighborhood. It seems to resemble the spruce, rising from 160 to 180 feet, and being from four to six in diameter, straight, round, and regularly tapering. The bark is thin, of a dark color, much divided in small longitudinal interstices; the bark of the boughs and young trees is somewhat smooth, but not equal [in this respect] to the balsam-fir; the wood is white, very soft, but difficult to rive; the trunk is a simple, branching, and diffuse stem, not so proliferous as pines and firs usually are. It puts forth buds from the sides of the small boughs, as well as from their extremities; the stem terminates, like the cedar, in a slender pointed top. The leaves are petiolate; the foot-stalks short, acerose, rather more than half a line in width, and very unequal in length; the greatest length seldom exceeds one inch, while other leaves, intermixed on every part of the bough, do not exceed a quarter of an inch. The leaf has a small longitudinal channel on the upper disk, which is of a deep and glossy

---

[19] The second species of " fir " is the hemlock-spruce, *Tsuga mertensiana*.

green, while the under disk is of a whitish green. It yields
but little rosin. What is remarkable, the cone is not longer
than the end of a man's thumb; it is soft, flexible, of an
ovate form, and produced at the ends of the small twigs.

17. The third species[20] resembles in all points the Canadian balsam-fir. It grows from 2½ to 4 feet in diameter,
and rises to the height of 80 or 100 feet. The stem is simple,
branching, and proliferous. The leaves are sessile, acerous,
one-eighth of an inch in length and one-sixteenth in width,
thickly scattered on the twigs, adherent to the three under
sides only, gibbous, a little declining, obtusely pointed, soft,
and flexible. The upper disk is longitudinally marked with
a slight channel, and of a deep glossy green; the under is of
a pale green and not glossy. This tree affords, in considerable quantities, a fine deeply aromatic balsam, resembling
the balsam of Canada in taste and appearance. The small
pistils [?] filled, rise like a blister on the ($p.$ 157) trunk and
the branches. The bark that envelops these pistils is soft
and easily punctured; the general appearance of the bark is
dark and smooth, but not so remarkable for that quality as
the white pine of our country. The wood is white and soft.

18. The fourth species[21] in size resembles the second. The
stem is simple, branching, ascending, proliferous; the bark
is of a dark-reddish brown, thicker than that of the third species, divided by small longitudinal interstices, not so much
magnified as in the second species. In relative position the
leaves resemble those of the balsam-fir, excepting that they
are only two-thirds the width and little more than one-half
the length, and that the upper disk is not so green and
glossy. The wood yields no balsam and but little rosin.
The wood is white and tough, though rather porous.

19. The fifth species[22] in size resembles the second, and has

---

[20] The third species is uncertain, possibly *Thuja gigantea.*

[21] The fourth species is probably the great white fir, *Abies grandis.*

[22] The fifth species is the Douglas fir of Western North America, *Pseudotsuga douglasi*, also known as the red or yellow fir; and from this the fir of "low marshy grounds," as given beyond, is probably not specifically distinct.

a trunk simple, branching, and proliferous. The bark is thin, dark brown, divided longitudinally by interstices, and scaling off in thin rolling flakes. It yields but little balsam ; two-thirds of the diameter of the trunk, in the center, presents a reddish-white ; the remainder is white, porous, and tough. The twigs are much longer and more slender than in either of the other species ; the leaves are acerose, one-twentieth of an inch in width and one inch in length, sextile, inserted on all sides of the bough, straight, and obliquely pointed toward the extremities. The upper disk has a small longitudinal channel, and is of a deep green, but not so glossy as the balsam-fir. The under disk is of a pale green.

We have seen a species of this fir on low marshy grounds, resembling in all points the foregoing, except that it branches more diffusively. This tree is generally 30 feet in height, and two in diameter. The diffusion of its branches may result from its open situation, as it seldom grows in the neighborhood of another tree. The cone is 2½ (*p. 158*) inches in length and 3¾ in its greatest circumference. It tapers regularly to a point, and is formed of imbricated scales, of a bluntly rounded form. A thin leaf is inserted in the pith of the cone, which overlays the center and extends one-half inch beyond the point, of each scale.

20. The sixth species[23] does not differ [generically] from what is usually denominated the white pine [*Pinus strobus*] in Virginia. The unusual length of the cone seems to constitute the only difference. This is sometimes 16 or 18 inches in length, and about 4 in circumference. It grows on the north side of the Columbia, near the ocean.

21. The seventh and last species[24] grows in low grounds, and in places frequently overflowed by the tide, seldom

[23] The sixth species is the giant white pine of the Pacific, *Pinus lambertiana*, also known as Lambert's pine, and sugar-pine. It is a noble tree, sometimes 275 feet high, yielding a very valuable timber.

[24] The seventh species is a spruce, in the most approved nomenclature now placed in a genus *Picea* (as distinguished from *Abies*). The species is *P. sitchensis*, the tide-land spruce, found from Alaska to California, and specially well developed about the mouth of the Columbia, where it forms a belt of timber 10

rising higher than 35 feet, and not more than from 2½ to 4
in diameter; the stem is simple, branching, and proliferous;
the bark resembles that of the first species, but is more
rugged; the leaves are acerose, two-tenths of an inch in
width, three-fourths in length, firm, stiff, and a little acumi-
nated; they end in short pointed tendrils, gibbous, and
are thickly scattered on all sides of the branch, though they
adhere to the three under sides only; those inserted on the
under side incline sidewise, with upward points, presenting
the leaf in the shape of a sithe [scythe]; the others are
pointed upward, sextile, and, like those of the first species,
grow from the small triangular pedestals of a bark, spongy,
soft, and elastic. The under disk is of a deep glossy green, the
other of a pale whitish-green; the boughs retain the leaves
of a six years' growth; the bud-scales resemble those of the
first species; the cone is of an ovate figure, 3½ inches in
length and 3 in circumference, thickest in the middle, tapering and terminating in two obtuse points; it is composed of
small, flexible scales, imbricated, and of a reddish-brown
color. Each of these scales covers two small seeds, and is
itself covered in the center by a small, thin, inferior scale,
acutely pointed; these scales (*p. 159*) proceed from the sides
of the bough as well as from its extremities. This tree was
nowhere seen above the Wappatoo [island].

22. The stem of the black alder[25] arrives to a great size.
It is simple, branching, and diffuse; the bark is smooth, of
a light color, with white spreading spots, resembling those
of the beech; the leaf, fructification, etc., resemble precisely
those of the common alder of our country. The shrubs

---

or 15 miles broad. It attains a height of 140–180 feet, and furnishes a lumber of some special excellences. The description of it occupies Clark R 59–61,
Feb. 18th, 1806.

[25] This is *Alnus rubra*, also called red alder. It is one of two alders of the
Pacific coast, which frequently grow to be medium-sized trees; the other species
is *A. rhombifolia*. Alders belong with the oaks in the natural order *Cupuli-
feræ*. Black alder is one of the names given in the eastern parts of the United
States to *A. serrulata* and *A. incana*. The common European alder is *A. glu-
tinosa*.

grow separately from different roots, not in clusters like those of the United States. The black alder does not cast its leaf until the 1st of December. It is sometimes found growing to the height of 60 or 70 feet, and from 2 to 4 in diameter.

23.[26] There is a tree common to the Columbia river, below the entrance of Cataract river, when divested of its foliage much resembling the ash. The trunk is simple, branching, and diffuse; the leaf is petiolate, plain, divided by four deep lines; it resembles that of the palm, and is considerably lobate; the lobes terminate in from three to five angular points, and their margins are indented with irregular and somewhat circular incisures; the petiolate [petiole] is cylindrical, smooth, and seven inches long; the leaf itself eight inches in length, and twelve in breadth. This tree is frequently three feet in diameter, and rises from 40 to 50 feet. The fruit is a winged seed, somewhat resembling that of the maple.

24.[27] In the same part of the country there is also another growth, resembling the white maple, though much smaller, and seldom to be seen of more than six or seven inches in diameter. These trees grow in clusters, from 15 to 20 feet in height, from the same bed of roots, spreading and leaning outward; the twigs are long and slender; the stem is simple and branching; the bark in color resembles the white maple·; the leaf is petiolate, plain, scattered, nearly circular, with acute, angular incisures round the margin, of an inch in length, and from six to eight in number; the acute (*p. 160*) angular points so formed are crenate, three inches in length, and four in width; the petiole is cylindric, smooth, 1¼ inch in length; the fruit is not known.

25–33.[28] The undergrowth consists of honeysuckles; alder

[26] Is a maple, *Acer macrophyllum*, a fine species of California and Oregon, distinguished as the broad-leaved maple, and furnishing a wood much used for furniture. It is the "new timber" of p. 679, note.

[27] Is another maple, *Acer circinatum*, the vine maple of western parts of the United States, especially from Oregon to British America.

[28] Are to be sought in Clark P 112 and following pages.

[elder]; seven-bark or nine-bark; huckleberry; a shrub like the quillwood; a plant like the mountain-holly; a green-briar; and ferns.

25.[29] The honeysuckle common to the United States we found in this neighborhood. We first discovered this honeysuckle on the waters of the Kooskooskee, near the Chopunnish nation, and again below the grand rapids.

26. The alder [elder,[30] a species of] which is also common to our country, was found in great abundance in the woodlands, on this side [west] of the Rocky mountains. It differs in the color of its berry, this being of a pale sky-blue, while that of the United States [*Sambucus canadensis*] is of a deep purple.

27. The seven-bark,[31] or, as it is usually denominated, the nine-bark of the United States, is also [represented by another species] common to this country.

28. There is a species of huckleberry, common to the high lands, from the commencement of the Columbia valley to the seacoast, rising to the height of six or eight feet, branching and diffuse. The trunk is cylindrical, of a dark brown color; the collateral branches are green, smooth, and square, and put forth a number of alternate branches of the same color, from the two horizontal sides only. The fruit is a small deep purple berry, held in much esteem by the natives. The leaf is pale green, small, three-fourths of an inch in length, and three-eighths in width, oval, terminating more acutely at the apex than at the insertion of the foot-

---

[29] This honeysuckle is wholly uncertain, for the description does not suffice to assure us that it is even of the genus *Lonicera*.

[30] Misprinted "alder" for elder. This is *Sambucus glauca*, a large species of western parts of the United States, attaining a height of 25 feet, and bearing a bluish edible berry. The elders belong to the honeysuckle family, order *Caprifoliaceæ*, but are typical of the tribe *Sambuceæ*.

[31] "Seven-bark" and "nine-bark" are names of a rosaceous plant, *Spiræa opulifolia*, sometimes placed in another genus than *Spiræa* (Niellia). A related species is the hardhack, *S. tomentosa*, pink-flowered; and the representative of the hardhack on the Pacific coast is *S. douglasi*, the Douglas hardhack, one of the most showy of American shrubs. This last is what the authors mean by seven-bark.

stalk; the base is nearly entire, but slightly serrate; the
foot-stalks are short ; their relative position is alternate, two-
ranked, proceeding from the horizontal sides of the boughs
only. [This huckleberry seems to be *Vaccinium ovatum*].

29, 30.[32] There are two species of shrubs, first seen at the
grand rapids of the Columbia, and which have since been
seen elsewhere; they grow in rich dry grounds, usually in
the (*p. 161*) neighborhood of some water-course; the roots
are creeping and cylindrical.

29. The stem of the first species is from 12 to 18 inches
in height, about as large as an ordinary goose-quill, simple,
unbranched, and erect ; its leaves are cauline, compound,
and spreading ; the leaflets are jointed, and oppositely pinnate, in three pairs terminated by one [leaflet] sextile,
widest at the base, tapering to an acuminate point ; it is 1¼
inch in its greatest width, and 3¼ inches in length ; each
point of the margin is armed with a subulate thorn ; these
thorns are 13 to 17 in number, veined, glossy, carinated
and wrinkled ; their points obliquely tending toward the
extremity of the common foot-stalk.

30. The stem of the second species is procumbent, about
the size of that of the first species, jointed, and unbranched ;
its leaves are cauline, compound, and oppositely pinnate ;
the rib is 14 to 16 inches in length, cylindric, and smooth ;
the leaflets are 2½ inches long, one inch wide, and of the
greatest width one-half inch from the base ; this they regularly surround, and from the same point taper to an acute
apex, usually terminated with a small subulate thorn ; they
are jointed and oppositely pinnate, consisting of six pairs
terminated by one [leaflet] ; sessile, serrate, ending in a
small subulate spine, from 25 to 27 in number ; they are
smooth, plain, deep green, all obliquely tending toward the
extremity of the foot-stalk ; they retain their green all
winter.

The large-leaved thorn [33] has a leaf about 2½ inches long,

---

[32] Have not been identified.

[33] May be some species of wild rose. Clark Q 99–101, April 8th, 1806, has this

which is petiolate and conjugate; the leaflets are petiolate,
acutely pointed, having their margins cut with unequal and
irregular incisures. The shrub, which we had once mistaken
for the large-leaved thorn, resembled the stem of that shrub,
excepting the thorn; it bears a large three-headed leaf.

31. The briar[34] is of the class Polyandria and order poligymnia [*Polygynia*]. The flowers are single; the peduncle
is long and cylindrical; the calyx is a perianth of one leaf,
five-cleft, and acutely pointed; the pe- (*p. 162*) rianth proper
is erect, inferior in both petals and germen [ovary]; the
corolla consists of five acute, pale scarlet petals, inserted on
the receptacle, with a short and narrow cleft; the corolla is
smooth, moderately long, situated at the base of the germen,
permanent, and in shape resembling a cup; the stamens, or
filaments, are subulate, inserted into the receptacle, unequal,
and bent inward, concealing the pystilium [pistils]; the
anther is two-lobed and inflated, situated on the top of the
filament of the pystilium; the germ is conical, imbricated,
superior, sessile, and short; the styles are short, compared
with the stamens, capillary, smooth, and obtuse; they are
distributed over the surface of the germ, and deciduous.
This green-briar grows most abundantly in rich dry lands, in
the vicinity of a water-course, and is found in small quantities in piny lands at a distance from the water. In the former situation the stem is frequently of the size of a man's
finger, and rises perpendicularly four or five feet; it then
descends in an arch, and becomes procumbent, or rests on
some neighboring plant; it is simple, unbranched, and cylindric; in the latter situation it grows much smaller, and is
usually procumbent. The stem is armed with sharped [*sic*]
and forked briars; the leaf is petiolate, ternate, resembles in
shape and appearance that of the purple raspberry so com-

---

note about the large-leaved thorn, "to correct an error which I have heretofore
made with respect to this shrub."

[34] The green-briar (not well-named, for green-briar is commonly said of *Smi-
lax*) is a bramble, *Rubus ursinus*, well described and readily recognized. The
word misspelled "poligymnia" in the text is in the MS. "Pollygynia."

mon to the Atlantic States; the fruit is a berry resembling the blackberry in all points, eaten when ripe by the natives, and held in much esteem, though it is not dried for winter consumption. This shrub was first discovered at the entrance of Quicksand river; it grows so abundantly in the fertile valley of the Columbia, and on the islands, that the country is almost impenetrable; it retains its verdure late in summer.

32, 33.[35] Besides the fern already described as furnishing a nutritious root, there are two other plants [not] of the same species [though of the same order *Filices* and suborder *Polypodiaceæ*], which may be divided into the large and the small.

32. The large fern rises three or four feet; the stem is a common (*p. 163*) footstalk [stipe] proceeding immediately from the radix [root-stock, which is] somewhat flat, about the size of a man's arm, and covered with innumerable black coarse capillary radicles issuing from every part of its surface. One of these roots will send forth from 20 to 40 of these common footstalks, bending outward from the common center; their ribs are cylindric, and marked longitudinally their whole length with a groove on the upper side; on either side of this groove, and a little below its edge, the leaflets are inserted; these are shortly petiolate for about two-thirds the length of the middle rib, commencing from the bottom, and thence to the extremity are sessile; the rib is terminated by a single undivided lanceolate leaflet; the leaflets are from two to four inches in length, have a small acute angular projection, and are obliquely cut at the base; their upper surface is smooth and of a deep green; the under surface is of a pale green, and covered with brown

---

[35] The large fern here described is quite different from *Pteris aquilina* var. *lanuginosa*, noted on p. 822. It is *Aspidium munitum*, one of the wood-ferns or shield-ferns, about 40 species of which are found in the United States. They are so named from the form of the indusium or covering of the fructification. The best-known is the Christmas shield-fern, *A. acrostichoides*, native of eastern North America, from Canada to Florida, and often used in Christmas decorations. The small fern is probably *Polypodium scouleri*.

protuberances [sori] of a woolly appearance, particularly near the central fiber; the leaflets are alternately pinnate, and in number from 110 to 140; they are shortest at the two extremities of the common footstalk, largest in the center, gradually lengthening and diminishing as they succeed each other.

33. The small fern rises likewise with a common footstalk from the radix, from four to eight in number and from four to eight inches long; the central rib is marked with a slight longitudinal groove throughout its whole length; the leaflets are oppositely pinnate for about one-third of the length of the common footstalk from the bottom, thence alternately pinnate; the footstalk terminates in a simple, undivided lanceolate leaflet; the leaflets are oblong, obtuse, convex, absolutely entire, and the upper disk is marked with a slight longitudinal groove; near the upper extremity these leaflets are decursively pinnate, as are all those of the large fern. Both of these species preserve green during the winter.

[*II. Zoölogy.*]

The quadrupeds of this country, from the Rocky mountains to the Pacific ocean, may be conveniently divided into (*p. 164*) the domestic and the wild animals. The first [division] embraces the horse and the dog only.

[*Domestic Animals.*]

1. The horse [*Equus caballus*] is confined principally to the nations inhabiting the great plains of the Columbia, extending from lat. 40° to 50° N., and occupying the tract of territory lying between the Rocky mountains and a [Cascade] range of mountains which passes the Columbia river about the Great Falls; [that is,] from long. 116° to 121° W.[36] The Shoshonees, Choppunish, Sokulks, Escheloots, Eneshures, and Chilluckittequaws all enjoy the benefit of

---

[36] That is, the country between the Bitter-root ranges and the Cascade range. Text had "from longitude sixteen to one hundred and twenty-one west," which slip I correct. Area approx. 22,000 sq. miles of "bunch-grass country."

that docile, noble, and generous animal, and all of them, except the last three, possess immense numbers.

They appear to be of an excellent race, lofty, elegantly formed, active and durable; many of them appear like fine English coursers; some of them are pied with large spots of white, irregularly scattered, and intermixed with a dark brown bay; the greater part, however, are of an uniform color, marked with stars and white feet, and resemble in fleetness and bottom, as well as in form and color, the best blooded horses of Virginia. The natives suffer them to run at large in the plains, the grass of which affords them their only winter subsistence, their masters taking no trouble to lay in a winter's store for them; notwithstanding, they will, unless much exercised, fatten on the dry grass afforded by the plains during the winter. The plains are rarely, if ever, moistened by rain, and the grass is consequently short and thin. The natives, excepting those of the Rocky mountains, appear to take no pains in selecting their male horses to breed: indeed, those of that class appear much the most indifferent. Whether the horse was originally a native of this country or not, the soil and climate appear to be perfectly well adapted to the nature of this animal. Horses are said to be found wild in many parts of this extensive country. The several tribes of Shoshonees who reside toward Mexico, on the waters of the Multnomah river, particularly one of them, called Shaboboah,[37] have (*p. 165*) also a great number of mules, which the Indians prize more highly than horses. An elegant horse may be purchased of the natives for a few beads or other paltry trinkets, which, in the United States, would not cost more than one or two dollars. The abundance and cheapness of horses will be extremely advantageous to those who may hereafter attempt the fur-trade to the East Indies by the way of the Columbia river and the Pacific ocean.

2. The dog [*Canis familiaris*] is unusually small, about the

[37] *Sic*—compare the name So-so'-bu-bar, of note *, p. 554, apparently the same word.

size of an ordinary cur; he is usually party-colored, among which [dogs] black, white, brown, and brindle are the colors most predominant. The head is long, the nose pointed, the eye small, the ear erect and pointed, like that of the wolf; the hair is short and smooth, excepting on the tail, where it is long and straight, like that of the ordinary cur. The natives never eat the flesh of this animal, and he appears to be in no other way serviceable to them than in hunting the elk.

[*Wild Animals.*]

The second division comprehends [among others] the brown, white, or grisly bear; the black bear; the common red deer; the black-tailed fallow-deer; the mule-deer; the elk; the large brown wolf; the small wolf of the plains; the large wolf of the plains; the tiger-cat; the common red fox; the silver fox; the fisher or black fox; the large red fox of the plains; the kit-fox, or small fox of the plains; the antelope; the sheep; the beaver; the common otter; the sea-otter; the mink; the seal; the raccoon; the large gray squirrel; the small gray squirrel; the small brown squirrel; the ground-squirrel; the braro; the rat; the mouse; the mole; the panther; the hare; the rabbit; the polecat or skunk.[38]

1. First the brown, white, or grisly [grizzly] bear, which seems to be of the same family [same species, *Ursus horribilis*[39]], with an accidental variation of color only, inhabits

[38] I leave this singularly drawn-up list in its original disorder, and without comment here, as the several species succeed one another in the same disorder on the following pages, where each one is identified as it occurs.

[39] The grizzly bear is the most notable discovery made in zoölogy by Lewis and Clark. Their accounts are very full, as we have already seen (pp. 288, 298, 306, 307, 309, 310, 342, 370, 371, 381, 392, 393), and shall see again in several places. This bear was found to be so numerous and so fierce, especially in the Upper Missouri region, as to more than once endanger the lives of the party, and form an impediment to the progress of the Expedition. Our authors carefully distinguish the grizzly, in all its color-variations, from the black bear (*Ursus americanus*); they are at pains to describe it minutely and repeatedly, laying special stress, for specific characters, upon its great size in all its dimensions, its general build and the form of the feet and claws, the peculi-

the timbered parts of the Rocky mountains. These are rarely found on the westerly side, and are more common below the Rocky mountains, on the plains or on their borders, amidst copses of brush and underwood, and near the water-courses. We are unable to (*p. 166*) learn that they inhabit at all the woody country bordering on the coast as far in the interior as the [Cascade] range of mountains which passes the Columbia between the Great Falls and the rapids [Cascades] of that river.

2. The black bear [*Ursus americanus* [40]] differs in no respect from that common to the United States. They chiefly inhabit timbered parts of the Rocky mountains, and likewise the borders of the great plains of the Columbia. They are sometimes found in that tract which lies between those plains and the Pacific ocean. One of our hunters saw one of this species, which was the only one we have discovered since our residence at Fort Clatsop.

3, 4, 5. The deer are of three kinds: the common red deer, the black-tailed fallow-deer, and the mule-deer.

arity of the scrotum, together with the inability of this species to climb trees, its great ferocity, and its remarkable tenacity of life. Their remarks are for the most part judicious and pertinent, establishing the species as distinct from the black bear ; and have been confirmed by subsequent investigators. The differences had long been known to the Indians, and are correctly set forth, as for example under dates of May 14th and 31st, which see beyond ; the point being that the grizzly, in all its variety of color, is different from the black bear, some color-varieties of which latter are nevertheless like some of those of the grizzly. Lewis and Clark's accounts furnished the basis of the technical names *Ursus horribilis*, first given in 1815 by George Ord, in Guthrie's Geography, 2d Am. ed., pp. 291, 299, and since almost universally adopted by naturalists ; *U. ferox*, used by Sir John Richardson in the Fauna Boreali Americana, 1829, I. p. 24, pl. i ; and *U. canescens*, used by Hamilton Smith in Griffith's edition of Cuvier's Règne Animal, 1827, II. p. 229, and V. p. 112, with a plate prepared from one of Lewis and Clark's specimens. The adjectives "grisly" and "grizzly" are used indiscriminately by our authors ; but it may be observed that *grisly* means horrible, terrible, fearful, and the like, while *grizzly* means of a grizzled gray color. Both designations are pertinent ; the former is rendered by the Latin word *horribilis*, and is preferable, because it applies to all the color-variations of the animal ; but "grizzly" is the adjective most in use.

[40] See preceding note on the grizzly bear ; also, pp. 150, 320. The black bear, like the grizzly, runs into color-variations, the best marked of which

3. The common red deer [*Cariacus virginianus macru-rus* [41]] inhabit the Rocky mountains in the neighborhood of the Chopunnish, about the Columbia, and down this river as low as where tide-water commences. They do not appear to differ essentially from those of the United States, being the same in shape, size, and appearance. The tail is, however, different, which is of an unusual length, far exceeding that of the common deer. Captain Lewis measured one, and found it to be 17 inches long.

4. The black-tailed fallow-deer [*Cariacus columbianus* [42]] are peculiar to this coast, and are a distinct species, partaking equally of the qualities of the mule [-deer] and the common deer. Their ears are longer, and their winter coat is darker than those of the common deer; the receptacle of the eye [larmier, crumen, or suborbital gland] is more conspicuous; their legs are shorter, their bodies thicker and larger. The tail is of the same length with that of the common deer, the

---

is a light reddish-brown; which variety is known as the "cinnamon" bear (*Ursus cinnamomeus*). A bear of this kind closely resembles, as far as color goes, some of the brownest varieties of the grizzly—a fact which has caused great though needless confusion. It is only necessary to remember that there are some "cinnamon" bears which are a variety of the species *Ursus americanus*, and other "cinnamon" bears which are a variety of the species *Ursus horribilis*. The common black bear was known to science long before the grizzly was discovered. It was named *Ursus americanus* by the celebrated Russian naturalist, Peter S. Pallas, in his Spicilegia Zoölogica, 1780, XVI. pp. 6–24, and was described as the black bear by Thomas Pennant in his History of Quadrupeds, 1781, No. 174, and again in his Arctic Zoölogy, 1784, I. p. 57.

[41] The character of that deer which represents *Cariacus virginianus* west of the Rocky Mountains is equivocal. As Lewis and Clark correctly state, it does not appear to differ essentially—that is, specifically, from the common deer of the United States. The great length of tail assigned (17 inches) does not hold good in all cases, the tail being usually but 12 or 14 inches long, and thus little if any longer than that of *C. virginianus*. Naturalists now incline to agree with our authors that the Pacific slope red deer is only a variety; and it is consequently called *C. virginianus macrurus* (after a name bestowed by C. S. Rafinesque in 1817, Amer. Monthly Mag. I. p. 436). This animal was named *C. leucurus* by David Douglas in 1829 (Zoöl. Journ. IV. p. 330). (See back, pp. 121, 715; also, Clark R 62.)

[42] This deer is a discovery made by Lewis and Clark, who describe it carefully, and fully distinguish it from both the Virginian deer, *C. virginianus*, and the

hair on the under side white, and on its sides and top of a deep jetty black; the hams resemble in form and color those of the mule [-deer], which it likewise resembles in its gait. The black-tailed deer never runs at full speed, but bounds with every foot from the ground at the same time, like the mule-deer. He sometimes inhabits the woodlands, but more (*p. 167*) often the prairies and open grounds. It may be generally said that he is of a size larger than the common deer and less than the mule-deer. The flesh is seldom fat, and in flavor is far inferior to any other of the species [genus].

5. The mule-deer [*Cariacu macrotis*[43]] inhabit both the

mule-deer, *C. macrotis.* Unfortunately, however, it was mistaken for a variety of the latter by Sir John Richardson, in 1829, on the occasion of its receiving its first technical name, this author calling it *Cervus macrotis* var. *columbianus,* in the Fauna Boreali-Americana, I. p. 255, pl. 20. To add to this confusion, as time wore on, and the mule-deer became well-known to hunters and travelers, it acquired the name of "black-tailed" deer—though the tail is white, only tipped with black. Moreover, though the true black-tailed deer of Lewis and Clark only inhabits west of the Rocky mountains, the so-called black-tailed deer (*C. macrotis*) is also found there, as well as east of these mountains. Hence, a "black-tailed" deer west of the Rockies, may be either *Cariacus columbianus* or *C. macrotis ;* but east of those mountains can only be *C. macrotis.* It would be much better, were it possible, to confine the name "black-tail" to *C. columbianus,* and call *C. macrotis* mule-deer ; but people will go on miscalling these deer to suit themselves. In 1848, the late Titian R. Peale (U. S. Expl. Exp. p. 59) dedicated the true Columbian black-tailed deer to Captain Lewis, as *Cervus lewisii ;* and in 1851-53, Audubon and Bachman renamed it *C. richardsonii,* after Sir John Richardson, in their Quadrupeds of N. Am. II. p. 211, and III. p. 27, pl. cvi. (See p. 122, note there, and also following note. See Clark R 63.)

[43] Yet another discovery of Lewis and Clark—a noble deer, superior in size to either of the foregoing, and only inferior in this respect to the elk. The authors called it the mule-deer, not with any implication of hybridity, but from the great size of the ears. To the same feature it owes its first technical name, *Cervus macrotis,* given in 1823 by Mr. Thomas Say, in Major Long's Expedition to the Rocky Mts. II. p. 88. This animal is quite different from any other deer of North America, and there never need have been any such misunderstanding as did arise (see preceding note). It got its preoccupied and inapt name "black-tail" by way of distinction from the common deer (*Cariacus virginianus*), on whose tail there is no black, and without any reference whatever to the black-tailed *C. columbianus.* The best character to distinguish *C. macrotis* is neither

seacoast [of the Pacific] and the plains of the Missouri, and likewise the borders of the Kooskooskee river, in the neighborhood of the Rocky mountains. It is not known whether they exist in the interior of the great plains of the Columbia, or on the lower borders, near the mountains which pass the river above the great falls. The properties of this animal have already been noticed [*e.g.*, at pp. 121, 122].

6. The elk [*Cervus canadensis*⁴⁴] is of the same species with that which inhabits much the greater part of North America. They are common to every part of this country, as well the timbered lands as the plains, but are much more

tail nor ears, but horns. The antlers are doubly dichotomous, or twice-forked— that is, the main beam forks in two nearly equal branches, and each branch forks in two nearly equal tines or points. Whereas, in *C. virginianus* (which is *not* black-tailed), and also in *C. columbianus* (which is black-tailed), the antlers agree in having a single regularly curved beam, from one side of which all the tines or points spring successively. Thus, though there is only one species of deer of the genus *Cariacus* in eastern North America—the common *C. virginianus*—there are three species in the West, namely : *C. virginianus macrurus*, the western variety of the last-named ; *C. columbianus*, the true black-tailed deer ; and *C. macrotis*, the so-called black-tailed deer, or true mule-deer—precisely as originally determined by our authors, to whom we owe the discovery of all three.

⁴⁴ It is unfortunate that this animal, *Cervus canadensis*, should have acquired the name of "elk." It was known by no other to Lewis and Clark. We may suppose that the term was already fixed in their day, and certainly the animal has been generally so called from their day to ours. To understand the transfer of this name from one European animal, not found in America, to a quite different American animal, we must know : first, that our "elk," so-called, is a true *Cervus*, and a near relative of the great red deer or stag, hart, and hind of Europe, *C. elaphus ;* second, that "elk" is the proper name only of a European animal, *Alces machlis*, which can hardly be distinguished from our moose ; whence it follows that if "elk" be applicable to any American animal, it should be applied to the moose, and not to *Cervus canadensis*. Both the European elk and the American moose have broad, flat, low, palmated antlers, and are otherwise very different from the European stag and the American so-called elk, both of which have long, high, cylindric antlers of many slender tines. Our animal should be (but will never generally be) called by the distinctive Indian name *wapiti*. It was technically named *Cervus wapiti* by Professor B. S. Barton in 1809 (Trans. Amer. Philos. Soc. VI. p. 70), and *Cervus major* by Mr. Geo. Ord in 1815 (Guthrie's Geogr., 2d Am. ed. II. pp. 292, 306); but it had previously been named *C. elaphus canadensis* by Erxleben, Syst. Anim. 1777, p. 305, and Boddaert, Elench. Anim. 1784, p. 135.

abundant in the former than in the latter. In the month of March we discovered several which had not cast their horns, and others of which the new horns had grown to the length of six inches. The latter were in much the best order, and hence we draw the inference that the leanest elk retain their horns the longest.

7, 8. The wolves [45] are either the large brown wolf, or the wolf of the plains, of which last there are two kinds [species], the large and the small. The large brown wolf inhabits the woody countries on the borders of the Pacific, and the mountains which pass the Columbia river between the great falls and rapids, and resembles in all points that of the United States. The large [*Canis lupus occidentalis*] and small [*Canis latrans*, the coyote] wolves of the plains principally inhabit the open country and the woodlands on their borders. They resemble, both in appearance and habit, those of the Missouri plains. They are by no means abundant in the plains of the Columbia, as they meet there but very little game for their subsistence.

[45] The authors are not so fortunate in treating the wolves as they are in handling the bears and the deer, since they separate the single large species which exists into two, and do not sufficiently discriminate one of these two from the distinct small species. Their "large brown wolf" of the wooded Columbian region is the brown color-variety of the common wolf, *Canis lupus occidentalis* (*C. nubilus* of Say, 1823). Their "large wolf of the plains" is the same in any of its color-variations, which range from black through various grizzled and brindled shades to whitish—the case being nearly parallel with that of the grizzly bear. These large wolves, of whatever color, are commonly also called "buffalo-wolf" and "timber-wolf." While the buffalo remained they were very numerous, but of late years their numbers have been greatly reduced by the business of the wolfers, who systematically destroyed them with strychnine for the sake of the pelts. On the other hand, the "small wolf of the plains" is a totally different animal, the coyote, *Canis latrans;* which, however, is by no means confined to the plains, and is still common in many parts of the West. This species varies less in coloration than the large wolves do, and some varieties of the latter are scarcely distinguishable by color alone from the coyote. The best account given by Lewis and Clark of the coyote is at p. 297, where it is fully described under the name of the "small wolf or burrowing-dog of the prairies": see also p. 122. This animal received no technical name till 1823, when it was called *C. latrans* by Say, in Long's Exped. R. Mts. I. p. 168. (Clark R 66.)

9. The tiger-cat [*Lynx rufus fasciatus*[46]] inhabits the borders of the plains, and the woody country in the neighborhood of the Pacific. (*p. 168*) This animal is of a size larger than the wild-cat [*L. rufus*] of our country, and much the same in form, agility, and ferocity. The color of the back, neck, and sides is reddish-brown, irregularly variegated with small spots of dark brown. The tail is about two inches long, and nearly white, except the extremity, which is black; it terminates abruptly, as if it had been amputated. The belly is white, beautifully variegated with small black spots; the legs are of the same color with the sides, and the back is [*sic*—but read legs are] marked transversely with black stripes; the ears are black on the outer side, covered with fine, short hair, except at the upper point, which is furnished with a pencil of hair, fine, straight, and black, three-fourths of an inch in length. The hair of this animal is long and fine, far exceeding that of the wild-cat of the United States, but inferior in that quality to that of the bear [*sic*—read Louservia, Clark R 68] of the northwest. The skin of this animal is in great demand among the natives, for of this

[46] Under the misleading name tiger-cat, but with minute accuracy, is thus described the lynx of the Columbia, discovered by our authors. This is quite distinct from the Canada lynx, *Lynx canadensis*, and has often been considered also a different species from the bay lynx, *L. rufus*, of which, however, it appears to be a local race. It was first named *Lynx fasciatus* by C. S. Rafinesque, in 1817 (Amer. Monthly Mag. II. p. 46), through a misunderstanding of the meaning of Lewis and Clark, where they are made in the above text to say " the back is marked transversely with black stripes"; for they mean that the legs are of the same color as the back and sides, but that the legs are furthermore crossed by black stripes—which is correct. (See Baird, Mamm. N. Am. 1857, p. 98, where " back " was attempted to be taken to mean back or inner side of the legs, in support of the name *fasciatus*—which would not be wrong, but was not what L. and C. meant.) A description of the "tyger cat" occupies Clark R 66–68, Feb. 21st, 1806, where the matter is easily settled. The words in question stand : "the legs are of the same colour with the sides and back, marked transversely with stripes of black." So, also, Lewis J 87. There is a still worse blunder in the above paragraph, where the authors are made to say that the fur of this lynx is inferior to that of the " *bear* of the northwest." Clark R 68 has : " Louservia of the N.W.," by which he means loup-cervier, *i. e.*, the Canada lynx, *Lynx canadensis*, the length and fineness of whose fur had struck him when he was among the Mandans. (See p. 211, note there ; also, pp. 734, 755.)

they form their robes; it requires four to make up the complement.

10–14. Of the foxes,[47] we have seen several species.

10. The large red fox [*Vulpes macrurus*] of the plains, and the [11.] kit-fox [*V. velox*] or small red fox of the plains, are the same which are found on the banks of the Missouri. They are found almost exclusively in the open plains, or on the tops of brush [*i. e.*, brushy hills] within the level country.

12. The common red fox [*Vulpes fulvus*] of the United States inhabits the country bordering the coast, nor does this animal appear to have undergone any alteration.

13. The black fox [*Mustela pennanti*[48]], or, as it is termed in the neighborhood of Detroit, the fisher, is found in the woody country bordering on the coast. How it should have

[47] This account of the foxes is sufficient for satisfactory identification. The "large red fox of the plains" is certainly that representative of the common red fox which was called *Vulpes macrourus* by Baird, in Stansbury's Exp. Great Salt Lake, pub. June, 1852, p. 309, and *V. utah* by Audubon and Bachman, in Proc. Acad. Nat. Sci. Phila. V. pub. July, 1852, p. 114, and Quad. N. Am. III. 1854, p. 255, pl. cli. Both the common fox and the long-tailed have their parallel color-variations to cross, silver and black; and the silver fox noticed in a following paragraph (No. 14) is of course the same as the "large red fox," though it is nominally a species called *V. argentatus* (after Shaw, 1800). The kit-fox, *V. velox*, is entirely distinct from all the other American foxes, having in fact its nearest relative in the Asiatic corsac. The swift fox, as it is also called, is noticed on previous pages of this work, and is one of our authors' discoveries; but it did not receive a technical specific name till 1823, when it was called *Canis velox* by Say, Long's Exp. R. Mts. I. p. 487 (later *Vulpes velox* of Audubon and Bachman, Quad. N. Am. 1851, II. p. 13, pl. lii).

[48] The animal here described is not a fox at all, nor even belonging to the same family (*Canidæ*). It is a member of the family *Mustelidæ*, and its nearest relative is the marten or sable. It is a remarkable species, peculiar to North America, and had been known for many years before it was noticed by Lewis and Clark. It was originally named as *Mustela pennanti* by Erxleben, Syst. Anim. 1777, p. 479, and the following year was renamed *M. canadensis* by Schreber, Säugethiere, III. p. 492, pl. 144. But it had already been known and described, years before it acquired a technical designation, as the pekan (so Buffon, 1765). Pennant called it the fisher in his several works, 1771–1784, for some unexplained reason or from erroneous information, as it does not catch fish. We may also be permitted to doubt that raccoons are its usual food. The original description occupies Clark R 68, 69, and is easily recognized.

acquired this appellation it is difficult to imagine, as it certainly does not prey upon fish. These animals are extremely strong and active, and admirably expert in climbing; this they perform with the greatest ease, and bound from tree to tree in pursuit of the squirrel or raccoon, their most usual food. Their color is jetty black, excepting a small white spot upon (*p. 169*) the breast; the body is long, the legs are short, resembling those of the ordinary turn-spit dog. The tail is remarkably long, not differing in other particulars from that of the ordinary fox.

14. The silver fox [*Vulpes macrurus* var. *argentatus*[49]] is an animal very rare, even in the country he inhabits. We have seen nothing but the skins of this animal, and those were in the possession of the natives of the woody country below the Columbia falls, which makes us conjecture it to be an inhabitant of that country exclusively. From the skin it appeared to be of the size of the large red fox of the plains, resembling that animal in form, and particularly in the dimensions of the tail. The legs Captain Lewis conjectured to be somewhat larger. It has a long deep lead-colored fur, for foil [*sic*—read, or poil], intermixed with long hairs, either of a black or white color at the lower part [roots], but invariably white at the top [tips], forming a most beautiful silver-gray. Captain Lewis thought this the most beautiful of the whole species [genus], excepting one which he discovered on the Missouri near the natural walls.

15. The antelope [*Antilocapra americana* [50]] inhabits the

[49] The silver fox is described in Clark R 69, Feb. 21st, 1806. As already stated, this animal is simply a color-variety of one of the large red foxes. See a preceding note. In the above text, the words "for foil," are a misprint; the clause should read "fur, or poil," etc. Clark R 10 has: "a long fine deep *poil*, the *poil* is of a dark lead colour," etc. *Poil* is French, same word as Latin *pilus*, hair, fur, or, as we say, *pile* (nap, as of velvet, etc.). It used to be a common furriers' term, and often occurs in the codices.

[50] It is not a little singular that an animal so large and conspicuous as the antelope—one which, moreover, yielded in those years only to the buffalo itself in its great abundance, should not have been scientifically named and described when this book was originally published, in 1814. Lewis and Clark were not its discoverers nor first describers, as the animal had long before been mentioned

great plains of the Columbia; it resembles [is the same as] those found on the banks of the Missouri, and indeed in every part of the untimbered country; but they are by no means so abundant on this as on the other side of the Rocky mountains. The natives in this place make themselves robes of the skins, and preserve the hair entire. In the summer and autumn, when the salmon begin to decline, the majority of the natives leave the sides of the river, and reside in the open plains, to hunt the antelope, which they pursue on horseback and shoot with their arrows.

16. The sheep [that is, the mountain goat, *Haplocerus montanus*[51]] is found in many places, but mostly in the timbered parts of the Rocky mountains. They live in greater numbers on that chain of mountains which forms the commencement of the woody country on the coast and passes the Columbia between the falls and rapids. We have only seen the skins of these animals, which the natives dress with the wool, and the blankets which they manufacture from the (*p. 170*) wool. The animal from this evidence appears to

by the Spaniard Hernandez, and after him was treated by a long series of writers; among whom Umfreville, Le Raye, Pike, Gass, etc., shortly preceded L. and C. But the first technical name, *Antilope americana*, was imposed by George Ord in 1815 (Guthrie's Geog., 2d Am. ed. II. pp. 292, 308), and a second, *Antilocapra americana*, was bestowed by the same naturalist in 1818, in the Bulletin de la Société Philomathique, p. 146; in both cases upon material furnished by Lewis and Clark. The figure given in Doughty's Cabinet of Natural History, II. p. 49, pl. 5, in 1833, was from a specimen of Lewis and Clark's collecting, in Peale's museum at Philadelphia. Our authors may, therefore, be credited with first making the interesting animal well known to naturalists. They repeatedly notice it in the course of this work, where it is usually called " goat ": see pp. 34, 109, 116, 496, and *passim*. But it is not a goat of any sort, nor indeed is it an antelope in any proper sense, but alone constitutes a separate natural family, *Antilocapridæ*, intermediate in some respects between the *Bovidæ* (cattle, sheep, goats, and antelopes) and the *Cervidæ* (deer). It has hollow horns, like the bovine ruminants, yet these horns are forked, and also shed like the antlers of the *Cervidæ*—a singular fact, first established by Dr. C. A. Canfield of Monterey, Cala., Apr. 10th, 1858, but first published by A. D. Bartlett, P. Z. S., for 1865. There are many other peculiarities. The pronghorn or prongbuck has of late years become much restricted, both in numbers and in extent of distribution, and seems likely to share the fate of the buffalo. See Clark R 71, Feb. 22d, 1806.

[51] It is unfortunate that the authors call this animal " the sheep," when it is *not*

be of the size of our common sheep, and of a white color; the wool is fine on many parts of the body, but in length not equal to that of our domestic sheep. On the back, and particularly on the top of the head [read neck], this is intermixed with a considerable proportion of long straight hairs. From the Indian accounts these animals have erect pointed horns; one of our engagees informed us that he had seen them in the Black Hills, and that the horns were lunated like those of our domestic sheep [a mistake]. We have nevertheless too many proofs to admit a doubt of their existence in considerable numbers on the mountains near the coast. [See also text of April 10th, beyond.]

17. The beaver [*Castor canadensis*] of this country is large and fat; the flesh is very palatable, and at our table was a real luxury. On the 7th of January, 1806, our hunter [Drewyer] found a beaver in his traps, of which he made a bait for taking others. This bait will entice the beaver to the trap from as far as he can smell it, which may be fairly stated to be at the distance of a mile, as their sense of smelling is very acute. To prepare beaver bate [bait], the castor

a sheep, and also that they do not notice in this connection the bighorn, which *is* a sheep, and one with which, moreover, they had become perfectly familiar on the Upper Missouri, as they mention it repeatedly as the " bighorn " or " big-horned animal," and describe it unmistakably. (See pp. 34, 613.) The error of calling this goat a sheep led Mr. Ord to give it the technical name *Ovis montana*, when in 1815 he came to apply scientific designations to various animals procured or noticed by Lewis and Clark, in Guthrie's Geography, 2d Am. ed. II. pp. 292, 309. Our authors' description is clear and unquestionable; they are the actual discoverers and first describers of this remarkable animal, which I now recognize as a member of the nemorhedine group of ruminants, and as finding its nearest allies in the goral and related Asiatic forms. It was first placed in the goat genus, *Capra*, and called *C. columbiana*, by Desmarest, Dict. Class. III. p. 580; then *C. montana*, by Dr. R. Harlan, in 1825, in his Fauna Americana, p. 253. This was much better than calling it *Ovis montana* (the correct designation of the bighorn); but the peculiarities of the animal are so great that a separate genus *Aploceros* was formed for its reception by Hamilton Smith in 1827; and it has since been generally known to naturalists as *Haplocerus montanus* (with correction of the originally faulty form of the generic word), or *H. columbianus*. It is also now known as *Mazama montana*, after Rafinesque. A description occupies Clark R 72–74, Feb. 22d, 1806. See especially pp. 34, 613, 678, and notes there, for the goat; and for the bighorn, see pp. 214, 326, 327, 420.

or bark-stone is first gently pressed from the bladder-like bag
which contains it, into a phial of four ounces, with a large
mouth.   Five or six of these stones are thus taken, to which
must be added a nutmeg, 12 or 15 cloves, and 30 grains of
cinnamon, finely pulverized and stirred together, with as
much ardent spirits added to the composition as will reduce
the whole to the consistency of mustard. This must be
carefully corked, as it soon loses its efficacy if exposed to
open air.   The scent becomes much stronger in four or five
days after preparation, and, provided proper precaution is
exercised, will preserve its efficacy for months.   Any strong
aromatic spices will answer, their sole virtue being to give
variety and pungency to the scent of the bark-stone.   The
male beaver has six stones, two of which contain a substance
much like finely pulverized bark, of a pale yellow color, in
smell resembling tanners' oose [ooze]; these are called bark-
stones, or (*p. 171*) castors.   Two others, which like the bark-
stones resemble small bladders, contain pure strong oil of
a rank smell, and are called the oil-stones; the other two
are the testicles.   The bark-stones are two inches in length;
the others are somewhat smaller, of an oval form, and lie in
a bunch together, between the skin and the root of the tail,
with which they are closely connected and seem to communicate.   The female brings forth once in a year only, and
has sometimes two and sometimes four at a birth, which
usually happens in the latter end of May and the beginning
of June; at this time she is said to drive from the lodge
the male, which would otherwise destroy the young.   They
propagate like fowl, by the gut [*per anum*], and the male
has no other sexual distinction that we could discover.

   18. The common otter [*Lutra canadensis*] has already
been described, and this species does not differ from those
inhabiting the other parts of America.

   19. The sea-otter [*Enhydris marina*] resides only on the
seacoast, or in the neighborhood of salt-water.   When fully
grown he arrives at the size of a large mastiff dog.   The
ears and eyes [are remarkably small, Lewis J 90], particularly

the former, which are not an inch in length, thick, pointed, fleshy, and covered with short hair; the tail is ten inches long, thick at the point of insertion, and partially covered with a deep fur on the upper side ; the legs are very short; the [hind [52]] feet, which have five toes each, are broad, large, and webbed; the legs are covered with fur, the feet with short hair. The body of this animal is long, and of the same thickness throughout ; from the extremity of the tail to the nose it measures five feet. The color is a uniform dark brown ; but when in good order and season, perfectly black. This animal is unrivaled for the beauty, richness, and softness of the fur; the inner part of the fur, when opened, is lighter than the surface in its natural position ; intermixed with the fur are some black and shining hairs, which are rather longer, and add much to its beauty; the fur about the ears, nose, and eyes, in some of this species, presents a lighter color, sometimes a brown (*p. 172*). The young are often seen of a cream-colored white about the nose, eyes, and forehead, which are always much lighter than their other parts ; their fur is, however, much inferior to that of the full-grown otter.

20. The mink [*Putorius vison*] inhabits the woody country bordering on the coast, and does not differ in any point from those of the United States.

21. Seals [53] are found on this coast in great numbers, and

[52] Irrespective of the number of digits, the description in the text only applies to the hind feet, which are remarkably long, broad, and flat, like a seal's flippers. The fore feet are extremely small, like a cat's paws—in fact, the toes are so short, and so closely bound together, as to suggest a stump left after amputation. Likewise, what is said of the tail is not what the authors meant—which is, that the fur of the upper side is specially long. There is also an ellipsis in the text, which I supply from the codex, regarding the eyes and ears. " The natives called the infant otter *Spuck*, and the full grown, or such as had obtained a coat of good fur, *E-luck'-ke*," Lewis J 91. The sea-otter is also described Clark R 75-78, Feb. 23d, 1806.

[53] The account hardly suffices for the identification of any species. The pinnipeds which are known to occur on the Pacific coast, at or near the mouth of the Columbia, are several species of the two families, *Otariidæ* or eared seals, and *Phocidæ* or ordinary seals. Of the former there are : 1. The great *Eumeto-*

as far up the Columbia river as the Great Falls, but none have been discovered beyond them. The skins of such as Captain Lewis examined were covered with a short, coarse, stiff, and glossy hair of a reddish-brown color. This animal, when in the water, appeared of a black color, sometimes spotted with white. We believe that there are several species of this animal to be found in this country, but we could not procure a sufficient number to make the examination; the skins were precisely of the same kind as our countrymen employ in the manufacture of trunks.

22. The raccoon [*Procyon hernandezi?*] inhabits woody countries bordering on the coast, in considerable numbers. These are caught by the natives with snares or pitfalls, but they hold the skins in little or no estimation, and very seldom make them into robes.

22-27. The squirrels we have seen are:

22. The large gray squirrel [*Sciurus fossor* [54]]. This animal appears to be an inhabitant of a narrow tract of country, well covered with white-oak timber, on the upper side of the mountains just below Columbia Falls. This animal we have only found in those tracts which have been covered with

pias stelleri, or so-called sea-lion. 2. The medium-sized *Zalophus californianus*, a very well-known species, still common on the rocks at the entrance of the Bay of San Francisco, as well as on those off Monterey, and therefore familiar objects. Both of these are hair-seals. 3. The northern fur-seal, or sea-bear, *Callorhinus ursinus*, whose pelt is of such commercial value, for sealskin sacks and the like, that it has lately occasioned much diplomatic correspondence between the United States and the United Kingdom, respecting a *modus vivendi*, pending final arbitration of the dispute. Of the *Phocidæ* the only Columbian species is *Halicyon richardsi* of J. E. Gray, 1864, or *Phoca pealei* of T. Gill, 1866 ; but this alleged species has never been satisfactorily distinguished from the common harbor seal or sea-calf, *Phoca vitulina*. Seals are noted R 79, 80.

[54] As remarked by Professor Baird, it is singular that an animal described with such particularity as this squirrel was not scientifically named by those early authors, as Ord, Rafinesque, and Harlan, who imposed technical names upon other species of Lewis and Clark's. But the large gray squirrel seems to have been first named *Sciurus fossor* by T. R. Peale, in 1848, in his Zoölogy of the United States Exploring Expedition under Commander Charles Wilkes, U. S. N. In 1852 it was renamed *S. heermanni* by Dr. John L. LeConte, after Dr. A. L. Heerman (Pro. Acad. Nat. Sc. Philada. p. 140). See Clark R 85.

[such] timber, for in countries where pine is most abundant he does not appear. He is much superior in size to the common gray squirrel, and resembles in form, color, and size the fox-squirrel [*Sciurus cinereus*] of the Atlantic States. The tail exceeds the whole length of the body and head; the eyes are dark; the whiskers long and black; the back, sides, head, tail, and outward part of the legs are all of a blue-colored gray ; the breast, (*p. 173*) belly, and inner part of the body [limbs], are all of a pure white ; the hair is short, like that of the fox-squirrel, though [not] much finer, and intermixed with a portion of fur. The natives hold in high estimation the skin of this animal, which they use in forming their robes. He subsists on the acorn and filbert, which last grows in great abundance in the oak country.

23. The small gray squirrel [*Sciurus richardsoni*[55]] is common to every part of the Rocky mountains where timber abounds.   He differs from the small brown squirrel [*S. douglasi*] in color only.   The back, sides, neck, head, tail, and outer side of the legs are of a brownish lead-colored gray; the tail is slightly touched with a dark reddish color near the extremity of some of the hairs ; the throat, breast, belly, and inner parts of the legs are of the color of a tanner's ooze ; a narrow stripe of black commences behind each shoulder and enters longitudinally about three inches between the colors of the sides and belly.   Their habits are precisely those of the small brown squirrel, and like them they are extremely nimble and active.

24. There is also a species of squirrel, evidently distinct,

[55] This is obviously one of the *S. hudsonius* group ; but the question might be raised whether it be *S. richardsoni* or *S. fremonti*. It is mainly a question of locality, and this our authors state only in general terms.   Since, however, they crossed the habitat of the northern species rather than of the southern, it will be best to let the identification stand as I first made it in 1876.   This western representative of our familiar chickaree or red squirrel was noticed by Richardson, Fauna Boreali-Americana, I. p. 190 (1829), as *S. hudsonius* var. B, and subsequently named *S. richardsoni* by Dr. John Bachman, in the Proceedings of the Zoölogical Society of London for 1838, p. 100.   See Clark R 89.

which we have denominated the burrowing-squirrel [*Spermophilus columbianus* [56]]. He inhabits these plains, and somewhat resembles those found on the Missouri. He measures one foot and five inches in length, of which the tail comprises 2½ inches only; the neck and legs are short; the ears are likewise short, obtusely pointed, and lie close to the head, with the aperture larger than will generally be found among burrowing animals. The eyes are of a moderate size; the pupil is black, and the iris of a dark, sooty brown; the whiskers are full, long, and black. The teeth, and, indeed, the whole contour [read color—so Clark Q 121], resemble those of the squirrel. Each foot has five toes; the two inner ones of the fore feet are [*i. e.*, the inner one of each fore foot is]

[56] Notwithstanding that the authors' description of what they call their "burrowing-squirrel" in this place is one of the most elaborate and minute of the series, it has occasioned much confusion of synonymy and woeful misunderstanding. The original is Clark Q 120–124, May 27th, 1806; locality Quamash flats, on the Kooskooskee. The first author who took up this account was Mr. George Ord, who thought the animal was a marmot, and called it *Arctomys columbianus*, basing his species entirely upon Lewis and Clark. This he did in Guthrie's Geogr., 2d Am. ed. II. pp. 292 and 303, in 1815. Next, in 1817, that rattle-headed genius C. S. Rafinesque, thought he had discovered in Lewis and Clark's description of the toes or claws (badly worded and incomplete in the text, as shown by my square brackets in the text) a singularity which caused him to make a new genus and species of this animal, which he called *Anisonyx brachiura*, or the "short-tail unequal-claw," in the Amer. Monthly Mag. II. p. 45. Then Dr. Harlan (Fn. Amer. 1825, p. 304,) replaced the animal in the genus *Arctomys*, but adopted Rafinesque's specific designation respelled, giving the name *Arctomys brachyura*. Subsequently Audubon and Bachman (Quad. N. Amer. III. 1853, p. 32, pl. cvii) described and figured a certain specimen, in the Zoölogical Society of London, as *Arctomys lewisii*, thus dedicating a species to Captain Lewis.

In 1855, in the Proceedings of the Philadelphia Academy of Natural Sciences, p. 334, Professor S. F. Baird described a kind of prairie-dog or species of *Cynomys*, from west of the Rocky mountains, as *C. gunnisonii*, after the lamented Lieutenant Gunnison, who was massacred with his party during the exploration of one of the routes for the then future Pacific Railroad. Later, in 1857, Professor Baird discussed the relationships of his *Cynomys gunnisonii* with the burrowing-squirrel of Lewis and Clark, and brought the *Arctomys lewisii* of Audubon and Bachman into the question.

In 1874, when my friend Professor J. A. Allen, now the distinguished curator of mammals and birds in the American Museum of Natural History of New York, prepared his first review of the *Sciuridæ* for the Proceedings of the Boston

remarkably short, and equipped with blunt nails ; the remaining toes [claws] on the front feet are long, black, slightly curved, and sharply pointed [; the outer and inner toes of the hind feet are not short, yet they are by no means as long as the three toes in the center of the foot, which are remarkably long, but the nails are not as long as those of the fore feet, though of the same form and color, Clark Q 121, 122]. The hair of the tail is thickly inserted on the sides only, which gives (*p. 174*) it a flat appearance, and a long oval form ; the tips of the hairs forming the outer edges of the tail are white, the other extremity [*i. e.*, the bases of these hairs] of a fox-red ; the under part of the tail resembles an iron-gray ; the upper is of a reddish-brown ; the lower part of the jaws, the under part of the neck, [and the] legs and feet, from the body and belly downward, are of a light brick-red ;

Society of Natural History, he came to the conclusion that all the names above noted belonged to the same animal ; that this animal was the burrowing-squirrel now under discussion ; that it was a species of *Cynomys ;* and that, restoring Mr. Ord's specific name as prior to all others, its proper name was *Cynomys columbianus.* This conclusion I adopted in my original commentary on Lewis and Clark, in the Bulletin of the U. S. Geol. and Geogr. Surv. of the Territories, 2d ser., No. 6, Feb. 1876, p. 436.

But it seems that we were both wrong, and that Baird had been on a wrong scent. For *this* burrowing-squirrel is not a prairie-dog of any species, but a true spermophile, belonging to the genus *Spermophilus.* It is identical with the animal described by Sir John Richardson (Fn. Bor.-Am. I. 1829, p. 161) under the name of *Arctomys (Spermophilus) parryi* var. *β. erythrogluteia*, which name was later changed by Professor Allen (Monogr. *Rodentia* N. Am., 1877, p. 841) to *Spermophilus empetra* var. *erythroglutæus.* Applying the rules for the rectification of synonymy, the technical name of Lewis and Clark's burrowing-squirrel becomes *Spermophilus columbianus*, as given by Dr. C. H. Merriam in the Fauna published by the U. S. Agricultural Department, No. 5, 1891, pp. 39–42.

We must not overlook the fact, however, that Lewis and Clark speak of a "burrowing-squirrel" in earlier parts of their narrative, before they had got across the Rockies. That is certainly not the animal which is described in the present place, for this one does not inhabit the Missouri region. The spermophile which I found most abundant in the Upper Missouri region, especially about Milk river and the adjoining parts of British America, is *Spermophilus richardsoni*, which much resembles a prairie-dog in habits and general appearance, but is smaller and lighter colored. This is the actual implication of "burrowing-squirrel" as earlier used in this work. See the notes, pp. 271, 349, for this species; and pp. 271, 405, for another one.

the nose and eyes are of a darker shade of the same color ;
the upper part of the head, neck, and body are of a curious
brown-gray, with a slight tinge of brick-red ; the longer hairs
of these parts are of a reddish-white color at their extremities,
and falling together give this animal a speckled appearance.
These animals form in large companies, like those on the
Missouri, occupying with their burrows sometimes 200 acres
of land ; the burrows are separate, and each possesses, perhaps, ten or twelve of these inhabitants. There is a little
mound in front of the hole, formed of the earth thrown out
of the burrow, and frequently there are three or four distinct
holes forming one burrow, with these entrances around the
base of the little mound. These mounds, sometimes two feet
in height and four in diameter, are occupied as watch-towers
by the inhabitants of these little communities. The squirrels, one or more, are irregularly distributed on the tract they
thus occupy, at the distance of 10, 20, or sometimes from 30
to 40 yards. When anyone approaches they make a shrill,
whistling sound, somewhat resembling tweet, tweet, tweet—
the signal for their party to take the alarm and retire into
their intrenchments. They feed on the roots of grass, etc.

25. The small brown squirrel [*Sciurus douglasi*[57]] is a beau-

---

[57] This "small brown squirrel" is another of the *Sciurus hudsonius* or chickaree group, which ought to have been enumerated after No. 23. It is quite a
distinct form, evidently recognized as such by Lewis and Clark, but received no
technical name till years afterward. Then, however, it was four times in succession named by different authors, as four distinct species. The first name
dates 1838, when the Rev. Dr. John Bachman called this squirrel *Sciurus dou-
glassii*, in the Proceedings of the Zoölogical Society of London for that year,
p. 99. The same gentleman also called it *S. townsendii*, in the Journal of the
Philadelphia Academy of Sciences, VII. 1839, p. 63. In 1842 Mr. J. E. Gray
of the British Museum renamed it *S. belcheri*, in the Annals and Magazine of
Natural History, X. p. 263. Once more, Professor S. F. Baird, in the Proceedings of the Philadelphia Academy for 1855, p. 333, redescribed this squirrel as
S. suckleyi, dedicating it to my friend the late Dr. George Suckley, U. S. A.,
who, in connection with the late Mr. George Gibbs, did so much to develop the
natural history of Washington and Oregon, and took some of his specimens in
the very tracks of Lewis and Clark. Thus it appears that three different naturalists dedicated this innocent chickaree to four different persons, at a great sacrifice
of science to synonymy.

tiful little animal, about the size and form of the red squirrel [*Sciurus hudsonius*] of the eastern Atlantic States and
western lakes.   The tail is as long as the body and neck,
formed like that of the red squirrel; the eyes are black;
the whiskers long and black, but not abundant; the back,
sides, head, neck, and outer part of the legs are of a reddish-brown; the throat, breast, belly, and inner part of the
legs (*p. 175*) are of a pale red; the tail is a mixture of black
and fox-colored red, in which the black predominates in
the middle, and the other [color] on the edges and extremity; the hair of the body is about half an inch long, and
so fine and soft it has the appearance of fur; the hair of
the tail is coarser, and double in length.   This animal subsists chiefly on the seeds of various species of pine, and is
always found in the pine country.

26. The ground-squirrel [*Tamias townsendi* [58]] is found in
every part of this country, as well in the prairies as in the
woodlands; it is one of the few animals which we have seen
in every part of our journey [west of the Bitter-root moun-
tains], and differs in no respect [in some respects] from those
of the United States [*Tamias striatus*].

27. There is still another species, denominated by Captain
Lewis the barking-squirrel [*Cynomys ludovicianus* [59]], found
in the plains of the Missouri.   This animal commonly weighs
three pounds; the color is a uniform bright brick-red and
gray, the former predominating; the under sides of the neck
and belly are lighter than the other parts of the body; the
legs are short, and the breast and shoulders wide; the head

[58] The little animal here noted, but not described, is a chipmunk of the genus
Tamias, quite near though not exactly the same as the common hackee of the
United States, with which the authors consider it identical.   Though they give
no description, we may presume, from the locality, that *Tamias townsendi* is the
species they actually have in view, as this is common in the region whose animals
are particularly described in the present chapter.   For an entirely different
animal, called ground-squirrel earlier in this work, see notes, pp. 271, 405.

[59] This paragraph gives one of the best descriptions of the prairie-dog, *Cynomys ludovicianus*, now known to almost everyone from the frequent popular
accounts of travelers, if not by actual observation.   It has been several times

is stout and muscular, terminating more bluntly, wider and
flatter than that of the common squirrel; the ears are short,
and have the appearance of amputation; the jaw is furnished
with a pouch to contain food, not so large as that of the
common squirrel; the nose is armed with whiskers on each
side; a few long hairs are inserted on each jaw, and directly
over the eyes; the eye is small and black. Each foot has
five toes; the two outer ones [*i. e.*, the lateral toes on each
side of each foot] are much shorter than those [three which
are] in the center. The two inner [*i. e.*, the second and
third toe of each forefoot] toes of the forefeet are long, sharp,
and well adapted to digging and scratching. From the
extremity of the nose to the end of the tail this animal measures one foot and five inches, of which the tail occupies four
inches. Notwithstanding the clumsiness of his form, he is
remarkably active, and burrows in the ground with great
rapidity. These animals burrow and reside in their little
subterraneous villages like the burrowing-squirrel [*Spermophilus columbianus*]. To these apartments, though six or
eight usually associate (*p. 176*) together, there is but one
entrance. They are of great depth; Captain Lewis once
[Sept. 7th, 1804] pursued one to the depth of ten feet, but
did not reach the end of the burrow. They [the prairie-dogs]
occupy in this manner several hundred acres of ground; when
at rest their position is generally erect on their hinder feet
and rump; they sit with much confidence, and bark at the
intruder as he approaches, with a fretful and harmless intrepidity. The note resembles that of the little toy-dog; the
yelps are in quick and angry succession, attended by rapid

noticed in the work already, particularly at p. 111, under date of Sept. 7th, 1804,
when it seems to have first attracted the authors' observation by its singularity,
and they tried to drown one out of its hole (see note there). The animal was first
technically named in 1815, by Ord, who called it *Arctomys ludoviciana*. Rafinesque soon after instituted the genus *Cynomys*, and called it *C. socialis* and *C.
grisea*, making two species of one. Then, in 1820, it was named *Arctomys
missouriensis* by someone in Warden's Description of the U. S., V. p. 627, and
in 1825 another name, *Arctomys latrans*, was bestowed by Dr. R. Harlan, on
p. 306 of his Fauna Americana.

and convulsive motions, as if they [the animals] were determined to sally forth in defense of their freehold.   They feed
on the grass of their village, the limits of which they never
venture to exceed.   As soon as the frost commences, they
shut themselves up in their caverns, and continue [to hiber-
nate] until the spring opens.   The flesh of this animal is not
unpleasant to the taste.

28. Sewellel [*Haplodon rufus* [60]] is a name given by the
natives to a small animal found in the timbered country on
this coast.   It is more abundant in the neighborhood of the
Great Falls and rapids of the Columbia than on the coast
which we inhabit.   The natives make great use of the skins
of this animal in forming their robes, which they dress with
the fur on, and attach them together with sinews of the elk

[60] The sewellel is one of the most remarkable animals discovered by Lewis and
Clark.   Fortunately they gave it a name by which it could be called, and which
has passed into our language.   I put it in the Century Dictionary in the form in
which it here occurs, and which therefore may be accepted as the correct spelling.   It will be observed that Captain Lewis never saw the animal itself, but
only the robes made of its skin by the natives.   It seems by the later researches
of George Gibbs into the unspellable jargon of the Columbia River Indians, that
" sewellel " is their name for the robes, mistaken by Captain Lewis for the name
of the animal which furnishes the skin, and that the latter is " show'tl " in Nis-
qually.   The animal is about the size of the muskrat, and of much the same
color ; in fact, it greatly resembles a muskrat minus the long scaly tail and without webbed feet.   It is the typical representative of a family *Haplodontidæ*,
intermediate in some respects between the squirrel and the beaver families.   It
was first technically named *Anisonyx rufa* by Rafinesque (Amer. Monthly Mag.
II. 1817, p. 45).   In 1829 Sir John Richardson renamed it *Aplodontia leporina*
in the Zoölogical Journal, IV. p. 335 ; and this naturalist described and figured
it fully in the Fauna Boreali-Americana, 1829, p. 211, pl. 18 C, figs. 7 to 14.   Correcting the faulty orthography of this generic name, and coupling it with the
prior specific name given by Rafinesque, I called the animal *Haplodon rufus*,
in the Monographs of N. Am. *Rodentia*, 1877, p. 557, where its anatomy, as well
as external characters, is given at length, with all that was then known of its history.   This name is the one by which it has since been known to naturalists.   I
understand that the whites on the Columbia call it the " mountain boomer "—a
queer name, which I hear applied to the red squirrel (*Sciurus hudsonius*) by the
natives of the mountains of North Carolina, where I happen to be penning this
note (Aug. 9th, 1892).   There is a second species of sewellel in California, *Haplodon major*.   The *original* description is Clark R 92, Feb. 26th, 1806, where
sewellel is said to be the Chinook and Clatsop name.   See p. 776, note.

or deer. The skin, when dressed, is from 14 to 18 inches
long and from 7 to 9 in width. The tail is always separated
from the skin by the natives when making their robes [the
tail is a mere stump, which the natives would hardly take the
trouble to remove, and which Captain Lewis probably over-
looked]. This animal mounts a tree and burrows in the
ground, precisely like a squirrel. The ears are short, thin,
pointed, and covered with a fine short hair, of a uniform reddish-brown; at the bottom or base the long hairs, which
exceed the fur but little in length, as well as the fur itself,
are of a dark color next to the skin for two-thirds of their
length. Of this animal the fur and hair are very fine, short,
thickly set and silky; the ends of the fur and tips of the
hair are of a reddish-brown, and that color predominates in
the usual appearance of the animal. Captain (*p. 177*) Lewis
offered considerable rewards to the Indians, but was never
able to procure one of these animals alive.

29. The braro [61] [blaireau, *Taxidea americana*], so called
from the French engagees, appears to be an animal [not] of
the civet species, and much resembles the common badger
[of Europe, *Meles taxus*]. These animals inhabit the open
plains of the Columbia, sometimes those of the Missouri, and
are sometimes found in the woods. They burrow in hard
grounds with surprising ease and dexterity, and will cover
themselves in a very few moments. They have five long
fixed [non-retractile] nails on each foot; those on the fore
feet are much the longest, and one of those on each hind
foot is double, like that of the beaver. They weigh from 14
to 18 pounds; the body is long in proportion to its thickness; the fore legs are remarkably large and muscular,
formed like those of the turn-spit dog, and, as well as the
hind legs, are short. These animals are broad across the
shoulders and breast; the neck is short; the mouth is wide,
furnished with sharp, straight teeth [incisors] both above
and below, and with four sharp, straight-pointed tusks

[61] A long description of the " braro " or badger, *Taxidea americana*, occupies
Clark R 95–102, Feb. 26th, 1806. See note [31], p. 64.

[canines], two in the upper and two in the lower jaw.   The
eyes are black and small ; whiskers are placed in four points
on each side, near the nose and on the jaws near the opening of the mouth ; the ears are short, wide, and oppressed
[appressed], as if a part had been amputated.   The tail is
four inches in length, the hair of which is longest at the
point of junction with the body, growing shorter until it
ends in an acute point.   The hairs of the body are much
shorter [read longer, as Clark R 98] on the sides and rump
than those on any other part, which gives the body an apparent flatness, particularly when the animal rests upon his
belly ; the hair is upward of three inches in length, especially
on the rump, where it extends so far toward the point of the
tail that it conceals the shape of that part, and gives to the
whole of the hinder parts of the body the appearance of a
right-angled [acute-angled, Clark R 99] triangle, of which
the point of the tail forms the acute angle ; the small quantity of coarse fur intermixed with the hair is of a pale reddish-yellow.

(*p. 178*) 30. The rat[62] which inhabits the Rocky moun-

[62] This account of " the rat " makes neither sense nor syntax ; it is so badly
mangled from the codex that I can by no ingenuity so bracket the text so as to
make it read as intended by the authors.   I must therefore edit the codex, and
annotate *that*.   Clark R 102, 103, Feb. 26th, 1806, has a perfectly intelligible
account of *Neotoma cinerea* and *N. floridana*, but not a word of finding the
" ordinary house-rat " (*Mus decumanus*) anywhere on the Expedition.   It is as
follows : " The rat in the Rockey Mountain, on its waist [west] side, are like
those in the upper part of the Missouri in and near those mountains and have
the distinguishing trait of possessing a tail covered with hair like other parts of
the body.   One of those we caught at the White Bear Islands in the beginning of
July last [see note [17], p. 400] and [it] was there described.   I have seen the nest of
those in the neighbourhood [Fort Clatsop], but not the animal.   I think it most
probable that they are like those of the Atlantic states or at least [by which I
mean] the native rat [*Neotoma floridana*] of our country which have no [such
great development of] hair on the tail [as *N. cinerea* has].   This species [*N.
floridana :* see p. 11] we found on the Missouri as far up it as the woody
country extended ; it is as large as the common European house rat [*Mus decumanus*] or rather larger," etc.   This is as clear as a bell.   1. *Neotoma floridana*,
the native wood-rat, which Lewis and Clark knew in the Atlantic States as
different from the imported house-rat, and which they found extending up the

tains, like those on the borders of the Missouri in the neighborhood of the mountains, has the distinguishing trait of possessing a tail covered with hair like the other parts of the body [see p. 400]. These animals are probably of the same species [genus] with those of the Atlantic States, which have not this characteristic distinction; the ordinary house rat we found on the banks of the Missouri, as far up as the woody country extends, and the rat, such as has been described [on p. 11], Captain Lewis found in the State of Georgia, and also in Madison's cave in Virginia.

31. The mouse [63] which inhabits this country are [is not] precisely the same with those which inhabit the United States.

32. The mole.[64] This animal differs in no [in many a] respect from the species so common in the United States.

33. The panther [cougar, *Felis concolor* [65]] is found indifferently, either on the great plains of the Columbia, the west-

Missouri as far as the woody country—correct. 2. *Neotoma cinerea*, which they first found at the Great Falls, with a hairy tail almost as bushy as a squirrel's— correct again. 3. A rat about Fort Clatsop, which they never saw, but which they judged, from its nests, to be a species of *Neotoma*—quite right; for the bushy-tailed rat of the Pacific slope is *N. cinerea occidentalis*, a mere variety of No. 2, first described from Cooper's MSS. by Baird, from Shoalwater bay, Wash. (Proc. Acad. Nat. Sci. Phila. 1855, p. 335). 4. The house-rat, *Mus decumanus*—merely mentioned for the purpose of contrasting *N. floridana* with it.

[63] Useless to attempt any identification of "the mouse." Several species of native mice, of more than one genus, occur in this region, none of which is precisely the same as *Hesperomys leucopus*, or *Vesperimus americanus*, of the Atlantic States.

[64] The common mole of the Columbia is *Scapanus townsendi*, which differs not only specifically but also generically from that of the eastern parts of the United States, *Scalops aquaticus*. But the distinctions are mainly cranial and dental, and would therefore not be likely to strike the casual observer. This mole was first technically named *Scalops townsendii* by the Rev. Dr. John Bachman of South Carolina (Journ. Acad. Nat. Sci. Phila. VIII. 1839, p. 58), and dedicated to Mr. J. K. Townsend, who with Mr. Thomas Nuttall, the distinguished botanist, collected extensively of the fauna and flora of the Columbia, 1834–5.

[65] The "panther," *Felis concolor*, whose name is often corrupted by mountaineers into "painter," would have been better called cougar or puma, both of which are native South American names exclusively pertinent to this species, while the panther is the same as the leopard, an old-world spotted cat of large

ern side of the Rocky mountains, or the coast of the Pacific. He is the same animal that is so well known on the Atlantic coast, and most commonly found on the frontiers or unsettled parts of our country. He is very seldom found; and when found, so wary that it is difficult to reach him with a musket.

34. The hare [*Lepus campestris*[66]] on this side of the Rocky mountains inhabits the great plains of the Columbia. Eastward of those mountains they inhabit the plains of the Missouri. They weigh from 7 to 11 pounds. The eye is large and prominent; the pupil is of a deep sea-green, occupying one-third of the diameter of the eye; the iris is of a bright yellowish and silver color; the ears are placed far back and very near each other, which the animal can, with surprising ease and quickness, dilate and throw forward, or contract and hold upon his back, at pleasure. The head, neck, back, shoulders, thighs, and outer part of the legs are of a lead color; the sides, as they approach the belly, become gradually more white; the belly, breast, and inner part of the legs and thighs are white, with a light shade of (*p. 179*) lead color; the tail is round and bluntly pointed,

size, found in no part of America. Our cougar is whole-colored, and somewhat resembles a small lioness; it is hence often known in the West as the mountain lion. Clark R 103, Feb. 27th, 1806.

[66] The large hare thus described (Clark R 104-110, Feb. 28th, 1806), is one of several species called "jack-rabbits" and "jackass-rabbits" in the West, where they abound, and are conspicuous by reason of their size and the great length of their ears and limbs. This species is *Lepus campestris*, which turns white in winter, and is the characteristic form in Dakota, Montana, etc. It was originally described by our authors, but wrongly treated by Dr. R. Harlan, in his Fauna Americana, 1825, p. 310, as a mere variety of the American varying hare, *L. virginianus*. Dr. Richardson also considered it the same (Fn. Bor.-Am. I. 1829, p. 224). It was first described as distinct by Dr. Bachman, in the Journal of the Philadelphia Academy, VII. 1837, p. 340, where it is named as above. Two years afterward the same gentleman renamed it *L. townsendii*, in Vol. VIII. of the same Journal, and gave a figure (pl. 2).

In crossing the mountains Lewis and Clark no doubt met with that variety of the varying hare which is now known to naturalists as *Lepus americanus washingtonianus;* but if so they did not distinguish it from the foregoing, though it is quite a different species.

covered with white, soft, fine fur, not quite so long as on the other parts of the body; the body is covered with a deep, fine, soft, close fur. The colors here described are those which the animal assumes from the middle of April to the middle of November; the rest of the year he is pure white, except the black and reddish-brown of the ears, which never change. A few reddish-brown spots are sometimes intermixed with the white at this season [February 26th, 1806], on the head and the upper part of the neck and shoulders. The body of the animal is smaller and longer, in proportion to its height, than the rabbit's; when he runs, he conveys his tail straight behind in the direction of his body; he appears to run and bound with surprising agility and ease; he is extremely fleet, and never burrows or takes shelter in the ground when pursued. His teeth are like those of the rabbit [cottontail, *Lepus sylvaticus*], as is also his upper lip, which is divided as high as the nose. His food is grass and herbs; in winter he feeds much on the bark of several aromatic herbs growing on the plains. Captain Lewis measured the leaps of this animal, and found them commonly from 18 to 21 feet. They are generally found separate, and are never seen to associate in greater numbers than two or three.

35. The rabbit [*Lepus artemisia* [67]] is [not] the same with those of our own country; it is found indifferently, either in the prairies or the woodlands, but is not very abundant.

36. The polecat [skunk, *Mephitis mephitica* [68]] is also found

[67] The rabbit which Lewis and Clark state to be the same as the common molly-cottontail (*Lepus sylvaticus*) of the United States is the sage-rabbit (*L. artemisia*), which abounds in the sage-brush regions of the West. But their mistake is very natural and pardonable, as the two differ so little that naturalists often discuss whether they are really different species, or only varieties of the same species. Like several other hares or rabbits of the West, this one was first named by Dr. Bachman, in the Journal above cited, VII. p. 345, pl. 22 (1837), where it is named *L. nuttallii*, after Thomas Nuttall; and was renamed by him *L. artemisia* in the succeeding volume of that Journal, p. 94 (1839). Clark R 110.

[68] The animal called polecat, here and elsewhere in this work, is the common skunk, *Mephitis mephitica;* but a skunk by any other name would smell the

in every part of this country.   They are very abundant on some parts of the Columbia, particularly in the neighborhood of the Great Falls and narrows of that river, where they live in the cliffs along the river, and feed on the offal of the Indian fisheries.   They are of the same species as those found in the other parts of North America.

The birds [69] which we have seen between the Rocky mountains and the Pacific may be divided into two classes, the terrestrial and the aquatic.   In the former class are to be arranged :

(*p. 180*) 1. The [sharp-tailed] grouse or prairie-hen [*Pediocætes columbianus*].   This is peculiarly an inhabitant of the great plains of the Columbia, and does not differ from those of the upper portion of the Missouri.   The tail is pointed, the feathers in the center being much longer than those on the sides.   This species differs essentially in the formation of the plumage from those [pinnated grouse, *Tympanuchus americanus*] of the Illinois, which have their tales [tails] composed of feathers of an equal length.   In the winter season this bird is booted to the first joint of the toes; the toes are curiously bordered on their lower edges with narrow hard scales, which are placed very close to each other, and extend horizontally about one-eighth of an inch on each side of the toes, adding much to the broadness of the feet—a security which bounteous nature has furnished them for passing over the snows with more ease ; and what is very remarkable, in the summer season these scales drop from the feet. This bird has four toes on each foot.   The color is a mixture of dark brown, reddish- and yellowish-brown, with white confusedly mixed.   In this assemblage of colors the reddish-brown prevails most on the upper parts of the body, wings, and tail, and the white on the belly and the lower parts of

same.   The misnomer is a very common one.   The polecat, properly so called, is a European animal, not found in America, and a species of another genus, *Putorius fœtidus*.   A still more misleading designation of the skunk is that of " Alaska sable," by which its manufactured pelts are known to commerce.   Clark R 110.

[69] Clark R 111, Fort Clatsop, March 1st, 1806.

the breast and tail.   These birds associate in large flocks in autumn and winter, and even in summer are seen in companies of five or six.   They feed on insects, grass, and leaves of various shrubs in the plains, and on the seeds of several species of speth [70] and wild rye, which grow in richer soils. In winter their food consists of the buds of the willow and cottonwood, and native berries.

2. The cock of the plains [sage-grouse, *Centrocercus urophasianus* [71]] is found on the plains of the Columbia in great abundance, from the entrance of the southeast fork of the Columbia to that of Clark's river.   It is about 2¾ inches the size of our ordinary turkey. [72]   The beak is large, short,

[70] *Sic*—read spilt.   The description of the bird occupies Clark R 111–114, and on p. 114 we read: ". . . seeds of several species of spilts and wild rie."   Spilt or spelt is properly a kind of cultivated wheat, *Triticum spelta*, of a different species or variety from *T. sativum* (*vulgare*).   What plant Clark actually had in view cannot be said.   The wild rye mentioned is presumably a species of *Elymus*.   The account of the bird is excellent ; it furnished the original basis of *Phasianus columbianus*, Ord, Guthrie's Geogr., 2d. Am. ed. II. 1815, p. 317, whence *Pediocætes columbianus* of D. G. Elliot, Proc. Acad. Nat. Sci. Philada. 1862, p. 403, and *Pedioecetes phasianellus* var. *columbianus* of Coues, Birds N.W. 1874, p. 40, which see for the relationships of the U. S. form to that of Arctic America, named by Linnæus *Tetrao phasianellus* (after G. Edwards' pl. 117), and by Suckley *P. kennicottii*.   The question whether the Columbian bird is a species or a subspecies is still discussed : but is immaterial to the positive identification of L. and C.'s grouse here described, and already frequently mentioned on these pages.   Clark's remark about the shedding of the fringes of the toes is an acute observation.   Various other birds moult such horny appendages ; some even shed the whole horny case of the beak periodically.   Some mammals (lemmings) similarly drop overgrown parts of their claws.

[71] Another notable discovery of L. and C., already noticed in these pages, now formally described ; basis of *Tetrao urophasianus*, Bonaparte, Zoöl. Journ. III. 1828, p. 214, and Am. Orn. III. 1830, p. 212, pl. 21, fig. 2 ; also, type of genus *Centrocercus*, Swainson, Fn. Bor.-Am. II. 1831, p. 358, with pl. col'd. lviii, the most accurate ever published.   The designation "cock of the plains" still holds ; and, as the Prince remarked, forms an excellent antithesis to "cock of the woods," by which name the European capercaillie, *Tetrao urogallus*, is commonly known.   The orig. descr. occupies Clark R 115–120 ; the remark about the gizzard or "maw" is a close and correct observation.

[72] A blunder of the types : read, "about two-thirds the size of a turkey," Clark R 116.

covered [feathered], and convex, the upper exceeding the
lower chop; the nostrils are large, and the back [beak is]
black; the color is a uniform mixture of a dark brown, resembling the dove's, and a reddish- and yellowish- (*p. 181*)
brown, with some small black specks. In this mixture the
dark brown prevails, and has a slight cast of the dove-color;
the wider side [inner webs] of the large feathers of the wings
are of a dark brown only. The tail is composed of 19 [20]
feathers; that [pair which is] inserted in the center is the
longest; the remaining nine on each side gradually diminish.
The tail, when folded, comes to a very sharp point, and
appears proportionately long, when compared with the other
parts of the body. In the act of flying, the tail resembles
that of the wild pigeon [*Ectopistes migratorius*], although
the motion of the wings is much like that of the pheasant
[ruffed grouse] and [other] grouse. This bird has four toes
on each foot, of which the hindmost is the shortest; the
leg is covered with feathers to about half the distance
between the knee [heel] and foot [bases of the toes]. When
the wing is expanded there are wide openings between its
[primary] feathers, the plumage [their webs] being too narrow to fill up the vacancy; the wings are short in comparison with those of the grouse or pheasant. The habits of this
bird resemble those of the [sharp-tailed] grouse, excepting
that his food is the leaf and buds of the pulpy-leaved
thorn [greasewood, *Sarcobatus vermiculatus ;* but sage-brush
(species of *Artemisia*) probably meant]. Captain Lewis did
not remember to have seen this bird but in the neighborhood of that shrub, which [but] they sometimes feed on the
prickly-pear. The gizzard is large, much less compressed
and muscular than in most fowls, and perfectly resembles
a maw. When this bird flies he utters a cackling sound,
not unlike that of the dunghill fowl. The flesh of the
cock of the plains is dark, and only tolerable in point of
flavor, being not so palatable as that of either the pheasant or grouse. The feathers about the head [neck] are
pointed and stiff; short, fine, and stiff about the ears; at

the base of the beak several hairs are to be seen. This bird is invariably found in the plains.

3–5. The pheasant:[73] of which we distinguish the large black and white pheasant; the small speckled pheasant; the small brown pheasant.

3. The large black and white pheasant [adult male of *Dendragapus franklini*[74]] differs but little from those of the United States; the brown is rather brighter and has a more reddish tint. This bird has 18 [usually 16] (*p. 182*) feathers in the tail, of about six inches in length. He is also booted to the toes. The two tufts of long black feathers, [one] on each side of the neck, so common in the male of this species [meaning the ruffed grouse, *Bonasa umbellus*] inhabiting the United States, are no less [read, are not at all] observable in this pheasant. The feathers on the body are of a dark brown, tipped with white and black, in which mixture the black predominates; the white [ones] are irregularly intermixed with those of the black and dark brown in every part, but in greater proportion about the neck, breast, and

[73] No descriptions in L. and C. have teased naturalists more than those here given of the three "pheasants." As they stand in the text, they are an odd jumble, utterly irreconcilable with what we know of these birds. I could make nothing of them in 1876, and gave the matter up, supposing the authors had written from memory and confused several species (see my remarks, Bull. U. S. Geol. Surv., 2d. ser., No. 6, Feb. 8, 1876, p. 440). Now I am pleased but not surprised to find that the only trouble is a mistakenly edited text ; the codices are all right, as usual. Correcting the original print by Clark R the difficulty vanishes, and our authors' meaning stands out in bold relief. See the following notes.

[74] The description, as it stood, mixed up characters of the genus *Canace* (or *Dendragapus*) with those of *Bonasa*. As it now stands, emended, we clearly recognize another discovery made by Lewis and Clark. This bird was new to science in 1814 ; it was first technically named *Tetrao franklini* by David Douglas, who dedicated it to Sir John Franklin, in Linn. Trans. XVI. 1829, p. 139. He had rediscovered it in the mountains of Washington and Oregon. Bonaparte figured the male in Am. Orn. III. 1830, pl. xxx, as a variety of *Tetrao canadensis* ; but the best figure is Swainson's, pl. lxi. of the Fn. Bor.-Am. (1831, opp. p. 348). Clark R 121–124 is faithful and graphic—there is not a single clause of it irreconcilable with the characters of Franklin's grouse. It is true that he gives the tail-feathers as "18," the normal number being 16 ; but I

belly; this mixture makes this bird resemble much that kind of dunghill fowl which the housewives of our country call Domminicker [Dominique]. On the breast of some [specimens] of this species the white predominates. The [absences of] tufts on the neck leave a space about 2½ inches long and one inch in width [on each side], where no feathers grow, though concealed by the plumage connected with the higher and under [hind and front] parts of the neck; this space enables them to contract or dilate the feathers on the neck with more ease. The eye is dark; the beak is black, curved, somewhat pointed, and the upper exceeds the under chop; a narrow vermilion stripe runs above each eye, not [very] protuberant, but uneven with a number of minute rounded dots [papillæ]. This bird feeds on wild fruits, particularly the berry of the sacacommis, and exclusively resides in that portion of the Rocky mountains watered by the Columbia.

4. The small speckled pheasant [adult female, and young, of *Dendragapus franklini*[75]] resides in the same country with the foregoing, and differs only in size and color. He is half the size of the black and white pheasant, associates

know the number is exceptionally 18, or 14 (see my Key N. A. Birds, 1814, p. 578). The worst blunder of the text is in crediting the bird with tufts or tippets on the neck, like those of the ruffed grouse ; whereas Clark R 123 reads : " They are *not* furnished with tufts of long feathers on the neck as our pheasants [*Bonasa umbellus*] are," and then speaks of the bare spaces on the neck resulting from the absence of these ruffs ! Again, Clark R 122 says the marking of the bird " gives it very much the appearance of that kind of dunghill fowls which the henwives call *dominecker*"—a very pat simile, for the blotches and chains of white spots in the black and dark brown recall that breed of poultry. Once more, as to the locality : Clark R 121 says that " this species is peculiar to that [part] of the Rocky mountains watered by the Columbia river, at least we did not see them after leaving the mountains "; clearly meaning the Bitter-root and other ranges of Idaho, where Franklin's grouse is a common and the most characteristic species of its genus.

[75] Clearly so, by Clark R 124, 125, though the description is not so good as that of the male, and the sexual differences in size and color are somewhat exaggerated. But they are very striking, as well illustrated on Swainson's pl. lxii. representing the female (supposed to be a variety of the Canada grouse). Mention of the dark meat serves to clinch the case, as in all the species of *Bonasa* the flesh is white.

in much larger flocks, and is very gentle. The black is more predominant, and the dark brown feathers are less frequent in this than in the larger species; the mixture of white is more general on every part. This bird is smaller than our pheasant, and the body is more round. The flesh of both this species [and the preceding] is dark, and, with our means of cooking, not well flavored. [Clark R 124.]

5. The small brown pheasant [Oregon or red ruffed grouse, *Bonasa umbellus* **fuscus**[76]] is an inhabitant of the same country, and is of the same size and shape as the speckled (*p. 183*) pheasant, which he likewise resembles in his habits. The stripe above the eye in this species is scarcely perceptible ; it is, when closely examined, of a yellow or orange color, instead of the vermilion of the other species. The color is a uniform mixture of dark yellowish-brown with a slight aspersion of brownish-white on the breast, belly, and feathers underneath the tail ; the whole appearance has much the resemblance of the common quail [*Ortyx virginiana*]. This bird is also booted to the toes. The flesh of this is preferable to the other two [and that of the breast is as white as that of the Atlantic Coast, *i. e.*, of the ruffed grouse, *Bonasa umbellus*, Clark R 127].

6. The buzzard [Californian vulture, *Pseudogryphus californianus*] is, we believe, the largest bird of North America. One which was taken by our hunters (*i. e.*, Shannon) was not in good condition, yet the weight was 25 pounds.   Between

---

[76] No question in this case ; identification absolute, and consequently requiring a rectification of the synonymy of that variety of the ruffed grouse commonly called *Bonasa umbellus sabinei*. For L. and C. are the discoverers and first describers of the Oregon ruffed grouse ; and on the present paragraph was exclusively based the *Tetrao fusca* of Ord, Guthrie's Geog., 2d Am. ed. 1815, II. p. 317. As I remarked in 1876, there was nothing in the original account which forbade us to suppose it intended for this bird ; though in the then uncertainty regarding L. & C.'s three "pheasants" I did not venture upon an identification of any of them. Now that all doubt has been removed by examination of the codices, Ord's name must take its rightful priority ; and this grouse become known as *Bonasa umbellus* **fuscus** (Ord) Coues. (Mr. David Douglas did not describe his *Tetrao sabini* till 1829, in Trans. Linn. Soc. XVI. p. 137 : see my Birds N. W. 1874, p. 421.)

the extremities of the wings the bird measured 9 feet 2 inches; from the extremity of the beak to the toes, 3 feet 9½ inches; from the hip to the toes, 2 feet; the circumference of the head was 9¾ inches; that of the neck 7½ inches; that of the body inclusive of [read exclusive of the wings, Clark P 122] 2 feet 3 inches; the diameter of the eye 4½ tenths of an inch [note ³³, p. 712]. The iris is of a pale scarlet red, and the pupil of a deep sea-green. The head and part of the neck are uncovered by feathers; the tail is composed of 12 feathers of equal lengths, each of the length of 14 inches; the legs are uncovered and not entirely smooth. The toes are four in number, three forward, and that in the center much the longest; the fourth is short, inserted near the inner of the three other toes, and rather projecting forward. The thigh [leg] is covered with feathers as low as the knee [heel]; the tops or upper parts of the toes are imbricated with broad scales, lying transversely; the nails are black, short, and bluntly pointed. The under side of the wing is covered with white down and feathers; a white stripe about two inches in width marks the outer part of the wing, embracing the lower points of the plumage covering the joints of the wing [*i. e.*, tips of the wing-coverts]; the remainder [of the plumage] is of a deep black. The skin of the beak and head to the joining (*p. 184*) of the neck is of a pale orange color; the other part, destitute of plumage, is of a light flesh-color. It is not known that this bird preys upon living animals; we have seen him feeding on the remains of the whale and other fish thrown upon the coast by the violence of the waves. This bird was not seen by any of the party until we had descended the Columbia river below the Great Falls. He is believed to be of the vulture genus, although the bird lacks some of the characteristics, particularly the hair on the neck and the plumage on the legs [of certain old world vultures. Above description in Clark P 122–124].

7. The [Oregon] robin [*Hesperocichla nævia*] is an inhabitant of the Rocky mountains. The beak is smooth, black, and convex; the upper chop exceeds the other in length,

and a few small black hairs garnish the sides of its base ; the eye " is of a uniform deep sea-green color ; the legs [tarsi], feet [toes], and talons [claws], are [not] white, of which the front one [toe], including the talon, is of the same length as the leg ; these [claws] are slightly imbricated, curved, and sharply pointed. The crown, from the beak to the neck, embracing more than half the circumference of the neck, the back, and tail, are all of a dark bluish-brown ; the two outer feathers of the tail are dashed with white near their tips, imperceptible when the tail is folded ; a fine black forms the ground of the wings ; two stripes of the same color pass on either side of the head from the base of the beak to the junction, and embrace the eye to its upper edge ; a third stripe of the same color passes from the side of the neck to the tip [carpal angle] of the wings and across the croop [breast], in the form of a gorget ; the throat, neck, breast, and belly are of a fine brick-red, tinged with yellow ; a narrow stripe of this color commences just above the center of each eye and extends backward to the neck till it comes in contact with the black stripe before mentioned, to which it seems to answer as a border ; the feathers forming the first and second ranges of the coverts of the two joints of the wing next to the body are beautifully tipped with this brick-red, as is also each large feather of the wing, on the short side [outer webs] of its plumage [primaries]. (*p. 185*) This beautiful little bird feeds on berries. The robin is an inhabitant exclusively of the woody country ; we have never heard its note, which the coldness of the season may perhaps account for.

The leather-winged bat, so common to the United States, likewise inhabits this side of the Rocky mountains. [A misplaced paragraph, duplicated beyond.]

8. The crow [*Corvus caurinus*] and [9. The] raven [*Corvus*

---

[77] It is a personal peculiarity of the writer of this chapter to discover " sea-green " in the eyes (pupils) of various birds, all of whose pupils are black ; and curiously also, he does not notice the green eyes (irides) of the cormorant described beyond.

carnivorus] is exactly the same in appearance and note as that on the Atlantic, except that it [the crow] is much smaller on the Columbia.

10–12. The hawks too of this coast do not [in all cases] differ from those of the United States.   We here see [10.] the large brown hawk [*Buteo borealis calurus* or *B. swainsoni*], [11.] the small or sparrow-hawk [*Falco sparverius*], and [12.] one of an intermediate size [*Circus hudsonius*], called in the United States the hen-hawk, which has a long tail and blue wings, and is extremely fierce and rapid in its flight. The hawks, crows, and ravens are common to every part of this country, their nests being scattered on the high cliffs, along the whole course of the Columbia and its southeastern branches.

13. The large blackbird [blue-headed grackle, *Scolecophagus cyanocephalus*] is [not] the same with those of our country, and is found everywhere in this country.

14. The large hooting-owl [*Bubo virginianus saturatus*] we saw only on the Kooskooskee under the Rocky mountains.   It is the same in form and size with the owl of the United States, though its colors, particularly the reddish-brown, seem deeper and brighter.

15–16. The turtle-dove [*Zenaidura carolinensis*] and the robin [*Merula migratoria*] (except the Columbian robin already described) are the same as those of the United States, and are found in the plains as well as in the common broken country.

17. The magpie [*Pica pica hudsonica*] is most commonly found in the open country, and resembles [is the same as] those of the Missouri, already described.

18–20. The large [pileated] woodpecker or laycock [logcock, *Ceophlœus pileatus*], the [red-shafted] lark-woodpecker [*Colaptes mexicanus*], and the common small [black and] white wood-pecker, with a red head [*Sphyropicus ruber*], are the inhabitants exclusively of the timbered lands, and [the first of these] differ[s] in no respect from birds of the same species in the United States.   [See also note to No. 28.]

(*p. 186*) 21. The lark [*Sturnella neglecta*], which is found in the plains only, and is not unlike what is called in Virginia the old-field lark [*S. magna*], is the same with those already described as seen on the Missouri.

22–23. The flycatcher is of two species.

22. The first is [the western winter-wren, *Anorthura hiemalis pacificus*] of a small body, of a reddish-brown color; the tail and neck are short, and the beak is pointed; some fine black specks are intermingled with the reddish-brown. This is of the same species with that which remains all winter in Virginia, where it is sometimes called the wren.

23. The second species has recently[78] returned, and emigrates during the winter. The colors of this bird are a yellowish-brown on the back, head, neck, wings, and tail; the breast and belly are of a yellowish-white; the tail is in the same proportion as that of the wren [?], but the bird itself is of a size smaller [larger?] than the wren; the beak is straight, pointed, convex, rather large at the base, and the chops are of equal length. The first species is smaller, and in fact the smallest bird which Captain Lewis had ever seen, excepting the humming-bird [*Trochilus colubris*.] Both of these species are found exclusively in the woody country.

24, 25. Corvus.[79] The blue crested [jay, *Cyanocitta stelleri* and *C. s. annectens*] and the small white-breasted [*Perisoreus*

[78] Clark R 132, date of March 4th. This is perhaps a flycatcher of the genus *Empidonax* ; but of what species we cannot conjecture.

[79] Two genera and more than two species of jays are here indicated. I. The blue jay, with a crest, of the Columbian coast region, is Steller's, *Cyanocitta stelleri*, in its typical form ; but as the text extends to the corresponding bird of the "Rocky" mountains, it brings in also the variety *annectens*. 2. The small white-breasted (misprinted "white-crested" in the M'Vickar ed. 1842) corvus might be taken for the Californian jay, *Aphelocoma californica*, which is blue, with white under parts, and no crest. But this species is not found in the piny country of the northern mountains to which the text refers. Hence, by exclusion, we discover that a species of *Perisoreus* is our "small white-breasted corvus." That one which the explorers found in the mountains of Idaho is *P. canadensis capitalis*, a variety of the familiar Canada jay, moose-bird, or whisky-jack. That which they found in the coast region is *P. obscurus*, technically distinct, but so little different from the other that it has usually been regarded as the same.

canadensis capitalis and *P. obscurus*] corvus are both natives of the piny country, and invariably found as well on the Rocky mountains as on this coast. They have already been described.

26, 27. The snipe. The common snipe [*Gallinago wilsoni* or *delicata*] of the marshes, and the common sand-snipe [*Tringoides macularius* or *Actitis macularia*] are of the same species as those so well known in the United States. They are by no means found in such abundance here as they are on the coast of the Atlantic.

The leathern-winged bat,[80] so familiar to the natives of the United States, is likewise found on this side of the Rocky mountains.

28. The [black and] white woodpecker[81] likewise frequents these regions, and reminds our party of their native country by his approaches. The head of this bird is of a deep red color, (*p. 187*) like that of the United States. We have conjectured that he has lately returned, as he does not abide in this country during the winter. The large [pileated] woodpecker [*Ceophlœus pileatus*], and the [red-shafted] lark-woodpecker [*Colaptes mexicanus*], which are found in this country, resemble those of the United States.

29. The black woodpecker [Lewis', *Asyndesmus torquatus*] is found in most parts of the Rocky mountains, as well as in

---

[80] This is a duplicated paragraph from p. 874, and very much out of place there and here alike, as a bat is not a bird. The case may simply be dropped, especially as the species of bat intended is not identifiable.

[81] No "white" woodpecker inhabits North America. There is a white-*headed* woodpecker (*Xenopicus albolarvatus*) in the Rocky mountains ; but the one above noticed is particularly said to have a deep red head. We must also observe that this whole paragraph is in substance a duplication of that on p. 875, where the same three woodpeckers (Nos. 18–20) are noticed. Here, therefore, as before, for "white," I read "black and white"; and from the further mention of the red head I identify the species as *Sphyropicus ruber*. This identification is strengthened by the mention of the migratory habit of the bird ; for another black and white woodpecker of this region, with the head partly red, is *Picus villosus harrisi*, a stationary bird. The only entirely black (blue-black) and white woodpecker with an entirely red head is our familiar *Melanerpes erythrocephalus*, which does not occur on the Columbia.

the western and southwestern mountains. He is about the size of the lark-woodpecker, or turtle-dove, though his wings are longer than the wings of either of those birds. The beak is one inch in length, black, curved at the base, and sharply pointed; the chops are the same in length [*i. e.*, the under mandible equals the upper mandible in length]; around the base of the beak, including the eye and a small part of the throat, there is a fine crimson-red: the neck, as low down as the crook [croop—breast] in front, is of an iron-gray; the belly and breast present a curious mixture of white and blood-red, which has much the appearance of paint where the red predominates; the top of the head, the back, the sides, and the upper surface of the wings and tail exhibit the appearance of a glossy green, in a certain exposure to the light; the under sides of the wings and tail are of a sooty black; the tail is equipped with ten feathers [and one pair of rudimentary feathers], sharply pointed, those in the center the longest, being about 2½ inches in length; the tongue is barbed and pointed, of an elastic and cartilaginous substance; the eye is rather large, the pupil black, and the iris of a dark and yellowish-brown. The bird in its actions when flying resembles the small red-headed woodpecker [*Melanerpes erythrocephalus*] common to the United States, and likewise in its notes. The pointed tail renders essential service when the bird is sitting and retaining his resting position against the perpendicular side of a tree. The legs and feet are black, covered with wide imbricated scales; he has four toes on each foot, two in the rear and two in front, the nails of which are much curved and pointed remarkably sharp. He feeds on bugs and a variety of insects. [Clark Q 124–126, May 27th, 1806: see note [15], p. 428.]

(*p. 188*) 30. The calamut [calumet] eagle [*Aquila chrysaëtos*[82]] sometimes inhabits this side of the Rocky mountains. This information Captain Lewis derived from the natives, in

[82] Under date of March 11th, 1806, Clark Q 57–60 has this description of the "Callamet" eagle, which has been copied or compiled repeatedly, by various writers, with more or less pertinent comment; and the calumet eagle, thus

whose possession he had seen the plumage.   These are of
the same species with those of the Missouri, and are the
most beautiful of all the family of eagles in America.   The
colors are black and white, and beautifully variegated.   The
tail-feathers, so highly prized by the natives, are composed
of twelve broad feathers of unequal lengths, which are white,
except within two inches of their extremities, where they
immediately change to a jetty black ; the wings have each a
large circular white spot in the middle, which is only visible
when they are extended ; the body is variously marked with
black and white.   In form they resemble the bald eagle, but
they are rather smaller, and fly with much more rapidity.
This bird is feared by all his carnivorous competitors, which,
on his approach, leave the carcass instantly, on which they
had been feeding.   The female breeds in the most inaccessible parts of the mountains, where she makes her summer
residence, and descends to the plains only in the fall and
winter seasons.   The natives are at this season on the watch ;
and so highly is this plumage prized by the Mandans, Minnetarees, and Ricaras, that the tail-feathers of two of these
eagles will be purchased by the exchange of a good horse or
gun, and such accouterments.   Among the Great and Little
Osages, and those nations inhabiting the countries where the
bird is more rarely seen, the price is even double that above

famed, has often been supposed to be a distinct species.   Then, however, the
trouble was to find any North American eagle which answered to the description—the fact being that there is none.   Just criticism of the passage clears up
all doubts.   1st. The description is based primarily upon the common golden
eagle of North America, *Aquila chrysaëtos*.   2d. It is not accurate in all
particulars.   3d. It includes a venerable vague tradition of the king vulture,
Sarcorhamphus papa.   4th, and especially, any eagle whose tail-feathers suit an
Indian for decorative purposes is *ipso facto* a "calumet" eagle ; and the bald
eagle, *Haliaëtus leucocephalus*, when it is changing its tail from black to white,
answers the Indian's purpose as well as it does Lewis and Clark's description.
I have myself more than once seen forlorn and dilapidated bald eagles cooped in
Indian villages, having been taken from the nest to be reared and kept till
they should acquire the party-colored tail-feathers desired for ornamentation.
A "calumet eagle," zoölogically speaking, is as much of a myth as the famous
"wakon-bird"—though both be "great medicine."   See pp. 138, 173, and
notes there.

mentioned. With these feathers the natives decorate the stems of their sacred pipes or calumets, whence the name of the calumet eagle is derived. The Ricaras have domesti-cated this bird in many instances, for the purpose of obtain-ing its plumage. The natives, on every part of the conti-nent, who can procure the feathers, attach them to their own hair and the manes and tails of their favorite horses, by way of ornament. They also decorate their war-caps or bonnets with these feathers.

(*p. 189*) As to the aquatic birds of this country, we have to repeat the remark that, as we remained near the coast during the winter only, many birds common both in the summer and autumn might have retired from the cold, and been lost to our observation [Clark R 135]. We saw, how-ever, the large blue and brown herron [heron], the fishing-hawk, the blue-crested fisher, several species of gulls, the cormorant, two species of loons, brant of two [three: see on] kinds, geese, swan, and several species of ducks.

31. The large blue and brown herrons [herons, *Ardea hero-dias*], or cranes, as they are usually termed in the United States, are found on the Columbia below tide-water. They differ in no respect from the same species of bird in the United States.[83] The same may be observed of

32. The fishing-hawk [*Pandion haliaëtos carolinensis*], with the crown of the head white, and the back of a mealy white, and of

33. The blue-crested kingfisher [*Ceryle alcyon*], both of which are found everywhere on the Columbia and its tribu-tary waters; though the fishing-hawk is not abundant, par-ticularly in the mountains.

34–37. Of gulls [84] we have remarked four species on the

---

[83] " Large blue or brown herrons, or cranes " is an equivocal statement. As, however, the great blue heron, *Ardea herodias*, is very commonly miscalled " crane " in the United States; and as, moreover, Lewis and Clark usually call the brown crane, *Grus canadensis*, by its proper name, sand-hill crane, we may safely identify their bird as being the heron just said.

[84] Clark R 137, March 7th, 1806, has an account to be transcribed, as the Biddle text omits it: " There are 4 species of larus or Gull on this coast and

coast and the river, all [but one of them different from those which are] common to the United States.

38. The cormorant [*Phalacrocorax dilophus cincinnatus*] is, [im]properly speaking, a large black duck that feeds on fish. Captain Lewis could perceive no difference between this bird and those ducks [cormorants] which inhabit the Potomack and other rivers on the Atlantic coast. He never remembered to have seen those inhabiting the Atlantic States so high up the river as they have been found in this quarter. We first discovered the corvus [*sic*—read cormorant] on the Kooskooskee, at the entrance of Chopunnish river; they increased in numbers as we descended, and formed much the greatest portion of the water-fowl which we saw until we reached the Columbia at the entrance of the tides. They abound even here, but bear no proportion to the number of other water-fowl seen at this place.

39–40. The loon: there are two species of loons.

39. The speckled loon,[85] found on every part of the rivers

river. 1st. A small species about the size of a pigeon, white except some black spots about the head & a little brown on the but [for butt, meaning the carpal angle] of the wings [*i. e.*, *Chroicocephalus philadelphia*, No. 34]. 2nd species somewhat larger, of a light brown colour with a whiteish or mealy coloured back [*i. e.*, young *Larus glaucescens*, No. 35]. 3d species, the large Gray Gull or white Larus with a greyish brown black [back] and light grey belly and breast about the size of a well grown pullet or rather larger ; the wings are remarkably long in proportion to the size of the body and its under chap towards the extremity is more gibbous and protuberant than in either of the other species [*i. e.*, young *Larus occidentalis*, No. 36]. 4th. A white gull about the size of the second with a remarkable [formation] adjoining the head and at the base of the upper chap. Their [this] is an elevated orning [for awning, meaning the nasal tubes] of the same substance with the beak which forms the nostrils," etc. Then reference is made to Journal No. 10 (Codex J), where at this date is a pen-and-ink figure of the head and beak of the Pacific fulmar petrel, *Fulmarus glacialis glupischa*, making No. 37.

[85] This is a species of *Colymbus* or *Urinator*, but may be any one of three or four. The bird actually meant, however, is probably the Pacific diver, *C.* or *U. pacificus*, which is the commonest loon along the coast of Oregon and California ; it is a very near relative of the black-throated diver, *C.* or *U. arcticus*. The common loon of the United States is *C. torquatus* or *U. imber;* the red-throated is *C. septentrionalis* or *U. lumme*.

of this country. (*p. 190*) They are [nearly] of the same size, color, and form with those of the Atlantic coast.

40. The second species [of " loon " is the Western grebe, *Æchmophorus occidentalis*,[86] which] we found at the falls of the Columbia, and thence downward to the ocean. This bird is not more than half the size of the speckled loon ; the neck is long, slender, and white in front ; the plumage on the body and back of the head and neck is of a dun or ash color ; the breast and belly are white ; the beak is like that of the speckled loon ; and, like the loon, it cannot fly, but flutters along the surface of the water, or dives for security when pursued.

41–43. The brant are of three kinds : the white, the brown, and the pied.

41. The white brant [snow-goose, *Chen hyperboreus*[87]] are very common on the shores of the Pacific, particularly below the [tide-]water, where they remain in vast numbers during the winter. They feed, like the swan and geese, on the grass, roots, and seeds which grow in the marshes. This bird is about the size of the brown brant, or a third less than the common Canadian wild goose ; the head is rather larger and the beak, thicker than that of the wild goose, shorter and of much the same form, but of a [pinkish-] yellowish-white color, except the edges of the chops, which are frequently of a dark brown. The legs and feet are of the same

---

[86] This is the original and an easily recognizable description of this bird, which was not formally characterized till many years afterward, when, in 1858 (Birds N. Am. p. 894), Mr. G. N. Lawrence, of New York, named it *Podiceps occidentalis*. I instituted the genus *Æchmophorus* for its reception in 1862 (Proc. Acad. Nat. Sci. Phila. p. 229). Lewis and Clark's statement that neither loons nor grebes can fly is erroneous.

[87] Already repeatedly mentioned and unmistakably characterized in this work, as the explorers found it in various parts of the Missourian and Columbian watersheds. It had already been long known to science, having been originally described and figured in 1767 by Pallas (Spicilegia Zoölogica, pl. 65) and Zoographia Rosso-Americana, II. 1811, p. 227. The western species or variety is smaller than that of the Atlantic States, and was named *Anser albatus* by Cassin, Pr. Acad. Nat. Sci. Phila. 1856, p. 41, and 1861, p. 73. This is Pallas' bird, and the one L. and C. here have in view.

form [as those] of the goose, and of a pale flesh-color.
The tail is composed of 16 feathers of the same length as
those of the goose and brown brant are, and bearing about
the same proportion in point of [their relative] lengths.
The eye is of a dark color, and nothing remarkable in size.
The wings are larger, when compared with those of the
goose, but not so much so as in the brown brant.   The color
of the plumage is a pure uniform white, except the large
feathers at the extremity of the wings, which are black; the
large feathers at the first joint of the wing, next to the body,
are white.   The note of this bird differs essentially from
that of the goose; it more resembles that of the brown
brant, but is somewhat different; it is like the note of a
young domestic goose that has not perfectly attained its full
sound.   The flesh of this bird is exceedingly fine, preferable
to either the goose or brown brant.

(*p. 191*) 42. The brown brant [*Bernicla brenta*] are much
of the same color, form, and size as the white, only that
their wings are considerably longer and more pointed.
The plumage of the upper part of the body, neck, head,
and tail, is much the color of the Canadian goose, but
somewhat darker, in consequence of some dark feathers
irregularly scattered throughout; they have not the same
white on the neck and sides of the head as the goose, nor is
the neck darker than the body; like the goose, they have
some white feathers on the rump at the joining of the tail;
the back is dark, and the legs and feet also dark with
a greenish cast; the breast and belly are of a lighter color
than the back, and also irregularly intermixed with dark
brown and black feathers, which give it a pied appearance.
The flesh is darker and better than that of goose.   The
habits of these birds resemble those of the goose, with this
difference, that they do not remain in this climate in such
numbers during the winter as the other, and that they set
out earlier in the fall season on their return to the south,
and arrive later in the spring, than the goose.   There is
no difference between this bird and that called simply the

brant, so common on the Lakes and on the Ohio and Mississippi.

43. The pied brant [*Anser albifrons gambeli*] weigh about 8½ pounds; they differ from the ordinary pied [read brown] brant in their wings, which are neither so long nor so pointed. The base of the beak is for a little distance white, suddenly succeeded by a narrow line of dark brown; the remainder of the head, neck, back, wings, and tail, all except the tips of the feathers, are of a bluish-brown [like that] of the common wild goose; the breast and belly are white, with an irregular mixture of black feathers, which give those parts a pied appearance [whence this goose is commonly called "speckle-belly" in California]. From the legs back underneath the tail, and around its junction with the body above, the feathers are white. The tail is composed of 18 feathers, the longest in the center, measuring (*p. 192*) six inches with the barrel of the quill; those on the sides of the tail are something shorter, and bend with the extremities inward toward the center of the tail; the extremities of these feathers are white. The beak is of a light flesh-color; the legs and feet, which do not differ in structure from those of the goose or brant of other species, are of an orange color. The eye is small, the iris of a dark yellowish-brown, the pupil black. The note is much that of the common brown brant, from which in fact the birds are not to be distinguished at a distance, although they certainly are of a distinct species. The flesh is equally palatable with that of common brown brant. They do not remain here during the winter in such numbers as the bird above mentioned. This bird is here denominated the pied brant, on account of the near resemblance, and for want of another appellation.

44, 45. The geese [88] are either the large or small kinds.

[88] It is hardly necessary to say that the distinction Lewis and Clark make between "geese" and "brant" is not sound, because all brant are geese, though only some geese are brant. Besides, they do not adhere to their own classification, for their "pied brant" is a typical goose, and their geese, both

The large goose [*Bernicla canadensis occidentalis*] resembles our ordinary wild or Canadian goose; the small [*B. hutchinsi*] is rather less than the brant, which it resembles in the head and neck, where it is larger in proportion than that of the goose ; the beak is thicker and shorter ; the note like that of a tame goose. In all other points it resembles the large goose, with which it associates so frequently that it was some time before it was discovered to be of a distinct species.

46, 47. The swan [89] are of two kinds, the large and the small. The large swan [*Cygnus (Olor) buccinator*] is [not] the same common to the Atlantic States. The small [*Cygnus (Olor) columbianus*] differs only [mainly] from the large in size and in note ; it is about one-fourth less, and its note is entirely different. It cannot be justly imitated by the sound of letters ; it begins with a kind of whistling sound, and terminates in a round full note, louder at the end ; this note is [not] as loud as that of the large species ; whence it [this small swan] might be denominated the whistling swan ; its habits, color, and contour appear to be precisely those of the larger species. These birds were first found below the great narrows of the Columbia, near the Chilluckittequaw nation ; they were very abundant in this neighborhood, and

large and small, are more like brant than they are like ordinary geese, since they belong to the genus *Bernicla* and not to the genus *Anser*. " Brant" is a name which ought to be restricted to *Bernicla brenta*, and one or two closely related species, as the black brant of North America, *B. nigricans*, and the barnacle goose, *B. leucopsis*, of Europe. Our common wild goose, *B. canadensis*, is a member of the same genus *Bernicla;* besides which we have Hutchins' goose, *B. hutchinsi*, and some others of this group. Then the so-called white brant (a name etymologically as appropriate as would be the phrase " white coal") represents another genus, *Chen*. A third genus, represented by the several geese which Lewis and Clark describe, is *Anser* itself, to which belongs their " pied brant," which is the American white-fronted goose, *Anser albifrons gambeli*. To this genus belongs the common wild goose of Europe, *A. ferus*, with several others, among them the original stock of the domestic goose.

[89] By their difference in size and in voice our two species of swans are correctly discriminated by Lewis and Clark, who also give to the smaller species the name " whistling" swan, by which it has ever since been generally called, in distinction

remained with the party all winter; (*p. 193*) in number they exceeded those of the larger species in the proportion of five to one.

48–56. Of ducks, we enumerate many kinds: the duckin-mallard; the canvas-back duck; the red-headed fishing-duck; the black and white duck; the little brown duck [not further noticed]; the black duck; two species of divers; the blue-winged teal [; and another species, No. 56].

48. The duckinmallard [*Anas boscas*], or common large duck, which resembles the domestic duck, is very abundant, and found in every part of the river below the mountains; they remain here all winter, but during this season do not continue much above tide-water.

49. The canvas-back duck [*Aristonetta vallisneria*] is a most beautiful fowl, most delicious to the palate; it is found in considerable numbers in this neighborhood. It is of the same species with those of the Delaware, Susquehannah, and Potomack, where it is called the canvas-back duck, and in James' river [Virginia] it is known by the name of the shelled drake [sheldrake]. From this last mentioned river, it is said, however, that they have almost totally disappeared. To the epicure of those parts of the United States, where this game is in plenty, nothing need be said in praise of its exquisite

from the large " trumpeting " swan. By an editorial slip, however, they are made to say that the larger species (the trumpeter, named *Cygnus buccinator* by Sir John Richardson, Fn. Bor.-Am. II. 1831, p. 464) is the same as that common on the Atlantic coast; the fact being that it is their other species (the whistling swan) which is common on this coast. But this does not prejudice the main point of the nomenclatural case, namely, that in 1815 Mr. George Ord (Guthrie's Geog., 2d Am. ed. II. p. 319) based his *Anas* [*Cygnus*] *columbianus* exclusively upon the whistling swan of Lewis and Clark—that is, upon the *smaller* of the two species, which is also common on the Atlantic coast, and was named *Cygnus americanus* by Dr. Sharpless in Doughty's Cab. Nat. Hist. I. 1830, p. 185, pl. 16. The slip our editor made does not effect the case of Ord, to whose name *columbianus* I restored its rightful priority over *americanus* of Sharpless (see Birds N.W. 1874, p. 546). Our common American or whistling swan is therefore to be known as *Cygnus* (*Olor*) *columbianus*, while the trumpeter retains the specific designation bestowed by Richardson, and is called *Cygnus* (*Olor*) *buccinator*. Both these species belong to the subgenus *Olor*, having no knob on the beak, which is the most obvious distinction of *Olor* from *Cygnus* proper.

flavor, and those on the banks of the Columbia are equally delicious. We saw nothing of them until after we reached the marshy islands [at the mouth of the Columbia].

50. The red-headed fishing-duck [*Mergus serrator*] is common to every part of the river, was likewise found in the Rocky mountains, and was the only duck discovered in the waters of the Columbia within those mountains. They feed chiefly on craw-fish [species of *Cambarus*, perhaps *C. gambeli*], and are the same in every respect as those on the rivers and the mountains bordering on the Atlantic ocean.

51. The black and white duck [*Charitonetta albeola*], is small, a size larger than the teal. The male is beautifully variegated with black and white ; the white occupies the sides of the head, the breast, back, tail, feathers of the wings, two tufts of feathers which cover the upper part of the wings when folded, and likewise the neck and head ; the female is darker. This is believed to be the same species of duck (*p. 194*) common to the Atlantic coast, called the butter-box. The beak is wide and short, and, as well as the legs, of a dark color ; the flesh is extremely well flavored. In form it [this duck] resembles the duckinmallard, though not more than half the size of that bird. It generally resorts to grassy marshes, and feeds on grass-seeds, as well as roots.

52. The black duck [coot, *Fulica americana*] is about the size of the blue-winged teal ; the color is a dusky black ; the breast and belly are somewhat lighter, and of a dusky brown. The legs stand longitudinally with the body, and the bird, when on shore, stands very erect ; the legs and feet are of a dark brown. It has four toes on each foot, [including] a short one at the heel ; the long toes are in front, unconnected with the [by a] web ; the webs are attached to each side of the several joints of the toes, and divided by several sinews [sinus] at each joint, the web assuming in the intermediate part an elliptical form. The beak is about two inches long, straight, fluted on the sides, and tapering to a sharp point ; the upper chop is the longest, and bears on its base, at its junction with the head, a little conic protuberance of a

cartilaginous substance, being of a reddish-brown at the point; the beak is of an ivory color; the eye dark. These ducks [coots] usually associate in large flocks, are very noisy, and have a sharp, shrill whistle; they are fat and agreeably flavored; feed principally on moss and vegetable productions of the water; they are not exclusively confined to the water at all seasons. Captain Lewis has noticed them on many parts of the Ohio and Mississippi rivers.

53–54. The divers [grebes [90]] are the same with those of the United States. The smaller species have some white feathers about the rump, with no perceptible tail, and are very acute and quick in their motions; the body is of a reddish-brown; the beak sharp and somewhat curved, like that of the pheasant; the toes are not connected, but webbed [pinnate], like those of the black duck [coot]. The larger species are about the size of the teal, and can fly a short distance, which the smaller but seldom attempt; they have a short tail; their color is also a uniform (*p. 195*) brick reddish-brown; the beak is straight and pointed; the feet are of the same form with [those of] the other species; the legs remarkably thin and flat, one edge being in front. The food of both species is fish, and their flesh is unfit for use.

55. The blue-winged teal [*Querquedula discors*] is an excellent duck, and in all respects the same as those of the United States.

56. One of our hunters killed a duck [*Fuligula collaris* [91]]

---

[90] In this misplaced paragraph Lewis and Clark describe two species of grebes, neither with desirable precision. But identification may be made with some confidence. Since they notice a particular difference in the beaks of the two species, it is probable that the birds are of two genera; and the smaller bird, with a beak "like that of the pheasant," is doubtless of the genus *Podilymbus;* the species is therefore the common pied-billed grebe or dabchick of America, *Podilymbus podiceps.* As the other is said to be larger, with a straight pointed beak, it is probably the red-necked grebe, *Podiceps* (or *Colymbus*) *holbœlli.* I formerly thought it might be meant for *Æchmophorus occidentalis*, but that species is fully accounted for at No. 40.

[91] Clark Q 81–83, Lewis K 10, Deer island, Mar. 28th, 1806. The printed description, though lengthy and minute, has hitherto proved a stumbling-block. The early commentators all blinked it, and I let it go for nothing in 1876. But

which appeared to be a male.   It was of a size less than the duckinmallard; the head, the neck as low as the croup, the back, tail, and coverts of the wings are all of a deep fine black, with a slight mixture of purple about the head and neck; the belly and breast are white; some long feathers which lie underneath the wings, and cover the thighs, are of a pale dove-color, with fine black specks; the large feathers of the wings are of a dove-color; the legs are dark; the feet are composed of four toes, of which three in front are connected by a web; the fourth is short and flat, and placed high on the heel behind the leg; the tail is composed of 14 short pointed feathers; the beak of this duck is remarkably wide, and two inches in length; the upper chop

the account in the codex is unmistakable.   This is the ring-necked scaup duck, whose beak is so remarkably colored, but whose neck does not always show the orange-brown ring.   L. and C. are again discoverers of a new species; for this duck was unknown to science in 1806.   It was first described as *Anas collaris* by Edw. Donovan, Nat. Hist. Brit. Birds, VI. 1809, and figured on his pl. cxlvii; next as *A. fuligula*, by Alex. Wilson, Am. Orn. VIII. 1814, p. 66, pl. lxvi; next as *A. rufitorques* by C. L. Bonaparte, Journ. Acad. Nat. Sci. Phila. III. 1824, p. 381.   By coupling Donovan's earliest specific name, *collaris*, with the proper generic term *Fuligula*, we have the present scientific designation of the interesting species—one which is widely distributed in North America, and has also been found in Europe.

Now glancing back over the botany and zoölogy of this most important but equally unlucky chapter—seeing some paragraphs duplicated—some misplaced— all in confusion—sentences mangled beyond recognition—clauses omitted—grammar defied—the clear sense of the codices often knocked senseless—seeing all this, so different from Mr. Biddle's usual handiwork, I suspect that here is where one Paul Allen, said on the title-page of the original edition to have "prepared for the press" this work, threw the ponderosity and opacity of his stupendous ignorance and incapacity.   Refer to note [17], p. 400, for explanation of the fact that Mr. Biddle systematically passed over the natural history matter of the codices, in expectation of Prof. Barton's work upon them.   I imagine that, disappointed in this, when he had finished his narrative and become absorbed in important political and financial affairs, he injudiciously allowed Paul Allen to try a bungler's hand at what remained to be done, with the result of trying our patience sorely.   No one has ever been able to discover what Paul Allen had to do with this book; we only know that his alleged "services" were secured by Mr. Biddle for $500.   Scape-goats come high, at that figure; but as this one was bought and paid for before 1814, he is entirely available in the light of this History, and may be turned to some account after all.

exceeds the under one, both in length and width, insomuch
that when the beak is closed, the under chop is entirely concealed by the upper; the tongue-indentures on the margins
of the chops are like those of the mallard; the nostrils are
large, longitudinal, and connected; a narrow stripe of white
garnishes the base of the upper [read under—Clark Q 82]
chop; this is succeeded by a pale sky-blue color, occupying
about an inch, which again is succeeded by a transverse stripe
of white, and the extremity is a fine black; the eye is moderately large, the pupil black, and [the iris] of a fine orange
color; the feathers on the crown of the head are larger than
those on the upper part of the neck and other parts of the
head, which gives it the appearance of being crested.

The fish which we have had an opportunity of seeing are:
the whale, porpoise, skait [skate], flounder, salmon, red char,
two species of salmon-trout, mountain or speckled trout,
bottlenose, anchovy, and sturgeon.[92]

(*p. 196*) 1. The whale [93] is sometimes pursued, harpooned,
and taken by the Indians, although it is much more frequently killed by running afoul of the rocks in violent
storms, and thrown on shore by the action of the wind and
tide. In either case, the Indians preserve and eat the blub-
ber and oil; the bone [baleen] they carefully extract and
expose to sale.

[92] Clark Q 61, date March 11th, 1806, has: " Beside the fish allready mentioned we have the following, viz the Whal Porpis Skaite flounder Salmon   red
charr two species of salmon trout Speckle trout, a species Simelar to One of
those noticed on the Missouri within the mountains called in the E. S. [Eastern
States] the bottle nose."

[93] In our day it seems odd to see the whale heading a list of fishes, with the porpoise too—both these being warm-blooded mammals. But our authors, if chal-
lenged, could have cited very high authority for this classification—even some
editions of the Systema Naturæ of Linnæus. I have left the two paragraphs
where I find them, with this remark by way of clearing my editorial skirts.
Lewis and Clark do not indicate any particular species of whale, though we see
that they had a whalebone-whale in view. We are therefore free to suppose the
notice to be inclusive of the *Balænidæ* and *Balænopteridæ* of the North Pacific,
of which there are several species, one of the most notable being the gray
whale, *Rhachianectes glaucus*, which, as its generic name implies, frequents the
coast and even the lagoons. See note [4], p. 750.

2. The porpoise [*Phocæna vomerina*] is common on this coast, and as far up the river as the water is brackish. The Indians sometimes gig them, and always eat their flesh when they can procure it.

3. The skait [skate,[94] *Raia inornata* or *R. binoculata*] is also common in salt-water; we saw several of them which had perished, and were thrown on shore by the tide.

4. The flounder[95] [*Pleuronectes* or *Platichthys stellatus*] is also well known here, and we have often seen them left on the beach after the departure of the tide. The Indians eat this fish, and think it very fine. These several species of fish are [not] the same with those on the Atlantic coast.

5, 6. The common salmon and the red char are the inhabitants of both the sea and rivers.[96]

5. The former [the quinnat, *Oncorhynchus chavicha*] are usually the largest, and weigh from 5 to 15 pounds. They extend into all the rivers and little creeks on this side of the continent, and to them the natives are much indebted for their subsistence. The body of the fish is from 2½ to 3 feet long, and proportionably broad; it is covered with imbricated scales of a moderate size, and [is variegated with irregular black spots on its sides and (Clark Q 64)] gills; the eye is large, the iris of a silvery color, the pupil black. The rostrum or nose extends beyond the under jaw; both

[94] Clark I 94, Jan. 7th, on the beach near the salt-works : " I saw a singular species of fish which I had never before seen. One of the men call this fish a Skaite, it is properly a Thornback." This is most probably *Raia inornata*. The large thornback ray of the N.W. coast, described as *R. cooperi* by Girard, P. R. R. Rep. X. 1859, p. 372 ; Suckley, *op. cit.* XII. pt. ii. 1860, p. 367, is the adult *R. binoculata*.

[95] Several genera and species of flounder or flatfish are found on this coast. That above named, as indicated by L. and C., is by far the largest and most important, as well as the one usually called " flounder." It attains a weight of 15 to 20 pounds, and alone constitutes half the catch of the Pacific coast flounders. (See Jordan and Goss, Rep. Comm. Fish, 1886, p. 297.)

[96] A pernicious activity of various misguided ichthyologists has resulted in making more than 30 nominal species, of several baseless genera, of Pacific coast *Salmonidæ*, all but five species of one genus of which are now allowed by judicious naturalists to lapse into innocuous desuetude, as the alleged specific characters have proved to be simply variations due to sex, age, season, and the

jaws are armed with a single series of long teeth, which are subulate and inflected near the extremities of the jaws, where they are also more closely arranged ; there are some sharp teeth of smaller size and some sharp points [*sic*, read and same shape, Clark Q 65] placed on the tongue, which is thick and fleshy. The fins of the back are two ; the first is placed nearer the head than the ventral fins, and has several rays ; the second [the adipose fin] is placed far back, near the tail, and has no rays. The flesh of this (*p. 197*) fish, when in order, is of a deep flesh-colored red, and of every shade from that to an orange yellow; when very meager it is almost white. The roes of this fish are in high estimation among the natives, who dry them in the sun, and preserve them for a great length of time; they are of the size of a small pea, nearly transparent, and of a reddish-yellow cast; they resemble very much, at a little distance, our common garden currants, but are more yellow. Both the fins and belly of this fish are sometimes red, particularly in the male.

6. The red char [blue-backed salmon, *Oncorhynchus nerka*] are rather broader, in proportion to their length, than the common salmon. The scales are also imbricated, but rather larger; the rostrum exceeds the under jaw more, and the teeth are neither so large nor so numerous as those of the

fresh or spent condition of the fish. The single genus is *Oncorhynchus*, whose five established species are : 1. *O. chavicha* or *quinnat*, the quinnat or king salmon, most properly so called, and *the* salmon of the Columbia, as always understood when no other is specified. It ranks easily first in commercial importance ; many millions of pounds' weight are anually taken on the Columbia alone. This is the "common salmon" of our text (No. 5). 2. *O. nerka*, the blue-backed salmon, of a silvery color, blue on the back, ranking second in commercial value. In the fall the males redden, and are known in the interior as the redfish. This is the "red char" of our text (No. 6). See note [2], p. 545, which would have been better placed on p. 493, as the salmon there mentioned was doubtless this species. 3. *O. kisutch*, the silver salmon. This is the "white salmon-trout" of our text (No. 7). 4. *O. keta*, the dog-salmon. 5. *O. gorbuscha*, the hump-backed salmon. Excepting the first, these are all rather small fishes of from three to six or eight pounds' weight ; but the quinnat averages over 20, and has been known to attain a weight of 100 pounds.

[quinnat] salmon. Some of these chars are almost entirely red on the belly and sides; others are much more white than the salmon, and none of them are variegated with the dark spots which mark the body of the other [the quinnat]; their flesh, roes, and all other particulars, with regard to their form, are those of the salmon.

7, 8. Of the salmon-trout we observe two species, differing only in color; they are seldom more than two feet in length, and narrow in proportion to their length, much more so than the salmon or red char. [7. *Oncorhynchus kisutch,* the silver-salmon.[97]] In the first species the jaws are nearly of the same length, and are furnished with a single series of small straight subulate teeth, neither so long nor as large as those of the salmon. The mouth is wide; the tongue is also furnished with some teeth; the fins are placed much like those of the salmon. At the Great Falls [of the Columbia] we found this fish of a silvery-white color on the belly and sides, and a light bluish-brown on the back and head. [8. *Salmo gairdneri,* the steelhead salmon trout.[98]] The second species is of a dark color on its back; its sides and belly are yellow, with transverse

[97] The accounts of the two species of "salmon-trout," one of the genus *Salmo* itself, and the other of *Oncorhynchus,* are so dovetailed together that they cannot be well disengaged in separate paragraphs without too much transposition. The paragraph is therefore left to stand as in the original text. There is no real ambiguity if the sentences are duly weighed; though I think that the sentence beginning "The Indians," etc., is an interpolation which belongs elsewhere. The white "salmon-trout" of the text (No. 7) is no other than the well-known silver salmon, *Oncorhynchus kisutch.* It is recognizably described in print; and it is *figured* unmistakably in Lewis J 133. See last and next note.

[98] Lewis and Clark's dark-colored salmon-trout (No. 8) was identified by Sir John Richardson with a fish taken by Dr. Gairdner from the Katpootl or Cathlapootl (now Lewis') river, and named *Salmo clarkii,* Fn. Bor.-Am. III. 1836, p. 224, in honor of Captain Clark, its original describer. The same author, in the Addenda on Fishes, p. 308, notes that his *S. clarkii* is probably the same fish as the ultai of new Caledonia. (See Suckley, P. R. R. Reps. XII. pt. ii. 1860, p. 344, where *S. clarkii* is treated as a distinct species.) The common steelhead is, however, specifically identical with Richardson's *S. gairdneri,* Fn. Bor.-Am. III. 1836, p. 221; and the latter name is now adopted.

stripes of dark brown; sometimes a little red is intermixed with these colors on the belly and sides toward the head. The eye, flesh, and roe are like those described of the salmon. The white species [No. 7], found below the falls, were in excellent order when the salmon were entirely out of season and (*p. 198*) not fit for use. They associate with the red char in little rivulets and creeks. The Indians say that the salmon begin to run early in May. This white salmon-trout is about 2 feet 8 inches long, and weighs 10 pounds. The eye is moderately large; the pupil black, with a small admixture of yellow; iris of a silvery white, a little turbid near its border with a yellowish-brown. The fins are small in proportion to the fish; they are bony, but not pointed, except the tail [caudal] and back [dorsal] fins, which are pointed a little; the prime back [first dorsal] fin and the ventral [anal] fin contain each 10 rays, those of the gills [pectorals] 13, that of the tail 12; the small [adipose] fin, placed near and above the tail, has no bony rays, but is a tough, flexible substance covered with smooth skin; it is thicker in proportion to its width than in the salmon. The tongue is thick and firm, beset on each border with small subulate teeth in a single series; the [jaw-] teeth and the mouth are as before described. Neither this fish nor the salmon is caught with the hook, nor do we know on what they feed.

9. The mountain or speckled trout [*Salmo purpuratus*] are found in the waters of the Columbia within the mountains; they are the same with those found in the upper part of the Missouri, [see note [20], p. 367] but are not so abundant in the Columbia as in that river. We never saw this fish below the mountains; but, from the transparency and coldness of the Kooskooskee, we should not doubt of its existence in that stream as low as its junction with the southeast branch [Lewis' river] of the Columbia.

10. The bottlenose is the same with that before mentioned [p. 458] on the Missouri, and is found exclusively within the mountains. [Perhaps *Catostomus longirostris*.]

11. The anchovy [*Thaleichthys pacificus*[99]], which the natives call olthen, is so delicate a fish that it soon becomes tainted unless pickled or smoked. The natives run a small stick through the gills and hang it up to dry in of the smoke their lodges, or kindle small fires under it for the purpose of drying. It needs no previous preparation of gutting, and will be cured in twenty-four hours. The natives do not appear to be very scrupulous about eating them when a little fetid.

[99] In the orig. ed. this paragraph on the "anchovy" appears on p. 201 of Vol. II., at the end of the chapter, separated from the rest of the fishes by the mollusks, reptiles, etc. I transpose it to its proper connection. If it were an anchovy, the species might be that described as *Engraulis mordax* by Girard, Proc. Acad. Nat. Sci. Phila. VII. 1854, pp. 138, 154, and P. R. R. Rep. X. 1859, p. 333; also treated by Suckley in the same Report, XII. pt. ii. 1860, p. 365 ; now known as *Stolephorus mordax*. But it is no anchovy ; *olthen* is the same word as *uthlecan* or *eulachon*, which is an entirely different fish—the candle-fish, *Thaleichthys pacificus*. It is surprising that no description is here given of this remarkable fish, which has been already mentioned in these pages, and is described and *figured* in the codices. The candlefish, so named from its fatness, is a small salmonoid related to and resembling the caplin (*Mallotus villosus*). It was unknown to science when discovered by L. and C.; it was first technically named *Salmo* (*Mallotus*) *pacificus* by Sir John Richardson in 1836 in the Fauna Boreali-Americana, and later described as *Thaleichthys stevensi* by Girard, P. R. R. Rep. X. 1859, p. 325, pl. lxxv. figs. 1–4 (as *Osmerus stevensi*): see also Suckley, *op. cit.* p. 348, and same plate. The original description occupies Clark R 80–84, Feb. 24th, 1806, as follows : "Sturgeon and a Species of small fish which now begin to run, and are taken in great quantities in the Columbia river, about 40 miles above us by means of skiming or scooping nets, See likeness Journal 10 [Codex J 93, where Lewis copies the description and where is a full length figure] which I have drawn with my pen, and will serve to give a general Idea of the fish the rays of the fins are bony but not sharp, tho' some what pointed, the small [adipose] fin on the back next to the tail has no rays of bone being a thin membranis pellicle, the fins next to the gills have 11 rays each those of the abdomen have eight each, those of the pinna ani are 20 & 2 half formed in front, that of the back has 11 rays all the fins are of a white colour the back is of a dusky bluish colour, and that of the lower parts of the sides and belly is of a Silvery White, no spots on any Part the first bone of the gills next behind the eye is of a bluish cast and the second of a light golded colour nearly white, the puple of the eye is black and the iris of a silver white the under Jaw exceeds the upper, and the mouth opens to great extent, folding like that of the herring it has no teeth, the abdomen is obtuse and smothe in this differing from the herring, shad, anchovy &c. of the Mallacapterygious Order and class clupia, to which however I think it more nearly allied than to any other, altho' it has not

Of shellfish [mollusks] we observe the clam, periwinkle, common mussel, cockle, and a species [*Placunanomia macroschisma*] with a circular, flat shell.

1. The clams [*Mytilus edulis* [100]] of this coast are very small; the shell consists of two valves, which open with hinges; it is smooth, thin, of an oval form like that of the common mussel, and of a sky-blue color. It is about 1½ inch in length, and hangs in clusters to the moss [seaweed] of the rocks; the natives (*p. 199*) sometimes eat them.

2. The periwinkles,[101] both of the river [*Melaniidæ, Limnæ-*

their acute and serrate abdomen, and the under Jaw exceeding the upper, the scales of this little fish are so small and thin, that without minute inspection you would suppose they had none, they are filled with roes of a pure white colour, and have scarcely any alimentary Duck [duct] I find them best when cooked in Indian stile which is by roasting a number of them together on a wooden spit without any Previous Preparation whatever, they are so soft that they require no additional sauce, I think them superior to any fish I ever tasted, even more delicate and lucious than the white fish [*Coregonus*] of the lakes, which heretofore formed my standard of excellence among the fishes."

The sturgeon mentioned in the beginning of this extract is also singularly omitted in the present instance, by editorial oversight. It has been heretofore noticed in these pages, as one of the important food-fishes, and should have been here formally introduced, as the codices have much to say about it, and it is a distinct species which was new to science in 1806—another of the many uncredited discoveries of our almost inexhaustible authors. The Columbia sturgeon was first formally characterized as *Acipenser transmontanus*, by Richardson, Fn. Bor.-Am. III. 1836, p. 278, pl. xcvii. fig. 2, and has since been treated by unnumbered authors. It attains a length of 10 to 15 feet, runs far up the Columbia and even the Snake river, and has great commercial value.

[100] The " clams " of the text are evidently this species of salt-water mussels, of the family *Mytilidæ*, as we see by the statement of their hanging in clusters on the rocks, whereas clams, properly so called, live in the sand and spin no byssus. For certain species of *Mytilus*, see also note [18], p. 731. A notable true clam of Oregon and Washington is a species of *Mactridæ*, named *Lutraria maxima* by Middendorff, Beit. Mal. Russ. III. 1849, p. 66, pl. xix. figs. 1–4, and *L. capax* by Dr. A. A. Gould, Proc. Bost. Soc. Nat. Hist. III. 1850, p. 217. This is of large size, up to 7½ inches in width, very abundant, and an important article of food with the Indians, who preserve the meat by drying and smoking it in their lodges.

[101] Periwinkles, most properly so called, are small sea-snails of the family *Littorinidæ*, and particularly of the genus *Littorina*, several species of which are found on the Oregon and Washington coasts, as *L. sitchana* and *L. scutulata*. But the name is loosely applied to many other small univalves. Periwinkles " of the river " may be melanians of the genus *Goniobasis*.

idæ, etc.,] and the ocean [*Littorinidæ*], are similar to those found in the same situation on the Atlantic coast.

3. The common mussels [102] of the river are also the same with [similar to] those on the rivers of the Atlantic coast.

4. The cockle [or thin clam, *Macoma nasuta*, of the family *Tellinidæ*] is small, and much resembles that of the Atlantic.

5. There is also an animal [103] that inhabits a shell perfectly circular, about three inches in diameter, thin and entire on the margin, convex and smooth on the upper side, plain on the under part, and covered with a number of minute capillary fibers, by means of which it attaches itself to the sides of the rocks. The shell is thin, and consists of one [large and one small] valve; a small circular aperture is formed in the center of the under shell. The animal is soft and boneless.

The pellucid, jelly-like substance called the sea-nettle [or jelly fish, *Cyanea* sp?] is found in great abundance along the strand, where it has been thrown up by the waves and tide.

There are two species of the fuci thrown up in that manner. The first species, at one extremity, consists of a large vesicle or hollow vessel, which will contain from one to two gallons; it is of a conic form, the base of which forms the extreme end, and is convex and globular, bearing at its center some short, broad, and angular fibers; the substance is about the consistence of the rind of a citron melon, and three-quarters of an inch thick; the rind is smooth. From the small extremity of the cone a long, hollow, cylindric, and regularly tapering tube extends to 20 and 30 feet, and is then terminated with a number of branches, which are flat, half an inch in width, and rough, particularly on the edges, where they are furnished with a number of little ovate vesicles, or bags, of the size of a pigeon's egg. This plant

---

[102] Here the reference is to fresh-water bivalves of the family *Unionidæ*. Among the Oregon and Washington members of this family are a species of *Margaritana* identified with *M. margaritifera* by various authors, and several of *Anodonta*, as *A. angulata*, *A. oregonensis*, and *A. wahlametensis* of Dr. Isaac Lea. The most notable species is *A. nuttalliana*.

[103] *Placunanomia macroschisma*, a bivalve of the family *Anomiidæ*. The "under shell" of the text is the small (right) valve, with a hole near the hinge.

seems to be calculated to float at each extremity, while the little end of the tube, whence the branches proceed, lies deepest in the water. [This is *Nereocystis lutkeana*.]

The other [same?] species, seen on the coast toward the Killamucks, resembles a large pumpkin; it is solid, and its specific gravity is greater than water, though it is sometimes thrown out by the waves. It is of (*p. 200*) a yellowish-brown color; the rind is smooth, and its consistence is harder than that of the pumpkin, but easily cut with a knife. There are some dark brown fibers, rather harder than any other part, which pass longitudinally through the pulp or fleshy substance which forms the interior of this marine production.

[Among] the reptiles of this country are the rattlesnake [*Crotalus lucifer*], the garter-snake, the lizard, and snail.[104]

The garter-snake [*Eutœnia pickeringi* or *concinna*] appears to [does] belong to the same family [*Colubridœ*] with the common garter-snakes of the Atlantic coast; and, like those snakes, they inherit no poisonous qualities. They have 160

[104] Comment is needless on the disorder of this chapter, at a climax here, where reptiles come after jellyfishes and seaweeds, which latter themselves should have appeared in the botanical division instead of coming between acalephs and snakes. I have already noted my transfer of one fish (anchovy or olthen), from the tail of the chapter to a more suitable connection; but I do not like to transfer the herpetological matter, as to do so would throw out the original pagination, scrupulously preserved in the present edition. Yet I cannot forbear to stigmatize the blunder of including the "snail"—which every school-child knows to be a mollusk—among reptiles, and then saying nothing about it. For all I can discover, this happened simply because it is described in Clark R 116 and Lewis J 123 in connection with certain reptiles. The notice is an important one: "The snail is numerous in the woody country on this coast; these are in shape like those of the United States, but are at least five times their bulk." Here is the original description of *Helix fidelis*, J. E. Gray, Proc. Zoöl. Soc. London, 1834, p. 67, of which L. and C. were the discoverers.

In connection with this land-snail, I may call attention to a remarkable sea-snail of this region, *Natica* (or *Lunatia*) *lewisi*, a fine large species representing on the Pacific Coast our common Atlantic *N.* (or *L.*) *heros*. This was first named and dedicated to Captain Lewis by Dr. A. A. Gould, Proc. Bost. Soc. Nat. Hist. II. 1847, p. 239, and thus two years before Middendorff renamed it *Natica herculea*, in his Beit. Mal. Russ. II. 1849, p. 97, pl. vii. figs. 5, 6, 7. "The name of the first explorer and collector in Oregon merited such a perpetuation," says Dr. Wm. Cooper, P. R. R. Rep. XII. pt. ii, p. 373, 1860.

scuta on the abdomen, and 70 on the tail; those on the abdomen, near the head and jaws, as high as the eye, are of a bluish-white, which, as it recedes from the head, becomes of a dark brown; the field of the back and sides is black; a narrow stripe of a light yellow runs along the center of the back; on each side of this stripe there is a range of small transversely oblong spots of a pale brick-red, diminishing as they recede from the head, and disappearing at the commencement of the tail.   The pupil of the eye is black, with a narrow ring of white bordering on its edge; the remainder of the iris is of a dark yellowish-brown.

The horned lizard [*Phrynosoma douglasi*], called, and for what reason we never could learn,[105] the prairie buffalo, is a native of these plains, as well as those on the Missouri. They are of the same size, and much the same in appearance as the black lizard;[106] the belly is, however, broader, the tail shorter, and the action much slower.   The color is generally

[105] Obviously from its horns, and from the way it hunches or humps itself up when irritated.   " A species of Lizzard call[ed] by the French engages prarie buffaloe are native of these [Columbian] plains as well as those of the Missouri. I have called them the horned lizzard," Clark Q 132, May 29th, 1806.

[106] This species has never been identified, as the text furnished no clew whatever.   It is twice noticed in the codices.   " The dark lizzard we Saw at the commencement of the woody Country, below the great narrows and falls of the Columbia," Clark R 162.   " the black or dark brown lizard we saw at the rock fort Camp [Dalles] at the commencement of the woody Country, below the great narrows and falls of the Columbia ; they are also the same with those of the United States."   A species of the same size as the horned lizard, and not distinguished by the authors from the lizard with which they were familiar in Virginia (*Sceloporus undulatus*, the common brown fence-lizard), may be identifiable as *Sceloporus occidentalis* or *S. graciosus*, both of which are known to occur at the Dalles.

In this connection I must call attention to one of the many serious omissions from the text of this chapter of species described in the codices, among which is one of those remarkable tailed batrachians which are popularly known as " fish with legs."   Lewis J 123 has : " There is a species of water lizzard of which I saw one only just above the grand rapids of the Columbia.   it is about 9 inches long the body is reather flat and about the size of a mans finger covered with a soft skin of a dark brown colour with an uneven surface covered with little pimples the neck and head are short, the latter terminating in an accute angular point and flat.   the forefeet each four toes.   the hinder ones five unconnected with a web

brown, intermixed with yellowish-brown spots. The animal
is covered with minute scales, interspersed with small horny
points, like blunt prickles, on the upper surface of the body;
the belly and throat resemble those of the frog, and are of a
light yellowish-brown; the edge of the belly is likewise beset
with small horny projections, imparting to those edges a serrate appearance. The eye is small and dark; above and
behind the eyes there are several projections of the bone;
their ex- (*p. 201*) tremities being armed with a firm black
substance, they resemble the appearance of horns sprouting
from the head. These animals are found in greatest numbers in the sandy open plains, and appear in the greatest
abundance after a shower of rain. They are sometimes
found basking in the sunshine, but conceal themselves in
little holes of the earth in much the greatest proportion of
the time. This may account for their appearance in such
numbers after rain, as their holes may thus be rendered
untenantable.

and destitute of tallons. it's tail was reather longer than the body and in form
like that of the Muskrat, first rising in an arch higher than the back and decending
lower than the body at the extremity, and flated [flattened] perpendicularly.
the belly and under part of the neck and head were of a brick red every other
part of the colour of the upper part of the body or dark brown. the mouth was
smooth, without teeth." This description answers accurately to the characters
of the warty salamander of Oregon and Washington—yet another hitherto un-
recognized discovery of Lewis and Clark's—*Triton torosus* of Eschscholtz, Zoöl.
Atlas, V. 1833, p. 12, pl. xxi. fig. 15; *T. granulosus* of Skelton, Amer. Jour.
Sci. VII. 1849, p. 202; *Notophthalmus torosus*, Baird, Journ. Acad. Nat. Sci.
Phila. I. 1850, p. 254; *Taricha torosa*, J. E. Gray, Cat. Amphib. Brit. Mus.
II. 1850, p. 25, and Girard, U. S. Expl. Exped. Herpet. 1858, p. 5; called also
Molge torosus, and now known as *Diemyctylus torosus*,

CHAPTER XXVI.

HOMEWARD BOUND ON COLUMBIAN TIDE-WATER.

Alarm felt for means of subsistence at Fort Clatsop—Determination to expedite the return journey—Clothing sufficient, but little merchandise left—Weather-bound—Chief Como-wool—Chief Delashelwilt—Certificates—Muster-rolls and other papers left with the Indians —Official bulletin posted at Fort Clatsop reaches Philadelphia via Canton—Fort Clatsop evacuated March 23d, 1806—Meriwether Bay left—Point William doubled—Cathlamah village—Seal islands—Canoe claimed, but a compromise effected—Clatsops, Skilloots, and Cathlamahs—Camp on a small creek—Chief Wallale—Chief Sahawacap—Fanny's island—Skilloots—Coweliskee river—Hullooetells—Deer island—Quathlapotles—Towah-nahiooks or Chawahnahiooks river—Quathlapotle island—Frogs and snakes—Wappatoo island—Clanaminimums, Claxtars, Cathlacumups, Clahnaquahs, Multnomahs, and Shotos—Image-canoe island—Shahalas—Diamond and White Brant islands—Quicksand and Seal rivers—Mt. Hood sighted—Unwelcome news—Halt to hunt for provisions—Cashooks—Captain Clark's exploration of the Multnomah river, and report—Nechacolees and Neer-chokioos—Mts. Regnier, St. Helen's, Hood, and Jefferson sighted—Clackamos and Nemal-quinners—Cashooks, Neerchokioos, Shahalas, and Nechacolees—An Indian map copied and preserved—The Expedition in camp opposite Quicksand (Sandy) river.

MARCH 22d, 1806.[1]   Many reasons had determined us to remain at Fort Clatsop till the 1st of April.   Besides the want of fuel in the Columbian plains, and the impracticability of passing the mountains before the beginning of June, we were anxious to see some of the foreign traders, from whom, by means of our ample letters of credit, we might have recruited our exhausted stores of merchandise. About the middle of March, however, we had become seriously alarmed for the want of food ; the elk, our chief dependence, had at length deserted their usual haunts in our

---

[1] The Biddle narrative is here resumed from the same date, Mar. 22d, on p. 792, where it was dropped to intercalate my new Chap. xxiv., between Biddle's Chaps. xxiii. and xxv.   At present date some of the matter given in regular diary form in Chap. xxiv. is summarily retraversed ; but that could only have been avoided by cutting out the end of Chap. xxiii. and the beginning of the present chapter—which of course would have been objectionable.   One of the Clatsop codices, Clark I, ended with Jan. 29th ; the other, Lewis J, with Mar. 20th ; both will have been disposed of as soon as certain matters, drawn from entries in Lewis J relating to the evacuation of the fort, are finished.   The narrative then proceeds from Mar. 23d with a new codex, Lewis K, running Mar. 21st–May 23d, 1806.

neighborhood and retreated to the mountains. We were too poor to purchase other food from the Indians, so that we were sometimes reduced, notwithstanding all the exertions of our hunters, to a single day's provision in advance. The men, too, whom the constant rains and confinement had rendered unhealthy, might, we hoped, be benefited by leaving the coast and resuming the exercise of traveling. We therefore determined to leave Fort Clatsop, ascend the river slowly, consume the month of (*p. 203*) March in the woody country, where we hoped to find subsistence, and in this way reach the plains about the 1st of April, before which time it will be impossible to attempt crossing them ; for this purpose we began our preparations.

During the winter we had been very industrious in dressing skins, so that we now had a sufficient quantity of clothing, besides between 300 and 400 pairs of moccasins. But the whole stock of goods on which we are to depend, for the purchase either of horses or of food, during the long tour of nearly 4,000 miles, is so much diminished that it might all be tied in two handkerchiefs. We have in fact nothing but six blue robes, one of scarlet, a coat and hat of the United States Artillery uniform, five robes made of our large flag, and a few old clothes trimmed with ribbon. We therefore feel that our chief dependence must be on our guns, which fortunately for us, are all in good order, as we had taken the precaution of bringing a number of extra locks, and one of our men proved to be an excellent artist in that way. The powder had been secured in leaden canisters, and though on many occasions they had been under water, it remained perfectly dry, and we now found ourselves in possession of 140 pounds of powder, and twice that quantity of lead, a stock quite sufficient for the route homeward.

After much trafficking, we at last succeeded in purchasing a canoe for a uniform coat and half a carrot of tobacco, and took a canoe from the Clatsops, as a reprisal for some elk which some of them had stolen from us in the winter. We were now ready to leave Fort Clatsop, but the rain prevented us for several days from calking the canoes, and we were forced to wait for calm weather before we could attempt to pass Point William.   In the meantime we were visited by many of our neighbors, for the purpose of taking leave of us. The Clatsop [chief] Commowool has been the most kind and hospitable of all the Indians in this quarter ; we therefore gave him a certificate of the kindness and at- (*p. 204*) tention which we had received from him, and added a more substantial proof of our gratitude, the gift of all our houses and furniture.   To the Chinnook chief Delashelwilt we gave a certificate of the same kind ; we also circulated among the natives several papers, one of which we also posted up in the fort, to the following effect :

"*The object of this list is, that through the medium of some civilized person, who may see the same, it may be made known to the world, that the party consisting of the persons whose names are hereunto annexed, and who were sent out by the Government of the United States to explore the interior of the continent of North America, did penetrate the same by the way of the Missouri and Columbia rivers, to the discharge of the latter into the Pacific ocean, where they arrived on the 14th day of November, 1805, and departed the 23d day of March, 1806, on their return to the United States by the same route by which they had come out.*" [2] *

[2] This paper is given literally from Lewis J 137, on p. 816, which see.   The date of Nov. 14th, assigned in the document as that of reaching the Pacific Ocean, is that on which Captain Lewis, having left the main party camped inside Point Ellice, went on to Cape Disappointment.   See p. 708.

* By a singular casualty, this note fell into the possession of Captain Hill, who, while on the coast of the Pacific, procured it from the natives.   This note accompanied him on his voyage to Canton, whence it arrived in the United States.   The following is an extract of a letter from a gentleman at Canton to his friend in Philadelphia :

"*Extract of a letter from —— to ——, in Philadelphia.*
"CANTON, *January*, 1807.

"I wrote you last by the Governor Strong, [Captain] Cleveland, for Boston ; the present is by the brig Lydia, [Captain] Hill, of the same place.

"Captain Hill, while on the coast, met some Indian natives **near the mouth**

On the back of some of these papers we sketched (*p. 205*)
the connection of the upper branches of the Missouri and
Columbia rivers, with our route, and the track which we
intended to follow on our return. This memorandum was
all that we deemed it necessary to make ; for there seemed
but little chance that any detailed report to our government, which we might leave in the hands of the savages, to
be delivered to foreign traders, would ever reach the United
States. To leave any of our men here, in hopes of their procuring a passage home in some transient vessel, would too
much weaken our party, which we must necessarily divide
during our route; besides that, we shall most probably be
there ourselves sooner than any trader, who, after spending
the next summer here, might go on some circuitous voyage.

The rains and wind still confined us to the fort ; but
at last our provisions dwindled down to a single day's stock,
and it became absolutely necessary to remove. We therefore sent a few hunters ahead, and stopped the boats as well
as we could with mud.

Sunday, March 23d, 1806.[3]   The canoes were loaded, and

of the Columbia river, who delivered to him a paper, of which I enclose you a
copy. It had been committed to their charge by Captains Clarke and Lewis, who
had penetrated to the Pacific ocean. The original is a rough draft with a pen
of their outward route, and that which they intended returning by. Just below
the junction of Madison's river, they found an immense fall of three hundred
and sixty-two [a gross exaggeration—see the text where the Great Falls of
the Missouri are described, beginning at p. 383] feet perpendicular. This, I
believe, exceeds in magnitude any other known. From the natives Captain Hill
learned that they were all in good health and spirits ; had met many difficulties
on their progress, from various tribes of Indians, but had found them about the
sources of the Missouri very friendly, as were those on the Columbia river and
the coast." (Original Note.)

[3] There is, of course, no question of this date. Gass gives the same day and
hour. But in a letter of Clark's, elsewhere printed, it stands March 27th in two
places. (By a curious coincidence, the date of evacuating Fort Mandan, April
7th, 1805, is misprinted April 17th in Jefferson's Message to Congress of Feb.
19th, 1806.) The spot thus left has never been lost sight of. It was fixed with
absolute precision, of course became historical, and has been marked on most
maps ever since. We frequently hear of it in books of travel, etc. Thus Ross
Cox, an Astorian by sea in the " Beaver," who reached the Columbia in April,

at one o'clock in the afternoon we took final leave of Fort Clatsop. The wind was still high, but the alternative of remaining without provisions was so unpleasant that we hoped to be able to double Point William. We had scarcely left the fork when we met Delashelwilt and a party of 20 Chinnooks, who, understanding that we had been trying to procure a canoe, had brought one for sale. Being, however, already supplied, we left them, and after getting out of Meriwether's bay, began to coast along the south side of the river. We doubled Point William without any injury, and at six o'clock reached, at the distance of 16 (*p. 206*) miles from Fort Clatsop, the mouth of a small [John Day⁴] creek, where we found our hunters. They had been fortunate enough to kill two elk, but at such a distance that we could not send for them before the next morning,

March 24th, when they were brought in for breakfast. We then proceeded [at half-past nine]. The country is covered with a thick growth of timber; the water, however, is

1812, visited the spot: " the logs of the houses were still standing, and marked with the names of several of the party." The Narrative of J. K. Townsend, a noted naturalist and associate of Nuttall, which was pub. Phila., 1839, gives another glimpse (1834). " Oct. 14th, I walked to-day around the beach to the foot of Young's bay. . . to see the remains of the house in which Lewis and Clark's party resided. . . The logs of which it was composed are still perfect, but the roof of bark has disappeared, and the whole vicinity is overgrown with thorn and wild currant bushes. . . One of Mr. Birnie's children found a few days since a large silver medal, which had been brought here by Lewis and Clark, and had probably been presented to some chief, who lost it. On one side was a head, with the name ' Th. Jefferson, President of the United States, 1801,' on the other, two hands interlocked, surrounded by a pipe and tomahawk ; and above, the words ' Peace and Friendship,' " (p. 256). This is a perfect identification of the medal. A little later, in the forties or early fifties, there was a saw-mill on the site. Thus we read in Mrs. F. F. Victor's book, pub. S. F'sco., 1872 : " Not only have sixty years effaced all traces of their encampment, but a house, which stood on the site in 1853, has quite disappeared, the site being overgrown with trees 20 feet in height. Of a saw-mill which furnished lumber to San Francisco in the same year, nothing now remains except immense beds of half rotten sawdust, embedding one or two charred foundation timbers. A dense growth of vegetation covers the whole ground." The present aspect of the place is better known than what might be discovered by digging in the right spot.

⁴ Kekemahke river or creek of Nov. 27th, 1805, p. 722, which see.

shallow to the distance of four miles from shore; and although there is a channel deep enough for canoes on the south side, yet as the tide was low we found some difficulty in passing along. At one o'clock we reached the Cathlamah village,[5] where we halted for about two hours, and purchased some wappatoo and a dog for the invalids. This village we have already described as situated opposite the Seal islands; on one of these the Indians have placed their dead in canoes, raised on scaffolds above the reach of the tide. These people seem to be more fond of carving in wood than their neighbors, and have various specimens of their taste about the houses. The broad pieces supporting the roof, and the board through which doors are cut, are the objects[6] on which they chiefly display their ingenuity, and are ornamented with curious figures, sometimes representing persons in a sitting posture supporting a burden.

On resuming our route among the Seal islands, we mistook our way, which an Indian observing, he pursued us and put us into the right channel. He soon, however, embarrassed us by claiming the canoe we had taken from the Clatsops, and which he declared was his property. We had found it among the Clatsops, and seized it as a reprisal for a theft committed by that nation; but being unwilling to do an act of injustice to this Indian, and having no time to discuss the question of right, we compromised with him for an elk-skin, with which he returned perfectly satisfied. We continued our route along the shore, and after making 15 miles camped at an old village of nine houses, opposite the lower village of the Wahkiacums.[7] Here we were overtaken by two Chinnooks,

[5] Where is now Warren's Landing: see pp. 705, 721. Hugging the south shore, they pass camp of Nov. 26th, going along highlands which set a little back of the river, and past some small creeks or sluices, among which are two called Bear and Big; Warren's creek at the Landing.

[6] Such objects are now commonly called totem-posts. They are found among the Indians of the whole northwest coast, often of immense size and carved in the most fantastic manner. Some fine specimens may be seen in the U. S. National Museum at Washington.

[7] For the village, *opposite* which is camp, see p. 701. Camp in Clatsop Co.,

who (*p. 207*) came to us after dark and spent the night at our camp. We found plenty of wood for fires, which were quite necessary, as the weather had become cold.

March 25th. This morning proved so disagreeably cold that we did not set out before seven o'clock, when, having breakfasted, we continued along [the channel between Tenasillihee island and] the south side of the river. The wind, however, as well as a strong current, was against us, so that we proceeded slowly. On landing for dinner at noon [at or near Clifton], we were joined by some Clatsops, who had been on a trading voyage to the Skilloots, and were now on their return loaded with dried anchovies, wappatoo, and sturgeon. After dinner we crossed the river [at head of Tenasillihee island] to a large [Puget] island along the [north] side of which we continued about a mile, till we reached a single house [about present site of Cathlamet] occupied by three men, two women, and the same number of boys, all of the Cathlamah nation. They were engaged in fishing or trolling for sturgeon, of which they had caught about a dozen, but they asked so much for them that we were afraid to purchase. One of the men purchased the skin of a sea-otter in exchange for a dressed elk-skin and a handkerchief. Nearly adjoining this house was another party of Cathlamahs, who had been up the river on a fishing excursion, and been successful in procuring a large supply, which they were not disposed to sell.

We proceeded on to the head of the [Puget] island, and then crossed to the north[8] side of the river. Here the coast formed a continued swamp for several miles back, so that it

Ore., by Point Samuel (Katalamat, Katlamet or Cathlamet Point, p. 721), near lower end of Tenasillihee island ; across the river is Skumaquea creek : see Nov. 7th, p. 700 and notes there.

[8] Read south. "Continued our rout up the [Puget] Island to it's head and passed to the south side," Lewis K 4. This is confirmed by the statement just beyond that they camped at the entrance of a small creek *opposite* camp of Nov. 6th, 1805, which last was on the right (going down river). To-night's camp is in a marsh on the right hand going up, left bank or south side, in Columbia Co., Ore.; across the river are the bold headlands of Cape Horn (see p. 700, Nov. 6th).

was late in the evening before we were able to reach a spot fit for our camp. At length we discovered the entrance of a small creek, opposite the place [near Cape Horn] where we were camped on the 6th of November. Though the ground was low and moist, yet the spot was sheltered from the wind, and we resolved to pass the night there. We had made 15 miles. Here we found another party of Cathlamahs, who had established a temporary residence for the purposes of fishing sturgeon and taking seal, in both of which they had been successful. They gave us some of the flesh (*p. 208*) of the seal, which was a valuable addition to the lean elk. The low grounds which we passed are supplied with cottonwood, and the tree resembling the ash, except in its leaf, with red willow, broad-leaved willow, seven-bark, gooseberry, green-briar, and the large-leaved thorn.[9] The wind was very high toward evening, and continued to blow so violently in the morning,

March 26th, that we could not set out before eight o'clock. In the meantime, finding that one of our neighbors the Cathlamahs, by name Wallale, was a person of distinction, we gave him a medal of small size, with which he was invested with the usual ceremonies. He appeared highly gratified, and requited us with a large sturgeon. The wind having abated, we proceeded to an old village, where we halted for dinner, having met on the way Sahawacap,[10] the principal chief of all the Cathlamahs, who was on his return from a trading voyage up the river with wappatoo and fish, some of which he gave us, and we purchased a little more. At dinner we were overtaken by two Wahkiacums, who have been following us for 24 hours, with two dogs, for which they are importuning us to give them some tobacco ; but, as

[9] Cottonwood, *Populus trichocarpa;* the tree resembling the ash, etc., is the broad-leaved maple, *Acer macrophyllum;* the red willow is probably a species of *Cornus;* the seven-bark is the Douglas hardhack, *Spiræa douglasi;* the gooseberry is an uncertain species of *Ribes;* the green-briar, *Rubus ursinus ;* the large-leaved thorn, *Cratægus douglasi.*

[10] " Sâh-hâh-wâh-cap," Lewis K 5, where the above-named Wallale, moreover, is Wal-lal'-le.

we have very little of that article left, they were obliged to go off disappointed. We received at the same time an agreeable supply of three eagles and a large goose, brought in by the hunters. After dinner we passed along the north shore opposite a high, fine bottom and dry prairie, at the upper end of which, near a grove of white-oak trees, is an island which we called Fanny's [11] island. There were some deer and elk at a distance in the prairie; but, as we could not stay to hunt, we continued till late in the evening, when we camped on the next [now Fisher's] island above Fanny's. According to the estimate we made in descending the river,[12] which we begin, however, to think was short, our journey of to-day was 18 miles. Some Indians came to us, but we were occupied in procuring wood, which we found it difficult to obtain in sufficient quantity for our purposes, and they therefore did not remain long.

(*p. 209*) *March 27th.* We set out early, and were soon joined by some Skilloots, with fish and roots for sale. At ten o'clock we stopped to breakfast at two houses of the

[11] " Elegant and extensive bottom on the South side and an island near it's upper point which we call Fanny's Island and bottom," Lewis K 6. Fanny's island is now Grim's, about 2 m. long; and the upper end of Fanny's bottom is shown as Oak Point by Commander Wilkes on the U. S. Exploring Expedition map of 1841. Captain Clark's youngest sister Frances is the lady thus complimented. For identifications of the various islands and other points of to-day's voyage, see p. 699 and note there. Wallace's island, now large and well marked, on the south side, between Puget island and Fanny's or Grim's, may not have been isolated in 1805-6 ; it is not recognizably noticed in the History. On the other hand, Grim's stands out very distinctly, nearer the south than the north shore, a little below Green Point, with the small Gull island at its lower end, near which Nequally and Negisticook creeks fall in on the Washington side, opposite the upper (Oak) point of Fanny's bottom. Opposite Green Point, Ore., is Cleveland's Landing, Wash.; next above are Fisher's and Walker's islands. To-night's camp is on the former one of these.

[12] " Agreeably to our estimate as we decended the river, we came 16 m. [March] 23 d., 16 m. the 24th., 15 m. the 25th., and 18 m. the 26th., tho' I now think our estimate in decending the river was too short," Lewis K 7. Miles look and feel differently going up and down a river! According to the down-river estimates here recapitulated, and thought too short, the Expedition has ascended 65 miles from Fort Clatsop. See last note.

same nation, where we found our hunters [Drewyer and J. and R. Fields], who had not returned to camp last night; they had killed nothing. The inhabitants seemed very kind and hospitable. They gave almost the whole party as much as they could eat of dried anchovies, wappatoo, sturgeon, quamash, and a small white tuberous root, two inches long and as thick as a man's finger, which, when eaten raw, is crisp, milky, and of an agreeable flavor. The Indians also urged us to remain with them all day, to hunt elk and deer, which they said were abundant in the neighborhood; but as the weather would not permit us to dry and pitch our canoes, we declined their offer and proceeded.

At the distance of two miles [further] we passed the entrance of Coweliskee river [see p. 698, Nov. 6th]. This stream discharges itself on the north side of the Columbia, about three miles above a remarkably high rocky knoll,[13] the south side of which it washes in passing, and which is separated from the northern hills by a wide bottom of several miles in extent. The Coweliskee is 150 yards wide, deep and navigable, as the Indians assert, for a considerable distance; it most probably waters the country west and north of the range of mountains which crosses the Columbia between the Great Falls and rapids. On the lower side of this river, a few miles from its entrance into the Columbia, is the principal village of the Skilloots, a numerous people, differing,

[13] Mt. Coffin, 240 feet high—a very conspicuous object, immediately on the river's edge, isolated by lowlands from the "northern hills," mentioned in the text, one of which is Mt. Solo, 400-500 feet high. It is a wonder no name was given to this rock, as various less striking formations were duly christened by the explorers. Mt. Coffin has been so called for many years. This and Coffin Rock (on the Oregon side, four or five miles above the mouth of the Cowlitz river) were from time immemorial places of deposit of the dead aborigines, and owe their English names to being thus "Memaloose Alahee." We should err, however, if we translated this term by graveyard, sepulcher, or the like, in the concrete sense of burial-ground. It means the place of the departed—happy hunting-grounds, lucky fishery, spirit-world, ghostland, other side of Jordan, Tartarus, Hades—or what you may choose to call that which you imagine you will go to when you die. Near mouth of the Cowlitz is Cottonwood island; opposite the mouth is Rainier (town); Cedar Landing 1½ m. below this.

however, neither in language, dress, nor manners from the Clatsops, Chinnooks, and other nations at the mouth of the Columbia. With the Chinnooks they have lately been at war, and though hostilities have ceased, yet they have not resumed their usual intercourse ; so that the Skilloots do not go as far as the sea, nor do the Chinnooks come higher up than the Seal islands, the trade between them being carried on by the Clatsops, Cathlamahs, and Wahkiacums, their mutual friends. On this same river, above the Skilloots, resides the nation called Hullooetell,[14] of (*p. 210*) whom we learnt nothing, except that the nation was numerous. Late in the evening we halted[15] at the beginning of the bottom-land below [Elallah or] Deer island, after having made 20 miles. Along the low grounds on the river were the cotton-wood [*Populus trichocarpa*], sweet-willow, oak, ash [*Fraxinus oregana*], broad-leaved ash [maple, *Acer macrophyllum*], and a growth resembling the beech ; while the hills were occupied almost exclusively by different species of fir ; the black alder [*Alnus rubra*] was common to the hills as well as the low grounds. During the day we passed a number of fishing-camps on both sides of the river, and were constantly attended by small parties of the Skilloots, who behaved in the most orderly manner, and from whom we purchased as much fish and roots as we wanted on very moderate terms. The night continued as the day had been, cold, wet, and disagreeable.

March 28th. We left our camp at an early hour, and by nine o'clock reached an old Indian village on the left [north] side of Deer island. Here we found a party of our men whom we had sent on yesterday to hunt, and who now returned after killing seven deer in the course of the morning,

---

[14] " Hul-loo-et-tell," Lewis K 8 ; nothing further known of them ; probably a Salishan tribe. They reappear in the Estimate as Hullooellel.

[15] In Columbia Co., Ore., at or near Enterprise Landing, a couple of miles above Coffin Rock and about a mile below Hunter's ; immediately opposite is Sandy island and town of Kalama, Cowlitz Co., Wash. Deer island shows large on Clark's map, where it is charted by its present name. See pp. 696, 697.

out of upward of a hundred which they had seen. They were the common fallow-deer with long tails [*Cariacus virginianus macrurus*], and though very poor are better than the black-tailed fallow-deer of the coast [*C. columbianus*], from which they differ materially. Soon after our arrival the weather became fair, and we therefore immediately hauled the boats on shore, and having dried them by means of large fires put on the pitch. We also took this opportunity of drying our baggage; and as some of the hunters had not yet returned, it was deemed advisable to pass the night at our present camp. This island, which has received from the Indians the appropriate name of Elalah [Elallah], or Deer island, is surrounded on the water-side by an abundant growth of cottonwood, ash, and willow, while the interior consists chiefly of prairies interspersed with ponds. These afford refuge to great numbers of geese, ducks, large swan [*Cygnus buccinator*], sandhill cranes, a few canvas-backed ducks [*Aristonetta vallisneria*], and particularly (*p. 211*) the duckinmallard [*Anas boscas*], the most abundant of all. There are also great numbers of snakes [16] resembling our garter-snakes in appearance, and like them not poisonons. Our hunters brought in three deer, a goose, some ducks, an eagle, and a tiger-cat [*Lynx rufus fasciatus*]. Such is the extreme voracity of the vultures [*Pseudogryphus californianus*], that they had devoured in the space of a few hours four of the deer killed this morning; and one [J. Fields] of our men declared that they had besides dragged a large buck about 30 yards, skinned it, and broken the backbone. [17] We were visited

---

[16] " On this island there are a greater number of snakes, than I had ever seen in any other place ; they appeared almost as numerous as the blades of grass ; and are a species of Garter snake," Gass, p. 192. Lewis K 10,11, this date, has the long description of the duck, No. 56 of Chap. xxiv., and also a good diagnosis of the garter-snakes, which were then new to science. This species was not rediscovered till the Wilkes Exploring Expedition, during which specimens were taken at Puget Sound, on which Baird and Girard based the name *Eutænia pickeringi*, after Dr. Charles Pickering, the collector (Serp. N. A. 1853, p. 27).

[17] " When our men went for the deer, they found that the fowls had devoured four of the carcases entirely, except the bones," Gass, p. 192, March 28th.

during the day by a large canoe with ten Indians of the Quathlapotle [18] nation, who reside about 17 miles above us. We advanced only five miles to-day. [19]

Saturday, March 29th. At an early hour we proceeded along the side of Deer island and halted for breakfast at the upper end of it, which is properly the commencement of the great Columbian valley. We were here joined by three men of the Towahnahiook [20] nation, with whom we proceeded, till at the distance of 14 [?] miles from our camp of last evening we reached a large inlet or arm of the river, about 300 yards wide, up which they went to their villages. A short distance above this inlet a considerable river empties from the north side of the Columbia. Its name is Chawahnahiooks.[21] It is about 150 yards wide, and at present

[18] One of the tribes of Upper Chinooks, of the Chinookan family, also spelled Quathlahpotle by L. and C. The name is usually spelled Cathlapotle, and has been very generally applied to the river now called Lewis'. See note [22], p. 914.

[19] And were camped on the north side of Deer island, about opposite the two small islands, Martin's and Burke's, behind which Burris creek falls in on the Washington side. Deer island is 5 m. long by 1½ at widest part, somewhat lozenge-shaped, and only separated from the Oregon side by a narrow slough.

[20] Mistake here. " We were joined by three men of the Clam-nah-min-na-mun nation," Lewis K 12, Mar. 29th. Towahnahiook, supposing that to be the word, would indicate the Towahha, a Salishan tribe. In 1867 there were 97 of them left, all on the Lummi Reservation, Wash.

[21] " This stream the natives call Cah-wâh-na-hi-ooks," Lewis K 12. So on the codex-map, K 29 ; Chah-wah-na-hi-ooks on Clark's map of 1814 ; in the Estimate, Tahwahnahiooks. However this gibberish word be spelled, I have reason to think that L. and C. were under some misapprehension in using it as the name of the present river. Unless there be some radical etymological distinction between Towahnahiooks and Chawahnahiooks, the same is the name of the Des Chutes river, on the Oregon side above the Dalles, as we have already seen (p. 657). The last note shows that there was a mistake in the text about the Indians met here. The native name of the river now in question, or at any rate of its main fork, is the same as that of the Indians next above mentioned— Quathlapotle, now usually Cathlapotle, to be found charted in some such form on various maps of comparatively modern dates. Perhaps in consequence of all this uncertainty, this stream is now called Lewis' river. It is a large forked stream, both the main branches of which, called North and South Fork of Lewis' river, arise in the mountains of Skamania Co., Wash., drain westward, through this and Clark Co., and only unite a little above the mouth of their conjoined courses. At the mouth of Lewis' river is also the mouth of an entirely separate stream,

discharges a large body of water, though the Indians assure us that a short distance above its mouth the navigation is obstructed by falls and rapids.   Three miles beyond the inlet is an island [Bachelor's] near the north shore of the river, behind the lower end of which is a village of Quath-lapotles,[22] where we landed about three o'clock.   The village consists of 14 large wooden houses. The people themselves received us very kindly, and voluntarily spread before us wappatoo and anchovies; but as soon as we fin-ished enjoying this hospitality, if it deserve that name, they began to ask us for presents.   They were, however, per-fectly satisfied with the small articles which we distributed according to custom, and equally pleased with (*p. 212*) our purchasing some wappatoo, twelve dogs, and two sea-otter skins. We also gave the chief a small medal, which he, however, soon transferred to his wife.   After remaining some time we embarked, and coasting along this island, which after the nation we called Quathlapotle island, camped for the night in a small prairie on the north side of the Columbia, having made by estimate 19 miles.[23]   The river is rising fast.

Lake or Calapooya river, which rises about Vancouver, especially in a lake there, and runs nearly parallel with the Columbia for some 20-25 miles.   This double disemboguement takes place at the lower point of Bachelor's island, immediately opposite Warrior Point—which point is the sharp lower end of the immense Wappatoo island of L. and C. (now Sauvie), just above town of St. Helen's, Columbia Co., Ore.   Between the Warrior point of Wappatoo or Sauvie island and the Oregon mainland is the "large inlet or arm" of the text—that is, Scap-poose bay, into which runs the great Willamette slough, some 20 miles long, with its other end in the Willamette or Multnomah river, thus delimiting Wappatoo island.   Near the entrance of this inlet are the town and the creek called Milton (originally named as a British fur-trading post).   See p. 696, Nov. 5th.

[22] Or Cathlapotles.   They were a tribe of the Chinookan stock, who spoke the Katlamat dialect.   Their name is from Gátlap'otlh, derived from that of the river Náp'otlh (Yah-kotl on Stevens' map No. 3, as S. fork of Lewis' river). See also last note.

[23] As the Columbia here runs about north, camp was rather on the east (right bank, left hand going up), in Clark Co., Wash.   Distances seem overestimated to-day, and this camp can hardly be fixed within two or three miles.   It must have been in the vicinity of Fale's Landing, as it was not far from camp of Nov. 4th.   See p. 695.

In the course of the day we saw great numbers of geese, ducks, and large and small swans [*Cygnus buccinator* and *C. columbianus*], which last are very abundant in the ponds where the wappatoo grows, as they feed much on that root. We also observed the crested kingfisher [*Ceryle alcyon*], and the large and small blackbird ; and this evening heard, without seeing, the large hooting-owl. The frogs [*Rana pretiosa ?*], which we have not found in the wet marshes near the entrance of the Columbia, are now croaking in the swamps and marshes with precisely the same note as in the United States. The garter-snakes [*Eutænia pickeringi*] appear in vast quantities, and are scattered through the prairies in large bundles of 40 or 50 entwined round each other. Among the moss on the rocks we observed a species of small wild onions [Clark Q 85] growing so closely together as to form a perfect turf, and equal in flavor to the shives [chives or cives, *Allium schœnoprasum*] of our gardens, which they resemble in appearance also.

Sunday, March 30th. Soon after our departure we were met by three Clanaminamums,[24] one of whom we recognized as our companion yesterday. He pressed us very much to visit his countrymen on the inlet, but we had no time to make the circuit, and parted. We had not proceeded far before a party of Claxtars[25] and Cathlacumups[26] passed us in

[24] In the Estimate printed Clannarminnamuns. Preferable spelling Clannahminnamun, as Lewis K 15. These were a Chinookan tribe, here enumerated among the " Wappatoo " Indians ; their village is charted on the codex-map on Wappatoo island. They probably became extinct as a separate body about 1840.

[25] So Lewis K 15 ; in the Estimate printed Clackstar. Here we have some entirely different Indians. These are the Tlatscanai, an Athapascan tribe, belonging to the Pacific group of Athapascan stock, which formerly resided on a small stream on the northwest side of Wappatoo Island, and hence were enumerated by Lewis and Clark among their " Wappatoo " Indians. According to Dr. George Gibbs, whose informant was an old Indian, the Tlatscanai " formerly owned the prairies on the Tsihalis (Chehalis) at the mouth of the Skukumchuck, but, on failure of game, left the country, crossed the Columbia river, and occupied the mountains to the south "—which statement is noted by Powell as too uncertain to be depended upon. There is a river and town of this name in Oregon south of the Columbia.

[26] Cathlahcumups, Lewis K 15, or Cathlacumups, as here and in the Estimate,

two canoes, on their way down the river; and soon after we were met by several other canoes, filled with persons of different tribes on each side of the river. We also passed several fishing-camps on Wappatoo [27] island, and then halted for breakfast on the north side of the river, [28] near our camp of the 4th of November. Here we were visited by several canoes from two villages on Wappatoo island; the first, about (*p. 213*) two miles above us, is called Clahnaquah; [29] the other, a mile above them, has the name of Multnomah. After higgling, much in the manner of those on the seacoast, these Indians gave us a sturgeon with some wappatoo and

were a tribe of Chinookan stock, simply known as mentioned by Lewis and Clark. Codex-map charts their village on west bank of Scappoose bay.

[27] An interesting " find " in the codices is a never-published map, Lewis K 28, 29—a pen-and-ink sketch in Clark's hand. It shows the Columbia from the Cahwahnahiooks (Lewis') to the Quicksand (Sandy) river, a long reach of the Multnomah, Mt. Jefferson, etc., with the residences of the various tribes in these parts. Some of the intricate geography about the mouths of the Multnomah is clearly displayed. Wappatoo island is a conspicuous feature of this map; it is of course much more accurately charted than as appears on Clark's published map of 1814, and a dozen or more other islands, large and small, are filled in. The reader will recall how much use Lewis and Clark made of this name " Wappatoo "—for the plant, for the great island now in mention, for a whole group of Indians—they even called the whole region between the Cascade and Coast ranges Wappatoo valley, before they named it the Columbia valley, and it is conspicuously so lettered on Clark's map of 1814. The island has had many names, as a whole, being called Multnomah and Willamette in all their shifty spellings, but seems to pass now usually as Sauvie or Sauvie's island. Similarly, the slough which isolates it is variously called; on one map before me it is marked Warrior's Branch. I do not see how any such terms are better than the original distinctive and highly appropriate name Wappatoo given by L. and C., which should by all means be restored. The island is big enough to have quite a geography of its own. Its most conspicuous feature is perhaps the large sheet of water called Sturgeon lake.

[28] " 5 miles above Quathlahpotle [Bachelor's] Island on the N.E. side we halted for breakfast," Lewis K 16. On the codex-map this island shows well, next above the mouth of Cahwahnahiooks (Lewis') river, with village of Quathlapotles marked on the mainland back of the island.

[29] Clan-nah-quah, Lewis K 16; Clannahqueh of the Estimate; elsewhere Clahnaqua. A band of Chinookan stock, only known as here noted by L. and C. The same is to be said of the Shotos next named. These are located on the codex-map on Lake (or Calapooya) river, and the " pond " near where they lived is shown there.

pashequaw in exchange for small fish-hooks. As we proceeded we were joined by other Indians, and on coming
opposite the Clahnaquah village were shown another village
about two miles from the river on the northeast side, and
behind a pond running parallel with it. Here they said the
tribe called Shotos resided. About four o'clock the Indians
all left us. Their chief object in accompanying us appeared
to be to gratify curiosity; but though they behaved in the
most friendly manner, most of them were prepared with
their instruments of war. About sunset we reached a beautiful prairie, opposite the middle of what we had [Nov. 4th:
see p. 694] called Image-canoe island, and having made 23
miles, camped for the night.[30] In the prairie is a large pond
or lake, and an open grove of oak borders the back part.
There are many deer and elk in the neighborhood, but they
are very shy; and the annual fern, which is now abundant
and dry, makes such a rustling as the hunters pass through
it that they could not come within reach of the game, and
we obtained nothing but a single duck.

March 31st. We set out very early, and at eight o'clock,
landed on the north side of the river and breakfasted.
Directly opposite is a large wooden house, belonging to the
Shahala[31] nation, the inhabitants of which came over to see
us. We had observed in descending the river last year [Nov.
4th], that there were at the same place 24 other houses,
built of wood and covered with straw, all of which are now
destroyed. On inquiry the Indians informed us that their
relations, whom we saw last fall, usually visit them at that
season for the purpose of hunting deer and elk, and collecting wappatoo, but that they had lately returned to their
permanent residence at the rapids—we presume in order to

[30] At or near present site of the historic Fort Vancouver, and present location
of Vancouver, county seat of Clark Co., Wash. The "large pond or lake" of
the text is now called Lake Vancouver, which discharges into Lake or Calapooya river, a little lower down on which is the other "pond" of the text, where
the Shotos resided.

[31] "Ne-er-cho-ki-oo Tribe of the Shâ-hâ-la Nation," located on the codex-map,
Lewis K 28, on the S. side of the Columbia, as per text. See note [23], p. 761.

prepare for the salmon season, as that fish will soon begin
(*p. 214*) to run. At ten o'clock we resumed our route along
the north side of the river, and having passed Diamond and
Whitebrant islands, halted for the night at the lower point of
a handsome prairie. Our camp,[32] which is 25 miles from
that of last night, is situated opposite the upper entrance of
Quicksand [Sandy] river; a little below [camp] a stream [Seal
or Washougal river] from the north empties into the Columbia, near the head of Whitebrant island. It is about 80 yards
wide, and at present discharges a large body of very clear
water, which near the Columbia overflows its low banks and
forms several large ponds. The natives inform us that this
river is of no great extent, rises in the mountains near us
[about Saddle Peak, in Skamania Co., Wash.], and at a mile
from its mouth is divided into two nearly equal branches,
both of which are incapable of being navigated, on account
of their numerous falls and rapids. Not being able to learn
any Indian name, we called it Seal river [p. 690, Nov. 3d],
from the abundance of those animals near its mouth. At
the same place we saw a summer-duck [*Aix sponsa*], or wood-
duck, as it is sometimes called; it is the same with that of
the United States, and the first we have seen since entering
the Rocky mountains last summer. The hunters, who had
been obliged to halt below Seal river on account of the
waves being too high for their small canoe, returned after
dark with the unwelcome news that game was scarce in that
quarter.

Tuesday, April 1st. Three Indians followed us yesterday

[32] Text is ambiguous as to whether camp was above or below the mouth of
Seal (Washougal) river. Lewis K 19 has: "continued our rout along the N. side
of the river passed diamond island and whitebrant island to the lower point of a
handsom prarie opposite to the upper entrance of the quicksand river; here we
encamped having traveled 25 miles to-day. a little below the upper point of the
whitebrant Island Seal river discharges," etc. Camp is therefore a little above
the mouth of the Washougal, at which is now town of La Camas, Clark Co.,
Wash., and back of this is a place called Fern Prairie—recalling what is said of
ferns in yesterday's itinerary. For rivers and islands named to-day, see p. 690,
Nov. 3d. On Wilkes' map, 1841, Seal river is marked Evet's; and Quicksand
river, Quichel's.

and camped near us last night. On putting to them a variety of questions relative to their country, they assured us that Quicksand river, which we had hitherto deemed so considerable, extends no further than the southwest side of Mount Hood, which is S. 85° E., 40 miles distant from this place; and it is moreover navigable for a very short distance only, in consequence of falls and rapids, and that no nation inhabits its borders. Several other persons affirmed that it rose near Mount Hood, and Sergeant Pryor, who was sent [with two men] for the purpose of examining it, convinced us (*p. 215*) of the truth of their statement. He found the river 300 yards wide, though the channel was not more than 50 yards wide and about 6 feet deep. The current was rapid, the water turbid; the bed of the river was formed entirely of quicksand; the banks very low, and at present overflowed. He passed several islands, and at 3½ miles' distance a creek from the south, 50 yards wide; his furthest course was six miles from the mouth of the river, but there it seemed to bend to the east, and he heard the noise of waterfalls. If Quicksand river then does not go beyond Mount Hood, it must leave the valley a few miles from its entrance, and run nearly parallel with the Columbia. There must, therefore, be some other large river [*i. e.*, the Multnomah [33]], which we have not yet seen, to water the extensive country between the mountains of the coast and Quicksand river; but the Indians could give us no satisfactory information of any such stream.

Whilst we were making these inquiries a number of canoes came to us, and among the rest a number of families were descending the river. They told us that they lived at the Great Rapids, but that a great scarcity of provisions there

[33] This largest of all tributaries of the Columbia, below the Snake, was actually missed both ways by the Expedition, owing to the situation of its principal mouth behind islands—some of the small islands now about the mouth of the river are Hayden's (or Shaw's), Pearcy's, Ramsay's, Coon, and Nigger Tom— though they correctly noted the sluice of its lower opening (see note [21], p. 914, Mar. 29th). But now they infer that there must be some such river, and to-morrow Captain Clark is coming back to look the matter up. See Apr. 3d, beyond.

had induced them to come down in hopes of finding subsistence in this fertile valley. All those who lived at the rapids,
as well as the nations above them, were in much distress for
want of food, having consumed their winter store of dried
fish ; and not expecting the return of the salmon before the
next full moon, which will happen on the 2d of May, this
intelligence was disagreeable and embarrassing. From the
falls to the Chopunnish nation the plains afford no deer, elk,
or antelope on which we can rely for subsistence. The
horses are very poor at this season, and the dogs must be in
the same condition if their food, the fish, has failed ; so that
we had calculated entirely on purchasing fish. On the other
hand, it is obviously inexpedient to wait for the return of the
salmon, since in that case we might not reach the Missouri
before the ice would prevent our navigating it. We might
besides hazard the loss of our horses, for the (*p. 216*) Chopunnish, with whom we left them, intend crossing the [Bitter-
root and Rocky] mountains as early as possible, which is
about the beginning of May, and would take our horses with
them, or suffer them to disperse ; in either of which cases the
passage of the mountains will be almost impracticable. We,
therefore, after much deliberation, decided to remain here
till we could collect meat enough to last us till we reach the
Chopunnish nation, and to obtain canoes from the natives as
we ascend, either in exchange for our periogues or by purchasing them with skins and merchandise. These canoes
may in turn be exchanged for horses with the natives of the
plains, till we obtain enough to travel altogether by land.
On reaching the southeast branch [Lewis' river] of the Columbia, four or five men shall be sent on to the Chopunnish to
have our horses in readiness. Thus we shall have a stock of
horses sufficient to transport our baggage and to supply us
with provisions, for we now perceive that they will form our
only certain resource for food.

The hunters returned from the opposite side of the river
with some deer and elk, which were abundant there, as were
also the tracks of the black bear ; while on the north side we

could kill nothing. In the course of our dealings to-day we purchased a canoe from an Indian, for which we gave six fathoms of wampum beads. He seemed perfectly satisfied and went away, but returned soon after, canceled the bargain, and giving back the wampum requested that we would restore him the canoe. To this we consented, as we knew this method of trading to be very common and deemed perfectly fair.

April 2d. Being now determined to collect as much meat as possible, two parties, consisting of nine men, were sent over the river to hunt; three were ordered to range the country on this side, while all the rest were employed in cutting and scaffolding the meat which we had already. About eight o'clock several canoes arrived to visit us, and among the rest were two young men who were pointed out as Cas- (*p. 217*) hooks.[34] On inquiry, they said that their nation resided at the falls of a large river which empties into the south side of the Columbia a few miles below us, and they drew a map[35] of the country with a coal on a mat. In order to verify this information, Captain Clark persuaded one of the young men, by a present of a burning-glass, to accompany him to this river, in search of which he immediately set out with a canoe and seven of our men. After his departure other canoes arrived from above, bringing families of women and children, who confirmed the accounts of a scarcity of provisions. One of these families, consisting of ten or twelve persons, camped near us and behaved perfectly well. The hunters on this side of the [Columbia] river returned with only the skins of two deer, the animals being too poor for use.

April 3d. A considerable number of Indians crowded

[34] Cash-hooks, Lewis K 20, elsewhere Cushooks: see notice of them in the Estimate, which is about all that is known of these Indians, who were probably of Chinookan stock. See the Nemalquinner note, p. 924.

[35] This map, transferred by Clark to paper, now occupies Lewis K 28, 29. It traces Clark's trip of Apr. 2d and 3d, marks his camp on the Multnomah, locates the tribes named in the text of Apr. 30th, and shows many other interesting points. See note [27], p. 916, and note [42], p. 927.

about us to-day, many of whom came from the upper part of the river. These poor wretches confirm the reports of scarcity among the nations above ; which, indeed, their appearance sufficiently proved, for they seemed almost starved, and greedily picked the bones and refuse meat thrown away by us.

In the evening [6 p. m.] Captain Clark returned from his excursion. On setting out yesterday at half-past eleven o'clock, he directed his course along the south side of the [Columbia] river, where, at the distance of eight miles, he passed a village of the Nechacohee [36] tribe, belonging to the Eloot nation. The village itself is small, and being situated behind Diamond island, was concealed from our view as we passed both times along the northern shore. He continued till three o'clock, when he landed at the single house already mentioned [p. 917] as the only remains of a village of 24 straw huts. Along the shore were great numbers of small canoes for gathering wappatoo, which were left by the Sha-halas, who visit the place annually. The present inhabitants of the house are part of the Neerchokioo tribe of the same [Shahala] nation. On entering one of the apartments of the house, Captain Clark offered several articles to the Indians in ex- (*p. 218*) change for wappatoo ; but they appeared sullen and ill-humored, and refused to give him any. He therefore sat down by the fire opposite the men, and taking a port-fire match from his pocket, threw a small piece of it into the flame ; at the same time he took his pocket-compass, and by means of a magnet, which happened to be in his inkhorn, made the needle turn round very briskly. The match now took fire and burned violently, on which the Indians, terrified at this strange exhibition, immediately brought a quantity of wappatoo and laid it at his feet, begging him to put out

[36] So on the codex-map, Lewis K 28, which locates the village opposite Dia-mond island ; Nechacokee of the Estimate ; also Nechecolee, and better Necha-coke. A Chinookan tribe, only known as given by Lewis and Clark. The same is to be said of the Neerchokioo next named. For Eloot in the above paragraph read Echeloot, and see note [11], p. 672.

the bad fire, while an old woman continued to speak with great vehemence, as if praying and imploring protection. Having received the roots, Captain Clark put up the compass, and as the match went out of itself tranquillity was restored, though the women and children still took refuge in their beds and behind the men. He now paid them for what he had used, and after lighting his pipe and smoking with them, continued down the river.

He now found what we had called Image-canoe island to consist of three islands, the one in the middle concealing the opening between the other two in such a way as to present to us on the opposite side of the river the appearance of a single island. At the lower point of the third, 13 miles below the last village, he entered the mouth of a large river, which is concealed by three small islands in its mouth from those who descend or go up the Columbia. This river, which the Indians call Multnomah, from a nation of the same name residing near it on Wappatoo island, enters the Columbia 140 miles from the mouth of the latter river, of which it may justly be considered as forming one-fourth, though it has now fallen 18 inches below its greatest annual height. From its entrance Mount Regnier [37] bears nearly north, and Mount St. Helen's [Helena] north, with a very high humped mountain [Mount Adams, Yakima Co., Wash.] a little to the east of it, which seems to lie in the same chain with the conic-pointed mountains before mentioned. Mount Hood bore due east, and (*p. 219*) Captain Clark now discovered to the southeast a mountain which he had not yet seen, to which he gave the name of Mount Jefferson [Wasco Co., Ore.] Like Mount St. Helen's, its figure is a regular cone, covered with snow; it is probably of equal height with that mountain, though being more distant, so large a portion of it does not appear above the range of mountains which lie between these and this point.

Soon after entering the Multnomah he was met by an old

[37] Mt. Rainier, so called, 14,444 ft. high, whose right and true name is *Tacoma*, as proven and insisted by the Tacoma Academy of Science.

Indian descending the river alone in a canoe. After some conversation with him the pilot informed Captain Clark that this old man belonged to the Clackamos nation,[38] who reside on a river 40 miles up the Multnomah.   The current of this latter river is as gentle as that of the Columbia; its surface is smooth and even, and it appears to possess water enough for the largest ship, since, on sounding with a line of five fathoms, he could find no bottom for at least one-third of the width of the stream.   At the distance of seven miles he passed a sluice or opening on the right,[39] 80 yards wide, which separates Wappatoo island from the continent by emptying into the inlet below.   Three miles further up he reached a large wooden house on the east side, where he intended to sleep, but on entering the rooms he found such swarms of fleas that he preferred lying on the ground in the neighborhood.   The guide informed him that this house is the temporary residence of the Nemalquinner[40] tribe of the Cushook nation, who reside just below the falls of the Mult-nomah, but come down here occasionally to collect wappa-too.   It was 30 feet long, and 40 deep, built of broad boards,

[38] First "Clark-á-mus Nation, 11 towns," on Clark's codex-map, Lewis K 28, strung along a river headed straight from Clark's Mt. Jefferson, and brought into the Multnomah "40 miles up."   Printed also Clarkamus in the Estimate.   On Clark's map, 1814, printed Clack-a-mus, and the river from Mt. Jefferson denoted as Clackamus.   Elsewhere Clackamus, etc.; preferably now Clackama, pl. Clackamas ; latter form is present name of the county in Oregon next south of Multnomah Co., and of a town in that county on the railroad between Oregon City and Portland.   The Clackama is one of the best known Upper Chinookan tribes.   There are or were lately left some 50 or 60 of these Indians at the Grande Ronde Agency in Oregon.

[39] On his right as he ascended the Multnomah or Willamette.   This is the upper opening of the great sluice of the same name, whose lower end debouches in Scappoose bay by Warrior Point.   See note [21], p. 914.   The solitary Nemal-quinner house he presently observes was standing about the present site of St. John, five or six miles below Portland.

[40] So on the codex-map, Lewis K 28, and Clark's camp on the Multnomah there marked.   The locality which Clark makes ten miles up river is certainly not so far—probably about St. John.   The two miles farther he goes to-morrow would bring him about Waud's Bluff and Swan Island, whence it is still three or four miles to Portland.   No more is known of the Nemalquinners than L. and C. give.   They were of Chinookan stock.

covered with the bark of white cedar; the floor on a level
with the surface of the earth, and the arrangement of the
interior like those near the seacoast. The inhabitants had
left their canoes, mats, bladders, train-oil, baskets, bowls, and
trenchers lying about the house at the mercy of every visi-
tor—a proof, indeed, of mutual respect for the property of
each other, though we have had very conclusive evidence
that the property of white men is (*p. 220*) not deemed equally
sacred. The guide informed him further that a small distance above were two bayous, on which were a number of
small houses belonging to the Cushooks, but that the inhabitants had all gone up to the falls of the Multnomah for the
purpose of fishing.

Early next morning Captain Clark proceeded up the river,
which, during the night, had fallen about five inches. At
the distance of two miles [41] he came to the center of a bend
under the high lands on the right side, from which its course,
as could be discerned, was to the E.S.E. At this place the
Multnomah is 500 yards wide, and for half that distance
across the cord of five fathoms would not reach the bottom.
It appears to be washing away its banks, and has more sand-
bars and willow points than the Columbia. Its regular, gentle
current, the depth, smoothness, and uniformity with which
it rolls its vast body of water, prove that its supplies are at
once distant and regular; nor, judging from its appearance
and courses, is it rash to believe that the Multnomah and its
tributary streams water the vast extent of country between
the western mountains and those of the seacoast, as far, perhaps, as the waters of the Gulf of California. About eleven
o'clock he reached the house of the Neerchokioo, which he
found to contain eight families; but they were all so much

---

[41] The end of his reconnoissance, though the text leaves this to be discovered.
For at 11 o'clock a. m. he had *descended* the Multnomah, and got up the
Columbia as far as the house of the Neerchokioo which stood on the Oregon side
of the latter river; at 3 p. m. he was at the Nechecolee village, opposite
Diamond island, and soon afterward reached camp. The hiatus in the text is
between the words "Gulf of California" and "About eleven o'clock."

alarmed at his presence, notwithstanding his visit yesterday, that he remained a very few minutes only. Soon after setting out he met five canoes filled with the same number of families belonging to the Shahala nation. They were descending the river in search of subsistence, and seemed very desirous of coming alongside of the boat; but as there were 21 men on board, and the guide said that all these Shahalas, as well as their relations at the house which we had just left, were mischievous, bad men, they were not suffered to approach. At three o'clock he halted for an hour at the Nechecolee house, where his guide resided.

This large building is 226 feet in front, entirely (*p. 221*) above ground, and may be considered as a single house, because the whole is under one roof; otherwise it would seem more like a range of buildings, as it is divided into seven distinct apartments, each 30 feet square, by means of broad boards set on end from the floor to the roof. The apartments are separated from each other by a passage or alley four feet wide, extending through the whole depth of the house, and the only entrance is from this alley, through a small hole about 22 inches wide, and not more than 3 feet high. The roof is formed of rafters with round poles laid on them longitudinally. The whole is covered with a double row of the bark of the white cedar, extending from the top 18 inches over the eaves, and secured as well as smoothed by splinters of dried fir, inserted through it at regular distances. In this manner the roof is made light, strong, and durable. Near this house are the remains of several other large buildings, sunk in the ground, and constructed like those we had seen at the great narrows of the Columbia, belonging to the Eloots, with whom these people claim an affinity. In manner and dress these Nechecolees differ but little from the Quathlapotles and others of this neighborhood; but their language is the same used by the Eloots, and though it has some words in common with the dialects spoken here, yet the whole air of the language is obviously different. The men, too, are larger, and both sexes better

formed than among the nations below; and the females are
distinguished by wearing larger and longer robes—which are
generally of deer-skin dressed in the hair—than the neighboring women.   In the house were several old people of both
sexes, who were treated with much respect, and still seemed
healthy, though most of them were perfectly blind.   On
inquiring the cause of the decline of their village, an old
man, the father of the guide, and a person of some distinction, brought forward a woman very much marked with the
smallpox, saying that when a girl she was very near dying
with the disorder which had (*p. 222*) left those marks, and
that all the inhabitants of the houses now in ruins had fallen
victims to the same disease.   From the apparent age of the
woman, connected with her size at the time of her illness,
Captain Clark judged that the sickness must have been about
30 years ago, the period about which we have supposed that
smallpox prevailed on the seacoast.   He entered into a long
conversation with regard to the adjacent country and its
inhabitants, which the old man explained with great intelligence, and then drew with his finger, in the dust, a sketch of
Multnomah river and Wappatoo island.   This Captain Clark
copied [42] and preserved.   He now purchased five dogs, and
taking leave of the Nechecolee village, returned to camp.

[42] To be incorporated with the Cashook map mentioned on p. 921, and in
note [35] there : see also note [27], p. 916.

CHAPTER XXVII.

THE COLUMBIA FROM SANDY RIVER TO THE DALLES.

Detention to hunt—Particular account of Multnomah river, etc.—Wappatoo island and inlet—Wappatoo-roots—Wappatoo or Columbia valley—Large firs—Botany and zoölogy—Clackstars, Cathlacumups, Cathlanahquiahs, Cathlacomatups, Clannaminimuns, Clahnaquahs, Quathlapotles, Shotos, Cathlahaws, all Multnomah Indians—Clackamos river and Indians—Cushooks and Chahcowahs—Calahpoewahs—Characters of the Multnomah nations—A bear killed—The voyage resumed April 6th—Detention by the weather—Hunters sent out—Wahclellahs and Clahclellahs—Chilluckittequaws—Beacon rock—Brant island—Clahclellahs—Rocky Mountain goat—The Grand Rapids or Cascades—Tedious and laborious towing—Thievish Wahclellahs—Collision with them—Their good chief—Eloots—Loss of a canoe—Seven miles in three days—The long portage made—Yehhuhs and their village—Cruzatte's river—Canoe creek—Weocksockwillacums—Smackshops—Sepulcher rock—Cataract river—Quinett creek—Labiche's river—Account of the Columbia from the Rapids to the Narrows (Cascades to the Dalles)—Attempt to procure horses.

FRIDAY, April 4th, 1804. The hunters were still out in every direction. Those [Gass' party] from the opposite side of the river returned with the flesh of a bear [killed by Collins] and some venison, but that of six deer and an elk which they had killed was so meager and unfit for use that they had left it in the woods. Two other deer were brought in; but as the game seemed poor we dispatched a large party [Gibson, Shannon, Howard, and Wiser] to some low grounds on the south, six miles above us, to hunt there until our arrival. As usual many of the Indians came to our camp, some descending the rivers with their families, and others from below, with no object except to gratify their curiosity.

The visit of Captain Clark to the Multnomahs enabled us to combine all that we had seen or learned of the neighboring countries and nations. The most important spot is Wappatoo island, a large extent of country lying between the Multnomah and an arm of the Columbia, which [latter, now called Willamette Slough] we have called Wappatoo inlet, and separated from the mainland by a sluice 80 yards wide, which at the distance (*p. 224*) of seven miles up the

Multnomah connects that river with the inlet. The island thus formed is about 20 miles long, and varies in breadth from five to ten miles; the land is high, extremely fertile, and on most parts supplied with a heavy growth of cottonwood, ash, large-leaved ash, and sweet-willow; the black alder common to the coast having now disappeared.

But the chief wealth of this island consists of the numerous ponds in the interior, abounding with the common arrowhead (sagittaria sagittifolia [*Sagittaria variabilis*]) to the root of which is attached a bulb growing beneath it in the mud. This bulb, to which the Indians give the name of wappatoo, is the great article of food, and almost the staple article of commerce on the Columbia. It is never out of season; so that at all times of the year the valley is frequented by the neighboring Indians who come to gather it. It is collected chiefly by the women, who employ for the purpose canoes from 10 to 14 feet in length, about 2 feet wide and 9 inches deep, and tapering from the middle, where they are about 20 inches wide. They are sufficient to contain a single person and several bushels of roots, yet so very light that a woman can carry them with ease. She takes one of these canoes into a pond where the water is as high as the breast, and by means of her toes separates from the root this bulb, which on being freed from the mud rises immediately to the surface of the water, and is thrown into the canoe. In this manner these patient females remain in the water for several hours, even in the depth of winter. This plant is found through the whole extent of the valley in which we now are, but does not grow on the Columbia farther eastward.

This valley is bounded westward by the mountainous country bordering the coast, from which it extends eastward 30 miles in a direct line, till it is closed by the range of mountains crossing the Columbia above the Great Falls. Its length from north to south we are unable to determine, but we believe that the valley must extend to a great distance.

It is in fact the only desirable situation for a (*p. 225*) settlement on the western side of the Rocky mountains, and being naturally fertile, would, if properly cultivated, afford subsistence for 40,000 or 50,000 souls. The highlands are generally of a dark rich loam, not much injured by stones; though waving they are by no means too steep for cultivation, and a few miles from the river they widen, at least on the north side, into rich extensive prairies. The timber on them is abundant, and consists almost exclusively of the several species of fir already described, some of which grow to a great height. We measured a fallen tree of that species, and found that, including the stump of about six feet, it was 318 feet in length, though its diameter was only three feet. The dogwood [*Cornus nuttalli*] is also abundant on the uplands ; it differs from that of the United States in having a much smoother bark and in being much larger, the trunk attaining a diameter of nearly two feet. There is some white cedar of a large size, but no pine of any kind. In the bottom-lands are the cottonwood, ash, large-leaved ash, and sweet-willow. Interspersed with these are the pashequaw, shanataque, and compound fern, of which the natives use the roots ; the red flowering currant abounds on the upland, while along the river-bottoms grow luxuriantly the watercress, strawberry, cinquefoil, narrow-dock, sand-rush, and flowering pea, which latter is not yet in bloom. There is also a species of bear's-claw now blooming, but the large-leaved thorn has disappeared, nor do we see any longer the huckleberry, the shallun, or any of the other evergreen shrubs which bear berries, except that species the leaf of which has a prickly margin.

Among the animals we observe the martin, small geese, small speckled woodpecker with a white back [*Picus villosus harrisi*], blue-crested corvus [*Cyanocitta stelleri*], ravens, crows, eagles, vultures, and hawks. The mellow bug, long-legged spider, butterfly, blowingfly, and tick, have already made their appearance, but none [some] of all these are distinguished from animals (*p. 226*) of the same sort in the

United States. The mosquitoes, too, have resumed their visits, but are not yet troublesome.[1]

The nations which inhabit this fertile neighborhood are very numerous. Wappatoo inlet extends, 300 yards wide, for ten or twelve miles to the south, as far as the hills, near which it receives the waters of a small creek[2] whose sources are not far from those of the Killamuck [Tillamook] river. On that creek resides the Clackstar[3] nation, a numerous people of 1,200 souls, who subsist on fish and wappatoo, and who trade by means of the Killamuck river with the nation of that name on the seacoast. Lower down the inlet, toward the Columbia, is the tribe called Cathlacumup. On the sluice which connects the inlet with the Multnomah are the tribes Cathlanahquiah and Cathlacomatup: on Wappatoo island, the tribes of Clannahminamun and Clahnaquah.

[1] The plants and animals grouped under Apr. 4th are mainly as per Clark Q 90, 91, Lewis K 31, where "mellow" bug is for "mellon" bug, *i. e.*, melon-bug, here meaning *Diabrotica soror*, the Pacific coast representative of our common chrysomelid, *D. duodecimpunctata*.

[2] Apparently the Scappoose, Columbia Co., Ore. Clark's codex-map, Lewis K 28, charts it, and marks the Clackstar village at its mouth. The several other tribes named in this paragraph are also there laid down. An old post of the Hudson's Bay Company was located hereabouts, named Milton. It gave name also to a creek falling into Skapoosh or Scappoose bay.

[3] For Indians already mentioned, whose names recur in this paragraph, see preceding notes in the last chapter. For Clackstars, see note [25], p. 915.

The Cathlanaquiahs (so in the Estimate also, but Cath-lah-nah-quiah on the codex-map) were a small body of Chinookan stock, speaking the Katlámet dialect, on the S. W. side of Wappatoo island. The name is more properly Gatlá-nakoa-iq, from the river Nakoáiq.

The Cathlacomatups of the text are charted on the codex-map as Cath-lah-com-mah-tup.

The Shoto village is charted on the codex-map on the north bank of Lake river, at a place where this river widens into a slough or narrow pond, a short distance west of Lake Vancouver.

The Cathlahaws were also a Chinookan tribe.

The Chahcowahs, in the Estimate Charcowahs, also Charcowas, were another Chinookan tribe located as stated in the text. Their village is charted Char-cow-ah on the codex-map already often cited, on the Multnomah, next above the Cashooks, just beyond some mountains through which the river is represented as passing, on its left bank opposite mouth of a small river making from the east, considerably south of the Clackamas.

Immediately opposite, near the Towahnahiooks [Chawah-nahiooks river, *i. e.*, Lewis'], are the Quathlapotles ; higher up on this side of the Columbia, the Shotos. All these tribes, as well as the Cathlahaws, who live somewhat lower on the river, and have an old village on Deer Island, may be considered as parts of the great Multnomah nation, which has its principal residence on Wappatoo island, near the mouth of the large river to which they give their name. Forty miles above its junction with the Columbia, it receives the waters of the Clackamos, a river which may be traced through a woody and fertile country to its sources on Mount Jefferson, almost to the foot of which it is navigable for canoes. A nation of the same name resides in 11 villages along its borders ; they live chiefly on fish and roots, which abound in the Clackamos and along its banks, though they sometimes descend to the Columbia to gather wappatoo, where they cannot be distinguished by dress, manners, or language from the tribes of Multnomahs. Two days' journey from the Columbia, or about 20 miles beyond the entrance of the Clackamos, are the falls of the Multnomah.[4] At this place are the permanent residences of the Cushooks (*p. 227*) and Chahco-wahs, two tribes who are attracted to that place by the fish, and by the convenience of trading, across the mountains and down Killamuck river, with the nation of Killamucks, from whom they procure train-oil. These falls are occasioned by the passage of a high range of mountains, beyond which the country stretches into a vast level plain, wholly destitute of timber. As far as the Indians with whom we conversed had ever penetrated that country, it is inhabited by a nation called Calahpoewah,[5] a very numerous people whose villages,

---

[4] Not to be confounded with the beautiful cascade on the Oregon side of the Columbia, *now* called Multnomah Falls, nor with a place there of the same name. These are below the Cascades of the Columbia, and we shall soon pass them, going up river. See p. 937.

[5] Cal-lah-po-é-wah, Clark, in K 28; 15 villages charted. These are entirely different from any of the other tribes mentioned in this paragraph. Though classed by Keane as Chinooks, they belong to a different linguistic stock, now called the Kalapooian family, to which they give name. The Calahpoewah of Lewis and

nearly 40 in number, are scattered along each side of the Multnomah, which furnishes them with their chief subsistence—fish and the roots along its banks.

All the tribes in the neighborhood of Wappatoo island we have considered as Multnomahs—not because they are in any degree subordinate to that nation, but as they all seem to regard the Multnomahs as the most powerful. There is no distinguished chief, except the one at the head of the Multnomahs; and they are, moreover, linked by a similarity of dress, manners, houses, and language, which, much more than the feeble restraints of Indian government, contribute to make one people. These circumstances also separate them from nations lower down the river. The Clatsops, Chinnooks, Wahkiacums, and Cathlamahs understand each other perfectly; their language varies, however, in some respects from that of the Skilloots; but on reaching the Multnomah Indians, we found that though many words were the same as, and a great number differed only in the mode of accenting them from, those employed by the Indians near the mouth of the Columbia, yet there was a very sensible variation of language.

The natives of this valley are larger and rather better shaped than those of the seacoast; their appearance is generally healthy, but they are afflicted with the common disease of the Columbia—soreness of the eyes. To whatever [cause] this disorder may be imputed, it is a great national calamity; at all ages their eyes are sore (*p. 228*) and weak; the loss of one eye is by no means uncommon; in grown

---

Clark are a main tribe of the Kalapooiah of Scouler (Journ. Roy. Geogr. Soc. London, XI. 1841, p. 225), and of the Kalapuya of Hale (U. S. Expl. Exped. VII. 1846, pp. 217, 564), and other authors; they are the Calapooya of Bancroft (Nat. Races, III. 1882, pp. 565, 629). The various tribes of the Kalapooian family inhabited the valley of the Willamette river in Oregon, up to the headwaters of that stream; but they were cut off from the Columbia by Chinook tribes, so that Lewis and Clark only knew them from Indian information. Six or eight tribes of this family have been recognized. A mere handful survive, all at the Grande Ronde Agency in Oregon, as far as is known. The census of 1890 gives 171 in all, of which the Calapooyas themselves are 22.

persons total blindness is frequent, and almost universal in old age. The dress of the men has nothing different from that used below; but they are chiefly remarked by a passion for large brass buttons, which they fix on a sailor's jacket, when they are so fortunate as to obtain one, without regard to any arrangement. The women also wear the short robe already described; but their hair is most commonly braided into two tresses falling over each ear in front of the body, and instead of the tissue of bark, they employ a piece of leather in the shape of a pocket handkerchief, tied around the loins. This last is their only and ineffectual defense when the warmth of the weather induces them to throw aside the robe.

The houses are in general on a level with the ground, though some are sunk to the depth of two or three feet into the ground, and like those near the coast are adorned or disfigured by carvings or paintings on the posts, doors, and beds. They do not possess any peculiar weapon except a kind of broad-sword made of iron, from three to four feet long, the blade about four inches wide, very thin and sharp at all its edges as well as at the point. They have also bludgeons of wood in the same form; both kinds generally hang at the head of their beds. These are formidable weapons.

Like the natives of the seacoast, they are also very fond of cold, hot, and vapor baths, which are used at all seasons, for the purpose of health as well as pleasure. They, however, add a species of bath peculiar to themselves, by washing the whole body with urine every morning.

The mode of burying the dead in canoes is no longer[6] practiced by the natives here. The place of deposit is a vault formed of boards, slanting like the roof of a house from a pole supported by two forks. Under this vault the dead are placed horizontally on boards, on the surface of the

[6] Meaning that the Expedition is "no longer" in a region where canoe-burial is practiced—not that the Multnomah or Wappatoo Indians have desisted from any former scaphotaphic custom.

earth, and carefully covered with mats. Many bodies are
here laid on each other, to the height of three or four
corpses ; and different articles, which were most esteemed
by the dead, are (*p. 229*) placed by their side, their canoes
themselves being sometimes broken to strengthen the vault.

The trade of all these inhabitants is in anchovies and sturgeon, but chiefly in wappatoo, to obtain which the inhabitants, both above and below them on the river, come at all
seasons, and supply in turn beads, cloth, and various other
articles procured from the Europeans.

April 5th. We dried our meat as well as the cloudy
weather would permit. In the course of his chase yesterday, one of our men [Collins], who had killed the bear, found
the den of another with three cubs in it. He returned [with
Gass and Windsor [7]] to-day in hopes of finding her, but
brought only the cubs, without being able to see the dam ;
and on this occasion Drewyer, our most experienced hunts-
man, assured us that he had never known a single instance
where a female bear, which had once been disturbed by a
hunter and obliged to leave her young, returned to them
again. The young bears were sold for wappatoo to some of
the many Indians who visited us in parties during the day
and behaved very well. Having made our preparations of
dried meat, we set out next morning,

April 6th, by nine o'clock, continued along the north side
of the river for a few miles, and then crossed the river to
look for the hunters who had been sent forward day before
yesterday. We found them at the upper end of the bottom
with some Indians—for we are never freed from the visits of
the natives. They had killed three elk, and wounded two
others so badly that it was still possible to get them. We

[7] Gass, p. 194, says under date of April 3d that, being out hunting with some
of the men, he " saw 3 small cubs in a den, but the old bear was not with them."
April 4th, p. 194, he makes another entry : " I went out with two more to the
den where we saw the cubs, to watch for the old bear ; we stayed there till dark
and then encamped about a quarter of a mile off, and went back early in the
morning ; but the old one was not returned : so we took the cubs and returned to
camp."

therefore landed [on the south side, after coming ten miles], and having prepared scaffolds and secured the five elk, we camped for the night.[8] The following evening,

April 7th,[9] the weather having been fair and pleasant, we had dried a sufficient quantity of meat to serve us as far as the Chopunnish, with occasional supplies, if we can procure them, of roots, dogs, and horses. In the course of the day several parties of Shahalas, from a village eight miles above (*p. 230*) us, came to visit us, and behaved themselves very properly, except that we were obliged to turn one of them from the camp for stealing a piece of lead. Everything was now ready for our departure; but in the morning,

April 8th, the wind blew with great violence, and we were obliged to unload our boats, which were soon after filled with water.[10] The same cause prevented our setting out to-day; we therefore dispatched several hunters around the neighborhood, but in the evening they came back with nothing but a duck. They had, however, seen some of the blacktailed or jumping fallow-deer [*Cariacus columbianus*], like those about Fort Clatsop, which are scarce near this place,

[8] Not edited with Biddle's habitual precision. Lewis K 32 says that the distance made to-day was ten miles ; camp was pitched on the south ; the Expedition is therefore in Multnomah Co., Ore., about ten miles above the mouth of Quicksand or Sandy river, somewhere above Cape Horn, and in view of Beacon rock; but I cannot fix the spot. It was about the end of the low country on the Oregon side—for all the route of Apr. 9th from this camp to Beacon rock was between precipices. See Nov. 2d, pp. 688, 689.

[9] Clark Q 93–99, this date, has a long description of a " bird like a quail," which he killed to-day, but of which there is no notice anywhere in the Biddle text. Perhaps it was passed over because it was not recognized—and no wonder, for here is probably the first description ever penned of the beautiful mountain quail of California, *Oreortyx picta*, unknown to science till described as *Ortyx picta* by Douglas, Trans. Linn. Soc. of London, XVI. 1829, p. 143. The description is clear and unmistakable ; it is copied in Lewis K 42–44, where it is stated that this bird was killed by R. Fields. Lewis says that he preserved the skin; also, that another specimen was shot by Captain Clark.

[10] Gass notes this, and adds, p. 196: " Some of the men are complaining of rheumatick pains ; which are to be expected from the wet and cold we suffered last winter, during which from the 4th of November 1805 to the 25th of March 1806, there were not more than 12 days in which it did not rain, and of these but 6 were clear."

where the common long-tailed fallow-deer are most abundant. They had also observed two black bears [*Ursus americanus*], the only kind that we have discovered in this quarter. A party of six Indians camped at some distance, and late at night the sentinel stopped one of the men, an old man who was creeping into camp in order to pilfer; he contented himself with frightening the Indian, and then giving him a few stripes with a switch, turned out the fellow, who soon afterward left the place with all his party.

April 9th. The wind having moderated, we reloaded the canoes and set out by seven o'clock. We stopped to take up the two hunters [R. and J. Fields] who left us yesterday, but were unsuccessful in the chase, and then proceeded to the Wahclellah village, situated on the north side of the river, about a mile below Beacon rock. During the whole of the route from camp we passed along under high, steep, and rocky sides of the mountains, which now close on each side of the river, forming stupendous precipices, covered with fir and white cedar. Down these heights frequently descend the most beautiful cascades,[11] one of which, a large creek, throws itself over a perpendicular rock 300 feet above the water, while other smaller streams precipitate themselves from a still greater elevation, and evaporating (*p. 231*) in a mist, collect again and form a second cascade before they reach the bottom of the rocks. We stopped to breakfast at this village. We [*i. e.*, John Colter] here found the tomahawk which had been stolen from us on the 4th of last November. They assured us they had bought it of the Indians below; but as the latter had already informed us that the Wahclellahs had such an article, which they had stolen, we made no difficulty about retaking our property.

This village appears to be the wintering-station of the Wahclellahs and Clahclellahs, two tribes of the Shahala

[11] There are five such cascades within a few miles of each other on the Oregon side, named Multnomah, Bridal Veil, Latourelle, Horsetail, and Oneonta. The first-named is the most striking and best-known, having a total fall of 600 feet or more, divided into two sections. These cascades were noted on p. 678.

nation [note [23], p. 761]. The greater part of the first tribe have lately removed to the falls of the Multnomah, and the second have established themselves a few miles higher up the Columbia, opposite the lower point of Brant island, where they take salmon, that being the commencement of the rapids.[12] They are now in the act of removing, and are carrying off with them not only the furniture and effects, but the bark and most of the boards of their houses. In this way nine have been lately removed. There are still 14 standing, and in the rear of the village are the traces of 10 or 12 others of more ancient date. These houses are either sunk in the ground or on a level with the surface, and are generally built of boards and covered with cedar-bark. In the single houses there is generally a division near the door, which is in the end; or, in case the house be double, opens in the narrow passage between the two. Like those we had seen below at the Neerchokioo tribe, the women wear longer and larger robes than their neighbors the Multnomahs, and suspend various ornaments from the cartilage of the nose; the hair is, however, worn in the same sort of braid, falling over each ear; and the truss [breech-clout[13]] is universal from Wappatoo island to Lewis' river. The men also form their hair into two cues by means of otter-skin thongs, which fall over the ears so as to give that extraordinary width to the face which is here considered so ornamental. These people seemed very unfriendly, and our numbers alone seemed to secure us from (*p. 232*) ill treatment.

While we were at breakfast the grand chief of the Chilluckittequaws [note [12], p. 673] arrived, with two inferior chiefs, several and men and women of his nation. They were returning home after trading in the Columbian valley, and

---

[12] See the plate of the "Great Shoot or Rapids" (Cascades) where "Village" is lettered, at head of Strawberry island, on the Washington side, opposite lower point of Brant island. Here, it will be remembered, was our camp of Nov. 1st (see this date, p. 685); and here is now town of Cascades.

[13] "A number of the Indians visit us daily; and the females in general have that leather covering round their loins, which is somewhat in the form of a truss," Gass, p. 195, Apr. 5th.

were loaded with wappatoo and dried anchovies, which, with some beads, they had obtained in exchange for chappelell, bear-grass, and other small articles. As these people had been very kind to us as we descended the river, we endeavored to repay them by every attention in our power. After purchasing, with much difficulty, a few dogs and some wappatoo from the Wahclellahs, we left them at two o'clock, and passing under the Beacon rock reached, in two hours, the Clahclellah village.

Beacon rock,[14] which we now observed more accurately than as we descended, stands on the north side of the river, insulated from the hills. The northern side has a partial growth of fir or pine. To the south it rises in an unbroken precipice to the height of 700 feet, where it terminates in a sharp point, and may be seen at the distance of 20 miles below. This rock may be considered as the commencement of tide-water, though the influence of the tide is perceptible here in autumn only, at which time the water is low. What the precise difference at those seasons is, we cannot determine; but on examining a rock which we lately passad, and comparing its appearance with that which we observed last November, we judge the flood of this spring to be twelve feet above the height of the river at that time. From Beacon rock, as low as the marshy islands, the general width of the river is from one to two miles, though in many places it is still greater.

On landing at the Clahclellahs' we found them busy erecting their huts, which seem to be of a temporary kind only, so that most probably they do not remain longer than the salmon season. Like their countrymen, whom we had just left, these people were sulky and ill-humored, and so much on the alert to pilfer that we were obliged to keep them at a distance from our baggage. As (*p. 233*) our large canoes

---

[14] Beacon Rock does not seem to be now so called, or to have ever been generally known by the name. I have yet to find it on any map. I have once found it marked Castle Rock (as I suppose), and am informed that it is now commonly called Pyramid mountains. See p. 688.

could not ascend the rapids on the north side, we passed to the opposite shore and entered the narrow channel which separates it from Brant island. The weather was very cold and rainy, and the wind so high that we were afraid to attempt the rapids this evening; therefore, finding a safe harbor, we camped for the night. The wood in this neighborhood has lately been on fire, and the firs have discharged considerable quantities of pitch, which we collected for some of our boats. We saw to-day some turkey-buzzards [*Cathartes aura*], which are the first we have observed on this side of the Rocky mountains.

April 10*th.* Early in the morning we dropped down the channel to the lower end of Brant island, and then drew our boats up the rapid.[16] At the distance of a quarter of a mile we crossed over to the village of Clahclellahs, consisting of six houses, on the opposite side. The river is here about 400 yards wide, and the current so rapid that although we employed five oars for each canoe, we were borne down a considerable distance. While we were at breakfast one of the Indians offered us two sheep-skins for sale; one, which

---

[16] *The Columbian Cascades.*—L. and C. do not use the term "Cascades" in any of its present senses. Until their narrative has been mastered, their graphic and faithful descriptions may not be grasped by the casual reader, because the same descriptive terms, "falls" "shoots," "rapids," "narrows," etc., repeatedly occur in connection with the obstructions to navigation in entirely different and widely separated places along the river. Moreover, the familiar word "Dalles" does not occur in their work. Perhaps a few words serving as stepping-stones may help the reader to make the portage of these difficult places.

At this point the Expedition has reached the head of tide-water, 50 miles above Vancouver, which is six miles above the mouth of the Multnomah. They are in the heart of the Cascade range, which stretches north-south, and through which the Columbia has burst its way from east to west. Here the sleepless sentinel, Beacon Rock, challenges further progress, as the river rushes through the last contraction of its water-way to the sea. The whole of this strait-jacketing is "The Cascades." The actual distance is about 4½ miles. But the pitch is not uniformly continuous for this distance. Consequently "The Cascades" is divisible into conveniently recognized sections. The pitch is greatest at the head of The Cascades, where the river makes a double rectangular bend around a rocky point on the Oregon shore. This point is now called the "Upper Cascades"; here is also now the place on the Oregon side called "Cascade Locks"; here is

was the skin of a full-grown sheep,[16] was as large as that of a common deer; the second was smaller, and the skin of the head, with the horns remaining, was made into a cap, highly prized as an ornament by the owner. He, however, sold the cap to us for a knife, and the rest of the skin for those of two elk; but as they observed our anxiety to purchase the other skin, they would not accept the same price for it, and as we hoped to procure more in the neighborhood, we did not offer a greater. The horns of the animal were black, smooth, and erect; they rise from the middle of the forehead, a little above the eyes, in a cylindrical form, to the height of four inches, where they are pointed. The Clahclellahs informed us that these sheep are very abundant on the heights and among the cliffs of the adjacent mountains; and that these two had been lately killed out of a herd of 36, at no great distance from the (*p. 234*) village.

We were soon joined by our hunters with three black-tailed fallow-deer [*Cariacus columbianus*]; and having purchased a few white salmon, proceeded on our route. The south side of the river is impassable, and the rapidity of the current, as well

likewise the "head of the rapids" of L. and C., their "great shoot or rapid" and their "portage": see the plate. Here they camped on an island, Oct. 30th, going down, and here they will camp, on the Washington mainland, Apr. 12th, going up. These "Upper Cascades" make about a mile—a stretch included in the "portage" of L. and C., and itself divisible into their "great shoot" at its head, 2,000 feet long, with a fall of 21 feet, and their "bad rapid" at its foot. All the rest of the contracted water-way, or about 3½ miles, answers to the name of "Lower Cascades." The lower end of this long pitch is the "foot of the rapids," between the head of Strawberry island (camp Nov. 1st) and the heel of Brant island (camp Apr. 9th). Here on the Washington side is now "Cascades" (town). A mail-boat ascends without difficulty, through a 2,000 foot rapid with a velocity of eight miles an hour, to the head of Bradford island. The engineering plan of improvement was to flank the Upper Cascades with a 3,000-foot canal and clear out the Lower Cascades by blasting. The total fall, from the head of the Upper to the foot of the Lower Cascades was found to be 45 feet at high water, 36 feet at low water; total distance between these points, 23,000 feet. An annual flood occurs in June with precise periodicity. (Compare the corresponding note about the "Dalles," 50 miles further up river, p. 954.)

[16] As presently appears, these "sheep" were the mountain goat, *Haplocerus montanus*. See p. 850, and note there.

as the large rocks along the shore, renders the navigation of even the north side extremely difficult. During the greater part of the day it was necessary to draw the boats along the shore, and as we have only a single tow-rope that is strong enough, we are obliged to bring them one after the other. In this tedious and laborious manner, we at length reached the portage on the north side, and carried our baggage to the top of a hill, about 200 paces distant, where we camped[17] for the night. The canoes were drawn on shore and secured, but one of them having got loose, drifted down to the last [Clahclellah] village, the inhabitants of which brought her back to us—an instance of honesty which we rewarded with a present of two knives. It rained all night and next morning,

April 11th, so that the tents, and the skins which covered the baggage, were wet. We therefore determined to take the canoes first over the portage, in hopes that by the afternoon the rain would cease, and we might carry our baggage across without injury. This was immediately begun by almost the whole party, who in the course of the day dragged four of the canoes to the head of the rapids, with great difficulty and labor. A guard, consisting of one sick man [Bratton] and three who had been lamed by accidents, remained with Captain Lewis [and a cook] to guard the baggage. This precaution was absolutely necessary to protect it from the Wahchellahs [*sic*], whom we discovered to be great thieves, notwithstanding their apparent honesty in restoring our boat; indeed, so arrogant and intrusive have they become that nothing but our numbers, we are convinced, saves us from attack. They crowded about us while we were taking up the boats, and one of them had the insolence to throw stones down the bank at two of our men.

We now found it necessary to depart from our mild and

---

[17] See the plate, dotted line marked " Portage 2 Miles "; camp on the hill 200 paces back of the lower end of this line, at *foot* of the portage, at *head* of which, two miles above, on an island, was camp of Oct. 30th. See p. 680, and note there.

pacific course of conduct. On returning to the ..ead of the portage, many of them met our men and seem- (*p. 235*) ed very ill-disposed. Shields had stopped to purchase a dog, and being separated from the rest of the party, two Indians pushed him out of the road, and attempted to take the dog from him. He had no weapon but a long knife, with which he immediately attacked them both, hoping to put them to death before they had time to draw their arrows; but as soon as they saw his design they fled into the woods. Soon afterward we were told by an Indian who spoke Clatsop, which we had ourselves learned during the winter, that the Wahclellahs had carried off Captain Lewis' dog to their village below. Three men well armed were instantly dispatched in pursuit of them, with orders to fire if there was the slightest resistance or hesitation. At the distance of two miles they came within sight of the thieves, who, finding themselves pursued, left the dog and made off.[18] We now ordered all the Indians out of our camp, and explained to them that whoever stole any of our baggage, or insulted our men, should be instantly shot; a resolution which we were determined to enforce, as it was now our only means of safety.

We were visited during the day by a chief of the Clahclellahs, who seemed mortified at the behavior of the Indians, and told us that the persons at the head of their outrages were two very bad men who belonged to the Wahclellah tribe, but that the nation did not by any means wish to displease us. This chief seemed very well-disposed, and we had every reason to believe was much respected by the neighboring Indians. We therefore gave him a small medal and showed him all the attention in our power,[19] with which he appeared very much gratified; and we trust his inter-

[18] " They also stole an ax from us, but scarcely had it in their possession before Thompson detected them, and wrest it from them," Lewis K 53.

[19] Even to an exchange of tomahawks, Lewis K 53. " He had in his possession a very good pipe tomahawk which he informed us he had received as a present from a trader who visited him last winter overland (pointing to the N.W.), whome he called Swippeton ; he was pleased with the Tommahawk of Capt. C. in consequence of it's having a brass bowl and Capt. C. gratified him

position may prevent the necessity of our resorting to force against his countrymen.

Many Indians from the villages above passed us in the course of the day, on their return from trading with the natives of the valley; among others, we recognized an Eloot [Echeloot], with ten or twelve of his nation who were on their way home to the Long Narrows of the Columbia. These (*p. 236*) people do not, as we are compelled to do, drag their canoes up the rapids, but leave them at the head as they descend, and carrying their goods across the portage, hire or borrow others from the people below. When the trade is over they return to the foot of the rapids, where they leave these boats and resume their own at the head of the portage. The labor of carrying the goods across is equally shared by the men and women, and we were struck by the contrast between the decent conduct of all the natives from above, and the profligacy and ill-manners of the Wahclellahs. About three-quarters of a mile below our camp is a burial-ground, which seems common to the Wahclellahs, Clahclellahs, and Yehhuhs. It consists of eight sepulchers on the north bank of the river.[20]

April 12th. The rain continued all night and this morning. Captain Lewis now took with him all the men fit for duty, and began to drag the remaining periogue over the rapids. This has become much more difficult than when we passed in the autumn; at that time there were in the whole distance of seven miles only three difficult points; but the water is now very considerably higher, and during all that distance the ascent is exceedingly laborious and dangerous; nor would it be practicable to descend, except by letting down the empty boats by means of ropes. The route over this part, from the foot to the head of the portage, is about three miles; the canoes which had been already dragged up

by an exchange. as a further proof of his being esteemed by the white trader he gave us a well backed baked saylor's bisquit which he also informed us he had received from Swippeton." This is the " Swipton " of p. 790.

[20] See " 8 Vaults " marked on the plate, and for description see p. 682.

immediately above the rapids, but who had now emigrated to the opposite shore, where they generally take salmon. Like their relations, the Wahclellahs, they have taken their houses with them, so that only one is now standing where the old village was. We observe, generally, that the houses which have the floor on a level with the earth are smaller, and have more the appearance of being temporary than those which are sunk in the ground; whence we presume that the former are the dwellings during spring and summer, while the latter are reserved for the autumn and winter. Most of the houses are built of boards and covered with bark, though some of the more inferior kind are constructed wholly of cedar-bark, kept smooth and flat by small splinters fixed crosswise through the bark, at the distance of 12 or 14 inches apart. There is but little difference in appearance between these (*p. 238*) Yehhuhs, Wahclellahs, Clahclellahs, and Neerchokioos, who compose the Shahala nation. On comparing the vocabulary of the Wahclellahs with that of the Chinnooks, we found that the names for numbers were precisely the same, though the other parts of the language were essentially different. The women of all these tribes braid the hair, pierce the nose, and some of them have lines of dots reaching from the ankle as high as the middle of the leg. These Yehhuhs behaved with great propriety, and condemned the treatment we had received from the Wahclellahs. We purchased from one of them the skin of a sheep [goat, *Haplocerus montanus*] killed near this place, for which we gave in exchange the skins of a deer and an elk. These animals, he tells us, usually frequent the rocky parts of the mountains, where they are found in great numbers. The bighorn [*Ovis montana*] is also an inhabitant of these mountains, and the natives have several robes made of their skins. The mountains near this place are high, steep, and strewed with rocks, which are principally black. Several species of fir, white pine, and white cedar, form their covering, while near the river we see cottonwood, sweet-willow, a species of maple, broad-leaved ash, purple haw, a small species of cherry, purple currant, gooseberry, red-willow, vining[24] and white-berry honeysuckle, huckleberry, sacacommis, two kinds of mountain holly, and the common ash.

April 13th. The loss of our periogue yesterday obliges us to distribute our loading between the two canoes and the two remaining periogues. This being done we proceeded along the north side of the river, but soon finding that the increased loading rendered our vessels difficult to manage, if not dangerous in case of high wind, the two periogues only continued on their route, while Captain Lewis, with the canoes, crossed over to the Yehhuh village, with a view of purchasing one or two more canoes. The village now consisted of 11 houses, crowded with inhabitants, and about 60 fighting men. They were very well disposed, and we found no difficulty in procuring two small canoes, in exchange (*p. 239*) for two robes and four elk-skins. He also purchased with deer-skins three dogs—an animal which has now become a favorite food, for it is found to be a strong, healthy diet, preferable to lean deer or elk, and much superior to horseflesh in any state. With these he proceeded along the south side of the river, and joined us in the evening. We had gone along the north shore as high as Cruzatte's [Wind: p. 679] river, to which place we had sent some hunters [Drewyer and R. and J. Fields] day before yesterday, and where we were detained by the high winds. The hunters, however, did not join us, and we therefore, as soon as the wind had abated, proceeded on for six miles, where we halted[25] for Captain Lewis, and in the meantime went out to hunt. We [Shields] procured two black-tailed fallow-deer, which seemed to be the only kind inhabiting these mountains. Believing that the hunters were still below us, we dispatched [Sergeant Pryor and two men in] a small canoe back for them, and in the morning,

[24] That is, twining like a vine.

[25] This camp, unspecified for position, was on the north side, in Skamania Co., Wash., and by text six miles above Cruzatte's or Wind river. It is therefore not much short of Little White Salmon river, a considerable stream which is passed without mention both ways. See note [19], p. 678.

April 14*th*, they all joined us, with four more deer. After breakfast we resumed our journey, and though the wind was high during the day, yet by keeping along the northern shore we were able to proceed without danger. At one o'clock we halted for dinner at a large village situated in a narrow bottom, just above the entrance of Canoe creek.[26] The houses are detached from each other, so as to occupy an extent of several miles, though only 20 in number. Those which are inhabited are on the surface of the earth, and built in the same shape as those near the rapids ; but there were others at present evacuated, which are completely under ground. They are sunk about eight feet deep, covered with strong timbers and several feet of earth in a conical form. On descending by means of a ladder through a hole at the top, which answers the double purpose of a door and a chimney, we found that the house consisted of a single room, nearly circular and about 16 feet in diameter.

The inhabitants, who call themselves Weocksockwillacum,[27] differ but little from those near the rapids, the chief (*p. 240*) distinction in dress being a few leggings and moccasins, which we find here like those worn by the Chopunnish. These people have ten or twelve very good horses, which are the first we have seen since leaving this neighborhood last autumn. The country below is, indeed, of such a nature as to prevent the use of this animal, except in the Columbian valley ; and there they would [not[28]] be of great service, for the inhabitants reside chiefly on the river side, and the country is too thickly wooded to suffer them to hunt game on horseback. Most of these, they inform us, have

[26] White Salmon river, on the boundary between Skamania and Klikitat counties, Wash. See note [17], p. 677.

[27] First Lewis K 61, We-ock-sock, Wil-la-cum (as two words, capitals, and comma between); a Chinookan band, of which our only information is as in the text.

[28] This self-contradictory sentence is as follows in Lewis K 62 : " The country below this place will not permit the uce of this valuable animal except in the Columbian vally—and there the present inhabitants have no uce for them as they reside immediately on the river and the country is too thickly timbered to admit them to run the game with horses if they had them."

been taken in a warlike excursion which was lately made against the Towanahiooks, a part of the Snake nation living in the upper part of the Multnomah, to the southeast of this place.   Their language is the same with that of the Chilluckittequaws.   They seemed inclined to be very civil, and gave us in exchange some roots, shapelell [*sic*], filberts, dried berries, and five dogs.

After dinner we proceeded and, passing at the distance of six miles the high cliffs on the left, camped at the mouth of a small run on the same [north [29]] side.   A little above us is a village, consisting of about 100 fighting men of a tribe called Smackshops,[30] many of whom passed the evening with us. They do not differ in any respect from the inhabitants of the village below.   In hopes of purchasing horses we did not set out next morning,

April 15*th*, till after breakfast.   In the meantime we exposed our merchandise and made them various offers ; but as they declined bartering, we left them and soon reached Sepulcher rock,[31] where we halted a few minutes.   The rock itself stands near the middle of the river, and contains about two acres of ground above high water.   On this surface are scattered 13 vaults constructed like those below the rapids, some of them more than half filled with dead bodies.   After

[29] This " small run " I have not succeeded in identifying satisfactorily.   Several such runs make in on the Washington side between White Salmon or Canoe and Klikitat or Cataract river, and one of them is about the right distance above the former ; but its name I have not learned.   The Major's creek of note [16], p. 677, seems a little too high up for the one here in question.   Camp should be in the vicinity of the present town of White Salmon.   Hood's or Labiche's river, from the south, has been passed without notice.

[30] See note [12], p. 673, and " Smacshop 300 souls " of Clark's 1814 map.

[31] Sepulcher island of p. 677, where located three miles below Cataract (Klikitat) river.   Those marked " Grave Rocks " on Wilkes' map of 1841 seem to be too low down for the place in mention here, but may be the same " Memaloose Alahee," incorrectly located.   Such rocks have been used from time out of mind for sepulture by Klikitats and other Indians.   One of them, whose location is given as 13 miles below the Dalles, has lately become noted through a whim of old " Vic " Trevett, an Oregon pioneer, who wished his body to be placed there. He died at San Francisco in January, 1883 ; his wishes were carried out in the following March, and over his bones is now a handsome monument.

satisfying our curiosity with these venerable remains, we
returned to the northern shore, and proceeded to a village
at the distance of four miles.   On land- (*p. 241*) ing, we
found that the inhabitants belonged to the same nation we
had just left; as they also had horses, we made a second
attempt to furnish a few of them ; but with all our dexterity
in exhibiting our wares, we could not induce them to sell,
as we had none of the only articles which they seemed
desirous of procuring—a sort of war-hatchet, called by the
northwest traders an eye-dog.   We therefore purchased two
dogs, and taking leave of these Weocksockwillacums, proceeded to another of their villages, just below the entrance
of Cataract [Klikitat : p. 667, Oct. 29th] river.   Here too we
tried in vain to purchase some horses, nor did we meet with
more success at two villages of Chilluckittequaws, a few
miles further up the river.   At three in the afternoon we
came to the mouth of Quinett creek,[32] which we ascended a
short distance, and camped for the night at the spot we had
called Rock fort.[33]   Here we were soon visited by some of
the people from the Great Narrows and Falls ; and on our
expressing a wish to purchase horses, they agreed to meet
us to-morrow on the north side of the river, where we would

[32] Before called Quenett river ; see note [8], p. 669.   A name of this creek, not
before noted, is Wasco (as Stevens' map No. 3, with The Dalles called Was-
copam).   Winquat and Kaclasco are also given as names of the place.

[33] Gass notes, p. 199, "*Tuesday* 15*th* . . . passed a place where there was a village in good order last fall when we went down ; but it has been lately torn down,
and again erected at a short distance from the old ground where it formerly stood.
The reason of this removal I cannot conjecture, unless [it is] to avoid the fleas,
which are more numerous in this country than any insects I ever saw."   His
editor notes a passage from A. McKenzie : "We had however the curiosity to
visit the houses (of a deserted village) which were erected upon posts ; and we
suffered very severely from the indulgence of it ; for the floors were covered with
fleas, and we were immediately in the same condition, for which we had no remedy but to take to the water.   There was not a spot round the houses, free from
grass, that was not alive, as it were, with this vermin."   This night's camp,
"Rock fort " in the text, is called " Rock camp" by Gass, and elsewhere Fort
Rock, or Fort Rock camp.   See note [8], p. 669.   Before there was any Dalles
City, an establishment here was called Fort Dalles, on Mill (Wasco) creek.
From this stream eastward, toward the Des Chutes, comes a remarkable set of

open a traffic. They then returned to their villages to collect the horses.

April 16*th*. In the morning Captain Clark crossed with
nine men and a large part of our merchandise, in order to
purchase twelve horses to transport our baggage, and some
pounded fish as a reserve during the passage of the Rocky
mountains. The rest of the men were employed in hunting
and preparing saddles.

From the Rapids [*i. e.*, Cascades] to this place, and indeed
as far as the commencement of the Narrows [*i. e.*, Dalles],
the Columbia is from half a mile to three-quarters in width,
and possesses scarcely any current. Its bed consists principally of rock, except at the entrance of Labiche [Hood: see
p. 677] river, which takes its rise in Mount Hood, from which,
like Quicksand river, it brings down vast quantities of sand.
During the whole course of the Columbia from the Rapids to
the Chilluckittequaws are the trunks of many large pine-trees
standing erect in the water, (*p. 242*) which is 30 feet deep at
present, and never less than ten. These trees could never
have grown in their present site, for they are all very much
doated [*sic* [34]], and none of them vegetate; so that the only

streams, known as Three-mile, Five-mile, Eight-mile and Fifteen-mile, according to their successive distances by the trail from Dalles. The first of these, also
called Holman creek, is a separate stream, falling into the Columbia. The
other three are branches of one stream which falls into the Columbia. That
one of these two disemboguements which occurs immediately below the " great
basin "at the foot of the Long Narrows, is clearly charted on Clark's unpublished
codex-map, H 3. This map also marks the first creek on the Oregon side below
Dalles, now known as Chenoweth or Cheneweth.

[34] An archaic and probably disused form of *doted*, meaning decayed, as a tree.
The verb as used in this sense is classed as an English provincialism by the
editor of the Century Dictionary, who also marks *doted*, adj., as obsolete. But
I fear my much esteemed friend and collaborator is mistaken on this point, for
the word is not a rare locution in some parts of our country. I have heard it in
North Carolina, where it is said of trees dead at the top, that they are *doted*, or
have *doted*. The word is also applied to lumber prepared from wood not exactly
decayed, but unsound to the extent of being not springy and tough enough.
The Columbia river phenomenon which L. and C. were the first white men to
note is well marked enough to be sometimes charted. Thus the Wilkes' map
of 1841 shows a place in the river legended " Rotten Pine Stumps."

reasonable account which can be given of this phenomenon is that at some period, which the appearance of the trees induces us to fix within 20 years, the rocks from the hillsides have obstructed the narrow pass at the rapids, and caused the river to spread through the woods. The mountains, which border as far as Sepulcher rock, are high and broken, and its romantic views occasionally enlivened by beautiful cascades rushing from the heights, forming a deep contrast with the firs, cedars, and pines which darken their sides. From Sepulcher rock, where the low country begins, the long-leaved pine is the almost exclusive growth of timber; but our present camp is the last spot where a single tree is to be seen on the wide plains, which are now spread before us to the foot of the Rocky [*i. e.*, Bitter-root] mountains. It is, however, covered with rich verdure of grass and herbs, some inches in height, which forms a delightful and exhilarating prospect, after being confined to the mountains and thick forests on the seacoast. The climate too, though we are only on the border of the plains, is here very different from that we have lately experienced. The air is drier and more pure, and the ground itself is as free from moisture as if there had been no rain for the last ten days. Around this place are many esculent plants used by the Indians; among which is a currant, now in bloom, with a yellow blossom like that of the yellow currant of the Missouri, from which, however, it differs specifically. There is also a species of hyacinth [*Camassia esculenta*] growing in the plains, which presents at this time a pretty flower of a pale blue color, and the bulb of which is boiled, baked, dried in the sun, and eaten by the Indians. This bulb, of the present year, is white, flat in shape, and not quite solid; it overlies and presses closely that of the last year, (*p. 243*) which, though much thinner and withered, is equally wide, and sends forth from its sides a number of small radicles.

Our hunters obtained one of the long-tailed deer [*Cariacus virginianus macrurus*] with the young horns about two inches long, and [J. Fields] a large black or dark brown

pheasant, such as we had seen on the upper part of the Missouri.[35] They [R. Fields] also brought in a large gray squirrel
[*Sciurus fossor*], and two others [*Sciurus* sp?] resembling it
in shape, but smaller than the common gray squirrel of the
United States, and of a pied gray and yellowish-brown color.
In addition to this game, they had seen some antelopes and
the tracks of several black bears, but no appearance of elk.
They had seen no birds, but [J. Fields] found three eggs of
the party-colored corvus [common magpie, *Pica pica hudsonica*[36]]. Though the salmon has not yet appeared, we have
seen less scarcity than we apprehended from the reports we
had heard below. At the rapids the natives subsist chiefly
on a few white salmon-trout which they take at this time,
and considerable quantities of a small indifferent mullet of
an inferior quality. Beyond that place we see none except
dried fish of the last season; nor is the sturgeon caught by
any of the natives above the Columbia, their whole stores
consisting of roots and fish either dried or pounded.

Captain Clark had, in the meantime, been endeavoring to
purchase horses, without success; but they promised to trade
with him if he would go up to the Skilloot village, above the
Long Narrows. He therefore sent over to us for more
merchandise, and then accompanied them in the evening to
that place, where he passed the night. The next day,

April 17*th*, he sent [Willard and Cruzatte] to inform us
that he was still unable to purchase any horses, but intended
going as far as the Eneeshur village to-day, whence he would
return to meet us to-morrow at the Skilloot village. In the
evening the principal chief of the Chilluckittequaws came to
see us, accompanied by twelve of his nation, and hearing
that we wanted horses, promised to meet us at the Narrows
with some for sale.

[35] Clark Q 106–108, this date, has a long description. The bird is the dusky
grouse, *Dendragapus obscurus*, probably of the variety *fuliginosus*.

[36] Clark Q 108, this date, has a page of description of these three eggs of the
" [party-] coloured corvus."

CHAPTER XXVIII.

THE COLUMBIA FROM THE DALLES TO WALLAWALLA RIVER.

FRIDAY, April 18th, 1806.[1] We set out this morning after an early breakfast, and crossing the river continued along the north side for four miles, to the foot of the first rapid. Here it was necessary to unload and make a portage of seven paces over a rock, round which we then drew the empty boats by means of a cord and the assistance of setting-poles. We then reloaded, and at the distance of five miles reached the basin at the foot of the Long Narrows. After unloading and arranging the camp we went up to the Skilloot village, where we found Captain Clark. He had not been able to procure more than four horses, for which he was obliged to give double the price of those for-

---

[1] *The Dalles of the Columbia.*—No phrase is more familiar than this, in connection with the great river, but none has become so elastic, and its various applications deprive it of a desirable precision. As a word, " dalles " is a French plural, the English of which is flagstones, such as we lay down for a sidewalk along a street. One may even hear of " those dalles," *i. e.*, flat rocks in the river serving for stepping-stones. " Dalles " are also the characteristic and celebrated columnar basaltic rock-formations through which the river passes for many miles. " Dalles "

merly purchased from the Shoshonees and the first tribe of
Flatheads [Ootlashoots: p. 582]. These, however, we hoped
might be sufficient, with the aid of the small canoes, to
convey our baggage as far as the villages near Muscleshell
rapid, where horses are cheaper and more abundant, and
where we may probably exchange the canoes for as many
horses as we want. The Skilloots have a (*p. 245*) number
of horses, but they are unwilling to part with them, though
at last we laid out three parcels of merchandise, for each of
which they promised to bring us a horse in the morning.
The Long Narrows have a much more formidable appear-

are likewise the course of the river through such formations, and the river itself
during such courses, *i. e.*, the river runs through " dalles," and is " dalles " in
running through them. In this sense there are various " dalles " on the Columbia ; the Cascades are " dalles," etc. Finally, there is at one spot a town called
" The Dalles," with a big T, or " Dalles City," with a big C, to make it look
bigger than it ever was, even before its recent destruction by fire. But by common geographical and engineering consent " the Dalles " has a technical sense
which specifies one certain stretch of the river, including the " Great Falls,"
" Short Narrows," and " Long Narrows " of L. and C., with certain bad rocky
places and " rapids "—altogether a distance of about 14 miles. At the head of this
reach is their " Great Falls," now called Celilo Falls ; and here is Celilo City, on
the Oregon side. At the foot of this reach is their Fort Rock camp ; and here is
(or was) Dalles City, on the Oregon side. At the " Great " or Celilo Falls the
pitch is 47 feet at a low stage of the water. About three miles below are the Ten
Mile Rapids (so reckoned for distance from a point below), half a mile long, with
a pitch at low water of $7\frac{1}{3}$ feet per mile, where the river runs through a trough
formed by high vertical basaltic walls, about 200 feet apart. These are the
" Short Narrows " of L. and C., also known as the " Short Dalles," " Little
Dalles," etc. Below here is a stretch of rapid water for some 1,800 feet, with a
pitch of 11 feet per mile. Lower down are the Dalles Rapids, $1\frac{1}{2}$ miles long,
with pitch of 10 feet per mile, where the river runs through another basaltic
trough with vertical walls from 125 to 350 feet apart. Here are the " Long
Narrows " of L. and C., also known as the " Long Dalles," " Great Dalles," etc.
The distance between the Dalles Rapids and Celilo Falls is about six miles. The
total descent of the river from Celilo City to Dalles City in low water is $81\frac{1}{2}$ feet ;
in mean high water, $62\frac{1}{2}$ feet. The rise of surface from l. w. to mean h. w. is at
the head of Celilo Falls 18 ft.; at head of Dalles Rapids, $7\frac{1}{3}$ ft.; at foot of do.,
49 ft., making navigation impossible. Transportation is effected on the Washington side, from a point below the foot of Dalles Rapids to a point above the
head of Celilo Falls.

Such, in brief, are the obstacles which the Expedition has now to surmount,
with great difficulty and labor, though with less danger, than they were overcome

ance than when we passed them in the autumn, so that it would, in fact, be impossible either to descend or go up them in any kind of boat.[2] As we had therefore no further use for the two periogues, we cut them up for fuel.

April 19*th.* Early in the morning all the party began to carry the merchandise over the portage. This we accomplished, with the aid of our four horses, by three o'clock in the afternoon, when we formed our camp a little above the Skilloot village. Since we left them in the autumn they have removed their village a few hundred yards lower down the river, and have exchanged the cellars, in which we then found them, for more pleasant dwellings on the surface of the ground. These are formed by sticks, covered with mats and straw, and so large that each is the residence of several families. They are also much better clad than any of the natives below, or than they were themselves last autumn. The dress of the

---

in descending the river. (See back, pp. 658–668.) As stated in note [4], p. 658, Clark's map of the Great Falls was engraved : see the plate. But it should be particularly recorded here, that his equally good map of the Dalles, covering the whole reach from Celilo (or Great) Falls to some distance beyond Dalles City (or Fort Rock camp) was never engraved. This continuously occupies pp. 2, 3, of Codex H, on a scale of 426 poles to the inch : it is legended " A Sketch of the Long & Short Narrows of the Columbia River &c." The codex has penciled memorandum " Begin to engrave at words ' Great Falls,' " and there is another penciling where the engraver was to stop; the intention being to take in p. 3 exactly, but omit p. 2, as p. 3 has the important parts of the drawing, viz., the Falls and both the Narrows. But if ever engraved, the sketch was never published. This is a great pity, for the drawing is beautifully executed, and would have been very useful, besides doing Captain Clark as much credit as his famous map of the Great Falls of the Missouri. It is very clear ; and besides the topographic and hydrographic details, it shows the Indian villages and the explorers' camps along this whole stretch of the Columbia.

[2] " *Friday* 18*th* . . . proceeded on with great difficulty and danger to the foot of the long narrows; and expect to be able to take the canoes no further.—Here we met one of the men from Captain Clarke with 4 horses. In coming up, one of our small canoes got split so that we were obliged to carry the load two miles to this place. Wood here is very scarce, as the Columbia plains have commenced. Several men went up to the village with their buffalo robes, to dispose of them for horses. Could we get about 12 horses we would be able to go by land." Gass, p. 200.

men consists generally of leggings, moccasins, and large robes; many of them wear shirts in the form used by the Chopunnish and Shoshonees, highly ornamented, as well as the leggings and moccasins, with porcupine quills. Their modesty is protected by the skin of a fox or some other animal, drawn under a girdle and hanging in front like a narrow apron. The dress of the women differs but little from that worn near the rapids; both sexes wear the hair over the forehead as low as the eyebrows, with large locks cut square at the ears, and the rest hanging in two cues in front of the body. The robes are made principally of the skins of deer, elk, bighorn, wolf, and buffalo, while the children use the skins of the large gray squirrel [*Sciurus fossor*]. The buffalo is procured from the nations higher up the river, who occasionally visit the Missouri; indeed, the (*p. 246*) greater proportion of their apparel is brought by the nations to the northwest, who come to trade for pounded fish, copper, and beads. Their chief fuel is straw, southern-wood, and small willows. Bear-grass, the bark of the cedar, and silk-grass are employed in various articles of manufacture.

The whole village was filled with rejoicing to-day at having caught a single salmon, which was considered as the harbinger of vast quantities in four or five days. In order to hasten their arrival the Indians, according to custom, dressed the fish and cut it into small pieces, one of which was given to each child in the village. In the good humor excited by this occurrence they parted, though reluctantly, with four other horses, for which we gave them two kettles, reserving only a single small one for a mess of eight men. Unluckily, however, we lost one of the horses by the negligence of the person [Willard] to whose charge he was committed. The rest were, therefore, hobbled and tied; but as the nations here do not understand gelding, all the horses but one were stallions; this being the season when they are most vicious, we had great difficulty in managing them, and were obliged to keep watch over them all night. In the afternoon Captain Clark set out with four men for the Eneeshur village at the

ried on horseback. We had intended setting out at the same time, but one of our horses broke loose during the night, and we were under the necessity of sending several men in search of him. In the meantime the Indians, who were always on the alert, stole a tomahawk, which we could not recover, though several of them were searched. Another fellow was detected in carrying off a piece of iron, and kicked out of camp. Captain Lewis, then addressing the Indians, declared that he was not afraid to fight them ; for if he chose, he might easily put them to death and burn their village ; that he did not wish to treat them ill if they did not steal; and that though, if he knew who had the tomahawk, he would take away the horses of the thieves, yet he would rather lose the property altogether than take the horse of an innocent man. The chiefs who were present at this harangue hung their heads and made no reply.[4] At ten o'clock the (*p. 248*) men [a man, Windsor] returned with the horse, and soon after an Indian, who had promised to go with us as far as

---

[4] Gass, p. 201, notes the fracas thus : "*Monday 21st.* . . While we were making preparations to start, an Indian stole some iron articles from among the men's hands, which so irritated Captain Lewis that he struck him ; which was the first act of the kind that had happened during the expedition. The Indians however did not resent it, otherwise it is probable we would have had a skirmish with them." "I detected a fellow in stealing an iron socket of a canoe pole and gave him several severe blows and made the men kick him out of camp. I now informed the indians that I would shoot the first of them that attempted to steal an article from us," Lewis K 73. It has always seemed to me there was some natural demoralizing agency at the Dalles and Cascades of the Columbia. Certainly the tribes at these points were thievish and murderous from their first contact with white men, as recorded in these pages, till they were finally broken up in very late years. The difficulty of passing these points, where navigation was necessarily interrupted, was taken every advantage of by the wily savages, who infested these places as bandits do mountain passes, and played on the Columbia the part of the Sioux on the Missouri—that of river-pirates. It seems to have been rather a local than a tribal matter—that is, no tribe could resist the temptation and opportunity that offered at the portages. Books of Columbian travel and adventure are full of such incidents, and much blood has been spilled in these places. Our heroes were more fortunate than many another party, as they only had to kick some of the Indians out of camp, with threats of more decisive action. I think the present is the only occasion on which either of the captains was forced to assault and battery.

the Chopunnish, came with two horses, one of which he politely offered to carry our baggage. We therefore loaded nine horses, and giving the tenth to Bratton, who was still too sick to walk, about ten o'clock left the village of these disagreeable people. At one o'clock we arrived at the village of the Eneeshurs, where we found Captain Clark, who had been completely unsuccessful in his attempt to purchase horses, the Eneeshurs being quite as unfriendly as the Skilloots. Fortunately, however, the fellow who had sold a horse and afterward lost him at gambling, belonged to this village, and we insisted on taking the kettle and knife which had been given to him for the horse, if he did not replace it by one of equal value. He preferred the latter [alternative], and brought us a very good horse. Being here joined by the canoes and baggage across the portage,[5] we halted half a mile above the town, and took dinner on some dogs; after which we proceeded on about four miles and camped at a village of Eneeshurs, consisting of nine mat huts, a little below the mouth of the Towahnahiooks.[6] We obtained

[5] The narrative hardly makes it plain enough that this is the portage of the Great Falls of the Columbia. Gass, p. 202 says: "*Monday 21st* . . . About 3 in the afternoon we arrived at the Great Falls of Columbia, where we met with Captain Clarke and the men that were with him. Here we got another horse; carried our canoes and baggage round the falls and halted for dinner." We must also bear in mind that from this point the main party proceeds *by land*, along the north bank of the river, in Washington, though some men are still navigating two canoes which were hauled over the portage.

[6] The Des Chutes river, a little above the Great Falls, in Oregon, the largest branch of the Columbia between the Multnomah or Willamette and the Snake. There is, of course, no real confusion between this and Lewis' river in Washington; but the ungainly Indian names of the two which Lewis and Clark use are so similar, and both are so variously spelled, that some forms of the names of each have in fact been misprinted or otherwise misused for the other. See Clark's map, 1814, where the Des Chutes (in Oregon) is inscribed To-war-na-he-ooks, and Lewis' (in Washington), Chah-wah-na-hi-ooks. Lewis K 74 has "Clark's river" for the Des Chutes, but with "Towanahiooks" interlined with red ink. See note [3], p. 657, and note [13], p. 992. The name Des Chutes is of course a part of the French term rivière des chutes. Other forms from this are Shutes, Shute's and Shoots; also, Falls river. Thus the U. S. Ex. Exp. map of 1841 marks "Falls or Shutes R." Stevens' map No. 3 charts it as Wanwauwie river, and gives the next creek above it, on the same (Oregon) side as Oonmauwie.

from these people a couple of dogs and a small quantity of fuel, for which we were obliged to give a higher price than usual. We also bought a horse with his back so much injured that he can scarcely be of much service to us; but the price was some trifling article, which in the United States would cost about a dollar and a quarter. The dress, manners, and language of the Eneeshurs differ in no respect from those of the Skilloots. Like them, too, these Eneeshurs are inhospitable and parsimonious, faithless to their engagements, and in the midst of poverty and filth retain a degree of pride and arrogance which render our numbers our only protection against insult, pillage, and even murder. We are, however, assured by our Chopunnish guide, who appears to be a very sincere, honest Indian, that the nations above will treat us with much more hospitality.

(*p. 249*) *April 22d.* Two of our horses broke loose in the night and straggled to some distance, so that we were not able to retake them and begin our march before seven o'clock. We had just reached the top of a hill near the village, when the load of one of the horses ["Charbono's"] turned, and the animal taking fright at a robe which still adhered to him, ran furiously toward the village; just as he came there the robe fell, and an Indian hid it in his hut. Two men went back after the horse, which they soon took; but the robe was still missing, and the Indians denied having seen it.⁷ These repeated acts of knavery now exhausted our patience. Captain Lewis therefore set out for the village, determined to make them deliver up the robe or to burn the village to the ground. This disagreeable alternative was rendered unnecessary, for on his way he met one of our men [Labiche], who had found the robe in an Indian hut hid behind some baggage.

⁷ " Being now confident that the indians had taken it I sent the Indian woman [Sacajawea] on to request Capt. C. to halt the party and send back some of the men to my assistance being deturmined either to make the indians deliver the robe or birn their houses. they have vexed me in such a manner by such repeated acts of villany that I am quite disposed to treat them with every severyty, their defenseless state pleads forgivness so far as rispects their lives," Lewis K 75.

We resumed our route and soon after halted at a hill, from the top of which we enjoyed a commanding view of the range of mountains in which Mount Hood stands, and which continue south as far as the eye can reach, with their tops covered with snow. Mount Hood itself bears S. 30° W., and the snowy summit of Mount Jefferson S. 10° W. Toward the south and at no great distance we discern some woody country, and opposite this point of view is the mouth of the Towahnahiooks. This river receives, at the distance of 18 or 20 miles, a branch from the right,[8] which takes its rise in Mount Hood, while the main stream comes in a course from the southeast, and 10 or 15 miles[9] is joined by a second branch, from Mount Jefferson. From this place we proceeded with our baggage in the center, escorted both before and behind by those of the men who were without the care of horses: and having crossed a plain eight miles in extent, reached a village of Eneeshurs, consisting of six houses. Here we bought some dogs on which we dined near the village, and having purchased another horse, went up the river four miles further, to another Eneeshur village of seven mat-

[8] That is, from the observer's point of view, facing the mouth of the river. The stream from Mt. Hood flows eastwardly, into the west (left) side of the Des Chutes. Clark charts it as "Skimhoox R." The main stream from Mt. Hood to the Des Chutes is now called White river, two tributaries of which, Tygh (Tyigh, Tyee, Tysch, etc.) and Badger creeks, seem to correspond best with the forked stream on Clark's map. The "point of view" of the text is probably at the place marked "High Rocks," on Wilkes' 1841 map, and I should imagine the tributaries of the Des Chutes river which the text indicates could be settled by determining what streams can be sighted from this spot. Lewis K 76 again calls the Des Chutes "Clark's" river, but the codex has "Towarnahiooks" red-inked in. On this unlucky slip, see note[6], p. 960, and note[13], p. 992.

[9] Further up the Des Chutes river from the mouth of that branch which rises in Mt. Hood. This second western affluent of the Des Chutes, "from Mt. Jefferson," is marked "Kies-how-e R." on Clark's map. A stream which comes nearest the position assigned by the text is that one (north of the Mutton mountains) on or near which is the place called Wapinitia ; but this seems to be too small for Clark's Kieshowe river. Other and larger streams draining eastwardly from Mt. Jefferson and vicinity into the Des Chutes are : 1. Warm Spring river or Wannassee creek. 2. Chittike or Shitike. 3. Sicksickawa, Siksikawa, Psuc-secque, etc. 4. Metolius or Mptolyas. But these four are south of the Mutton mountains and entirely too far away to answer to the text.

(*p. 250*) houses. Our [Chopunnish] guide now informed us
that the next village was at such a distance that we could not
reach it this evening, and as we should be able to procure
both dogs and wood at this place, we determined to camp.[10]
We here purchased a horse, and engaged for a second
in exchange for one of our canoes ; but as these were on the
opposite side of the river, and the wind was very high, they
were not able to cross before sunset, at which time the Indian
had returned home to the next village above. This evening, as well as at dinner time, we were obliged to buy wood
to cook our meat, for there is no timber in the country, and
all the fuel is brought from a great distance. We obtained
as much as answered our purposes on moderate terms ; but
as we are too poor to afford more than a single fire, and lie
without any shelter, we find the nights disagreeably cold,
though the weather is warm during the daytime.

April 23*d.* Two of the horses strayed away in consequence of [Charbono's] neglecting to tie them as [he] had
been directed. One of them was recovered, but as we had
a long ride to make before reaching the next village, we
could wait no longer than eleven o'clock for the other. Not
being found at that time we set out, and after marching for
twelve miles over the sands of a narrow rocky bottom on
the north side of the river, came to a village near Rock rapid,
at the mouth of a large [Rock [11]] creek, which we had not

[10] Klikitat Co., Wash., some twelve miles above the Des Chutes river, but a
short distance below the John Day (Lepage's). For the latter, to be passed to-
morrow without mention, see note [3], p. 655, to which add that this river is also
called Mah-hah on Stevens' map No. 3. Some points on the river passed to-day
are Hellgate and Columbus.

[11] The most considerable stream on the Washington side since the Klikitat or
Cataract river ; missed in coming down the Columbia Oct. 21st. The maps
before me agree to call it Rock creek, excepting Stevens' No. 3, which marks
it " Camill Cr." Rock rapid of the text is still called Rock Creek rapids, after
the name of the creek, thus fairly attributable to L. and C., though our authors
do not thus formally designate the stream in mention. Other rapids which have
been passed in this reach of the Columbia since leaving those (Lower, Middle,
and Upper) about the mouth of the John Day, are Indian and Squally Hook.
(See pp. 655, 654.) The last-named are near a turn of the river, perhaps the

observed in descending.   It consisted of twelve temporary huts of mat, inhabited by a tribe called Wahhowpum,[12] who speak a language very similar to that of the Chopunnish, whom they resemble also in dress, both sexes being clad in robes and shirts as well as leggings and moccasins.   These people seemed much pleased to see us, and readily gave us four dogs and some chapelell and wood in exchange for small articles, such as pewter buttons, strips of tin, iron, and brass, and some twisted wire, which we had previously prepared for our journey across the plains.   These people, as well as some more living in five huts a little below them, were waiting the return (*p. 251*) of the salmon.   We also found a Chopunnish returning home with his family and a dozen young horses, some of which he wanted us to hire; but this we declined, as in that case we should be obliged to maintain him and his family on the route.   After arranging the camp we assembled all the warriors, and having smoked with them, the violins were produced, and some of the men danced.   This civility was returned by the Indians in a style of dancing such as we had not yet seen.   The spectators formed a circle round the dancers, who, with their robes drawn tightly round the shoulders, and divided into parties of five or six men, perform by crossing in a line from one

original " Squally hook," above which, from about the point Rock creek falls in, there is a straight stretch of the Columbia which used to be called "the long reach."   On this are now places called Blalock's and Lang's Landing ; it ends above, about Arlington, in a bend which used to be charted as " Longreach Elbow."   In the course of the long reach, Chambers' creek falls in, at a place called Chapman's, on the north, nearly opposite Lang's Ldg.   The same stretch includes Owyhee rapids (see p. 654), given as 10 miles above Rock Creek rapids. The river is much obstructed by rocks, some of which came to be specified as Hieroglyphic Rocks, from the fact that the Indians used them for petrography, or the pictographic illustration of events in their history.

[12] " Wah-how-pums 1000 Souls," Clark's map, located above " R. la Page " ; elsewhere spelled Wahowpum.   These are different Indians from any of the Chinookan stock of which our travelers saw so much lower down the Columbia. As indicated by the remark that they " speak a language very similar to that of the Chopunnish," etc., the Wahhowpums were the Klikitats, a tribe of the Shahaptian linguistic stock or family, which stock included as more prominent tribes, the Nez-percé, Umatilla, Wallawalla, and other Indians.

side of the circle to the other. All the parties, performers as well as spectators, sing, and after proceeding in this way for some time, the spectators join, and the whole concludes by a promiscuous dance and song. Having finished, the natives retired at our request, after promising to barter horses with us in the morning. The river is by no means so difficult of passage nor obstructed by so many rapids as it was in the autumn, the water being now sufficiently high to cover the rocks in the bed.

April 24th. We began early to look for our horses, but they were not collected before one o'clock. In the meantime we prepared saddles for three new horses which we purchased from the Wahhowpums, and agreed to hire three more from the Chopunnish Indian, who was to accompany us with his family. The natives also had promised to take our canoes in exchange for horses; but when they found that we were resolved on traveling by land they refused giving us anything, in hopes that we would be forced to leave them. Disgusted at this conduct, we determined rather to cut them to pieces than suffer these people to enjoy them, and actually began to split them, on which they gave us several strands of beads for each canoe. We had now a sufficient number of horses to carry our baggage, and therefore proceeded wholly by land.[13] At two o'clock we set out, and pass- (*p. 252*) ing between the hills and the northern shore of the river, had a difficult and fatiguing march over a road alternately sandy and rocky. At the distance of four miles we came to four huts of the Metcowwee [14] tribe, two miles further the same number of huts, and after making twelve miles from our last night's camp halted [15] at a larger village of five huts of Metcowwees.

[13] Gass, p. 203, thus notes the end of the navigation of the Columbia: "We sold our two small canoes; . . . at 2 o'clock we all started by land on the north side of the river, . . . we entered the low country, the great and beautiful plains of Columbia." The Wahowpums he calls "Wal-la-waltz" and "Wal-a-waltz."

[14] Or Meteowwee; preferably Met'how. This was a Salishan tribe.

[15] The mileage assigned (12 m. from Rock creek camp) should bring the Expedition about opposite present site of Arlington, above Chambers' creek (un-

As we came along many of the natives passed and repassed without making any advances to converse, though they behaved with distant respect. We observed in our route no animals except the killdeer [*Ægialites vociferus*], the brown lizard [*Sceloporus* sp.], and a moonax [*Arctomys flaviventer*], which the people had domesticated as a favorite. Most of the men complain of a soreness in their feet and legs, occasioned by walking on rough stones and deep sands after being accustomed for some months past to a soft soil. We therefore determined to remain here this evening, and for this purpose bought three dogs and some chapelell, which we cooked with dry grass and willow boughs. The want of wood is a serious inconvenience, on account of the coolness of the nights, particularly when the wind sets from Mount Hood, or in any western direction; those winds being much colder than the winds from the Rocky mountains. There are no dews on the plains, and from appearances we presume that no rain has fallen for several weeks. By nine o'clock the following morning,

April 25th, we collected our horses and proceeded 11 miles to a large village of 51 mat houses, where we purchased some wood and a few dogs, on which we made our dinner. The village contained about 700 persons of a tribe called Pishquitpah,[16] whose residence on the river is only during the spring and summer, the autumn and winter being passed in hunting through the plains and along the borders of the mountains. The greater part of them were at a distance from the river as we descended, and never having seen white men before, they flocked round us in great numbers; but though they were exceedingly curious (*p. 253*) they treated us with great respect, and were very urgent that we should spend the night with them. Two principal chiefs were pointed out by our Chopunnish companion, and acknowledged by the tribe; we therefore invested each of

noticed), and a little below Wood creek (Pine creek of Symons: see note [26], p. 652).

[16] Or Pisquow, a Salishan tribe also; " 2,600 souls " charted by Clark.

them with a small medal. We were also very desirous of
purchasing more horses; but as our principal stock of merchandise consists of a dirk, a sword, and a few old clothes,
the Indians could not be induced to traffic with us. The
Pishquitpahs are generally of good stature and proportion,
and as the heads of neither males nor females are so much
flattened as those lower down the river, their features are
rather pleasant. The hair is braided in the manner practiced by their western neighbors; the generality of the men
are dressed in a large robe, under which is a shirt reaching
to the knees, where it is met by long leggings, and the feet
are covered with moccasins; others, however, wear only the
truss and robe. As they unite the occupations of hunting
and fishing, both sexes ride very dexterously, their caparison
being a saddle or pad of dressed skin, stuffed with goat's
hair, and from which wooden stirrups are suspended; and a
hair rope tied at both ends to the under jaw of the animal.
The horses, though good, suffer much, as do in fact all
Indian horses, from sore backs.

Finding them not disposed to barter with us, we left the
Pishquitpahs at four o'clock, accompanied by 18 or 20 of
their young men on horseback. At the distance of four
miles, we passed, without halting, five houses belonging to
the Wollawollahs [Wallawallas]; and five miles further,
observing as many willows as would answer the purpose of
making fires, availed ourselves of the circumstance by camp-
ing[17] near them. The country through which we passed bore

[17] A good early start to-day, without any trouble in catching their opinionative
and vagarious Indian ponies, and a good stretch of 20 miles. Passed Wood
creek (Pine creek of Symons) at once, then camp of Oct. 20th (see the date, p.
652, note there), then Pine creek (Olive creek of Symons); all these on the N. side.
Next is Willow creek, as might be expected from mention of this tree or bush in
the text. This is a considerable stream on the *south*, but passed unnoticed both
ways, unless it be indicated in the text of p. 652, as I there observe. It was
certainly not altogether missed, for this is one of two streams in Oregon, which
Clark charts without name, between "R. La Page," and "You-ma-lolam R.,"
i.e., between the John Day and Yumatilla. Willow creek is also called Hokes-
pam on Stevens' map No. 3, and is Quesnell's river of Wilkes' map, 1841.
Next beyond Willow creek is Cedar creek; somewhat beyond which, and some-

the same appearance as that of yesterday. The hills on both sides of the river are about 250 feet high, generally abrupt and craggy, and in many places presenting a perpendicular face of black, hard, and solid rock. From the top of these hills, (*p. 254*) the country extends in level plains to a very great distance, and though not as fertile as the land near the falls, produces an abundant supply of low grass, which is an excellent food for horses. This grass must indeed be unusually nutritious; for even at this season of the year, after wintering on the dry grass of the plains, and being used with greater severity than is usual among the whites, many of these horses are perfectly fat, nor have we, indeed, seen a single one which was poor. In the course of the day we killed several rattlesnakes,[18] like those of the United States, and saw many of the common as well as the horned lizard.[19] We also killed six ducks, one of which proved to be of a different species[20] from any we had yet seen, being distinguished by yellow legs, and feet webbed like those of the duckinmallard [*sic—Anas boseas*]. The Pishquitpahs passed the night with us; at their request the violin was played, and some of

what short of the place on the Oregon side called Castle Rock, camp is pitched. The proportion of 20 m. to-day, and 28 m. to-morrow, which brings the Expedition almost to Yumatilla, fixes this camp very closely ; and the estimated distances agree remarkably well with reliable modern measurement. This is specially satisfactory along a reach of the river which the text passes so cursorily.

[18] There are two distinct species of rattlesnakes along the Columbia. The one most like the common *Crotalus horridus*, " of the United States," is *C. lucifer* of Baird and Girard, Serps. N. A. 1853, p. 6 (orig. descr. Proc. Acad. Nat. Sci. Phila. VI. 1852, p. 177), and doubtless the one here in mention. The other is Say's *C. confluentus*, of very wide distribution in the West. See p. 898.

[19] *Phrynosoma douglasi*, commonly called horned frog or horned toad, though the designation of Lewis and Clark is much better, as the animals are lizards and neither frogs nor toads : see pp. 899, 1019, for description. The " common " lizard was doubtless a species of *Sceloporus :* see pp. 899, 900.

[20] This is the shoveler duck, *Spatula clypeata*. Clark Q 110 has, at this date : " The Curloos are abundant in the Plains and are now laying their eggs. Saw the Kilde [*Ægialites vociferus*], the brown Lizzard [*Sceloporus* sp.] and a moonac which the natives had petted." This word " moonac," on p. 564 " moonax," is a name of the woodchuck or ground-hog in Virginia, reflected in the specific name of *Arctomys monax ;* and the animal intended to be designated by Clark is doubtless the yellow-bellied marmot, *Arctomys flaviventer*.

the men amused themselves with dancing. At the same
time we succeeded in obtaining two horses at nearly the
same prices which had already been refused in the village.

April 26th. We set out early [along the north bank of the
river]. At the distance of three miles the river hills become
low, and retiring to a great distance leave a low, level, extensive plain, which on the other side of the river began 13
miles lower. As we were crossing this plain, we were overtaken by several families traveling up the river with a number of horses; though their company was inconvenient, for
the weather was warm, the roads were dusty, and their
horses crowded in and broke our line of march, yet we were
unwilling to displease the Indians by any act of severity.
The plain possesses much grass and a variety of herbaceous
plants and shrubs; but after going twelve miles we were
fortunate enough to find a few willows, which enabled us to
cook a dinner of jerked elk and the remainder of the dogs
purchased yesterday. We then went on 16 miles further,
and six miles above our camp of the 19th of October (*p. 255*)
camped [21] in the rain, about a mile below three houses of
Wollawollahs.[22] Soon after we halted an Indian boy took a

[21] This camp is immediately below the mouth of the Yumatilla river, but on the
Washington side. The statement in reference to the camp of Oct. 19th does
good service in fixing the latter, which was left somewhat uncertain in going
down river (see p. 649, and note there). Some of the points passed to-day
are : Castle Rock ; Canoe Encampment rapids ; Long island, whose foot is 14
miles above the mouth of Willow creek ; opposite this island, a place called
Coyote, on the Oregon side ; and on the Washington side, a considerable creek,
which, when it runs, drains some country curiously called Horse Heaven ; town
of Scott, at mouth of a small creek on the Washington side ; then Grande
Ronde Landing, 13 m. above above the foot of Long island; and finally Devil's
Bend, 4 m. below Yumatilla river, where are rapids of the same name.

[22] Here Lewis K 82 has Wollâh Wollâhs ; Clark Q 112 has Wallow Wallows ;
map has Wollaw Wollah ; Clark elsewhere Woller Woller. As earlier observed
in this work, the codices vary greatly in this slippery word, more than 20 forms
of which are also found in print. Accepted forms are now Walla Walla, or
Walla-walla, or Wallawalla. In several languages *walla* means running water,
and reduplication of a word diminutizes it ; so *Wallawalla* is the small rapid
river. (Compare Koos-koos-kee, note [24], p. 1002.) For these Indians, see
note [38], p. 605.

piece of bone, which he substituted for a fish-hook, and caught several chub[23] nine inches long.

Sunday, April 27th. We were detained till nine o'clock, before a horse ["Charbono's" again] which broke loose in the night could be recovered. We then passed, near our camp, a small river called Youmalolam[24] and proceeded through a continuation,[25] till at the distance of 15 miles the abrupt and rocky hills, 300 feet high, return to the river. These we ascended and then crossed a higher plain for nine miles, when we again came to the water-side. We had been induced to make this long march because we had but little provision, and hoped to find a Wollawollah village, which our guide had told us we should reach when next we met the river. There was, however, no village to be seen; and as both men and horses were fatigued, we halted, and collecting some dry stalks of weeds and the stems of a plant resembling southern-wood, cooked a small quantity of jerked meat for dinner. Soon after we were joined by seven Wollawollahs, among whom we recognized a chief by the name of Yellept,[26] who had visited us on the 19th of October, when we gave him a medal with the promise of a larger one on our return. He appeared very much pleased at see-

[23] *Mylochilus caurinus :* description, Lewis K 83 and Clark Q 111, given at this date, with a sketch of the apparatus with which the boy took the fish.

[24] Emptying into the Columbia from the south, in county of the same name ; now usually rendered Yumatilla or Umatilla ; on Clark's map as in the text, but hyphenated. A dozen different spellings have had currency, as Umatella, Umatalla, Umatallow, Youmatalla, Yourmatalla, Umatillah, Umatillah, Emmitilly, etc., and without labialization Euatallah, Utalla, Utilla, etc. It is the first considerable stream in Oregon below the Wallawalla, and the second such above the John Day. At its mouth is town of same name, and opposite is Crimea, Klikitat Co., Wash. Its main western fork is Bitter creek, a name sometimes extended to the whole river, and given as "Butter" on the G. L. O. map of 1879, and on that of Symons, 1881. Certain Astorians who had survived their horrible experiences in the Snake river .region struck the Columbia here, and were the first white men on the spot after L. and C. There is a local tradition that some of them were also at Lewiston next after our explorers.

[25] *I. e.*, a country like that of yesterday, Lewis K 84.

[26] Accent Yel-lept' ; Yelleppit of p. 645 ; his medal found last year on an island about mouth of Wallawalla river (James Wickesham, *in lit.*)

ing us again, and invited us to remain at his village three or four days, during which he would supply us with the only food they had, and furnish us with horses for our journey.   After the cold, inhospitable treatment we have lately received, this kind offer was peculiarly acceptable ; and after a hasty meal we accompanied him to his village, six miles above, situated on the edge of the low country, about twelve miles below the mouth of Lewis' river.[27]

Immediately on our arrival Yellept, who proved to be a man of much influence, not only in his own but in the neighboring nations, collected the inhabitants, and having made a harangue, the purport of which was to induce the nations to (*p. 256*) treat us hospitably, he set them an example by bringing himself an armful of wood, and a platter containing three roasted mullets.   They immediately assented to one part, at least, of the recommendation, by furnishing us with an abundance of the only sort of fuel they employ, the stems of shrubs growing in the plains. We then purchased four dogs, on which we supped heartily, having been on short allowance for two days past.   When we were disposed to sleep, the Indians retired immediately on our request, and indeed, uniformly conducted themselves with great propriety.   These people live on roots, which are very abundant in the plains, and catch a few salmon-trout ; but at present they seem to subsist chiefly on a species of mullet, weighing from one to three pounds.   They informed us that opposite the village there was a route which led to the mouth of the Kooskooskee, on the south side of Lewis' river ;[28]

[27] Yakima Co., Wash., nearly or exactly opposite mouth of Wallawalla river, on N. side of which latter was *old* Fort Wallawalla and is now town of Wallula. Some of the features of the country passed to-day are : A gulch called Juniper cañon—"Jumper" on some maps.   A little lower down, on the same side, is a similar formation known as Spring-water cañon.   Above Juniper cañon, about halfway thence to Wallawalla river, are Bull Run rapids.   Hereabouts is the point on the Columbia where the great river comes from wholly within Washington to be henceforth to the sea the boundary between that State and Oregon. See p. 644, note [19].

[28] That is, a route across the country south of Lewis' river from the point where

that the road itself was good, and passed over a level country well supplied with water and grass ; and that we should meet with plenty of deer and antelope. We knew that a road in that direction would shorten the distance at least 80 miles, and as the report of our guide was confirmed by Yellept and other Indians, we did not hesitate to adopt that course. They added, however, that there were no houses or permanent residences of Indians on the road ; it was therefore deemed prudent not to trust wholly to our guns, but to lay in a stock of provisions.

April 28th. We therefore purchased ten dogs. While this trade was carried on by our men, Yellept brought a fine white horse and presented him to Captain Clark, expressing at the same time a wish to have a kettle ; but on being informed that we had already disposed of the last kettle we could spare, he said he would be content with any present we should make in return. Captain Clark therefore gave his sword, for which the chief had before expressed a desire, adding 100 balls, some powder, and other small articles, with which he appeared perfectly satisfied. (*p. 257*) We were now anxious to depart, and requested Yellept to lend us canoes for the purpose of crossing the river. But he would not listen to any proposal of leaving the village. He wished us to remain two or three days ; and would not let us go to-day, for he had already sent to invite his neighbors,

---

the Expedition now is to the mouth of the Kooskooskee. The Expedition, being opposite the mouth of Wallawalla river, where this falls into the Columbia, proposes to cross the Columbia here, leave this river to the north, and make straight across country to the mouth of Clearwater river. This direct route is like going along the string of a bow instead of along the arc of the bow itself, and so cuts off a good deal, besides saving all the northing of the Columbia itself from the mouth of the Wallawalla to that of the Snake. We must remember that at lat. 46° on the Columbia, this river ceases to separate Washington from Oregon, and that hence eastward the boundary runs along the parallel of 46° N., thus leaving the main course of the Wallawalla, as well as the route of the Expedition, in Washington. The route is thus entirely south of the Snake, and goes eastward (mainly along Touchet river) via Dayton, Columbia Co., Wash., to Lewiston, Nez-percé Co., Idaho. In Washington they will traverse Wallawalla, Columbia, and Garfield counties, and touch the northern border of Asotin Co.

the Chimnapoos,[29] to come down this evening and join his people in a dance for our amusement. We urged in vain that, by setting out sooner, we would the earlier return with the articles they desired ; for a day, he observed, would make but little difference. We at length mentioned that, as there was no wind, it was now the best time to cross the river, and we would merely take the horses over and return to sleep at their village. To this he assented ; we then crossed with our horses, and having hobbled them, returned to their [the Indians'] camp.

Fortunately, there was among these Wollawollahs a pris-oner belonging to a tribe of Shoshonee or Snake Indians, residing to the south of the Multnomah and visiting occasion-ally the heads of Wollawollah creek. Our Shoshonee woman, Sacajawea, though she belonged to a tribe near the Missouri, spoke the same language as this prisoner ; by their means we were able to explain ourselves to the Indians, and answer all their inquiries with respect to ourselves and the object of our journey. Our conversation inspired them with much confidence, and they soon brought several sick persons, for whom they requested our assistance. We splintered [Cap-tain Clark splinted] the broken arm of one, gave some relief to another, whose knee was contracted by rheumatism, and administered what we thought beneficial for ulcers and erup-tions of the skin on various parts of the body, which are very common disorders among them. But our most valuable medicine was eye-water, which we distributed, and which, indeed, they required very much ; the complaint of the

[29] See note [15], p. 637, and p. 643.   Lewis K 85 has Chym-nâh'-pos.   Clark's map charts " Chim nah pun 2000 Souls " on the Tapetete (Yakima) river and two of its branches called Nock-tock and Se-lar-tar, next below the Wah-nâ-â-cha.   The latter is the Wenatchee, Wainape, or Wenatshapam river, also called Piss-cows, Piscous, Pischous, Pisquouse, etc.   Some names of the Yakima which I neglected to note on p. 641 are, besides Tapatele and Tapatelle, Yaka man, Eyakama, Eyakema, Eyakemah, and Ekama.   In the Estimate the name of these Indians is printed Chimnahpum ; now usually Chimnapum.   They are supposed to have been a branch of the Yakima tribe of the Shahaptian family. A river is named after these Indians.

eyes, occasioned by living on the water and increased by the fine sand of the plains, being universal.

(*p. 258*) A little before sunset, the Chimnapoos, amounting to 100 men and a few women, came to the village, and joining the Wollawollahs, who were about the same number of men, formed themselves in a circle round our camp and waited very patiently till our men were disposed to dance, which they did for about an hour, to the tune of the violin. We then requested to see the Indians dance. With this they readily complied, and the whole assemblage, amounting, with the women and children of the village, to several hundred, sang and danced at the same time. The exercise was neither very violent nor very graceful ; for the greater part of them were formed into a solid column around a kind of hollow square, stood on the same place, and merely jumped up at intervals, to keep time to the music. Some, however, of the more active warriors, entered the square and danced round it sidewise, and some of our men joined in the dance, to the great satisfaction of the Indians. The dance continued till ten o'clock.

April 29th. Yellept supplied us with two canoes, in which we crossed [the Columbia from west to east] with all our baggage, by eleven o'clock ; but the horses having strayed to some distance, we could not collect them in time to reach any fit place to camp if we began our journey, as night would overtake us before we came to water. We therefore thought it advisable to camp about a mile from the Columbia, on the mouth [30] of the Wollawollah river. This is a handsome

---

[30] Having passed from Yakima to Wallawalla Co. in crossing the Columbia to site of Wallula and old Fort Wallawalla, which was established at the mouth of the river of the same name in 1818, and was also called Fort Nez-percé. It is thus a very old post—among the very earliest fur-trading establishments after Astoria and that myrionymous place which David Stuart founded in 1811, called by L. and C. Otchenaukane, by Ross Coxe, Oakinacken, Oakanazan, Oakinagan, and Oakanagan ; by others, Okunoakan, Okenakan, Okanagan, Okinagan, Okonagan, Okinikaine, Okinakane, Okenagen, Oknagen, Oknagan, and doubtless in other ways, which have not come under my observation. Captain Bonneville was at Wallawalla in 1833-34, Townsend and Nuttall in Sept., 1834, with the

stream, about 50 yards wide and 4½ feet in depth ; its waters, which are clear, roll over a bed composed principally of gravel mixed with sand and mud, and though the banks are low they do not seem to be overflowed. It empties into the Columbia 12 or 15 miles from the entrance of Lewis' [Snake] river, just above a range of high hills crossing the Columbia. Its sources, like those of the Towahnahiooks, Lapage. You-malolam, and Wollawollah,[31] come, as the Indians inform us, from the north side of a range of mountains [the Blue mountains] which (*p. 259*) we see to the east and southeast, and which, commencing to the south of Mount Hood, stretch in a northeastern direction to the neighborhood of a southern branch of Lewis' river,[32] at some distance from the Rocky mountains. Two principal branches, however, of the Tow-ahnahiooks [Des Chutes] take their rise [respectively] in Mount Jefferson and Mount Hood, which, in fact, appear to separate the waters of the Multnomah and the Columbia.[33] They [the Blue mountains], are 65 or 70 miles from this place, and, though covered with snow, do not seem high.

Wyeth expedition, and J. C. Fremont in 1843. It is supposed to be 325 miles up the Columbia from the sea. It stands on the southern border of a large irregular depression in which the Yakima and the Snake meet the Columbia, supposed to have been the bed of a prehistoric body of water called by Symons "Ancient Lake Lewis." New Fort Wallawalla is some 30 miles eastward, on one of the branches of Wallawalla river ; and there is also the county seat, Wallawalla, the chief city of the "Valley of many Waters," pop. about 8,000. The people generally make the most of the name by writing it as two words. It was first settled in 1856, after the Indian massacre of whites at the old Waiilatpu mission in this place, Nov., 1847 ; the site was selected for the county seat and lots were laid out in 1859 ; the city was chartered by act of territorial legislature Jan. 11th, 1862. The altitude of the place is given as 978 feet. The U. P. R. R., and the Washington and Columbia R. R. go through the city.

[31] Thus naming in order the Des Chutes, John Day, Yumatilla, and Wallawalla, the four principal affluents of the Columbia, on the Oregon side, east of the Cascade range and west of Snake river. But the text is so pointed that I could not make it read as intended without recasting. It obviously means that the sources of the Wallawalla, like those of the other three rivers named, come, etc.

[32] This "southern branch of Lewis' river" is, in fact, the main Snake river, marked on Clark's map as the "South Fork of Lewis's R." See note [58], p. 621.

[33] That is, the Cascade range of mountains, of which Mts. Hood and Jefferson are conspicuous peaks, divides off the Multnomah watershed, between the Cas-

To the south of these mountains the Indian prisoner says there is a river [*i. e.*, the Multnomah], running toward the northwest, as large as the Columbia at this place, which is nearly a mile. This account may be exaggerated ; but it serves to show that the Multnomah must be a very large river, and that with the assistance of a southeastern branch of Lewis' river, passing round the eastern extremity of that chain of mountains in which Mounts Hood and Jefferson are so conspicuous, waters the vast tract of country to the south, till its remote sources approach those of the Missouri and Rio del Norde.[34]

Near our camp is a fish-weir, formed of two curtains of small willow-switches, matted together with wythes [withes] of the same plant, and extending across the river in two parallel lines six feet asunder. These are supported by several parcels of poles, in the manner already described as in use among the Shoshonees, and are either rolled up or let down at pleasure for a few feet, so as either to suffer the fish to pass or detain them. A seine of 15 or 18 feet in length is then dragged down the river by two persons, and the bottom drawn up against the curtain of willows. They also employ a smaller seine, like a scooping-net, one side of which is confined to a semicircular bow five feet long, and half the size of a man's arm, and the other side is held by a strong rope, which, being tied at both ends to the bow, forms the chord to the semicircle. This is used by one person, but the only fish which they can take at this time is a mullet, [probably *Ptychochilus oregonensis*] from four to five pounds in weight; this is the chief subsist- (*p. 260*) ence of a village of twelve houses of Wollawollahs, a little below us on this river, as well as of others on the opposite side of the Columbia.

In the course of the day we gave small medals to two

cade and Coast ranges, from the southern watershed of the Columbia east of the Cascade range. The sentence is parenthetical, interrupting the mention of the Blue mountains.

[34] I print this last sentence with its original punctuation, which leaves it ambiguous ; but it is all conjecture from Indian information, and hardly worth the attention necessary for its rectification. See any modern map of Oregon.

inferior chiefs, each of whom made us a present of a fine horse. We were in a poor condition to make an adequate acknowledgment for this kindness, but gave several articles, among which was a pistol, with some hundred rounds of ammunition. We have, indeed, been treated by these people with an unusual degree of kindness and civility. They seem to have been successful in their hunting during the last winter; for all of them, but particularly the women, are much better clad than when we saw them last; both sexes among the Wollawollahs, as well as the Chimnapoos, being provided with good robes, moccasins, long shirts, and leggings. Their ornaments are similar to those used below; the hair is cut on the forehead, and cues fall over the shoulders in front of the body; some have some small plaits at the ear-locks, and others tie a bundle of the docked foretop in front of the forehead. They were anxious that we should repeat our dance of last evening; but as it rained and the wind was high, we found the weather too cold for such amusement.

April 30th. Although we had hobbled and secured our new purchases, we found some difficulty in collecting all our horses. In the meantime we purchased several dogs and two horses, besides exchanging one of our least valuable horses for a very good one belonging to the Chopunnish who is accompanying us with his family. The daughter of this man is now about the age of puberty; being incommoded by the disorder incident to that age, she is not permitted to associate with the family, but sleeps at a distance from her father's camp, and on the route always follows at some distance alone. This delicacy or affectation is common to many nations of Indians, among whom a girl in that state is separated from her family, and forbidden to use any article of the household or kitchen furniture, or to engage in any oc- (*p. 261*) cupation. We have now 23 horses, many of which are young and excellent animals, but the greater part of them are afflicted with sore backs. The Indians in general are cruel masters; they ride very hard, and the saddles are so badly constructed that it is almost impossible to

ing Rock fort [at Dalles], an abundance of firewood. The growth consists of cottonwood, birch, crimson haw, red and sweet willow, choke-cherry, yellow currants, gooseberry, the honeysuckle with a white berry, rosebushes, seven-bark, and sumac, together with some corn-grass and rushes. The advantage of a comfortable fire induced us, as the night was come, to halt at this place. We were soon supplied by Drewyer with a beaver and an otter, of which we took only a part of the beaver, and gave the rest to the Indians. The otter is a favorite food, though much inferior, at least in our estimation, to the dog, which they will not eat. The horse is seldom eaten, and never (*p. 262*) except when absolute necessity compels them, as the only alternative to dying of hunger. This fastidiousness does not, however, seem to proceed so much from any dislike to the food, as from attachment to the animal itself; for many of them eat very heartily of the horse-beef which we give them.

Thursday, May 1st, 1806. At an early hour in the morning we collected our horses, and after breakfast set out about seven o'clock and followed the road up the creek [Touchet river]. The low grounds and plains presented the same appearance as that of yesterday, except that the latter were less sandy. At the distance of nine miles the Chopunnish Indian, who was in front, pointed out an old unbeaten road to the left, which he informed us was our shortest route. Before venturing, however, to quit our present road, which was level, and not only led us in the proper direction, but was well supplied with wood and water, we halted to let our horses graze till the arrival of our other guide, who happened to be at some distance behind. On coming up he seemed much displeased with the other Indian, and declared that the road we were pursuing was the proper one; that if we decided on taking the left road, it would be necessary to remain till to-morrow morning, and then make an entire day's march before we could reach either water or wood. To this the Chopunnish assented, but declared that he himself meant to pursue that route; we therefore gave him some

powder and lead which he requested.   Four hunters whom
we had sent out in the morning joined us while we halted,
and brought us a beaver for dinner.

We then took our leave of the Chopunnish at one o'clock,
and pursued our route up the creek, through a country similar to that we had passed in the morning.   But at the distance of three miles the hills on the north side became lower,
and the bottoms of the creek widened into a pleasant
country, two or three miles in extent.   The timber is now
more abundant, and our guide tells us that we shall not want
either wood or game from this place as far (*p. 263*) as the
Kooskooskee.   We have already seen a number of deer, of
which we killed one, and observed great quantities of curlew,
as well as some cranes, ducks, prairie larks, and several species of sparrows common to the prairies.   There is, in fact,
very little difference in the general face of the country here
from that of the plains on the Missouri, except that the latter are enlivened by vast herds of buffalo, elk, and other
animals, which give them an additional interest.   Over these
wide bottoms we continued on a course N. 75° E. till, at
the distance of 17 miles from where we dined, and 26 from
our last camp, we halted for the night.[36]

We had scarcely camped when three young men came up
from the Wollawollah village, with a steel trap, which had
been left behind inadvertently, and which they had come a
whole day's journey in order to restore.   This act of integrity was the more pleasing because, though very rare among
Indians, it corresponds perfectly with the general behavior
of the Wollawollahs, among whom we had lost carelessly
several knives, which were returned as soon as found.   We
may, indeed, justly affirm that, of all the Indians whom we
have met since leaving the United States, the Wollawollahs
are the most hospitable, honest, and sincere.

[36] The estimated total of 40 miles from camp near the mouth of Wallawalla
river by way of the Touchet leaves the Expedition short of 118° W. long., and
therefore still in Wallawalla Co., but near Columbia Co.   A person familiar
with the locality could almost pitch a tent where Lewis and Clark sleep to-night,
between Prescott and Waitesburg.

CHAPTER XXIX.

OVERLAND EAST OF THE COLUMBIA AND ALONG THE KOOSKOOSKEE TO COMMEARP CREEK.

The Expedition continues overland toward the Kooskooskee along the Touchet river with the Wallawalla guides—Character of the country—Camass in bloom—An esculent umbelliferous plant—Kimooenim creek—Sudden appearance of Bighorn, a Chopunnish chief and old friend, who joins the party—Bad weather—A creek which falls into Lewis' river—Southwest mountains—Halt at a Chopunnish village—Advice of old guides to ascend the Kooskooskee on the north side—This route to be adopted—Sequestration of Chopunnish menstruants—The party reaches the Kooskooskee and proceeds up that river—Captain Clark receives a gray mare for a bottle of eye-wash—His reputation as a medicine-man grows, and is turned to account—Indian impudence—Old Chopunnish guide found again—Colter's creek—Cut-nose, a Chopunnish chief—Further practice of medicine—Indian prejudices removed—Skeetsomish Indians—Out of provisions—Colter's creek—The party crosses the Kooskooskee to its south side—Joined by Cut-nose and a Shoshonee—Snow-capped mountains in prospect—Hunters bring in game—Indian map-making—Chief Twisted-hair—Quarrel between Cut-nose and Twisted-hair—Other Indian rivalries and jealousies—Chief Broken-arm—Horses and saddles left last autumn recovered—Camp on Commearp creek at Broken-arm's house—Hospitality of the Indians—Chief Hohastilpilp—Council with the four principal Chopunnish chiefs through five different languages—Its happy result promoted by the practice of medicine—Satisfactory state of Indian affairs.

FRIDAY, May 2d, 1806. We despatched two hunters ahead; but the horse we had yesterday purchased from the Chopunnish, though closely hobbled, contrived to break loose in the night, and went back to rejoin his companions. He was overtaken and brought to us about one o'clock, when we set forward. For three miles we followed a hilly road on the north side of the [Touchet] creek, opposite a wide bottom, where a branch [1] falls in from the southwest mountains, which, though covered with snow, are about 25 miles distant, and do not appear high. We then entered an extensive level bottom, with about 50 acres of land, well covered with pine near the creek, and with the long-leaved pine (*p. 265*) occasionally on the sides of the hills along its banks. After cross-

---

[1] Coppie creek (Copei of Symons, Kapyo of Stevens), falling in about a mile west of Waitesburg. The next branch from the south is Hookie creek (with which compare Imaheim creek of Stevens' large map) ; Waitesburg is at or by its mouth, and here a railroad comes up from Wallawalla City.

ing the creek at the distance of seven miles from our camp,
we repassed it seven miles further, near the junction of one of
its branches from the northeast. The main stream here bears
to the south, toward the [Blue] mountains, where it rises; its
bottoms then become narrow, as the hills are higher.² We
followed the course of this northeast branch in a direction N.
45° E. for 8¾ miles; when, having made 19 miles,³ we halted
in a little bottom on the north side. The [Pelat] creek is
here about four yards wide, and as far as we can perceive it
comes from the east; but the road here turns from it into
the high [1,500 to 2,000 feet] open plain. The soil of the
country seems to improve as we advance, and this afternoon
we see in the bottoms an abundance of quamash in bloom.
We killed nothing but a duck, though we saw two deer at a
distance, as well as many sand-hill crows [cranes], curlews,
and other birds common to the prairies, and there is much
sign of both beaver and otter along the creeks. The three
young Wollawollahs continued with us. During the day we
observed them eating the inner part of the young succulent
stem of a plant [*Heracleum lanatum*] very common in the
rich lands on the Mississippi, Ohio, and its branches. It is
a large, coarse plant with a ternate leaf, the leaflets of which
are three-lobed and covered with a woolly pubescence, while
the flower and fructification resemble those of the parsnip.
On tasting this plant we found it agreeable, and ate heartily
of it without any inconvenience.

May 3d. We set out at an early hour and crossed the
high plains, which we found more fertile and less sandy than
below; yet, though the grass is taller, there are very few
aromatic shrubs. After pursuing a course N. 25° E. for

---

² Dayton, county seat of Columbia Co., Wash., is situated at the main forks
of Touchet (Toosha) river. The N. E. branch is Pelat, Patit, or Patita creek, up
which the Expedition goes for some miles before striking over for the Tukanon.

³ The text appears to not agree with itself, for 7+7+8¾=22¾ miles. Gass
say 15 miles for May 2d. Lewis K 96 has: "Steered East 3 m. [from camp] over
a hilly road along the N. side of the creek, . . . a branch falls in on S. side. N.
75° E. 7 [miles]. . . [crossed] the creek at 4 m. on this course. N. 45° E.
9 m. repassed the creek at 4 m. [on this course] and continued up a N. E. branch

twelve miles, we reached the Kimooenim.[4] This creek rises
in the southwest [Blue] mountains, and though only twelve
yards wide discharges a considerable body of water into
Lewis' [the Snake] river, a few miles above the narrows.
Its bed is pebbled, (*p. 266*) its banks are low, and the hills
near its sides high and rugged ; but in its narrow bottoms
are found some cottonwood, willow, and the underbrush
which grows equally on the east branch of the Wollawollah.
After dining at the Kimooenim [which we now crossed], we
resumed our journey over the high plains, in the direction
N. 45° E. and reached, at the distance of three miles, a small
[Pataha] branch of that creek, about five yards wide. The
land in its neighhorhood is composed of a dark rich loam ;
its hill-sides, like those of the Kimooenim, are high ; its
bottoms narrow, possessing little timber. This increased,
however, in quantity as we advanced along the north side
of the [Pataha] creek for 11 miles. At that distance we were
agreeably surprised by the appearance of Weahkoonut,
[We-ark-koomt, Lewis K 97], the Indian whom we had called
Bighorn from the circumstance of his wearing a horn of that
animal suspended from his left arm. He had gone down
with us last year along Lewis' river, and was highly serviceable in preparing the minds of the natives for our reception.
He is, moreover, the first chief of a large band of Chopunnish ; and hearing that we were on our return, had come
with ten of his warriors to meet us. He now turned back
with us, and we continued up the bottoms of the creek for
two miles, till the road began to leave the creek [to the right]

of the same which falls in about a mile below where we passed [crossed] the main
creek. . . We passed the small creek [*i.e.*, the N.E. branch] at 8¾ miles from
the commencement of this course and encamped on the N. side in a little
bottom, having made 19 miles." Thus the discrepancy is only seeming, not
actual ; for the 7+7+ 8¾ is not intended to represent the total distance traveled.
Camp is 8¾ miles up the north side of Pelat creek, in Columbia Co.

    [4] The Tukanon : see note [8], p. 629, for this badly and much-named stream. A
curious name of it I lately noticed is "Two Canon." The Expedition strikes it
at Marengo or Maringo, about on the boundary between Columbia and Garfield
counties, and some 20–25 miles above its mouth. The branch of it reached three
miles further on is the Pataha (Pat-tah-haha of Stevens' large map).

and cross the hills to the plains. We therefore camped for
the night in a grove of cottonwood, after a disagreeable
journey of 28 miles.[5] During the greater part of the day
the air was keen and cold, and it alternately rained, hailed,
and snowed ; but, though the wind blew with great violence,
it was fortunately from the southwest, and on our backs.
We had consumed at dinner the last of our dried meat and
nearly all that was left of the dogs ; so that we supped very
scantily on the remainder, and had nothing for to-morrow.
Weahkoonut, however, assured us that there was a house
on the river at no great distance, where we might supply
ourselves with provisions. We now missed our guide and
the Wollawollahs, who left us abruptly this morning and
never (*p. 267*) returned.

Sunday, May 4th. After a disagreeable night, we collected our horses at an early hour and proceeded, with a
continuation of the same weather. We are now nearer the
southwest mountains, which appear to become lower as they
advance toward the northeast. We followed the road over
the plains, N. 60° E. for four miles to a ravine, where was the
source of a small [branch of Alpowa] creek, down the hilly
and rocky sides of which we proceeded for eight miles to its
entrance into Lewis' river, about 7½ miles above [below[6]]

[5] Here the Expedition is in Garfield Co., Wash., east of Pomeroy and Patah
City, and only about twelve miles from the Snake river at the mouth of Alpowa
creek, where is Silcott. For this creek, see note [2], p. 625.

[6] I think we must here read *below* for "above." Seven and a half miles
above the mouth of Clearwater river, on Snake river, would be in the vicinity of
the town of Asotin. The same distance *below* the mouth of the Clearwater
would seem to be necessarily the place to strike the Snake river by the route
they had taken. This reading is confirmed in every particular by Gass (p. 208,
May 4th), who says that they kept down a creek, *i. e.*, Alpowa, " until we came
to Lewis's river, some distance *below* the forks of Koos-koos-ke," *i. e.*, confluence
of the Clearwater with the Snake. Then he says that after lunch they " proceeded *up* the *south* side of Lewis's river about three miles," where they crossed
it. Snake river here runs approximately east-west ; above the mouth of the
Clearwater it runs south-north. So Gass' compass-points as well as his *up*-river
direction agree with what I make out. Furthermore, May 5th, after they had
crossed from the south to the north bank of the Snake, still below the mouth of
the Clearwater, Gass says, p. 209 : " About 10 o'clock we passed the forks, and

the mouth of the Kooskooskee. Near this place we found the house which Weahkoonut had mentioned, where we halted for breakfast. It contained six families, so miserably poor that all we could obtain from them were two lean dogs and a few large cakes of half-cured bread, made of a root resembling the sweet potato, of all which we contrived to form a kind of soup. The soil of the plain is good, but it has no timber. The range of southwest mountains is about 15 miles above us, but continues to lower, and is still covered with snow to its base. After giving passage to Lewis' [Snake] river, near their northeastern extremity, they terminate in a high [1,500 to 1,000 feet] level plain between that river and the Kooskooskee. The salmon not having yet called them to the rivers, the greater part of the Chopunnish are now dispersed in villages through this plain, for the purpose of collecting quamash and cows [see note, May 12th], which here grow in great abundance, the soil being extremely fertile, in many places covered with long-leaved pine, larch, and balsam-fir, which contribute to render it less thirsty than the open, unsheltered plains.

After our repast we continued our route along the west [*up*, (Lewis' K 99 has " up") the south] side of the river, where, as well on the as opposite shore, the high hills

kept along the north side of Koos-kooskee," *i. e.*, passed by the mouth of the Clearwater and kept along its north bank, which they could not have done without crossing the Clearwater had they come *down* the east (right hand) bank of the Snake.

P. S., Apr. 2d, 1893. I penned the above note in August, 1892, before I knew the codices existed, and having no map at hand but a common school atlas. I saw that by the text they must fetch out at Asotin, but could not see how they got there ; so my friend Gass was a friend indeed, to fortify me. Having later studied out the route with good maps, and traced it through Prescott, Waitesburg, Dayton, Marengo, Pomeroy, Patah, and Alpowa, I was sure the Expedition struck the Snake at Silcott, and not at Asotin (Hashoteen). Now for the codex, Lewis K 99 : " Down this creek N. 75⁰ E. 8 ms. to it's entrance into Lewis's river 7¾ ms. BELOW [capitals mine, as I am happy to say] the entrance of the Kooskooske." At this point where the Snake is reached, at the mouth of Alpowa creek, is Silcott or Selkirk ; across the Snake was a place called Red Wolf. The Expedition goes up the Snake on its S. side 3 m., crosses to its N. side, and goes up along this to the Kooskooskee.

approach it closely, till at the distance of three miles we halted opposite two houses. The inhabitants consisted of five families of Chopunnish, among whom were Tetoh, or Sky, the younger of the two chiefs who had accompanied us in the autumn to the Great Falls (*p. 268*) of the Columbia, and also our old pilot, who had conducted us down the river to the Columbia. They both advised us to cross [Snake river] here and ascend the Kooskooskee on the northeast side [north bank], this being the shortest and best route to the forks of that river, where we should find Twisted-hair, in whose charge we [had] left our horses, and to which place they promised to show us the way. We did not hesitate to accept this offer, and therefore crossed with the assistance of three canoes; but, as night was coming on, we purchased a little wood and some roots of cows, and camped,[7] though we had made only 15 miles. The evening proved cold and disagreeable, and the natives crowded round our fire in such numbers that we could scarcely cook or even keep ourselves warm. At these houses of the Chopunnish we observed a small hut with a single fire, which we were informed is appropriated for women who are undergoing the operation of the menses; there they are obliged to retreat; the men are not permitted to approach within a certain distance of them, and when anything is to be conveyed to those deserted females, the person throws it to them 40 or 50 paces off, and then retires. It is singular,[8] indeed, that among the nations

[7] At place of ferriage, on the north bank of the Snake, in Whitman Co., Wash. 4½ miles west of and below the mouth of the Kooskooskee.

[8] Here as in some other places linger the traces of those rampant superstitions in which the explorers had been raised, and which may have affected their editor too, since he allowed such misapprehensions in print. The similarity is simply because the "nations of this wilderness" and of the Sinaitic wilderness were about on a par in savagery. According to the scraps of mythology and history which reach us in the O. T., the cosmogony and theogony of the nomadic hordes of Arabia, *e. g.*, Gen. i., ii., etc., is no funnier than that of the Osages, p. 13, or Mandans, p. 208; the Mandan medicine-stone, p. 236, and the Chilluckittequaw medicine-bag, p. 675, are duplicates of that "ark" which was so mysteriously connected with hæmorrhoids and mice; while the buffalo-dance, p. 221, is so much like one of the sprees recorded of the man who was after Jehovah's own

of this wilderness, there should be found customs and rites so nearly resembling those of the Jews. It is scarcely necessary to allude more particularly to the uncleanness of Jewish females and the rites of purification.

May 5th. We collected our horses and at seven o'clock set forward alone ; for Weahkoonut, whose people reside above on the west side of Lewis' river, continued his route homeward when we crossed to the huts. Our road was across the plains for 4½ miles, to the entrance of the Kooskooskee.[9] We then proceeded up [the north bank of] that river, and at five miles reached a large mat-house, but could not procure any provisions from the inhabitants ; though on reaching another, three miles beyond, we were surprised at the liberality of an Indian, who gave Captain Clark a very elegant (*p. 269*) gray mare, for which all he requested was a phial of eye-water.

Last autumn, while we were camped at the mouth of the Chopunnish river, a man who complained of a pain in his knee and thigh was brought to us in hopes of receiving relief. The man was to appearance recovered from his disorder, though he had not walked for some time. But that we might not disappoint him, Captain Clark, with much ceremony, washed and rubbed his sore limb, and gave him some volatile liniment to continue the operation, which either caused or did not prevent his recovery. The man gratefully circulated our praises, and our fame as physicians was increased by the efficacy of some eye-water which we gave at the same time. We are by no means displeased at this new resource for obtaining subsistence, as they [Indians] will give us no provisions without merchandise, and our stock is now very much reduced. We cautiously abstain

heart, that the " deadly parallel " could be drawn there more closely than in the present instance of menstruant females. But no such monstrosity in the way of a god, as Jehovah is represented by his apologists to have been, blackens any page of Lewis and Clark ; to match that, we should have to magnify the atrociousness of Le Borgne, p. 242 *seq.*

[9] The Expedition has passed from Whitman Co., Wash., into Nez-percé Co., Idaho, and now goes by the present site of Lewiston : see note [57], p. 620.

from giving them any but harmless medicines; and as we cannot possibly do harm, our prescriptions, though unsanctioned by the faculty, may be useful and are entitled to some remuneration.

Four miles beyond[10] this house we came to another large one, containing ten families, where we halted and made our dinner on two dogs and a small quantity of roots, which we did not procure without much difficulty. Whilst we were eating, an Indian standing by, looking with great derision at our eating dogs, threw a poor half-starved puppy almost into Captain Lewis' plate, laughing heartily at the humor of it. Captain Lewis took up the animal and flung it with great force into the fellow's face; and seizing his tomahawk, threatened to cut him down if he dared to repeat such insolence. He immediately withdrew, apparently much mortified, and we continued our repast of dog very quietly. Here we met our old Chopunnish guide, with his family; and soon afterward one of our horses, which had been separated from the rest in charge of Twisted-hair, and had been in this neighborhood for several weeks, was caught and restored to us.

After dinner we pro- (*p. 270*) ceeded to the entrance of Colter's [Potlatch, p. 617] creek, at the distance of four miles; and having made 20½ miles, camped on the lower side of it. Colter's creek rises not far from the Rocky mountains, passes in the greater part of its course through a country well supplied with pine, and discharges a large body of water; it is about 25 yards wide, with pebbled bed and low banks. At a little distance from us are two Chopunnish

[10] Past a point opposite the mouth of Lapwai creek, for which see note ²³, p. 619, and add: Lapwai is said to be from Nez-percé *lap-pit*, "two," and *wai-tash*, "country," thus meaning place of division, or boundary, and the creek to have actually separated certain Upper and Lower Nez-percés, the distinction between whom was, that the former used to go to the buffalo-country, and the latter never did. There is a reasonableness in this distinction with a difference, and according P. B. Whitman it is etymologically correct. The golden rule in etymology is, to take it for granted that any given etymology is wrong, until it is proved to be right.

houses, one of which contains eight families, and the other, which is by much the largest we have ever seen, is inhabited by at least 30. It is rather a kind of shed built, like all the other huts, of straw and mats in the form of the roof of a house, 156 feet long and about 15 wide, closed at the ends, and having a number of doors on each side. The vast interior is without partitions, but the fire of each family is kindled in a row along the middle of the building, about ten feet apart.

This village is the residence of one of the principal chiefs of the nation, who is called Neeshnepahkeook, or Cut-nose, from the circumstance of having his nose cut from the stroke of a lance in battle with the Snake Indians. We gave him a small medal; though he is a great chief, his influence among his own people does not seem to be considerable, and his countenance possesses very little intelligence. We arrived very hungry and weary, but could not purchase any provisions, except a small quantity of the roots and bread of the cows. They had, however, heard of our medical skill, and made many applications for assistance, but we refused to do anything unless they gave us either dogs or horses to eat. We soon had nearly fifty patients. A chief brought his wife with an abscess on her back, and promised to furnish us with a horse to-morrow if we would relieve her. Captain Clark, therefore, opened the abscess, introduced a tent, and dressed it with basilicon. We also prepared and distributed some doses of flour of sulphur and cream of tartar, with directions for its use. For these we obtained several dogs, but too poor for use, (*p. 271*) and therefore postponed our medical operations till the morning. In the meantime a number of Indians, besides the residents of the village, gathered about us or camped in the woody bottom of the creek.

In the evening we learned, by means of a Snake Indian who happened to be at this place, that one of the old men had been endeavoring to excite prejudices against us, by observing that he thought we were bad men, and came here, most probably, for the purpose of killing them. In order to remove such impressions, we made a speech, in which, by means of the Snake Indian, we told them of our country and all the purposes of our visit. While we were engaged in this occupation, we were joined by Weahkoonut [Big-horn], who assisted us in effacing all unfavorable impressions from the minds of the Indians.

May 6th. Our practice [of medicine] became more valuable. The woman declared that she had slept better than at any time since her illness. She was therefore dressed a second time, and her husband, according to promise, brought us a horse, which we immediately killed. Besides this woman, we had crowds of other applicants, chiefly afflicted with sore eyes, and after administering to them for several hours, found ourselves once more in possession of a plentiful meal; for the inhabitants began to be more accommodating, and one of them even gave us a horse for our remedies to his daughter, a little girl who was afflicted with rheumatism. We also exchanged one of our horses with Weahkoonut, by the addition of a small flag,[11] which procured us an excellent sorrel horse.

We here found three men of a nation called Skeetsomish,[12]

[11] Here is mention of a flag which was certainly left among the Indians; others are elsewhere spoken of in similar terms; any one of these might easily have passed to other hands. See the note about the Cayuses, p. 1038.

[12] These are a Salishan tribe, now called Skitsnish, but better known as the Cœur d'Alêne Indians. Clark charts " Sketsomish 2600 Souls " on a river just west of his " Wayton Lake," *i. e.*, Lac Cœur d'Alêne. This river is a branch of Spokan, Spokane, Spokain or Spokein river; it is called by Clark Lau-taw (same word as Lahtoo, now generally spelled Latah); and another Indian name is given by Mullan as Nedlewhauld or Nedwauld. Symons charts it as Hangman's creek, because Col. Wright hung some Indians there in 1858. Skitsnish, Skitsuish, Sketchhugh, etc., is a name both of these Indians and their lake. This is according to Clark's map of 1814, with " Lau-taw R." emptying into " Clark's river " etc.; but the actual implication of the " large river " of the text, at whose " falls " these Indians are said to live, is the Spokane itself, running from Cœur d'Alêne lake into the Columbia, having the noted Spokane falls, and receiving Latah river from the south. (See codex-map M 1, 2.) As to the curious French name, Cœur d'Alêne, meaning literally " heart of awl," and figuratively pointed-heart, *i. e.*, small-hearted, stingy, etc., various legends are current, all

who reside at the falls of a large [Spokane] river emptying
into the north [east] side of the Columbia.   This river takes
its rise from a large [Cœur d'Alêne] lake in the mountains,
at no great distance from the falls where these natives live.
We shall designate this river, hereafter, by the name of
Clark's river,[13] as we do not know its Indian appellation, and
we are the first whites who have (*p. 271*) ever visited [any
one of] its principal branches; for the Great Lake river mentioned by Mr. Fidler, if at all connected with Clark's river,
must be a very inconsiderable branch.   To this [that other,
the Des Chutes] river, moreover, which we have hitherto
[once, p. 960] called Clark's river, which rises in the southwest mountains, we restored the name of Towahnahiooks
[see notes, pp. 657 and 960], the name by which it is known

to be rejected on general principles. See Symons' Report, 1882, p. 127, citing
A. N. Armstrong, 1856, and Ross Coxe, 1832. Were I disposed to add to the
stock of stories, I should compare the phrase with Crèvecœur and various other
geographical names which commemorate French misery in the West. Very
likely some persons in this locality went hungry till not only were their bellies
pinched as in a vise, but their hearts were pierced with sorrow as with an awl.

[13] There is great confusion concerning this river, now proposed to be called
Clark's.   On Clark's map Wayton Lake, *i. e.*, Cœur d'Alêne, and a river
thence to " Clark's river," are laid down, and this river is moreover marked by
the word " Falls." This is the river now called the Spokane. North of this, on
Clark's map, is no other lake marked.   But a large river is there charted by the
name of " Ki-hi-a-nan R.," and run into " Lau-taw R."   This we may suppose to
be a hint of the large stream now known as Colville river ; but if so, it is laid
down so far out of the way that no such identification can be made. North of
both these questionable rivers is charted the great Clark's Fork of the Columbia,
with approximate accuracy, though with no body of water to represent Pend
d'Oreille lake.   On the much reduced and variously modified map in the
M'Vickar ed. of 1842, the river which runs from *this* lake to the Columbia is
marked " Saleesh R." (Salish).   This is the true " Clark's Fork of the Columbia," as now known, which before it enters Pend d'Oreille Lake is the Missoula,
and certain headwaters of which (Bitter-root or St. Mary's river) were first called
Clark's river by the Expedition on p. 584.   But the river marked Clark's on the
reduced M'Vickar map is that one now known as the Kootenai. Thus what
the text here proposes to call Clark's river is the Spokane ; what is marked on
the M'Vickar map as Clark's river is the Kootenai ; but what they really intend
to name Clark's river is the continuation of the Missoula through Pend d'Oreille
lake into the Columbia. This identification is confirmed by the further remark
that they are the first whites who have visited its principal branches. They were

to the Eneeshurs.   In dress and appearance the Skeetsomish were not to be distinguished from the Chopunnish, but their language is entirely different—a circumstance which we did not learn till their departure, when it was too late to procure from them a vocabulary.

About two o'clock we collected our horses and set out, accompanied by Weahkoonut, with ten or twelve men and a man who said he was the brother of Twisted-hair.   At four miles we came to a single house of three families, but could not procure provisions of any kind; and five miles further we halted for the night near another house, built like the rest, of sticks, mats, and dried hay, and containing six families.   It was now so difficult to procure anything to eat that our chief dependence was on the horse which we received yesterday [in return] for medicine; but to our great

---

never on any branches of the Spokane or Kootenai.   All this is perfectly well understood by modern geographers, who have seen the clear intent of this unlucky paragraph, penned by Captain Lewis, not by "Lewis and Clark," mainly upon Indian information, which was either incorrect in itself or incorrectly apprehended—whence all this confusion.   The case is still further complicated by the fact that Captain Lewis once took a notion to apply Captain Clark's name to the *Des Chutes* river—the Towahnahiooks of our text—and did not give it up till this date of May 6th is reached.   But "Clark's river," as a name of the Des Chutes, should never have been allowed to appear in print at all; the present occasion for repudiating it should never have arisen.   In the codex this name is repeatedly deleted in red ink by Captain Clark's hand, and "Towahnahiooks" interlined, as I have already pointed out.   Under all the circumstances I find it necessary to cite the codex in this place.   Lewis K 105, May 6th, has: "The river here [here in the above text, May 6th] called Clark's river is that which we have heretofore [see *passim anteà*] called the Flathead river.   I have thus named it in honour of my worthy friend and fellow traveller Capt. Clark. for this stream we know no indian name and no whiteman but ourselves was ever on it's principal branches.   the river which Fidler calls the great lake river may possibly be a branch of it.   but if so it is but a very inconsiderable branch and may as probably empty itself into the Skeetsomish [*i. e.*, into the Lau-taw or Spokane, here given another name which does not appear in the text] as into that [Clark's] river.   the stream which I have heretofore [see p. 960] called Clark's river has it's three principal sources in mountains Hood, Jefferson, and the Northern side of the S.W. mountains and is of course a short river.   This river I shall in future call the To-wannahiooks it being the name by which it is called by the Eneshur nation."

disappointment he broke the rope by which he was confined, made his escape, and left us supperless in the rain.[14]

May 7th. Weahkoonut and his party left us, and we proceeded up the river with the brother of Twisted-hair as a
guide. The Kooskooskee is now rising fast; the water is
clear and cold; and as all the rocks and shoals are covered navigation is safe, notwithstanding the rapidity of
the current. The timber begins about the neighborhood
of Colter's creek, and consists chiefly of long-leaved pine.
After going four miles, we reached a house of six families,
below the entrance of a small [Bed-rock] creek, where our
guide advised us to cross the river, as the route was better
and game more abundant near the mouth of the Chopun-
(*p. 273*) nish. We therefore unloaded, and by means of a
single canoe passed to the south side in about four hours,
during which time we dined. An Indian of one of the houses
now brought two canisters of powder, which his dog had discovered underground in a bottom some miles above. We
immediately knew them to be the same we had buried last
autumn; as he had kept them safely, and had honesty
enough to return them, we rewarded him inadequately, but
as well as we could, with a steel for striking fire. We set
out at three o'clock, and pursued a difficult stony road for
two miles, when we left the river and ascended the hills on
the right, which begin to resemble mountains. But when
we reached the heights, we saw before us a beautiful level
country, partially ornamented with long-leaved pine, and
supplied with an excellent pasture of thick grass and a
variety of herbaceous plants, the abundant productions of a
dark, rich soil. In many parts of the plain, the earth is
thrown up into little mounds, by some animal,[15] whose habits

[14] Camp, as given nine miles above Colter's or Potlatch creek, should be on N.
bank of the Kooskooskee, four miles below Bed-rock creek, for which see note [50],
p. 617, Oct. 7th. How they lost their supper is best explained in Lewis K 105:
"I directed the horse which we had obtained for the purpose of eating to be led
as it was yet unbroke, in performing this duty a quarrel ensued between Drewyer
and Colter."

[15] The pocket-gopher of this region, a species of *Thomomys* known as the

most resemble those of the salamander [*Geomys tuza:* see
p. 263]; but though these tracks are scattered over all the
plains from the Mississippi to the Pacific, we have never
yet been able to obtain a sight of the animal itself.

As we entered the plain Neeshnepahkeeook, the Cut-nose,
overtook us, and after accompanying us a few miles turned
to the right to visit some of his people, who were gathering
roots in the plain. Having crossed the plain a little to the
south of east, we descended a long steep hill, at the distance
of five miles, to a [Jack's] creek, six yards wide, which empties
into the Kooskooskee.[16] We ascended this little stream for
a mile and camped at an Indian establishment of six houses,
which seem to have been recently evacuated. Here we
were joined by Neeshnepahkeeook and the Shoshonee who
had interpreted for us on the 5th.

camass-rat from its fondness for the bulbs of the camass (quamash, *Camassia
esculenta*). The species is uncertain, and cannot be determined without specimens from this very locality. My *Thomomys clusius*, Proc. Phila. Acad. 1875,
p. 138, was described originally from Bridger's Pass, Wyo., and has since been
found to be the common gopher of the Snake river plains and some other Idahoan localities. A variety of this, *T. clusius fuscus*, has lately been described
from the mountains of Idaho, as different from that of the sage-brush plains
and valleys (Fauna No. 5, 1891, p. 69). When L. and C. speak of the "tracks"
of gophers, they do not mean the footprints of the animals, but the heaps of
loose earth they everywhere throw up in the course of their burrowing.

[16] Gass says, p. 210, May 7th, that after crossing to the south side of the Kooskooskee, "We then proceeded over a large hill and struck a small creek, about
5 miles below the place where we made our canoes in October last." But it is
impossible for the Expedition to be only "about five miles" from the mouth of
the Chopunnish river at this moment. This creek, "six yards wide," has
never been identified: that is because the text does not fully give the codex,
where we find the required data for identification, and a name too, Lewis K
307: "Through the plain and down a steep and lengthey hill to a creek
which we called Musquetoe Creek in consequence of being infested with swarms
of those insects on our arrival at it. this is but an inconsiderable stream about
6 yds. wide, heads in the plains at a small distance and discharges itself into the
Kooskooke [*sic*] 9 miles by water below the entrance of the Chopunnish river.
we struck this creek at the distance of 5 ms. from the point at which we left the
river our cours being a little to the S. of East. ascending the creek one mile on
the S.E. side we arrived at an indian incampment," etc. This is Jack's creek,
for which see note [50], p. 617. (Examine in this connection Stevens' Pepuennemah and Ahleah creeks ; also Canister run of Clark I 6.)

of a falling-trap, constructed on the same plan with those common to the United States. We gave Neeshnepah-keeook and his people some of our game and horse-beef, besides the entrails of the deer, and four fawns which we found inside of two of them. They did not eat any of them perfectly raw, but the entrails had very little cook-ing; the fawns were boiled whole, and the hide, hair, and entrails all consumed. The Shoshonee was offended at not having as much venison as he wished, and refused to interpret; but as we took no notice of him, he became very officious in the course of a few hours, and (*p. 275*) made many efforts to reinstate himself in our favor. The mother [*sic*—read brother: but see p. 1000] of Twisted-hair, and Neeshnepahkeeook, now drew a sketch, which we preserved, of all the waters west of the Rocky mountains. They make the main southern branch [*i. e.*, the Snake itself] of Lewis' river much more extensive than the other [*i. e.*, Salmon river], and place a great number of Shoshonee vil-lages on its western side. [See codex-map, Clark M 1, 2.]

Between three and four o'clock in the afternoon we set out, in company with Neeshnepahkeeook and other Indians, the brother of Twisted-hair having left us. Our route was up a high steep hill to a level plain with little wood, through which we passed in a direction parallel to the [Kooskooskee] river for four miles, when we met Twisted-hair and six of his people. To this chief we had confided our horses and a part of our saddles last autumn, and we therefore formed very unfavorable conjectures on finding that he received us with great coldness. Shortly afterward he began to speak in a very loud, angry manner, and was answered by Neeshnepahkeeook. We now discovered that a violent quarrel had arisen between these chiefs, on the subject, as we afterward understood, of our horses. But as we could not learn the cause, and were desirous of terminating the dispute, we interposed, and told them we should go on to the first water and camp. We therefore set out, followed by all the Indians, and having reached, at two miles' dis-

tance, a small stream[19] running to the right, we camped with
the two chiefs and their little bands, forming separate camps
at a distance from each other.   They all appeared to be in
an ill humor; and as we had already heard reports that the
Indians had discovered and carried off our saddles, and that
the horses were very much scattered, we began to be uneasy,
lest there should be too much foundation for the report.
We were therefore anxious to reconcile the two chiefs as
soon as possible, and desired the Shoshonee to interpret
for us while we attempted a mediation, but he peremptorily
refused to speak a word.   He observed that it was a quarrel
between the two chiefs, and he had therefore no right to
inter- (*p. 276*) fere; nor could all our representations, that
by merely repeating what we said he could not possibly be
considered as meddling between the chiefs, induce him to
take any part in it.

Soon afterward Drewyer returned from hunting, and was
sent to invite Twisted-hair to come and smoke with us. He
accepted the invitation, and as we were smoking the pipe
over our fire he informed us that according to his promise
on leaving us at the falls of the Columbia, he had collected
our horses and taken charge of them as soon as he reached
home. But about this time Neeshnepahkeeook and Tunnachemootoolt (Broken-arm) who, as we passed, were on
a war-party against the Shoshonees on the south branch of
Lewis' river, returned; and becoming jealous of him, because
the horses had been confided to his care, were constantly
quarreling with him. At length, being an old man and unwilling to live in perpetual dispute with these two chiefs, he
had given up the care of the horses, which had consequently
become very much scattered. The greater part of them

[19] " A little branch which run to the wright, . . . having traveled 6 miles to-
day," Lewis K 112.   The trail is not plain, and if they proceeded parallel with
the Kooskooskee, a stream called Big Cañon river (see note [50], p. 617) remains to
be accounted for, unless this " little branch" be it, or a branch of it. But that
should run from their right to their left as they went eastward.   They are making
for the Upper Kooskooskee, which they appear to strike at a point four miles
above the mouth of the Chopunnish river, or its North fork, as we presently see.

were, however, still in this neighborhood; some in the forks between the Chopunnish and Kooskooskee, and three or four at the village of Broken-arm, about half a day's march higher up the [latter] river. He added that, on the rise of the river in the spring, the earth had fallen from the door of the cache and exposed the saddles, some of which had probably been lost; but as soon as he was acquainted with the situation of them, he had them buried in another deposit, where they now are. He promised that if we would stay to-morrow at his house, a few miles from this place, he would collect such of the horses as were in the neighborhood, and send his young men for those in the forks over the Kooskooskee. He moreover advised us to visit Broken-arm, who was a chief of great eminence, and that he would himself guide us to his dwelling. We told him that we meant to follow his advice in every respect; that we had confided our horses to his charge, and expected that he would deliver them to us, on which we should willingly pay him the (*p. 277*) two guns and ammunition we had promised. With this he seemed very much pleased, and declared that he would use every exertion to restore our horses. We now sent for Cut-nose, and after smoking for some time, took occasion to express to the two chiefs our regret at seeing a misunderstanding between them. Neeshnepahkeeook told us that Twisted-hair was a bad old man, and wore two faces; for instead of taking care of our horses, he had suffered his young men to hunt with them, so that they had been very much injured, and that it was for this reason that Broken-arm and himself had forbidden him to use them. Twisted-hair made no reply to this speech, after which we told Neeshnepahkeeook of our arrangement for to-morrow. He appeared very well satisfied, and said that he would himself go with us to Broken-arm, who expected that we would see him, and who had "two bad horses for us"—an expression by which was meant that he intended making us a present of two valuable horses. That chief, he also informed us, had been apprised of our want of provisions, and sent four young men to meet us with a supply; but having taken a different road, they had missed us. After this interview we retired to rest at a late hour.

May 9th. After sending out several hunters, we proceeded through a level, rich country, similar to that of yesterday, for six miles, when we reached the house of Twisted-hair, situated near some larch-trees and a few bushes of balsam-fir. It was built in the usual form, of sticks, mats, and dried hay; and although it contained no more than two fires and twelve persons, was provided with the customary appendage [20] of a small hut, to which females in certain situations were to retreat.   As soon as we halted [21] at this place, we went with Twisted-hair to the spot where he had buried our saddles, and two young Indians were dispatched after our horses.   Our hunters joined us with nothing but a few pheasants, the only deer which they killed having been lost in the river.   We therefore dined on soup made of the roots [22]

[20] "An appendage of the solitary lodge, the retreat of the tawny damsels when nature causes them to be driven into coventry," Lewis K 115.

[21] "We halted as had been previously coucerted, and one man [Willard] with 2 horses accompayed the twisted hair to the canoe camp about 4 ms. in quest of the saddles." This is the clearest indication I can discover of the whereabouts of the party, and even this is not given in the text. Canoe camp (see p. 612) was on the south side of the Kooskooskee, opposite the confluence of the Chopunnish. The camp of Twisted-hair, when we first made his acquaintance (p. 607), was on an island in the Kooskooskee near the mouth of Village, Flores, or Jim Ford's creek. For a small matter, the itinerary of May 7th–9th is troublesome. We have to set camp to-night in an open plain, short (west) of the Kooskooskee, not far from opposite the mouth of the creek just named, at a point given as 4 m. south of Canoe camp, yet only 16 miles north of Commearp creek hills, as we are told.

[22] Clark Q 116–118, this date: "a root called the *quawmash* and *cows* are esteemed.   The cows is a knobbed root of an irregular form, rounded, not unlike the gensang this root they collect rub off a thin black rind which covers it and pounding it expose it in cakes to the sun," etc.   Lewis K 116, same date: "These cakes are about an inch and ¼ thick and 6 by 18 in width when dried they either eat this bread alone without any further preparation, or boil it and make a thick musilage ; the latter is most common and much the most agreeable.   the flavor of the root is not very unlike the gensang.—this root they collect as early as the snows disappear in the spring and continue to collect it until the quawmash supplys its place which happens about the latter end of June."

(*p. 278*), which we purchased of the Indians. Late in the afternoon, Twisted-hair returned with about half the saddles we had left in the autumn, and some powder and lead which were buried at the same place. Soon after, the Indians brought us 21 of our horses, the greater part of which were in excellent order, though some had not yet recovered from hard usage, and three had sore backs. We were, however, very glad to procure them in any condition. Several Indians came down from the village of Tunnachemootoolt and passed the night with us. Cut-nose and Twisted-hair seem now perfectly reconciled, for they both slept in the house of the latter. The man who had imposed himself upon us as a brother of Twisted-hair also came and renewed his advances, but we now found that he was an impertinent, proud fellow, of no respectability in the nation, and we therefore felt no inclination to cultivate his intimacy. Our camp was in an open plain, and soon became very uncomfortable, for the wind was high and cold, and the rain and hail, which began about seven o'clock, changed in two hours to a heavy fall of snow, which continued till after six o'clock,

May 10*th*, the next morning, when it ceased, after covering the ground eight inches deep and leaving the air keen and cold. We soon collected our horses, and after a scanty breakfast of roots set out on a course S. 35° E.[23] across

The true ginseng is a plant of the order *Araliaceæ* (related to the *Umbelliferæ* and containing the ivy), *Panax ginseng*, a native of China; what the authors mean is the corresponding species common in the United States, *P. quinquefolia*. Both are commercial products of much value, owing to their medicinal repute. The plant whose root is here called *cows*, elsewhere *cowas*, is the same as *cowish*, given in the Century Dictionary as a plant found in the valley of the Columbia river, "probably some species of *Peucedanum*." But it certainly is the well-known *Peucedanum cous*. The "quamash and cows" noted at May 4th are thus given by Gass under date of May 12th: "We also got bread made of roots, which the natives call Cow-as, and sweet roots which they call Commas." The Rev. Mr. M'Vickar renders "cows" by "cow-weed."

[23] A course approximately parallel with the Upper Kooskooskee, up which the Expedition proceeds, but in the plains a little distance west of this river, some points of which may here be noted. The South fork or American river comes north through a gap in Mt. Idaho. Five or six miles below this cañon is Jackson's bridge; about 15 miles by river further north, the South fork joins the

the plains, the soil of which being covered with snow, we could only judge from observing that near the ravines, where it had melted, the mud was deep, black, and well supplied with quamash. The road was very slippery; the snow stuck to the horses' feet and made them slip down very frequently. After going about 16 miles we came to the hills of Commearp creek, which are 600 feet in height, but the tops of which only are covered with snow, their lower parts as well as the bottoms of the creek having (*p. 279*) had nothing but rain while it snowed in the high plains. On descending these hills to the creek, we reached, about four o'clock, the house of Tunnachemootoolt, where was displayed the flag we had given him, raised on a staff. Under this we were received with due form, and then conducted a short distance [24] to a good spot for a camp on Commearp creek.

Middle fork, or main course of the Kooskooskee; whence the united streams take the name of Upper Kooskooskee, and flow about 30 miles to the confluence of the North fork or Chopunnish river (where was Canoe camp, and whence the river becomes the Lower Kooskooskee). The general course of the Upper Kooskooskee, from the junction of the South and Middle forks to the North fork, is about N. 28° W. The principal obstructions to navigation in this course are the following rapids : at 27 miles above the North fork, Indian Billy's, half a mile long, 14 ft. fall; at 23 miles, Reuben's, 500 ft. long, 3 ft. fall; at 19 miles, Miner's, 1000 ft., 15 ft. fall ; at 17½ miles, Carlton's, 350 ft. long ; at 16½ miles, Cañon, 500 ft. long; at 16 miles, Sixteen-mile, 1000 ft. long, 15 ft. fall ; at 15 miles, Granite, 350 ft. long ; at 10 miles, Grier's, 700 ft. long, 3 ft. fall ; at 7 miles, Ford's, 400 ft. long, 3 ft. fall ; at 1½ miles, Slew Gundy ; at mouth of the river, or junction of the North fork, Cobblestone bar. (See Report of Philip G. Eastwick, 1878.) The principal affluents of the Upper Kooskooskee are : first, Kamai, Komeyer, or Commearp creek, now Lawyer's Cañon creek, from the west, the only considerable stream on this side, falling in a few miles north of the confluence of the South and Middle fork ; then, from the east, Collins' creek, Nahwah river or Lo Lo fork ; Village, Flores, or Jim Ford's creek ; and Rockdam or Oro Fino creek.

[24] A very short distance—"about 80 yds.," Lewis K 119 ; for the spot see note [1], p. 1009. As already stated, note [33], p. 601, the creek whose name is spelled "Commearp" in L. and C. is otherwise known as Kamai and Komeyer creek, and now usually called Lawyer's Cañon creek. It is the only considerable tributary of the Upper Kooskooskee from the west, and its course, as far as it goes, separates Nez-percé Co., Idaho, from Idaho Co. on the south—the Upper Kooskooskee separating these same counties as far down as Collins' creek, whence to the Chopunnish river the Upper Kooskooskee separates Nez-percé from Sho-

We soon collected the men of consideration, and after smoking, explained how destitute we were of provisions. The chief spoke to the people, who immediately brought two bushels of dried quamash-roots, some cakes of the roots of cows, and a dried salmon-trout ; we thanked them for this supply, but observed that, not being accustomed to live on roots alone, we feared that such diet might make our men sick, and therefore proposed to exchange one of our good horses, which was rather poor, for one that was fatter, and which we might kill. The hospitality of the chief was offended at the idea of an exchange ; he observed that his people had an abundance of young horses, and that if we were disposed to use that food we might have as many as we wanted. Accordingly, they soon gave us two fat young horses, without asking anything in return, an act of liberal

shone Co. Since passing the site of Lewiston the Expedition has been entirely within Nez-percé Co.; and they may be said simply to have followed up the Kooskooskee thus far—first on its north bank eastward to Bed-rock creek, then along its south bank eastward to near where its North fork comes in, then turning S.S.E. along its west bank to Commearp creek. Near the mouth of this creek, but across the Kooskooskee, in Idaho Co., is a place which passes for a town by the name of Kamai or Kamia. A very few miles below the mouth of Commearp creek, on the Kooskooskee, is the terminus of both the Northern and Southern Nez-percé trails through Idaho, as laid down by Stevens—the former being the Mullan trail of 1854, as we have seen (p. 601), and the latter the Tinkham trail of Nov., 1853. The present name of " Lawyer's " creek and cañon has a history. Lawyer was an Indian who became famous mainly because his father was the man who kept Lewis and Clark's horses during the winter of 1805–6. He claimed to remember the explorers perfectly well. His name occurs more than once in books, as for example in Stevens' Report, p. 198. Chief Lawyer was living about 20 years ago, and we pick up this personal link of the Expedition in the book (pub. 1872) of Mrs. Victor, who was introduced to Lawyer by Mr. Perrin B. Whitman, nephew of the missionary, Dr. Marcus Whitman, slain in the Wallawalla massacre of the whites at Waiilatpu Mission, Nov. 29th, 1847. Lawyer told her that L. and C. had misunderstood the meaning of the word " Kooskooskee"; that the Indians, being questioned concerning this river, and seeing that the object of the explorers was to reach the " river of the west " i. e., the Columbia, told them that the Clearwater was not that great river, but was " Kooskooskee," i. e., a smaller river ; though what the real name of the Clearwater was Lawyer could not say. See p. 596, note [28], and p. 616—seeming to indicate that there was some hitch about the name, upon which Mrs. Victor's story bears quite plausibly.

hospitality much greater than any we have witnessed since crossing the Rocky mountains, if it be not in fact the only really hospitable treatment we have received in this part of the world. We killed one of the horses, and then telling the natives that we were fatigued and hungry, and that as soon as we were refreshed we would communicate freely with them, began to prepare our repast.

During this time, a principal chief, called Hohastilpilp, came from his village about six miles distant, with a party of 50 men, for the purpose of visiting us. We invited him into our circle; he alighted and smoked with us, while his retinue, who had five elegant horses, continued mounted at a short distance. While this was going on, the [other[25]] chief had a large leathern tent spread for us, and desired that we would make that our home whilst we (*p. 280*) remained at his village. We removed there; and having made a fire, we cooked a supper of horse-beef and roots, collected all the distinguished men present, and spent the evening in explaining who we were, the objects of our journey, and giving answers to their inquiries. To each of the chiefs, Tunnachemootoolt and Hohastilpilp, we gave a small medal, explaining the use and importance [of medals] as honorary distinctions among both the white and the red men. Our men are delighted at once more having made a hearty meal. They have generally been in the habit of crowding the houses of the Indians and endeavoring to purchase provisions on the best terms they could; for the inhospitality of the country was such that, in the extreme of hunger, they were often obliged to treat the natives with but little ceremony; but this Twisted-hair had told us was disagreeable. Finding these people so kind and liberal, we ordered our men to treat them with great respect and not to throng round their

[25] Tunnachemootoolt, at whose village they were. They simply made the chief's large tent their headquarters and did not " remove " six miles to Hohastilpilp's village, as the text might suggest. The medal they gave the former chief was the small one with Jefferson's likeness; Hohastilpilp received one of the " sewing " medals, struck during the presidency of Washington. Lewis K 119.

fires; so that they now agree perfectly well together. After our council the Indians felt no disposition to retire, and our tent was crowded with them all night.

May 11*th.* We arose early and breakfasted again on horse-flesh. This village of Tunnachemootoolt is in fact only a single house, 150 feet long, built after the Chopunnish fashion, with sticks, straw, and dried grass. It contains 24 fires, about double that number of families, and might perhaps muster 100 fighting men. The usual outhouse, or retiring-hut for females, is not omitted. Their chief subsistence is roots, and the noise made by the women in pounding them gives the hearer the idea of a nail factory. Yet, notwithstanding so many families are crowded together, the Chopunnish are much more cleanly in their persons and habitations than any people we have met since we left the Ottoes on the river Platte.

In the course of the morning a chief named Yoompahkatim, a stout, good-looking man about forty years of age, (*p. 281*) who had lost his left eye, arrived from his village on the south side of Lewis' river. We gave him a small medal; and finding that there were present the principal chiefs of the Chopunnish nation, Tunnachemootoolt, Neeshnepahkeeook, Yoompahkatim and Hohastilpilp, whose rank is in the order they are mentioned, we thought this a favorable moment to explain to them the intentions of our government.

We therefore collected the chiefs and warriors, and having drawn a map of the relative situation of our country on a mat with a piece of coal, detailed the nature and power of the American nation, its desire to preserve harmony between all its red brethren, and its intention of establishing trading-houses for their relief and support. It was not without difficulty, nor till after nearly half the day was spent, that we were able to convey all this information to the Chopunnish, much of which might have been lost or distorted in its circuitous route through a variety of languages; for in the first place, we spoke in English to one of our men,

who translated it into French to Chaboneau; he interpreted it to his wife in the Minnetaree language; she then
put it into Shoshonee, and the young Shoshonee prisoner
explained it to the Chopunnish in their own dialect. At
last we succeeded in communicating the impression we
wished, and then adjourned the council; after which we
amused them by showing the wonders of the compass,
spy-glass, magnet, watch, and air-gun, each of which attracted its share of admiration. They said that after we
had left the Minnetarees last autumn, three young Chopunnish had gone over to that nation, who had mentioned
our visit and the extraordinary articles we had with us; but
they had placed no confidence in it [this relation] until
now. Among other persons present was a youth, son
of the Chopunnish chief, of much consideration, killed
not long since by the Minnetarees of Fort de Prairie. As
soon as the council was over, he brought a very fine mare
with a colt, and begged us to accept them as a proof that
he meant to (*p. 282*) pursue our advice, for he had
opened his ears to our councils, which had made his heart
glad.

We now resumed our medical labors, and had a number
of patients afflicted with scrofula, rheumatism, and sore eyes,
to all of whom we administered very cheerfully, as far as
our skill and supplies of medicine would permit. We also
visited a chief who has for three years past so completely
lost the use of his limbs that he lies like a perfect corpse in
whatever position he is placed; yet he eats heartily, digests
his food very well, has a regular pulse, and retains his flesh—
in short, were he not somewhat pale from lying so long out
of the sun, he might be mistaken for a man in perfect health.
This disease does not seem to be common; we have seen
only three cases of it among the Chopunnish, who alone are
afflicted with it. The scrofulous disorders we may readily
conjecture to originate in the long confinement to vegetable
diet, which may perhaps also increase the soreness of the
eyes; but this strange disorder baffles at once our curiosity

and our skill.   Our assistance was again demanded early the next morning,

May 12th, by a crowd of Indians, to whom we gave eye-water.   Shortly after, the chiefs and warriors held a council among themselves, to decide on their answer to our speech; and the result was, as we were informed, that they confided in what we had told them, and resolved to follow our advice.   This resolution once made, the principal chief, Tunnachemootoolt, took a quantity of flour of the roots of cows, and going round to all the kettles and baskets, in which his people were cooking, thickened the soup into a kind of mush.   He then began a harangue, making known the result of the deliberations among the chiefs; and after exhorting them to unanimity, concluded by an invitation to all who agreed to the proceedings of the council to come and eat, while those who would not abide by the decision of the chiefs were requested to show their dissent by not partaking of the feast.   During this animated harangue, the women, (*p. 283*) who were probably uneasy at the prospect of forming this new connection with strangers, tore their hair and wrung their hands, with the greatest appearance of distress.   But the concluding appeal of the orator effectually stopped the mouth of every malcontent; the proceedings were ratified, and the mush was devoured with the most zealous unanimity.[26]

The chiefs and warriors then came in a body to visit us, as we were seated near our tent; and at their instance, two young men, one of whom was the son of Tunnachemootoolt and the other the youth whose father had been killed by the Pahkees, presented to each of us a fine horse.   We caused the chiefs to be seated, and gave every one of them a flag, a pound of powder and 50 balls, and a present of the same kind to the young men from whom we had received the horses.   They invited us into the tent, and told us that

---

[26] " I was told by one of our men who was present, that there was not a dissenting voice on this great national question, but all swallowed their objections, if any they had, very cheerfully with their mush," Lewis K 123.

they wished to answer what we had told them yesterday;
but that many of their people were at that moment waiting
in great pain for our medical assistance. It was therefore
agreed that Captain Clark, who is the favorite physician,
should visit the sick, while Captain Lewis would hold the
council; which was accordingly opened by an old man, the
father of Hohastilpilp. He began by declaring that the
nation had listened with attention to our advice, and had
only one heart and one tongue in declaring their determination to follow it. They knew well the advantages of peace,
for they valued the lives of their young men too much to
expose them to the dangers of war; and their desire to live
quietly with their neighbors had induced them last summer
to send three warriors with a pipe to the Shoshonees, in the
plains of the Columbia south of Lewis' river. These minis-
ters of peace had been killed by the Shoshonees, against
whom the nation immediately took up arms. They had met
them last winter and killed 42 men, with the loss of only
three of their own party; so that having revenged their
deceased brethren, they would no longer make war on the
Shoshonees, but receive them as friends. As to (*p. 284*)
going with us to the plains of the Missouri, they would be
very willing to do so, for though the Blackfoot Indians and
the Pahkees had shed much of their blood, they still wished
to live in peace with them. But we had not yet seen either
of these nations, and it would therefore be unsafe for them
to venture, till they were assured of not being attacked by
them. However, some of their young men would accompany us across the mountains, and if they could effect a
peace with their enemies, the whole nation would go over
to the Missouri in the course of next summer. On our proposal that one of the chiefs should go with us to the country
of the whites, they had not yet decided, but would let us
know before we left them. But at all events, the whites
might calculate on their attachment and their best services;
for though poor, their hearts were good. The snow was,
however, still so deep on the mountains that we should

CHAPTER XXX.

CAMP CHOPUNNISH, ON THE UPPER KOOSKOOSKEE.

The Kooskooskee crossed—Camp Chopunnish, on its east bank—Hospitality of the Chopunnish—Characteristics of different bears—Indian cooking of bear's meat—Gelding stallions—Various occupations—Indian honesty—Game scarce—Bad weather—The surrounding
country and its productions—Account of the Chopunnish—Their dress and ornaments—
Their amiable character—Mode of burial—Reptiles of the country—Horned lizards—Various
insects—Indian hunting and fishing—Medical practice—The commissary deficient—Much
sickness—Heroic hydropathy—Hunters out—Sweating an Indian chief—Indian natural history of bears—Important trade for provisions—Story of the stolen tomahawk—Sergeant
Ordway's hunting-party returns—The Tommanamah, or East fork of Lewis' river—Indian
express to Traveler's-rest creek—Propositions respecting the accompanying of the party
by Indians.

TUESDAY, May 13th, 1806. Our medical visits occupied us till a late hour, after which we collected our
horses and proceeded for two miles in a southeastern direction, crossing a branch from the right at the distance of a
mile. We then turned nearly north, and crossing an extensive open bottom a mile and a half wide, reached the bank
of the Kooskooskee.[1] Here we expected the canoe which
they had promised ; but though a man had been dispatched
with it at the appointed time, he did not arrive before sunset. We therefore camped, with a number of Indians who
had followed us from the village, and in the morning,

May 14th, after sending out some hunters, transported
the baggage by means of the canoe, and then drove our
horses into the river, over which they swam without accident, though it is 150 yards wide and the current very rapid.
We then descended the river about (*p. 287*) half a mile, and
formed our camp on the spot which the Indians had recom-

---

[1] " We followed the [Commearp] creek downwards about two miles, passing a
stout branch at 1 m. which flowed in on the right [from the south]. our course
S.E. we now entered an extensive open bottom of the Kooskooske R. through
which we passed nearly N. about 1½ miles, and halted on the [west] bank of the
river," Lewis K 127. This fixes two points with precision ; for the text has not
hitherto shown us just how far up they struck Commearp creek on the 10th.

mended.² It was about 40 paces from the river, and formerly an Indian habitation; but nothing remained but a circle 30 yards in diameter, sunk in the ground about 4 feet, with a wall around it of nearly 3½ feet in height. In this place we deposited our baggage, and around its edges formed our tents of sticks and grass. This situation is in many respects advantageous. It is an extensive level bottom, thinly covered with long-leaved pine, with a rich soil affording excellent pasture, and supplied, as well as the high and broken hills on the east and northeast, with the best game in the neighborhood; while its vicinity to the river makes it convenient for the salmon, which are now expected daily. As soon as we camped, Tunnachemootoolt and Hohastilpilp, with about twelve of their nation, came to the opposite side and began to sing, this being the usual token of friendship on such occasions. We sent the canoe for them, and the two chiefs came over with several of the party, among whom were the two young men who had given us the two horses in behalf of the nation. After smoking some time, Hohastilpilp presented to Captain Lewis an elegant gray gelding, which he had brought for the purpose, and was perfectly satisfied at receiving in return a handkerchief, 200 balls, and four pounds of powder.

The hunters killed some pheasants, two squirrels, and [Collins] a male and a female bear, the first of which was large, fat, and of a bay color; the second meager, grizzly, and of smaller size. They were of the species [*Ursus horribilis*] common to the upper part of the Missouri, and might well be termed the variegated bear, for they are found occasionally of a black, grizzly, brown, or red color. There is every

---

² The Expedition is to remain here in camp on the east bank of the Upper Kooskooskee or Clearwater river until June 10th, or nearly a month, to wait for the melting of the snows on the Bitter-root mountains, which they have to cross. Thus it is the place of the next longest residence of the Expedition, after Fort Mandan and Fort Clatsop. It does not seem to have ever received a name, and may therefore be called Camp Chopunnish. We have the exact location, in Idaho Co., Idaho; and distances from various notable points will appear in the narrative in due course.

reason to believe them to be of precisely the same species. Those of different colors are killed together, as in the case of these two, and as we found the white and bay associated together on the Missouri; and some nearly white were seen in this neigh- (*p. 288*) borhood by the hunters. Indeed, it is not common to find any two bears of the same color; and if the difference in color were to constitute a distinction of species, the number would increase to almost twenty. Soon afterward the hunters killed a female bear with two cubs. The mother was black, with a considerable intermixture of white hairs and a white spot on the breast. One of the cubs was jet black, and the other of a light reddish-brown or bay color. The foil[3] of these variegated bears are [is] much finer, longer, and more abundant than that of the common black bear; but the most striking differences between them are that the former are larger and have longer tusks, and longer as well as blunter talons; that they prey more on other animals; that they lie neither so long nor so closely in winter-quarters; and that they never climb a tree, however closely pressed by the hunters. These variegated bears, though specifically the same with those we met on the Missouri, are by no means so ferocious; probably because the scarcity of game and the habit of living on roots may have weaned them from the practices of attacking and devouring animals. Still, however, they are not so passive as the common black bear, which is also to be found here; for they have already fought with our hunters, though with less fury than those on the other side of the mountains.

A large part of the meat we gave to the Indians, to whom it was a real luxury, as they scarcely taste flesh once in a month. They immediately prepared a large fire of dried wood, on which was thrown a number of smooth stones from the river. As soon as the fire went down and the stones were heated, they were laid next to each other in a level position, and covered with a quantity of branches of

[3] Misprint for *poil*, clearly and correctly written, Clark Q 119, meaning, of course, the hair or pelage. See note [49], p. 849.

pine, on which were placed flitches of the bear ; thus placed, the boughs and the flesh alternated for several courses, leaving a thick layer of pine on the top. On this heap was then poured a small quantity of water, and the whole was covered with earth to the depth of four inches. After remaining in this state about three hours the meat was taken off ; it was (*p. 289*) really more tender than that which we had boiled or roasted, though the strong flavor of the pine rendered it disagreeable to our palates. This repast gave them much satisfaction ; for though they sometimes kill the black bear, yet they attack very reluctantly the furious variegated bear, and only when they can pursue him on horseback through the plains and shoot him with arrows.

The stone-horses we found so troublesome that we endeavored to exchange them for either mares or geldings ; but though we offered two for one, the Indians were unwilling to barter. It was therefore determined to castrate them ; and being desirous of ascertaining the best method of performing this operation, two were gelded in the usual manner, while one of the natives tried the experiment in the Indian way, which he assured us was much the better plan, without tying the string of the stone, but carefully scraping the string clean and separating it from the adjoining veins before cutting it. All the horses recovered ; but we afterward found that those on which the Indian mode had been tried, though they bled more profusely at first, neither swelled nor appeared to suffer as much as the others, and recovered sooner ; so that we are fully persuaded that the Indian method is preferable to our own.

May 15*th.* As we shall now be compelled to pass some time in this neighborhood, a number of hunters[4] were sent

[4] " Reubin Fields in surching for his horse saw a large bear at no great distance from camp. Several men went in pursuit of the bear : they followed his trail a considerable distance, but could not come up with him. Labuishe and Shannon set out with a view to establish a hunting-camp and continuing several days ; two others accompanied them in order to bring in the three bears which Labuish had killed. Drewyer and Cruzatte were sent up the river ; Sheilds R. Fields and Willard hunted in the hills near camp," Lewis K 133.

different directions, and the rest were employed in completing the camp. From this labor, however, we exempted five of the men, two of whom are afflicted with colic, the others complaining of violent pains in the head ; all which are occasioned, we presume, by the diet of roots to which the men have recently been confined. We secured the baggage with a shelter of grass and made a kind of bower of the under part of an old sail, the leathern tent being now too rotten for use, while the men formed very comfortable huts in the shape of an awning of a wagon, by means of willow-poles and grass. Tunnachemootoolt and his young men left (*p. 290*) us this morning on their way home ; and soon after we were visited by a party of 14 Indians on horseback, armed with bows and arrows, going on a hunting-excursion. Their chief game is deer, and wherever the ground will permit the favorite hunt is on horseback ; but in the woodlands, where this is impracticable, they make use of a decoy. This consists of the skin of the head and the upper part of the neck of the deer, kept in its natural shape by a frame of small sticks on the inside. As soon as the hunter perceives a deer he conceals himself, and with his hand moves the decoy so as to represent a real deer in the act of feeding, which is done so naturally that the game is seduced within reach of his arrows.[5]

We also exercised our horses by driving them together, so as to accustom them to each other, and incline them the less to separate. The next morning,

May 16*th,* an Indian returned with one of them, which had strayed away in the night to a considerable distance— an instance of integrity and kindness by no means singular among the Chopunnish. Hohastilpilp, with the rest of the

[5] Such decoying of game is practiced by various Indians, as by the Apaches and others in Arizona. There I have seen the hunters wear the stuffed head of an antelope, and throw over their shoulders a dressed hide of the same, daubed with colored earth in imitation of the natural color of the animal ; then, stooping or going on all-fours, they counterfeited the natural appearance of the game so exactly as to be very deceptive at a little distance.

natives, left us to-day. The hunters who have as yet come in brought nothing except a few pheasants, so that we still place our chief reliance on the mush made of roots, among which cows and quamash are the principal ones; with these we use a small onion, which grows in great abundance, and which corrects any bad effects they may have on the stomach. The cows [*Peucedanum cous*] and quamash incline to produce flatulency; to obviate which we employ a kind of fennel,⁶ called by the Shoshonees yearhah, resembling anniseed [anise-seed] in flavor, and a very agreeable food.

In the course of the day two other hunters [Drewyer and Cruzatte] brought in a deer. The game, they said, was scarce; but they [*i. e.*, Drewyer] had wounded three bears as white as sheep. The hunters who left us yesterday also came in to-night, with information that at the distance of five or six miles [northward] they attempted to cross Collins'⁷ creek to the other side, where game is (*p. 291*) most abundant, but that they could not ford it with their horses, on account of its depth and the rapidity of the current.

May 17th. It rained during the greater part of the night, and our flimsy covering being insufficient for our protection, we lay in the water most of the time. What was more unlucky, our chronometer became wet, and in consequence somewhat rusty; but by care we hope to restore it. The rain continued nearly the whole day; on the high plains the snow is falling, and already two or three inches in depth. The bad weather confined us to camp and kept the Indians from us; so that, for the first time since we left the narrows of the Columbia, a day has passed without our being visited by any of the natives.

---

⁶ *Carum gairdneri*, commonly called "yamp," as noted on p. 552, *q. v.*

⁷ A statement of importance as collateral evidence for the identification of Collins' creek with the Nahwah river or Lo Lo Fork of the Kooskooskee, as heretofore made upon other data. There always used to be a sort of cloud over the title of this stream; but that has now been fully cleared up. See p. 601, and note there.

The country along the Rocky[8] mountains, for several hundred miles in length and about 50 in width, is a high, level plain, in all its parts extremely fertile, and in many places covered with a growth of tall long-leaved pine. This plain is chiefly interrupted near the streams of water, where the hills are steep and lofty;[9] but the soil is good, being unincumbered by much stone and possessing more timber than the level country. Under shelter of these hills, the bottom-lands skirt the margin of the rivers, and though narrow and confined, are still fertile and rarely inundated. Nearly the whole of this wide-spread tract is covered with a profusion of grass and plants, which are at this time as high as the knee. Among these are a variety of esculent plants and roots, acquired without much difficulty, and yielding not only a nutritious but a very agreeable food. The air is pure and dry; the climate is quite as mild as, if not milder than, [that of] the same parallels of latitude in the Atlantic States, and must be equally healthy; for all the disorders which we have witnessed may fairly be imputed more to the nature of the diet than to any intemperance of climate. This general observation is of course to be qualified, since in the same tract of country the degrees of the combination of heat and cold obey the influence of situa- (*p. 292*) tion. Thus the rains of the low grounds near our camp are snows

[8] Perhaps it is worth while here to note, that as long as the Expedition is in Idaho, " Rocky mountains " means the Bitter-root and collateral ranges, as our authors never specified these by name, but treated as " Rocky " all the vertebræ in the spinal column of the continent. Their locutions concerning the several ranges they crossed may be roundly reduced to—1. Black hills : everything mountainous east of the Rockies. 2. Rocky mountains : all the other mountain chains in Montana, and all the ranges in Idaho, collectively. 3. Mountains between the Columbian plains and Columbian valley, *i. e.*, the Cascade range. 4. Mountains between the Columbia valley and the Pacific, *i. e.*, the Coast range.

[9] Not meaning that the general level of the country rises into " steep and lofty hills " along the water-courses, but that the plains are there rifted into precipitous crevasses or cañons. Such formations are highly characteristic of the general area drained by the Snake river system. Some of these vast chasms, along the Snake itself and Salmon river, are second in formidable magnitude only to the Grand Cañon of the Colorado.

in the high plains; the sun shines with intense heat in the confined bottoms, but the plains enjoy a much colder air, and the vegetation is there retarded at least 15 days, while at the foot of the mountains the snows are still many feet in depth; so that within 20 miles of our camp we observe the rigors of winter cold, the cool air of spring, and the oppressive heat of midsummer. Even on the plains, however, where the snow has fallen, it seems to do but little injury to the grass and other plants, which, though apparently tender and susceptible, are still blooming at the height of nearly 18 inches through the snow. In short, this district affords many advantages to settlers, and if properly cultivated, would yield every object necessary for the subsistence and comfort of civilized man.

The Chopunnish themselves are in general stout, well formed, and active; they have high, and many of them aquiline, noses; the general appearance of the face is cheerful and agreeable, though without any indication of gayety and mirth. Like most Indians, they extract their beards; but the women only pluck the hair from the rest of the body. That of the men is very often suffered to grow, nor does there appear to be any natural deficiency in that respect; for we observe several men who, had they adopted the practice of shaving, would have been as well supplied as ourselves. The dress of both sexes resembles that of the Shoshonees, and consists of a long shirt reaching to the thigh, leggings as high as the waist, moccasins, and robes—all of which are formed of skins.

Their ornaments are beads, shells, and pieces of brass attached to different parts of the dress, or tied around the arms, neck, wrists, and over the shoulders; to these are added pearls [10] and beads suspended from the ears, and a single shell of wampum through the nose. The head-dress

[10] Bits of mother-of-pearl, the shell of the abalone, most probably; perhaps, however, an inferior sort of pearls from a kind of pearl-mussel, *Margaritana margaritifera*, which could be procured from the Indians of the lower Columbia. The wampum here in mention is a tooth-shell of *Dentalium* or a related genus.

of the men is a bandeau of fox or otter-skin, either with or without the fur, and sometimes an ornament tied to a (*p. 293*) plait of hair, falling from the crown of the head; that of the women is a cap without a rim, formed of bear-grass and cedar-bark; while the hair itself, of both sexes, falls in two rows down the front of the body. Collars of bears' claws are also common. But the personal ornament most esteemed is a sort of breastplate, formed of a strip of otter-skin six inches wide, cut out of the whole length of the back of the animal, including the head; this being dressed with the hair on, a hole is made at the upper end, through which the head of the wearer is placed, and the skin hangs in front with the tail reaching below the knee, ornamented with pieces of pearl, red cloth, and wampum or, in short, any other fanciful decoration. Tippets also are occasionally worn. That of Hohastilpilp was formed of human scalps and adorned with the thumbs and fingers of several men slain by him in battle.

The Chopunnish are among the most amiable men we have seen. Their character is placid and gentle, rarely moved to passion, yet not often enlivened by gayety. Their amusements consist in running races and shooting with arrows at a target; they partake also of the great and pre-vailing vice of gambling. They are, however, by no means so much attached to baubles as the generality of Indians, but are anxious to obtain articles of utility, such as knives, tomahawks, kettles, blankets, and awls for [making] mocca-sins. They have also suffered so much from the superiority of their enemies that they are equally desirous of procuring arms and ammunition, which they are gradually acquiring; for the band of Tunnachemootoolt have already six guns, which they acquired from the Minnetarees.

The Chopunnish bury their dead in sepulchers formed of boards, constructed like the roof of a house. The bodies are rolled in skins and laid one over another, separated by a board only, both above and below. We have sometimes seen their dead buried in wooden boxes, and rolled in skins in the manner above mentioned. They sacrifice their horses, (*p. 294*) canoes, and every other species of property to their dead; the bones of many horses are seen lying round their sepulchers.

Among the reptiles common to this country are the two species of innocent snakes already described and the rattle-snake, which last is of the same species [*Crotalus confluentus*] as that of the Missouri, and though abundant here, is the only poisonous snake we have seen between the Pacific and the Missouri. Besides these there are the common black lizard [*Sceloporus* sp.] and the horned lizard. Of frogs there are several kinds, such as the small green tree-frog [*Hyla regilla*]; the small frog [*Chorophilus triseriatus*, like one which is] common in the United States, which sings in the spring of the year; a species of frog [toad, *Bufo columbiensis*] frequenting the water, much larger than the bullfrog, and in shape between the delicate length of the bullfrog and the shorter and less graceful form of the toad, like which last, however, its body is covered with little pustules, or lumps. We have never heard it make a noise of any kind. Neither the toad [*Bufo americanus*], bullfrog [*Rana catesbiana*], moccasin [*Ancistrodon piscivorus*], nor copperhead [*A. contortrix*] is to be found here. Captain Lewis killed a snake [*Pityophis* sp.] near the camp 47 inches in length and much the color of the rattlesnake; no poisonous tooth [fang] was to be found; it had 218 scuta [gastrosteges] on the abdomen, and 59 squamæ [urosteges], or half-formed scuta, on the tail; the eye was of moderate size, the iris dark yellowish-brown, and the pupil black; there was nothing remarkable in the form of the head, which was not so wide across the jaws as that of the poisonous class of snakes usually is.

There is a species of lizard, which we have called the horned lizard [*Phrynosoma douglasi*], about the size of and much resembling in figure the ordinary black lizard. The belly is, notwithstanding, broader, the tail shorter, and the action much slower than the ordinary lizard. It crawls like the toad, and is of a brown color, interspersed with yellowish-brown spots. It is covered with minute shells [scales], interspersed with little horny projections like prickles on the upper part of the body. The belly and throat resemble the frog's, and are of a light yellowish- (*p. 295*) brown; the edge of the belly is regularly beset with horny projections, which give both edges a serrate figure. The eye is small and of a dark color. Above and behind the eyes are several projections of bone [horn], which, being armed at the extremities with a firm black substance, have the appearance of horns sprouting from the head; [this] has induced us to call it the horned lizard. These animals are found in great abundance in the sandy parts of the plains, and after a shower of rain are seen basking in the sun. For the greatest part of the time they are concealed in holes. They are found in great numbers on the banks of the Missouri, and in the plains through which we have passed above the Wollawollahs. [Compare p. 899.]

Most of the insects common to [or resembling those of] the United States are seen in this country: such as the butterfly, the common house-fly [*Musca domestica*], the blowing-fly [*Lucilia cæsar*, or a related species], the horse-fly [*Tabanus atratus?*], except one species of it, the gold-colored ear-fly [*Chrysops* sp.], the place of which is supplied by a fly of a brown color, which attaches itself to the same part of the horse and is equally troublesome. There are likewise nearly all the varieties of beetles known in the Atlantic States, except the large cow-beetle [*Copris carolina*], and the black beetle commonly called the tumble-bug [*Canthon lævis*]. Neither the hornet, the wasp, nor the yellow-jacket inhabits this part of the country; but there is an insect [*Vespa diabolica*] resembling the last of these, though much larger, which is very numerous, particularly in the Rocky mountains and on the waters of the Columbia; the body and abdomen are yellow, with transverse circles of black; the head is black, and the wings, which are four in number, are of a dark brown color. Their nests are built in the ground and resemble that of the hornet, with an outer covering to the comb.

These insects are fierce and sting very severely, so that we found them very troublesome in frightening our horses as we passed the mountains. The silkworm [*Attacus polyphemus* or *cecropia*] is also found here, as well as the humble-bee [*Bombus*], though the honey-bee [*Apis mellifica*] is not.

(*p. 296*) *May* 18*th.* Twelve hunters set out this morning after bear, which are now our chief dependence; but as they are now ferocious, the hunters henceforward never go except in pairs. Soon after they left us, a party of Chopunnish erected a hut on the opposite side of the river in order to watch for salmon, which are expected to arrive every day. For this purpose they have constructed with sticks a kind of wharf, projecting about ten feet into the river and three feet above its surface, on the extremity of which one of the fishermen exercised himself with a scooping-net, similar to that used in our country; but after several hours' labor he was unsuccessful. In the course of the morning three Indians called at our camp and told us that they had been hunting near the place where we met the Chopunnish last autumn, and which is called by them the Quamash grounds; [11] but after roaming about for several days had killed nothing. We gave them a small piece of meat, which they said they would keep for their small children, who they said were very hungry, and then, after smoking, took leave of us. Some of our hunters [Drewyer, J. and R. Fields, and Lepage] returned almost equally unsuccessful. They had gone over the whole country between Collins' creek and the Kooskooskee, to their junction, a distance of ten miles, without seeing either deer or bear, and at last brought in a single hawk and a salmon dropped by an eagle. This last was not in itself considerable, but gave us hopes of soon seeing that fish in the river, an event which we ardently desire; for though the

[11] Here indicating the low country first reached by Captain Clark Sept. 20th, when he was leading the Expedition out of the mountains : see p. 603, and note [34], p. 602. But several widely separated spots where camass grew are called " Quamash flats " and " Quamash glades " in the course of the narrative. Three such places are so lettered on Clark's map, 100 miles and more apart.

rapid rise of the river denotes a great decrease of snow on the mountains, yet we shall not be able to leave our camp for some time.[12]

May 19*th.* After a cold, rainy night, during a greater part of which we lay in the water, the weather became fair; we then sent some men [Hall, Potts, Wiser, Thompson, and "Charbono"] to a village above us, on the opposite side, to purchase some roots. They carried with them for this purpose a small collection of alls [awls], knitting-pins, and armbands, with which they obtained several bushels of the root of cows, and some bread of the same mate- (*p. 297*) rial. They were followed, too, by a train of invalids from the village [*i. e.*, Thompson soon returned with four men, eight women, and a child], who came to ask for our assistance. The men were generally afflicted with sore eyes; but the women had besides this a variety of other disorders, chiefly rheumatic, a violent pain and weakness in the loins, which is a common complaint among them; one of them seemed much dejected, and as we thought, from the account of her disease, hysterical. We gave her 30 drops of laudanum, and after administering eye-water, rubbing the rheumatic patients with volatile liniment, and giving cathartics to others, they all thought themselves much relieved and returned highly satisfied to the village. We [J. and R. Fields] were fortunate enough to retake [that] one of the horses on which we [Captain Lewis] had crossed the Rocky mountains in the autumn, and which had become almost wild since that time.

May 20*th.* Again it rained during the night and the greater part of this day. Our hunters were out in different directions; but though they saw a bear and a deer or two, they only killed one of the latter, which proved to be of the mule-deer species.[13]

[12] " I am pleased at finding the river rise so rapidly; it no doubt is attributeable to the melting snows of the mountains; that icy barier which separates me from my friends and Country, from all which makes life esteemable.—patience, patience—," Lewis K 138.

[13] According to Lewis K 141, this date, both the captains lay in the wet all

May 21st. Finding the rain still continue we left our ragged sail tent and formed a hut with willow-poles and grass. The rest of the men were occupied in building a canoe for present use, as the Indians promise to give us a horse for it when we leave them. We received nothing from our hunters except a single sand-hill crane [*Grus canadensis*], which species is very abundant in this neighborhood, and consumed at dinner the last morsel of meat we had. As there seems but little probability of our procuring a stock of dried meat, and fish is as yet an uncertain resource, we made a division of all our stock of merchandise, so as to enable the men to purchase a store of roots and bread for the mountains. We might ourselves collect these roots, but as there are several species of [water-] hemlock [14] growing among the cows [*Peucedanum cous*], difficult to be distinguished from that plant, we are afraid to suffer the men to collect them, lest the party be poisoned (*p. 298*) by mistaking them. On parceling out the stores, the stock of each man was found to consist of only one awl and one knitting-

night, their covering being insufficient. Drewyer and the brothers Fields set out on a hunt toward the mountains. Shannon and Colter came in unsuccessful ; they had wounded a bear and a deer yesterday, but night coming on, were unable to procure them, and a snow-fall obliterated their tracks. It was Labiche who killed the mule-deer. Yesterday he had left Cruzatte and Collins on the creek named for the latter, where they were to await his return ; late this evening he set out with Lepage to join them, and resume the hunt in the morning. Frazier returned at 5 p. m. with a good stock of eatables he had bought at the village for brass buttons ; and the men, observing how fond the Indians are of these articles, are now cutting them off their clothes to trade for bread of cows.

[14] The plant which the authors have here in mind is the common cowbane, *Cicuta maculata*, a poisonous umbelliferous plant of wide distribution in the United States, where it is also known as water-hemlock and poison-hemlock. The reference is useful in identifying " cows " as *Peucedanum cous*—a plant so similar to this that the two might be confounded with disastrous results. The European water-hemlock is *Cicuta virosa*. The true hemlock of Eurasiatic countries is another umbellifer, *Conium maculatum*, also poisonous. The juice which Socrates is said to have drunk to his death was one of these two, most likely the last-named. Hemlock as applied to a coniferous tree means the hemlock-spruce, or American fir, *Tsuga canadensis*, whose sprays are likened to the dissected foliage of the umbelliferous *Conium*. For the identification of cows or cous, see note [22], p. 999.

pin, half an ounce of vermilion, two needles, a few skeins of thread, and about a yard of ribbon—a slender means of bartering for our subsistence; but the men have been so much accustomed to privations that now neither the want of meat nor the scanty funds of the party excites the least anxiety among them.

May 22d. We availed ourselves of the fair weather to dry our baggage and store of roots; and being still without meat, killed one of our colts, intending to reserve the other three for the mountains. In the afternoon we were amused by a large party of Indians, on the opposite side of the river, hunting on horseback. After riding at full speed down the steep hills, they at last drove a deer into the river, where we shot it; two Indians immediately pursued it on a raft and took it. Several hunters,[1] who had gone to a considerable distance near the mountains, returned with five deer. They had purchased also two red salmon-trout, which the Indians say remain in this river during the greater part of the winter, but are not good at this season, as it in fact appeared, for they were very meager. The salmon, we understand, have now arrived at no great distance, in Lewis' river; but some days will yet elapse before they come up to this place. This, as well as the scarcity of game, made us wish to remove lower down; but on examination we found that there was no place in that

---

[1] The brothers Fields, Drewyer, Gibson, and Shields. The text is very brief in the narrative at Camp Chopunnish; the codex has probably three times as much to say of incidents and occupations—the latter chiefly hunting and trading. There was also a good deal of sickness in camp, owing to the diet. Sacajawea's baby was teething and had cholera infantum and the mumps, which kept both captains " walking the floor," so to speak, all night. Captain Lewis' fine horse, so recently gelded, managed to hitch his lariat about the parts, and injured himself so seriously that the chances seemed against his recovery; he was shot on June 2d. There are also some singularly regular entries of the men (privates) who were each day " permitted " to go to the village, and were not inquired about. Most probably the Chopunnish tribe did not deteriorate under the circumstances. Certain traditions of Idaho, relating to a well-known half-breed who was still living about twenty years ago, are a part of the unwritten history of the Expedition. The paternal name in this case is spelled with five letters in the codex.

direction calculated for a camp, and therefore resolved to remain in our present position. Some uneasiness has been excited by a report that two nights ago a party of Sho-shonees had surrounded a Chopunnish house, on the south side of Lewis' river; though the inhabitants, having dis-covered their intentions, had escaped without injury.

May 23d.[16] The hunters were sent out to make a last effort to procure provisions; but after examining the whole country between Collins' creek and the Kooskooskee, they (*p. 299*) found nothing except a few pheasants of the dark brown kind [see p. 872]. In the meantime we were visited by four Indians, who had come from a village on Lewis' river, at the distance of two days' ride, for the purpose of procuring a little eye-water. The extent of our medical fame is not a little troublesome; but we rejoice at any circumstance which enables us to relieve these poor crea-tures, and therefore willingly washed their eyes, after which they returned home.

May 24th. This proved the warmest day we have had since our arrival here. Some of our men visited the village of Broken-arm, and exchanged some awls, which they had made of the links of a small chain belonging to one of their steel traps, for a plentiful supply of roots.

Besides administering medical relief to the Indians we are obliged to devote much of our time to the care of our own invalids. The child of Sacajawea is very unwell; and with one of the men [Bratton] we have ventured an experi-ment of a very robust nature. He has been for some time sick, but has now recovered his flesh, eats heartily, and digests well, but has so great a weakness in the loins that he cannot walk or even sit upright without extreme pain. After we had in vain exhausted the resources of our art, one of the hunters [Shields] mentioned that he had known persons in similar situations to be restored by violent sweats, and at

---

[16] Codex K ends at this date on p. 147, so far as the journal is concerned, though there are a few more folios of a meteorological register, etc. The Biddle narrative continues directly with Lewis L.

the request of the patient, we permitted the remedy to be applied. For this purpose a hole about four feet deep and three in diameter was dug in the earth, and heated well by a large fire in the bottom of it. The fire was then taken out, and an arch formed over the hole by means of willow-poles, and covered with several blankets so as to make a perfect awning. The patient being stripped naked, was seated under this on a bench, with a piece of board for his feet, and with a jug of water sprinkled the bottom and sides of the hole, so as to keep up as hot a steam as he could bear. After remaining 20 minutes in this situation, he was taken out, immediately plunged twice in cold water, and brought back (*p. 300*) to the hole, where he resumed the vapor bath. During all this time he drank copiously a strong infusion of horse-mint, which was used as a substitute for seneca-root, which our informant said he had seen employed on these occasions, but of which there is none in this country. At the end of three-quarters of an hour he was again withdrawn from the hole, carefully wrapped, and suffered to cool gradually. This operation was performed yesterday; this morning he walked about and is nearly free from pain. About 11 o'clock a canoe arrived with three Indians, one of whom was the poor creature who had lost the use of his limbs, and for whose recovery the natives seem very anxious, as he is a chief of considerable rank among them. His situation is beyond the reach of our skill.[17] He complains of no pain in any peculiar limb, and we therefore think his disorder cannot be rheumatic, as his limbs would have been more diminished if his disease had been a paralytic affection. We had already ascribed it to his diet of roots, and had recommended his living on fish and flesh, and using the cold bath every morning, with a dose of cream of tartar or flowers of sulphur every third day. These prescriptions seem to have been of little avail, but as he thinks himself

[17] " I am confident that this would be an excellent subject for electricity and much regret that I have it not in my power to supply it," Lewis L 3.

somewhat better for them, we concealed our ignorance by giving him a few drops of laudanum and a little portable soup, with a promise of sweating him, as we had done our own man. On attempting it, however, in the morning, *May 25th*, we found that he was too weak to sit up or be supported in the hole. We therefore told the Indians that we knew of no other remedy except frequent perspirations in their own sweat-houses, accompanied by drinking large quantities of the decoction of horse-mint, which we pointed out to them. Three hunters set out to hunt toward Quamash flats [of p. 603], if they could pass Collins' creek. Others crossed the river for the same purpose, and one of the men was sent to a village on the opposite side, about eight miles above us. Nearly all the inhabitants were either hunting, digging roots, or (*p. 301*) fishing in Lewis' river, from which they had brought several fine salmon. In the course of the day some of our hunters wounded a female bear with two cubs, one of which was white and the other perfectly black.

The Indians who accompanied the sick chief are so anxious for his safety that they remained with us all night ; and in the morning,

May 26th, when we gave him some cream of tartar and portable soup, with directions how they were to treat him, they still lingered about us in hopes we might do something effectual, though we desired them to take him home.

The hunters [J. and R. Fields] sent out yesterday returned with Hohastilpilp and a number of inferior chiefs and warriors. They passed [crossed] Commearp creek at the distance of 1½ miles, and a larger creek three miles beyond; they then went on [southward] till they were stopped by a large creek [18] ten miles above camp, [*i. e.*, higher up the

[18] This is very satisfactory as to the distance from camp assigned, and yields a ready identification. This "large creek," too large for the hunters to cross, is the South fork of the Kooskooskee, otherwise known as American river, which, coming almost due north through a chasm in Mt. Idaho, joins the main or Middle fork of the Kooskooskee, from the east, at a point about or within ten miles from Camp Chopunnish. On American river, five or six miles above its

Kooskooskee], and finding it too deep and rapid to pass, they returned home. On their way they stopped at a village four miles up the second creek, which we have never visited, and where they purchased bread and roots on very moderate terms; an article of intelligence very pleasing at the present moment, when our stock of meat is again exhausted. We still have, however, agreeable prospects; for the river is rising fast, as the snows visibly diminish, and we saw a salmon in the river to-day. We also completed our canoe [and put her in the water; she appears to answer very well, and will carry about 12 persons, Lewis L 5.

May 27th. The horse which the Indians gave us some time ago had gone astray; but in our present dearth of provisions we searched for him and killed him. Observing that we were in want of food, Hohastilpilp informed us that most of the horses which we saw running at large belonged to him or his people, and requested that whenever we wished any meat we would make use of them without restraint. We have, indeed, on more than one occasion, had to admire the generosity of this Indian, whose conduct presents a model of what is due to strangers in distress.[19] A party was sent to (*p. 302*) the village discovered yesterday, and returned with a large supply of bread and roots. Sergeant Ordway and two men were also dispatched to Lewis' [Snake] river, about half a day's ride to the south, where we

mouth, was fought the well-remembered battle of July 11th and 12th, 1877, and under Mt. Idaho was established Camp Howard, named for General Oliver O. Howard, who conducted the Nez-percé campaign. But I am entirely at a loss for the "larger [than Commearp] creek" of the text; none of the maps before me yields even a conjecture as to what *this* stream can be.

[19] These Indians have excited admiration from that day to this for various virtues that are becoming in men, and our soldiers in the Nez-percé war found another Hohastilpilp in the celebrated chief Joseph. A good story, possibly with some foundation in fact, is told of an Indian who exhibited another "model of what is due to strangers in distress." In the thick of the fight, a wounded soldier suddenly found a Nez-percé bending over him, as he supposed to dispatch him and lift his hair. His hair naturally rose of its own motion in this extremity of terror; observing which, the Indian remarked: "O! bother your scalp—I don't want that; fork over your ammunition."

expected to obtain salmon, which are said to be very abundant at that place. The three men who had attempted to go to the Quamash flats returned with five deer; but though they had proceeded some distance up Collins' creek, it continued too deep for them to cross. The Indians who accompanied the chief were so anxious to have the operation of sweating him performed under our inspection that we determined to gratify them by making a second attempt. The hole was therefore enlarged, and the father of the chief, a very good-looking old man, went in with him and held him in a proper position. This strong evidence of feeling is directly opposed to the received opinion of the insensibility of savages, nor are we less struck by the kindness and attention paid to the sick man by those who are unconnected with him; which is the more surprising, as the long illness of three years might be supposed to have exhausted their sympathy. We could not produce as complete a perspiration as we desired; after he was taken out he complained of suffering considerable pain, which we relieved with a few drops of laudanum, and he then rested well. The next morning,

May 28th,[20] he was able to use his arms; he feels better than he has done for many months, and sat up during the greater part of the day.

We sent to the village of Tunnachemootoolt for bread and roots, and a party of hunters set out to hunt up a creek

[20] At this date Clark Q 126–132 has two long ornithological descriptions. One of these, pp. 126–129, is of *Picicorvus columbianus*, elsewhere cited in substance. The other is more important, for it has never been used, and brings a new bird into the results of the Expedition. "Our hunters brought us a large hooting owl," etc., differing from those of the United States, with long silky plumage of a dark iron-gray, etc., the head "1 Foot 10 Inches" in circumference, with a remarkable facial disk, etc., pp. 129–132. This is clearly the great gray owl, *Scotiaptex cinerea*, better known as *Syrnium cinereum*. Both these descriptions are also in Lewis L 10, 11. Under date of May 27th, Clark Q 122–124, and Lewis L 7, 8, have the long description of the burrowing-squirrel, *Spermophilus columbianus*, which should have been brought in here, as this is the locality where the animal was first noticed. The same may be said of other zoölogical matter in the Chopunnish codices.

[American river] about eight miles above us. In the evening, another party, who had been so fortunate as to find a
ford across Collins' creek, returned from the Quamash flats
with eight deer, of which they saw great numbers, though
there were but few bears.   Having now a tolerable stock of
meat, we were occupied during the following day,

(*p. 303*) *May 29th*, in various engagements in the camp.
The Indian chief is still rapidly recovering, and for the first
time during the last twelve months had strength enough to
wash his face. We had intended to repeat the sweating
to-day, but as the weather was cloudy, with occasional rain,
we declined it. This operation, though violent, seems
highly efficacious; for our own man [Bratton], on whom the
experiment was first made, is recovering his strength very
fast, and the restoration of the chief is wonderful.   He continued to improve, and on the following day,

May 30th,[21] after a very violent sweating, was able to move
one of his legs and thighs, and some of his toes ; the fingers
and arms being almost entirely restored to their former
strength.   Parties were sent out as usual to hunt and trade
with the Indians.   Among others, two of the men, who had
not yet exchanged their stock of merchandise for roots,
crossed the river for that purpose in our boat.   But as they
reached the opposite shore, the violence of the current
drove the boat broadside against some trees; she immediately filled and went to the bottom.   With difficulty one of
the men [Potts] was saved, but the boat itself, with three
blankets, a blanket-coat, and their small pittance of merchandise, was irrevocably lost.

May 31st. Two men visited the Indian village, where
they purchased a dressed bear-skin, of a uniform pale reddish-brown color, which the Indians called yackah, in con-

---

[21] At this date Clark Q 139 has : " Found some Onions on the high plains of a
different species from those near the borders of the river, as they are also from the
Shive or small Onion noticed below the falls of the Columbia, they are as large as
a nutmeg, generally grow double, connected by the same tissue of radicles ; each
bulb has two long linior [linear] flat solid leaves, the peduncle is solid celindric

tradistinction to hohhost, or white bear. This remark induced us to inquire more particularly into their opinions as to the several species of bears; we therefore produced all the skins of that animal which we had killed at this place, and also one very nearly white which we had purchased. The natives immediately classed the white, the deep and the pale grizzly red, the grizzly dark brown—in short, all those with the extremities of the hair of a white or frosty color, without regard to the color of the ground of the foil [*sic*], under the name of hohhost. They assured us that (*p. 304*) they were all of the same species with the white bear; that they associated together, had longer nails than the others, and never climbed trees. On the other hand, the black skins, those which were black with a number of entirely white hairs intermixed, or with a white breast, the uniform bay, the brown, and the light reddish-brown, were ranged under the class yackah, and were said to resemble each other in being smaller, in having shorter nails than the white bear, in climbing trees, and in being so little vicious that they could be pursued with safety. This distinction of the Indians seems to be well founded, and we are inclined to believe: 1st, that the white, grizzly, etc., bear of this neighborhood forms a distinct species [*Ursus horribilis*], which, moreover, is the same with that of the same color on the upper part of the Missouri, where the other species is not found; 2d, that the black, reddish-brown, etc., is a second species [*U. americanus* and its var. *cinnamomeus*], equally distinct from the white bear of this country and [only varietally different] from the black bear of the Atlantic and Pacific oceans, which two last seem to form only one species. The common black bear is indeed unknown in this country; for the bear of which we are speaking, though in

and crowned with an umbel of from 20. to 30. flowers. This onion is exceedingly crisp and delicately flavoured, indeed I think more sweet & less strong than any I ever tasted, it is not yet perfectly in bloom, the parts of the flower are not distinct." Lewis L 16 has the same description, which appears to indicate *Allium tolmiei.*

most respects similar, differs from it in having much finer, thicker, and longer hair, with a greater proportion of fur mixed with it, and also in having a variety of colors, while the common black bear has no intermixture or change of color, but is of a uniform black.   [See pp. 841, 842.]

In the course of the day the natives brought us another one of our original stock of horses, of which we have now recovered all except two ; these, we are informed, were taken by our Shoshonee guide [Toby, and his son] when he [they] returned home.   They amount to 65, most of them fine, strong, active horses, in excellent order.

Sunday, June 1st, 1806.   Two of our men, who had been up the river to trade with the Indians, returned quite unsuccessful.   Nearly opposite the village, their horse fell with his load down a steep cliff into the river, across which he swam.   An Indian on the opposite side drove him back to (*p. 305*) them ; but in crossing most of the articles were lost and the paint melted.   Understanding their intentions, the Indians attempted to come over to them, but having no canoe, were obliged to use a raft, which struck on a rock, upset, and the whole store of roots and bread were destroyed. This failure completely exhausted our stock of merchandise ; but the remembrance of what we suffered from cold and hunger during the passage of the Rocky mountains makes us anxious to increase our means of subsistence and comfort, since we have again to encounter the same inconvenience.   We therefore created a new fund, by cutting off the buttons from our clothes and preparing some eye-water and basilicon, to which were added some phials and small tin boxes in which we had once kept phosphorus.   With this cargo two men [M'Neal, York] set out in the morning,

June 2d, to trade, and brought home three bushels of roots and some bread, which, in our situation, was as important as the return of an East India ship.   In the meantime, several hunters [Collins, Shields, Shannon, and R. and J. Fields] went across Collins' creek to hunt on the Quamash grounds.   The Indians informed us that there were great quantities of moose [22] to the southeast of the east branch of Lewis' river, which they call the Tommana-mah [Salmon [23] river]. We had lately heard that some Indians, who reside at a distance on the south side of the Kooskooskee, are in possession of two tomahawks, one of which was left at our camp on Mosquito [24] creek, and the other stolen while we were camped at the Chopunnish [river, in Canoe camp] last autumn. This last we were anxious to obtain, in order to give to the relations of our unfortunate companion, Sergeant Floyd, to whom it once belonged. We therefore sent Drewyer yesterday with Neeshnepah-keeook and Hohastilpilp, the two chiefs, to demand it. On their arrival, it seemed that the present owner, who had pur-chased it from the thief, was himself at the point of death; so that his relations were unwilling to give it up, as they meant to bury it in the grave with the deceased. But the influence of Neeshnepahkeeook (*p. 306*) at length succeeded ; they consented to surrender the tomahawk on receiving two

---

[22] A notable statement. For what a moose is, as different from an elk, see note [44], p. 845. Here Lewis and Clark lead all the naturalists, as usual ; for the American moose, *Alces machlis americanus* or *A. americanus*, had no scientific standing in their day. Nor has the fact here stated of its inhabiting Idaho been given due weight. I hardly know where to turn for another Idahoan reference, till 1860, when Dr. Geo. Suckley (P.R.R. Rep. XII. pt. ii, p. 133) speaks of a pair of moose-horns procured " in the most eastern part of Washington territory, near the St. Mary's valley," *i. e.*, in Idaho, not far from Camp Chopunnish ! The U. S. National Museum also has antlers taken by Dr. C. H. Merriam in 1872 in Idaho near the Wyoming border (Fauna No. 5, 1801, p. 79). *Moose* is an Algonkin word, found also as *moosis, musu, muswa, mouswah*, etc., said to mean " wood-eater." The animal is the *orignal* of French naturalists.

[23] Heretofore called the Pawnashte : see p. 622. We presently hear more of this river, when Sergeant Ordway reports his reconnoissance : see on. The sergeant and his party were the first white men who ever saw Salmon river about its mouth, as Captain Clark and his men were the first to see it at and below the confluence of the Lemhi. Sergeant Ordway should be fully recognized in this matter of exploring about the mouth of Salmon river. He went some 70 miles and back on this trip—thus quite as far as Captain Clark did on upper reaches of the river, though the bearing of the Ordway scout upon the course of the Expedition obviously had less weight.

[24] Name here first in the text without the slightest indication of what it means : but see note [16], p. 994, where we picked the name out of the codex as indicating

strands of beads and a handkerchief from Drewyer, and from each of the chiefs a horse, to be killed at the funeral of the deceased, according to the custom of the country.

Soon after their return, Sergeant Ordway and his party, [Frazier and Wiser] for whose safety we had become extremely anxious, came home from Lewis' river, with some roots of cows and 17 salmon. The distance, however, from which they were brought was so great that most of the fish were nearly spoiled; but such as continued sound were extremely delicious, the flesh being of a fine rose-color with a small mixture of yellow, and so fat that they were cooked very well without the addition of any oil or grease.

When they set out May 27th, they hoped to reach the salmon-fishery in the course of that day; but the route by which the guides led them was so circuitous that they rode 70 miles before they reached their place of destination, in the evening of the 29th. After going [west] for 20 miles up Commearp creek, through an open plain, broken only by the hills and timber along this creek, they then entered a high, irregular, mountainous country, the soil of which was fertile and well supplied with pine. Without stopping to hunt, though they saw great quantities of deer and some of the bighorn, they hastened [about southwest] for 30 miles across this district to the Tommanamah, or east branch of Lewis' river; and not finding any salmon, descended that stream [southerly] for 20 miles, to the fishery at a short distance below its junction with the south branch [main Snake river].

Jack's creek. Respecting this and its mate, Big Cañon creek, I may observe further, that Stevens' large map lays down a pair of streams, lettered Pepuennemah and Ahleah, which may be compared with Jack's and Big Cañon, respectively. But if they are the same, they are far out of proper position, being run into the Kooskooskee from the S. W., *above* and not below the mouth of the Chopunnish river or North fork. What makes me imagine that they may represent Jack's and Big Cañon, is, that they are in about the right relative position to each other, and that no such streams do fall into the Kooskooskee from the S.W. or W. between the Chopunnish river and Commearp (Stevens' Komeyer) creek.

Both these forks appear to come from or enter a mountainous country. The Tommanamah itself, they said, was about 150 yards wide; its banks, for the most part, were formed of solid perpendicular rocks, rising to a great height; as they passed along some of its hills they found that the snow had not yet disappeared, and the grass was just springing up. During its whole course it presented one (*p. 307*) continued rapid, till at the fishery itself, where the river widens to the space of 200 yards, the rapid is nearly as considerable as the great rapids of the Columbia. Here the Indians have erected a large house of split timber, 150 feet long and 35 feet wide, with a flat roof; at this season it is much resorted to by the men, while the women are employed in collecting roots. After remaining a day and purchasing some fish, they returned home.

June 3d. Finding that the salmon have not yet appeared along the shores, as the Indians assured us they would in a few days, and that all the salmon which they themselves use are obtained from Lewis' river, we began to lose our hopes of subsisting on them. We are too poor, and at too great a distance from Lewis' river, to purchase fish at that place, and it is not probable that the river will fall sufficiently for us to take them before we leave this place. Our Indian friends sent an express to-day over the mountains to Traveler's-rest [creek], in order to procure intelligence from the Oot-lashoots, a band of [Tushepaw] Flatheads who wintered on the east side of the mountains, and the same band which we first met on that river [Sept. 4th]. As the route was deemed practicable for this express, we also proposed setting out; but the Indians dissuaded us from attempting it, as many of the creeks, they said, were still too deep to be forded, the roads very deep and slippery, and there was no grass as yet for our horses; but [said that] in 12 or 14 days we should no longer meet with the same obstacles. We therefore determined to set out in a few days for Quamash flats, in order to lay in a store of provisions, so as to cross the mountains about the middle of the month.

[*June 4th* and *5th.*[25]]   For the two following days we continued hunting in our own neighborhood, and by means of
our own exertions, and trading with the Indians for trifling
articles, succeeded in procuring as much bread and roots,
besides other food, as will enable us to subsist during the
passage of the moun- (*p. 308*) tains.   The old chief in the
meantime gradually recovered the use of his limbs, and our
own man [Bratton] was nearly restored to his former health.
The Indians who had been with us returned, and invited us
to their village on the following day,

June 6th,[26] to give us their final answer to a number of pro-
posals which we had made to them.   Neeshnepahkeeook
then informed us that they could not accompany us, as we
wished, to the Missouri; but that in the latter end of the
summer they meant to cross the mountains and spend the
winter to the eastward.   We had also requested some of
their young men to go with us, so as to effect a reconcilia-

---

[25] Clark Q 146, June 5th, 1806, has : "The corn [cord] grass so called in the
Southern States and the foxtail in Virginia a third species resembles the cheet
tho' the horses feed on it very freely a fourth and most prevalent species is a
grass which appears to be the same called the blue grass."   This is said to be
now seeding, 9-12 inches high, affording excellent pasturage, bearing frost well,
and would, no doubt, be valuable for hay.   The absence of "greensward" is
also noted.   The grasses of the United States with which Captain Clark com-
pares the species he observed here are : cord-grass, a kind of marsh-grass of the
genus *Spartina ;* foxtail, species of *Alopecurus,* as *A. pratensis ;* cheet, cheat or
chess, *Bromus secalinus* or another species of brome-grass ; and blue-grass,
the well-known *Poa pratensis.*   As to the latter, the red-topped blue-grass,
Poa tenuifolia, of Montana, Idaho, etc., is no doubt the species in mention
as affording a valuable pasturage.   The chess may be *B. breviaristatus.*

Lewis L 26, 27, same date : "Among the grasses of this country I observe a
large species [*Phragmitis communis*] which grows in moist situations ; it rises to
the height of 8 or 10 feet ; the culm is jointed, hollow, smooth, as large as a
goos quill, and more firm than ordinary grasses ; the leaf is linear, broad and
rough ; it has much the appearance of the maden [maiden ? meadow ?] cain [cane]
as it is called in the State of Georgia, and retains its virdure until late in the fall.
This grass propagates principally by the root, which is horizontal and perennial.
A second species grows in tussocks and rises to the hight of six or eight feet ; it
seems to delight in the soil of the river bottoms."

[26] The earliest description of the Louisiana tanager (*Piranga ludoviciana*) ever
penned is in Clark Q 148-151, and Lewis L 29, June 6th, 1806.   So here is the

tion between them and the Pahkees, in case we should meet
these last. He answered that some of their young men
would go with us, but they had not yet been selected for that
purpose, nor could they be until a general meeting of the
whole nation, who were to meet in the plain on Lewis' river,
at the head of Commearp [creek]. This meeting would
take place in ten or twelve days, and if we set out before
that time, the young men should follow us. We therefore
depend but little on their assistance as guides, but hope to
engage for that purpose some of the Ootlashoots near Traveler's-rest creek. Soon after this communication, which
was followed by a present of dried quamash, we were visited
by Hohastilpilp and several others, among whom were the
two young chiefs who had given us horses some time ago.

original locality of this species. It is described as seven inches long, the tail 2½,
the beak thick and heavy, the plumage " remarkably delicate ; that of the neck
and head is of a fine orange yellow & red, the latter predominates on the top of the
head and around the base of the beak . . . the red has the appearance of being
laid over a ground of yellow, the breast, sides, rump and some long feathers
which lie between the legs and extend under the tail are of a fine orange yellow ;
the tail, back and wings are black except a small stripe of yellow on the outer
part of the middle joint of the wings," etc. The description is clear and unmistakable. This is one of the three species named by Wilson (Am. Orn. III. 1811,
p. 27, pl. 20, fig. 1) from specimens procured by the Expedition—the other two
being Lewis' woodpecker and Clark's crow, both figured on the same plate.

CHAPTER XXXI.

AGAIN IN THE BITTER-ROOT MOUNTAINS.

Preparation to visit Quamash flats—Willetpo Indians—Diversions and traffic with the Indians —The mountains reported impassable till July—Present state of the Kooskooskee—The party sets out for Quamash flats June 10th—Collins' creek—Camp on the flats near where the Chopunnish were first met last autumn—Vegetation described—Hunting—Laborious progress to an east branch of Collins' creek—Hungry creek reached and descended—Ascent of the ridge which divides the Chopunnish and main Kooskooskee watershed —Rigors of winter in June—Doubts and difficulties—The repulse—Return to Hungry creek —Drewyer and Shannon dispatched to hasten arrival of Indian guides—Return to Collins' creek—Determination to fall back on Quamash flats—Other deliberations—Snow ten feet deep—Query: As a last resource to attempt the main S.W. branch of Lewis' river and thence over to Madison or Gallatin river?—Collins' creek passed—Camp at last September's camp—Camp again on Quamash flats—Success in hunting—Drewyer and Shannon return with three Indian guides—The return to Collins' creek—To Hungry creek—To the ascent of the mountain—Route through deep snow to camp of Sept. 18th—Visit of a Chopunnish who wishes to go to the falls of the Missouri—Indian landmark on the crest of the mountain—Sagacity of Indian guides—Descent of the mountain, across two branches of the Chopunnish river—Camp of Sept. 16th reached—Another mountain crossed—Descent to headwaters of the Kooskooskee—Recovery of the road—The hot springs on a branch of Traveler's-rest creek reached June 29th.

SATURDAY, June 7th, 1806.[1] The two young chiefs returned after breakfast to their camp on Commearp creek, accompanied by several of our men, who were sent to purchase ropes and bags for packing, in exchange for some parts of an old seine, bullets, old files, and pieces of iron. In the evening they returned with a few strings, but no bags. Hohastilpilp crossed the river in the course of the day, and brought with him a horse, which he gave to one of our men, who had previously made him a present of a pair of Canadian shoes, or shoe-packs. We were all occupied in preparing packs and saddles for our journey; and as we intend to visit the Quamash flats on the 10th, in order to lay in a store of provisions for the journey over the mountains, we do not suffer the men to disturb the game in that neighborhood.

[1] Clark Q 152–155 and Lewis L 31, 32, describe a kind of cherry of this place and date.

June 8th. Cut-nose visited us this morning with ten or twelve warriors ; among these were two belonging to a band of Chopunnish we had not yet seen, who call themselves Willetpos,² and reside on the south side of Lewis' (*p. 310*) river. One of them gave us a good horse which he rode, in exchange for one of ours which was unable to cross the mountains, on receiving a tomahawk in addition. We were also fortunate in exchanging two other horses of inferior value for others much better, without giving anything else to the purchaser. After these important purchases, several foot-races were run between our men and the Indians; the latter, who are very active and fond of these races, proved themselves very expert, and one of them was as fleet as our

---

² My friend Mr. A. J. Hill of St. Paul, Minn., a deep delver in historico-geographical matters, calls my attention to a certain relation, "important if true," which goes to show that L. and C. met with the Indians now known as Cayuses. The Narrative of Commander Charles Wilkes, U. S. N. of the U. S. Expl. Exped. IV. p. 395, speaks of an old man who took a flag, *given by L. and C. to the Cayuse,* to the Grande Ronde, and had it planted there by a party of Cayuses and Wallawallas, with the result of a permanent peace with the Shoshones. L. and C. certainly left flags in various places (note ¹¹ p. 990) ; they probably first met with Cayuses when among the Wallawallas ; and the Willetpos of above text (Y-e-let-pos, Lewis L 32 : compare Yellept′ and Yelleppit, pp. 645, 970) were doubtless Cayuses, here first mentioned by name. These were Indians of a different stock from the Wallawallas, being Waiilatpuans. Waiilatpu is also spelled Wailatpu, Willetpoo, etc., and in some form became a tolerably familiar word, because a mission of this name was established in 1836, by Dr. Marcus Whitman, in the present locality of Fort Wallawalla and Wallawalla City. The Cayuse lived along the Columbia between the Umatilla and the Snake, and especially on the Wallawalla river. They were also called Cailleux, Kiuse, Kiuze (Kinze by misprint), etc. There was another tribe of Waiilatpuans, the Molele or Molale or Mollale, who lived in the Cascade range, south of the Columbia, about Mts. Hood and Jefferson. Hale established his linguistic family on these two tribes, U. S. Expl. Ex. VI. 1846, pp. 199, 214, 569 ; so Gallatin, Trans. Am. Ethn. Soc. II. 1848 ; Bancroft, Nat. Races, III. 1882, p. 565, etc. The Indian Report for 1889 returned 31 Molales on Grande Ronde Reservation, and the same Report for 1888 returned 401 Cayuses on the Umatilla Reservation ; " but Mr. [H. W.] Henshaw was able to find only six old men and women upon the Reservation in August, 1888, who spoke their own language. The others, though presumably of Cayuse blood, speak the Umatilla tongue " (Powell, Rep. U. S. Bureau Ethnol. for 1885–86, pub. 1891, p. 128).

swiftest runners.   After the races were over, the men divided themselves into two parties and played prison bass [base], an exercise which we are desirous of encouraging, before we begin the passage over the mountains, as several of the men are becoming lazy from inaction.   At night these games were concluded by a dance.

One of the Indians informed us that we could not pass the mountains before the next full moon, or about the 1st of July; because, if we attempted it before that time, the horses would be forced to travel without food three days on the top of the mountains.   This intelligence was disagreeable, for it excited a doubt as to the most proper time for crossing the mountains; but having no time to lose, we are determined to risk the hazards, and start as soon as the Indians generally consider it practicable, which is about the middle of this month.

June 9th.   Our success yesterday encouraged us to attempt to exchange some more of our horses whose backs were unsound, but we could dispose of one only.   Hohastilpilp, who visited us yesterday, left us with several Indians for the plains near Lewis' river, where the whole nation are about to assemble.   Broken-arm, too, with all his people, stopped on their way to the general rendezvous at the same place.   Cut-nose, or Neeshnepahkeeook, borrowed a horse and rode down a few miles after some young eagles.   He soon returned with two of the gray kind, nearly grown, which he meant to raise for the sake of the feathers.   The young chief who some time since made us a present of (*p. 311*) two horses, came with a party of his people and passed the night with us.

The river, which is about 150 yards wide, has been discharging vast bodies of water; but notwithstanding its depth, the water has been nearly transparent, and its temperature quite as cold as our best springs.   For several days, however, the river has been falling, and is now six feet lower than it has been, a strong proof that the great body of snow has left the mountains.   It is, indeed, nearly at the same height as when we arrived here ; a circumstance which the Indians consider as indicating the time when the mountains may be crossed. We shall wait, however, a few days, because the roads must still be wet and slippery, and the grass on the mountains will be improved in a short time. The men are in high spirits at the prospect of setting out, and amused themselves during the afternoon with different games.

June 10*th*. After collecting our horses, which took much time, we set out at eleven o'clock for Quamash flats. Our stock of horses is now very abundant, each man being well mounted, with a small load on a second horse, and several supernumerary ones in case of accident or want of food. We ascended the river-hills, which are very high, and three miles in extent, our course being N. 22° E.; then turning to N. 15° W. for two miles, till we reached Collins' creek. This was deep and difficult to cross ; but we passed without any injury, except wetting some of our provisions, and then proceeded due north for five miles to the eastern edge of Quamash flats, near where we first met the Chopunnish last autumn. We camped [3] on the bank of a small stream, in a point of woods bordering the extensive level and beautiful prairie, which is intersected by several rivulets ; and which, as the quamash is now in blossom, presents a perfect resemblance of lakes of clear water.

[3] "*Tuesday* 10*th*. We collected all our horses, but one, and set out accompanied by several of the natives, travelled about 12 miles and arrived at what we call Com-mas flat, where we first met the natives after crossing the Rocky Mountains last fall. Here we encamped and some hunters went out. The com-mas grows in great abundance on this plain, and at this time looks beautiful, being in full bloom with flowers of a pale blue color." Gass, p. 233.

Quamash flats is west of Weippe prairie, upon which Captain Clark descended from the mountains Sept. 20th (see p. 603 and note there), followed by the Expedition two days later (p. 609). Camp is now on Village (Flores or Jim Ford's) creek, or a branch of it, five miles north of Nahwah river or Lo Lo fork, at a point I suppose to be about the present site of Fraser (town)—some six or eight miles N.W. of town of Weippe, and about the same distance N. of E. of Lo Lo P. O., which is at the mouth of the river of the same name. It might be located still more closely by one familiar with the place.

A party of Chopunnish, who had overtaken us a few miles above, halted for the night with us, and mentioned that they (*p. 312*) too had come down to hunt in the flats, though we fear they expect we will provide for them during their stay.

The country through which we passed is generally free from stone, extremely fertile, and supplied with timber, consisting of several species of fir, long-leaved pine, and larch. The undergrowth is choke-cherry near the water-courses, and scattered through the country are black alder, a large species of red root [?] now in bloom, and a plant resembling the pawpaw in its leaf, bearing a berry with five valves of a deep purple color. There were also two species of sumach, the purple haw [*Viburnum pauciflorum*], seven-bark, service-berry, gooseberry, the honeysuckle bearing a white berry [*Symphoricarpus racemosus*], and a species of dwarf pine, ten or twelve feet high, which might be confounded with a young pine of the long-leaved species [*Pinus ponderosa*], except that the former bears a cone of a globular form, with small scales, and that its leaves are in fascicles of two, resembling in length and appearance those of the common pitch-pine. We also observed two species of wild rose [*Rosa nutkana* and *R. sayi ?*], both quinquepetalous, both of a damask-red color, and similar in the stem; but one of them is as large as the common red rose of our gardens; its leaf is somewhat larger than that of the other species of wild rose; and the apex [*sic*—read apples, *i. e.*, the haws or mature fruits], as we saw them last year, were more than three times the size of the common wild rose.

We saw many sand-hill cranes, some ducks in the marshes near camp, and a greater number of burrowing-squirrels [*Spermophilus columbianus*], some of which we killed, and found as tender and well-flavored as our gray squirrels.

June 11th.[4] All our hunters set out by daylight; but on their return to dinner, had killed nothing except a black bear

---

[4] Clark Q 156–163 and Lewis L 36–41 give at this date a minute description of the " quawmash," *Camassia esculenta :* see note [35], p. 603. The botanical notes of the paragraph above are on immediately preceding folios of the same codices.

and two deer. Five of the Indians also began to hunt, but they were quite unsuccessful, and in the afternoon returned to their village. Finding that the game had become shy and scarce, the hunters set out after dinner with orders to stay out during the night, and hunt at a greater distance from the camp, in ground less frequented. But the next (*p. 313*) day [*June* 12*th*⁵] they returned with nothing except two deer. They were therefore again sent out, and about noon the following day [*June* 13*th*⁶], seven of them came in with eight deer out of a number which, as well as a bear, they had wounded but could not take. In the meantime we had sent two men [R. Fields and Willard] forward about eight miles to a [Weippe] prairie on this side of Collins' creek, with orders to hunt till our arrival. Two other hunters [Labiche and Cruzatte] returned toward night ; they had killed only one deer, which they had hung up in the morning, and which had been devoured by the buzzards [*Cathartes aura*]. An Indian, who had spent the last evening with us, exchanged a horse for one of ours, which being sick, we gave a small ax and a knife in addition. He seemed very much pleased, and set out immediately to his village, lest we should change our minds and give up the bargain, which is perfectly allowable in Indian traffic. The hunters resumed

⁵ Gass makes a notable entry at this date, p. 224. "The magpie is also plenty here, and woodpeckers of a different kind from any I had before seen. They are about the size of a common red-headed woodpecker ; but are all black except the belly and neck, where the ends of the feathers are tipped with a deep red, but this tipping extends to so short a distance on the feathers, that at a distance the bird looks wholly black." The point is that here is the original appearance in print of Lewis' woodpecker, four years before it was described and figured as *Picus torquatus* by Wilson in 1811 (Amer. Orn. III. p. 31, pl. 20, fig. 3) and seven years before Lewis and Clark's own description appeared. See note ¹⁵, p. 428, and p. 877.

⁶ Important memorandum at this date, Lewis L 42 : "We made a digest of the Indian Nations West of the Rocky mountains which we have seen and of whom we have been repeated[ly] informed by those with whome we were conversant. they amount by our estimate to 69,000 Souls"—with "about 80,000" red-inked under the other figures. By this we learn just when and where the "Estimate of the Western Indians" which is printed in the Appendix was originally drafted.

the chase in the morning [*June 14th*], but the game is now so scarce that they [*i. e.*, Colter] killed only one deer. We therefore cut up and dried all the meat we had collected, packed all our baggage, and hobbled our horses to be in readiness to set out. But in the morning,

June 15*th*, they had straggled to such a distance that we could not collect them without great difficulty, and as it rained very hard, we waited till it should abate. It soon, however, showed every appearance of a settled rain, and we therefore set out at ten o'clock.[7] We crossed the prairie [passed a little prairie, Lewis L 43] at the distance of eight [8½] miles, [to] where we had sent our hunters, [R. Fields and Willard] and found two deer which they had hung up for us. At 2½ miles further we overtook these two men at Collins' creek. They had killed a third deer, and had seen one large [black] and another white bear. After dining, we proceeded up this creek about half a mile [passing it three times], then crossing through a high broken country for about ten [for 10½] miles, reached an easterly branch of the same creek, near which we camped in the bottom [near a small prairie], after a ride of 22 miles. The rains during the day made the roads very slippery, which, joined to the quantity of fallen timber, rendered our progress slow and laborious to the (*p. 314*) horses, many of which fell, though without suffering any injury. The country through which we passed has a thick growth of long-leaved pine, with some pitch-pine, larch, white pine, white cedar or arbor vitæ [*Thuja occidentalis*] of large size, and a variety of firs. The undergrowth consists chiefly of reed-root [so Lewis L 44] from six to ten feet in height, with the other species already enumerated. The soil is in general good, and has

---

[7] The Expedition is now about to attempt the passage of the "Rocky" mountains, *i. e.*, of the Bitter-root ranges, to Traveler's-rest creek, by the same route they came last autumn—as nearly as they can. For this trail, see back, date of Sept. 11th, p. 592, and following page with notes, and compare as we proceed. A few new points will come up; for the rest, this reference must suffice. As already stated, there is no very serviceable map of this huge nest of mountains. Stevens' No. 3 is on the whole the best.

somewhat of a red cast, like that near the Southwest mountain in Virginia. We saw in the course of our ride the
speckled woodpecker [*Picus villosus hyloscopus*], the logcock
or large woodpecker [*Ceophlœus pileatus*], the bee-martin
[*Tyrannus carolinensis*], and found the nest of a humming-
bird [*Selasphorus platycercus* [8]], which had just begun to lay
its eggs.

June 16th. We readily collected our horses, and having
taken breakfast, proceeded at six o'clock up the [easterly
branch of Collins'] creek, through handsome meadows of
fine grass, and a great abundance of quamash. At the distance of two miles we crossed this creek, and ascended a
ridge in a direction toward the northeast. Fallen timber
still obstructed our way so much that it was eleven o'clock
before we had made seven miles, to a small branch of Hungry creek. In the hollows and on the north sides of the
hills large quantities of snow still remain, in some places to
the depth of two or three feet. Vegetation is proportionally retarded, the dog-tooth violet being just in bloom, and
the honeysuckle, huckleberry, and a small species of white
maple beginning to put forth their leaves. These appearances, in a part of the country comparatively low, are ill
omens of the practicability of passing the mountains. But
being determined to proceed, we halted [9] merely to take a
hasty meal, while the horses were grazing, and then resumed
our march. The route was through thick woods and over
high hills, intersected by deep ravines and obstructed by
fallen timber. We found much difficulty also in following
the road, the greater part of it being covered with snow,
which lies in great masses eight or ten feet deep, and would

[8] Credit Lewis and Clark with the discovery of this species, which was unknown
to science until described as *Trochilus platycercus* by Swainson, Philos. Mag. I.
1827, p. 441, from Mexico, and was only very recently reported from Idaho again.

[9] This nooning was at "a handsome little glade" on the "small branch"
of Hungry creek, Lewis L 44—a statement which may help to identify the
spot. This branch of Hungry creek is named Fish creek on June 24th, which
see: see also June 18th. The codex also says that "this morning Windsor
busted his rifle near the muzzle."

be impassable were it not so firm as to bear our horses. Early in the evening (*p. 315*) we reached Hungry creek, at the place where Captain Clark had left a horse for us as we passed on September 19th; and finding a small glade with some grass, though not enough for our horses, we thought it better to halt for the night, lest by going further we should find nothing for the horses to eat. Hungry creek is small at this place, but deep, and discharges a torrent of water, perfectly transparent and cold as ice. During the 15 miles of our route to-day the principal timber was the pitch-pine, white pine, larch, and fir. The long-leaved pine extends but a small distance on this side of Collins' creek, and the white cedar does not reach beyond the branch of Hungry creek on which we dined. In the early part of the day we saw the columbine, the bluebell, and the yellow flowering-pea in bloom. There is also in these mountains a great quantity of angelica, stronger to the taste and more highly scented than that common in the United States. The smell is very pleasant, and the natives, after drying and cutting the plants into small pieces, wear them in strings around their necks.

June 17th. We find lately that the air is pleasant in the course of the day; but notwithstanding the shortness of the night, it becomes very cold before morning. At an early hour we collected our horses and proceeded down the [Hungry] creek, which we crossed twice with much difficulty and danger, in consequence of its depth and rapidity. We avoided two other crossings of the same kind, by crossing over a steep and rocky hill. At the distance of seven miles the road begins the ascent of the main ridges which divide the waters of the Chopunnish and [main] Kooskooskee rivers.[10] We followed it up a mountain for about three

[10] This is the first distinct statement in the text that the route is on a divide between the watershed northward of the North fork of the Kooskooskee and the main watershed southward. The outward route made it evident that they were on an extended divide, but what one the explorers could not say, as they knew nothing of what was before them or on either hand. See note [31], p. 600.

miles, when we found ourselves enveloped in snow from 12 to 15 feet in depth, even on the south side of the mountain, with the fullest exposure to the sun. Winter now presented itself in all its rigors; the air was keen and cold, no vestige of vegetation was to be seen, and our hands and feet benumbed.

We halted at the sight of this new difficulty. We already knew that to wait till the snows (*p. 316*) of the mountains had dissolved, so as to enable us to distinguish the road, would defeat our design of returning to the United States this season. We now found also that as the snow bore our horses very well, traveling was infinitely easier than it was last fall, when the rocks and fallen timber had so much obstructed our march. But it would require five days to reach the fish-weirs at the mouth of Colt [-killed] creek, even if we were able to follow the proper ridges of the mountains; and the danger of missing our direction is exceedingly great while every track is covered with snow. During these five days, too, we have no chance of finding either grass or underwood for our horses, the snow being so deep. To proceed, therefore, under such circumstances, would be to hazard our being bewildered in the mountains, and to insure the loss of our horses; even should we be so fortunate as to escape with our lives, we might be obliged to abandon all our papers and collections. It was therefore decided not to venture any further; to deposit here all the baggage and provisions for which we had no immediate use; and, reserving only subsistence for a few days, to return while our horses were yet strong to some spot where we might live by hunting, till a guide could be procured to conduct us across the mountains. Our baggage was placed on scaffolds and carefully covered, as were also the instruments and papers, which we thought it safer to leave than to risk over the roads and creeks by which we came.

Having completed this operation, we set out at one o'clock; and treading back our steps, reached Hungry creek, which we ascended for two miles till, finding some

scanty grass, we camped." The rain fell during the greater
part of the evening, and as this was the first time that we
have ever been compelled to make any retrograde movement, we feared that it might depress the spirits of the
men; but though they were somewhat dejected at the
circumstance, the obvious necessity precluded all repining.
During the night our horses straggled in search of food to a
considerable distance among (*p. 317*) the thick timber on
the hillsides, nor could we collect them till nine o'clock the
next morning,

June 18*th*. Two of them were, however, still missing, and
we therefore directed two of the party [Shields and Lepage]
to remain and hunt for them. At the same time, we dispatched Drewyer and Shannon to the Chopunnish [Indians],
in the plains beyond the Kooskooskee, in order to hasten
the arrival of those Indians who had promised to accompany us; or at any rate, to procure a guide to conduct us to
Traveler's-rest [creek]. For this purpose they took a rifle,
as a reward to anyone who would engage to conduct us, with
directions to increase the reward, if necessary, by an offer of

---

[11] Gass thus records this disheartening day, p. 226: "*Tuesday* 17*th*. We early
continued our march ; took down Hungry creek about six miles, and then took
up a large mountain. When we got about half way up the mountain the ground
was entirely covered with snow three feet deep ; and as we ascended it still
became deeper, until we arrived at the top, where it was 12 or 15 feet deep ;
but it in general carried our horses. Here there was not the appearance of a
green shrub, or anything for our horses to subsist on ; and we know it cannot
be better for four days march, even could we find the road or course, which
appears almost impossible, without a guide perfectly acquainted with the mountains. We therefore halted to determine what was best to be done, as it
appeared not only imprudent but highly dangerous to proceed without a guide of
any kind. After remaining about two hours we concluded it would be most
advisable to go back to some place where there was food for our horses. We
therefore hung up our loading on poles, tied to and extended between trees,
covered it all safe with deer skins, and turned back melancholy and disappointed."
There was perhaps no more critical day in the history of the Expedition than
this, and certainly none when the spirits of the party were at a lower ebb. The
outlook was four or five days of 10 to 15 feet deep snow, no guide, no road,
and no forage ; it would have been madness to proceed ; it was wisdom to retire
from frowning " Old Baldy."

two other guns, to be given immediately, and ten horses, at the falls of the Missouri.

We then resumed our route. In crossing Hungry creek one of the horses fell and rolled over with the rider [Colter], who was driven for a considerable distance among the rocks; but he fortunately escaped without losing his gun or suffering any injury. Another of the men [Potts] was cut very badly, in a vein in the inner side of the leg, and we had great difficulty in stopping the blood. About one o'clock we halted for dinner at the glade, on a branch [Fish creek] of Hungry creek, where we had dined on the 16th inst. Observing much track of deer, we left two men [R. and J. Fields] at this place to hunt, and then proceeded to Collins' creek, where we camped [12] in a pleasant situation, at the upper end of the meadows, two miles above our camp of the 15th inst. The hunters were immediately sent out, but they returned without having killed anything, though they saw some few tracks of deer, very great appearance of bear, and what is of more importance, a number of what they thought were salmon-trout in the creek. We therefore hope, by means of these fish and other game, to subsist at this place without returning to Quamash flats, which we are unwilling to do, since there is in these meadows [where we are now] great abundance of good food for our horses.

June 19*th*. The hunters renewed the chase at a very early hour, but they brought only a single fish at noon. (*p. 318*) The fishermen [Gibson and Colter] were more unsuccessful, for they caught no fish, and broke their two Indian gigs. We, however, mended them with a sharp piece of iron, and toward evening they took a single fish; but instead of find-

---

[12] Gass, p. 227, gives the mishaps of to-day tersely : "We started about eight o'clock, and found the road very slippery and bad. Two men went on ahead to the village to enquire for a guide, and two more remained to look for two horses that could not be found. We proceed on with four men in front to cut some bushes out of the path ; but did not go very far till one of the men cut himself very badly with a large knife ; when we had to halt and bind up his wound. We went again forward, and in crossing the creek the horse of one of our men fell with him, threw him off, hurt his leg and lost his blanket."

Determined as we now are to reach the United States, if (*p. 319*) possible, this winter, it would be destructive to wait till the snows have melted from the road. The snows have formed a hard, coarse bed without crust, on which the horses walk safely without slipping; the chief difficulty, therefore, is to find the road. In this we may be assisted by the circumstance that, though generally ten feet in depth, the snow has been thrown off by the thick and spreading branches of the trees, and from round the trunk; while the warmth of the trunk itself, acquired by the reflection of the sun, or communicated by natural heat of the earth, which is never frozen under these masses, has dissolved the snow so much that immediately at the roots its depth is not more than one or two feet. We therefore hope that the marks of the baggage rubbing against the trees may still be perceived; and we have decided, in case the guide cannot be procured, that one of us will take three or four of our most expert woodsmen, several of our best horses, and an ample supply of provisions, go on two days' journey in advance, and endeavor to trace the route by the marks of the Indian baggage on the trees, which we would then mark more distinctly with a tomahawk. When they should have reached two days' journey beyond Hungry creek, two of the men were to be sent back to apprise the rest of their success, and if necessary to cause them to delay there; lest, by advancing too soon, they should be forced to halt where no food could be obtained for the horses. If the traces of the baggage be too indistinct, the whole party is to return to Hungry creek, and we will then attempt the passage by ascending the main southwest branch of Lewis' river through the country of the Shoshonees, over to Madison or Gallatin river. On that route, the Chopunnish inform us, there is a passage not obstructed by snow at this period of the year. That there is such a passage we also learned from the Shoshonees whom we first met on the east fork of Lewis' river; but they represented it as much more difficult than that by which we came, being obstructed by high, steep, rugged (*p. 320*)

mountains, followed by an extensive plain, without either
wood or game. We are, indeed, inclined to prefer the
account of the Shoshonees, because they would have certainly recommended that route had it been better than the
one we have taken; and because there is a war between the
Chopunnish and the Shoshonees who live on that route, the
former are less able to give accurate information of the state
of the country. This route, too, is so circuitous that it
would require a month to perform it; we therefore consider
it as the extreme resource. In hopes of soon procuring a
guide to lead us over a more practicable route, we collected
our horses at an early hour in the morning,

June 21st, and proceeded toward Quamash flats. The
mortification of being obliged to tread back our steps rendered still more tedious a route always so obstructed by
brush and fallen timber that it cannot be passed without
difficulty, and even danger to our horses. One of these
poor creatures wounded himself so badly in jumping over
fallen logs that he was rendered unfit for use, and sickness
has deprived us of the service of a second.[14] At the pass of
Collins' creek we met two Indians, who returned with us
about half a mile to the spot where we had slept last September, and where we now halted to dine and let our horses
graze. These Indians had four supernumerary horses, and
were on their way to cross the mountains. They had seen
Drewyer and Shannon, who they said would not return for
two days. We pressed them to remain with us till that
time, in order to conduct us over the mountains; to which
they consented, and deposited their stores of roots and
bread in the bushes at a little distance. After dinner we left
three men [Gass and R. and J. Fields] to hunt till our return,

---

[14] Great trouble with the horses. Captain Lewis', the one that was gelded,
was shot June 2d. Yesterday Bratton's horse strayed away, probably back to
Quamash flats, and left this invalid afoot. "Thompson's horse is either choked
this morning or has the distemper very badly . . . an excellent horse of Cruzatte's snagged [impaled] himself so badly in the groin in jumping over a parsel
of fallen timber that he will evidently be of no further service," Lewis L 54.

and then proceeded; but we had not gone further than two miles when the Indians halted in a small prairie, where they promised to remain at least two nights, if we did not over-take [return to] them sooner. We left them, and about seven in the evening found ourselves at our old camp on Quamash flats; and were glad to find that the four (*p. 321*) hunters, whom we had sent ahead, had killed a deer for supper.

Sunday, June 22d. At daylight all the hunters set out, and having chased through the whole country, were much more successful than we even hoped, for they brought in eight deer and three bears. Hearing that salmon were now abundant in the Kooskooskee, we dispatched a man [White-house] to our old camp [Camp Chopunnish] above Collins' creek, for the purpose of purchasing some with a few beads which were found accidentally in one of our waistcoat pockets. He did not return in the evening, nor did we hear from Drewyer and Shannon, who we begin to fear have had much difficulty in engaging a guide; and we were equally apprehensive that the two Indians [left yesterday] might set out to-morrow for the mountains. Early in the morning,

June 23d, therefore, we dispatched two hunters [Frazier and Wiser] to prevail on them, if possible, to remain a day or two longer; if the Indians persisted in going on, the hunters were to accompany them with the three men [left June 21st] at Collins' creek, and mark [15] the route as far as Trav-eler's-rest [creek], where they were to remain till we joined them by pursuing the same road.

Our fears for the safety of Drewyer, Shannon, and White-house were fortunately relieved by their return in the after-

---

[15] "And *blaize* the trees well as they proceeded," Lewis L. 56. "To blaze" is such a common phrase, I have wondered why it never occurs in our text. This, however, is the first time I have noticed it in any codex. On the same page in Lewis L is a more unusual expression : "the does now having their fawns the hunters can *bleat* them up," *i. e.*, toll or decoy them by imitating the bleating of a fawn.

noon [but Colter is still absent]. The former brought three Indians, who promised to go with us to the falls of the Missouri, for the compensation of two guns. One of them is the brother of Cut-nose, and the other two had each given us a horse, at the house of Broken-arm; and as they are men of good character, respected in the nation, we had the best prospect of being well served. We therefore secured our horses near the camp, and at an early hour next morning,

June 24th, set out on a second attempt to cross the mountains. On reaching Collins' creek, we found only one of our men [Frazier], who informed us that a short time before he arrived there yesterday, the two Indians, tired of waiting, had set out, and the other four of our men [Gass, Wiser, and R. and J. Fields] had accompanied them (*p. 322*) as they were directed. After halting, we went on to Fish creek, the branch of Hungry creek where we had slept on the 19th inst. Here we overtook two [Gass and Wiser] of the party who had gone on with the Indians, and had been fortunate enough to persuade them to wait for us. During their stay at Collins' creek, they [R. and J. Fields] had killed only a single deer, and of this they had been very liberal to the Indians, whom they were prevailing upon to remain; so that they were without provisions, and two [R. and J. Fields] of them had set out for another branch of Hungry creek, where we shall meet them to-morrow.

In the evening the Indians, in order as they said to bring fair weather for our journey, set fire to the woods. As these consisted chiefly of tall fir-trees, with very numerous dried branches, the blaze was almost instantaneous; and as the flame mounted to the tops of the highest trees, it resembled a splendid display of fire-works.

June 25th. One of our guides complained of being sick —a symptom by no means pleasant, for sickness is generally with an Indian the pretext for abandoning an enterprise which he dislikes. He promised, however, to overtake us; we therefore left him with his two companions, and set out at an early hour. At eleven o'clock we halted for dinner at the [another [16]] branch of Hungry creek, where we found our two men [R. and J. Fields], who had killed nothing. Here too we were joined rather unexpectedly by our guides, who now appeared disposed to be faithful to their engagements. The Indian was indeed really sick, and having no other covering than a pair of moccasins and an elk-skin dressed without the hair, we supplied him with a buffalo-robe. In the evening we arrived at Hungry creek, and halted for the night about a mile and a half below our camp of the 16th inst.

June 26th. Having collected our horses and taken breakfast, we set out at six o'clock; and pursuing our former route [of June 17th], at length began to ascend, for the second time,[17] (*p. 323*) the ridge of mountains. Near the snowy region we killed two of the small black pheasant [*Dendragapus franklini*] and one of the speckled pheasant [the same species]. These birds generally inhabit the higher parts of the mountains, where they feed on the leaves of pines and firs; both of them seem solitary and silent birds, for we have never heard either of them make a noise in any situation, and the Indians inform us that they do not drum or produce a whirring sound with their wings [as do the ruffed grouse of the genus *Bonasa*]. On reaching the top of the mountain [N.E. of Hungry creek, Lewis L 59], we found our deposit [made June 17th] untouched. The snow in the neighborhood has melted nearly four feet since the 17th inst. By measuring it accurately, and comparing it by a

[16] This branch appears to be nameless, and remains to be identified. Here Lewis L 58 has: "At this place I met with a plant the root of which the Shoshones eat. it is a small knob root, a good deel in flavor an consistency like the Jerusalem artichoke [*Helianthus tuberosus*]. it has two small oval smooth leaves placed opposite on either side of the peduncle just above the root. the scape is only about 4 inches long, is round and smooth. the roots of this plant formed one of those collections of roots which Drewyer took from the Shoshones last summer," *i. e.*, Aug. 22d : see p. 544.

[17] The Expedition has now been 12 days (since June 14th) back and forth between Quamash flats and the mountains. They have meanwhile traversed the route three times—east, west, and east again—and now for the second time run up against the snowy barrier.

mark which we then made, the general depth we discover
to have been 10 feet 10 inches, though in some places still
greater ; but at this time it is about seven feet.

It required two hours to arrange our baggage and prepare
a hasty meal, after which the guides urged us to set off, as
we had a long ride to make before reaching a spot where
there was grass for our horses. We mounted, and following
their steps, sometimes crossed abruptly steep hills, then
wound along their sides near tremendous precipices, where,
had our horses slipped, we should have been lost irrecover-
ably. Our route lay on the ridgy mountains which separate
the waters of the Kooskooskee and Chopunnish, above the
heads of all the streams, so that we met no running water.
The whole country was completely covered with snow,
except that occasionally we saw a few square feet of earth, at
the roots of some trees around which the snow had dissolved.
We passed our camp of Sept. 18th [1805]; late in the evening
reached the deserted [desired] spot, and camped near a good
spring of water.[18] It was on the steep side of a mountain,
with no wood and a fair southern aspect, from which the
snow seems to have melted for about ten days, and given
place to an abundant growth of young grass, resembling
greensward. There is also another species of grass, not
unlike a flag, with a broad succulent leaf, which is confined
to the upper parts of the highest mountains. It (*p. 324*) is
a favorite food of the horses, but at present is either covered with snow or just making its appearance. There is a
third plant peculiar to the same regions, a species of whortleberry. There are also large quantities of a species of bear-

---

[18] Gass notes, p. 230 : "*Thursday 26th*. We had a foggy morning; proceeded
on early ; and found the banks of snow much decreased : at noon we arrived at the
place where we had left our baggage and stores. The snow here had sunk 20
inches. We took some dinner, but there was nothing for our horses to eat.
We measured the depth of snow here, and found it 10 feet 10 inches. We proceeded over some very steep tops of the mountains and deep snow ; but the
snow was not so deep in the drafts between them ; fortunately we got in the
evening to the side of a hill where the snow was gone ; and there was very good
grass for our horses."

grass, which, though it grows luxuriantly over all these mountains, and preserves its verdure during the whole winter, is never eaten by horses.

In the night there came to the camp a Chopunnish, who had pursued us with a view to accompanying us to the falls of the Missouri. We now learned that the two young Indians whom we had met on the 21st and detained several days, were going merely on a party of pleasure to the Ootla-shoots, or, as they call them[selves], Shallees,[19] a band of Tushepahs, who live on Clark's river near Traveler's-rest [creek]. Early the next morning,

June 27th, we resumed our route over the heights and steep hills of the same great ridge. At eight miles' distance we reached an eminence where the Indians have raised a conic mound of stone, six or eight feet high, on which is fixed a pole made of pine, about 15 feet long. Here we halted and smoked for some time at the request of the Indians, who told us that, in passing the mountains with their families, some men are usually sent on foot from this place to fish at the entrance of Colt [-killed[20]] creek, whence they rejoin the main party at the Quamash glade on the head of the Kooskooskee. From this elevated spot we have a commanding view of the surrounding mountains, which so completely inclose us that, though we have once [in Sept., 1805] passed them, we almost despair of ever escaping from them without the assistance of the Indians. The marks on the trees, which had been our chief dependence, are much fewer and more difficult to be distinguished than we had supposed. But our guides traverse this trackless region with a kind of instinctive sagacity; they never hesitate, they are never embarrassed; and so undeviating is their step, that

[19] Elsewhere Shalees, Shalles, and Shahlees. Otherwise Ootlashoots, Utla-shoots, Oatlashoots, etc.: see note [10], p. 582, and note [11], p. 583.

[20] See note [25], p. 596, where "Colt-killed" is the name given to this creek. Observe also that the "Quamash glade" here in mention—one of several similiar spots of the same name—is the Summit prairie of note [24], p. 595. Lewis L 61 says that the stone mound above mentioned was one mile short of their camp of Sept. 17th—a good point made for the identification of the latter. See p. 599.

wherever the snow has disappeared, for even a hundred
paces, we find the summer (*p. 325*) road. With their aid the
snow is scarcely a disadvantage ; for though we are often
obliged to slip down, yet the fallen timber and the rocks,
which are now covered, were much more troublesome when
we passed in the autumn. Traveling is indeed comparatively pleasant, as well as more rapid, the snow being hard
and coarse, without a crust, and perfectly hard enough to
prevent the horses sinking more than two or three inches.
After the sun has been on it for some hours it becomes
softer than it is early in the morning ; yet they are almost
always able to get a sure foothold.

After some time we resumed our route, and at the distance
of three miles descended a steep mountain ; then crossing
two branches of the Chopunnish river, just above their
forks, we began to mount a second ridge. Along this we
proceeded for some time, and then, at the distance of seven
miles, reached our camp of the 16th of September [1805[21]].
Near this place we crossed three small branches of the
Chopunnish, and then ascended a second dividing ridge,
along which we continued for nine miles, when the ridge
became somewhat lower, and we halted for the night in a
position similar to that of our camp last evening.

We had now traveled 28 miles without taking the loads
from our horses or giving them anything to eat, and as the
snow where we halted had not much dissolved, there was
still but little grass. Among the vegetation we observed
great quantities of the white lily [22] with reflected petals, which

[21] See note [28], p. 598, Sept. 16th, and note [29], p. 599, Sept. 17th. Streams
there noted as passing to the explorers' then right hand, *i. e.*, northward, are here
again in mention, and now regarded, no doubt correctly, as affluents of the
Chopunnish or *North* fork of the Kooskooskee. Yet on no contemporaneous
map I have seen, does a single such tributary touch the Lo Lo trail. It is true
that the Stevens' No. 3, which dots in the 1854 Mullan trail, lays down several
such northward streams, but these are only charted at their heads, without any
connections lower down. Lewis and Clark's trail in these mountains should be
carefully studied in the making of the future correct map of Idaho.

[22] " Yellow lilly," Lewis L 62. Codex also notes : " Potts's legg, which has

is now in bloom, and in the same forwardness as it was in the plains on the 10th of May. As for ourselves, the whole stock of meat being gone, we distributed to each mess a pint of bear's oil, which, with boiled roots, made an agreeable dish. We saw several black-tailed or mule-deer [*Cariacus macrotis*], but could not get a shot at them, and were informed that there is an abundance of elk in the valley near the fishery on the Kooskooskee. The Indians also assert that on the mountains to our right are large numbers of what they call white buffalo or mountain sheep [*Haplocerus montanus*]. Our horses strayed to some distance to look for food, and in the morning,

(*p. 326*) *June 28th*, when they were brought up, exhibited rather a gaunt appearance. The Indians, however, promised that we should reach some good grass at noon, and we therefore set out after an early breakfast. Our route lay along the dividing ridge and across a very deep hollow, till at the distance of six miles we passed our camp of the 15th of September [1805 : see note [27], p. 597]. A mile and a half further we passed the road from the right, immediately on the dividing ridge, leading by the fishery. We went on, as we had done during the former part of the route, over deep snows; when, having made 13 miles, we reached the side of a mountain just above the fishery; which having no timber and a southern exposure, the snow had disappeared, leaving an abundance of fine grass. Our horses were very hungry as well as fatigued, and as there was no other spot within reach this evening where we could find any food for them, we determined to camp, though it was not yet midday. But as there was no water in the neighborhood, we melted snow for cooking.

Sunday, June 29th.[23] We continued along the ridge which we have been following for several days, till at the end of

been much swolen and inflamed for several days is much better this evening and gives him but little pain. we applyed the pounded roots and leaves of the wild ginger from which he found great relief."

[23] Clark Q 165, this date describes the "lady-slipper or mockerson flower, it is in shape and appearance much like ours [*i. e.*, a common orchid of the genus

five miles it terminated; and bidding adieu to the snows
in which we have been imprisoned, we descended to the
main branch of the Kooskooskee. On reaching the water-
side, we found a deer which had been left for us by two
hunters who had been dispatched at an early hour to the
warm springs, and which proved a very seasonable addition
to our food; for having neither meat nor oil, we were
reduced to a diet of roots, without salt or any other addition. At this place, about a mile and a half from the spot
where Quamash²⁴ creek falls in from the northeast, the Kooskooskee is about 30 yards wide, and runs with great velocity
over a bed which, like those of all the mountain streams, is
composed of pebbles. We forded the river and ascended
for two miles the steep acclivities of a mountain, on the
summit of which we found coming in from the right the old
road which we had passed on our route (*p. 327*) last autumn.
It was now much plainer and more beaten, which the
Indians told us was owing to the frequent visits of the
Ootlahshoots from the valley of Clark's river to the fishery,
though there was no appearance of their having been here
this spring. Twelve miles from our camp we halted to graze
our horses on the Quamash flats, on the creek of the same
name [Quamash, *i. e.*, Glade creek]. This is a handsome
plain of fifty acres in extent, covered with an abundance of
quamash, and seems to form a principal stage or camp for
the Indians in passing the mountains. We saw here several
young pheasants, and killed one of the small black kind,
[*Dendragapus franklini*] which is the first we have observed
below the region of snow. In the neighborhood were also
seen the tracks of two barefooted Indians, which our companions supposed to be Ootlashoots, who had fled in distress

Cypripedium], only that the corolla is white marked with small veins of a pale red
longitudinally on the inner side." This species is *Cypripedium montanum*.

²⁴ Here a new name merely for the Glade creek of note²⁴ , p. 595, and note²³,
p. 594: see there. The Quamash flats about to be mentioned in this paragraph are
the same as the Quamash glade of p. 1056, June 27th, but of course not the flats
named Quamash which were finally left on June 24th. Lewis L 65 notes that
to-day's nooning was two miles past the camp of Sept. 13th.

from the Pahkees.   Here we discovered that two of the horses were missing.   We therefore sent two men [Colter and J. Fields] in quest of them, and then went on seven miles further to the warm springs, where we arrived early in the afternoon.   The two hunters [Drewyer and R. Fields] who had been sent forward in the morning had collected no game, nor were several others, who went out after our arrival, more successful.   We therefore had a prospect of continuing our usual diet of roots, when late in the afternoon the men returned with the stray horses, and a deer for supper.

These warm springs are situated at the foot of a hill on the north side of Traveler's-rest creek,[25] which is ten yards wide at this place.   They issue from the bottoms, and through the interstices of a gray freestone rock, which rises in irregular masses round their lower side.   The principal spring, which the Indians have formed into a bath by stopping the run with stone and pebbles, is about the same temperature as the warmest bath used at the hot springs in Virginia.   On trying, Captain Lewis could with difficulty remain in it 19 minutes, and then was affected with a profuse perspiration.   The two other springs are much hotter, the temperature being equal to that of the warmest of the hot springs (*p. 328*) in Virginia.   Our men, as well as the Indians, amused themselves with going into the bath; the latter, according to their universal custom, going first into the hot bath, where they remain as long as they can bear the heat, then plunging into the creek, which is now of an icy coldness, and repeating this operation several times, but always ending with the warm bath.

[25] More exactly, on the north side of the southern one of two main headwaters which compose this creek : see note [23], p. 594, and note [22], p. 592.   This southern branch is first named Hotspring creek, Lewis L 7.   Here we are once more on a perfectly well-known spot, to be found on any fairly good map.   The Expedition has to-day crossed over the main divide or ridge of the Bitter-root mountains, and has consequently passed from Idaho into Montana, but is still on the Pacific watershed.   On this point see note [9], p. 580.

CHAPTER XXXII.

DIVISION OF THE EXPEDITION: CAPTAIN LEWIS' EXPLORATION OF BIG BLACKFOOT AND MARIA'S RIVERS.

Down Traveler's-rest creek to its mouth—Halt to plan and prepare for further operations—Captain Lewis and nine men to pursue a direct route to the Missouri, then explore Maria's river—Captain Clark and the rest of the party to go by a new route to the Jefferson, descend this to the Three Forks, and thence proceed with a detachment of this party to explore the Yellowstone, while Sergeant Ordway, with nine men, descends the Missouri, the thus separated parties to reunite at or below the mouth of the Yellowstone—Animals and plants of the vicinity—Indian guides to accompany Captain Lewis—The two parties separate July 3d—Captain Lewis proceeds north down the west side of Clark's river—The Indian guides show the "River of the Road to Buffalo" and depart—Sufferings from mosquitoes—Joined by a Palloatpallah—Up east branch of Clark's river to the Cokahlarishkit—Up this river to Werner's creek—Seaman's creek—North fork of the Cokahlarishkit—Prairie of the Knobs—(Hence there is a southerly Indian route to Dearborn's river)—The river followed up to its two forks—That one which goes N. 75° E. taken—The north side of this fork followed for 12 miles; two ridges crossed N. 15° E. for four miles; a bottom to the right followed for seven miles; a ridge ascended N. 45° E. through an easy gap—Here is "Lewis' and Clark's Pass" across the Great Divide—Fort mountain bears N.E. about 20 miles—Camp near a source of Dearborn's river—Shishequaw mountain—Shishequaw creek—Medicine river—First buffalo seen on the return journey—Elk and bear shot—Hunters sent down Medicine river—Captain Lewis goes to White Bear islands at the head of the Great Falls of the Missouri—Drewyer sent for horses lost—Cache at White Bear islands opened—Drewyer returns with the lost horses—M'Neal's adventure with a bear—Myriads of mosquitoes—Sergeant Gass and his men left here to await Sergeant Ordway's party, which is coming down the Jefferson and Missouri—Captain Lewis, with Drewyer and J. and R. Fields, sets out to explore Maria's river—He proceeds N. 10° W. to strike the river at the point to which he ascended it in 1804—Tansy river reached in 20 miles—Vast herds of buffalo—Buffalo creek, a tributary of Maria's river—Maria's river—Hunters sent down this river six miles to the point to which it was ascended in 1804—Captain Lewis proceeds up this river.

MONDAY, June 30th, 1806. We dispatched some hunters ahead, and were about setting out, when a deer came to lick at the springs; we killed it, and being now provided with meat for dinner, proceeded along [down] the north side of the [Traveler's-rest] creek, sometimes in the bottoms and over the steep sides of the ridge, till, at the distance of 13 miles, we halted at the entrance of a small stream where we had stopped on the 12th of September [see p. 593 [1]]. Here we observed a road to the right, which the

[1] "At one mile from the [hot] springs we passed a stout branch of the creek on the north side and at noon having travelled 13 ms. we arrived at the entrance

Indians inform us leads to a fine, extensive valley on Clark's river, where the Shallees or Ootlashoots occasionally reside. After permitting our horses to graze, we went on along a road much better than any we have seen since entering the mountains; so that before sunset we made 19 [more] miles, and reached our old camp[2] [of Sept. 9th and 10th, 1805] on the south side of the creek, near its entrance into Clark's river. In the course of the day we killed six deer, of which there are (*p. 330*) great numbers, as well as bighorn and elk, in this neighborhood. We also obtained a small gray squirrel [*Sciurus fremonti ?*] like that on the coast of the Pacific, except that its belly was white. Among the plants was a kind of lady's slipper or moccasin-flower [*Cypripedium montanum*], resembling that common in the United States, but with a white corolla, marked with longitudinal veins of a pale red color on the inner side.

Tuesday, July 1st.[3] We had now made 156 miles[4] from

of a second Northern branch of the creek where we had nooned it on the 12th. of Sept. last," Lewis L 66. For verb "to noon," see Lew Wallace, Ben-Hur, p. 459.

[2] "*June 30th.* We halted for dinner at the same place, where we dined on the 12th of Sept. 1805, as we passed over to the Western Ocean. . . . In the evening we arrived at [that point on] Travellers'-rest creek where the party rested two days last fall, and where it empties into Flat-head (called Clarke's) river." Gass, p. 232. See pp. 588–592 and notes there, esp. note [20], p. 590.

[3] At this date Clark Q 166–169, and Lewis L 72, 73, both have the long description of the barking-squirrel or prairie-dog of the Missouri, *Cynomys ludovicianus*, which is given in the natural history chapter (No. 27, p. 859).

[4] This reduces somewhat the former estimates of 190 or 184 miles from the mouth of Traveler's-rest creek to the Chopunnish forks of the Kooskooskee (Canoe camp: see p. 612). It will be useful to give the never-published courses and distances of the return journey, for comparison with those of the outward journey over the same trail. I edit them as concisely as possible from Lewis L 70, 71. From Quamash flats:

"East 11 ms. to Collins' cr., 25 yds. wide, passing a small prairie at 9 ms.; road hilly, thickly timbered.

"N. 45° E. 13 ms. to the crossing of Fish cr., 10 yds. wide, passing a small cr. at 6 ms.

"N. 75° E. 9 ms. to a small branch of Hungry cr.; road along a ridge with much windfall; some snow at end of this course.

"N. 22½° E. 5 ms. to the heads of the main branch of Hungry creek; road hilly, some snow.

the Quamash flats to the mouth of Traveler's-rest creek. This being the point where we proposed to separate, it was resolved to remain a day or two in order to refresh ourselves and the horses, which have borne the journey extremely well and are still in fine order, but require some little rest. We had hoped to meet here some of the Ootlashoots, but no tracks of them could be discovered. Our Indian companions express much anxiety lest they should have been cut off by the Pahkees during the winter, and mention the tracks of the two barefooted persons as a proof of how much the fugitives must have been distressed.

" N. 75° E. 3 ms. down Hungry cr. on its N. side, passing 2 small branches on its N. side, the 1st at ½ m., the 2d at 1½ ms. further.

" N. 75° E. 3 ms. still down the N. side of Hungry cr. to the foot of the mtn., passing 3 N. branches and 1 S. branch of this cr.

" N. 45° E. 3 ms. to the top of the mtn. where we deposited baggage on the 17th June.

" N. 45° E. 15 ms. to an open prairie on the side of a mtn., having kept the dividing ridge between waters of the Kooskooskee and Chopunnish rivers.

" N. 45° E. 28 ms. to an open prairie on the S. side of mtn., having kept the same dividing ridge, though you ascend many steep mtns., and descend many deep hollows.

" East 3 ms. to the end of a ridge where you descend to a deep hollow ; much windfall from a fire and a S.W. storm.

" N. 45° E. 10 ms. along a snowy ridge to a large open hillside, passing at 4½ ms. the road which turns off to the right and leads by the fishery at entrance of Colt-killed cr.

" N. 45° E. 12 ms. to the Quamash flats at the head of a branch of the Kooskooskee, passing the Kooskooskee, 35 yds. wide, at 5 ms. on this course. . . at 7 ms. fell again into the road which leads by the fishery about 4 ms. above the mouth of Quamash [Glade] cr.

" N. 4 ms. to the Hotspring cr. or the main branch of Traveler's-rest cr.

" N. 20° E. 3 ms. down this branch, to the hot springs on its N. side.

" N. 20° E. 3 ms. down the cr., passing a N. branch 8 yds. wide at 1 m., also the cr. itself twice a short distance below the N. branch.

" N. 45° E. 10 ms. down the N. side of Trav.-r. cr., to entrance of another N. branch 8 yds. wide ; a road leads up this branch.

" N. 60° E. 9 m. down N. side same cr., to the prairie of this cr. and valley of Clark's river.

" East 9 m. to our camp on S. side of Trav.-r. cr., crossing it 1 m. above camp and 2 m. above its mouth.

" 156 miles."

We now formed the following plan of operations:[5] Captain Lewis, with nine men, is to pursue the most direct route to the falls of the Missouri, where three of his party [Thompson, Goodrich, and McNeal] are to be left to prepare carriages for transporting the baggage and canoes across the portage. With the remaining six,[6] he will ascend Maria's river to explore the country and ascertain whether any branch of it reaches as far north as latitude 50°, after which he will descend that river to its mouth. The rest of the men will accompany Captain Clark to the head of Jefferson river, which Sergeant Ordway and a party of nine men will descend, with the canoes and other articles deposited there. Captain Clark's party, which will then be reduced to ten [men and Sacajawea], will proceed to the Yellowstone, at its nearest approach to the Three Forks of the Missouri. There he will build canoes, go down that river with seven of his party, and wait at its mouth till the rest of the party join him. Sergeant Pryor, with two others, (*p. 331*) will then take the horses by land to the Mandans.

---

[5] Gass' report of this project is (p. 233): "Here the party is to be separated; some of us are to go straight across to the falls of the Missouri, and some to the head waters of Jefferson river, where we left the canoes. At the falls we expect to be subdivided, as Capt. Lewis, myself and four or five men intend to go up Maria's river as far as the 50th degree of latitude, and a party to remain at the falls to prepare harness and other things necessary for hauling our canoes and baggage over the portage. Perhaps Capt. Clarke, who goes up the [Clark's] river here [at Traveler's-rest] may also take a party and go down the Riviere Jaune, or Yellow-stone river." The sergeant accompanied Captain Lewis to the falls of the Missouri, but did not go on the exploration of Maria's river, as he was left in charge of the men at the falls. The plan here sketched was carried out to the letter, with the following main exceptions: 1. Captain Lewis did not go as far north as 50°, nor indeed to 49°, as Maria's river was found not to head as far north as he had supposed; besides, an Indian fight forced him to beat a precipitate retreat to the Missouri. 2. Captain Clark and his party descended the Jefferson with Sergeant Ordway's detachment, before he went over to the Yellowstone by way of the Gallatin. 3. The project devised for Sergeant Pryor was defeated by the Crows, who stole all his horses.

[6] "I now called for the volunteers to accompany me on this rout, many turned out, from whom I scelected Drewyer, the two Fieldses, Werner, Frazier, and Sergt. Gass," Lewis L 68. But the last three of these were left at the falls.

From that nation he will go to the British posts on the Assiniboin with a letter to Mr. [Alexander] Henry,[7] to procure his endeavors to prevail on some of the Sioux chiefs to accompany him to the city of Washington.

Having made these arrangements, this and the following day [*July 2d*] were employed in hunting and [by Shields in] repairing our arms. We were successful in procuring a number [13] of fine large deer, the flesh of which was exposed to dry. Among other animals in this neighborhood are the dove [*Zenaidura carolinensis*], black woodpecker [*Asyndesmus torquatus*], lark-woodpecker [*Colaptes mexicanus*], logcock [*Ceophlœus pileatus*], prairie-lark [*Eremophila alpestris* var.], sand-hill crane [*Grus canadensis*], prairie-hen with the short and pointed tail [*Pediœcetes columbianus*], the robin [*Merula migratoria*], a species of brown plover [*Podasocys montanus ?*] a few curlews, small blackbirds [cowbirds, *Molothrus ater*], ravens, hawks, and a variety of sparrows, as well as the bee-martin [*Tyrannus carolinensis*,] and several species of *Corvus*. The mosquitoes have been excessively troublesome since our arrival. The Indians assert that there are great numbers of the white buffalo or mountain sheep [*Haplocerus montanus*[8]], on the snowy heights of the mountains west of Clark's river. They generally inhabit the rocky and most inaccessible parts of the mountains; but they are not fleet, and easily killed by hunters.

The plants which most abound in this valley are the wild

---

[7] " Mr. Henry," interlined " Haney," Lewis L 69. This is the " Mr. Haney " of p. **212** : see note **36** there. He is no other than the famous Alexander Henry, (the Fort Henry and Lake Henry man, who was drowned at mouth of the Columbia in **1811** or **1814**, and was the nephew of another Alexander Henry). Through the kindness of the Rev. Dr. Edw. D. Neill, of Macalester College, St. Paul, Minn., I have been favored with the valuable unpublished MS., fcp. pp. **1-186**, of this Mr. Henry, giving the history of his visit to the Mandans, July 7th to Aug. 14th, 1806, thus in the interval between Lewis and Clark's leaving and returning to these Indians. It is full of interesting matter which has never seen the light, and has a good deal to say of our explorers besides.

[8] At date of July 1st, 1806, Clark Q 165 has : " The Indians inform us that there are a great number of White Buffaloe, or Mountain Sheep of the snowy heights of the mountains, west of Clark's river."

rose, the honeysuckle with a white berry, the seven-bark, service-berry, elder, aspen, alder, choke-cherry, and both the narrow- and broad-leaved willow. The principal timber consists of long-leaved pine, which grows as well in the river-bottoms as on the hills; the firs and larches are confined to the higher parts of the hills; while on the river itself is a growth of cottonwood, with a wider leaf than that of the upper part of the Missouri, though narrower than that which grows lower down that river. There are also two species of clover in this valley; one with a very narrow, small leaf and a pale red flower; the other with a white flower, and nearly as luxuriant in its growth as our red clover.

The Indians who had accompanied us intended leaving us in order to seek their friends, the Ootlashoots; but we (*p. 332*) prevailed on them to accompany Captain Lewis a part of his route, so as to show him the shortest road to the Missouri, and in the meantime amused them with conversation and running races, on foot and with horses, in both of which they proved themselves hardy, athletic, and active. To the chief Captain Lewis gave a small medal and a gun, as a reward for having guided us across the mountains; in return the customary civility of exchanging names passed between them, by which the former acquired the title of Yomekollick, or White Bearskin Unfolded.[9] The Chopunnish, who had overtaken us on the 26th, made us a present of an excellent horse for the good advice we gave him, and as a proof of his attachment to the whites, as well as of his desire to be at peace with the Pahkees.

July 3d. All our preparations being completed, we saddled our horses, and the two parties, who had been so long companions, now separated with an anxious hope of soon meeting, after each had accomplished the destined purpose.[10]

[9] So the Biddle text; but Lewis L 74 has: " I was called Yo-me-kol-lick which interpreted is *the white bearskin foalded.*"

[10] The narrative here divides in two. Captain Lewis' continues through the present and the following chapter; then Captain Clark's occupies the next two chapters. The two parties were separated for more than a month—July 3d to August 12th. The beginning of the present narrative of Captain Lewis' ex-

The nine men and five Indians who accompanied Captain Lewis proceeded in a direction due north, down the west side of Clark's river.   Half a mile from camp we [had] forded Traveler's-rest creek, and 2½ miles further passed a western branch of the [main fork of Clark's, *i. e.*, St. Mary's or the Bitter-root] river; a mile beyond this was a small creek on the eastern side [of the same], and a mile lower down, the entrance of the eastern [Hellgate] branch of the [same] river. This stream [Hellgate river] is from 90 to 125 yards wide; and its water, which is discharged through two channels, is more turbid than that of the main river.   The latter is 150 yards in width, and waters an extensive level plain and prairie, which on their lower parts are ornamented with long-leaved pine and cottonwood, while the tops of the hills are covered with pine, larch, and fir.   We proceeded two miles further to a place where the Indians advised us to cross;

ploration occupies Codex L 75-81, July 3d and 4th.   Then the codex is blank to p. 99, July 15th.   For some reason not evident, the narrative of July 5th-14th was never copied by Lewis into this " red book."   Most fortunately, however, we have it on the loose sheets of note-paper on which it was originally penned in the field—the very sheets he had in his pocket when he started on this trip. They are in bad order, ragged on the edges and much stained—I suppose from the wetting they got when Captain Lewis fell into the river, as noted beyond. This most precious of all the fragmentary codices, now forming Codex La, I also call the " Pass Codex," because it gives the discovery of the famous pass now known as Lewis and Clark's, which Captain Lewis and his men made July 7th.   I shall cite it fully, and it will set at rest forever some doubtful points which have occasioned much discussion.   As a climax of good luck, I find, furthermore, a never-published sketch map of Lewis' whole route from Traveler's-rest creek through the Pass to the Missouri.   This invaluable map, plotted by Captain Clark from Captain Lewis' courses and distances, etc., in Codex La, occupies Clark N 149, 150—two pages of one of the "red books," facing each other, and when laid out flat measuring 14½ × 4⅞ inches.   *This* is the map mentioned in note ⁸, p. 802.   It is full of detail, and gives a clearer idea of Captain Lewis' trail than can be derived from any published map whatsoever. Aside from this, the best map I know of from which to study the route along Big Blackfoot river to the Pass and beyond, is the large one of Governor Stevens' (see " Route of Lt. Donelson in 1853," as there laid down, with various collateral routes, Cadotte's Pass, etc.).   But this is not to be compared for detail with Clark's pen-and-ink sketch.   The G. L. O. of 1892, Montana, and the milit. map, Dept. Dakota, 1891, give the most detail of any I have examined.

but having no boats, and timber being scarce, four hours were spent in collecting timber to make three small (*p. 333*) rafts; on which, with some difficulty and danger, we passed the river [*i. e.*, crossed the Missoula itself, from west to east, below the confluence of St. Mary's and Hellgate rivers]. We then drove our horses into the water; they swam to the opposite shore, but the Indians crossed on horseback, drawing at the same time their baggage alongside of them in small basins of deer-skins. The whole party being now re-assembled, we continued [up the Missoula and the north side of Hellgate river] for three miles and camped about sunset at a small [Hellgate] creek.[11] The Indians now showed

[11] Emptying into Hellgate river from the north, four or five miles due west of Missoula City. The *route* of July 3d is perfectly plain, but the *distances* involve some discrepancies not easily disposed of. In this matter the text is true to the codices, which therefore require examination, as it is not clear how Captain Lewis reached to-night's camp in so few miles. First for Lewis L 77: "North 7 m. down the west side of Clark's river to the place at which we passed it. forded travelersrest C. ½ a mile below our camp, passed a branch on west side at 2½ m. further, also at 1 m. further [still] passed the entrance of a small creek on the E. side of Clark's river, and two miles short of the extremity of this course passed the entrance of the east [Hellgate] branch of Clark's river which discharges itself in two channels." This allows only *five* miles from camp on Traveler's-rest creek to the confluence of Hellgate with St. Mary's river. Next lap is: "N. 75° E. 7 m. through a handsome level plain to the point at which the east branch [Hellgate] enters the mountain or where the hills set in near it on either side. We halted and encamped 5 miles short of the extremity of this course," *i. e.*, only went two or three miles after crossing the Missoula, and camped at the small creek which there makes in from the north. The end of this course would have been site of Missoula City, four or five miles further east: see July 4th. Codex La 1, written on the spot, has the identical courses and distances, but calls the east branch of Clark's river, *i. e.*, Hellgate, by the name of "Cokahlar ishkit, or Buffalo river," as Captain Lewis did not learn till next day that "the river of the road to buffalo" he was to take was only a branch of Hellgate, not this river itself. Now turning again to Codex L, for incidents of to-day, we find on p. 76 an account of the ferriage of the Missoula on rafts, during which Captain Lewis was swept overboard: "I remained myself with two men who could scarcely swim untill the last; by this time the raft by passing so frequently, had fallen a considerable distance down the [Missoula] river to a rapid and difficult part of it crouded with several small islands and willow bars which were now overflown; with these men I set out on the raft and was soon hurried down with the current a mile and a half before we made shore, on our approach to the shore the raft sank and I was drawn off the raft by a brush and

us a road at no great distance, which they said would lead up the [north bank of the] eastern [Hellgate] branch of Clark's river, and [thus to] another river called Cokalahishkit [elsewhere Cohahlarishkit], or River of the Road to Buffalo, thence to Medicine river and the falls of the Missouri. They added that, not far from the dividing ridge of the waters of Clark's river and the Missouri, the roads forked; and though both led to the falls, the left-hand route was the best. The route was so well beaten that we could no longer mistake it; and having now shown us the way, they were anxious to go in quest of their friends, the Shahlees [or Shallees]; besides which they feared, by venturing further with us, to encounter the Pahkees; for we had this afternoon seen a fresh track of a horse, which they supposed to be a Shahlee scout. We could not insist on their remaining longer with us; and as they had so kindly conducted us across the mountains, we were desirous of giving them a supply of provisions; we therefore distributed to them half of three deer, and the hunters were ordered to go out early in the morning in hopes of adding to the stock.

The horses suffered so dreadfully from the mosquitoes that we were obliged to kindle large fires and place the poor ani-

swam on shore the two men remained on the raft and fortunately effected a landing at some little distance below. I wet the chronometer by this accident which I had placed in my fob as I conceived for greater security. I now joined the party, and we proceeded with the indians about 3 ms. to a small creek and encamped at sunset." With this narrative compare for distances, etc., the account of July 3d given by Gass, p. 234: "Captain Lewis and his party went down Clarke's river, and Captain Clarke with the rest of the party went up it. We proceeded on down Clarke's river about *twelve miles*, [which is about right] when we came to the forks [confluence of Hellgate with St. Mary's river], and made three rafts to carry ourselves and baggage over. The river here is about 150 yards wide, and very beautiful. We had to make three trips with our rafts, and in the evening got all over safe; when we moved on up the north [Hellgate] branch, which is on our way over to the falls of the Missouri, and after travelling a mile and a half camped for the night. . . This north branch of the river is called by the natives Is-quet-co-qual-la, which means the road to the buffalo." Gass here transposes the syllables of this Indian name: reversed it would be Co-qual-la-is-quet, the Cokalahishkit of the L. and C. text, which Gass, like Lewis La, takes the main Hellgate river to be.

mals in the midst of the smoke. Fortunately, however, it became cold after dark, and the mosquitoes disappeared.

Friday, July 4th. The hunters accordingly set out; but returned unsuccessful about eleven o'clock. In the meantime we were joined by a young man of the Palloatpallah[12] tribe, who had set out a few days after us, and had followed us alone across the mountains—the same who had attempted to pass the mountains in June, while we were on the Kooskoos- (*p. 334*) kee, but had been obliged to return. We now smoked a farewell pipe with our estimable companions, who expressed every emotion of regret at parting with us; which they felt the more, because they did not conceal their fears of our being cut off by the Pahkees. We also gave them a shirt, a handkerchief, and a small quantity of ammunition. The meat which they received from us was dried and left at this place, as a store during the homeward journey. This circumstance confirms our belief that there is no route[13] along Clark's river to the Columbian plains so near or so good as that by which we came; for, though these people mean to go for several days' journey down that river, to look for the Shalees [Shallees or Shahlees: see note *anteà*, p. 1056, and see Ootlashoots, p. 582], yet they intend returning home by the same pass of the mountains through which they have conducted us. This route is also used by all the nations whom we know west of the mountains who are in the habit of visiting the plains of the Missouri; while on the other side all the war-paths of the Pahkees which fall into this valley of Clark's river concenter at Traveler's-rest, beyond which these people have never ventured to the west.

[12] "The band [of the Chopunnish nation] with which we have been most conversant call themselves pel-lote-pal-ler," Lewis L 32. "A man of the Pallotepellows," interlined "Pelloatpallahs," Lewis L 78. These are the Paloos, a Shahaptian tribe; the name is from Tlpélekc, a Chihalish word translated, "slough covered with trees." The corresponding Chinook word is Gitlápeleks. (*Fide* U. S. Bur. Ethnol.) Compare "Selloatpallah 3,000 Souls," charted by Clark on the north bank of the Snake near the Columbia.

[13] The Northern Pacific Railroad now passes by this route.

Having taken leave of the Indians, we mounted our horses and proceeded up the eastern [Hellgate] branch of Clark's river through the level plain in which we were camped.   At the distance of five miles we crossed a small creek [14] 15 yards wide, and entered the mountains.   The [Hellgate [15]] river is here closely confined within the hills for two miles [further], when the bottom widens into an extensive prairie, and the river is 110 yards in width.   We went three miles further, over a high plain succeeded by a low and level prairie, to the entrance of the Cokalahishkit. [16]   This river empties from the

[14] Site of Missoula City, Mont., county town of county of same name, at the mouth of Rattlesnake creek, on N. bank of Hellgate river, about halfway between the mouth of this river and the mouth of the Cokalahishkit or Big Blackfoot river, which falls into Hellgate river from the N.E.   The place just east of the city where the river is confined in a sort of cañon for two miles, as the text says, is the Hellgate or Hell's Gate which gives name to the river, and the name is thus explained by some : Father De Smet left his St. Mary's (Bitter-root) valley Aug. 16th, 1846, and camped that night at the mouth of Big Blackfoot river.   He went by way of this defile, which he called *Porte de l'Enfer* (Gate of Hell), as he says, from its being "the principal entrance by which parties of marauding Blackfeet reach the lands of our neophytes."   This sounds reasonable enough, especially in connection with the name, "Big Blackfoot," of the river along which came from the buffalo-country the heathen wolves upon the lamblike or sheepish converts of the good shepherd's flock.   For each of the rivers here in mention, see next notes.

[15] The river so named, probably from the circumstance given in the last note, is that large stream, some 130 miles long, whose confluence with the Bitter-root or St. Mary's river composes the Missoula, a little distance west of Missoula City. It runs in Deer Lodge Co., at first northerly, then westerly to enter Missoula Co., and with its numerous tributaries drains the S.E. portion of the large area between the main Rocky Mountain and the Bitter-root ranges.   It heads in the former range, with Missourian waters ; its principal valley is Deer Lodge, so called as being a long famous resort of such game ; one of its most notable branches is Little Blackfoot river (falling in at Garrison, below Deer Lodge City), which heads in and about Mullan's Pass, by which the railroad comes westward from Helena.   The largest tributary is the Big Blackfoot, the mouth of which Captain Lewis is now approaching, and up which he goes : see next note.

[16] Name of the "river of the road to buffalo" variant in the text, and still more so in the codices ; usually as here spelled.   This river is now called the Blackfoot, and distinctively Big Blackfoot.   It heads in the main Rocky mountains, about Lewis and Clark's, Cadotte's, and other defiles, by several affluents ; runs with a general course nearly due west, though very crookedly, and falls into the Hellgate from the N.E. a little east of the gorge called Hellgate, some

northeast, is deep, rapid, and about 60 yards wide, with banks which, though not high, are sufficiently bold to prevent the water from overflowing.   The eastern branch of Clark's river is 90 yards wide above the junction, but below it spreads to 100.   The waters of both are turbid, though the Cokalahishkit is (*p. 335*) the clearer of the two ; the beds of both are composed of sand and gravel, but neither of them is navigable on account of the rapids and shoals which obstruct their currents.   Before the junction of these streams, the country had been bare of trees; but as we turned up the north branch of [Hellgate river—that is, up [17]] the Cokalahishkit, we found a woody country, though the hills were high and the low grounds narrow and poor.   At the distance of eight miles in a due east course we camped in a bottom, where there was an abundance of excellent grass.   The evening proved fine and pleasant, and we were no longer annoyed by mosquitoes.   Our only game were two squirrels, one of the kind common to the Rocky mountains, the second a ground-squirrel of a species we had not seen before.   Near the place where we crossed Clark's river, we saw at a distance some wild horses; which are said, indeed, to be very numerous on this river, as well as on the heads of the Yellowstone.

July 5th.   Early in the morning we proceeded for 3½ miles, in a direction N. 75° E.; then inclining to the south,[18]

15 miles above the mouth of the main river.   The Big Blackfoot drains northerly parts of the Hellgate basin ; its valley is about 75 miles long, with a width of from half a mile to twelve miles.   See note at Prairie of the Knobs, beyond.

[17] A slip of the text here, because the Cokalahishkit is the north branch of Hellgate river, and has itself no north branch here which could be gone up. The mistake could also be corrected by reading " north side " for " north branch," as Lewis L 80: " Continued my rout up the N. side of the Cokahlahishkit river."   The original Codex La has : " East 8 m. up the buffaloe road river or Co-kah-lah-, ishkit."   One mile short of the mouth of this river, La 2 notes " a small branch " from the north, which is duly laid down on Clark's map, N 150, but is not noticed in the text.   Camp is on the north side of the Big Blackfoot, at the distance said above its mouth.   The third return of the Fourth of July is suffered to pass without allusion to this anniversary.

[18] Read north—the inclination was from N. 75° E. to N. 25° E., Lewis La 3.

crossed an extensive, beautiful, and well-watered valley nearly
12 miles in length, at the extremity of which we halted
for dinner.[19] Here we obtained a great quantity of quamash
and shot an antelope from a gang of females, which at this
season herd together, apart from the bucks. After dinner
we followed the course of the river eastward for six miles,
to the mouth of a creek 35 yards wide, which we called
Werner's[20] creek. It comes in from the north, and waters a
high, extensive prairie, the hills near which are low, and supplied with the long-leaved pine, larch, and some fir. The
road then led N. 22° W. for four miles,[21] soon after which
it again turned N. 75° E. for 2½ miles, over a handsome
plain watered by Werner's creek, to the river; this we followed on its eastern direction, through a high prairie,
rendered very unequal by a vast number of little hillocks

[19] No fewer than *five* creeks are passed before dinner and thus before Werner's
creek is reached—all duly noted on Lewis La 3, and duly charted on Clark N
150, but omitted from the text ! La 3 has : " Set out at 6 A.M.—steered N. 75°
E. 3½ m. passed a stout C. [on] N. side at 2½ m. another on S. side at 3½ m. . .
N. 25° E. 12 m. passing a small creek at one m. on S. side, . . . also another
creek 12 yds. wide at ½ a mile further on N. side, and another 8 yds. wide on N.
side at 5 ms. further. One ½ m. short of the extremity of this course arrive at
a high prarie on N. side from one to three miles in width extending up the river.
halted and dined in the mouth of a little drane on the left of the plain." One of
these two creeks on the S., between the first two on the N., is Union creek ; on
this is a place called Potomac. I can find no names for any of the other four—
three of them N. and one S. Further along the river, on the boundary between
Missoula and Deer Lodge Co., before Werner's creek is reached, Elk creek falls
in from the S., on which are places called Sunset and Yreka.

[20] Named for Private William Werner of the party : compare p. 303. This is
the largest branch of Big Blackfoot river thus far reached, and the first one
named by Captain Lewis ; it is the Clearwater river of G. L. O. 1892, and
apparently " Littlewater cr." of Symons. With it are connected several sheets
of water, one of them called Clearwater lake.

[21] " To a high insulated knob just above the entrance of a creek 8 yards wide
which discharged itself into Werner's creek," Lewis La 3, 4—a datum which
assists in identifying this creek, and which should not have been omitted.
Observe that this last course, " N. 22° W. 4 miles," is no advance eastward, but
takes the party away from the river. On the next course, N. 75° E. 2½ miles,
Werner's creek is crossed at the first mile. "leaving a high prairie hill to the
right separating the plain from the river," Lewis La 4—another item which should
not have been omitted from the text ; codex-map and Stevens' both show it.

and sink-holes, and at three miles' distance camped near
(*p. 336*) the entrance of a large creek, 20 yards wide, to
which we gave the name of Seaman's [22] creek. We had seen
no Indians, though near camp were the concealed fires of a
war-party, who had passed about two months ago.

July 6th. At sunrise we continued our course eastward
along the river. At seven miles' distance we passed the
North fork [23] of the Cokalahishkit, a deep and rapid stream 45
yards in width, and like the main branch itself somewhat
turbid, though the other streams of this country are clear.
Seven miles further the river enters the mountains, and here
end those extensive prairies on this side, though they widen
in their course toward the southeast, and form an Indian
route to Dearborn's river [see beyond], and thence to the
Missouri. From the multitude of knobs irregularly scattered through them, Captain Lewis called this country the
Prairie of the Knobs.[24] They abound in game, as we saw

[22] A name I believe not found elsewhere in this History, and to the personality
of which I have no clew. " East 3 m. to the entrance of a large creek 20 yds.
wide called Seaman's Creek, passing a creek at 1 m. 8 yds. wide," Lewis La 4.
Here are two creeks within three miles of each other, the first and smallest nameless, both N.; " at the head of these two creeks high broken mountains stand at
the distance of 10 m. forming a kind of cove generally of open untimbered
country," Lewis La 4. The codex-map, Stevens, and the G. L. O. 1892, agree
exactly in laying down these two creeks, the larger of which Clark N 150 letters
" Seamons "; this is that whose main west fork the G. L. O. letters " Stanley
cr.," it is the Clear creek of Symons, and apparently " Moncure cr." of Dept.
Dakota map. Camp is on it, near a place marked Woodworth by Symons. (Beyond Seaman's creek is one unnoted by L. and C., charted nameless by Stevens,
and marked " Lightning Cr." on the G. L. O.; on a branch of this is Ovanda.)

[23] Salmon Trout creek of Stevens' large map and of present geography—the
largest northern affluent of the Big Blackfoot. " Passed the N. fork of the
Cokahlarishkit River at 7 ms. it is 45 yards wide deep and rapid. had some
difficulty in passing it. Passed a large crooked pond at 4 ms. further," Lewis
La 4. This pond is charted on Clark N 150, but I have not seen it elsewhere.

[24] " These plains I called [" *knob plains* " erased] the prarie of the knobs from a
number of knobs being irregularly scattered through it," Lewis La 4. This area
later became known as the Blackfoot prairie ; also, as Stevens' prairie, having been
crossed by some of Governor I. I. Stevens' party in 1853–55 : see P.R.R. Rep.
XII. pt. i. 1860, p. 121. Governor Stevens twice passed along in Captain Lewis'
tracks, and under date of July 20th, 1855, we find him paying the tribute he

antelopes, deer, great numbers of burrowing-squirrels, some
curlews, bee-martins, woodpeckers, plovers, robins, doves,
ravens, hawks, ducks, a variety of sparrows, and yesterday
observed swans on Werner's creek. Among the plants we
observed the southernwood, and two other species of shrubs,
of which we preserved specimens.

On entering the high grounds we followed the course of
the river through the narrow bottoms, thickly timbered
with pine and cottonwood intermixed, and variegated with
the bois-rouge [redwood], which is now in bloom, the common small blue flag, and pepper-grass. At a distance of 3½
miles we reached the two forks [25] of the river mentioned by
the Indians. They are nearly equal in width, and the road
itself here forks and follows each of them. We followed
that which led us in a direction N. 75° E., over a steep high
hill, then along a wide bottom to a thickly wooded side of a
hill, where the low grounds are narrow, till we reached a
large creek,[26] eight miles from the forks and 25 from our last
camp. Here we halted for the night [in the vicinity of Lin-
coln]. In the course of the day the track of the In- (*p. 337*)

never grudged : " As I moved up the valley I began to realize the fidelity of the
description of Lewis and Clark, who speak of the whole prairie of the Blackfoot,
over which our day's journey led to-day, as the Prairie of the Knobs. On a map
of the usual scale, these knobs or little ridges are too small to be represented,
as the slightest mark on the map would exaggerate them," P.R.R. Rep. XII.
pt. i. 1860, p. 212.

[25] Before reaching the two forks, and within two miles of them, Lewis La 6
notes " a creek on N. side 12 yds. wide, shallow and clear." The alleged situation of these forks, where the road also forked, does not correspond closely
with that in which they are laid down on any map before me, on all of which
the forks seem to be considerably lower. Clark N 150 charts *two* sizable streams
coming into Big Blackfoot from the S.E.—one falling in opposite the " crooked
pond " above mentioned, the other about in position to correspond to the " two
forks " of our text. The former of these is the stream laid down on modern
maps as Nevada creek, heading with some northern affluents of Little Blackfoot
river, and connecting on the main divide with some affluents of Little Prickly-
pear creek (see note [10], p. 422), near which is Marysville.

[26] This " large creek " is one of several into which the main stream now breaks
up within a few miles. Camp is on its west bank " some little distance above
its mouth," Lewis La 6, in the vicinity of a place called Lincoln. The creek is

dians, whom we supposed to be Pahkees, continued to grow fresher, and we passed a number of old lodges and camps. At seven o'clock the next morning,

Monday July 7th,[27] we proceeded through a beautiful plain [Belly prairie] on the north side of the river, which seems here to abound in beaver. The low grounds possess much timber, and the hills are covered chiefly with pitch-pine, that of the long-leaved kind having disappeared since we left the Prairie of the Knobs.

thus identified, though I have no name for it. It is a good ways short of Lander's creek. As Captain Lewis will cross the Continental Divide to-morrow, I give Gass' account, p. 236, of the approach to the famous "Lewis and Clark's Pass." "*July 6th*. Having gone about seven miles we crossed a north branch of the Coqual-la-isquet, which is 40 yards wide and was mid-rib deep on our horses, with a rapid current. About seven miles up the valley [Prairie of Knobs] we passed a beautiful small lake [the "crooked pond"] ; where the river and road leaves the valley and bears towards the northeast between two hills not very large. We kept up the river, through a small brushy valley about the eighth of a mile wide, for a mile and a half, and then halted for dinner. . . At 1 o'clock we proceeded on, passed a number of handsome streams which fall into the river, and a number of old Indian lodges. As we advance the valley becomes more extensive, and is all plain. At night we encamped on a beautiful creek, having travelled 25 miles."

[27] Lewis La 6, 7, this date : "N. 75° E. 6 m. with the road through a level beatifull plain on the north side of the river. . . crossed a branch of the creek 8 yds. wide on which we [were] encamped at ¼ m. also passed a creek 15 yards wide at ¼ [of a mile] further. . . North 6 ms.—passed the main creek at a mile [and a] ½ and kept up it on the wrighthand side through handsom plain bottoms to the foot of a ridge which we ascended the main stream boar [bore] N.W. and W. as far as I could see it a wright hand fork falls into this [main] creek at 1 m. above the commencement of this course. [N.B. This "main creek" is Lander's creek of Stevens' and modern maps. It leads toward but not into the Pass. Captain Lewis crossed it near its mouth and kept up its east side 4½ miles. The "right hand fork" which he observed is really the main Blackfoot.] N. 15° E. 8 miles over two ridges [away from Lander's creek] and again striking the wrighthand fork at 4 ms. then continued up it on the left hand [west] side. . . N. 10° E 3 m. up the same creek on the east side [of it, having crossed it at the beginning of this course], through a handsome narrow plain. N. 45° E. 2 m. passing the dividing ridge between the waters of the Columbia and Missouri rivers at ¼ of a mile. from this gap which is low and an easy ascent on the W. side the fort mountain bears North East, and appears to be distant about 20 miles. The road for one and ¾ miles decends the hills and continues down a branch [of an affluent of Dearborn's river]. N. 20° W. 7 ms. over sev-

At the distance of twelve miles we left the river, or rather the creek, and having for four miles crossed, in a direction N. 15° E., two ridges, again struck to the right, which we followed through a narrow bottom, covered with low willows and grass, and abundantly supplied with both deer and beaver. After seven miles we reached the foot of a ridge, which we ascended in a direction N. 45° E., through a low gap of easy ascent from the westward, and on descending it were delighted to discover that this was the dividing ridge between the waters of the Columbia and those of the Missouri.

eral hills and hollows along the foot of the mountain hights passing five small rivulets [all tributaries of Dearborn's river] running to the wright . . . encamped on a small run under the foot of the mountain." It will be observed that this account is much more detailed and precise than the published text, particularly in the sentences I have italicized, hitherto our main guide to and through this Pass. The actual trail is luminous on Clark N 150, where the word "Gap" indicates the Pass. The Gass Journal of course antedated the History, so far as publication was concerned.

Gass makes the Pass in these terms, p. 236 : "Continued our journey early along the valley, which is very beautiful with a great deal of clover in its plains. Having gone about five miles, we crossed the main [Lander's] branch of the river, which comes in from the north ; and up which the road goes about five miles further and then takes over a hill towards the east. On the top of this hill there are two beautiful ponds, of about three acres in size. We passed over the ridge and struck a small stream, which we at first thought was of the headwaters of the Missouri, but found it was not. [This is the one that also deceived Stevens : see below.] Here we halted for dinner, and after staying three hours proceeded on four miles up the branch, when we came to the dividing ridge between the waters of the Missouri and Columbia ; passed over the ridge and came to a fine spring, the waters of which run into the Missouri. We then kept down this stream or branch about a mile ; then turned a north course along the side of the dividing ridge for 8 miles, passing a number of small streams or branches [tributaries of Dearborn's river], and at 9 o'clock at night encamped, after coming 32 miles."

Lewis and Clark's Pass was examined by Mr. F. W. Lander, C. E., in 1853, and hence the "main creek" of our text, which leads up toward but not into it, was dedicated to him by Governor Stevens ; see P. R. R. Rep. XII. pt. i. 1860, p. 122. The Pass was also made by Mr. James Doty in July, 1854, en route from Fort Benton to Fort Owen and return : *op. cit.*, pp. 186, 187. Mr. Doty named Lander's creek. Both gentlemen were of Governor Stevens' party. On July 22d, 1855, Governor Stevens himself approached the Pass from the west, desiring to establish certain connections which his assistants had left to be made. Going up the valley 4½ miles he came to a small creek which he supposed flowed

From this gap Fort mountain is about 20 miles in a north-eastern direction. We now wound through the hills and hollows of the mountains, passing several rivulets which run to the right, and at the distance of nine miles from the gap camped, after making 32 miles. We procured some beaver, and this morning saw some signs and tracks of buffalo, from which it seems those animals do sometimes penetrate to a short distance within the mountains.

July 8th. At three miles from our camp we reached a stream[28] issuing from the mountains to the southwest; though it only contains water for a width of 30 feet, yet its

from the Pass, but which on the contrary soon gave out. *Even this rivulet is charted on Clark N* 150 ! Continuing northward Governor Stevens soon fell into the trail which passed from Lander's creek to the stream which did flow from the Pass, and of which he was in search. His Report says :

"Starting now from the point where the trail from Lander's Fork strikes the stream flowing from Lewis and Clark's Pass, we continued up the latter stream for five miles, passing over the most remarkable valley that I have ever seen in the immediate region of a mountain divide. [Plate lxii. represents this valley.] Its width and the declivities of the ground were remarkably uniform ; the valley not less than half a mile wide ; the bottom—excepting a small portion of the lower part, where were beaver dams—always above the freshets, until we came to a point where I halted for a few moments in order to observe with the barometer. Here there was a fork in the stream, the left hand branch coming immediately from Lewis and Clark's Pass, and the larger and right hand fork coming from the north some little distance, judging from the quantity of water in the stream. We now kept up the left hand fork, and passed over Lewis and Clark's Pass, where many observations were taken, both of the immediate basis of the divide on either slope and at the summit. This divide can be arranged for wagon roads with gentle declivities on either side. Little or no timber would have to be cut away. We found grass on both sides of the mountain, as well as near its summit. Going down the eastern base on our right, and some little distance below the trail, was a fine stream of water, a tributary of the Dearborn, and about a mile and a quarter from the summit we came to another tributary connecting with this, coming from the north. It is on this tributary that a railroad line must be laid in order to tunnel the mountain in the shortest and most practicable line." (P. R. R. Rep. XII. Pt. i. 1860, pp. 213–215.)

[28] Main course of the North fork of Dearborn's river. Lewis La 8 : " N. 25° W. 3½ m. to the top of a hill from thence we saw the Shishequaw mountain about 8 m. distant, immediately before us. Passed [" *Torrent*" erased and interlined] Dearborne's river at 3 m." This explains "we called it Dearborn's river," in the text—for this was named July 18th, 1805 : see p. 421. It means that Captain Lewis did not know this was a fork of Dearborn's river, and therefore gave it a

bed is more than three times that width, and from the appearance of the roots and trees in the neighboring bottom, must
sometimes run with great violence. We called it Dearborn's
river. Half a mile further we observed from a height Shishequaw [29] mountain, a high, insulated moun- (*p. 338*) tain of a
conic form, standing several miles in advance of the eastern
range of the Rocky mountains, here about eight miles from
us and immediately on our road, which was in a northwest
direction. But as our object was to strike Medicine [Sun]
river, and hunt down to its mouth to procure skins for the
food [30] and gear necessary for the three men who are to be
left at the falls, none of whom are hunters, we determined to
leave the road. We therefore proceeded due north through
an open plain, till we reached Shishequaw creek, a stream
about 20 yards wide, with a considerable quantity of timber
in its low grounds. Here we halted and dined, and now
felt, by the luxury of our food, that we were approaching
once more the plains of the Missouri, so rich in game. We
saw a great number of deer, antelope, goats, wolves, and
some barking-squirrels, and for the first time caught a distant
prospect of two buffaloes. After dinner we followed the
Shishequaw for 6½ miles [thus past Augusta and Florence],
to its entrance into Medicine river, and went along the

new name—Torrent river—which was suppressed when the final determination
was made. But this is an appropriate name for the North fork.

[29] Heart mountain of Stevens' large map, now known as Haystack Butte,
standing between two forks (Smith's and Elk) of the South fork of Medicine or
Sun river ; places called Cecil and Racine Ford in the vicinity. Shishequaw
creek of the text is this South fork, which Captain Lewis strikes at or near town
of Augusta and follows down to its mouth. Shishequaw mountain has sometimes been thought to be that isolated butte now called Tip-top mountain, by
which a certain Spring creek passes to fall into Sun river. But this is much
further east. Captain Lewis held a trail nearly north from the Pass—one course,
indeed, being given as N. 25° W. See the position of "Shishequaw R." on
Clark's map of 1814. The trail there dotted is *not* that by which Captain Lewis
came, but a shorter hypothetical one, dotted on Clark N 149 with the words :
"This is the nearest and best rout," and finally "adopted" as the route of the
Expedition. See Stevens' pl. lxiii, at points marked *a* and *b*.

[30] *Sic*—read, " in order to procure the necessary skins to make geer [boat-gear],
and meat for the three men," etc., Lewis La 9.

banks [south bank] of this river for eight miles, when we
camped [31] on a large island.   The bottom continued low,
level, and extensive; the plains too are level; but the soil
of neither is fertile, as it consists of a light-colored earth,
intermixed with a large proportion of gravel; the grass in
both is generally about nine inches high.   Captain Lewis
here shot a large and remarkably white wolf.   We had now
made 28 miles, and set out early the next morning,

July 9th; but the air soon became very cold, and it began
to rain.   We halted for a few minutes in some old Indian
lodges; but finding that the rain continued we proceeded,
though we were all wet to the skin, and halted for dinner at
the distance of eight miles [about on W. border of Fort
Shaw Milit. Res.].   The rain, however, continued and we
determined to go no further.   The river is about 80 yards
wide, with banks which, though low, are seldom overflowed;
the bed is composed of loose gravel and pebbles; the water
is clear and rapid, but not so much so as to impede navigation.   The bottoms are hand- (*p. 339*) some, wide, and level,
and supplied with a considerable quantity of narrow-leaved
cottonwood.   During our short ride we killed two deer and
a buffalo, and saw a number of wolves and antelopes.

July 10th.   We set out early, and continued through a
country similar to that of yesterday, with bottoms of wide-
leaved cottonwood occasionally along the borders, though
for the most part the low grounds are without timber.   In
the plains are great quantities of two species of prickly-pear
now in bloom.   Gooseberries of the common red kind are
in abundance and just beginning to ripen, but there are
no currants.   The river has now widened to 100 yards;
it is deep, crowded with islands, and in many parts rapid.
At the distance of 17 miles,[32] the timber disappears totally
from the river-bottoms.   About this part of the river, the

[31] In making the Pass, Captain Lewis went from Deer Lodge into Lewis and
Clark Co.   At this camp Sun river divides the latter from Choteau Co., and, as
camp is on an island, it is between these two counties.   To-morrow he will
pass into Cascade Co.

[32] At this point Captain Lewis has passed the site of Fort Shaw, has traversed the

wind, which had blown on our backs, and constantly put
the elk on their guard, shifted round ; we then shot three
of them and a brown bear.   Captain Lewis halted to skin
them, while two of the men took the pack-horses forward to
seek for a camp.   It was nine o'clock before he overtook
them, at the distance of seven miles, in the first grove of
cottonwood.   They had been pursued as they came along
by a very large bear, on which they were afraid to fire, lest
their horses, being unaccustomed to the gun, might take
fright and throw them.   This circumstance reminds us of
the ferocity of these animals, when we were last near this
place, and admonishes us to be very cautious.   We saw vast
numbers of buffalo below us, which kept up a dreadful bellowing during the night.   With all our exertions we were
unable to advance more than 24 miles, owing to the mire
through which we are obliged to travel, in consequence of
the rain.   The next morning, however,

July 11th, was fair, and enlivened by great numbers of
birds, which sang delightfully in the clusters of cottonwood.   The hunters were sent down Medicine river to hunt
elk, while Captain Lewis crossed the high plain, in a direction (*p. 340*) [S.] 75° E., to Whitebear islands, a distance
of eight miles, where the hunters joined him.   They had
seen elk ; but in this neighborhood the buffalo are in such
numbers that, on a moderate computation, there could not
have been fewer than 10,000 within a circuit of two miles.
At this season they are bellowing in every direction, so as
to make an almost continued roar ; this at first alarmed
our horses, which, being from the west of the mountains,
are unused to the noise and appearance of these animals.
Among the smaller game are the brown thrush, pigeons,
doves, and a beautiful bird called the buffalo-pecker.[33]

Military Reservation of that name, and is already beyond Sun River Crossing.   He
proceeds to camp on S. bank, below entrance of Big Muddy creek from the N.

[33] The bird properly so called is African, and not found elsewhere.   The bird
meant is the cowbird, or cow blackbird, *Molothrus ater*, which has the same
habit of alighting on the backs of cattle to pick the ticks or other insects which
infest their hides.

Immediately on our arrival we began to hunt, and by three in the afternoon had collected a stock of food and hides enough for our purpose. We then made two canoes, one in the form of a basin, like those used by the Mandans, the other consisting of two skins, in a form of our own invention. They were completed the next morning,

July 12*th*, but the wind continued so high that it was not till toward night that we could cross the [Missouri] river in them, and make our horses swim. In the meantime, nearly the whole day was consumed in search after our horses, which had disappeared last night, and seven of which were not recovered at dark, while Drewyer was still in quest of them. The river is somewhat higher than it was last summer, the present season being much more moist than the preceding one, as may be seen in the greater luxuriance of the grass.

July 13*th*. We formed our camp this morning at our old station,[34] near the head of the Whitebear islands, and immediately went to work in making gear. On opening the cache, we found the bear-skins entirely destroyed by water, which, in a flood of the river, had penetrated to them. All the specimens of plants were unfortunately lost; the chart of the Missouri, however, remained unhurt, and several articles contained in trunks and boxes had suffered but little injury; but a phial of laudanum had lost its stopper, and (*p. 341*) run into a drawer of medicines, which it spoiled beyond recovery. The mosquitoes have been so troublesome that it was impossible even to write without the assistance of a mosquito-bier. The buffalo are leaving us fast on their way to the southeast.

July 14*th*. We continued making preparations to transport our articles, and as the old deposit was too damp, we secured the trunks on a high scaffold, covered with skins, among the thick brush on a large island—a precaution against any visit from the Indians, should they come before the main

[34] On the east (right) bank of the Missouri, formed June 22, 1805: see p. 387; and for the cache there, made July 10th, see p. 408.

party arrives here. The carriage-wheels were in good order, and the iron frame of the boat had not suffered materially. The buffalo have nearly disappeared, leaving behind them a number of large wolves, which are prowling about us.

July 15*th.*[35] To our great joy Drewyer returned to-day from a long search after the horses ; for we had concluded, from his long stay, that he had probably met with a bear and with his usual intrepidity attacked the animal; in which case, if by any accident he should have been separated from his horse, his death would be almost inevitable. Under this impression, we had resolved to set out to-morrow in quest of him, when his return relieved us from our apprehensions. He had searched for two days before he discovered that the horses had crossed Dearborn's river, near a spot where was an Indian camp, which seemed to have been abandoned about the time the horses were stolen, and which was so closely concealed that no trace of a horse could be seen within the distance of a quarter of a mile. He crossed the river and pursued the track of these Indians westward, till his horse became so much fatigued that he despaired of overtaking them, and then returned. These Indians we suppose to be a party of Tushepaws, who have ventured out of the mountains to hunt buffalo. During the day we were engaged in drying meat and dressing skins.

At night M'Neal, who had been sent in the morning to examine the (*p. 342*) cache at the lower end of the portage, returned ; but had been prevented from reaching that place by a singular adventure. Just as he arrived near Willow run, he approached a thicket of brush in which was a white bear, which he did not discover till he was within ten feet of him. His horse started, and wheeling suddenly round, threw M'Neal almost immediately under the bear, which started up instantly. Finding the bear raising himself on his hind feet to attack him, he struck him on the head with the

---

[35] The fragmentary Codex La ends with a few words at this date, breaking off at the midst of a sentence. The narrative now returns to Lewis L 99, beginning with same date—nothing is lost.

butt end of his musket; the blow was so violent that it broke
the breach of the musket and knocked the bear to the
ground.   Before he recovered, M'Neal, seeing a willow-tree
close by, sprang up, and there remained while the bear closely
guarded the foot of the tree until late in the afternoon.   He
then went off; M'Neal being released came down, and having found his horse, which had strayed off to the distance of
two miles, returned to camp.[36]   These animals are, indeed, of
a most extraordinary ferocity, and it is matter of wonder
that in all our encounters we have had the good fortune to
escape.   We are now troubled with another enemy, not
quite so dangerous, though even more disagreeable : these
are the mosquitoes, who now infest us in such myriads that
we frequently get them into our throats when breathing,
and the dog even howls with the torture they occasion.

Having now accomplished the object of our stay, Captain
Lewis determined to leave Sergeant Gass, with two men
[Frazier and Werner] and four horses, to assist the party
[Sergeant Ordway's] who are expected [to come down the
Jefferson and Missouri in the canoes which we left at the
Two Forks] to carry our effects over the portage, whilst he,
Drewyer, and the two Fields, with six horses, proceeded to
the sources of Maria's river.[37]   Accordingly, early in the
morning,

July 16*th*, Captain Lewis descended in a skin-canoe to the

[36] One of the most comical pictures (though all are very funny) in the Philadelphia editions of Gass' Journal represents this incident, with M'Neal com-
fortably seated in the fork of a tree, at the foot of which the bear stands guard,
with an expression of resolution equal to the occasion.   M'Neal's horse is in the
distance, but the bear is between, and M'Neal seems the personification of patience
on a monument.   This artistic effort is inscribed : " An American having struck a
Bear but not killed him, escapes into a Tree."   For the cache which M'Neal
examined at Portage creek, see June 18th, p. 378.

[37] This paragraph is puzzling, as it only accounts, apparently, for six men, and
Captain Lewis had nine with him : see July 1st, p. 1064.   The point is that
Captain Lewis had detailed three men, Thompson, Goodrich, and M'Neal,
whom he had all along intended to leave here at the falls, and had intended to
take the other six on with him to Maria's river.   But *of these six* he now decides
to leave Gass, Frazier and Werner at the falls, with Thompson, Goodrich, and

lower side of Medicine river, where the horses had previously been sent, and then rode with his party to the falls of 47 feet, where he halted for two hours to dine, and took a sketch of the falls. In the afternoon they proceeded to the Great Falls, near which they slept under a (*p. 343*) shelving rock, with a happy exemption from mosquitoes. These falls have lost much of their grandeur since we saw them, the river being much lower now than at that time ; though they still form a most sublime spectacle. As we came along we met several white bears, but they did not venture to attack us. There were but few buffalo, however, the large[r number] having principally passed the river, directing their course downward. There are, as usual, great numbers of goats and [or] antelopes dispersed through the plains, and large flocks of geese [*Bernicla canadensis*], which raise their young about the entrance of Medicine river. We observe here also the cuckoo [*Coccygus erythrophthalmus*], or, as it is sometimes called, the raincraw [raincrow], a bird which is not known either within or west of the Rocky mountains.[38]

July 17th. After taking a second draught of the falls, Captain Lewis directed his course N. 10° W., with an intention of striking Maria's river at the point to which he had ascended it in 1804 [*sic*—read June 4th–8th, 1805]. The country is here spread into wide and level plains, swelling like the ocean, in which the view is uninterrupted by a single

M'Neal, taking only Drewyer and the brothers Fields to Maria's river with himself. Thus the nine are all " present or accounted for "—as sergeants say to their commissioned officers. (Lewis L 100, this date.)

[38] *Wednesday, 16th,* Gass notes Captain Lewis' departure for Maria's river, and states that he was left with two men [*i. e.,* Frazier and Werner, *besides* Thompson, Goodrich and M'Neal] and four horses to repair the trucks they had uncached, and have things ready to bring over the portage and down the Missouri, when Sergeant Ordway's party, which was then with Captain Clark, should arrive with the canoes and baggage uncached at the Two Forks of Jefferson river. Gass was ordered to wait with his party at the mouth of Maria's river till Sept. 1st, or until Captain Lewis should come there, which was expected to be Aug. 5th ; but if the latter did not reach the mouth of this river by Sept. 1st, Gass was to wait no longer, but go down the Missouri and join Captain Clark at or below the mouth of the Yellowstone.

tree or shrub, and is diversified only by the moving herds
of buffalo. The soil consists of a light-colored earth, intermixed with a large proportion of coarse gravel without sand,
and is by no means so fertile as either the plains of the Columbia or those lower down the Missouri. When dry it
cracks, and is hard and thirsty, while in its wet state it is as
soft and slimy as soap. The grass is naturally short, and at
this time is still more so from the recent passage of the
buffalo.

Among the birds that we met was the party-colored plover
[avocet, *Recurvirostra americana :* see p. 291], with the head
and neck of a brick-red, a bird which frequents the little
ponds scattered over the plains. After traveling 20 miles we
reached Tansy [39] river, and as we could not go as far as Maria's
river this evening, and perhaps not find either wood or water
before we arrived there, we determined to camp. As we
approached the river, we saw the fresh track of a bleeding
buffalo, a circumstance by no means pleasant, as it indicated
that Indians had been hunting and were not far from us.
The tribes who princi- (*p. 344*) pally frequent this country
are the Minnetarees of Fort de Prairie and the Blackfoot
Indians, both of whom are vicious and profligate rovers; we
have therefore everything to fear from their stealing not
only our horses, but even our arms and baggage, if they are

[39] It will be remembered that Tansy river, so named by L. and C., and also
called by them Rose river, is the Teton, which falls into Maria's river : see note [5],
p. 356. This trail is across country, with nothing to go by but compass-points
uncorrected for magnetic variation, and the distance is only estimated.
"Twenty miles" seems short of any point where the Teton can be struck
from the Great Falls. We can only assume, therefore, that the river was reached
at its nearest approach to these falls—an assumption borne out by the details of
to-morrow's march. This would be about halfway between Perrysburg and
Valleux, both of which are places on the north bank of the Teton. The route
was about at right angles with the old Mullan trail from Fort Shaw to Fort Benton (a distance of 63 miles), and probably crossed this road in the vicinity of
Twenty-eight-mile spring. The Oksut or Teton ridge is passed in the left offing.
Captain Lewis, with perhaps more courage than prudence, has undertaken a
hazardous thing, with only three men at his back, even though these were the
pick of the whole party. We shall follow him with an eager, almost painful,
interest to a scene of bloodshed, a hair-breadth escape, and a precipitate retreat.

sufficiently strong. In order, therefore, to avoid, if possible, an interview with them, we hurried across the [Teton] river to a thick wood; and having turned out the horses to graze, Drewyer went in quest of the buffalo to kill it, and ascertain whether the wound was given by Indians, while the rest reconnoitered the whole country. In about three hours they all returned without having seen the buffalo or any Indians in the plains. We then dined, and two of the party resumed their search, but could see no signs of Indians; we therefore slept in safety. Tansy river is here about 50 yards wide, though its water occupies only 35 feet, and is not more than three in depth. It most probably arises [does arise] within the first range of the Rocky mountains; its general course is from east to west, and as far as we are able to trace it through wide bottoms, well supplied with both the long- and broad-leaved cottonwood. The hills on its banks are from 100 to 150 feet in height, and possess bluffs of earth, like the lower part of the Missouri; the bed is formed of small gravel and mud; the water is turbid and of a whitish tint; the banks are low, but never overflowed—in short, except in depth and velocity, it is a perfect miniature of the Missouri.

July 18th.[40] A little before sunrise we continued on a course N. 25° W. for six miles, when we reached the top of a high plain which divides the waters of Maria's and Tansy rivers, and a mile further reached a creek of the former, about 25 yards wide, though with no water except in occasional pools in the bed. Down this creek we pro-

[40] All of to-day's text requires correction by the codex, Lewis L 106, 107, as it is faulty in several particulars. The "high plain" is the general elevation which further eastward is called Bec d'Outard (or d'Otard) and in the west presents an elevation known as the Knee. Lewis' route here strikes obliquely the well-known Whoop-up trail which crosses between the Knee and the Bec. While at this height Captain Lewis notes by name various mountains which are in full view in different directions, as the Tower mountains (Sweetgrass hills) to the N., and others to the N.E., E., and S.E. " Our course led us nearly parallel with a creek of Maria's river which takes it's rise on these high plains at the place we passed them; at noon we struck this creek about 6 ms. from it's junction with

ceeded [N. 15° W.] for twelve miles through thick groves
of timber on its banks, passing such immense quantities of
buffalo that the whole seemed to be a single herd.   Accompanying them were great numbers of wolves, besides which
we saw some antelopes and hares [*Lepus campestris*].   After
dinner we left this creek, which we (*p. 345*) called Buffalo
creek, and crossing the plain [due north] for six miles, came
to Maria's river, where we camped in a grove of cottonwood
on its western [southern] side, keeping watch through the
night lest we should be surprised by Indians.   Captain Lewis
was now convinced that he was above the point to which he
had formerly ascended [in June, 1805], and feared that some
branch might come in on the north, between that point and
our present position.   Early in the morning, therefore,

July 19*th*, he dispatched two hunters [Drewyer and J.
Fields], who descended the river in a direction N. 80° E., till
they came to our former position [of June, 1805], at the distance of six miles, without seeing any stream except Buffalo creek [which they passed two miles below our present
camp, Lewis L 107].   Having completed an observation of
the sun's meridian altitude, Captain Lewis [crossed and]
proceeded along the north side of Maria's river.   The
bottoms are in general about half a mile wide ; they
possess considerable quantities of cottonwood timber, and
an underbrush consisting of honeysuckle, rosebushes, narrow-leaved willow, and the plant called by the engagees
buffalo-grease.   The plains are level and beautiful, but the
soil is thin and overrun with prickly-pears.   It consists of

Maria's river, where we found some cottonwood timber ; here we halted to
dine . . . . hence downwards there is a considerable quantity of timber," etc.,
L 106.   So there is no " twelve miles " of thick woods ; it was the buffalo that
were "thick" for this distance.   After dinner Captain Lewis left the creek,
which ran too easterly for his course, and went five or six miles due north to
Maria's river, which he struck only two miles above the point where the creek
fell into it.   This creek, named Buffalo in the text, seems to be that now charted
as Antelope creek ; and the branch of it down which the party went, to be
Piser or Piser's.   But the best maps are so widely discrepant here, that this
tentative identification is open to question.

a sort of white or whitish-blue clay, which after being trod-
den, when wet, by the buffalo, stands up in sharp, hard points,
which are as painful to the horses as the great quantity of
small gravel, which is everywhere scattered over the ground,
is in other parts of the plains. The bluffs of the river are
high, steep, and irregular, and composed of a sort of earth
which easily dissolves and slips into the water, though with
occasional strata of freestone near the tops. The bluffs of
the Missouri above Maria's river differ from these in consisting of a firm red or yellow clay, which does not yield to
water, and a large proportion of rock. The buffalo are not
so abundant as they were yesterday; but there are still
antelopes, wolves, geese, pigeons, doves, hawks, ravens,
crows, larks, and sparrows, though the curlew has disappeared.

At the distance of eight miles a large creek falls[41] in on
the south [?] side; seven miles beyond it is another, 30
yards wide, (*p. 346*) which seems to issue from three mountains [Three Buttes or Sweetgrass hills] stretching from east
to west, in a direction N. 10° W. from its mouth, and which,

[41] I can find no large creek on the *south* in anything like the required position,
and suspect a lurking error here, which I am unable to correct.   Text is true to
the codex, which has : " S. 80° W. 20 ms. up Maria's river to the place of our
encampment on its N. side.   Passed a large creek on South side with some
timber on its valley at 8 ms. also another large creek on N. side at 15 ms.   this
last is 30 yds. wide," etc.   This extract is from the formal " courses and distances" of to-day, L 108, but I observe that no creek from the *south* is mentioned
in the narrative of to-day, L 107, where we read : " up the N. side of the river
20 miles and encamped.   at 15 miles we passed a large creek on N. side," etc.
In fact, I am not satisfied with any identifications that I can offer, even pro-
visionally, thus far on Maria's river ; and the difficulty of adjustment with the
furthest point said to have been reached by Captain Lewis in 1805 is equally
great.   But the large creek from the *north*, reached at 15 miles of to-day's
20 mile march, is certainly Willow or Sweetgrass creek, the largest stream making south from the Three Buttes or Sweetgrass hills (the Broken mountains of
the text).   Now we know where the party is, though we do not see exactly how
they got there ; and we can confidently set their camp on the north bank of
Maria's river, five miles above the mouth of Sweetgrass creek (Clark's 1814 map
charts this creek, nameless : see the forked stream making in from the north
between the word " Maria's " and the letter " R.").

from their loose, irregular, and ragged appearance, we called
the Broken mountains. That in the center terminates in a
conic spire, for which reason we called it Tower mountain.[42]
After making 20 miles we halted for the night.

July 20th. We continued our route up the river, through
a country resembling that which we passed yesterday, except
that the plains are more broken, and the appearances of
mineral salts, common to the Missouri plains, are more
abundant than usual; these are discerned in all the pools,
which indeed at present contain the only water to be found
throughout the plains, and are so strongly impregnated as
to be unfit for any use, except that of the buffalo, which
seem to prefer it to even the water of the river. The low
grounds are well timbered, and contain also silk-grass, sand-
rush, wild liquorice, and sunflowers, the barbs [*sic*—read
latter, Lewis L 110] of which are now in bloom. Besides the
geese, ducks, and other birds common to the country, we
have seen fewer buffalo to-day than yesterday, though elk,
wolves, and antelopes continue in equal numbers; there is
also much appearance of beaver, but none of otter. At the
distance of six miles we passed a creek from the south [?];
18 miles further, one from the north [?], four miles beyond
which we camped.[43] The river is here 120 yards wide, and

[42] Tower mountain and the Broken mountains were so named, June 5th, 1805 :
see note [35], p. 349, and note [37], p. 350, where these elevations were identified as
the Three Buttes or Sweetgrass hills.

[43] Lewis L 110 : " S. 80° W. 28 ms. with the river in its course upwards to our
encampment of this evening on it's N. side. river 120 yds. wide and deep . . .
passed a creek on S. side at 6 ms. also another [at] 22 ms. on the N. side this
last has no water some little timber bed 15 yds. wide." Text and codex alike
reverse these creeks both as to distances and direction. The required adjustment is : At 18 miles from camp we passed opposite the mouth of a (dry) creek
from the *south ;* at 6 miles further we crossed a creek from the *north ;* 4 miles
beyond which we camped on the N. side of Maria's river, having made 28 miles.
This adjustment is borne out by the requirements of to-morrow's 15 miles to the
forks ; it is further justified by the relative positions of the two creeks charted
by Clark below Battle river ; and it is required by the known geography of the
region, unless the maps are wrong. Assuming its correctness, identifications are
easy : 1. The creek at " 18 " miles, from the south, without water, is that now
known as the Dry Fork of Maria's river ; old Fort Conrad was at its mouth, where

its water is but little diminished as we ascend. Its general course is very straight. From the apparent descent of the country to the north and above the Broken mountains, it seems probable that the south branch of the Saskashawan receives some of its waters from these plains[44], and that one of its streams must, in descending from the Rocky mountains, pass not far from Maria's river, to the northeast of the Broken mountains. We slept in peace, without being annoyed by mosquitoes, which we have not seen since we left the Whitebear islands.

also the Whoop-up trail crossed the river, and where the Canada and Great Falls R. R. now crosses, coming south from Milk river, past Sweetgrass, Rocky Ridge, and Rocky Springs, along Medicine Rock coulée. This latter is : 2. The other creek, from the north, falling in at " 22 " or at 24 miles of this day's journey ; on this is Shelby Junction, where the Great Northern Ry. crosses the other railroad just named, some 10 miles N.W. or N.N.W. of Old Fort Conrad. We pitch camp " four " miles above the mouth of this last creek or coulée, on the north bank of the Maria's river ; this point being about the same distance below a certain Shultz creek which makes in on the south, from Trunk Ridge, and will be passed unnoticed to-morrow. Maria's river is now running in " bad lands," as indicated by the statement in the text that " the plains are more broken."

[44] A conjecture which, however plausible it seemed then, is refuted by the facts as subsequently ascertained, for the whole Milk River country intervenes. See note [27], p. 345.

CHAPTER XXXIII.

CAPTAIN LEWIS' EXPLORATION OF MARIA'S RIVER : CONTINUED—REUNION OF THE EXPEDITION.

Forks of Maria's river—The North fork taken—Cooking with bois de vache—Sources of Maria's river in the Rocky mountains—Bad Indian sign—No game—Minnetarees of Fort de Prairie suspected to be in the vicinity—Determination to break camp, now named Camp Disappointment—Across country to a branch of Maria's river—Down this toward the forks—Unwelcome sight of a party of about 30 Indian horsemen—Friendly advances of Captain Lewis—Eight Indians advance and shake hands—They are Minnetarees— A colloquy—Camp together—Treachery of the Indians—Attempted robbery—R. Fields kills one Indian—Captain Lewis shoots another—The party wins horses in the fight— They make a forced march from Battle creek about 80 miles toward the Missouri— They (July 28th) meet Sergeant Ordway's and Sergeant Gass' parties coming down river together, and all proceed to their camp on the Missouri of May 29th, 1805—They descend the Missouri to the mouth of the Yellowstone (August 7th), where they find a note from Captain Clark, who had already reached this point and would wait for them below— They descend to White-earth river—Cruzatte shoots Captain Lewis by mistake for an elk— The party proceeds—They reach a camp of Dickson and Hancock—They learn that Captain Clark is below—Are overtaken by Colter and Collins—They proceed to Captain Clark's camp—Reunion of the Expedition on the Missouri, August 12th, 1806.

ONDAY, July 21st, 1806. At sunrise we proceeded along the northern side of the river for a short distance, when finding the ravines too steep, we crossed to the south ; but after continuing for three miles, returned to the north, and took our course through the plains, at some distance from the river. After making 15 miles, we came to the forks of the river, the largest branch of which bears S. 75° W. [about 30 miles] to the mountains, while the course of the other is N. 40° W. We halted for dinner; and believing, on examination, that the northern branch came from the mountains and would probably lead us to the most northern extent of Maria's ri- (*p. 348*) ver, we proceeded, though at a distance over the plains, till we struck it eight miles from the junction. This river [*i. e.*, the North fork, now called Cut-bank river] is about 30 yards wide ; the water clear, but shallow and unfit for navigation. It is closely confined between cliffs of freestone ; the adjacent country is

broken and poor. We crossed to the south side and proceeded [up this fork N. 25° W.] for five miles, till we
camped[1] under a cliff, where, not seeing any timber, we
made a fire of buffalo-dung, and passed the night.

July 22d. We went on [up the west side of Cut-bank
river]; but as the ground was now steep and unequal, and
the horses' feet were very sore, we were obliged to proceed
slowly. The river is still confined by freestone cliffs, till at
seven miles [N. 30° W. from camp] the country opens, is
less covered with gravel, and has some bottoms, though
destitute of timber or underbrush. The river here makes a
considerable bend to the northwest, so that we crossed the
plains [S. 80° W.] for 11 miles, when we again crossed the
river [from south to north]. Here we halted for dinner;
and having no wood, made a fire of the dung of buffalo, with
which we cooked the last of our meat, except a piece of
spoiled buffalo. Our course [N. 80° W.] then lay across a
level, beautiful plain, with wide bottoms near the bank of the
river. The banks are three or four feet high, but are not
overflowed. After [thus] crossing for ten miles a bend of

---

[1] Lewis L 112: "S. 80° W. 15 ms. with the river upwards. it forks at the
extremity of this course and the main or Southern branch bears S. 75° W. about
30 ms. to the mountains. N. 40° W. 6 ms. up the North branch, 30 yds. wide
confined closely between clifts of rocks, shallow rapid and not navigable. N.
25° W. 7 ms. still with the N. fork upwards. we struck the river [*i. e.* this N.
fork, Cut-bank river] at 2 miles from the Commencement of this Course, passed
[crossed] it and continued on it's South side." This is highly satisfactory for
distances, and serves also to strengthen the positions I have assigned for yesterday and the day before that. The two forks of Maria's river are now known as
Cut-bank river, the northern fork, and Two Medicine Lodge river, the southern
fork, the latter being the main stream. On striking these forks, Captain Lewis
has reached the S.E. corner of the present Blackfoot Indian Reservation, one
boundary of which meanders Cut-bank river northward, while another boundary
runs up Birch creek—which latter is the Battle creek of L. and C., as we shall
presently see. Captain Lewis follows up Cut-bank river 13 miles, and thus to
a point somewhat beyond the mouth of Snake creek from the east, where the
Grt. N. Ry. crosses. This Cut-bank crossing is scheduled as 25 miles west of
Shelby Junction by rail—in very close agreement with the L. and C. estimate
of 28 miles by the river from camp to-day. A little below the forks there is or
was a place on the river called Abbott.

the river toward the south, we saw, for the first time during the day, a clump of cottonwood trees in an extensive bottom ; and [having recrossed the river from its north to its south side] halted there for the night.[2]

This place is about ten miles below the foot of the Rocky mountains ; and being now able to trace distinctly that the point at which the river issued from those mountains was to the south of west, we concluded that we had reached its most northern point ; and as we have ceased to hope that any branches of Maria's river extend as far north as the 50th degree of latitude, we deemed it useless to proceed further, and rely chiefly on Milk and White-earth rivers for the desired boundary.   We therefore determined to remain here two days, for the purpose of making the necessary observations and resting our horses.

(*p. 349*) *July* 23*d*.   Drewyer was sent to examine the bearings of the river, till its entrance into the mountains,

___

[2] To appreciate the brackets in the text, compare Lewis L 114, as follows : " N. 30° W. 7 ms. with the river upwards. . . S. 80° W. 10 ms. through the plains, the river making a considerable bend to the wright or N.W. S. 75° W. 11 ms. through the plains on the N. side of the river which here made a considerable bend to the left or south. we passed the river to it's N. side at one mile from the commencement of this course and again recrossed it at the extremity of this course and encamped on its S. side." That is to say, the journey began and ended on the same (south) side of the river, which was twice crossed in the course of the 28 miles made to-day. Camp Disappointment is easy to locate, though it is not in the immediate vicinity of any named place. It is on the S. side of Cutbank river, a little west of the Riplinger road to Fort McLeod, and but little short of long. 113° W. The nearest named point is Blackfoot, a station on the Grt. N. Ry., some eight or ten miles southward, on Willow creek. The latitude is approximately 48° 40′ N.—the northernmost position ever reached by the Expedition—and thus about east of the Rocky Mountain passes severally called Flathead, Gunsight, and Cut-bank Pass ; the true Maria's Pass, through which the railroad goes, being considerably further south. The streams next north of the present station are some heads of Milk river, and north of these, though still south of 49°, are St. Mary's and Belly rivers, tributary to the Saskatchewan. Camp Disappointment is also about in the center of the present Blackfoot Reservation. Examine the position marked on Clark's map, where the two terminal forks of Maria's river are N. and S. forks of Cut-bank river, next below is Willow creek, and next below this, on the same side, is the true Maria's river, coming from Maria's pass, through which the railroad now goes.

which he found to be at the distance of ten miles, in a direction S. 50° W.   He had seen also the remains of a camp of
11 leathern lodges, recently abandoned, which induced us
to suppose that the Minnetarees of Fort de Prairie are
somewhere in this neighborhood—a suspicion which was
confirmed by the return of the hunters, who had seen no
game of any kind.   As these Indians have probably followed the buffalo toward the main branch of Maria's river,
we shall not strike it [this game] above the north branch.

The course of the mountains continues from southeast to
northwest; in which last direction from us the front range
appears to terminate abruptly at the distance of 35 miles.
Those which are to the southwest and more distinctly in
view, are of an irregular form, composed chiefly of clay,
with a very small mixture of rock, without timber; and
though low are yet partially covered with snow to their
bases.   The river itself has nearly doubled the volume of
water which it possessed when we first saw it below, a circumstance to be ascribed, no doubt, to the great evaporation and
absorption of the water in its passage through these open
plains.   The rock in this neighborhood is of a white color
and a fine grit, and lies in horizontal strata in the bluffs of
the river.   We attempted to take some fish, but could procure only a single trout.   We had, therefore, nothing to eat
except the grease which we pressed from our tainted meat
and [with which we] formed a mush of cows, reserving one
meal more of the same kind for to-morrow.   We have seen
near this place a number of the whistling-squirrel [*Spermophilus columbianus?*] common in the country watered by
the Columbia, but which we observed here for the first time
in the plains of the Missouri.   The cottonwood of this place
is similar to that of the Columbia.   Our observations this
evening were prevented by clouds.   The weather was clear
for a short time in the morning,

(*p. 350*) *July 24th*, but the sky soon clouded over, and it
rained during the rest of the day.   We were therefore
obliged to remain one day longer for the purpose of com-

pleting our observations. Our situation now became unpleasant from the rain, the coldness of the air, and the total absence of game; for the hunters could find nothing of a large kind, and we were obliged to subsist on a few pigeons and a kettle of mush made of the remainder of our bread of cows. This supplied us with one more meal in the morning,

July 25th, when, finding that the cold and rainy weather would still detain us here, two of the men were dispatched to hunt. They returned in the evening with a fine buck, on which we fared sumptuously. In their excursion they had gone [southward] as far as the main branch of Maria's river, at the distance of ten miles, through an open extensive valley, in which were scattered a great number of lodges lately evacuated.

July 26th. The weather was still cloudy, so that no observation could be made; and what added to our disappointment, Captain Lewis' chronometer stopped yesterday from some unknown cause, though when set in motion again it went as usual. We now despaired of taking the longitude of this place; and as our staying any longer might endanger our return to the United States during the present season, we therefore waited till nine o'clock, in hopes of a change of weather; but seeing no prospect of that kind, we mounted our horses, and leaving with reluctance our position, which we now named Camp Disappointment, directed our course across the open plains, in a direction nearly southeast.[3] At

[3] We must follow Lewis L 118 carefully, if we are to find where the fight took place. "I took my rout through the open plains S.E. 5 ms. passing a small creek at 2 ms. . . when I changed my direction to S. 75° E. for 7 ms. further and struck a principal branch of Maria's river 65 yds. wide, not very deep, I passed this stream to it's south side and continued down it 2 ms. on the last mentioned course, when another branch of nearly the same dignity formed a junction with it, coming from the S.W. . . . . I passed the S. branch just above it's junction, and continued down the river which runs a little N. of E. 1 m. and halted to dine." Captain Lewis thus comes down nearly with the Riplinger road already mentioned; he soon crosses Willow creek, a small tributary of Cut-bank river from the S.W., whose mouth he had not noticed in going up that river, as he was then on the N. side of it; he next crosses the line of the Grt.

12 miles' distance [having crossed Willow creek at two miles from camp] we reached [Two Medicine Lodge river] a branch of Maria's river, about 65 yards wide, which we crossed, and continued along its southern side for two miles, where it is joined by another branch [Badger river], nearly equal in size from the southwest, and far more clear than the north branch, which is turbid, though the beds of both are composed of pebbles. We now decided on pursuing this river [resulting from the confluence of Badger with Two Medicine Lodge] to its junction with (*p. 351*) that [North] fork of Maria's river which we had ascended, then cross the country obliquely to Tansy [Teton] river, and descend that stream to its confluence with Maria's river. We therefore crossed and descended the river; and at one mile below the junction, halted to let the horses graze in a fertile bottom, in which were some Indian lodges that appeared to have been inhabited during the past winter. We here discern more timber than the country in general possesses; for, besides an undergrowth of rose, honeysuckle, and redberry bushes, and a small quantity of willow timber, the three species of cottonwood, the narrow-leaved, the broad-leaved, and the species known to the Columbia, though here seen for the first time on the Missouri, are all united at this place. Game appears in greater abundance. We saw a few antelopes and wolves, and killed a buck, besides which we saw also two of the small burrowing-foxes [*Vulpes velox*] of the plains, about the size of the common domestic cat, and of a reddish-brown color, except the [tip of the] tail, which is black.

N. Ry. at a point in the vicinity of Carlow station, six miles E. of Blackfoot station; he then reaches Two Medicine Lodge river, which is the main fork of Maria's, at or near a point where a Mission was established; crosses this river here and follows down its S. bank to the confluence of Badger river, a short distance up which was a trading-post and is now the Blackfoot Indian Agency or Piegan P. O.; crosses Badger river at its mouth, and continues down the now united streams, which constitute the main or South fork of Maria's river, passed going up on the 21st. After dinner he will proceed three miles further down this stream, on its south side, and there encounter the hostiles.

At the distance of three miles we ascended the hills close to the river-side, while Drewyer pursued the valley of the river on the opposite side. But scarcely had Captain Lewis reached the high plain when he saw, about a mile on his left, a collection of about 30 horses. He immediately halted, and by the aid of his spy-glass discovered that one-half of the horses were saddled, and that on the eminence above the horses several Indians were looking down toward the river, probably at Drewyer. This was a most unwelcome sight. Their probable numbers rendered any contest with them of doubtful issue; to attempt to escape would only invite pursuit, and our horses were so bad that we must certainly be overtaken; besides which, Drewyer could not yet be aware that the Indians were near, and if we ran he would most probably be sacrificed. We therefore determined to make the most of our situation, and advance toward them in a friendly manner. The flag which we had brought in case of any such accident was therefore displayed, and we con- (*p. 352*) tinued slowly our march toward them. Their whole attention was so engaged by Drewyer that they did not immediately discover us. As soon as they did see us, they appeared to be much alarmed and ran about in confusion; some of them came down the hill and drove their horses within gunshot of the eminence, to which they then returned, as if to await our arrival. When we came within a quarter of a mile, one of the Indians mounted and rode at full speed to receive us; but when within a hundred paces of us, he halted. Captain Lewis, who had alighted to receive him, held out his hand and beckoned to him to approach; he only looked at us for some time, and then, without saying a word, returned to his companions with as much haste as he had advanced. The whole party now descended the hill and rode toward us. As yet we saw only eight, but presumed that there must be more behind us, as there were several horses saddled.ᵃ We how-

---

That did not necessarily follow. These Indians were a hunting-party, with spare ponies to exchange for those already ridden when about to run buffalo, just as an Englishman would ride his hack to the meet and then mount his

ever advanced, and Captain Lewis now told his two men that he believed these were the Minnetarees of Fort de Prairie, who, from their infamous character, would in all probability attempt to rob us; but being determined to die rather than lose his papers and instruments, he intended to resist to the last extremity, and advised them to do the same, and to be on the alert should there be any disposition to attack us. When the two parties came within a hundred yards of each other, all the Indians, except one, halted. Captain Lewis therefore ordered his two men to halt while he advanced, and after shaking hands with the Indian, went on and did the same with the others in the rear, while the Indian himself shook hands with the two men. They all now came up ; and after alighting, the Indians asked to smoke with us. Captain Lewis, who was very anxious for Drewyer's safety, told them that the man who had gone down the river had the pipe, and requested that as they had seen him, one of them would accompany R. Fields, to bring him back. To this they assented, and Fields went with a young man in search of Drewyer.

Captain Lewis now asked them by signs (*p. 353*) if they were the Minnetarees of the North, and was sorry to learn by their answer that his suspicion was too true. He then inquired if there was any chief among them. They pointed out three ; but though he did not believe them, yet it was thought best to please them, and he therefore gave to one a flag, to another a medal, and to a third a handkerchief. They appeared to be well satisfied with these presents, and now recovered from the agitation into which our first interview had thrown them ; for they were really more alarmed than ourselves at the meeting. In our turn, however, we became equally satisfied on finding that they were

hunter. Not far from this very spot, a party of which I was a member came as unexpectedly upon just such an outfit of Piegans, who, when they had satisfied their curiosity at our approach, mounted their led horses and were soon scouring the plain for buffalo. If there had been any more Indians than the eight Captain Lewis descried, they would have been on hand before next morning, and his whole party might have been cut off.

not joined by any more of their companions ; for we consider ourselves quite a match for eight Indians, particularly as these have but two guns, the rest being armed with only eye-dogs [or eye-daggs, Lewis L 127—a sort of war-hatchet] and bows and arrows. As it was growing late Captain Lewis proposed that they should camp together near the river; for he was glad to see them and had a great deal to say to them. They assented ; and being soon joined by Drewyer, we proceeded toward the river, and after descending a very steep bluff, 250 feet high, camped in a small bottom.[5]

Here the Indians formed a large semicircular tent of dressed buffalo-skins, in which the two parties assembled ; and by the means of Drewyer, the evening was spent in conversation with the Indians. They informed us that they were a part of a large band which at present were camped on the main branch of Maria's river, near the foot of the Rocky mountains, at the distance of a day and a half's journey from this place. Another large band were hunting buffalo near the Broken mountains, from which they would proceed in a few days to the north of Maria's river. With the first of these there was a white man. They added that from this place to the establishment on the Saskashawan at which they trade is only six days' easy march—that is, such a day's journey as can be made with their women and children ; so that we computed the distance at 150 miles. There

---

[5] Lewis L 122 : "we decended a very steep bluff about 250 feet high to the river where there was a small bottom of nearly ½ a mile in length and about 250 yards wide in the widest part, the river washed the bluffs both above and below us and through it's course in this part is very deep ; the bluffs are so steep that there are but few places where they could be ascended, and are broken in several places by deep nitches which extend back from the river several hundred yards, their bluffs being so steep that it is impossible to ascend them ; in this bottom there stand tree [three] solitary trees near one of which the indians formed a large simicircular camp of dressed buffaloe skins and invited us to partake of their shelter which Drewyer and myself accepted and the Fieldses lay near the fire in front." These topographical details fix the spot absolutely, when taken in connection with the broader geographical features already given. I do not think that the actual scene of the conflict has ever before been determined.

they carry the skins of wolves and (*p. 354*) beavers, to exchange for guns, ammunition, blankets, spirituous liquors,
and other articles of Indian traffic.   Captain Lewis in turn
informed them that he had come from a great distance up
the large river which runs toward the rising sun; that he
had been as far as the great lake where the sun sets; that
he had seen many nations, the greater part of whom were at
war with each other, but by his mediation were restored to
peace ; that all had been invited to come and trade with him
west of the mountains; that he was now on his way home,
but had left his companions at the falls, and come in search
of the Minnetarees, in hopes of inducing them to live at
peace with their neighbors, and to visit the trading-houses
which would be formed at the entrance of Maria's river.
They said that they were anxious to be at peace with the
Tushepaws ; but those people had lately killed a number of
their relations, as they proved by showing several of the
party who had their hair cut as a sign of mourning.   They
were equally willing, they added, to come down and trade
with us.   Captain Lewis therefore proposed that they should
send some of their young men to invite all their band to
meet us at the mouth of Maria's river, the rest of the party
to go with us to that place, where he hoped to find his men ;
offering them ten horses and some tobacco in case they
would accompany us.   To this they made no reply.   Finding them very fond of the pipe, Captain Lewis, who was
desirous of keeping a constant watch during the night,
smoked with them until a late hour.[6]   As soon as they
were all asleep, he woke R. Fields, and ordering him to
rouse us all in case any Indians left the camp, as they
would probably attempt to steal our horses, he lay down by
the side of Drewyer in the tent with all the Indians, while
the Fields were stretched near the fire at the mouth of it.

[6] Lewis L 124: "I plyed them with the pipe until late at night. . . I took
the first watch to-night and set up untill half after eleven ; the indians by this
time were all asleep [or feigned to be?].   I roused up R. Fields and laid down
myself ; . . . I fell into a profound sleep."

Sunday, July 27th. At sunrise, the Indians got up and crowded around the fire near which J. Fields, who was then on watch, had carelessly left his rifle, near the head of his brother, who was still (*p. 355*) asleep. One of the Indians slipped behind him, and, unperceived, took his brother's and his own rifle, while at the same time two others seized those of Drewyer and Captain Lewis. As soon as Fields turned, he saw the Indian running off with the rifles; instantly calling his brother, they pursued him for 50 or 60 yards; just as they overtook him, in the scuffle for the rifles R. Fields stabbed him through the heart with his knife. The Indian ran about fifteen steps and fell dead. They now ran back with their rifles to the camp. The moment the fellow touched his gun, Drewyer, who was awake, jumped up and wrested it from him. The noise awoke Captain Lewis,[7] who instantly started from the ground and reached for his gun; but finding it gone, drew a pistol from his belt, and turning saw the Indian running off with it. He followed him and ordered him to lay it down, which he did just as the two Fields came up, and were taking aim to shoot him; when Captain Lewis ordered

---

[7] The account of the sad affair is so close to the codex that there is little to add, but I give an extract in Captain Lewis' words, L 125 : " Drewyer who was awake saw the indian take hold of his gun and instantly jumped up and sized her and rested her from him but the indian still retained his pouch, his jumping up and crying damn you let go my gun awakened me I jumped up and asked what was the matter which I quickly learned when I saw drewyer in a scuffle with the indian for his gun, I reached to seize my gun but found her gone, I then drew a pistol from my holster and terning myself about saw the indian making off with my gun I ran at him with my pistol and bid him lay down my gun which he was in the act of doing when the Fieldses returned and drew up their guns to shoot him which I forbid. . . as soon as they found us all in the possession of our arms they ran and indeavored to drive off all the horses I now hollowed to the men and told them to fire on them if they attempted to drive off our horses, they accordingly pursued the main party who were driving the horses up the river and I pursued the man who had taken my gun who with another was driving off a part of the horses which were to the left of the camp, I pursued them so closely that they could not take twelve of their own horses but continued to drive one of mine with some others ; at the distance of 300 paces they entered one of those steep nitches in the bluff with the horses before them being nearly out of breath I could pursue no further, I called to them as I

them not to fire, as the Indian did not appear to intend any mischief.   He dropped the gun and was going slowly off when Drewyer came out and asked permission to kill him ; but this Captain Lewis forbade, as he had not yet attempted to shoot us.   But finding that the Indians were now endeavoring to drive off all the horses, he ordered [all] three of us to follow the main party, who were chasing the horses up the river, and fire instantly upon the thieves ; while he, without taking time to run for his shot-pouch, pursued the fellow who had stolen his gun and another Indian, who were driving away the horses on the left of the camp.   He pressed them so closely that they left twelve of their horses, but continued to drive off one of our own.   At the distance of 300 paces they entered a steep niche in the river-bluffs, when Captain Lewis, being too much out of breath to pursue them any further, called out, as he had done several times before, that unless they gave up the horse he would shoot them.   As he raised his gun one of the Indians jumped behind a rock and spoke to the other, who stopped (*p. 356*) at the distance of thirty paces.   Captain Lewis shot him in the belly.   He fell on his knees and right elbow ;

had done several times before that I would shoot them if they did not give me my horse and raised my gun, one of them jumped behind a rock and spoke to the other who turned arround and stoped at the distance of 30 steps from me and I shot him through the belly, he fell to his knees and on his wright elbow from which position he partly raised himself up and fired at me, and turning himself about crawled in behind a rock which was a few feet from him.   he overshot me, being bearheaded I felt the wind of his bullet very distinctly.   not having my shotpouch I could not reload my piece and as there were two of them behind good shelters from me I did not think it prudent to rush on them with my pistol which had I discharged I had not the means of reloading untill I reached camp ; I therefore returned leasurely towards camp."

The picture of " Captain Lewis shooting an Indian," which illustrates the affair in the Phila. eds. of Gass' Journal, gives him five men to four Indians ; he had but three to eight Indians.   In his personal encounter he was alone, with two Indians against him : " the Fieldses told me that three [two] of the indians whom they pursued swam the river one of them on my horse.   and that two others ascended the hill and escaped from them with a part of their horses, two I had pursued into the nitch one lay dead near camp and the eighth we could not account for but suppose that he ran off early in the contest," Lewis L **128**.

but raising himself a little, fired and then crawled behind a rock. The shot had nearly been fatal, for Captain Lewis, who was bareheaded, felt the wind of the ball very distinctly. Not having his shot-pouch, he could not reload his rifle ; and having only a single load for his pistol, he thought it most prudent not to attack the Indians, and therefore retired slowly to the camp. He was met by Drewyer, who, hearing the report of the guns, had come to his assistance, leaving the Fields to pursue the Indians. Captain Lewis ordered him to call out to them to desist from the pursuit, as we could take the horses of the Indians in place of our own ; but they were at too great a distance to hear him. He therefore returned to the camp ; and whilst he was saddling the horses, the Fields returned with four of our own, having followed the Indians until two of them swam the river and two others ascended the hills, so that the horses became dispersed.

We, however, were rather gainers by this contest, for we took four of the Indian horses, and lost only one of our own. Besides which, we found in the camp four shields, two bows with quivers, and one of the guns, which we took with us, as also the flag which we had presented to the Indians, but left the medal round the neck of the dead man, in order that they might be informed who we were. The rest of their baggage, except some buffalo-meat, we left ;[8] and as there was no time to be lost, we mounted our horses, and after ascending the river-hills, took our course through the beautiful level plains, in a direction a little to the south of east. We had no doubt but that we should be immediately pursued by a much larger party, and that as soon as intelligence was given to the band near the Broken mountains, they would hasten to the mouth of Maria's river to intercept us.

[8] In ashes. " While the men were preparing the horses I put four sheilds and two bows and quivers of arrows which had been left on the fire, with sundry other articles ; they left all their baggage at our mercy. they had but two guns and one of them they left the others were armed with bows and arrows and eyedaggs. the gun we took with us. I also retook the flagg, but left the medal about the neck of the dead man," Lewis L 127.

We hoped, however, to be there before them, so as to form a junction with our friends. We therefore pushed our horses as fast as we possibly could; fortunately for us, the Indian (*p. 357*) horses were very good, the plains perfectly level, without many stones or prickly-pears, and in fine order for traveling after the late rains. At eight miles from our camp we passed a stream 40 yards wide, to which, from the occurrence of the morning, we gave the name of Battle river.[9] At three o'clock we reached Rose [or Tansy] river, five miles above where we had formerly[10] passed it; and having now come by estimate 63 miles, halted for an hour and a half to refresh our horses. We then pursued our journey 17 miles further, when, as night came on, we killed a buffalo, and again stopped for two hours. The sky was now overclouded, but as the moon gave light enough to show us the

[9] "Battle R." is the only branch of Maria's river charted by Clark by name, except "Tansey R." Observe that the collision was not on *this* river, but the next above it, and that they struck Battle river eight miles from the scene its name commemorates. The place of action is intended to be represented by Clark at that point where the dotted trail is bent into an elbow: for the precise spot, see a preceding note. Battle river is now known as Birch river or creek, which for some distance forms the southern boundary of the Blackfoot Indian Reservation from Maria's river, near its forks, toward the main divide of the Rocky mountains. This stream was reached and crossed but a short distance above its mouth, whence a forced march was made straight for the Teton. Fortunately Captain Lewis and his men were thoroughly alive to the danger of their situation, and understood that their lives depended on putting as many miles as possible behind them, in order not to be overtaken and "wiped out" by the larger body of hostiles then in the country, who would get word of the fight in a few hours. They escaped unhurt; but the affair had far-reaching consequences. "In consequence of the death of this man at the hands of Captain Lewis, a treacherous and lurking hostility was excited in the breasts of the Blackfeet (and it is presumed still remains), which induced the American Fur Company to establish a strong fort, with a force of sixty men, at the mouth of Maria's river," Irving, quoted in the M'Vickar ed. of L. and C. 1842, II. p. 274. When I was at Fort Benton, in 1874, having come down from the Milk river region along Maria's river, an escort of cavalry was required for the safety of the party, and our scout (George Boyd) was full of bloody stories. Within his own knowledge were scores of dark deeds that never saw the light of history, and the memory of which has since perished with the participants.

[10] On the 17th inst. The estimate of 63 miles from the scene of action to the point thus indicated seems to me very close. The distance is certainly not over-

route, we continued through immense herds of buffalo for 20 miles, and then, almost exhausted with fatigue, halted at two in the morning,

July 28th, to rest ourselves and the horses. At daylight we awoke sore and scarcely able to stand; but as our own lives as well as those of our companions depended on our pressing forward, we mounted our horses and set out. The men were desirous of crossing the Missouri at Grog spring, where Rose river approaches so near the river, and passing down the southwest side of it, thus avoiding the country at the junction of the two rivers, through which the enemy would most probably pursue us. But as this circuitous route would consume the whole day, and the Indians might in the meantime attack the canoes at the point [*i. e.*, mouth of Maria's river], Captain Lewis told his party it was now their duty to risk their lives for their friends and companions; that he would proceed immediately to the point to give the alarm to the canoes; and if they had not yet arrived he would raft the Missouri, and after hiding the baggage, ascend the river on foot through the woods till he met them. He told them also that it was his determination, in case they were attacked in crossing the plains, to tie the bridles of the horses and stand together till they either routed their enemies, or sold their lives as dearly as possible.

To this they all assented, (*p. 358*) and we therefore con-

stated if, as I judge, they struck the Teton somewhere in the vicinity of Perrysburg. The codex says that after the halt they followed down Rose river in the bottoms, but finding it inconvenient to cross and recross the stream so often as they were obliged to, they left the bottoms and ascended the hills on the S.W. side. The 17 additional miles thus made should put them somewhere in the vicinity of Valleux; and 20 more by moonlight would bring them near Fort Benton. On resuming the march in the morning and before reaching Grog spring, at the narrow isthmus of the Cracon du Nez, the men proposed to put the Missouri between themselves and the hostiles before approaching the mouth of Maria's river. The insistence of Captain Lewis was, that the party should proceed direct to that point—the " point" of to-morrow text, left unspecified, being the mouth of Maria's river—to which the men who were coming down the Missouri in the canoes had been ordered to proceed and there await Captain Lewis' return from his reconnoissance.

tinued our route to the eastward, till at the distance of twelve miles we came near the Missouri, when we heard a noise which seemed like the report of a gun. We therefore quickened our pace for eight miles further, and about five miles from Grog spring heard distinctly the noise of several rifles from the river. We hurried to the bank, and saw with exquisite satisfaction our friends[11] coming down the river. They landed to greet us, and after turning our horses loose we embarked with our baggage, and went down to the spot where we had made a deposit. This, after reconnoitering the adjacent country, we opened; but, unfortunately, the cache had caved in, and most of the articles were injured. We took whatever was still worth preserving, and immediately proceeded to the point, where we found our deposits in good order.

By singular good fortune we were here joined by Sergeant Gass[12] and Willard from the falls, who had been ordered to bring the horses here to assist in collecting meat for the voyage, as it had been calculated that the canoes would reach this place much sooner than Captain Lewis' party. After a very heavy shower of rain and hail, attended with violent

[11] Sergeant Ordway's party, who had left Captain Clark at the Three Forks of the Missouri, to which they had come down the Jefferson, and navigated the Missouri to the Great Falls, made the portage there, and were now just in the nick of time to reinforce Captain Lewis. The latter says, L 130 : "On arriving at the bank of the river we had the unspeakable satisfaction to see our canoes coming down. We hurried down from the bluff on which we were and joined them striped our horses and gave them a final discharge imbarking without loss of time with our baggage. I now learned that they had brought all things safe, having sustained no loss nor met with any accident of importance. Wiser had cut his leg badly with a knife, and was unable in consequence to work. We decended the river opposite to our principal cash [cache] which we proceeded to open after reconnoitering the adjacent country."

[12] Gass' Journal gives fully the movements of his own and Sergeant Ordway's party. The latter joined him on the 19th, consisting of Ordway and nine men, who had come from Captain Clark's party down the Missouri from the Three Forks in the canoes. The whole were occupied with the portage of the Great Falls till the 27th, when most of them started down the Missouri in the canoes, and Gass and Willard set out overland for the mouth of Maria's river. They proceeded about 20 miles through the plains, and there struck Tansy or

thunder and lightning, we left the point, and giving a final discharge to our horses, went over to the island where we had left our red periogue, which, however, we found so much decayed that we had no means of repairing her.   We there-fore took all the iron work out of her, proceeded down the river 15 miles, and camped near some cottonwood trees, one of which was of the narrow-leaved species, and the first of that species we had remarked as we ascended the river.

Sergeant Ordway's party, which had left the mouth of Madison river on the 13th, had descended in safety to the White Bear islands, where they arrived on the 19th, and after collecting the baggage, left the falls on the 27th in the white periogue and five canoes; while Sergeant Gass and Willard set out at the same time by land with the horses, and thus fortunately all met together.

(*p. 359*) *July* 29th.   A violent storm of rain and hail came on last night ; and as we had no means of making a shelter we lay in the rain, and during the whole day continued so exposed.   The two small canoes [13] were sent ahead in order to hunt elk and buffalo, which are in immense quantities, so as to provide shelter as well as food for the party.   We then

Rose river, down which they passed for ten miles and camped.   " In our way we killed a buffalo and a goat [antelope].   The wolves in packs occasionally hunt these goats, which are too swift to be run down and taken by a single wolf. The wolves having fixed upon their intended prey and taken their stations, a part of the pack commence the chace, and running it in a circle are at certain intervals relieved by others.   In this manner they are able to run a goat down. At the Falls, where the wolves are plenty, I had an opportunity of seeing one of these hunts," Gass, p. 244.   "*July* 28th.   The morning was fine and pleasant, and at an early hour we proceeded down the river.   In our way we killed six goats or antelopes and seven buffaloes; and about one o'clock came to the point at the mouth of Maria's river, where we met with the party who had come down from the falls by water, and who had just arrived; and also unexpectedly with Captain Lewis and the three men who had gone with him.   They had joined the party descending the river this forenoon, after riding 120 miles since yesterday morning, when they had a skirmish with a party of the Prairie Grossventres or Bigbellied Indians who inhabit the plains up Maria's river," Gass, pp. 244, 245.

[13] The hunters in these canoes were the brothers Fields, Colter, and Collins. Camp of May 29th was " on the north, three-quarters of a mile above Slaughter river," for which and the Natural Walls see pp. 335, 338, and notes there.

proceeded very rapidly with the aid of a strong current, and after passing, at one o'clock, the Natural Walls, camped late in the evening at our former camp of the 29th of May, 1805. The river is now as high as it has been during the present season, and every little rivulet discharges torrents of water, which bring down such quantities of mud and sand that we can scarcely drink the water of the Missouri. The buffalo continue to be very numerous, but the elk are few. The bighorns,[14] however, are in great numbers along the steep cliffs of the river, and being now in fine order, their flesh is extremely tender, delicate, and well-flavored, resembling in color and flavor mutton, though it is not so strong. The brown curlew [*Numenius longirostris*] has disappeared, and has probably gone to some other climate after rearing its young in these plains.

July 30*th*. The rain still prevented us from stopping to dry our baggage ; we therefore proceeded with a strong current which, joined to our oars, enabled us to advance at the rate of seven miles an hour. We went ashore several times for the purpose of hunting, and procured several bighorns, two buffalo,[15] a beaver, an elk, and a female brown bear, whose talons were 6¼ inches in length. In the evening we camped on an island two miles above Goodrich's island [see note [10], p. 326]; and early in the morning,

July 31*st*, continued our route in the rain, passing, during the greater part of the day, through high pine hills, succeeded by low grounds abounding in timber and game. The buffalo are scarce, but we procured 15 elk, 14 deer, 2 bighorns, and a beaver. The elk are in fine order,

[14] Gass, p. 246, notes at this date that "Captain Lewis had four of these animals skeletonized, to take with him to the seat of government of the United States."

[15] While passing down this part of the Missouri in 1874, the Northern Boundary Survey, to which I was attached as surgeon and naturalist, found the buffalo and bighorns still very abundant. The buffalo were crossing the river, and their alarm at our flotilla of six Mackinaw boats sweeping down the river gave rise to a remarkable scene at a point where the banks were precipitous. We have all heard of the slaughter of buffalo by being urged over a precipice, but I fancy that the suicide of buffalo by their trying to climb cliffs too

particularly the males, who now herd together in (*p. 360*) small parties. Their horns have reached their full growth, but ill [still] retain the velvet or skin which covers them. Through the bottoms are scattered a number of lodges, some of which seem to have been built last winter, and were probably occupied by the Minnetarees of Fort de Prairie. The river is still rising, and more muddy than we have ever seen it. Late this night we took shelter from the rain in some old Indian lodges, about eight miles below the entrance of North-mountain creek, and then set out,

Friday, August 1st, 1806, at an early hour. We passed the Muscleshell[16] river at eleven o'clock, and 15 miles further landed at some Indian lodges, where we determined to pass the night ; for the rain still continued, and we feared that the skins of the bighorn would spoil by being constantly wet. Having made fires, therefore, and exposed them to dry, we proceeded to hunt.

August 2d was fair and warm, and we availed ourselves of this occasion to dry our baggage in the sun. Such is the immediate effect of fair weather that since last evening the river has fallen 18 inches. Two men [J. and R. Fields] were sent forward in a canoe to hunt ; and now, having reloaded our canoes, we resolved to go on as fast as possible.

August 3d. Accordingly we set out at an early hour, and without stopping as usual to cook dinner, camped in the evening two miles above our camp of May 12th, 1805. We were here joined by the two hunters, who had killed 29 deer since they left us. These animals are in great abun-

---

steep for them is not so well known. A herd of several hundred took the alarm at our approach, and rushed headlong up the bank. They got on very well for some distance—for buffalo can climb steeper places than one would suppose from their ungainly and unwieldy form ; but as they proceeded the way grew worse. Still those that were in the rear pressed so hard on the leaders of this climb that the latter could neither turn nor even stop ; several of them lost their footing, rolled down, end over end, in a cloud of dust, and then tumbled off the cliff to be dashed to pieces on the rocks below.

[16] Gass has this " Muscle shoal river," p. 247 ; Lewis L 135 has " Missel shell river."

dance in the river-bottoms, and very gentle. We passed
also a great number of elk, wolves, some bear, beaver,
geese, a few ducks, the party-colored corvus [magpie, *Pica
pica hudsonica*], a calumet eagle, some bald eagles, and red-
headed woodpeckers [*Melanerpes erythrocephalus*], but very
few buffalo. By four o'clock next morning,

August 4th, we were again in motion. At eleven we
passed the Bigdry [Big Dry] river, which has now a bold,
even, but shal- (*p. 361*) low current, 60 yards in width,
and halted for a few minutes at the mouth of Milk river.
This stream is at present full of water, resembling in color
that of the Missouri; and as it possesses quite as much
water as Maria's river, we have no doubt that it extends to
a considerable distance toward the north. We here killed
a very large rattlesnake. Soon after we passed several
herds of buffalo and elk, and camped at night two miles
below the Gulf,[17] on the northeast side of the river. For
the first time this season we were saluted with the cry of
the whippoorwill or goatsucker of the Missouri [*Phalænoptilus nuttalli*].

August 5th. We waited until noon in hopes of being
overtaken by two of the men [Colter and Collins], who had
gone ahead in a canoe to hunt two days ago, but who were
at a distance from the river as we passed them. As they did
not arrive by that time we concluded that they had passed
us in the night, and therefore proceeded until late, when
we camped about ten miles below Littledry [Little Dry[18]]
river. We again saw great numbers of buffalo, elk, antelope, deer, and wolves; also eagles and other birds, among
which were geese and a solitary pelican, neither of which can
fly at present, as they are now shedding the feathers of their
wings. We also saw several bears, one of them the largest,
except one, we had ever seen; for he measured nine feet

---

[17] That is, the so-called "Gulf in the Island Bend," located 13 miles below
Milk river. See note [15], p. 300.

[18] For this stream, so much confused with some others of similar names, see
note [14], p. 299.

from the nose to the extremity of the tail. During the
night a violent storm came on from the northeast with such
torrents of rain that we had scarcely time to unload the
canoes before they filled with water. Having no shelter we
ourselves were completely wet to the skin, and the wind
and cold air made our situation very unpleasant.

August 6th. We left early ; but after we had passed Porcupine river, were, by the high wind, obliged to lie by until
four o'clock, when the wind abating we continued, and at
night camped five miles below our camp of the 1st of May,
1805. Here (*p. 362*) we were again drenched by the rain,
which lasted all the next morning,

August 7th, but being resolved, if possible, to reach the
Yellowstone, a distance of 83 miles, in the course of the day,
we set out early, and being favored by the rapid current and
good oarsmen, proceeded with great speed. In passing
Martha's river,[19] we observed that its mouth is at present
a quarter of a mile lower than it was last year. Here we
find for the first time the appearance of coal-burnt hills and
pumice-stone, which seem always to accompany each other.
At this place also are the first elms and dwarf cedars in the
bluffs of the river. The ash first makes its appearance in
one solitary tree at Ash rapids, but is seen occasionally
scattered through the low grounds at Elk rapids, and thence
downward, though it is generally small. The whole country
on the northeast side, between Martha and Milk rivers, is
a beautiful, level plain, with a soil much more fertile than
that higher up the river. The buffalo, elk, and other animals[20] continue numerous, as are also the bears, which lie

---

[19] Lewis L 141: "At 8 A. M. we passed the entrance of Marthy's river which
has changed it's entrance since we passed it last year," Apr. 29th, 1805 : see note[3],
p. 289. This is an important note, as indicating what decided changes may
occur in the debouchure of rivers in a few months even. In reviewing Lewis
and Clark's work as a whole, the wonder may become—not an occasional doubt
that arises concerning the channels of the main rivers and the positions of the
mouths of their lesser tributaries—but the seldom erring certainty with which we
can fix points.

[20] "We also saw an unusual flight of white gulls about the size of a pigeon

in wait at the crossing-places, where they seize elk and the weaker cattle, and then stay by the carcass in order to keep off the wolves until the whole is devoured.   At four o'clock we reached the mouth of the Yellowstone, where we found a note [21] from Captain Clark, informing us of his intention of waiting for us a few miles below.   We therefore left a memorandum for our two huntsmen [Colter and Collins], whom we now supposed must be behind us, and then pursued our course till night came on ; and not being able to overtake Captain Clark, we camped [on the N.E. shore, in the next bottom above our camp of April 23d and 24th, 1805, Lewis L 143].

August 8th.   We set out in hopes of overtaking Captain Clark ; but after descending nearly to the entrance of White-

with the top of their heads black," Lewis L 142.   These were terns, and I think most probably *Sterna forsteri.*

[21] Gass says, p. 248 : "about 4 o'clock arrived at the mouth of the Yellow Stone river.   We found that Captain Clark had been encamped on the point some time ago, and had left it.   We discovered nothing to inform us where he was gone, except a few words written or traced in the sand, which were ' W. C. a few miles further down on the right hand side.' "   But the sergeant did not discover all there was to be found.   Lewis 142, 143 is more explicit: "At 4 P. M. we arrived at the entrance of the Yellowstone river.   I landed at the point and found that Capt. Clark had been encamped at this place and from appearances had left it about 7 or 8 days.   I found a paper on a pole at the point which mearly contained my name in the hand wrighting of Capt. C.   we also found the remnant of a note which had been attatched to a pear of Elk'shorns in the camp ; from this fragment I learned that game was scarce at the point and musquetoes troublesome which were the reasons given for his going on ;   I also learnt that he intended halting a few miles below where he intended waiting my arrival.   I now wrote a note directed to Colter and Collins provided they were behind, ordering them to come on without loss of time ; this note I wraped in leather and attatched to the same pole which Capt. C. had planted at the point ; this being done I instantly reimbarked and decended the river in the hope of reaching Capt. C's camp before night.   about 7 miles below the point on the S.W. shore I saw some meat that had been lately fleased [flensed] and hung on a pole. I directed Sergt. Ordway to go on shore [to] examine the place ; on his return he reported that he saw the tracks of two men which appeared so resent that he beleived they had been there to-day, the fire he found at the place was blaizing and appeared to have been mended up afresh or within the course of an hour past.   he found at this place a part of a Chinnook hat which my men recognized as the hat of Gibson."

earth [22] river without being able to see him, we were at a loss
what to conjecture. In this situation we landed, and began
to calk and repair the canoes, as well as prepare some skins
for clothing, for since we left the Rocky mountains we
(*p. 363*) have had no leisure to make clothes, so that the
greater part of the men are almost naked. In these occupations we pased this and the following day [*August 9th*[23]],
without any interruption except from the mosquitoes,
which are very troublesome; and then having completed
the repairs of the canoes, we embarked,

Sunday, August 10*th*, at five in the afternoon; but the
wind and rain prevented us going further than near the
entrance of Whiteearth river.[24]

August 11*th*. Being anxious to reach the Burnt hills by
noon, in order to ascertain the latitude, we went forward
with great rapidity; but by the time we reached that place,
it was 20 minutes too late to take the meridian altitude.

Having lost the observation, Captain Lewis observed on
the opposite side of the river a herd of elk on a thick sand-
bar of willows, and landed with Cruzatte to hunt them.
Each of them fired and shot an elk. They then reloaded
and took different routes in pursuit of the game; when, just
as Captain Lewis was taking aim at an elk, a ball struck him
in the left thigh, about an inch below the joint of the hip,

[22] "About 8 ms. by water and three by land above the entrance of White earth
river. not finding Capt. Clark I knew not what calculation to make with rispect
to his halting and therefore determined to proceed as tho' he was not before me
and leave the rest to the chapter of accidents," Lewis L 148. Codex L ends at
this date (though there are a few more pages of meteorological registration), with
a call for a "supplement." This additional matter makes Lewis Lb, a small
codex, running only Aug. 9th-12th, 1806. Captain Lewis was shot by Cruzatte
on the 11th; his wound soon became so painful that he could write no more;
and his entry of Aug. 12th is the last he ever made on the Expedition.

[23] The brothers Fields were sent to White-earth river, but saw no signs of
Captain Clark's party. "Colter and Collins have not yet overtaken us I fear
some missfortune has happened them for their previous fidelity and orderly
deportment induces me to beleive that they would not thus intentionally delay,"
Lewis Lb 1.

[24] Where they had camped before, Apr. 21st, 1805 : see note [42], p. 278.

and missing the bone, went through the left thigh and grazed
the right to the depth of the ball.   It instantly occurred to
him that Cruzatte must have shot him by mistake for an elk,
as he was dressed in brown leather, and Cruzatte had not a
very good eye-sight.   He therefore called out that he was
shot,[25] and looked toward the place from which the ball
came ; seeing nothing, he called on Cruzatte by name several
times, but received no answer.   He now thought that as
Cruzatte was out of hearing, and the shot did not seem to
come from more than 40 paces' distance, it must have been
fired by an Indian ; and not knowing how many might be
concealed in the bushes, he made toward the periogue, calling
out to Cruzatte to retreat, as there were Indians in the willows.   As soon as he reached the periogue he ordered the
men to arms, and mentioning that he was wound- (*p. 364*) ed,
though he hoped not mortally, by the Indians, bade them
follow him to relieve Cruzatte.   They instantly followed
for a hundred paces, when his wound became so painful and
his thigh stiffened in such a manner that he could go no
further.   He therefore ordered the men to proceed, and if

---

[25] " I called out to him damn you, you have shot me," etc., Lewis Lb 3.   In
respect to this painful incident, I had feared that the codex might reveal something even more regrettable than the accident itself, touching the relations
between Captain Lewis and one of his men.   But there is no trace of anything
of the sort ; the text is almost literally true to the codex, and we may dismiss
all suspicion that Cruzatte intended to shoot his captain.   " I do not believe
that the fellow did it intentionally, but after finding that he had shot me was
anxious to conceal his knowledge of having done so.   the ball had lodged in
my breeches which I knew to be the ball of the short rifles such as that he
had . . . with the assistance of Sergt. Gass I took off my cloaths and dressed
my wound myself as well as I could," Lewis Lb 4.

Gass, p. 249, narrates this accident : " In a short time Captain Lewis returned
wounded and very much alarmed ; and ordered us to our arms, supposing he
had been shot at by Indians.   Having prepared for an attack, I went out with
three men to reconnoitre and examine the bushes, which are very thick at this
place, and could see no Indians ; but after some time met with the man who
went out with Captain Lewis, and found on inquiry that he had shot him by
accident through the hips, and without knowing it pursued the game.   Having
made this discovery we returned to the periouge ; examined and dressed Captain Lewis's wound ; and found the ball, which had lodged in his overalls."

overpowered by numbers, to retreat toward the boats, keeping up a fire; then limping back to the periogue, he prepared himself with his rifle, a pistol, and the air-gun, to sell his life dearly in case the men should be overcome.

In this state of anxiety and suspense he remained for about 20 minutes, when the party returned with Cruzatte, and reported that no Indians could be seen in the neighborhood. Cruzatte was now much alarmed, and declared that he had shot an elk after Captain Lewis left him, but disclaimed every idea of having intentionally wounded his officer. There was no doubt that he was the person who gave the wound; yet as it seemed to be perfectly accidental, and Cruzatte had always conducted himself with propriety, no further notice was taken of it. The wound was now dressed, and patent lint was put into the holes; but though it bled considerably, yet as the ball had touched neither a bone nor an artery, we hope that it may not prove fatal. As it was, however, impossible for him to make the observation of the latitude of the Burnt hills, which is chiefly desirable, these being the most northern parts of the Missouri, he declined remaining till to-morrow, and proceeded till evening.[26] Captain Lewis could not now be removed without great pain, as he had a high fever. He therefore remained on board during the night, and early the next morning,

August 12*th*, proceeded with as much expedition as possible. Soon afterward we put ashore to visit a camp, which we found to be that of [Joseph] Dickson and [Forest] Hancock, the two Illinois traders, who told us that they had seen Captain Clark yesterday.[27] As we stopped with them, we

---

[26] When "we came within 8 miles of our encampment of the 15th of April 1805 and encamped on N.E. side. . . At 4 P. M. we passed an encampment which had been evacuated this morning by Capt. Clark, here I found a note from Capt. C. informing me that he had left a letter for me at at the entrance of the Yelow stone river, but that Sergt. Pryor who had passed that place since he left it, had taken the letter; that Sergt. Pryor having been robed of all his horses had decended the Yelowstone river in skin canoes and had overtaken him at this encampment," Lewis Lb 5.

[27] "They also informed me that they had left the Illinois in the summer

were overtaken by our two hunters, Colter and Collins, who had (*p. 365*) been missing since the 3d, and whose absence excited much uneasiness.   They informed us that, after following us the first day, they concluded that we must be behind, and waited for us during several days, when they were convinced of their mistake, and had then come on as rapidly as they could.   We made some presents to the two traders, and then proceeded, till at one o'clock we joined our friends and companions under Captain Clark.

1804 since which time they had been ascended [ascending] the Missouri, hunting and traping beaver ; that they had been robed by the indians and the former wounded last winter by the Tetons of the birnt woods . . . but were still determined to proceed. I gave them a short description of the Missouri, a list of distances to the most conspicuous streams and remarkable places on the river above and pointed out to them the places where the beaver most abounded. I also gave them a file and a couple of pounds of powder with some lead. these were articles they assured me they were in great want of. . . my wounds feel very stiff and soar this morning but gave me no considerable pain. there was much less inflamation than I had reason to apprehend there would be. I had last evening applied a poltice of peruvian barks. At 1 P. M. I overtook Capt. Clark and party and had the pleasure of finding them all well. as wrighting in my present situation is extreemly painfull to me I shall desist untill I recover and leave to my frind Capt. C. the continuation of our journal," Lewis Lb 7.

The meeting of Captain Lewis' party with the traders Dickson and Hancock, and his thus linking himself once more with the civilized world, is of course subsequent in time to the meeting of Captain Clark's party with the same white men, though thus prior in the course of the narrative. For various details of the happy reunion of the Expedition, at a point on the Missouri a little below Goatpen (Little Knife) creek, see the same date of Aug. 12th, p. 1175.

CHAPTER XXXIV.

CAPTAIN CLARK PROCEEDS TO EXPLORE THE YELLOWSTONE.

Captain Clark and party proceed south up the valley of Clark's river—Character of the valley —Fourth of July—They strike the camp of Sept. 7th, 1805—Flower creek—Clark's Pass of the Continental Divide—Glade creek, a branch of Wisdom river—Sacajawea acts as guide—Fish creek—Horses lost—Wisdom river—Its three forks—A hot spring in the plains —The extensive valley through which they have passed called Hot Springs valley— Willard's creek—Shoshone cove—Jefferson river at its Two Forks, where was the cache of August 20th, 1805—Avidity of the men for tobacco—Horses brought back by Sergeant Ordway—Ice—A division of the party ; one to go down the Jefferson in canoes with the baggage, Captain Clark and the others on horseback—Service-berry valley—Rattlesnake mountain—Beaver's Head valley—Three-thousand-mile island—Beaver's-head—Mouth of Wisdom river—Panther creek—Fields' creek—Camp of July 31st, 1805—Madison river, where Sergeant Ordway and the horses had just arrived—Gallatin river—Sergeant Ordway, with nine men in six canoes, starts down the Missouri—Captain Clark, with ten men, Sacajawea, her baby, and fifty horses, goes overland to the Yellowstone—They reach the three forks of Gallatin river—Cross the watershed between the Missouri and Yellowstone— Strike a tributary of the latter—Down this to the Yellowstone, at a point 48 miles from the Three Forks of the Missouri—Down the Yellowstone—This river described—Shields' river—Rivers-across—Otter river—Beaver river—Bratton's river—Indian fort—Accident to Gibson—Rose river—Canoes to be built—Twenty-four horses stolen by Crow Indians—Two canoes completed—Sergeant Pryor and two men to take the remaining horses to the Mandans on the Missouri—Captain Clark to descend the rest of the Yellowstone in the boats, July 23d.

THURSDAY, July 3d, 1806.[1]   On taking leave of Captain Lewis and the Indians, the other division, consisting of Captain Clark with 15 men and 50 horses, set out through the valley of Clark's river, along [up] the western side of which they rode in a southern direction. The valley is from 10 to 15 miles in width, tolerably level, partially

[1] The thread of narrative now loops back to this date on p. 1066 of Chap. xxxii, when the two parties separated at the mouth of Traveler's-rest creek, and continues through the present and the following chapter, till August 12th, when the Expedition is reunited on the Missouri, p. 1175. Captain Clark goes up the " main fork of Clark's river," *i.e.*, the Bitter-root or St. Mary's river, to Ross' Hole ; strikes over the Continental Divide there, by way of Clark's Pass, to certain headwaters of Wisdom or Big Hole river, whence he proceeds by Willard's creek to Shoshone cove and the Two Forks of the Jefferson ; thence down this river to the Three Forks of the Missouri, up the Gallatin, and over to the

covered with long-leaved and pitch-pine, with some cottonwood, birch, and sweet willow on the borders of the
streams. Among the herbage are two species of clover;
one the white clover common to the western parts of
the United States; the other much smaller, both in
leaf and blossom, than either the red or white clover,
and particularly relished by the horses. After crossing eight different streams, four of which were small,
we halted at the distance of 18 miles on the upper
side of a large creek, where we let our horses graze, and
(*p. 367*) after dinner resumed our journey in the same direction we had pursued during the morning, till at the distance
of 18 miles further, we camped [2] on the north side of a large
creek. The valley became more beautiful as we proceeded,
and was diversified by a number of small open plains,
abounding with grass and a variety of sweet-scented plants,
and watered by ten streams [3] which rush from the western
mountains with considerable velocity. The mountains
themselves are covered with snow about one-fifth from the
top, and some snow is still to be seen on the high points
and in the hollows of the mountains to the eastward. In
the course of our ride we saw a great number of deer, a

Yellowstone. The routes up the Bitter-root and down the Jefferson we have
been over before and may now pass cursorily; the rest of this journey is new,
and of great importance; it will therefore require studious attention, especially as
the text is entirely too summary. The codex we follow is Clark M, beginning
at p. 48, July 3d.

As to the composition of Captain Clark's detachment: The codex has "with
men," the number not being filled in, and the "15" of the text is a mistake.
There were 31 men, 1 woman, and 1 child on the Expedition: see p. 257. Captain Lewis was gone with 9 other men—Gass, Drewyer, the two Fields, Werner,
Frazier, M'Neal, Goodrich, and Thompson—leaving Captain Clark with 20 other
men, and the woman and child, all of whom started with him. This is confirmed
by the roster of Captain Clark's party, on July 13th: see note [16], p. 1131.

[2] In the vicinity of Corvallis, but on the other side of the river.

[3] Among the 18 creeks from the west of to-day's march may be named Big
Timber, Kootenay, Lower Big, Sweathouse, Fred Burr, Mill, and perhaps Upper
Big; the last is very likely the one on which was camp. The route is up the
left (west) bank of the river, which was passed down on its east bank, Sept. 8th
and 9th, 1805: see pp. 587-590, and notes there.

single bear, and some of the burrowing-squirrels [*Spermo-philus columbianus*] common about the Quamash flats.   The mosquitoes were very troublesome.

Friday, July 4th. Early in the morning three hunters were sent out.   The rest of the party having collected the horses and breakfasted, we proceeded at seven o'clock up the valley, which is now contracted to the width of from eight to ten miles, with a good proportion of pitch-pine, though its low lands, as well as the bottoms of the creeks, are strewn with large stones.   We crossed five creeks of different sizes, but of great depth, and so rapid that in pass-ing the last several of the horses were driven down the stream, and some of our baggage was wet.   Near this river we saw the tracks of two Indians, whom we supposed to be Shoshonees.   Having made 16 miles, we halted at an early hour for the purpose of doing honor to the birthday of our country's independence.   The festival was not very splen-did, for it consisted of a mush made of cows and a saddle of venison ; nor had we anything to tempt us to prolong it. We therefore went on till at the distance of a mile we came to a very large creek, which, like all those in the valley, had an immense rapidity of descent ; we therefore proceeded up for some distance, in order to select the most convenient spot for fording.   Even there, however, such was the vio- (*p. 368*) lence of the current that, though the water was not higher than the bellies of the horses, the resistance made in passing caused the stream to rise over their backs and loads.   After passing the creek we inclined to the left, and soon after struck the road which we had descended last year, near the spot where we dined on the 7th of Septem-ber [1805].   Along this road we continued on the west side of Clark's river, till at the distance of 13 miles, during which we passed three more deep, large creeks, we reached its western branch,[4] where we camped ; and having sent out

---

[4] The Nez-percé fork, which by uniting with the East (Ross') fork, composes the river up which we have come : see Sept. 7th, p. 586, and note there. " This being the day of the declaration of Independance of the United States and a

two hunters, dispatched some men to examine the best ford across the [west fork of the] river. The game to-day consisted of four deer ; though we also saw a herd of ibex, or bighorn. By daylight the next morning,

July 5*th*, we again examined the fords; and having discovered what we conceived to be the best, began the passage at a place where the river is divided by small islands into six different channels. We, however, crossed them all without any damage, except wetting some of our provisions and merchandise; and at the distance of a mile came to the eastern branch [Ross' fork], up which we proceeded about a mile, till we came into the old road we had descended in the autumn. It soon led us across this river, which we found had fallen to the same depth at which we found it last autumn, and along its eastern bank to the foot of the mountain nearly opposite Flower [5] creek. Here we halted to let our horses graze, near a spot where there was a fire still burning and the tracks of two horses, which we presumed to be Shoshonees; and having dried all our provisions, proceeded at about four o'clock across the mountain into the valley where we had first seen the Flatheads.[6] We crossed the river, which we perceived took its rise from a

Day commonly selebrated by my country, I had every disposition to selebrate the day, and therefore halted early and partook of a Sumptious Dinner of a fat saddle of venison and mush of cows (roots)," Clark M 50.

[5] " Flour Creek," Clark M 52—a name not before used. This is one of the small streams which make into Ross' fork from the south, between the Nez-percé fork and Camp creek.

[6] Ootlashoots of p. 582 (which see, and note there), first met with on Sept. 4th : for the route down Camp creek to their village, see that date, pp. 580, 581, and note [9] there. Captain Clark is again in Ross' Hole, in the crotch of the **Y**, as explained in the note just cited. To the S.W., the Bitter-root range, over which he came Sept. 4th, divides the waters of Clark's basin from those of Lewis' basin, both these being Pacific waters ; to the S.E., the Rocky mountains divide the Pacific waters of Clark's river from the Atlantic waters of Wisdom river and so of the Missouri. He proposes now to try the latter divide, and thus avoid the roundabout way the Expedition came last fall, by Salmon river and Fish creek. His last crossing of Ross' fork puts him on the south side of that river, at the mouth of Camp creek, in the vicinity of town of Sula. Clark M 52 is very explicit : " Crossed the mountain into the vally we first met with the flatheads. . .

high peaked mountain at about 20 miles to the northeast of the valley ; passed up it [*i. e.*, Camp creek, not Ross' fork] for two miles, and camped after a ride of 20 miles during the day.   As soon as we halted several men were dispatched in different directions to ex- (*p. 369*) amine the road ; from their report we concluded that the best path would be one [that continued] about three miles up the creek [and then turned to the left].   This is the road traveled by the Ootla-shoots, and will certainly shorten our route two days at least, besides being much better, as we had been informed by the Indians, than that by which we came last fall.

July 6th. The night was very cold, succeeded by frost in the morning ; and as the horses were much scattered, we were not able to set out before nine o'clock.   We then went along the [Camp] creek for three miles, and leaving to the right the path by which we came [down this creek] last fall, pursued the road taken by the Ootlashoots, up a gentle ascent to the dividing mountain[7] which separates the waters of the

crossed the river. . . Shields informed me that the Flathead indians passed up the small creek which we came down last fall about 2 miles above our encamp-ment of the 4th. and 5th. of Sept. I proceeded up this south branch [Camp creek] 2 miles and encamped on the E. side of the Creek, and sent out several men to examine the road.   Shields returned at dark and informed me that the best road turned up the hill from the creek 3 miles higher up, and appeared to be a plain beaten parth.   As the rout of the Ootlashoots can be followed it will evidently shorten our rout at least two days and as the indians informed me last fall [it is] a much better rout than the one we came out.   at all events I am deturmined to make the attempt and follow their trail if possible ; if I can prosue it, my rout will be nearer and much better than the one we came from the Shoshones, and if I should not be able to follow their road ; our rout can't pos-sibly be much wors."

   [7] Here is one of the most important geographical points of the whole route, as already sufficiently indicated : see preceding note, and note[9], p. 580.   It is sur-prising that no name was given by the explorers to this creek, by which the Expe-dition came down from Lewis' to Clark's waters, and by which Captain Clark went up from the Pacific to the Atlantic watershed.   "Camp creek" is the only name I find for it, on both military and civil maps of latest dates.   On crossing the ridge before him, which separates Missoula Co. from Beaver-head Co., Captain Clark will strike his Glade creek, a source of Wisdom river, a branch of the Jefferson.   Thus he makes what ought to be, if it is not, called **Clark's Pass.** Captain Lewis never made this pass, and Captain Clark never made "Lewis and

middle fork of Clark's river from those of Wisdom and Lewis rivers. On reaching the other side [on a course N. 80° E.] we came to Glade creek, down which we proceeded [S. 50° E. for seven miles], crossing it frequently into the glades on each side, where the timber is small, in many places destroyed by fire, and there are great quantities of quamash now in bloom. Throughout the glades are great numbers of holes made by the whistling- or burrowing-squirrel [*Spermophilus columbianus*]; and we killed a hare of the large mountain species [probably the snowshoe rabbit, *Lepus americanus bairdi*]. Along these roads there are also appearances of old buffalo-paths, and some old heads of buffaloes; as these animals have wonderful sagacity in the choice of their routes,

Clark's" Pass from the Big Blackfoot to Dearborn's river. Both captains together made the original pass of the Great Divide from a tributary of the Missouri over to the Lemhi river. Thus honors are easy on the three points at which the Expedition traversed the Continental backbone.

Clark's Pass is sometimes charted by this name. I noticed it lately on an atlas in a popular encyclopedia. It has, however, become better known as Gibbon's Pass (misprinted "Gibson's" on the latest G. L. O. map of Montana, 1892, where also Gibbonsville, on the forks of Fish creek, in Idaho, is lettered Gibsonsville : see note [6], p. 551). This name commemorates General John Gibbon, U. S. A., who fought Chief Joseph in the bloody battle of the Big Hole, Aug. 9th and 10th, 1877, and who lately gave me the particulars of the engagement, as well as of his route through this Pass to the scene of action. The fight was close by the confluence of Glade creek with the united stream of Pioneer and Ruby creeks (see note [7], p. 578). General Gibbon testified to the fidelity of Captain Clark's narrative, especially as given in the codex, which he examined with the greatest pleasure. He used in our conversation the name " Glade " creek, which, however, is lettered on no map I have seen ; nor do I know of any other name for this stream. I give here the formal courses and distances of July 6th, not hitherto published. Clark M 55, beginning at camp :

" On the course which we had decended the branch [Camp creek] of Clark's river to the first Flat heads or Oatlashshoot band the 4th. of Septr. 1805 .... 3.½ miles.

" Thence up a jintle stope [gentle slope] of the dividing mountains which seperates the waters of the [Wisdom river] from those of Lewis's & Clark's rivers leaving the old rout on which we came out to the right on a course nearly S.E............................. 3. miles.

" Thence N. 80° E. through a leavel piney Country on the top of the mountain to a glade at the head of a [Glade creek] branch which runs towards the Missouri..................................... 2.½ miles.

the coincidence of a buffalo [trail] with an Indian road was the strongest assurance that it was the best.

In the afternoon we passed along the hill-side north of the creek, till, in the course of six miles [N. 68° E.], we entered an extensive level plain. Here the tracks of the Indians scattered so much that we could no longer pursue a road; but Sacajaweah recognized the plain immediately. She had traveled it often during her childhood, and informed us that it was the great resort of the Shoshonees, who came for the purpose of gathering quamash and cows, and of taking beaver, with which the plain abounded; that Glade creek was a branch of Wisdom river; and that on reaching the higher part of the plain we should see a gap in the moun- (*p. 370*) tains, on the course to our canoes,[8] and from that gap a high point of mountain covered with snow. At the distance of a mile we crossed a large [Pioneer[9]] creek from the right, rising, as well as Fish creek, in a snowy mountain

"Thence S. 50° E. down the branch crossing it frequently & through small glades on either side of the branch the glades at some places ½ a mile wide with several small streams [one of them Trail creek, from the left] falling in on either side up which there is small glades to the narrows, N.S. [north side]..................... 7. miles.

"Thence N. 68° E. keeping down the North side of the creek on the side of the hill, the bottom of the creek small open and much fallen timber to an extensive bottom S. side..................... 4. miles.

"Thence S. 56° E. through an open Leavle [level] plain passing a large [Pioneer] creek from the right at one mile to a quawmash flatt through which a small [Swamp?] creek runs scattered through the bottom and Encamped... 6. miles.

"26 miles."

[8] Which had been cached Aug. 20th, 1805, at the Two Forks of Jefferson river.

[9] Heading in the Main Divide, S.E. of Brown's peak, and thus leading up to Big Hole Pass, the "gap" of the text, where it connects with the Datongo branch of Fish creek : see note [7], p. 578. The "gap" pointed out by Sacajawea, toward which Captain Clark is holding the course S. 56° E., is under Bald mountain, in the range W. and N.W. of Bannock City, which latter is on Willard's (Grasshopper : note [20], p. 501) creek. The "small creek" on which to-night's camp is pitched is one of numerous western tributaries of Wisdom river, not easy to specify by name—perhaps Swamp creek, near the mouth of which, on Wisdom river, is a place called Wisdom.

over which there is a gap. Soon after, on ascending a rising
ground, the country spreads into a beautiful plain [Big Hole
prairie] extending north and south, about 15 miles wide and
30 in length, surrounded on all sides by high points of mountains covered with snow, among which was the gap pointed
out by the squaw, bearing S. 56° E. We had not gone two
miles from the last [Pioneer] creek when we were overtaken
by a violent storm of wind, accompanied with hard rain, which
lasted an hour and a half. Having no shelter, we formed a
solid column to protect ourselves from the gust, and then
went on five miles to a small [Swamp?] creek; where, finding
some small timber, we camped for the night and dried ourselves. We here observed some fresh signs of Indians, who
had been gathering quamash. Our distance was 26 miles.

July 7th. In the morning our horses were so much
scattered that, although we sent out hunters in every direction to range the country for six or eight miles, nine of
them could not be recovered. They were the most valuable
of all our horses, and so much attached to some of their
companions that it was difficult to separate them in the daytime. We therefore presumed that they must have been
stolen by some roving Indians; and accordingly left a party
of five men [10] to continue the pursuit, while the rest went on
to the spot where the canoes had been deposited. We set
out at ten o'clock and pursued a course S. 56° E. across the

[10] Sergeant Ordway, with Shannon, Gibson, Collins, and Labiche. Clark M 56:
" At ½ past 10 A. M. I set out and proceeded on through an open rich valley
crossing four large creeks [western tributaries of Wisdom river] with extensive
low and mirey bottoms, and a small [Wisdom] river keeping the course I had
set out on S. 56° E. after crossing the river I kept up on the N.E. side, sometimes following an old road which frequently disappeared, at the distance of 16
miles [from camp] we arived at a Boiling Spring situated about 100 paces from
a large Easterly fork of the Small river in a leavel open vally plain and nearly
opposite and E. of the 3 forks of this little river which heads in the Snowey mountains to the S.E. and S.W. of the Springs." Thus is the spot fixed with admirable
precision ; which is fortunate, as the country along these reaches of Wisdom river
and its tributaries is still unsettled, and there are no modern names (that I
know of) for any of the streams passed thus far to-day. A place on Wisdom
river called Alamo is passed in the vicinity of the three forks.

valley, which we found to be watered by four large creeks, with extensive low and miry bottoms; and then reached [and crossed] Wisdom river, along the northeast side of which we continued, till at the distance of 16 miles we came to its three branches. Near that place we stopped for dinner at a hot spring situated in the open plain. The bed of the spring is about 15 yards in circumference, and compo- (*p. 371*) sed of loose, hard, gritty stones, through which the water boils in great quantities. It is slightly impregnated with sulphur, and so hot that a piece of meat about the size of three fingers was completely done in 25 minutes. After dinner we proceeded across the eastern branch, and along the north side of the middle branch for nine miles, when we reached the gap in the mountains, and took our last leave of this extensive valley, which we called Hotspring valley. It is indeed a beautiful country; though inclosed by mountains covered with snow, the soil is exceedingly fertile and well supplied with esculent plants; while its numerous creeks furnish immense quantities of beaver. Another valley, less extensive and more rugged, opened to our view as we passed through the gap; but as we had made 25 miles and night was advancing, we halted near some handsome springs which fall into Willard's [Grasshopper [11]] creek. After a cold night, during which our horses separated and could not be collected till eight o'clock in the morning,

July 8th, we crossed the valley along the southwest side of Willard's creek for twelve miles, when it entered the mountains; then turning S. 20° E. came to Shoshonee cove, after

---

[11] The trail after dinner was, Clark M 57 : S. 45° E. 5 ms. up the N.E. side of the middle fork of Wisdom river; then N. 50° E. 4 miles to the gap, crossing a small branch from the left at 2 miles, and camped. "After taking dinner and letting our horses graize 1 hour and a half we proceeded on, crossed this Easterly branch and up on the N. side of the middle fork 9 miles crossed it near the head of an Easterly branch and passed through a gap of a mountain on the Easterly side of which we encamped near some beautiful springs which fall into Willards creek," *ibid.* This sets the party in the pass S.W. of Bald mountain and N.W. of Bannock City, on an upper course of Willard's or Grasshopper creek, probably that now called Divide creek.

riding seven miles; whence we proceeded down the west branch [*i. e.*, Prairie creek [12]] of Jefferson river, and at the distance of nine miles reached its forks, where we had deposited our merchandise in the month of August [1805]. Most of the men were in the habit of chewing tobacco; and such was their eagerness to procure it after so long a privation that they scarcely took the saddles from their horses before they ran to the cave [cache], and were delighted at being able to resume this fascinating indulgence. This was one of the severest privations which we had encountered. Some of the men, whose tomahawks were so constructed as to answer the purposes of pipes, broke the handles of these instruments, and after cutting them into small fragments, chewed them; the wood having, by frequent smoking, become strongly im-(*p. 372*) pregnated with the taste of that plant. We found everything safe, though some of the goods were a little damp, and one of the canoes had a hole. The ride of this day was 27 miles in length, through a country diversified by low, marshy grounds and high, open, stony plains, terminated by high mountains, on the tops and along the northern sides of which the snow still remained. Over the whole were scattered great quantities of hyssop and different species of shrubs common to the plains of the Missouri.

We had now crossed the whole distance from Traveler's-rest creek to the head [Two Forks] of Jefferson river, which

[12] Clark M 58: "we proceeded on down Willards Creek on the S.W. side about 11 miles near which the Creek passes through the mountain, we then steered S. 20° E. to the West branch of Jefferson's river [*i. e.*, to Prairie creek] in Snake indian [Shoshone] Cove about 7 miles . . . and on down the fork . . . 9 miles to our encampment of 17 Augt." The detailed courses and distances are, M 59: S. 40° E. 11 miles down the creek on the S.W. side, passing several small branches of it from the mountains on the right; S. 20° E. 7 miles through a gap at 3 miles, then through a plain beyond this gap to the "west branch of Jefferson's river," *i. e.*, to Prairie creek in Shoshone cove; E. 4 miles down this creek, to a high point of land, striking their old trail; N. 45 E. 5° miles further down the creek to the Two Forks of the Jefferson. If the road to-day did not actually pass over the present site of Bannock City, it went at any rate but little west of that place. See note [20], p. 501, and for the road from Bannock into Shoshone cove see p. 483.

seems to form the best and shortest route over the mountains, during almost the whole distance of 164 miles.   It is, in fact, a very excellent road, which by cutting a few trees might be rendered a good route for wagons, with the exception of about four miles over one of the mountains, which would require some leveling.[13]

July 9th.   We were all occupied in raising and repairing the canoes, and making the necessary preparations for resuming our journey to-morrow.[14]   The day proved cold and windy, so that the canoes were soon dried.   We were here overtaken by Sergeant Ordway and his party, who had discovered our horses near the head of the creek on which we [had] camped ; though they were very much scattered, and endeavored to escape as fast as they could, he brought them back.   The squaw found to-day a plant which grows in the moist lands, the root of which is eaten by the Indians.   The stem and leaf as well as the root of this plant resemble the common carrot in form, size, and taste, though the color is of somewhat a paler yellow.   The night continued very cold.

July 10th.   In the morning a white frost covered the ground ; the grass was frozen, and the ice three-quarters of an inch thick in a basin of water.   The boats were now loaded, and Captain Clark divided his men into two bands, one to descend the (*p. 373*) river with the baggage, while he, with the other, proceeded on horseback [down the river, too, en route] to the Rochejaune [Yellowstone river].

[13] It seems almost incredible that the modesty or the indifference of the great explorer should have led him to dismiss this part of his route without further remark. A road for 164 miles, fit for wagons except at one point, across the great Continental Divide—we hardly realize what it meant to make that discovery in 1806. No one of the three Continental Divide passes made by the Expedition has as yet been utilized for a railroad ; but there will doubtless be one in time from Dillon to Missoula by the way of **Clark's Pass,** or near it, and practically on the route taken by Captain Clark in passing from Traveler's-rest creek to the Two Forks of the Jefferson.

[14] " I had the canoes repared men & lodes appotioned ready to embark to-morrow morning. I also formed. the party to accomp me to the river Rejhone [Roche-jaune] from applicants and apportioned what little baggage I intended to carry as also the spear [spare] horses," Clark M 60.

After breakfast the two parties set out, those on shore skirting the eastern side of Jefferson river, through Service [-berry] valley and over Rattlesnake mountain, into a beautiful and extensive country, known among the Indians by the name of Hahnahappapchah, or Beaverhead valley, from the number of those animals to be found in it, and also from a point of land resembling the head of a beaver. It [the valley] extends from Rattlesnake mountain as low as Frazier's creek, and is about 50 miles in length in a direct line; while its width varies from 10 to 15 miles, being watered in its whole course by Jefferson river and six different creeks.[15] The valley is open and fertile; besides the innumerable quantities of beaver and otter with which its creeks are supplied, the bushes of the low grounds are a favorite resort for deer; while on the higher parts of the valley are seen scattered groups of antelopes, and still further, on the steep sides of the mountains, are observed many bighorns, which take refuge there from the wolves and bears. At the distance of 15 miles the two parties stopped to dine; when Captain Clark, finding that the river became wider and deeper, and that the canoes could advance more rapidly than the horses, determined to go himself by water, leaving Sergeant Pryor with six men to bring on the horses. In this way they resumed their journey after dinner, and camped on the eastern side of the river, opposite the head of Three-thousand-mile island [see p. 482]. The beaver were basking in great numbers along the shore; there were also some young wild geese and ducks. The mosquitoes were very troublesome during the day, but after sunset the weather became cool and they disappeared.

July 11*th.* Captain Clark sent four men ahead to hunt, and after an early breakfast proceeded down a very narrow chan-

---

[15] " Jefferson's river in passing through this vally receives M'Neals creek, Track creek, Phalanthrophy river, Wisdom river, Fields river and Fraziers creek," Clark M 61,—thus merely picking out six of the principal tributaries, which are the " six creeks" of the text ! For these, beginning with Frazier's or South Boulder, see p. 454 *et seq.*

nel, rendered more difficult by a high southwest wind, which blew from the high snowy mountains in (*p. 374*) that quarter and met them in the face at every bend of the river, which now became very crooked. At noon they passed the high point of land on the left, to which Beaverhead valley owes its name, and at six o'clock reached Philanthropy river, which was at present very low. The wind now shifted to the northeast, and though high was much warmer than before. At seven o'clock they reached their camp, at the entrance of Wisdom river, of the 6th of August [see p. 465]. They found the river very high, but falling. Here they overtook the hunters, who had killed a buck and some young geese. Besides these they had seen a great number of geese and sand-hill cranes, and some deer. The beaver were in great quantities along the banks of the rivers, and through the night were flapping their tails in the water round the boats. Having found the canoe which had been left here as they ascended, they employed themselves,

July 12*th*, till eight o'clock in drawing out the nails and making paddles of the sides of it. Then leaving one of their canoes here, they set out after breakfast. Immediately below the forks [confluence of Wisdom with Jefferson river] the current became stronger than above, and the course of the river straighter, as far as Panther creek; after which it became much more crooked. A high wind now arose from the snowy mountains to the northwest, so that it was with much difficulty and some danger they reached, at three o'clock, the entrance of Fields' creek. After dining at that place, they pursued their course and stopped for the night below their camp of the 31st of July last. Beaver, young geese, and deer continued to be their game, and they saw some old signs of buffalo. The mosquitoes were still very troublesome.

July 13*th*. Early in the morning they set out, and at noon reached the entrance of Madison river, where Sergeant Pryor had arrived with the horses about an hour before. The horses were then driven across Madison and Gallatin rivers, and the whole party halted to dine and unload the canoes below the mouth of the latter.   Here the two par- (*p. 375*) ties separated.   Sergeant Ordway with nine men set out in six canoes to descend the [Missouri] river, while Captain Clark with the remaining ten, and the wife and child of Chaboneau, were to proceed by land, with fifty horses, to Yellowstone river.[16]   They set out at five in the afternoon from the forks [Three Forks] of the Missouri, in a direction nearly east; but as many of the horses had sore feet, they were obliged to move slowly, and after going four miles halted for the night on the [north] bank of Gallatin river [opposite Logan].

This is a beautiful stream, and, though the current is rapid and obstructed by islands near its mouth, is navigable for canoes.   On its lower side the land rises gradually to the foot of a mountain running almost parallel to it; but the country below it and Madison river is a level plain, covered at present with low grass, the soil being poor, and injured by stones and strata of hard white rock along the hill-sides. Throughout the whole, game was very abundant.   They procured deer in the low grounds; beaver and otter were seen in Gallatin river, and elk, wolves, eagles, hawks, crows, and geese at different parts of the route.   The plain was intersected by several great roads leading to a gap in the mountains,[17] about 20 miles distant, in a direction E.N.E.;

[16] Approximately by the present railroad route via Bozeman from Gallatin City to Livingston.   " My party now consists of the following persons viz : Serjeant N. Pryor, Jo. Shields, G. Shannon, William Bratton, Labiesh, Windser, H. Hall, Gibson, Interpreter Shabono his wife & child and my man york ; with 49 horses and a colt," Clark M 65.   This opportune statement informs us of the where-abouts of every person on the Expedition, now divided into three parties, numerically as nearly even as possible; for the nine men not accounted for by name here and in note [1], p. 1118, go with Sergeant Ordway down the Missouri to the Great Falls.   At this point Captain Clark starts over new ground ; and the whole of his Yellowstone Exploration is treated so summarily in the text that we must follow him mainly by the codex.

[17] The mountains directly before Captain Clark, to the east, are the Bridger range ; south of this is the Gallatin range ; between these two comes East Gallatin river, south of Bridger Peak and north of Mt. Ellis.   This is the gap

but the Indian woman, who was acquainted with the country, recommended a gap more to the southward. This
course Captain Clark determined to pursue; therefore, at
an early hour in the morning,

July 14th, he crossed Gallatin river in a direction S. 78°
E., and passing over a level plain, reached the Jefferson
[*sic*—read Gallatin again[18]] at the distance of six miles.
That river is here divided into many channels, which spread
for several miles through the low grounds, and are dammed
up by the beaver in such a manner that, after attempting
in vain to reach the opposite side, the party were obliged to
turn short about to the right, till with some difficulty they
reached a low but firm island, extending nearly in the course
they desired to follow. The squaw now assured Captain
(*p.376*) Clark that the large road from Medicine [Sun] river
to the gap [Bozeman Pass] they were seeking crossed the
upper part of this plain. He therefore proceeded four miles
up the plain and reached the main channel of the river [*i. e.,*
the West Gallatin], which is still navigable for canoes, though

"to the southward" which Sacajawea ("The indian woman who has been of
great service to me as a pilot through this country," Clark M 66) recommended
him to take. He very sensibly followed the advice of the remarkable little
woman, who never failed to rise to the occasion, even when it was mountains high.
He accordingly makes the Bozeman Pass between the ranges named, and strikes
the Yellowstone at its nearest point, by the most direct route. The other gap,
noted as bearing E.N.E., would have taken him over the Flathead Pass of the
Bridger range and so to Flathead creek and other upper tributaries of Shields'
river, a good deal north of his best route.

[18] A sad slip here, for which the codex gives no occasion. Captain Clark did
not cross the Gallatin in a direction "S. 78° E."; he simply crossed it the only way
he could, at Logan, and then proceeded S. 78° E. over the plain south of this
river till he struck *it* again—by no means the "Jefferson," which was behind
him, with the Madison intervening ! He went eastward south of the Gallatin
till he struck its "main channel," *i. e.,* West Gallatin river; this he forded, and
continued eastward till he struck East Gallatin river at its "three forks," *i. e.,*
where it is joined by two tributaries, Bridger creek, N., and Bozeman creek, S.,
in the immediate vicinity of Bozeman. Sacajawea's knowledge was certainly
extensive and accurate. The road to Medicine river, of which she informed Captain Clark, is the great highway from Fort Ellis or Bozeman to Gallatin City and
Helena, and thence to Fort Shaw on Sun river, now followed by the railroad for
the greater part of this whole distance.

much divided and dammed up by multitudes of beaver. Having forded this river, they passed through a little skirt of cottonwood to a low open plain, where they dined. They saw elk, deer, and antelope, and in every direction the roads made by the buffalo, as well as some old signs of them. The squaw informed them that a few years ago these animals were numerous, not only here, but even to the sources of Jefferson river, but of late they have disappeared ; for the Shoshonees, being fearful of going west of the mountains, have hunted this country with the more activity, and of course driven the buffalo from their usual haunts. After dinner the party continued, inclining to the south of east, through an open level plain [in passsing which Middle creek was crossed], till at the distance of twelve miles they reached the three forks of [East] Gallatin river. On cross- ing the southerly branch [Bozeman creek], they fell into the buffalo-road described by the squaw, which led them up the middle branch [main East Gallatin river] for two miles [toward Fort Ellis]. This branch is provided with immense quantities of beaver, but is sufficiently navigable for small canoes by unlading at the worst dams. After crossing it they went on a mile further, and camped [on a small branch of the middle fork, on the N.E. side [19]] at the beginning of the

[19] East of Bozeman, and about opposite Fort Ellis. This most interesting itinerary has to be pricked into the text. Except when he was floundering in the sluices among the islands of West Gallatin river, Captain Clark almost stepped off the very track of the N. P. R. R. from Logan to Bozeman, under the guidance of the faithful Sacajawea. The direct distance by rail is scheduled as 25 miles. Clark M 68 : " After dinner we proceeded on a little to the South of East through an open leavil plain to the three forks of the E. branch of Gallitines River at about 12 miles, crossed the most Southerly of those forks [Bozeman creek, at Bozeman] and struck an old buffalow road the one our Indn. woman meant which I kept continuing nearly the same course up the middle fork crossed it and camped on a small branch of the middle fork on the N.E. side at the commencement of the gap of the mountain." (See also formulated courses and distances, in next note.) Of the two forks of East Gallatin river, the northern one is Bridger creek, which flows south along the east side of Bridger range, past Hardscrabble, Ross' and Bridger's peaks, and thence west- ward through Bridger cañon to its confluence with East Gallatin river near Boze- man. The south fork is Bozeman creek, which arises in and about Mystic lake

gap in the mountain, which here forms a kind of a semicircle, through which the three branches of the river pass. Several roads come in from the right and left, all tending to the gap. A little snow still remains on a naked mountain to the eastward, but in every other direction the mountains are covered with great quantities.

July 15*th.* After an early breakfast they pursued the buffalo-road over a low gap [Rocky Cañon] in the mountain to the heads of the eastern [or middle] fork of Gallatin river, near which they had camped last evening; and at the distance of six miles reached the top of the dividing ridge [Bozeman Pass], which sepa- (*p.377*) rates the waters of the Missouri and the Yellowstone; on descending this ridge, they struck one of the streams [Billman's or Trail creek] of the latter river. They followed its course through an open country, with high mountains on each side, partially covered with pine and watered by several streams, crowded as usual with beaver-dams. Nine miles from the top of the ridge they reached the Yellowstone itself, about a mile and a half below [the point] where it issues [through Lower cañon] from the Rocky mountains.[20]

It now appeared that communication between the two

in the Gallatin range, and flows northwestward to its confluence just below Bozeman. The middle, main, or eastern fork comes from Bozeman Pass and vicinity through Rocky cañon, receiving in its course Meadow and Bear creeks and some lesser affluents. The Yellowstone affluent with which it connects on the other side of Bozeman Pass is Billman's or Trail creek. The altitude of the pass is about 5,800 feet. Places on the N. P. R. R. are Gordon, Chestnut, Mountain Side, Timber Line, West End, Muir City, Hopper's, and Coal Spur. On making the divide, the Captain Clark passes from Gallatin into Park Co.

[20] A mile or two above site of present town of Livingston, Park Co., Mont., some 45 miles north of Yellowstone National Park, where a branch of the N. P. R. R. runs up into the Park, and the main road keeps on to Bozeman, Gallatin City, etc. This is the point of nearest approach of the Yellowstone to headwaters of the middle fork of East Gallatin river. It is singular that Clark gives no names to the geographically important streams he discovered on this traverse. His distances are very near those since determined by accurate survey. I transcribe his hitherto unpublished "Course Distance & Remarks from the Three forks of Missouri to the River Rochejhone where it enters the Rocky mounts.," Clark M 70:

rivers was short and easy.   From the head of the Missouri
at its Three Forks to this place is a distance of 48 miles, the
greatest part of which is through a level plain ; indeed, from
the forks of the eastern branch of Gallatin river [*i. e.*, Three
Forks of East Gallatin river], which is there navigable for
small canoes, to this part of the Yellowstone, the distance is

"S. 85° E. 6 Miles through an open plain crossing a ridge to gallitines river,
it having made a bend to the S.W, Campd. . .

" S. 78° E. 6 Miles to a part of the river which is divided by numbers of beaver
dams on one channel of the river.   passed through an open leavel butifull
plain covered with low grass.   river making a bend to the N.E. from the
place [Logan] I crossed it this morning. . .

" S. 70° E. 6 Miles to the main principal stream [West Gallatin] of the river
which we crossed having crossed several streams near the crossing.   a leavel
firm plain on the Island.

" S. 78° E. 12 Miles to the most southerly [Bozeman creek] of the three Easterly
branches of the Easterly fork of Gallitines river.   passed through an open
leavel plain in which there is three [one of them is Middle creek] Small
streams of water from the snow mountains [Gallatin range] to the South. . .
marked my W.C. July 14th. 1806. with powder on a cotton tree at the
river.

" N. 80° E. 3 Miles to the entrance of a small branch which falls into the Middle branch of the East fork of Gallitine River having crossed the middle
branch at 2 miles, . . . encamped. . .

" N. 45° E. 3 Miles to the top of the mountain in a low gap [Rocky Cañon] passing up the [middle] branch [of Gallatin's river] on which we encamped
last night.

" East 3 Miles to the top of the dividing ridge [Bozeman Pass] between the
waters of the Missouri and those of the river Rochejhone, passing down a
small branch and at 2½ miles crossing a larger branch of the middle fork of
the East fork of Gallitins about ½ a mile above the branch I came down.
running to the right a road coms in from the left which passes through
a low gap of the mtn. from the most easterly branch of the East fork.

" S. 45° E. 1 mile down a small branch crossed two runs from the left passing
on the hillside to the left of the branch.

" N. 75° E. 8 Miles to the River Rochejhone passed down on the Northerly side
side of the said branch [Billman's or Trail creek] across which there is several beaver dams, crossed three small streams from the left with running
water one of which is crouded with beaver dams, a small stream [Coke
creek] com's in on the right at 6 ms.   Struck the Rochejhone ½ a mile
below the branch we came down and 1½ ms. below where it passes out of
the Rocky mountains. . . .

" Ms. 48."   (Gallatin City to Livingston is scheduled as 53 miles by rail.)

no more than 18 miles, with an excellent road over a high, dry country, with hills of inconsiderable height and no difficulty in passing. They halted three hours to rest their horses, and then pursued the buffalo-road along the [left [21]] bank of the river.

Although just leaving a high snowy mountain, the Yellowstone is already a bold, rapid, and deep stream, 120 yards in width. The bottoms of the river are narrow within the mountains, but widen to the extent of nearly two miles in the valley below, where they are occasionally overflowed; the soil gives nourishment to cottonwood, rose-bushes, honeysuckle, rushes, common coarse grass, a species of rye, and such productions of moist lands. On each side these low grounds are bounded by dry plains of coarse gravel and sand, stretching back to the foot of the mountains and supplied with a very short grass. The mountains on the east side of the river are rough, rocky, and still retain great quantities of snow; two other high snowy mountains may be distinguished, one bearing north 15 or 20 miles, the other nearly east. They have no covering except a few scattered pine, nor indeed was any timber fit for even a small canoe to be seen. At the distance of nine (*p. 378*) miles from the mountain, a river discharges into the Yellowstone from the northwest, under a high rocky cliff [Sheep Cliffs]. It rises from the snowy [Crazy] mountains in that direction; is about 35 yards wide; has a bold, deep current; is skirted by some cottonwoods and willow-trees; and, like the Yellowstone itself, seems to abound in beaver. They gave it the name of Shields' river,[22] after one of the party. Immedi-

[21] Past Livingston and Benson's Landing, between which places the N. P. R. R., coming up the Yellowstone along its south bank, crosses this river. Some small runs are passed before Shields' river is reached, two of them, both from the south, being called Chicken and Poison.

[22] Still so named; on Clark's map it is the first tributary of the Yellowstone to be marked by a name, "Shield R."; same in the codex; sometimes Shield's. It rises in the Crazy mountains, about Three Peaks, where are also the heads of Howard's or Sixteen-mile creek (see p. 440) and some southerly sources of the Musselshell, and flows E. of S. into the Yellowstone. Some of its tributaries

ately below is a very good buffalo-road, which obviously leads from its head, through a gap in the mountain, over to the waters of the Missouri. They passed Shields' river, and at three miles further, after crossing a high rocky hill, camped in a low bottom near the entrance of a small creek.[23] As they came through the mountains they had seen two black bears and a number of antelopes, as well as several herds of elk, between 200 and 300 in number; but had been able to kill only a single elk.

July 16*th*. A hunter [Labiche] was dispatched ahead, while the party collected the straggling horses. They then proceeded down the river, which is very straight and has several islands covered with cottonwood and willow; but they could not procure a single tree large enough for a canoe, and being unwilling to trust altogether to skin-canoes, Captain Clark preferred going on until they found some timber. The feet of the horses were now nearly worn to the quick, particularly the hind feet, so that they were obliged to make a sort of moccasin of green buffalo-skin, which relieved them very much in crossing the plains. After passing a bold creek[24] from the south, 20 yards wide,

are Cottonwood, Flathead, Fly, Pine, Brackett, Rock, Wood, Rabbit, Willow, and Falls creeks, in the order named from above downward. This stream and its tributaries drain between the Crazy mountains and Bridger range. There is a place called Shields at its mouth, and a little lower down the Yellowstone, on the opposite side, were the old Mission and the old Crow Agency. (For another Shields' river, see p. 375.)

[23] Unidentified. Several small streams come down from Sheep Cliffs. Camp is about opposite or rather above a large creek from the south or right, now called Skull or Mission (see next note); a little lower down are Lock and Greeley creeks, on the same side; between these is Elton station, on the N. P. R. R.

[24] Clark M 75, July 16th, from camp: " N. 80° E. 9 miles to a Bluff in a Stard. bend, the general course of the river very streight, passing several islands, most of them covered with Cotton trees and willow. passed *Stinking Cabin Creek* 20 yards wide bold current from the South which falls in on the Stard. Side timber up this cree[k] as far as I could see." Unfortunately this creek is noted only by direction, not for position, on this course of nine miles; it is charted by Clark, nameless. For all that appears to the contrary it might be either one of the three last named; but may be identifiable by its description. Distances are overestimated to-day, and must be adjusted with the first " 6½ " miles of

they halted for dinner on an island; then they went on till at night they camped near the entrance of another small stream,[25] having made 26 miles during the day. They saw some bears and great numbers of antelope and elk; but the soreness of their horses' feet rendered it difficult to chase them. One of the men caught a fish [*Pantosteus jordani*] which they had not seen before; it was eight inches long, and resembled a trout in form, but its mouth was like that of the sturgeon, and it (*p. 379*) had a red streak passing on each side from the gills to the tail. In the plains were but few plants except silk-grass, wild indigo, and sunflower, which are now all in bloom. The high grounds on the river are faced with a deep freestone rock, of a hard, sharp grit, which may also be seen in perpendicular strata throughout the plain.

July 17*th*. It rained during the night, and as the party had no covering but a buffalo-skin, they rose drenched with water. Pursuing their journey at an early hour, over the point of a ridge and through an open low bottom, they reached, at the distance of 6½ miles, a part of the river where two large creeks enter immediately opposite each other; one from the northwest, the other from the south of southwest. These Captain Clark called Rivers-across.[26]

to-morrow, which bring us to " Rivers-across "—the latter being an absolutely fixed point. I think that Stinking Cabin creek is actually Skull or Mission, the first one of the three from the south already mentioned, and thus much above McAdow's cañon. The next considerable creek from the south is Mendenhall's, at the mouth of which is Springdale, on the N. P. R. R., scheduled as 20 miles by rail below Livingston (following the curves of the river). Two creeks below Mendenhall's are Gage, N., and Antelope, S.; Duck creek, N., on which is Hunter's Hot Springs, is a very short distance above Mendenhall's.

[25] " A small creek on the Lard. side below which I incamped," Clark M 75. This is Little Timber creek.

[26] " Rivers a Cross," Clark M 77 ; " Rivers across," M 76 ; elsewhere Rivers Across ; in the orig. ed. the end of the line happened to come across the phrase, which was consequently hyphenated, and I preserve this form. It was a happy hit of Clark's. The odd term attracted attention to this pair of rivers, and proved more serviceable for identifying them than if he had named each of them—which he did not do. The one from the north is now known as Big Timber river or creek, and at 1½ miles above its mouth is now the town of Big Timber, on the N. P. R. R., scheduled as 15 miles by rail below Springdale. The other one

At 10½ miles further they halted for dinner below the entrance of a large creek on the northeast side, about 30 yards in width, which they named Otter[27] river. Nearly opposite this is another, to which they gave the name of Beaver[28] river. The waters of both are of a milky color, and the banks well supplied with small timber. The river is now becoming more divided by islands, and a number of small creeks fall in on both sides. The largest of these is about seven miles from Beaver river, and enters on the right ; they called it Bratton's[29] river, from one of the men. The highlands approach the river more nearly than before, but although their sides are partially supplied with pine and cedar, the growth is still too small for canoes. Buffalo are beginning to be more abundant, and to-day, for the first time on this river, they saw a pelican ; but deer and elk are now

of the pair, from the south, is Boulder river, considerably larger than Big Timber. It is formed by three main courses, East, Middle, and West, which head but little north of Yellowstone Park. Its main stream and East fork together delimit to some extent the present Crow Indian Reservation on the west. Within a mile below Rivers-across a considerable stream falls in on the north. This the text does not notice, but the codex does : " N. 76° E. 1½ miles to the entrance of a brook in the Lard. bend," Clark M 77. This is Medicine-bow creek of various civil and military maps before me, which I regret to find charted on the Big Timber sheet of the beautiful U.S. Geol. Surv. cartographs as Otter creek—for this is sure to be confounded with the Otter creek of our text : see on.

Before we pass to the next pair of rivers (Otter and Beaver) we must notice a curiously named creek which the text omits. At six miles beyond the last-named, and 7½ from Rivers-across, Clark M 77 has : " Thy Snag'd creek on the Stard. Side." For the explanation we must turn to Clark M 80, July 18th : "Gibson in attempting to mount his horse after shooting a deer this evening fell on a Snag and runt [ran] it nearly two inches into the muskeler part of his thy." Thigh-snagged creek is that now known as Little Deer or Upper Deer creek. It runs parallel with Lower Deer or Big Deer creek, about two miles above which it falls into the Yellowstone.

[27] Now Sweetgrass creek, at whose mouth is a place of same name, otherwise known as Harrison's Ferry.

[28] Now Lower Deer or Big Deer creek : see note above. Below this, and before Bratton's river is reached, the codex speaks of a " high clift " in a starboard bend, Clark M 78. This is the remarkable precipice, 4,230 ft. high, and thus several hundred feet above the river, called Gray Cliff or Greycliff.

[29] " Bratten R." of Clark's map. Bratton's is now Bridger's river or creek. It is not a large stream (smaller than Lower Deer creek), but somewhat notable

more scarce than before. In one of the low bottoms of the river was an Indian fort, which seemed to have been built last summer. It was built in the form of a circle, about fifty feet in diameter and five feet high, formed of logs lapping over each other, and covered on the outside with bark set up on end. The entrance was guarded by a work on (*p. 380*) each side of it, facing the river. These intrenchments, the squaw informs us, are frequently made by the Minnetarees and other Indians at war with the Shoshonees, when pursued by their enemies on horseback. After making 33 miles, the party camped near a point of woods in the narrow bottom of the river.

July 18*th.*[30] Before setting out they killed two buffaloes which ventured near the camp, and then pursued their route over the ridges of the high lands, so as to avoid the bends of the river, which now washes the feet of the hills. The face of the country is rough and stony, covered with immense quantities of prickly-pear. The river is nearly 200 yards wide, rapid as usual, with a bed of coarse gravel and round stones. The same materials are the basis of the soil in the

for the open character of the country east of it, permitting two trails northward from Stillwater river to meet at its mouth. The codex notices "a small brook on the Stard. side" three miles below Bratton's, which the text omits ; this is Work creek. The codex notices another creek from the south, three miles lower down, which Clark N 131 calls Weasel creek ; this is Hump creek, two miles below which is the N. P. R. R. station Reed Point, opposite a large island, nine miles by rail below Greycliff. To-day's camp is set two or three miles below this point.

[30] July 18th is barren in the text, but the codex is fruitful of notable points, as usual : see also Clark's map, where three streams, N., are charted, two of them by name, between Bratton's river and the Rosebud (Stillwater). He first passes White Beaver creek, N., which corresponds to the "Dry Cr." of his map. Below this he crosses the boundary between Park and Yellowstone counties. Next comes town of Merrill, scheduled ten miles below Reed Point, and near which the N. P. R. R. crosses the river to run on its N. side as far as Billings. Merrill is on Berry creek, which is the one Clark charts without name. Next comes the "Fort Cr." of Clark's map, which is Keyser's creek, falling into the Yellowstone about opposite the Rosebud, below Benson's Bluff, and above Stillwater, which town is eight miles by rail below Merrill. To-day's camp is on an island, near the mouth of the Rosebud.

high bottoms, with a mixture of dark brown earth. The river-hills are about 200 feet high, still faced with a dark freestone rock; the country back of them is broken into open waving plains. Pine is the only growth of importance; but among the smaller plants were distinguished purple, yellow, and black currants, which are now ripe and of an excellent flavor.

About eleven o'clock a smoke was descried to the S.S.E., toward the termination of the Rocky mountains, intended most probably as a signal of the Crow Indians, who have mistaken us for their enemies, or for friends to trade with them. They [we] could not, however, stop to ascertain the truth of this conjecture, but rode on; and after passing another old Indian fort, similar to that seen yesterday, halted for the night on a small island, 26 miles from the camp of last evening. One of the hunters [Gibson], attempting to mount his horse after shooting a deer, fell on a small piece of timber, which ran nearly two inches into the muscular part of his thigh. The wound was very painful; were it not for their great anxiety to reach the United States this season, the party would have remained till he was cured; but time was too precious to wait.

[*July* 19*th*.] The gentlest and strongest (*p. 381*) horse was therefore selected, and a sort of litter formed in such a manner as to enable the sick man to lie nearly at full length. They then proceeded gently, and at the distance of two miles passed a river entering from the southeast side, about 40 yards wide, called by the Indians Itchkeppearja, or Rose[31] river; a name which it deserves, as well from its beauty as from the roses which we saw budding on its borders. Soon afterward they passed another Indian

[31] A " Rose " or " Rosebud " river, the same with this, is still down on some maps ; but must not be confounded with the greatly larger Rosebud river, much farther down the Yellowstone, between Bighorn and Tongue rivers. The present Itchkeppearja river is charted by Clark as " Rosebud R." It is formed of three main courses, Big and Little Rosebud and Stillwater, whose conjoined waters now take the latter name, and flow into the Yellowstone nearly opposite Stillwater (town). The old Crow Agency was on the first-named of these branches.

fort on an island; and after making nine miles halted to let
the horses graze, and sent out a hunter to look for timber
to make a canoe, and procure, if possible, some wild ginger
to make a poultice for Gibson's thigh, which was now exceedingly painful, in consequence of his constrained position.
He returned, however, without being able to find either;
but brought back two bucks. He had a contest with two
white bears which chased him ; but being on horseback he
escaped, after wounding both of them. There are great
quantities of currants in the plains; but almost every blade
of grass for many miles has been destroyed by immense
swarms of grasshoppers,[32] which appear to be ascending the
river. After taking some refreshments they proceeded, and
found that the hills became lower on both sides; those on
the right overhanging the river in cliffs of a darkish yellow
earth, and the bottoms widening to several miles in extent.
The timber, though chiefly cottonwood, is becoming large.

They had not gone far when Gibson's wound became so
violently painful that he could no longer remain on horseback. He was therefore left with two men under the shade
of a tree, while Captain Clark went on to seek for timber.
At the distance of 18 [?] miles from his camp of last night he
halted near a thick grove of trees, some of which were large
enough for small canoes, and then searched all the adjacent
country till evening, when Gibson was brought on to the
camp.[33] The game of to-day consisted of six deer, seven elk,
and an antelope. The smoke which had been (*p. 382*) seen
on the 17th was again distinguished this afternoon, and one
of the party reported that he had observed an Indian on the
highlands on the opposite side of the river.

[32] *Caloptenus spretus*, the now famous Rocky Mountain locust or hateful grasshopper, which does almost incalculable damage to the crops.

[33] This camp, where the party will remain till the 24th, and the location of which
is to be sought, is given as 16 miles by land below the Itchkeppearja, and 29
river-miles above Clark's Fork. Certainly no such distance as 45 miles intervenes
between these two fixed points. The distance by rail from Stillwater to Laurel
is scheduled as only 24 miles. Reducing our figures by rule of three, but
taking into consideration that he reaches this camp by land, and then proceeds to

Sunday, July 20th. At daylight two good judges of timber [Pryor and Shields] were sent down the river in quest of lumber, but returned without being able to find any trees larger than those near camp; nor could they procure any for ax-handles except choke-cherry. Captain Clark determined therefore to make two canoes which, lashed together, might be sufficient to convey the party down the river, while a few men might lead the horses to the Mandan nation. Three axes were sharpened with a file, and some of the men proceeded to cut down two of the largest trees, on which they worked till night. The rest of the party were occupied in dressing skins for clothes, or in hunting, in which they were so fortunate as to procure a deer, two buffalo, and an elk. The horses being much fatigued, they were turned out to rest for a few days; but in the morning,

July 21st, 24 of them were missing. Three hunters [Shannon, Bratton, and "Shabono"] were sent in different directions to look for them; but all returned unsuccessful, and it now seemed probable that the Indians who had made the smoke a few days since had stolen the horses. In the meantime the men worked so diligently on the canoes that one of them was nearly completed. Late in the evening a very black cloud, accompanied with thunder and lightning, rose from the southeast, and rendered the weather extremely warm and disagreeable. The wind too was very high, but shifted toward morning,

July 22d, to the northeast, and became moderately cool.

navigate, we can hardly allow him more than twelve miles of actual advance to-day. This would bring him somewhat below Trout Rapids and the railroad station called Rapids, which latter is three miles below the point where Hensley creek falls in from the north. As no rapids are noted on the first day's voyage, July 24th, he was doubtless past this point. I give the last course, Clark M 84: "East 3 ms. on the course to a clump of large Cottonwood trees in a Lard. Bend passing several Islands river much divided and crooked. high yellow Bluffs on the Stard. Side under which part of the river passes. The bottoms wide and extensive on the Lard. Side. Encamped." Again, Clark N 131 has: "☞ Black bluffs opposit to the place Capt. C. built 2 canoes." These details may be found to fit a place on the north bank of the river, 1¾ miles below Rapids station, one mile above the entrance of Rye Grass creek from the south,

Three men [two, Pryor and "Shabono"] were dispatched in quest of the horses; but they came back without being able to discover even a track, the plains being so hard and dry that the foot makes no impression. This confirms the suspicion of their being stolen by the Indians, who would probably take them across (*p. 383*) the plains to avoid being pursued by their traces; besides the improbability of their voluntarily leaving the rushes and grass of the river-bottoms to go on the plains, where they could find nothing but a short dry grass. Four men [Pryor, Shannon, Bratton, and "Shabono"] were again sent out with orders to encircle the camp for a great distance; but they too returned with no better success than those who had preceded them. The search was resumed in the morning,

July 23d, when a piece of a robe and a moccasin were discovered not far from camp. The moccasin was worn out in the sole, still wet, and had every appearance of having been left but a few hours before. This sign was conclusive that the Indians had taken our horses, and were still prowling about for the remainder, which fortunately escaped last night by being on a small prairie surrounded by thick timber. At length Labiche, who is one of the best trackers, returned from a very wide circuit, and informed Captain Clark that he had traced the tracks of the horses, which were bending their course rather down the river toward the open plains, and [judging] from the tracks, were going very rapidly. All hopes of recovering them were now abandoned. Indians are not the only plunderers which surround camp;

half a mile above the entrance of Allen's creek from the north, and about the same below the upper end of Billing's ditch; if so, they serve to fix precisely the spot where Captain Clark first found cottonwoods large enough for canoes, and whence he proceeded wholly by water to St. Louis. These canoes, which Mr. Biddle on the 24th inst. takes the truly poetic license of calling "a little flotilla," were simply a pair of dug-outs lashed together with raw-hide; but they did wonderfully good service, and were not turned adrift till the morning of Sept. 20th, at the mouth of the Osage river, only 3½ days before the end of the Expedition. The place where they were built should have a name; and I propose to call it Camp Cottonwood.

for last night the wolves or dogs stole the greater part of the dried meat from the scaffold.   The wolves which constantly attend the buffalo, are here in great numbers, for this seems to be the commencement of the buffalo country.   Besides these are seen antelopes, pigeons, doves, hawks, ravens, crows, larks, sparrows, eagles, bank-martins, etc.; great numbers of geese, too, which raise their young on this river, have passed the camp.   The country consists of beautiful level plains, but the soil is thin and stony; both plains and low grounds are covered with great quantities of prickly pear.

At noon the two canoes were finished.   They are 28 feet long, 16 or 18 inches deep, and from 16 to 24 inches wide. Being lashed to- (*p. 384*) gether, everything was prepared for setting out to-morrow.   Gibson had now recovered. Sergeant Pryor[34] was directed, with Shannon and Windsor, to take our horses to the Mandans; and if he found that Mr. Henry was on the Assiniboin river, to go thither and deliver him a letter, the object of which was to prevail on the most distinguished chiefs of the Sioux to accompany him to Washington.

[34] This further subdivision of the party is given in Clark M 88 : " I gave Sergt. Pryor his instructions and a letter to Mr. Haney [*sic*] and derected that he G. Shannon & Windser take the remaining horses to the Mandans, where he is to inquire for Mr. H : Heney [*sic*] if at the establishment on the Assinniboin river to to take 12 or 14 horses and proceed on to that place and deliver Mr. Haney the letter which is with a view to engage Mr. Haney to provale on some of the best informed and most influential chiefs of the different bands of *Sieoux* to accompany us to the Seat of our Government with a view to let them see our population and resourses &c. which I believe is the surest garentee of Savage fidelity to any nation that of a Governmt. possessing the power of punishing promptly every aggression."

CHAPTER XXXV.

CAPTAIN CLARK DESCENDS THE YELLOWSTONE—REUNION OF THE EXPEDITION ON THE MISSOURI.

Sergeant Pryor to go by land along the Yellowstone—Captain Clark descends the river—Clark's fork—Beavers numerous—Large Indian lodge—Horse creek—Many buffalo—Sergeant Pryor arrives with the horses—Pryor's creek—Remarkable sculptured rock named Pompey's Pillar—Extensive prospect—The party reaches the mouth of the Bighorn—Last view of the Rockies, in sight since May—Elk creek—Windsor's river—Labiche's river—Various tributaries of the Yellowstone, including that now called the Rosebud—Tongue river—Buffalo shoals—Bear rapids—York's Dry river—Redstone (Powder) river—Wolf rapids—Coal river—Gibson's river—Progress obstructed by buffalo—Trouble with bears—Persecution by mosquitoes—Fields' creek—Camp at mouth of the Yellowstone, Aug. 3d, 1806—Review of the Yellowstone and its tributaries—Various Indian tribes noted—Driven away by mosquitoes, the party starts down the Missouri—White-earth river—Sergeant Pryor's party arrives and reports; the Indians had stolen their horses; they had gone to the Yellowstone near Pompey's Pillar, and come down that river in improvised bull-boats—The united parties proceed down the Missouri—They meet Messrs. Dickson and Hancock, and hear news—They go on (Aug. 11th) and next day will be overtaken below Goat-pen creek by Captain Lewis' party, thus reuniting the whole Expedition on the Missouri (Aug. 12th, 1806).

THURSDAY, July 24th, 1806. The canoes were loaded. Sergeant Pryor and his party set out with orders to proceed down [the left bank of the Yellowstone] to the entrance of Bighorn river, which was supposed to be at no great distance, where they should be taken in the boats across the Yellowstone. At eight o'clock Captain Clark embarked in the little flotilla, and proceeded very steadily down the river, which continues to be about 200 yards wide, and contains a number of islands, some of which are supplied with a small growth of timber. At the distance of a mile from camp, the river passes under a high bluff for about 23 [?] miles, when the bottoms widen on both sides. At the distance of 29 [?] miles, a river falls in from the south. This is the river [we] sup- (*p. 386*) posed to be the Bighorn; but afterward, when the Bighorn was found, the name of Clark's fork was given this stream.[1] It is a bold river, 150 yards

[1] Still so named ; to be found also as Clarke's, Clarck's and Clake's fork or river. "Proceeded on verry well to a riffle about 1 mile above the enterance

wide at the entrance, but a short distance above is contracted to 100 yards.   The water is of a light muddy color
and much colder than that of the Yellowstone; its general
course is south and east of the Rocky mountains.   There is
a small island situated immediately at the entrance; this or
the adjoining mainland would form a very good position
for a fort.   The country most frequented by beaver begins
here, and that which lies between this river and the Yellowstone is, perhaps, the best district for the hunters of that
animal.   About a mile before reaching this river, there is
a ripple in the Yellowstone, on passing which the canoes
took in some water.   The party therefore landed to bail the
boats, and then proceeded six miles [2] further to a large
island, where they halted to wait for Sergeant Pryor.

It is a beautiful spot with rich soil, covered with wild rye,
a species of grass, and some of another kind which the
Indians wear in plaits around the neck, on account of
a strong scent resembling that of vanilla. [3]   There is also
a thin growth of cottonwood scattered over the island.   In

of Clarks fork or *big horn river* a river 150 yds. wide comes in from
South we thought it the B. H. but aftds. when we found the B. H. we called it
Clarks fork a bold river washing plain—The Indians call this —— or ' The
Lodge where all dance,' " Clark M 90, where an original writing is interlined
in red ink as here quoted, but without deletion of the other text.   The missing
Indian name I suppose to be Ap-sah-soo-ha, as lettered on Clark's map, which
see.   This is by far the largest branch of the Yellowstone thus far met, and one
of the four largest tributaries of this noble river.   The town of Laurel is nearly
opposite its mouth ; above is Park City, on the N. P. R. R.   Young's Point was
passed early to-day ; also Valley creek, N.

[2] Vicinity of Cañon, Canon, or Canyon creek, from the north ; place of same
name at its mouth, nearly halfway between Laurel and Billings.   At a point up
this creek will be found on some maps the legend " Sturges Bat Field "—which
being interpreted means that here General Sturgis, U. S. A., had an Indian fight.
A short distance below Cañon creek a stream falls in on the right, from the
south.   Clark M 93 notes it exactly, at a point he makes 10½ miles below Clark's
fork : " A large brook in a Stard. Bend. opposite a stony bar."   This is now
called Blue creek—one of very many we find in the Yellowstone Codex, but of
which the text takes no notice.

[3] " A mixture of sweet grass which the Indians plat and ware around their
necks for its cent which is of a Strong sent like that of the vinella," Clark M 91.
This is the well-known holy-grass, *Hierochloa borealis*, also called seneca-grass.

the center is a large Indian lodge, which seems to have been built last summer. It is in the form of a cone, 60 feet in diameter at the base, composed of 20 poles, each 45 feet long and 2½ in circumference, and the whole structure covered with bushes. The interior was curiously ornamented. On the tops of the poles were feathers of eagles, and circular pieces of wood, with sticks across them in the form of a girdle; from the center was suspended a stuffed buffalo-skin; on the side fronting the door was hung a cedar-bush; on one side of the lodge, a buffalo's head; on the other, several pieces of wood stuck in the ground. From its whole appearance, it was more like a lodge for holding councils than an ordinary dwelling-house.

(*p. 387*) Sergeant Pryor not having yet arrived, they went on about 15½ [?] miles further to a small creek on the right, to which they gave the name of Horse [4] creek, and just below it overtook Sergeant Pryor with the horses. He had found it almost impossible, with two men, to drive on the remaining horses; for as soon as they discovered a herd of buffalo the loose horses, having been trained by the Indians to hunt, immediately set off in pursuit of them, and surrounded the herd with almost as much skill as their riders could have done. At last he was obliged to send one horseman forward to drive all the buffalo from the route. The horses were here driven across, and Sergeant Pryor again proceeded with an additional man [Hall [5]] to his party. The river is here

---

[4] " Hors creek falls in on Std.," Clark M 93. This is but little below Billings, county seat of Yellowstone Co., on left bank of the river, at or near mouth of Alkali creek, from the north. Here the N. P. R. R. crosses the Yellowstone, and the point is also notable as being about the head of steamboat navigation. A short distance below Alkali creek comes in Bitter creek, from the north. At 7½ miles below Horse creek the codex has a nameless brook from the *south*, which I cannot identify ; it is to be sought 10½ codex-miles above Pryor's fork, *i. e.*, in the vicinity of Huntley, or between Spring Butte, N., and Belle Butte, S.

[5] " H. Hall who cannot swim expressed a williness to proceed on with Sergt. Pryor by land, and as another man was necessary to assist in driving on the horses but observed he was necked [naked] I gave him one of my two remaining shirts a par of Leather Legins and 3 pr. of mockersons which equipt him completely and sent him on with the party by land to the Mandans," Clark M 92.

much more deep and navigable, and the current more regular, than above Clark's fork ; and though much divided by well-wooded islands, when collected the stream is between 200 and 300 feet in width. Along its banks are some beaver, and an immense number of deer, elk, and buffalo. Toward night they passed a creek [river] from the southeast, 35 yards wide, which they called Pryor's creek [river⁶] ; half a mile below which they camped, after making 69½ miles during the day.

*July 25th.*⁷ They resumed their voyage at sunrise, and

⁶ Still so named, and notable as delimiting on the west the present restricted Crow Indian Reservation, which until very recently extended west to Boulder creek (the southern one of the " Rivers-across "). This large stream comes north from the Pryor or Pryor's mountains in which it heads, and on which there is a pass called Pryor's Gap. Huntley station of the N. P. R. R. is on the river near its mouth. It is a slip of the text to call this stream Pryor's *creek :* for this, see next note.

⁷ To-day's text omits everything from Pryor's river to Pompey's Pillar, but the codex yields the required data. Within six miles from Pryor's river Clark M 97 has : " Passed rock creek (small) on the Lard. side." In fact two such streams fall in from the north in the distance given. These are now called Crooked and Razor, and one of them is the Rock creek of the codex. Clark actually charts both, though without names. Along the river here are rapids known as Hellgate and Little Giant. In the next course of five miles the codex has : " Passed the enterance of a small river on Stard. Side." This is Arrow creek ; Clermont at its mouth, nine miles by rail below Huntley station. This stream is called " Pryor's creek in the big bend," Clark N 131, where it is marked from the S.E., 11 miles below Pryor's river, in the tabular statement of Yellowstone points ; and Clark's map lays it down, nameless. L. and C. afford several other instances of such naming, where the distinction is between " creek " and " river " for different streams which they call by the same name. Again : within the next few miles Clark M 97 formally notes no fewer than *five* more small streams from the left or north, one of which he names Big Dry brook, N 131 ; and he notes also Tumbling Bluff, N 131, " on the Lard. Side which has sliped into the river and filled up ⅓ of the river." As to his distances, which certainly seem excessive, we must remember that what the text and codex both give is the *wake of his ungainly craft*—a couple of dug-out cottonwood logs lashed together—steered back and forth across the river amidst uncounted islands, and by no means to be taken as any sure indication of actual air-line advance, or even progress by land. It is most like the laborious ascent of the Expedition up Jefferson river, where the advance was ½, ⅓, even ¼ of the actual navigation. When we correctly adjust his wake's mileages between any two known points, we find that the creeks, bluffs, and islands fall into

passed a number of islands and small streams, and occasionally high bluffs composed of a yellow, gritty stone. A storm
of rain and high southwest wind soon overtook them, and
obliged them to land and form a sort of log hut, covered
with deerskins. As soon as it ceased they proceeded ; and
about four o'clock, after having made 49 miles, Captain
Clark landed to examine a very remarkable rock situated in
an extensive bottom on the right, 250 paces from the shore.[8]
It is nearly 400 paces in circumference, 200 feet high, and
accessible only from the northeast, the other sides being a
perpendicular cliff of a light-colored gritty rock. The soil
of the top is (*p. 388*) five or six feet deep, of good quality,
and covered with short grass. The Indians have carved the
figures of animals and other objects on the sides of the rock,
and on the top are raised two piles of stones.

From this height the eye ranges over a large extent of
variegated country : on the southwest, the Rocky mountains
covered with snow ; a low mountain about 40 miles distant,
bearing S. 15° E.; and in a direction N. 55° W., at the distance of 35 miles, the southern extremity of what are called
the Little Wolf [now Bull] mountains. The low grounds of
the river extend nearly six miles to the southward, when they
rise into plains reaching to the mountains, watered with a

their actual positions with admirable precision. I have heard L. and C.'s
Yellowstone narrative belittled by competent critics, who knew what they
were talking about, and justly complained that they could find little in it but
Pompey's Pillar, Rivers-across, and some of the largest tributaries. But
that does Captain Clark a cruel injustice. He missed very little, as we now
see by the many new points I am picking out of the codex ; and if I were
to transcribe his formal courses and distances in full, we should find almost
every bluff, bottom, and island, as well as almost every tributary. No part
of the whole Expedition is so inadequately represented in the published narrative as this Yellowstone exploration, which may not unfairly be regarded as
slurred.

[8] " And opposit to a large Brook on the Lard. Side I call baptiests creek,"
Clark M 98, after Baptiste Lepage ; " Baptist Cr." of Clark's map. This
stream, which the text should never have ignored, is now known as Pompey's
Pillar creek, from the remarkable rock about to be described. It comes S.E.
from the Bull mountains (the Little Wolf mountains of our text), and near its
mouth is a notable isolated elevation known as Pine Butte.

large creek; while at some distance below a range of high-
land, covered with pine, stretches on both sides of the river
in a direction north and south.   The north side of the river,
for some distance, is surrounded by romantic jutting cliffs;
these are succeeded by rugged hills, beyond which the
plains are again open and extensive.   The whole country
is enlivened by herds of buffalo, elk, and wolves.

After enjoying the prospect from this rock, to which Captain Clark gave the name of Pompey's Pillar,[9] he descended
and continued his course.   At the distance of six or seven
miles he stopped to get two bighorns, which were shot from
the boat; and while on shore saw in the face of the cliff on
the left, about 20 feet above the water, the fragment of a
rib of a fish, 3 feet long and nearly 3 inches round, incrusted
in the rock itself, and neither decayed nor petrified, but
very rotten [*i. e.*, brittle or friable from exposure to the
weather].   After making 58 miles they reached the entrance
of a stream on the right,[10] about 22 yards wide, which
discharges a great quantity of muddy water.   Here they

[9] "East to Pompys Tower," Clark M 97! "Pompeys Tower," Clark N 131!
"Pompey's Tower," Clark's map.   So our hero must have polished up his
classics later, or perhaps had a shine put on them by his editor.   "I marked
my name and the day of the month and year" on the rock, Clark M 95.   Mr. Peter
Koch, of Bozeman, and several other correspondents, have called my attention to
the fact that Captain Clark's sign manual is still legible.   I understand it to be in
the usual form of his signature, "Wm. Clark."   General John Gibbon, U. S. A.,
told me a few days ago that he had examined this inscription with care, and
judged from its weather-worn appearance that it was actually made by Clark's
hand, and not a recent forgery of some idle tourist.   Pompey's Pillar is now
also the name of a station on the N. P. R. R., scheduled as eight miles below
Clermont and seven above Bull Mountain station.

[10] Shannon's river or creek, Clark M 96, 98, and N 131, given in both codices
as nine miles below Pompey's Pillar.   This name should not have been suppressed, especially as it was the point on the Yellowstone at which Sergeant
Pryor's little party, having had all the horses they were driving to the Mandans
stolen by the Crows, made themselves "skin canoes," *i. e.*, bull-boats of buffalo-
hide, as duly noted in the codex, and floated in these down the Yellowstone.
At least three streams fall into the Yellowstone from the south between Pompey's
Pillar and Bull Mountain station.   Two of these are called Sand creek and Bull
Mountain creek.   Shannon's is doubtless the first one of these, heading about
Pine Ridge.   Forsyth's map miscalls it Pompey's Pillar creek.

camped rather earlier than usual, on account of a heavy squall, accompanied with some rain.   Early next morning,

July 26th, they proceeded.   The river is now much divided by stony islands and bars; but the current, though swift, is regular, and there are many very handsome islands covered with cottonwood.   On the left shore the bottoms (*p. 389*) are very extensive; the right bank is formed of high cliffs [White cliffs, Clark N 131] of a whitish gritty stone; beyond these, the country on both sides is diversified with waving plains, covered with pine.   At the distance of ten miles is a large creek on the right [left], about 40 yards in width, but containing very little water; in the course of the day are two smaller streams on the left [right], and a fourth [large] on the right [left ¹¹].   After coming 62 miles, they landed at the entrance of Bighorn ¹² river; but finding the point between the two [rivers] composed of soft mud and sand, liable to be overflowed, they ascended the Bighorn for half a mile, then crossed and formed a camp on its lower side. Captain Clark then walked up the river.

At the distance of seven miles, a creek 20 yards wide, which from the color of the water he called Muddy ¹³ creek, falls in on the northeast; a few miles further the river bends to the east of south.   The bottoms of the river are

¹¹ Text totally inadequate to any identification of these streams ; besides suppressing the names given by Captain Clark to the two large ones, text reverses all four from their proper positions !   1.   " A large creek 40 yds. wide on Lard. side I call Hall's R.," Clark M 101 ; also N 131, making it 10 m. below Shannon's river.   This is one now called Cañon or Cannon creek.   2.   " A small creek on the Stard.," Clark M 101.   This is Bull Mountain creek.   3. " A small brook on the Stard.," Clark M 101.   This will be found in the vicinity of Riverside station or Conway, but its name I do not know.   The creek hereabouts on the opposite (north) side is called Hubberd.   4.   " A large creek falls in on the Lard. side [I call it] Island brook," Clark M 101 ; also, N 131. This is given as " 16 " miles above the mouth of the Bighorn ; it is now called Buffalo creek.   It falls into the Yellowstone from the north, a short distance above Junction City and Custer.

¹² Engraved " Big Horn R." on Clark's 1814 map, and " Great Horn R." on that of the 1842 M'Vickar ed., where its main branch (the Little Bighorn) is styled " Lit. Horn R."

¹³ Charted by Clark, nameless ; now known as Tullock's fork of the Bighorn.

extensive, supplied chiefly with cottonwood trees, and variegated with great quantities of rose bushes. The current is regular and rapid; like the Missouri, it constantly changes, so as to wash away the banks on one side, leaving sand-bars on the other. Its bed contains much less of the large gravel than that of the Yellowstone; its water is muddier and of a brownish color, while the Yellowstone has a lighter tint. At their junction the two rivers are nearly equal in breadth, from 200 to 220 yards, but the Yellowstone contains much more water, being ten or twelve feet deep, while the depth of the Bighorn varies from five to seven feet. This is the river which had been described by the Indians as rising in the Rocky mountains, near the Yellowstone and the sources of the Platte, and then finding its way through the Cote Noir and the eastern range of the Rocky mountains.[14] In its long course it receives two [several] large

[14] The Bighorn is one of the three largest tributaries of the Yellowstone, Tongue and Powder rivers being the other two. All three rise in Wyoming; the Bighorn rises by numerous affluents in the Shoshone range and Wind River mountains, S.E. of the Yellowstone Park. Its southernmost affluents rise in the latter mountains about the South Pass, near the heads of the Sweetwater, a principal tributary of the North fork of the Platte. Across the main divide here are the eastern headwaters of Grand river, which joins Green river to form the Colorado of the West. But some far more interesting than these now well-known matters are found in the codex, concerning the *sources* of the Bighorn, as then understood. The text gives no hint of them, and they have not hitherto been published. First examine Clark's map of 1814, and trace "Colter's route in 1807," as there dotted from Pryor's fork over to Clark's fork, thence to the Yellowstone, up this and around Clark's Lake Eustis (which of course is Yellowstone Lake), thence around Clark's Lake Biddle (in which the Bighorn is made to head), thence over to heads of Clark's "Rio del Norte" (which is Green river), to *Colter's* river (which is the Big Sandy fork of Green river), to the Bighorn, to Salt fork, to the Boiling Spring on Stinking Water R., and so down Clark's fork again to Pryor's fork. For much, if not most of this information, the great geographer was undoubtedly indebted to Colter himself, who certainly discovered Lake Yellowstone (Eustis), and whose account of the Boiling Spring foreshadowed our knowledge of the famous Yellowstone geysers. Lake Biddle, in which Clark heads the Bighorn, may be one of those immediately south of Yellowstone Lake, in the Park; but is laid down more nearly in the position of Jackson Lake, under Mt. Moran, which is in the Snake river watershed. Stinking Water R. of Clark's map retains this name to-day. Clark N 125 has: "☞ From the Fort [*i. e.* Manuel Lisa's] or enterance of Bighorn River the Indians say a man on horseback

of Crows, and the Castahana, a small band of Snake Indians.[15]

Sunday, July 27th. They again set out very early, and on leaving the Bighorn took a last look at the Rocky mountains, which had been constantly in view from the 1st of May. The [Yellowstone] river now widens to the extent of from 400 to 600 yards; it is much divided by islands and sand-bars; its banks are generally low and falling in; it thus resembles the Missouri in many particulars, but its islands are more numerous, its waters less muddy, and the current is more rapid. The water is of a yellowish-white, and the round stones, which form the bars above the Bighorn, have given place to gravel. On the left side the river runs under cliffs of light, soft, gritty stone, varying in height from 70 to 100 feet, behind which are level and extensive plains. On the right side of the river are low extensive bottoms, bordered with cottonwood, various species of willow, rose-bushes, grapevines, redberry or buffalo-grease bushes, and a species of sumach; to these succeed high grounds supplied with pine, and still further on are level plains. Throughout the country are vast quantities of buffalo, which, as this is the running-season, keep up a continued bellowing. Large herds of elk also are lying on every point, so gentle that they may be approached within 20 paces without being alarmed. Several beaver were seen in the course of the day; indeed, there is a greater appearance of those animals than there was above the Bighorn. Deer, however, are by no means abundant, and antelopes, as well as bighorns, are scarce.

[15] Clark N 125 specifies as bands of Crows : " Ship-tâh-cha a band of Crow Indians of 150 Lodges and about 1500 soles rove on Bighorn River & Rochejhone. Ap-shâ-roo-kee a band of Crow Indians of 200 Lodges and about 2000 soles rove on the Tonge River, bighorn & River Rochejhone." The latter is of course the familiar name Absaroka. The codex further says : " Es-cup-scup-pe-âh a Band of Tushapaws speak their language and sometimes rove on the waters of the Rojhone, of about 80 Lodges 800 Soles." For the " Yep-pe Band of Snake Inds. 1000 Souls," see Clark's map ; which see also for the location of the Castahana tribe in the text, " 1500 Souls." See also pp. 58, 59 and notes there.

At 15 miles from Bighorn river they [had] passed a large dry creek on the left, to which they gave the name of Elk [16] (*p. 391*) creek, and halted for breakfast about three miles further, at the entrance of Windsor's [17] river, a stream from the left, which, though 50 yards wide, contains scarcely any water. At 48 miles from the Bighorn is the large bed of a stream, 60 yards wide, but with very little water. They called it Labiche's [18] river. Several other smaller streams,[19] or rather beds of creeks, were passed in the course of the day, and after coming 80½ miles, they camped on a large island.

July 28th. At daylight they proceeded down the smooth, gentle current, passing a number of islands and several creeks,

[16] Name since changed to Alkali creek ; charted without name by Clark, as the first stream below the Bighorn from the north. To reach it, he passed Allen's coulée, on the north or left, with a place by its mouth called Etchetah ; then two islands, a high cliff on the south, two more islands, and a bluff on the south ; and at the 15th mile of the text had passed Elk creek. All these points are duly codified, Clark M 103. The high ground on the right is Guy's bluffs ; the low ground on the left is Pease's bottom. On leaving the mouth of the Bighorn Captain Clark passed from Yellowstone into Custer Co., on his left ; but continues to have the Crow Indian Reservation on his right till he strikes long. 107° W. (A stream from the south is miscalled Alkali creek on Forsyth's map.)

[17] Windsor's river is charted by Clark, but unluckily lettered "Little Wolf R." by mistake. It is that stream from the north, opposite the mouth of which is now the town of Myers, on the N. P. R.R., ten miles below Bighorn station. This stream is now called Van Horn's or Pease's river or creek. I had the pleasure of Colonel Van Horn's acquaintance, and would be glad of any honor due him, but do not see how Private Richard Windsor can be rightly deprived of that which Captain Clark once bestowed upon him.

[18] By the codex this is 45 (not 48) miles below the Bighorn; is marked "Ork-ta-ha" on Lewis' map of 1806, where Clark laid it down upon Indian information, by an Indian name ; it is "Lebich R." of Clark's 1814 map ; "Labieshe's R.," Clark M 104 ; "Laabeech' R.," Clark N 132. It is now known as Sarpy or Sarpie's creek, from a trader who had a post below its mouth. The present town of Sanders, twelve miles by rail below Myers, is at its mouth, and will serve to identify the stream, which ought to bear the name which Clark gave it.

[19] "Several other small streams" are noted by Clark with his usual precision, and should not have been thus slighted in the text. First we have, from the south, a little below Windsor's, Van Horn's, or Pease's creek, a stream now called Box-elder ; of which, however, I find no mention in the codex. Next, the codex notes a cliff 60 feet high, "eight" miles below Windsor's river, on the north, and in connection with this cliff the codex speaks of two dry brooks, both above

which are now dry.   These are, indeed, more like torrents ;
and like the dry brooks of the Missouri, merely serve to
carry off the vast quantity of water which falls in the plains,
and bring also a great deal of mud, which contributes to the
muddiness of the Yellowstone.   The most distinguished of
these are :   At the distance of six miles, a creek 80 yards
in width, from the northwest, called by Indians Littlewolf[20]
river.   At 29 miles lower, another, on the left, 70 yards
in width, which they call Table creek, from several mounds
in the plains to the northwest, the tops of which resemble
a table.   Four miles further, a stream of more importance

Labiche's river. One of these is that now known as Froze to Death creek (see
milit. map, 1891, and G. L. O., 1892).   Then comes Labiche's or Sarpy's river,
on the south.   Next, the codex gives by name a *White* creek, on the north,
" seven " miles below Labiche's river, above a low cliff.   This is evidently the
creek that now rejoices in the name of Starved to Death creek.   This creek may
be identified by its position, on the north, in the vicinity of some white bluffs,
close to the meridian of 107° W. long., and so but little west of the eastern
boundary of the Crow Reservation, where was old Fort Sarpy, on the south
bank of the Yellowstone.   See Clark's map of 1814, and observe that both
" Froze " and " Starved " creeks are there charted, though neither by name—one
above, the other below, Labiche's river.   Next, in the course of " 20 " miles
further, Clark notes two creeks from the south, each 20 yards wide.   The last
of these may be identified by the present site of Howard, on the N. P. R. R.
ten miles by rail below Sanders.   Then he goes a little further, and camps on a
large island.

[20] "*Little Wolf river.*"   To-day's course is full of snags, of which let the
reader beware !   July 28th has never been satisfactorily explained.   The actual
geography, with which July 28th must be adjusted, is in its main features as follows : (1, 2) A pair of large rivers, N. and S., next below Howard ; (3, 4) a pair
of small rivers, N. and S., next below Forsyth ; (5) a large river, N.; (6, 7) a
pair of small rivers, N. and S., at Albright ; (8) the great Rosebud river, S.; (9)
a creek, S.; (10) a creek, N.; (11) a creek, S.; (12) a creek, S.   These twelve can
by no means be found in the text, but they are nearly all in the codex, and those
found there can be identified by Clark M 106, as follows :

(1) On breaking camp on the 28th, below Howard, Clark shortly comes to a
large river, 80 yards wide, from the N., " called by the Indians ————, or
Little Wolf river."   This blank means that he had not the Indian name at hand
or in mind.   This is the river he charted on Lewis' map of 1806 as " Little Wolf
Mt. C."   This is the river he charts on his map of 1814, but without a name—
by some inadvertency of the engraver the name " Little Wolf " having been
lettered in place of *Windsor's* river (the third one on the north above where we
now are).   But the true Little Wolf of the text, of the codex, and of the 1814

enters behind an island, from the south; it is about 100 yards in width, with a bold current of muddy water, and is probably the river called by the Indians the Little Bighorn. [Much further down there is] another stream, on the right, 25 yards wide, the Indian name of which is [not] Mashaskap. Nearly opposite to this creek they camped, after making 73 miles. The river during part of the route is confined by cliffs, which on the right are of a soft, yellowish, gritty rock, while those on the left are harder and of a lighter color. In some of these cliffs were several strata of coal of different thicknesses and heights above the water; but like that of the Missouri, it is of an inferior quality.

(*p. 392*) *July 29th.* During the night there was a storm

map, is easily identified as the Great Porcupine river of present maps, from the north, with the town of Ada near its mouth, with Castle Butte on the plain off its left bank, about ten miles from the Yellowstone, and with a large river from the *south* emptying nearly opposite its mouth. (Compare note [27], p. 1163.)

(2) *This last* is the "four miles further" stream "of importance" "behind an island" "from the south," "probably the river called by the Indians the Little Bighorn," of our text. It is the largest river from the south between Labiche's or Sarpie's and the Rosebud. Together with Little Wolf or Great Porcupine, it makes the first pair of rivers. It is correctly charted by Clark on his map of 1814 by the name of " Little Horn R.," nearly opposite his unlettered river, which, we have just seen, should have been lettered " Little Wolf." It is now known as Armell's, Emill's, Emmel's, Emmette's, etc., river—for which name see note [8], p. 324.

(3, 4) Passing Forsyth (ten miles by rail below Howard), we soon find a pair of creeks, one of which, on the north, is now called Short creek. I find this named in the codex " Table Brook " (*not* Table " creek," nor Table " river "), " 30 yards wide, on the Lard. side, nearly dry." This is a very exceptionable nomenclature with Clark. The other one of this pair, from the south, Clark simply notes as " a brook." Its name I do not know.

(5) Next comes in the codex " East 7 miles to a Stard. Bluff passed 3 islands and *Table river* on the Lard. side 70 yards wide some water." This fetches out exactly for Table *river* to be identified with Little Porcupine river. Clark's map of 1814 charts it, but without any name.

(6, 7) Reaching the vicinity of Albright, on the N. P. R. R., we find a pair of creeks, north and south, the former named Horse creek, with Old Rosebud near its mouth. These I cannot identify from the codex.

(8) The Rosebud river is reached, 100 yards wide. This was originally charted by Clark on the Lewis map of 1806 as " Mar-shas-kass R.," upon Indian information. It is the " Mar-shas-kap R." of his 1814 map. (The difference in

of thunder and lightning, with some rain ; a high northeast wind continued during the morning, and prevented the party from making more than 41 miles. The country resembles that passed yesterday; the dry beds of rivers continue, and large quantities of coal are seen in the sides of the cliffs. The [Yellowstone] river itself is now between 500 yards and half a mile in width, and has more sand and bars of gravel than above. Beaver are in great numbers ; in the course of the day some catfish and a soft-shelled turtle [*Aspidonectes spinifer*] were procured. In the evening they camped on the left, opposite the entrance of a stream called by the Indians Lazeka, or Tongue river.[21] This stream rises in the Cote Noir [Bighorn mountains], and is formed of two

spelling is simply because in Clark's MS. a *p* and a *ss* look alike.) It is the " Little Bighorn " of the codex, Clark M 105, 106, but not the " Little Horn " of his 1814 map. It is the " Little Bighorn " of the Biddle text, but not the " Mashaskap " of that text. (It must not be confounded with the Little Horn or Little Bighorn, a branch of the Bighorn.) This is a well-known river, heading in the Chetish or Wolf mountains, and winding northward into the Yellowstone in Custer Co. It runs through the North Cheyenne Indian Reservation in one part of its course. Old Fort Alexander was at or near its mouth.

(9) Below the Rosebud, the codex first notes " a brook on std. at 3 miles." This is the insignificant stream on which is present station Rosebud of the N. P. R. R., given as 14 miles by rail below Forsythe.

(10) The Codex next has : " passed a creek on Lard.," opposite which, on the south, is a cliff of " stone coal." This creek, from the north, is clearly Sand creek.

(11) Below Sand creek, " passed a large creek at 6 miles on the stard. side, & 2 Islds." This is clearly Sweeny creek. Clark N 132 names it " Wood Brook."

(12) Finally, we reach a creek " in the stard. bend behind an island," 14 or 15 miles by the codex below Sweeny creek. *This* is the " Mashaskap " of the text ! It is now called Graveyard creek. Here Clark camps on an island, close by the town of Hathaway, on the N. P. R. R., 11 miles by rail below Rosebud station ; and right here, no doubt, before he slept, he wrote the notes which enable us now to identify no fewer than twelve streams which he discovered, but concerning every one of which he has from that day to this been reported wrongly or not at all ! All his fine work of to-day buried in oblivion— *Graveyard creek !*

[21] Text of July 29th is sadly defective, in giving only Tongue river by name. To-day's voyage passes many coulées or runs, seven of which Clark notices, six of which he specifies, and one of which he names. " Passed three large Dry Brooks on the Stard. Side, and four on the Lard. Side," Clark M 107. Six

branches, one having its sources with the head of the Cheyenne, the other with one of the branches [*i. e.*, the Little
Bighorn] of the Bighorn. It has a very wide bed and a
channel of water 150 yards wide; but the water is of a light
brown color, very muddy and nearly milk-warm; it is shallow, and its rapid current throws out great quantities of
mud and some coarse gravel. Near the mouth is a large
proportion of timber, but the warmth of the water would
seem to indicate that the country through which it passes
is open and without shade.

of these can be located by the courses and distances, M 108, 109. These I give
in substance :

N. 25° W. five miles to a dry brook in a starboard bend near highlands ;
passed eight islands. This brook, from the north, is now called *Bull* creek ;
about opposite it is *Hawkins* creek, from the south.

E. three miles to a brook in a starboard bend, below a small island. This is
now *Tepee* creek. Then after nine miles—

E. six miles to a bluff starboard, having passed at five miles a large dry brook
starboard, " Turtle creek," named for *Aspidonectes spinifer*. This is also named
in Clark N 132, where the Yellowstone points are tabulated. This is the creek
at whose mouth is now the town of *Horton*, on the N. P. R. R., nine miles by
rail below Hathaway. Opposite this, on the north, is Kellogg creek.

N. 76° E. to a coal-bluff starboard ; passed a dry creek starboard. This is the
first or second from the south below Horton, nearly on the boundary of the
present military reservation of Fort Keogh ; probably that now called *Moon*
creek. Then, after a mile further—

N. four miles, passing a dry brook larboard and a dry brook starboard. Of this
pair, the one from the south is now *Indian* creek, on the military reservation ;
place called Lignite at its mouth.

Thence 10½ miles by the codex to Tongue river, past the site of the now
flourishing Fort Keogh (named for a friend of mine who perished in the Custer
fight), and camp on the north bank of the Yellowstone, opposite Miles City.
The last course notes " an island." This now called Reynolds' island. Some
bluffs or cliffs passed to-day, on the north, are now known as Sundown Buttes.
On the much reduced L. and C. map of the M'Vickar ed., 1842, is marked here
" Monnels Ft., 1807." I suppose this to be a misengravement for Manuel's,
i. e., Manuel Lisa's fort ; but it is not the Manuel's Fort of Clark's 1814 map,
this being at the mouth of the Bighorn : see note [14], p. 1154.

The Lazeka or Tongue is a great river, heading in the Bighorn Mountains of
Northern Wyoming, draining also the Wolf Mountains of Southern Montana,
and coursing in a general N.E. direction to the Yellowstone. The headwaters
of Powder river intervene between the eastern sources of Tongue river and the
western sources of the North fork of the Cheyenne.

July 30*th*. They set out at an early hour, and after passing, at the distance of twelve miles, the bed of a [Big Dry [22]]
river 100 yards wide, but nearly dry at present, reached two
miles below it a succession of bad shoals, interspersed with
a hard, dark brown, gritty rock, extending for six miles; the
last shoal stretches nearly across the river, and has a descent
of about three feet. At this place they were obliged to let
the canoes down by hand, for fear of their splitting on a
concealed rock; though when the shoals are known a large
canoe could with safety pass through the worst of them.
This is the most difficult part of the whole Yellowstone river,
and was called Buffaloe shoal, from the circumstance of one of
those animals be- (*p. 393*) ing found in them. The neighboring cliffs on the right are about 100 feet high; on the left
the country is low, but gradually rises, and at some distance
from the shore presents the first appearance of burnt hills
which have been seen on the Yellowstone. Below Buffaloe
shoals the river is contracted to the width of 300 or 400
yards, the islands are less numerous, and a few scattering
trees only are seen either on its banks or on the highlands.
Twenty miles from those shoals is a rapid, caused by a number of rocks strewed over the river; but though the waves
are high, there is a very good channel on the left, which
renders the passage secure. There was a bear standing on
one of these rocks, which occasioned the name of the Bear
[Yellow Bear, Clark N 132] rapid.[23] As they were descend-

---

[22] " Dry river," larboard, Clark M 111, N 132 ; " Big Dry R." Clark's map,
1814 ; a large water-course, coming from the north about opposite present town
of Dixon or Dickson, on the N. P. R. R., eight miles by rail below Miles City.
It is now known as Sunday creek. Near the town is an elevation, now called
Tower Butte, which did not escape Clark's eye ; for he notes here " a high
bluff." Within a mile or two begin the series of shoals or rapids called Buffalo
in the text, and still known by this name.

[23] Biddle gives nothing between Buffalo and Bear rapids, but the codex is
perfect. Omitting details, we find in Clark M 111, 112, as follows, after
passing Big Dry (now *Sunday*) creek : 1. A " dry brook," N. This is now
Sand creek. 2. A " large dry creek," N. This is now *Muster* creek, whose
mouth is about opposite Ainslie on the N. P. R. R. 3. A " large dry brook," S.
This is now *Cottonwood* creek. 4. A " dry brook," N. This now *Wolf* creek.

ing this rapid a violent storm from the northwest obliged
them to take refuge in an old Indian lodge near the mouth
of a river on the left, which has lately been very high, and
widened to the distance of a quarter of a mile; but though
its present channel is 88 yards wide, there is not more water
in it than would easily pass through a hole of an inch in
diameter. It was called York's Dry river.

As soon as the rain and wind had abated, they resumed
their journey, and at seven miles camped under a spreading
cottonwood on the left side, after making 48 miles. A mile
and a half above on the opposite side is a [Powder] river
containing 100 yards' width of water, though the bed itself
is much wider. The water is very muddy, and like its banks
of a dark brown color. Its current throws out great quantities of red stones; which circumstance, with the appearance of the distant hills, induced Captain Clark to call it the
Redstone, which he afterward found to be the meaning of
its Indian name, Wahasah.²⁴

July 31st. During the whole night the buffalo were
prowling about camp, and excited much alarm, lest in crossing the river they should tread on the boats and split them
to pieces. The party set out as usual, and at the dis- (*p. 394*)
tance of two miles passed a rapid of no great danger, which
they called Wolf²⁵ rapid, from seeing a wolf there. At this

5. " Bluffs on the larboard side." These are now known as the *Devil's Backbone.* 6. " A brook which discharges itself on the stard. side at White [or Yellow]
Bear rapids," which is exactly right. Bear rapids is still so called on various
maps, including Warren's. 7. York's Dry river. This is now known as *Custer's*
creek. Its mouth is in the vicinity of Blatchford and Morgan, on the N. P. R. R.
9. Finally, passed Wahasah or Redstone river, now *Powder*, and camped 1½
miles below its mouth, at the entrance of a small, dry creek on the north.

²⁴ "War-rak-sash or Powder R." of Lewis' map, 1806; " War-har-sa R." of
Clark's map, 1814, very badly charted ! " Wah-har-sop, Redstone River," Clark
N 132; " Redstone river," Clark M 112; "Chakadee Wakpa or Powder R."
of Warren's map. Powder river is the last great branch of the Yellowstone; it
heads in Central Wyoming, in connection with heads of the North Fork of the
Platte and of both North and South Forks of the Big Cheyenne, east of the Wind
River mountains, by two main forks, whose united course flows but little E. of N.
into the Yellowstone.

²⁵ Present name on most maps, probably through the influence of General

place commences a range of highlands [*i. e.*, Sheridan Butte[26]]. These highlands have no timber, and are composed of earth of different colors, without much rock, but supplied throughout with great quantities of coal or carbonated wood.   After passing these hills the country again opens into extensive plains, like those passed yesterday; the river is diversified with islands, and partially supplied with water by a great number of wide but nearly dry brooks.   Thus, 18 miles below camp is a shallow, muddy stream[27] on the left, 100 yards wide, supposed to be that known among the Indians by the name of Saasha, or Little-wolf river; five miles below, on the right side, is another river,[28] 40 yards wide and 4 feet in

G. K. Warren, U. S. A., who not only knew what Lewis and Clark's work was worth, but also appreciated what he owed to them, when he came to make that great map which, after Clark's, became the secure foundation of our present geographical knowledge of the whole country he charted.

[26] "A very high ruged hill or Mtn. on the Lard. Side opposit a timbered point," Clark M 114.   This is Sheridan Butte, opposite which is Stanley Point. The codex next notes "a dry brook on stard. side;" and there is one, which falls in by Stanley Point.   A few miles further Captain Clark comes by site of Terry, 39 miles by rail below Miles City.

[27] "A river 100 yds. wide on the Lard. Side. shallow and the water muddy, low bluffs Shabono R.," Clark M 114 ; "Shabonos R.," Clark N 132 ; "this river I take to be the one the Minitarrees Call little wolf or Sa-a-shah River," Clark M 113.   Clark charts it, N., between his "War-har-sa R." and his "Oahtaroup R.," but unluckily his draughtsman or engraver lettered it "York's Dry R.," instead of putting these words on the next stream above, where they belong.   This is the secret of Warren's affixing "York's R." to a wrong stream. The name of "Shabono" has never appeared in connection with this river and I am sorry to bring it to light, but I must read my codex faithfully as well as fervidly.   This 100-yard stream on the left, thus provided with four names already, was later called Maynadier's creek, which became "Mayradiers Cr." of the G. L. O. map, 1892.   It falls in about halfway between Terry and Fallon.   (Observe duplication here of "Little Wolf" river of p. 1157 : see note [20] there.)

[28] "This stream I call Oak-tarpon-er or Coal River," Clark M 113 ; "Oak-tar-pon-er or Stone Coal River," Clark N 132 ; "Oahtaroup Cr.," Clark's map. This is now O'Fallon's or Fallon's creek ; quite a large stream, falling in by town or station of same name, ten miles by rail below Terry.   Before Gibson's river of the text is reached, we have in the codex : 1. "A brook below the Lard. Bluff, passed a Stard. point," Clark M 114, *i. e.*, Sheepshead Bluffs and Ferry Point, with a creek from the left just there.   2. "Passed a brook on Stard. Side," Clark M 114.   There is one just above Bears or Barns (Burns') Bluffs.

depth, which from the steep coal-banks on each side they called Oaktaroup, or Coal river; and 18 miles further is a third stream of 60 yards' width, to which they gave the name of Gibson's [29] river. Having made 66 miles, they halted for the night.[30] Just as they landed, they saw the largest white bear that any of the party had ever before seen, devouring a dead buffalo on a sand-bar. They fired two balls into him; he then swam to the mainland and walked along the shore. Captain Clark pursued him and lodged two more balls in his body; but though he bled profusely he made his escape, as night prevented them from following him.

Sunday, August 1st.[31] A high wind from ahead made the

3. " A brook in the Lard. bend," Clark M 115.   This is Bad Route creek, opposite the bluffs said, and near De Russy's rapids.

[29] Glendive's creek of Warren, now usually called Cabin creek, falling in on the right a short distance above town of Milton, and about the same distance below a certain Five-mile creek, on the left, which I do not find in the codex. Warren seems to have identified it as Glendive's creek because it is charted too far down on Clark's map.

[30] But not before passing four more streams, duly noted in Clark 115. 1. A creek given as four m. below Gibson's river, on the left.   This is Clear creek, falling in by the Monroe rapids, nearly opposite Milton. 2. A creek on the right, next below Milton. 3. A creek on the right, below a bluff.   This is Cedar creek, below Cedar Bluffs.   It is called Catfish creek in Clark N 132, where tabulated as " eight " miles below Gibson's river (*i. e.*, Cabin creek). 4. " The entrance of a brook on the Lard. Side.   Encamped opposit on the Stard. Side," Clark M 115.   This is either Sand or Spring creek, on the left— most probably the latter, falling in below Edgerly island, a short distance above Glendive, where the N. P. R. R. turns away from the Yellowstone.

[31] The text for to-day is barren, and must be supplemented by the codex. Clark M 116 first notes : " a large brook in a Stard. Bend opposite to the head of an island, Pine brook."   This Pine brook is also tabulated in Clark N 132 as " 18 " miles below Gibson's river.   Whence it is clear that " Gibson's R." is charted too far down ; Gibson's river of the text is Cabin creek, as already said, but the stream so lettered on the map is in about the position of Glendive creek, which is the Pine creek here in mention, falling in on the right, a short distance below the town of the same name : see last note.   Within five miles Clark M 116 notes " a large brook " on the left (which is one of those falling in by Glendive Butte), and then one on the right ; beyond which he enters no stream to the place where the herd of buffalo obstructed the river.   Here he says, M 116 : " I was obliged to land to let the Buffalow cross over.   notwithstanding an

water rough and retarded their progress; and as it rained
during the whole day, their situation in the open boats was
very disagreeable. The country bears in every respect the
same appearance as that of yesterday, though there is some
ash timber in the bottom, and low pine and cedar on the
sides of the hills. The current of the river is less rapid,
has more soft mud, and is more obstructed by sand-bars;
and the rains have given an unusual quantity of water to the
(*p. 395*) brooks. The buffalo now appear in vast numbers.
A herd happened to be on their way across the river. Such
was the multitude of these animals that, though the river,
including an island over which they passed, was a mile wide,
the herd stretched, as thickly as they could swim, from one
side to the other, and the party was obliged to stop for an
hour. They consoled themselves for the delay by killing
four of the herd; and then [having] proceeded for the distance of 45 miles [in all to-day] to an island, below which
two other herds of buffalo, as numerous as the first, soon
after crossed the river [they camped on the right, at the
entrance of a small brook].

August 2d. The river is now about a mile wide, less rapid
and more divided by islands and bars of sand and mud than
hitherto; the low grounds too are more extensive, and contain a greater quantity of cottonwood, ash, and willow trees.
On the northwest is a low, level plain; on the southeast are

island of *half a mile in width* over which this gangue of Buffalow had to pass,"
etc. Then M 117 has "a wood in a Stard. Bend, psd. [passed] Buffalow Crossing C[reek]." This creek is tabulated in Clark N 132 as on the left, "29" m.
below Pine brook (Glendive creek). Clark also charts it, but without name:
see his map, first creek on the left above "Samuel R." All points being duly considered, we may pretty safely identify Buffalo-crossing creek with that one now
known as Thirteen-mile creek, on the left, falling in by the very large island
called Joe's, where also the present Box-elder creek falls in on the right. Clark
then passes "a dry creek on the Lard. side," and finally camps "at the enterance
of a small brook on the Stard. Side," after a total of "45" miles to-day. This
camp is probably not determinable with precision from any data we possess concerning the numerous islands and small streams in the vicinity. I suppose it
to be near Burns' creek; and this creek may be the never-identified "Samuel
R." of Clark's map: see next note.

some rugged hills, on which they saw, without being able to approach, some bighorns.   The buffalo and elk, as well as the pursuers of both, the wolves, are in great numbers.   On each side of the river are several dry brooks; but the only stream of any size is that they called Ibex [32] river, on the right, about 30 yards wide, and 16 miles from camp.   The bears, which gave so much trouble on the head of the Missouri, are equally fierce in this quarter.   This morning one of them, which was on a sand-bar as the boat passed, raised himself on his hind feet; and after looking at the party, plunged in and swam toward them.   He was received with three balls in the body; he then turned round and made for the shore. Toward evening another entered the water to swim across. Captain Clark ordered the boat toward the shore, and just as the bear landed, shot the animal in the head.   It proved to be the largest female they had ever seen, so old that its tusks were worn quite smooth.   The boats escaped with difficulty between two herds of buffalo which were cross-ing the river, and would probably have again detained the party.   Among the elk of (*p. 396*) this neighborhood are an unusual number of males, while higher up the river the numerous herds consist of females chiefly.   After making

[32] To-day we have over " eighty " miles to account for—certainly an excessive estimate.   The text affords but one point by which to check this long voyage, namely, Ibex river, which is given as " 16 " miles from last night's camp.   But the codex and map afford two points, namely, " Samuel R." and " Argalia Cr." (Ibex of the text).   Clark M 119 for Aug. 2d, begins : " N. 201 E. to a bluff point on the Stard. Side, passed 3 islands and several sand bars also a large creek on the Lard. side at 4 m."   This large creek on the left is tabulated in Clark N 132 as " Samuels creek," 30 yds. wide, 18 miles below Buffalo-crossing creek, and twelve miles above Ibex or Argalia creek.   By these *relative* distances, to which the absolute distances, both actual and alleged, can be adjusted, we may identify Samuel's creek with Burns' creek, and Ibex or Argalia creek with Smith's creek. The latter stream is described as " a small river 30 yds. wide with steep banks on the Stard. Side which I call Ibex River," Clark M 117.   This is the last stream Clark specifies during this voyage, excepting one brook on the right much further down.   The place where the buffalo were again crossing in great numbers is specified in Clark N 132 as " Buffalo Crossings, a low plain each side," tabulated as " 31 " miles below Ibex creek, and " 39 " miles above J. Fields' creek.   For the latter, see note [49], p. 284.

84 miles, they camped among some ash and elm trees on the right [two miles above the mouth of J. Fields' creek]. They, however, rather passed the night than slept there, for the mosquitoes were so troublesome that scarcely any of the party could close their eyes during the greater part of the time. They therefore set out early in the morning,

August 3d, to avoid the persecution of those insects. At the distance of two miles they passed Fields' creek, a stream 35 yards wide, which enters on the right, immediately above a high bluff which is rapidly sinking into the river. Here Captain Clark went ashore in pursuit of some bighorns, but the mosquitoes were so numerous that he was unable to shoot with certainty. He therefore returned to the canoes ; and soon after, observing a ram of the same animals, sent one of the hunters, who shot it ; it was preserved entire as a specimen. About two o'clock they reached, eight miles below Fields' creek, the junction of the Yellowstone with the Missouri, and formed a camp on the point where they had camped on the 26th of April, 1805.[33] The canoes were unloaded, and the baggage was exposed to dry, as many of the articles were wet and some of them spoiled.

The Rochejaune[34] or Yellowstone river, according to Indian information, has its remote sources in the Rocky mountains, near the peaks of the Rio del Norde, on the confines of New Mexico, to which country there is a good road during the whole distance along the banks of the Yellowstone. Its western waters are probably connected with those of Lewis' [main Snake] river, while its eastern branches approach the heads of Clark's river, the Bighorn, and the [North fork of the] Platte ; so that it waters the middle portion of the Rocky mountains for several hundred miles, from

[33] See note [47], p. 283. Clark M 121 checks the crew with which he descended in his two dug-outs lashed together from the point where Sergeant Pryor's party left him : "I had the following persons. John Shields, George Gibson, William Bratten, W. Labeech, Toust. Shabono his wife & child and my man York."

[34] The rest of the entry under Aug. 3d, describing the Yellowstone, etc., is in Lewis' hand in Clark M 122-124 ; the MS. resumes with Aug. 4th in Clark's hand.

northwest to southeast. During its whole course from the point at which Captain Clark reached it to the Missouri, a distance which he computed at 837 miles, this river is large and naviga- (*p. 397*) ble for periogues, or even batteaux, there being none of the moving sand-bars which impede the navigation of the Missouri, and only a single ledge of rocks, which, however, is not difficult to pass. Even its [main] tributary waters, [as] the Bighorn, Clark's fork [and the Powder, Rosebud] and Tongue river, may be ascended in boats for a considerable distance. The banks of the river are low, but bold, and nowhere subject to be overflowed, except for a short distance below the mountains. The pre-dominating color of the river is a yellowish-brown; that of the Missouri, which possesses more mud, is of a deep drab color; the bed of the former being chiefly composed of loose pebbles which, however, diminish in size in descend-ing the river, till after passing the Lazeka [Tongue river], they cease as the river widens, and mud and sand continue to form the greater part of the bottom. Over these the water flows with a velocity constantly and almost equally decreasing in proportion to its distance from the mountains. From the mountains to Clark's fork, the current may be estimated at 4½ miles per hour; thence as low as the Big-horn, at 3½ miles; between that and the Lazeka, at 3 miles; and from that river to Wolf rapid, at 2¾ miles; from which to its entrance [into the Missouri], the general rapidity is two miles per hour. The appearance and character of the country present nearly similar varieties of fertile, rich, open land. Above Clark's fork it consists of high, waving plains bordered by stony hills, partially supplied with pine; the middle portion, as low as Buffalo shoals, contains less tim-ber, and the number [of trees] diminishes still lower, where the river widens and the country spreads into extensive plains.

Like all the branches of the Missouri which penetrate the Rocky mountains, the Yellowstone and its streams, within that district of country beyond Clark's fork, abound in beaver and otter; a circumstance which strongly recommends the entrance of the latter river as a judicious position for the purposes of trade.[35] To an establishment at that place the Shoshonees, both within and west- (*p. 398*) ward of the Rocky mountains, would willingly resort, as they would be further from the reach of the Blackfoot Indians and the Minnetarees of Fort de Prairie, than they could be in trading with any [other] factories on the Missouri. The same motive of personal safety would most probably induce many of the tribes on the Columbia and Lewis, river to prefer this place to the entrance of Maria's river, at least for some years; and as the Crow and Paunch Indians, the Castahanahs, and the Indians residing south of Clark's fork, would also be induced to visit it, the mouth of the Yellowstone might be considered as one of the most important establishments for the western fur-trade. This too may be the more easily effected, as the adjacent country possesses a sufficiency of timber for the purpose—an advantage which is

[35] Old Fort Union long stood here, and was then replaced by Fort Buford, close by. Writing in 1842, M'Vickar notes in his ed. of Lewis and Clark, II. p. 303: "The American Fur Company have for many years had a fort [Union] at the mouth of the Yellowstone River, and one also [Benton] at the junction of the Teton and the Missouri, in the heart of the buffalo country. In the year 1832, a steamboat in the service of the company ascended the Missouri from St. Louis to the post at the mouth of the Yellowstone, which was higher than any steamboat had proceeded before. On board this boat, Mr. Catlin, well known as the founder and proprietor of the Indian Gallery, made his first excursion into the Indian country; and at this point, surrounded by different Indian tribes, and in daily intercourse with their chiefs, he commenced his indefatigable labors. In these labors he enthusiastically persevered for several successive years in the wide regions between the Great Northern Lakes and the Red river, the Rocky Mountains and the Mississippi. It is needless to say, that by his delineations of Indian life and manners, his portraits of the native chiefs, and the rich collections of his museum, he has done more than any other individual towards presenting the living image of a race which is seemingly fast passing away." This was true when written, and the praise of Catlin is doubly deserved now, when the Indians have changed during the half century (1842–92) in all things that the famous artist delineated. The priceless treasures of the Catlin art gallery, or a considerable portion of it, are now, and have for some years been, displayed in one of the rooms of the U. S. National Museum at Washington.

not found at any spot between Clark's fork and the Rocky mountains.

August 4th. The camp became absolutely uninhabitable in consequence of the multitude of mosquitoes; the men could not work in preparing skins for clothing, nor hunt in the timbered low grounds; there was no mode of escape, except by going on the sand-bars in the river, where, if the wind should blow, the insects do not venture; but when there is no wind, and particularly at night, when the men have no covering except their worn-out blankets, the pain they suffer is scarcely to be endured. There was also a want of meat, for no buffalo were to be found; and though elk are very abundant, yet their fat and flesh is more difficult to dry in the sun, and is also much more easily spoiled than the meat or fat of either deer or buffalo.

Captain Clark therefore determined to go on to some spot which should be free from mosquitoes and furnish more game. Having written a note to Captain Lewis, to inform him of his intention, and stuck it on a pole at the confluence of the two rivers, he loaded the canoes at five in the afternoon, proceeded down the river to the second point, and camped on a sand-bar; but here the mosquitoes seemed to be even more numerous than above. The face of the (*p.399*) Indian child is considerably puffed up and swollen with their bites; the men could procure scarcely any sleep during the night, and the insects continued to harass them next morning,

August 5th, as they proceeded. On one occasion Captain Clark went on shore and ascended a hill after one of the bighorns; but the mosquitoes were in such multitudes that he could not keep them from the barrel of his rifle long enough to take aim. About ten o'clock, however, a light breeze sprung up from the northwest, and dispersed them in some degree. Captain Clark then landed on a sand-bar, intending to wait for Captain Lewis, and went out to hunt. But not finding any buffalo, he again proceeded in the afternoon; and having killed a large white bear camped under a high bluff exposed to a light breeze from the southwest, which blew away the mosquitoes. About eleven o'clock, however, the wind became very high and a storm of rain came on, which lasted for two hours, accompanied with sharp lightning and loud peals of thunder.

August 6th. The party rose, very wet, and proceeded to a sand-bar below the entrance of Whiteearth river. Just above this place the Indians, apparently within seven or eight days past, had been digging a root which they employ in making a kind of soup. Having fixed their tents, the men were employed in dressing skins and hunting. They shot a number of deer; but only two of them were fat, owing probably to the great quantities of mosquitoes which annoy them while feeding.

August 7th. After some severe rain they proceeded at eleven o'clock, through intervals of rain and high wind, till six in the evening, when they camped on a sand-bar. Here they had a very violent wind for two hours, which left the air clear and cold, so that the mosquitoes completely disappeared.

(*p. 400*) *Sunday, August 8th.* Sergeant Pryor, accompanied by Shannon, Hall, and Windsor, arrived, but without the horses. They reported that on the second day after they left Captain Clark, they halted to let the horses graze near the bed of a large creek, which contained no running water; but soon afterward a shower of rain fell, and the creek swelled so suddenly that several horses, which had straggled across the dry bed of the creek, were obliged to swim back. They now determined to form their camp; but the next morning were astonished at not being able to find a single one of their horses. They immediately examined the neighborhood, and soon finding the track of the Indians who had stolen the horses, pursued them for five miles, where the fugitives divided into two parties. They now followed the largest party five miles further, till they lost all hopes of overtaking the Indians, and returned to the camp; and packing the baggage on their backs, pursued a

northeast course toward the Yellowstone.   On the following
night a wolf bit Sergeant Pryor through the hand as he lay
asleep, and made an attempt to seize Windsor, when Shannon discovered and shot him.   They passed over a broken
open country, and having reached the Yellowstone near
Pompey's pillar, determined to descend the river; for this
purpose they made two skin canoes,[36] such as they had seen
among the Mandans and Ricaras.   These are made in the
following manner: two sticks of an inch and a quarter in
diameter are tied together so as to form a round hoop,
which serves for the brim, while a second hoop, for the
bottom of the boat, is made in the same way; both are
secured by sticks of the same size from the sides of the
hoops, fastened by thongs at the edges of the hoops and at
the interstices of the sticks; over this frame the skin is
drawn closely and tied with thongs, so as to form a perfect
basin, 7 feet 3 inches in diameter, 16 inches deep, with 16
ribs of cross-sticks, and capable of carrying six or eight men
with their loads.   Being unacquainted with the river, they
thought it most (*p. 401*) prudent to divide their guns and
ammunition, so that in case of accident all might not be lost,
and therefore built two canoes.   In these frail vessels they
embarked, and were surprised at the perfect security in
which they passed through the most difficult shoals and
rapids of the river, without ever taking in water, even during
the highest winds.

In passing the confluence of the Yellowstone and Missouri, he [Sergeant Pryor] took down the note [which Captain Clark had posted] from the pole, supposing that Captain
Lewis had passed; and thus learning where the [Captain
Clark's] party was, pressed on in the skin canoes to join
them.   The day was spent in hunting, to procure a number

[36] Such " skin canoes " are commonly called bull-boats, from being made of
buffalo-hide ; they are well-known for the ease and security with which they may
be used.   Clark M 129 says that after the horses were stolen Sergeant Pryor's
party struck the Yellowstone at Pompey's Pillar.   This, then, was the point from
which they navigated the river, being all the while close in the wake of Captain
Clark's boats.

of skins to trade with the Mandans; for having now neither horses nor merchandise, our only resource, in order to obtain corn and beans, is a stock of skins, which those Indians very much admire.

August 9th. A heavy dew fell this morning. Captain Clark proceeded slowly down the river, hunting through the low grounds in the neighborhood after the deer and elk, till late in the afternoon he camped on the southeast side. Here they remained during the next day,

August 10th, attempting to dry the meat, while the hunters were all abroad; but they could obtain nothing except an antelope and one black-tailed deer; these animals being very scarce on this part of the river. In the low grounds of the river Captain Clark found to-day a species of cherry which he had never seen before, and which seems peculiar to this small district of country, though even here it is not very abundant. The men also dug up quantities of a large and very insipid root, called by the Indians hankee, and by the engagees, white-apple [pomme blanche, *Psoralea esculenta*]. It is used by them in a dry and pounded state, to mix with their soup; but our men boiled it and ate it with meat. In descending the river yesterday the squaw brought in a large well-flavored gooseberry, of a rich crimson color, and a deep purple berry of (*p. 402*) a species of currant common on the river as low as the Mandans, and called by the engagees Indian currant.

August 11th. Captain Clark set out early, and landed on a sand-bar about ten o'clock for the purpose of taking breakfast and drying the meat. At noon they proceeded about two miles, when they observed a canoe near the shore. They immediately landed, and were equally surprised and pleased at discovering two men by the names of Dickson and Hancock,[37] who had come from the Illinois on a hunting

[37] This meeting was of course prior in time to that noted on p. 1116, though so long subsequent in the narrative. These were the first white men any members of the Expedition had seen, except themselves, since they parted with the three French trappers at Goose creek, near the Little Missouri, April 13th, 1805 : see

excursion up the Yellowstone. They had left the Illinois in the summer of 1804, and had spent last winter with the Tetons, in company with a Mr. Ceautoin,[38] who had come there as a trader, and whom they [the Tetons] had robbed—rather, they had taken all his merchandise and given him a few robes in exchange. These men had met the boat which we had dispatched from Fort Mandan, on board of which, they were told, was a Ricara chief on his way to Washington ; and also another party of Yankton chiefs, accompanying Mr. Durion on a visit of the same kind. We were sorry to learn that the Mandans and Minnetarees were at war with the Ricaras, and had killed two of them. The Assiniboins too are at war with the Mandans. They have, in consequence, prohibited the Northwestern Company from trading to the Missouri, and even killed two of their traders near Mouse river ; they are now lying in wait for Mr. McKenzie of the Northwestern Company, who has been for a long time among the Minnetarees. These appearances are rather unfavorable to our project of carrying some of the chiefs to the United States ; but we still hope that, by effecting a peace between the Mandans, Minnetarees, and Ricaras, the views of our Government may be accomplished.

After leaving these trappers Captain Clark went on and camped nearly opposite the entrance of Goat-pen [Little Knife : see note [36], p. 274] creek, where the party were again assailed by their old enemies, the mosquitoes.

p. 270. Communication with the world was thus first resumed near the very spot where it had been last severed.

[38] The name "Ceautoin" of the text is questionable. Clark M 134 twice has "Coartang," once overlined "Qu : Ceautoin." It may possibly be meant for Chouteau.

CHAPTER XXXVI.

DOWN THE MISSOURI FROM THE LITTLE MISSOURI TO WHITE RIVER.

Captain Lewis' boats heave in sight, and the Expedition is now reunited—The Little Missouri passed—Many Indians met—Mandan village—Council with Black Cat, Le Borgne, Black Crow, etc., and overtures to take Indians to visit their Great Father in Washington—Private Colter asks and receives his discharge from the Expedition, to go trapping with Dickson and Hancock—Further Indian Councils—Le Borgne presented with the swivel—Big White agrees to go to Washington with his family—Chaboneau and his family discharged—Jessaume and his family engaged—Scene on departure of Big White—Fort Mandan reached—Chesshetah and Cannon-ball rivers—Obvious change in channel of the Missouri since 1804—Traders met—Information of the death of the Pawnee chief who had been to Washington—Council with Ricaras and Cheyennes—Speech of Gray-eyes—Visit to the Cheyenne village—Amenities of the occasion—Speech of Big White—Reconciliation of chiefs—Captain Lewis now first able to walk after his wound—Points passed to Lookout Bend—Cheyenne and Teton rivers—Loisel's fort on Cedar island—Tyler's river—Big Bend—First turkey sign—White river—Multitude of buffalo—Indian alarm—They were Black Buffalo's band of Tetons, who had been unruly in 1804—Overtures declined.

$\mathcal{T}$HURSDAY, August 12th, 1806. The party continued slowly to descend the river. One of the skin canoes was by accident pierced with a small hole ; they halted for the purpose of mending it with a piece of elk-skin, and also to wait for two of the party who were behind. While there, they were overjoyed at seeing Captain Lewis' boats heave in sight about noon.[1] But this feeling was changed into alarm on seeing the boats reach the shore without Captain Lewis, who they then learned had been wounded the day before, and (*p. 404*) was lying in the periogue. After giving

---

[1] The place where all the members of the Expedition were thus happily reunited is left a little hazy here and on p. 1117, but may be fixed precisely by Clark M 135, this date : " Proceeded on myself with the two wood and one skin canoe to a large bottom on the N.E. side above the head of Jins [red inked "Qu : an "] island and landed to take breakfast as well as to delay untill Shannon and Gibson should arive." These two men had been sent back to the last camp to recover a lost tomahawk, with which they returned at 2 p. m. This "Jins" is clearly written, but Captain Clark seems to have forgotten himself what name he meant, and so queries " an " island. This is undoubtedly the large island mentioned without name on p. 273 : see note[33] there. While the party were in the bottom on the N.E. side of the Missouri, at the head of this island, " at

his wound all the attention in our power, we remained here some time, during which we were overtaken by our two men, accompanied by Dickson and Hancock, who wished to go [back] with us as far as the Mandans.   The whole party being now happily reunited, we left the two skin canoes, and all embarked together, about three o'clock, in the boats. The wind was, however, very high from the southwest, accompanied with rain, so that we did not go far before we halted for the night on a sand-bar.   Captain Lewis' wound was still sore and somewhat painful.

August 13th.   We set out by sunrise, and having a very strong breeze from the northwest, proceeded rapidly.   At eight o'clock we passed the mouth of the Little Missouri. Some Indians were seen at a distance below in a skin canoe ; these were probably some Minnetarees on their return from a hunting-excursion, as we passed one of their camps on the southwest side, where they had left a canoe.   Two other Indians were seen far off on one of the hills, and we shall therefore soon meet with our old acquaintances, the Mandans.   At sunset we arrived at the entrance of Miry [2] river, and camped on the northeast side, having come, by the assistance of the wind and our oars, a distance of 86 miles. The air was cool, and the mosquitoes ceased to trouble us.

August 14th. [3]   We again set out at sunrise, and at length

meridian Capt. Lewis hove in sight with the party [Ordway's] which went by way of the Missouri as well as that which accompanied him from Travellers rest," Clark M 135.   The codex shows Captain Clark's alarm and anxiety at finding his comrade so sorely wounded ; describes the wound carefully, and furthermore exonerates Cruzatte—" this Crusat is nearsighted and has the use of but one eye, he is an attentive and industerous man and one whome we both have placed the greatest confidence in dureing the whole rout."   The codex continues, pp. 136–143, with an abstract of Captain Lewis' whole trip, including tabulated courses and distancces ; then the entry for Aug. 12th closes by fixing camp " on a large sand point from the S.E.," " a little below the enterance of Shabonos creek" : see p. 272.   " And now, (thanks to God) we are all together again in good health, except Captain Lewis, and his wound is not dangerous," is the fervent reflection of Sergeant Gass, p. 250.

   [2] " Myry river," Clark M 143 : see note [13], p. 261.

   [3] Codex M ends with the account of Aug. 14th, p. 146, though a few pages of meteorological register continue.   The last remark is "☞ see next book."   This

approached the grand[4] village of the Minnetarees, where the
natives had collected to view us as we passed. We fired
the blunderbuss several times by way of salute and soon
after landed on the bank near the village of the Mahahas or
Shoe[5] Indians, where we were received by a crowd of people
who came to welcome our return. Among these were the
principal chief of the Mahahas and the chief of the Little
Minnetaree village, both of whom expressed great pleasure
at seeing us again ; but the latter wept most bitterly. On
inquiry, it appeared that his tears were excited because the
(*p. 405*) sight of us reminded him of his son, who had been
lately killed by the Blackfoot Indians.

After remaining there a few minutes, we crossed to the

next book is Clark N, beginning Aug. 15th, and thus directly continuous. On
reaching the Mandans, Lewis and Clark just missed the Mr. Henry with whom
they so much desired to communicate that they had intended to send Sergeant
Pryor to his post on the Assiniboin. This gentleman had left Le Borgne's village
July 29th, 1806, and camped next day on Miry river, as I see by his MS., now in
my possession. (See note [7], p. 1065.) I shall make a few extracts from this
MS., on points touching the Expedition.

[4] The Henry MS. has, p. 76 : " We entered the great village of the Big
Bellies, which consists of about 130 huts. Here we found Messrs. Charles
Mackenzie and James Caldwell, who had left Rivière La Souris [Mouse river]
with a small assortment of goods in May last ; both the young men in the
service of the North West Co." Here is doubtless in mention the Mr. McKenzie
of note [29], p. 203, pp. 226, 232, etc.

[5] " The little Big Belly Village and the Saulteur Village situated on the south
side," Henry MS., p. 44. *Saulteur* is the name Mr. Henry uses throughout for
the Indians L. and C. call Soulier, Soulier Noir, and Shoe Indians : see note[7],
p. 183, and note[21], p. 198. July 21st, Mr. Henry proceeded " to the Saulteur
village, which consists of about 40 huts. These people are an entirely different
tribe from the Big Bellies and Mandanes ; their language resembles that of the
latter nation more than that of the former, and cannot be said to be the same.
The long intercourse they have had with those people may perhaps tend to this
similarity of languages, and from the proximity of these nations, they have acquired their manners and customs, though they still continue to live by themselves and not intermix with any other tribe. They have the character of a
brave and war-like set of people. They formerly sustained a three years' war with
their neighbours the Big Bellies, notwithstanding their villages are situated so
close to each other and the latter were then ten times their number. They
held out with the greatest resolution and disdained submitting ; when the others
finding it impossible to reduce them unless by a total extermination of the tribe,

Mandan village of Black Cat, where all the inhabitants seemed very much pleased to see us. We immediately sent Chaboneau with an invitation for the Minnetarees to visit us, and dispatched Drewyer to the lower village of the Mandans to bring Jesseaume[6] as an interpreter. Captain Clark, in the meantime, walked up to the village of Black Cat, where he smoked and ate with the chief. This village has been rebuilt since our departure, and is now much smaller; a quarrel having arisen among the Indians, in consequence of which a number of families had removed to the opposite side of the river. On the arrival of Jesseaume, Captain Clark addressed the chiefs. We spoke to them now, he said, in the same language we had used before; and repeated his invitation to accompany him to the United States, to hear in person the counsels of their Great Father, who can at all times protect those who open their ears to his counsels, and punish his enemies. Black Cat,[7] in reply,

they proposed to make peace," MS., pp. 73, 74. " We now came to the little Big Bellies Village (or Willow Indians) which is situated at the entrance of the Knife river which comes from the South and here enters into the Missourie, and is about one mile from the Saulteur village," Henry MS., p. 75. In note[8], p. 183, I might have adduced this name of " Willow" for these Indians ; Dr. Matthews discusses it in treating of them.

[6] Whose name Gass spells " Geesem," p. 253. " We found in this village a Canadian of the name of Jussaume ; it was this man who accompanied Captains Clark and Lewis the ensuing autumn down to Washington on their return from their voyage of discoveries to the Pacific Ocean as Interpreter for the Mandane Chief, Le Gros Blanc. This man has been a resident among the Indians for upwards of fifteen years, he speaks their language tolerably well, has a wife and family who dress in the same manner and style as the natives, as for himself he still retains the outward appearance of a Christian but his principles as far as I could observe are much worse than those of a Mandane ; he is possessed of every superstition natural to those people, nor is he different in every mean dirty trick which they have acquired from their intercourse with a set of worthless scoundrels who are generally accustomed to visit these parts," Henry MS., p. 58. In estimating Jessaume's character as here given, weigh the corn-deal of note[26], p. 200, at 90 to the 100 bushels bought. Mr. Henry sums him with fine scorn as " that old sneaking cheat Monsr. Jussaume, whose character is more despicable than the worst among the natives," MS., p. 156. " Jussome's squar" can be identified by note[8], p. 227.

[7] Otherwise Poscopsahe : see pp. 182, 183, 231, etc. The Henry MS., *passim*,

declared that he wished to visit the United States, and see his Great Father; but he was afraid of the Sioux, who had killed several of the Mandans since our departure, and who were now on the river below, and would intercept him if he attempted to go. Captain Clark endeavored to quiet his apprehensions by assuring him that he would not suffer the Sioux to injure one of our red children who should accompany us; they should return loaded with presents, and be protected at the expense of the United States.

The council was then broken up; after which we crossed and formed our camp on the other side of the river, where we should be sheltered from the rain. Soon afterward the chief of the Mahahas informed us that, if we would send to his village, we should have some corn. Three men were therefore dispatched, and soon returned loaded with as much as they could carry; they were followed by the chief and his wife, to whom we presented a few needles and (*p. 406*) other articles fit for women.

In a short time Le Borgne, the great chief of all the Minnetarees, came down, attended by several other chiefs; to whom, after smoking a pipe, Captain Clark made a harangue, renewing his assurances of friendship and the invitation to go with us to Washington. He was answered by Le

calls Black Cat by his French name, Chat Noir, and praises him highly for hospitality, etc., agreeing with our authors in estimating his good qualities. "About this time B^te La France made his appearance. This man had left the Rivière La Souris in May last [1806], equipped by the H. B. Co. with a small assortment for the purpose of trading. He now resided on the south side of the river at the great Mandane village, and hearing of the arrival of the white people he came over to us. He now informed the Black Cat, the chief, our kind host, who his guests were, and the cause of our visit, which was mere curiosity; he instantly retired to his family hut, brought out his flag and in a short time it was flying over the hut in which we were accommodated. This flag was given him by Captains Lewis and Clarke in 1804-5, they also gave him a silver medal and the same articles were also given to the principal chief of each of the other villages, also several very useful utensils were left among them. I saw the remains of an excellent large corn mill, which the foolish fellows had demolished on purpose to barb their arrows," Henry MS., pp. 51, 52, July 20th, 1806. For La France here in mention, see note [29], p. 203, and note [38], p. 213.

Borgne, who began by declaring that he much desired to visit his Great Father, but that the Sioux would certainly kill any of the Mandans who should attempt to go down the river. They were bad people, and would not listen to any advice. When he saw us last, we had told him that we had made peace with all the nations below ; yet the Sioux had since killed eight of his tribe, and stolen a number of their horses. The Ricaras too had stolen their horses, and in the contest his people had killed two of the Ricaras. Yet in spite of these dispositions he had always had his ears open to our counsels, and had actually made a peace with the Chayennes and the Indians of the Rocky mountains. He concluded by saying, that however disposed they were to visit the United States, the fear of the Sioux would prevent them from going with us.[8] The council was then finished.

Soon afterward an invitation was received from Black Cat, who, on Captain Clark's arrival at his village, presented him with a dozen bushels of corn, which he said was a large proportion of what his people owned. After smoking a pipe, he declared that his people were too apprehensive of the Sioux to venture with us. Captain Clark then spoke to the chiefs and warriors of the village. He told them of his anxiety that some of them should see their Great Father, hear his good words, and receive his gifts ; and requested them to fix on some confidential chief who might accompany us. To this they made the same objections as before ;

---

[8] Le Borgne feared nobody. The wily savage had not the slightest intention of going to Washington, and was simply amusing himself by talking "for buncombe." See pp. 242-244. But better than the portrait drawn of him there is the account given by Mr. Henry, who was his guest, and was treated with every consideration. One-eye was a moral monster, but he had other Napoleonic qualities which might have made him an almost equally great soldier, had his sphere of action been equally extensive. Mr. Henry calls him " His Excellency Le Borgne," with unconcealed sarcasm, and says that he breathed more freely after bidding him good-by. I have heard that his real name was Kakoakis—which would be middling good Greek for Wicked Point—and that he was finally killed by a chief named Etamingehisha or Red Shield ; but I have mislaid the reference, and cannot now verify the statement.

till at length a young man offered to go, and the warriors all assented to it. But the character of this man was known to be bad ; and one of the party with Captain Clark informed him that at the moment he [this Indian] had in his possession a knife which he had stolen. Captain (*p. 407*) Clark therefore told the chief of this theft, and ordered the knife to be given up. This was done with a poor apology for having it in his possession, and Captain Clark then reproached the chiefs for wishing to send such a fellow to see and hear so distinguished a person as their Great Father. They all hung down their heads for some time, till Black Cat apologized by saying that the danger was such that they were afraid of sending any one of their chiefs, as they considered his loss almost inevitable.

Captain Clark remained some time with them, smoking and relating various particulars of his journey ; and then left them to visit the second chief of the Mandans, Black Crow,[9] who had expressed some disposition to accompany us. He seemed well inclined to the journey, but was unwilling to decide till he had called a council of his people, which he intended to do in the afternoon. On returning to camp, Captain Clark found the chief of the Mahahas, and also the chief of the Little Minnetaree village. They brought a present of corn on their mules, of which they possess several, and which they procure from the Crow Indians, who either buy or steal them on the frontiers of the Spanish settlements. A great number of Indians visited us for the purpose of renewing their acquaintance, or of exchanging robes or other articles for the skins brought by our men.

In the evening we were applied to by one of our men, Colter, who was desirous of joining the two trappers who had accompanied us, and who now proposed an expedition up the river, in which they were to find traps and give him a share of the profits. The offer was a very advantageous one ; and, as he had always performed his duty, and his services might be dispensed with, we agreed that he might go, pro-

[9] This is the Kagohami or Little Raven of p. 182, etc.

vided none of the rest would ask or expect a similar indulgence. To this they cheerfully answered that they wished
Colter every success, and would not apply for liberty to
separate before we reached St. Louis. We, therefore, supplied him, as did his comrades also, with powder, lead,
(*p. 408*) and a variety of articles which might be useful to
him, and he left us the next day.[10]   The example of this man
shows how easily men may be weaned from the habits of
civilized life to the ruder but scarcely less fascinating manners of the woods. This hunter has been now absent for
many years from the frontiers, and might naturally be presumed to have some anxiety, or some curiosity at least, to return to his friends and his country ; yet, just at the moment
when he is approaching the frontiers, he is tempted by a hunting scheme to give up those delightful prospects, and go back
without the least reluctance to the solitude of the woods.

In the evening Chaboneau, who had been mingling with
the Indians and had learned what had taken place during
our absence, informed us that as soon as we left the Minnetarees they sent out a war-party against the Shoshonees,
whom they attacked and routed, though in the engagement they lost two men, one of whom was the son of the
chief of the Little Minnetaree village. Another war-party
had gone against the Ricaras, two of whom they killed. A
misunderstanding too had taken place between the Mandans
and Minnetarees, in consequence of a dispute about a woman,
which nearly occasioned a war; but at length a pipe was presented by the Minnetarees, and a reconciliation took place.

August 16*th.*   The Mandans had offered to give us some

[10] Uncertain whether this "next day" is Aug. 15th or 16th. Observe that
the text lacks Aug. 15th, the events of two days, Aug. 14th and 15th, being
given under one date.   Codices M and N break between these days, with certain unlucky inadvertences of the entries, making it impossible now to adjust
the two dates in question.   I think *most* of the matter given as of the 14th is
really of the 15th.   John Colter turns up Jan. 18th, 1811, near La Charette,
where he was met by the overland Astorians.   He had come from some upper
waters of the Missouri to St. Louis in a canoe, and gave many particulars of the
Indians, who had conceived an implacable hatred of the whites from Captain
Lewis' affair on Maria's river. See p. 254.

corn, and on sending this morning we found a greater quantity collected for our use than all our canoes would contain.
We therefore thanked the chief and took only six loads.
At ten o'clock the chiefs of the different villages came
down to smoke with us. We took this opportunity of endeavoring to engage Le Borgne in our interests by a present
of the swivel, which is no longer serviceable, as it cannot be
discharged from our largest periogue. It was loaded; and
the chiefs being formed into a circle round it, Captain
Clark addressed them with great ceremony. He said that
he had listened with much attention to what had (*p. 409*)
yesterday been declared by Le Borgne, whom he believed
to be sincere, and then reproached them with their disregard
of our counsels, and their wars on the Shoshonees and
Ricaras. Little Cherry, the old Minnetaree chief, answered
that they had long stayed at home and listened to our advice, but at last went to war against the Sioux because their
horses had been stolen and their companions killed; and
that in an expedition against those people they met the
Ricaras, who were on their way to strike them, and a battle ensued. But in future he said they would attend to our
words and live at peace. Le Borgne added that his ears
would always be open to the words of his Good Father, and
shut against bad counsel. Captain Clark then presented to
Le Borgne the swivel, which he told him had announced the
words of his Great Father to all the nations we had seen,
and which, whenever it was fired, should recall those which
we had delivered to him. The gun was discharged, and
Le Borgne had it conveyed in great pomp to his village.
The council then adjourned.

In the afternoon Captain Clark walked up to the village
of Little Crow, taking a flag which he intended to present
to him; but was surprised on being told by him that he had
given over all intention of accompanying us, and refused the
flag. He found that this was occasioned by jealousy between

[11] See pp. 182, 192, etc. " On our going down to the water side we found the
Chief of the Great Mandane Village, Le Gros Blanc. (It was this man who

him and the principal chief, [Shahaka [11] or] Big White; on the interference, however, of Jesseaume,[12] the two chiefs were reconciled, and it was agreed that Big White himself should accompany us with his wife and son.

August 17th. The principal chiefs of the Minnetarees came down to bid us farewell, as none of them could be prevailed on to go with us. This circumstance induced our interpreter, Chaboneau, with his wife and child, to remain here, as he could be no longer useful. Notwithstanding our offers of taking him with us to the United States, he said that he had there no acquaintance and no chance of making a livelihood; and that he preferred remaining among the In- (*p. 410*) dians. This man has been very serviceable to us, and his wife was particularly useful among the Shoshonees. Indeed, she has borne with a patience truly admirable the fatigues of so long a route, encumbered with the charge of an infant, who is even now only 19 months old. We therefore paid Chaboneau his wages,[13] amounting to $500.33, including the price of a horse

accompanied Messrs. Lewis & Clark the ensuing autumn down to Washington.) He was waiting with his own canoe to ferry over Mr. Chaboillez and me," Henry MS., July 20th, p. 54. " Mr. Chaboillez and his people, who consisted of an Indian, Mr. C.'s brother-in-law and Mr. Allen McDonnell took up their lodging with Hairy Horn; and our guide, MacrEacan, Straight Horn, and myself and my people V. and D. remained with Le Grand, who appeared to me to be a very civil fellow," *ibid.* See note [11], p. 187, and note [36], p. 212, for the name Chaboillez. The "MacrEacan" above noted is the M'Cracken of p. 187.

[12] "We sent for Mr. Jessomme and told him to use his influence to prevail on one of the Chiefs to accompany us and we would employ him [Jessaume, as an interpreter]. He informed us soon after that the bid [Big] White chief would go if we would take his wife & son & Jessoms wife & 2 children we were obliged to agree to do [it]," Clark N 89. Considering the relative size of the two families, the Frenchman seemed to have argued the case with Shahaka to his own advantage.

[13] It could hardly have occurred to anyone, in 1806, that Chaboneau's wife had earned *her* wages too. What Chaboneau's services were, except on some rare occasions when his wife interpreted to him, does not appear in the History to the naked eye. This individual remained among the Indians for many years. He was found by Maximilian in 1832–34; and he " candidly confessed " to the Prince of Wied that after a residence of 37 years among the Minnetarees, " he could never learn to pronounce their language correctly " (Matthews, p. 81). " Old Charbonneau," as Dr. Matthews styles him, must therefore have been a

and a lodge purchased of him; and soon afterward dropped down to the village of Big White, attended on shore by all the Indian chiefs, who went to take leave of him.

We found Big White surrounded by his friends, who sat in a circle smoking, while the women were crying. He immediately sent his wife and son, with their baggage, on board, accompanied by the interpreter and his wife and two children; and then, after distributing among his friends some powder and ball which we had given him, and smoking a pipe with us, he went with us to the river-side. The whole village crowded about us, and many of the people wept aloud at the departure of the chief. As Captain Clark was shaking hands with the principal chiefs of all the villages, they requested that he would sit with them one moment longer. Being willing to gratify them, he stopped and ordered a pipe; after smoking which they informed him that when they first saw us they did not believe all that we then told them; but having now seen that our words were all true, they would carefully remember them and follow our

fool as well as the coward and wife-beater that we know he was (pp. 270, 310, 395, 442, 497, etc.). But his linguistic accomplishments were equal to abuse of Sacajawea in more than one dialect, and interpreters received good pay in those days. I have examined the autograph notifications of drafts made by Captain Lewis in favor of most of the members of the Expedition, and the pay of the privates and non-commissioned officers was certainly very small in comparison. It may be interesting to give a specimen of these, copied from the original on file in the War Department. Out of twenty-eight examined, of most of which I hold copies, I select the following:

Louisville, November 9th, 1806.

Sir:

My bill of exchange No. 115 of this date in favor of Capt. William Clark for the sum of four hundred dollars is in part of monies due him for his services while on the late expedition to the Pacific Ocean, and which when paid will be charged to me on the faith of my final settlement with the United States relative to the said Expedition.

I have the honor to be with due consideration,

Your obt. Servt.
[signed] MERIWETHER LEWIS, Capt.
1st U. S. Regt. Infty.

Genl. HENRY DEARBORN,
    Secretary at War.

advice; he might tell their Great Father that the young men should remain at home and not make war on any people except in defense of themselves. They requested him to tell the Ricaras to come and visit them without fear, as they meant that nation no harm, but were desirous of peace with them. On the Sioux, however, they had no dependence, and must kill them whenever they made war-parties against their country. Captain Clark, in reply, informed them that we had never insisted on their not defending themselves, but requested only that they would not strike those whom we had taken by (*p. 411*) the hand; that we would apprise the Ricaras of their friendly intentions, and that, though we had not seen those of the Sioux with whom they were at war, we should relate their conduct to their Great Father, who would take measures for a general peace among all his red children. Le Borgne now requested that we would take good care of this chief, who would report whatever their Great Father should say; and the council being then broken up, we took leave with a salute from a gun, and proceeded.

On reaching Fort Mandan, we found a few pickets standing on the river-side, but all the houses, except one, had been burnt by an accidental fire. At the distance of 18 miles we reached the old Ricara village, where we camped on the southwest side, the wind being too violent and the waves too high to permit us to go any further. The same cause prevented us from setting out before eight o'clock the next day.

August 18th. Soon after we embarked, an Indian came running down to the beach, who appeared very anxious to speak to us. We went ashore, and found it was the brother of Big White, who was camped at no great distance, and hearing of our departure came to take leave of the chief. Big White gave him a pair of leggings, and they separated in a most affectionate manner. We then continued, though the wind and waves were still high. The Indian chief seemed quite satisfied with his treatment, and during the whole of his time was employed in pointing out the ancient monuments of the Mandans, or in relating their traditions. At length, after making 40 miles, we camped on the north-east side, opposite an old Mandan village, below the mouth of Chesshetah[14] river.

August 19th. The wind was so violent that we were not able to proceed until four in the afternoon, during which time the hunters killed four elk and twelve deer. We then went on for ten miles, and came-to on a sand-bar. The rain (*p. 412*) and wind continued through the night, and during the whole of the next day,

August 20th, the waves were so high that one man was constantly occupied in bailing the boats. We passed at noon Cannon-ball river; at three in the afternoon, the entrance of Wardepon[15] river, the boundary of the country claimed by the Sioux; and after coming 81 miles passed the night on a sand-bar. The plains are beginning to change their appearance, the grass becoming of a yellow color. We have seen great numbers of wolves to-day, and some buffalo and elk, though these are by no means so abundant as on the Yellowstone.

Since we passed in 1804, a very obvious change has taken place in the current and appearance of the Missouri. In places where at that time there were sand-bars, the current of the river now passes, and the former channel of the river is in turn a bank of sand. Sand-bars then naked are now covered with willows several feet high; the entrance of some of the creeks and rivers has changed in consequence of the quantity of mud thrown into them; and in some of the bottoms are layers of mud eight inches in depth.

August 21st. We rose after a night of broken rest, owing to the mosquitoes; and having put our arms in order, to be prepared for an attack, continued our course. We soon met three traders, two[16] of whom had wintered with us among the

---

[14] "Chis-che-tor River," Clark N 13 ; now Heart river: see note[51], p. 174.

[15] "Warreconne" creek of p. 170, which see, and note there.

[16] The names of both are given in two places, Clark N 17, but are uncertain.

Mandans in 1804, and were now on their way there. They had exhausted all their powder and lead; we therefore supplied them with both. They informed us that 700 Sioux had passed the Ricara towns on their way to make war against the Mandans and Minnetarees, leaving their women and children camped near the Big Bend of the Missouri, and that the Ricaras all remained at home, without taking any part in the war. They also told us that the Pawnee or Ricara chief, who went to the United States in the spring of 1805, died on his return near Sioux river.

(*p. 413*) We then left them, and soon afterward arrived opposite the upper Ricara villages. We saluted them with the discharge of four guns, which they answered in the same manner; on our landing we were met by the greater part of the inhabitants of each village, and also by a band of Chayennes who were camped on a hill in the neighborhood.

As soon as Captain Clark stepped on shore he was greeted by the two chiefs to whom we had given medals on our last visit; and as they, as well as the rest, appeared much rejoiced at our return and desirous of hearing from the Mandans, he sat down on the bank, while the Ricaras and Chayennes formed a circle round him. After smoking he informed them, as he had already done the Minnetarees, of the various tribes we had visited, and of our anxiety to promote peace among our red brethren. He then expressed his regret at their having attacked the Mandans, who had listened to our counsels, and had sent on a chief to smoke with them and to assure them that they might now hunt in the plains and visit the Mandan villages in safety, and concluded by inviting some of the chiefs to accompany us to Washington. The man whom we had acknowledged as the prin-

---

One looks like " Reevea " and Reevey—is it possibly same as the " Reevey's Prairie " man? The other is apparently Greinyea in one place, clearly Grienway in the other. Text omits to note that the other one of the three, " quite a young lad requested a passage down to the Illinois, we concented and he got into a canoe to an ore," *i. e.*, took an oar in one of our canoes, Clark N 17.

cipal chief when we ascended[17] now presented another, who he said was a greater chief than himself; to him, therefore, he had surrendered the flag and medal with which we had honored him. This chief, who was absent at our last visit, is a man of 35 years of age, stout, well-looking, and called by the Indians Gray-eyes.

He now made a very animated reply. He declared that the Ricaras were willing to follow the counsels we had given them, but a few of their bad young men would not live in peace, but had joined the Sioux and thus embroiled them with the Mandans. These young men had, however, been driven out of the villages, and as the Ricaras were now separated from the Sioux, who were a bad people and the cause of all their misfortunes, they now desired to be at peace with the Mandans, and would receive them with (*p. 414*) kindness and friendship. Several of the chiefs, he said, were desirous of visiting their Great Father; but as the chief who went to the United States last summer had not returned, and they had some fears for his safety, on account of the Sioux, they did not wish to leave home until they heard of him. With regard to himself, he would continue with his nation, to see that they followed our advice.

The sun being now very hot, the chief of the Chayennes invited us to his lodge, which was at no great distance from the river. We followed him, and found a very large lodge, made of 20 buffalo-skins, surrounded by 18 or 20 lodges, nearly equal in size. The rest of the nation are expected to-morrow, and will make the number of 130 or 150 lodges, containing from 350 to 400 men, at which the strength of the nation may be computed. These Chayennes are fine-looking people, of large stature, with straight limbs, high cheek-bones and noses, and of a complexion similar to that of the Ricaras. Their ears are cut at the lower part, but few wear ornaments in them; the hair is generally cut over the eyebrows, and small ornaments fall down the cheeks,

[17] For the Arikara villages, and the several chiefs made or recognized in Oct., 1804, see pp. 159–165.

the remainder being either twisted with horse or buffalo
hair and divided over each shoulder, or else flowing loosely
behind. Their decorations consist chiefly of blue beads,
shells, red paint, brass rings, bears' claws, and strips of otter-
skins, of which last they, as well as the Ricaras, are very
fond. The women are coarse in their features, with wide
mouths, and ugly. Their dress consists of a habit falling
to the midleg, made of two equal pieces of leather, sewed
from the bottom, with arm-holes, with a flap hanging nearly
halfway down the body, both before and behind. These
are burnt with various figures by means of a hot stick, and
adorned with beads, shells, and elk's tusks, which all Indians
admire. The other ornaments are blue beads in the ears ;
but the hair is plain and flows down the back. The summer dress of the men is a simple buffalo-robe, a cloth round
the waist, moc- (*p. 415*) casins, and occasionally leggings.
Living remote from the whites, they are shy and cautious,
but are peaceably disposed, and profess to make war against
no people except the Sioux, with whom they have been
engaged in contests immemorially. In their excursions they
are accompanied by their dogs and horses, which they possess in great numbers, the former serving to carry almost all
their light baggage.

After smoking for some time, Captain Clark gave a small
medal to the Chayenne chief, and explained at the same time
the meaning of it. He seemed alarmed at this present, and
sent for a robe and a quantity of buffalo-meat, which he
gave to Captain Clark, and requested him to take back the
medal ; for he knew that all white people were " medicine,"
and was afraid of the medal, or of anything else which the
white people gave to the Indians. Captain Clark then
repeated his intention in giving the medal, which was the
medicine his great father had directed him to deliver to all
chiefs who listened to his word and followed his counsels ;
and that as he [the chief] had done so, the medal was given
as a proof that we believed him sincere. He now appeared
satisfied and received the medal, in return for which he gave

double the quantity of buffalo-meat he had offered before.[18]
He seemed now quite reconciled to the whites, and requested that some traders might be sent among the Chayennes, who lived, he said, in a country full of beaver, but did
not understand well how to catch them, and were discouraged
from it by having no sale for them when caught.   Captain
Clark promised that they should be soon supplied with
goods and taught the best mode of catching beaver.

Big White, the chief of the Mandans, now addressed them
at some length, explaining the pacific intentions of his
nation; the Chayennes observed that both the Ricaras and
Mandans seemed to be in fault; but at the end of the council the Mandan chief was treated with great civility, and the
greatest harmony prevailed among them.   The great chief,
however, informed us that none of the Ricaras could be pre-
(*p. 416*) vailed on to go with us till the return of the other
chief; and that the Chayennes were a wild people, afraid to
go.   He invited Captain Clark to his house, and gave him
two carrots of tobacco, two beaver-skins, and a trencher of
boiled corn and beans.   It is the custom of all the nations on
the Missouri to offer to every white man food and refresh-
ment when he first enters their tents.

[18] Our friend Gass seems to have had a very sincere contempt for Indians
generally, whom no doubt he used to call "thim haythen nagurs" in his own
mess; and must have looked on the diplomatic medal business with amused dis-
dain.   The international amenities of to-day serve him for the reflection : " They
are a very silly superstitious people.   Captain Clarke gave one of their chiefs
a medal, which he gave back with a buffalo robe, and said he was afraid of white
people, and did not like to take any thing from them : but after some persuasion
he accepted the medal, and we left them," p. 254.   Whereupon Gass' editor, the
Irish pedagogue M'Keehan, acutely observes in a footnote : " We think that some
further proof is necessary to establish the weakness and superstition of these
Indians.   Had the chief persevered in his rejection of the medal, we, instead of
thinking him silly and superstitious, would have been inclined to the opinion,
that he was the wisest Indian on the Missouri."   As between these two views
of the situation, everyone is free to judge for himself.   The Henry MS., p. 81,
has another opinion of such performances.   Referring to Le Borgne's village, it
says : " In the year 1804-5, when Captains Lewis and Clark passed the winter
near this place, they presented the people here with Silver medals and Flags the
same as the Mandanes, but they [the Indians] pretended to say that these orna-

Captain Clark returned to the boats, where he found the chief of the lower village, who had cut off part of his hair, and disfigured himself in such a manner that we did not recognize him at first, until he explained that he was in mourning for his nephew, who had been killed by the Sioux. He proceeded with us to the village on the island, where we were met by all the inhabitants. The second chief, on seeing the Mandan, began to speak to him in a loud and threatening tone, till Captain Clark declared that the Mandans had listened to our councils, and that if any injury was done to the chief, we should defend him against every nation. This chief then invited the Mandan to his lodge, and after a very ceremonious smoking, assured Captain Clark that the Mandan was as safe as at home, for the Ricaras had opened their ears to our councils, as well as the Mandans. This was repeated by the great chief, and the Mandan and Ricara chiefs now smoked and conversed in great apparent harmony; after which we returned to the boats. The whole distance to-day was 29 miles.

August 22d. It rained all night, so that we all rose this morning quite wet, and were about proceeding, when Cap-

ments had conveyed bad medicine to them and their children, for it must be observed they are exceedingly superstitious, and therefore supposed they could not dispose of those articles better than by giving them to the other natives with whom they are frequently engaged in war, in hope that the ill-luck would be conveyed to them. They were all much disgusted at the high sounding language the American Captains bestowed upon themselves and their own nation, wishing to impress the Indians with an idea of their great power as warriors, and a powerful people that if once exasperated could instantly crush into atoms all the nations of the earth. This manner of proceeding did not agree with these haughty savages; they have too high an opinion of themselves to entertain the least idea of acknowledging any race of people in the universe to be their superior." From "Mr. Haney, who is a very sensible intelligent man," according to Lewis and Clark's estimate of him on p. 213, more sensible and intelligent reflections than these were to have been expected; but we must allow for the international jealousies and business rivalries which were soon to explode in the war of 1812; and no doubt the comprehensive paternalism which Lewis and Clark, as the vicars apostolic of Our Father which wast in Washington, D. C., displayed toward the Indians, looked very much as Mr. Henry says it did to the only eye of such an astute and atrocious savage as Le Borgne.

tain Clark was requested to visit the chiefs. They now made several speeches, in which they said that they were unwilling to go with us until the return of their countryman ; and that, though they disliked the Sioux as the origin of all their troubles, yet as they had more horses than they wanted, and were in want of guns and powder, they would be obliged to trade once more with the Sioux for those articles, after which they would break off all connection with them. (*p. 417*) He now returned to the boats ; and after taking leave of the people, who seemed to regret our departure, and firing a salute of two guns, we proceeded 17 miles and camped below Grouse island [see p. 156]. We made only 17 miles to-day, for we were obliged to land near Wetarhoo [Grand] river to dry our baggage ; besides which, the sand-bars are unusually numerous as the river widens below the Ricara villages. Captain Lewis is now so far recovered that he was able to walk a little to-day for the first time. While here we had occasion to notice that the Mandans as well as the Minnetarees and Ricaras keep their horses in the same lodges with themselves.

August 23d. We set out early ; but the wind was so high that, soon after passing the Sahwacanah,[19] we were obliged to go on shore and remain there till three o'clock, when a heavy shower of rain fell and the wind lulled. We then continued our route, and camped after a day's journey of 40 miles. While on shore we killed three deer and as many elk. Along the river are great quantities of grapes and choke-cherries, and also a species of currant which we have never seen before ; it is black, with a leaf much larger than that of other currants, and inferior in flavor to all of them.

Sunday, August 24th. We set out at sunrise, and at eight o'clock passed Lahoocat's island, opposite the lower point of which we landed to examine a stratum of stone, near the top of a bluff of remarkably black clay. It is soft, white, contains

[19] " Sar-war-kar-na-han," Clark N 29—the " Pork " river of p. 150 : see note there.

a very fine grit, and on being dried in the sun will crumble to pieces. The wind soon after became so high that we were obliged to land for several hours, but proceeded at five o'clock. After making 43 miles, we camped [20] at the gorge of the Lookout bend of the Missouri. The Sioux have lately passed in this quarter; and there is now very little game, and that so wild that we are unable to shoot anything. Five of the hunters were therefore sent ahead before daylight next morning,

(*p. 418*) *August 25th*, to hunt on Pawnee island, and we followed them soon after. At eight o'clock we reached the entrance of the Chayenne, where we remained till noon, in order to take a meridian observation. At three o'clock we passed the old Pawnee village near which we had met the Tetons in 1804, and camped in a large bottom on the northeast side, a little below the mouth of No-timber creek [see p. 143]. Just above our camp the Ricaras had formerly a large village on each side of the river; there are still seen the remains of five villages on the southwest side below the Chayenne, and one also on Lahoocat's island; but these have all been destroyed by the Sioux. The weather was clear and calm, but by means of our oars we made 48 miles. Our hunters procured nothing except a few deer.

The skirt of timber in the bend above the Chayenne is inconsiderable, scattered from 4 to 16 miles on the southwest side of the river, and the thickest part is from the distance of from ten to six miles of the Chayenne. A narrow bottom of small cottonwood trees is also on the northeast point, at the distance of four miles above the river. A few large trees and a small undergrowth of willows on the lower side bottom on the Missouri half a mile, and extend a quarter of a mile up the Chayenne; there is also a bottom of cottonwood timber in the part above the Chayenne. The

[20] " Encamped on the gouge [gorge] of the lookout bend of 20 miles around and ¾ through, a little above an old tradeing house and 4 miles above our outward bound encampment of the 1st of October 1804," Clark N 30, 31 : see pp. 149 and 151.

Chayenne discharges but little water at its mouth, which resembles that of the Missouri. [See note [8], p. 147.]

August 26th. After a heavy dew we set out, and at nine o'clock reached the entrance of Teton river, below which were a raft and a skin canoe, which induced us to suspect that the Tetons were in the neighborhood. The arms were therefore put in perfect order, and everything was prepared to revenge the slightest insult from those people, to whom it is necessary to show an example of salutary rigor. We, however, went on without seeing any of them, though we were obliged to land near Smoke creek for two hours, to stop (*p. 419*) a leak in the periogue. Here we saw great quantities of plums and grapes, not yet ripe. At five o'clock we passed Louisville's [21] fort, on Cedar island, twelve miles below which we camped, having been able to row 60 miles with the wind ahead during the greater part of the day.

August 27th. Before sunrise we set out with a stiff eastern breeze in our faces, and at the distance of a few miles landed on a sand-bar near Tylor's [or Tyler's] river and sent out the hunters, as this was the most favorable spot to recruit our stock of meat, now completely exhausted. But after a hunt of three hours they reported that no game was to be found in the bottoms, the grass having been laid flat by the immense number of buffaloes which recently passed over it; and, that they saw only a few buffalo bulls, which they did not kill, as they were quite unfit for use. Near this place we observed, however, the first signs of the wild turkey; not long afterward we landed in the Big Bend, and killed a fine fat elk, on which we feasted. Toward night we heard the bellowing of buffalo bulls on the lower island of the Big Bend. We pursued this agreeable sound, and after killing some of the cows, camped on the island, 45 miles from the camp of last night.

[21] Read *Loisel's* : see note [63], p. 126. Gass here prints " Landselle's," p. 266. " We proceeded on about 10 miles lower and encamped on the S.W. side opposit our outward bound encampment of the 21st. of Sept. 1804. a few miles above Tylors river," Clark N 33, 34. For Smoke creek, see p. 127 ; for Tyler's river, p. 125.

August 28th. We proceeded at an early hour, having previously dispatched some hunters ahead, with orders to join us at our old camp [Pleasant camp,[22] Sept. 16th, 17th, 1804] a little above Corvus creek, where we intended remaining one day, in order to procure the skins and skeletons of some animals, such as the mule-deer, the antelope, the barking-squirrel, and the magpie, which we were desirous of carrying to the United States, and which we had seen there in great abundance. After rowing 32 miles we landed at twelve o'clock, and formed a camp in a high bottom, thinly timbered and covered with grass, but not crowded with mosquitoes. Soon after we arrived the squaws and several of the men went to the bushes near the river, and brought great quantities of large, well-flavored plums of three different species. (*p. 420*) The hunters returned in the afternoon, having been unable to procure any of the game we wished, except the barking-squirrel; though they killed four common deer, and had seen large herds of buffalo, of which they brought in two. They resumed their hunt in the morning,

August 29th, and the rest of the party were employed in dressing skins, except two, who were sent to the village of the barking-squirrels, but could not see one of them out of their holes. At ten o'clock the skins were dressed; we proceeded, and soon passed the entrance of White river, the water of which is at this time nearly the color of milk. The day was spent in hunting along the river, so that we did not advance more than 20 miles;[23] but with all our efforts we were unable to kill either a mule-deer or an antelope, though we procured the common deer, a porcupine, and some buffaloes. These last animals are now so numerous that from an eminence we discovered more than we had ever seen before at one time; and if it be not impossible to

[22] Otherwise Crow Creek camp: see pp. 118–121, where the name Pleasant camp does not occur. But Gass has it at present date, p. 257. " The place we encamped the 16th. and 17th. of Sept. 1804 and which place the party had called pleasant camp," Clark N 36. To-day's camp is on the same spot.

[23] To-night's camp is "on the S.W. Side a little below our encampment of 13th Sept. 1804," Clark N 38, 39: see p. 116.

calculate the moving multitude which darkened the whole plains, we are convinced that 20,000 would be no exaggerated number.   With regard to game in general, we observe that the greatest quantities of wild animals are usually found in the country lying between two nations at war.

August 30*th*.   We set out at the usual hour, but after going some distance were obliged to stop for two hours, in order to wait for one of the hunters.   During this time we made an excursion to a large orchard of delicious plums, where we were so fortunate as to kill two buck elks.   We then proceeded down the river, and were about landing at a place where we had agreed to meet all the hunters, when several persons appeared on the high hills to the northeast, whom, by the help of the spy-glass, we distinguished to be Indians.   We landed on the southwest side of the river, and immediately after saw, on a height opposite to us, about 20 persons ; one of whom, from his blanket greatcoat and a handkerchief round his head, we supposed to be a (*p. 421*) Frenchman.   At the same time, 80 or 90 more Indians, armed with guns and bows and arrows, came out of a wood some distance below them, and fired a salute, which we returned.   From their hostile appearance we were apprehensive that they might be Tetons ; but as, from the country through which they were roving, it was possible that they were Yanktons, Pawnees, or Mahas, and therefore less suspicious [to be suspected], we did not know in what way to receive them.

In order, however, to ascertain who they were, without risk to the party, Captain Clark crossed, with three persons who could speak different Indian languages, to a sand-bar near the opposite side, in hopes of conversing with them. Eight young men soon met him on the sand-bar, but none of them could understand either the Pawnee or Maha interpreter.   They were then addressed in the Sioux language, and answered that they were Tetons, of the band headed by Black Buffaloe, Tahtackasabah.   This was the same who had attempted to stop us in 1804 ; and being now less anxious about offending so mischievous a tribe, Captain Clark told them that they had been deaf to our councils, had ill-treated us two years ago, and had abused all the whites who had since visited them. He believed them, he added, to be bad people, and they must therefore return to their companions; for if they crossed over to our camp we would put them to death. They asked for some corn, which Captain Clark refused; they then requested permission to come and visit our camp, but he ordered them back to their own people. He then returned, and all our arms were prepared, in case of an attack; but when the Indians reached their comrades, and informed their chiefs of our intention, they all set out on their way to their own camp; though some of them halted on a rising ground and abused us very copiously, threatening to kill us if we came across. We took no notice of this for some time, till the return of three of our hunters, whom we were afraid the Indians might have met. But as soon as they joined us we embarked; and to see what the Indians would at- (*p. 422*) tempt, steered near their side of the river. At this the party on the hill seemed agitated; some set out for their camp, others walked about, and one man walked toward the boats and invited us to land. As he came near, we recognized him to be the same who had accompanied us for two days in 1804, and who was considered a friend of the whites. Unwilling, however, to have any interview with these people, we declined his invitation; upon which he returned to the hill, and struck the earth three times with his gun, a great oath among the Indians, who consider swearing by the earth as one of the most sacred forms of imprecation.

At the distance of six miles we stopped [24] on a bleak sandbar; where, however, we thought ourselves safe from attack during the night, and also free from mosquitoes. We had now made only 22 miles; but in the course of the day had procured a mule-deer, which we much desired. About

[24] "In the middle of the river about 2 miles above our encampment on Mud Island on the 10th. Sept. 1804," Clark N 43 : see p. 113.

eleven in the evening the wind shifted to the northwest and it began to rain, accompanied with hard claps of thunder and lightning ; after which the wind changed to the southwest and blew with such violence that we were obliged to hold the canoes for fear of their being driven from the sandbar. The cables of two of them broke, and two others were blown quite across the river ; nor was it till two o'clock that the whole party was reassembled, waiting in the rain for daylight.

Sunday, August 31*st.* We examined our arms and proceeded with the wind in our favor. For some time we saw several Indians on the hills, but soon lost sight of them. In passing the Dome, and the first village of barking-squirrels, we stopped and killed two fox-squirrels, an animal which we had not seen on the river higher than this place. At night we camped[25] on the northeast side, after a journey of 70 miles. We had seen no game, as usual on the river ; but in the evening the mosquitoes soon discovered us.

[25] "A little below our Encampment of the 5th of Sept. on no preserve Island," Clark N 45. For No-preserves island, see p. 110.

CHAPTER XXXVII.

THE EXPEDITION RETURNS IN SAFETY TO ST. LOUIS.

MONDAY, September 1st, 1806. We set out early but were shortly compelled to put to shore for half an hour, till a thick fog disappeared. At nine o'clock we passed the entrance of the Quicurre [L'Eau qui Court—the Niobrara : see p. 107], which presents the same appearance as when we ascended, the water rapid and of a milky-white color. Two miles below several Indians ran down to the bank, and beckoned to us to land ; but as they appeared to be Tetons, and of a war-party, we paid no attention to them, except to inquire to what tribe they belonged ; as the Sioux interpreter did not understand much of the language they probably mistook his question. As one of our canoes was behind, we were afraid of an attack on the men, and therefore landed on an open commanding situation, out of the view of the Indians, in order to wait for the men.

We had not been in this position fifteen minutes when we heard several guns, which we immediately concluded were fired at the three hunters ; and being determined to protect them against any number of (*p. 424*) Indians, Captain Clark with fifteen men ran up the river, while Captain Lewis hobbled up the bank, and formed the rest of the party in such a manner as would best enable them to protect the boats. On turning a point of the river, Captain Clark was agreeably surprised at seeing the Indians remaining in the place where we left them, and our canoe at the distance of a mile. He went on a sand-bar; and when the Indians crossed, gave them his hand, and was informed that they had been amusing themselves with shooting at an old keg, which we had thrown into the river, and was floating down. We now found them to be part of a band of 80 lodges of Yanktons [1] [Yonktins, Gass], on Plum creek; we therefore invited them down to the camp, and after smoking several pipes told them that we had mistaken them for Tetons, and had intended putting every one of them to death, if they had fired at our canoe; but finding them to be Yanktons, who were good men, we were glad to take them by the hand as faithful children, who had opened their ears to our counsels. They saluted the Mandan with great cordiality; one of them declared that their ears had indeed been opened, and that they had followed our advice since we gave a medal to their great chief, and should continue to do so. We tied a piece of ribbon to the hair of each Indian, and gave them some corn. We made a present of a pair of leggings to the principal chief, and then took our leave, being previously overtaken by our canoe.

At two o'clock we landed to hunt on Bonhomme island, [2] but obtained a single elk only. The bottom of the northeast side is very rich, and so thickly overgrown with pea-vines and grass, interwoven with grape-vines, that some of the party who attempted to hunt there were obliged to leave it and ascend the plains, where they found the grass nearly as high as their heads. These plains are much richer below than above the Quicurre, and the whole country is now very beautiful. After making 52 miles against a head wind we stopped for the night on a sand-bar opposite Calumet bluff, (*p. 425*) where we had camped on the 1st of September, 1804, and where our flag-staff was still standing. We

[1] " One of the men with me knew one of the Indians to be the brother of young Durion's wife," Clark N 46. I suppose this young Durion to be Pierre— for whom and for his heroic squaw, see p. 21. Plum creek is the Plumb or White-paint creek of p. 107.

[2] " At this Island we brought 2 years together on [as] on the 1st of Septr. 1804 we Encamped at the lower point of this Island," Clark N 48 : see p. 102.

suffered very much from the mosquitoes, till the wind became so high as to blow them all away.

September 2d. At eight o'clock we passed Jacques[3] river, but soon after were compelled to land in consequence of the high wind from the northeast, and remain till sunset; after which we went on to a sand-bar 22 miles from our camp of last evening. While we were on shore we killed three buffaloes, and four prairie-fowls, which are the first we have seen in descending. Two turkeys were also killed, and were very much admired by our Indians, who had never seen that bird before. The plains continue level and fertile; in the low grounds there is much white oak, and some white ash in the ravines and high bottoms, with lyn [linden] and slippery-elm occasionally. During the night the wind shifted to the southwest and blew the sand over us in such a manner that our situation was very unpleasant. It lulled, however, toward daylight, when we proceeded,

September 3d. At eleven o'clock we passed the Redstone.[4] This river is now crowded with sand-bars which are very differently situated now from what they were when we ascended. Notwithstanding these and the head winds, we made 60 miles before night, when we saw two boats, and several men on shore. We landed and found a Mr. James Airs,[5] a partner of a house at Prairie de Chien, who had

---

[3] For the Jacques or James river, see p. 89. "Passed the River Jacques at 8 A.M. in the first bottom below on the N.E. side I observed the remains of a house which had been built since we passed up, this most probably was McClellins tradeing house with the Yanktons in the winter of 1804 & 5," Clark N 45. To-night's camp is not more closely located in the codex than in the text.

[4] Vermilion river, heretofore called Whitestone by L. and C. See p. 84, and note there.

[5] "A Mr. James Airs from Mackanaw by way of Prarie Dechien and St. Louis. this Gentleman is of the house of Dickson and Co.," Clark N 50, and lower on same folio, "Aires." Gass prints *Aird*, p. 258, which latter is correct. Pike's Journal of a Voyage to the Sources of the Mississippi, pub. 1810, notes on p. 9, under the date of Aug. 28th, 1805 : "Met with Mr. *Aird's* boats (which had pilots) fast on the rocks." And again, "a Mr. James *Aird*" is mentioned by Pike, along with M. Dubuque, Mr. Dickson, and Mr. Fisher, in a letter to General James Wilkinson, dated Prairie du Chien, Sept. 5th, 1805 (p. 4 of app. to pt. i

come from Mackinau by the way of Prairie de Chien and St. Louis, with a license to trade among the Sioux for one year. He had brought two canoes loaded with merchandise, but lost many of his most useful articles in a squall some time since [July 25th, 1806]. After so long an interval, the sight of anyone who could give us information of our country was peculiarly delightful, and much of the night was spent in making inquiries into what had occurred during our absence. We found Mr. Airs a very friendly and liberal gen- (*p. 426*) tleman ; when we proposed to him to purchase a small quantity of tobacco, to be paid for in St. Louis, he very readily furnished every man of the party with as much as he could use during the rest of the voyage, and insisted on our accepting a barrel of flour. This last we found very agreeable, although we have still a little flour which we had deposited at the mouth of Maria's river. We could give in return only about six bushels of corn, which was all that we could spare.

September 4th. We left Mr. Airs about eight o'clock, and after passing the Big Sioux river stopped at noon near Floyd's bluff. On ascending the hill we found that the grave of Floyd had been opened [by the Indians], and was now half uncovered. We filled it up, and then continued down to our old camp near the Maha village, where all our baggage, which had been wet by the rain of last night, was exposed to dry. There is no game on the river except wild geese and pelicans. Near Floyd's grave are some flourishing black-walnut trees, which are the first we have seen on our return. [We proceeded to the sand-bar on which we were

of his book). We must hear some of Mr. Aird's news : General Wilkinson at the moment in St. Louis, as Governor of Louisiana ; 300 American troops cantoned a short distance up the Missouri ; disturbances with the Spaniards in the "Nackatosh" country ; Spain had taken a U. S. frigate in the Mediterranean ; two British ships of war had fired on an American ship in the port of New York ; two Indians hanged in St. Louis for murder " and several others in jale." " Mr. Burr & Genl. Hambleton fought a Duel the latter was killed," etc., Clark N 51. This was of course the affair of honor between Aaron Burr and Alexander Hamilton, at Weehawken on the Hudson, opposite New York City, July 11th, 1804.

camped from the 13th to the 20th of August, 1804, near the
Maha village, having made 36 miles to-day, Clark N 52.]
At night we heard the report of several guns in a direction
toward the Maha village, and supposed it to be the signal of
the arrival of some trader [*i. e.*, Mr. McClellan, who we were
informed was on his way up to the Mahas, Clark N 53].
But not meeting him when we set out next morning,

September 5th, we concluded that the firing was merely to
announce the return of the Mahas to their village, this being
the season at which they return home from buffalo-hunting,
to take care of their corn, beans, and pumpkins.   The river
is now more crooked, the current more rapid and crowded
with snags and sawyers, and the bottoms on both sides are
well supplied with timber.   At three o'clock we passed Blue-
stone[6] bluff, where the river leaves the high lands and meanders through a low, rich bottom, and at night camped, after
making 73 miles.

September 6th.   The wind continued ahead, but the mosquitoes were so tormenting that to remain was more unpleasant than even to advance, however slowly ; we there- (*p. 427*)
fore proceeded.   Near the Little Sioux river we met a trading boat belonging to Mr. Augustus Chateau[7] of St. Louis.
with several men, on their way to trade with the Yanktons
at the Jacques river.   We obtained from them a gallon of
whisky, and gave each of the party a dram, which is the
first spirituous liquor any of them have tasted since the 4th
of July, 1805.   After remaining with them for some time,
we went on to a sand-bar, 30 miles from our last camp,
where we passed the night in expectation of being joined

[6] " Blue Stone bluff " Clark N 54—a name not used before : compare " Cobalt
bluffs " of p. 518.   But camp is readily fixed " on the S.W. Side on a Sand bar
at a cut-off a little below our Encampment of the 9th of August 1804," Clark N
54.   This cut-off is the Coupée à Jacques of p. 71, *q. v.*

[7] Gass has it " Shotto," p. 259.   " At the lower point of Pelecan Island a
little above the Petite River de Suoux we met a tradeing boat of Mr. Ag. Cho-
teaux. . . in care of a Mr. Henry Delorn [? De Launay]," Clark N 54.   This
was Colonel Auguste Chouteau, Sr., founder of the great mercantile house in
St. Louis.

by two of the hunters [the brothers Fields]. But as they did not come on, we set out next morning,

Sunday, September 7th, leaving a canoe with five men [Sergeant Ordway and four privates] to wait for them ; but had not gone more than eight miles, when we overtook them ; we therefore fired a gun as a signal for the men behind, which, as the distance in a direct line was about a mile, they readily heard and soon joined us. A little above Soldier's river we stopped to dine on elk, of which we killed three, and at night, after making 44 miles, camped on a sand-bar [about two miles below camp of Aug. 4th, 1804 : see p. 67], where we hoped in vain to escape from the mosquitoes. We therefore set out early next morning,

September 8th, and stopped for a short time at the Council bluffs to examine the situation of the place. We were confirmed in our belief that it would be a very eligible spot for a trading-establishment. Being anxious to reach the Platte, we plied our oars so well that by night we had made 78 [73] miles, and landed at our old White-catfish camp [of July 22d–26th, 1804 : see p. 52], twelve miles above that river. We had here occasion to remark the wonderful evaporation from the Missouri, which does not appear to contain more water, nor its channel to be wider, than at the distance of 1,000 miles nearer its source ; though within that space it receives about 20 rivers, some of them of considerable width, and a great number of creeks. This evaporation seems, in fact, to be greater now than when we ascended the river, for we are obliged to replenish the inkstand every day with fresh ink, nine-tenths of which must escape by evaporation.

(*p. 428*) *September 9th.* By eight o'clock we passed the Platte, which is lower than it was ; its waters are almost clear, though the channel is turbulent as usual. The sand-bars which obstructed the Misssouri are, however, washed away, and nothing is to be seen except a few remains of the bar. Below the Platte, the current of the Missouri becomes evidently more rapid, and the obstructions from fallen timber increase. The river-bottoms are extensive, rich, and covered with tall, large timber, which is still more abundant in the hollows of the ravines, where may be seen oak, ash, and elm, interspersed with some walnut and hickory. The mosquitoes, though still numerous, seem to lose some of their vigor. As we advance so rapidly, the change of climate is very perceptible; the air is more sultry than we have experienced for a long time, and the nights are so warm that a thin blanket is sufficient, though a few days ago two were not burdensome. Late in the afternoon we camped opposite [our camp of July 16th and 17th, which had been on] Baldpated prairie, after a journey of 73 miles.

September 10th. We again set out early and the wind being moderate, though still ahead, we came 65 miles to a sand-bar, a short distance [about four miles] above the Grand Nemaha [see p. 43]. In the course of the day we met a trader, with three men, on his way to the Pawnee Loups, or Wolf Pawnees, on the Platte. Soon after another boat[8] passed us with seven men from St. Louis, bound to the Mahas. With both of these trading-parties we had some conversation, but our anxiety to go on would not suffer us to remain long with them. The Indians, particularly the squaws and children, are weary of the long journey, and we are not less desirous of seeing our country and friends. We saw on the shore deer, raccoons, and turkeys.

September 11th. A high wind from the northwest detained us till after sunrise, when we proceeded slowly; for as the river is rapid and narrow, as well as more crowded with

[8] In the first of these boats was "a Mr. Alexander Lafass," qu. Faysseau? The name is again written, but differently, and I can make nothing of it. The second boat was in charge of "a Mr. La Craw," interlined La Croix, Clark N 59. L. and C. first learned at this moment of Pike's Expedition—the same that gave us Pike's Peak : "Mr. Pike and young Mr. Wilkinson [son of the general] had set out on an expedition up the Arkansaw river or in that direction," Clark N 59. I think that this string of boats the explorers met going up the river, even before they themselves were ready to lay down their own oars, was one of the most deeply significant circumstances in the whole narrative. It showed which way the "course of empire" was already taking—that way which Lewis and Clark had been, first of all our countrymen.

sand-bars and timber than above, much caution is necessary (*p. 429*) in avoiding these obstacles, particularly in the present low state of the water. The Nemaha seems less wide than when we saw it before, and Wolf river has scarcely any water. In the afternoon we halted above the Nadowa to hunt, and killed two deer ; after which we went on to a small island [near the N.E. side, " a few miles " below Nadowa island, Clark N 60: see p. 41], 40 miles from last night's camp. Here we were no longer annoyed by mosquitoes, which do not seem to frequent this part of the river ; after having been persecuted with these insects during the whole route from the falls, it is a most agreeable exemption. Their noise was very agreeably changed for that of the common wolves, which were howling in different directions, and of the prairie-wolves, whose barking resembles precisely that of the common cur dog.

September 12*th.* After a thick fog and a heavy dew we set out by sunrise, and at the distance of seven miles met two periogues, one of them [Chouteau's] bound to the Platte, for the purpose of trading with the Pawnees, the other on a trapping expedition to the neighborhood of the Mahas. Soon after we met the trading-party under Mr. M'Clelland ;[9] and with them was Mr. Gravelines, the interpreter whom we had sent with a Ricara chief to the United States. The chief had unfortunately died at Washington, and Gravelines was now on his way to the Ricaras, with a speech from the President, and the presents which had been made to the chief. He had also directions to instruct the Ricaras in agriculture. He was accompanied on this mission by old Mr. Durion, our former Sioux interpreter, whose object was to procure, by his influence, a safe passage for the Ricara presents through the bands of Sioux, and also to engage some

[9] At St. Michael's Prairie, Clark N 61 : see p. 40. The " M'Clelland " here named was Captain Robert M'Clellan, whom Captain Clark had known personally as a partisan under General Wayne. He is to be distinguished from a captain of artillery of the same name met Sept. 17th : see p 1210. Both these names occur in five or six different spellings in the codex. Joseph Gravelines will be remembered : see note [9], p. 258.

of the Sioux chiefs, not exceeding six, to visit Washington. Both of them were instructed to inquire particularly after the fate of our party, no intelligence having been received from us during a long time. We authorized Mr. Durion to invite ten or twelve Sioux chiefs to accompany him, particularly the Yanktons, whom we had found well disposed to our country. The (*p. 430*) afternoon being wet, we determined to remain with Mr. M'Clellan during the night; and therefore, after sending five hunters ahead, spent the evening in inquiries after occurrences in the United States during our absence. By eight o'clock next morning,

September 13*th*, we overtook the hunters; but they had killed nothing. The wind being now too high to proceed safely through timber stuck in every part of the channel, we landed and sent the small canoes ahead to hunt. Toward evening we overtook them and camped [on the N.E. side], not being able to advance more than 18 miles [below St. Michael's prairie]. The weather was very warm, and the rushes in the bottoms were so high and thick that we could scarcely hunt; but we were fortunate enough to obtain four deer and a turkey, which, with the hooting-owl, the common buzzard, crow, and hawk, were the only game we saw. Among the timber is the cottonwood, sycamore, ash, mulberry, papaw, walnut, hickory, prickly-ash, and several specimens of elm, intermixed with great quantities of grape-vines and three kinds of peas.

Sunday, September 14*th.* We resumed our journey. This being a part of the river to which the Kansas resort, in order to rob the boats of traders, we held ourselves in readiness to fire upon any Indians who should offer us the slightest indignity; as we no longer needed their friendship, and found that a tone of firmness and decision is the best possible method of making proper impressions on these freebooters. However, we did not encounter any of them; but just below the old Kansas village met three trading-boats from St. Louis, on their way to the Yanktons and Mahas. After leaving them we saw a number of deer, of which we killed five, and camped on an island [near the middle of the river, below our camp of July 1st, 1804: see p. 36], 53 miles from our camp of last evening.

September 15*th.* A strong breeze ahead prevented us from advancing more than 49 miles, to the neighborhood of [a short distance above] Hay-cabin creek. The Kansas river is very low at this time. About a mile below it we landed to view the situa- (*p. 431*) tion of a high hill, which has many advantages for a trading-house or fort; while on the shore we gathered great quantities of papaws and shot an elk. The low grounds are now delightful, and the whole country exhibits a rich appearance; but the weather is oppressively warm, and descending as rapidly as we do from a cool open country, [for the most part] between the latitudes of 46° and 49°, in which we have been for nearly two years, to the wooded plains in latitudes 38° and 39°, the heat would be almost insufferable were it not for the constant winds from the south and southeast.

September 16*th.* We set out at an early hour, but the weather soon became so warm that the men rowed but little. In the course of the day we met two trading-parties [10] on their way to the Pawnees and Mahas; and, after making 52 miles, remained on an island [a little above our camp of the 17th and 18th of June, 1804: see p. 26] till next morning,

September 17*th,* when we passed in safety the island of the Little Osage village. This place is considered by the navi-

[10] The second of these parties was that of "young Mr. Bobidoux," Clark N 66, *i. e.*, either Joseph or François Robidou, Robidoux, or Robadeau. These were brothers, and we find by St. Louis papers they were in business there in 1820, when they moved their store to Papin's brick house. Captain Clark was surprised to find a certain suspiciously loose license the young man had to trade with various Indians, without the Territorial seal or Gen. Wilkinson's signature. He was not acquainted with the autograph of the Territorial secretary, and was rather inclined to take charge of the youth. However, the trader was allowed to go, with a caution "against prosueing the steps of his brother in attempting degrade the American character in the eyes of the Indians." We may remember that he was at the moment in the hands of two of the most resolute and determined men who ever lived, each of whom became in turn for some years the Governor of all the United States' territory west of the Mississippi.

gators of the Missouri as the most dangerous part of it, the whole water being compressed for two miles within a narrow channel crowded with timber, into which the violence of the current is constantly washing the banks. At the distance of 30 miles we met Captain McClellan,[11] lately of the United States army, with whom we camped [four miles above Grand river, on the S.E. side]. He informed us that the general opinion in the United States was that we were lost; the last accounts which had been heard of us being from the Mandan villages. Captain McClellan is on his way to attempt a new trade with the Indians. His plan is to establish himself on the Platte, and after trading with the Pawnees and Ottoes, prevail on some of their chiefs to accompany him to Santa Fee, where he hopes to obtain permission to exchange his merchandise for gold or silver, which is there in abundance. If this be granted, he can transport his goods on mules or horses from the Platte to some part of Louisiana convenient to the Spanish settlements, where he may be met by the traders from New Mexico.

(*p. 432*) *September 18th.* We parted with Captain McClellan, and within a few [four] miles passed Grand river [note [52], June 13th, 1804], below which we overtook the hunters, who had been sent forward yesterday afternoon. They had not been able to kill anything, nor did we see any game except one bear and three turkeys, so that our whole stock of provisions is one biscuit for each person ; but as there is an abundance of papaws, the men are perfectly contented. The current of the river is more gentle than it was when we ascended, the water being lower, though still rapid in

[11] " M'Clanen " in Gass, who says that the captain " gave all our party as much whiskey as they could drink," p. 262. The critics call Gass' Journal "dry," but it is generally to the point, and never dryer than the sergeant's throat must have become by this time. For the officer here in mention, compare note [9], p. 1207. He had been a captain of Artillerists, with whom Captain Lewis was acquainted. " This gentleman informed us that we had been long sence given out [up] by the people of the US generally and almost forgotten— the President of the U. States had yet hopes of us," Clark N 67.

places where it is confined. We continued to pass through a very fine country for 52 miles, when we camped [on an island] nearly opposite Mine river.

September 19*th*. We worked our oars all day without taking time to hunt, or even landing, except once to gather papaws ; and at eight o'clock reached the entrance of Osage river, a distance of 72 miles [where we camped on the spot we had occupied June 1st and 2d, 1804: see p. 11]. Several of the party have been for a day or two attacked with a soreness in the eyes ; the eye-ball being very much swelled and the lid appearing as if burnt by the sun, and extremely painful, particularly when exposed to the light. Three of the men are so much affected by it as to be unable to row. We therefore turned one [12] of the boats adrift, and distributed the men among the other canoes, when we set out a little before daybreak,

September 20*th*. The Osage is at this time low, and discharges but a very small quantity of water. Near the mouth of the Gasconade, where we arrived at noon, we met five Frenchmen on their way to the Great Osage village. As we moved along rapidly we saw on the banks some cows feeding, and the whole party almost involuntarily raised a shout of joy at seeing this image of civilization and domestic life.

Soon after we reached the little French village of La Charette, which we saluted with a discharge of four guns and three hearty cheers. We landed and were recei- (*p. 433*) ved with kindness [13] by the inhabitants, as well as by some traders from Canada [two young Scotchmen in the employ of Mr. Aird], who were going to traffic with the Osages and Ottoes. They were all equally surprised and pleased at our arrival, for they had long since abandoned all hopes of ever seeing us return.

[12] " We left the two canoes lashed together which I had made high up the River Rochejhone, those canoes we set a drift," Clark N 71.

[13] It is almost too bad—but : " we purchased of a citizen two gallons of Whiskey for our party for which we were obliged to give Eight Dollars in Cash, an imposition on the part of that Citizen," Clark N 73.

These Canadians have boats for the navigation of the Missouri, which seem better calculated for the purpose than those in any other form.   They are in the shape of batteaux, about 30 feet long and 8 wide, the bow and stern pointed, the bottom flat, and carrying six oars only ; their chief advantage is their width and flatness, which saves them from the danger of rolling sands.

Having come 68 miles, and the weather threatening to be bad, we remained at La Charette till the next morning,

Sunday, September 21st, when we proceeded ; and as several settlements have been made during our absence, we were refreshed with the sight of men and cattle along the banks.   We also passed twelve canoes of Kickapoo Indians, going on a hunting-excursion.   At length, after coming 48 miles, we saluted, with heartfelt satisfaction, the village of St. Charles, and on landing were treated with the greatest hospitality and kindness by all the inhabitants of that place. Their civility detained us till ten o'clock the next morning,

September 22d,[14] when the rain having ceased, we set out for Coldwater creek, about three miles from the mouth of the Missouri, where we found a cantonment of troops of the United States, with whom we passed the day ; and then,[15]

---

[14] "We did not propose to proceed on untill after the rain was over, and continued at the house of Mr. Proulx. I took this oppertunity of writing to my friends in Kentucky &c. at 10 A.M. it seased raining and we colected our party and set out and proceeded on down to the Contommt. at Coldwater Creek about 3 miles up the Missouri on its Southern banks, at this place we found Colo. Hunt & a Lieut. Peters & one Company of Artillerists.   We were kindly received by the gentlemen of this place.   Mrs. Wilkinson, the Lady of the Gov. & Genl. we wer sorry to find in delicate health.   We were honored with a salute of guns and a harty welcom—at this place there is a publick store kept in which I am informed the U, S have 60000$ worth of indian goods," Clark N 75.

[15] Clark N 76 : " Tuesday 23d Septr. 1806.   We rose early took the Chief [Big White] to the publick store & furnished him with some clothes &c.   took an early brackfast with Colo. Hunt and set out decended to the Mississippi and down that river to St. Louis at which place we arived about 12 oClock. We suffered the party to fire off their pieces as a Salute to the Town.   We were met by all the village and received a harty welcom from it's inhabitants &c. here I found my old acquaintance Maj. W. Christy who had settled in this town in a public line as a Tavern Keeper.   He furnished us with store room for our bag-

September 23*d*, descended to the Mississippi, and round
to St. Louis, where we arrived at twelve o'clock ; and having
fired a salute, went on shore and received the heartiest and
most hospitable welcome from the whole village.

gage and we accepted of the invitation of Mr. Peter Choteau and took a room
in his house. We payed a friendly visit to Mr. Auguste Chotau and some of our
old friends this evening. As the post had departed from St. Louis Capt. Lewis
wrote a note to Mr. Hay in Kahoka [Cahokia] to detain the post at that place
until 12 to-morrow which was reather later than is usual time of leaveing it.

" Wednesday 24th of September, 1806. I sleped but little last night however we rose early and commencd wrighting our letters Capt. Lewis wrote one
to the presidend and I wrote Gov. Harrison and my friends in Kentucky and
sent of [off] George Drewyer with those letters to Kohoka & delivered them to
Mr. Hays &c. We dined with Mr. Chotoux to day and after dinner went to a
store and purchased some clothes, which we gave to a tayler and derected to be
made. Capt. Lewis in opening his trunk found all his papers wet, and some
seeds spoiled. [For two of Captain Lewis' letters to President Jefferson, of this
or nearly the same date, see note [47], p. 283. Two of Captain Clark's letters
were : one to his distinguished elder brother, General George Rogers Clark ; and
one to Governor William Henry Harrison, " hero of Tippecanoe," once President
of the United States, and grandfather of the late incumbent of that office. Both
of these were published, though I have never been able to ascertain where they
first appeared in print. Both are contained in the original (1809) London
edition of the *spurious* Lewis and Clark book, and subsquent editions of the
Apocrypha.]

' Thursday 25th of Septr. 1806. had all of our skins &c suned [sunned] and
stored away in a storeroom of Mr. Caddy Choteau, payed some visits of form,
to the gentlemen of St. Louis. in the evening a dinner & Ball.

" Friday 25th [26th] of Septr. 1806. a fine morning we commenced wrighting,
&c.," Clark N 78—finishing the narrative in the codex, and thus the History of
the Expedition.

APPENDIX I.

ESSAY ON AN INDIAN POLICY.

Observations and reflections on the present and future state of Upper Louisiana, in relation to the government of the Indian Nations inhabiting that country, and the trade and intercourse with the same. By Captain Lewis.

WITH a view to the more complete development of this subject, I have deemed it expedient, in the outset, to state the leading measures pursued by the provincial government of Spain in relation to this subject, and the evils which have flowed from those measures, as well to the Indians as to the whites, in order that we may profit by their errors, and be ourselves the better enabled to apply the necessary correctives to the remnant of evils which their practice introduced.

From the commencement of the Spanish provincial government in Louisiana, whether by the permission of the crown, or originating in the pecuniary rapacity of their governors general, this officer assumed to himself exclusively the right of trading with all the Indian nations in Louisiana, and therefore proceeded to dispose of this privilege to individuals, for certain specific sums; his example was imitated by the governors of Upper Louisiana, who made a further exaction. These exclusive permissions to individuals varied as to the extent of the country or nations they embraced and the period for which they were granted; but in all cases the exclusive licenses were offered to the highest bidder. Consequently, the sums paid by the individuals purchasing were quite as much as the profits of the trade would bear, and in (*p. 436*) many instances, from a spirit of opposition between contending applicants, much more was given than the profits of the traffic would ever justify. The individual, of course, became bankrupt.

This, however, was among the least of the evils flowing from this system to the Indians; it produced the evil of compelling him to pay such enormous sums for the articles he purchased that his greatest exertions would not enable him to obtain as much as he had previously been in the habit of consuming, and which he therefore conceived necessary to him; for as this system progressed the demands of the governors became more exorbitant, and the trader, to meet his engagements, exacted higher prices from the Indians, though the game became scarcer in their country. The morals of the Indians were corrupted by placing before him the articles which he viewed as of the first necessity to him, at such prices that he had it not in his power to purchase. He was therefore induced, in many instances, to take by force that which he had not the means of paying for; consoling himself with the idea that the trader was compelled of necessity to possess himself of the peltries and furs in order to meet his engagements with those from whom he had purchased his merchandise, as well as with those who had assisted him in their transportation, and that, consequently, he could not withdraw from their trade without inevitable ruin.

The prevalence of this sentiment among the Indians was strongly impressed on my mind by an anecdote related to me by a gentleman who had for several years enjoyed, under the Spanish government, the exclusive privilege of trading with the Little Osages. It happened that, after he had bartered with them for all the peltries and furs which they had on hand, they seized forcibly a number of guns and a quantity of ammunition which he had still remaining; he remonstrated with them against this act of violence, and concluded by declaring that never would he return among them again, nor would he suffer any person to bring them merchandise there- (*p. 437*) after. They heard him very patiently, when one of their leaders pertly asked him, if he did not return next season to obtain their peltries and furs, how he intended to pay the persons from whom he had purchased the merchandise they had then taken from him ?

The Indians believed that these traders were the most powerful persons in the nation; nor did they doubt their ability to withhold merchandise from themselves; but the great thirst displayed by the traders for the possession of their peltries and furs, added to the belief that they were compelled to continue their traffic, was considered by the Indians a sufficient guarantee for the continuance of their intercourse. The Indians, therefore, felt themselves at liberty to practice aggressions on the traders with impunity. Thus they governed the trader by what they conceived his necessities to possess their furs and peltries, rather than governing themselves by their own anxiety to obtain merchandise, as they may most effectually be by a well-regulated system.[1] It is immaterial to Indians how they obtain merchandise; in possession of a supply they feel independent. The Indians found by a few experiments of aggression on the traders that, as it respected themselves, it had a salutary effect; and though they mistook the legitimate cause of action on the part of the trader, the result being favorable to themselves, they continued their practice. The fact is that the trader was compelled to continue his trade under every disadvantage, in order to make good his engagements to the governors; for having secured their protection, they were safe both in person and property from their other creditors, who were, for the most part, merchants of Montreal.

The first effect of these depredations of the Indians was the introduction of a ruinous custom among the traders, of extending to them credit. The traders who visit the Indians on the Missouri arrive at their wintering stations from the latter end of September to the middle of October; they carry on their traffic until the latter end of (*p. 438*) March

---

[1] That is, Indians would take advantage of a trader's supposed necessities, whether they needed his goods or not, and could only be prevented from so doing by a well-regulated system of commerce.

or beginning of April. In the course of the season they possess themselves of every skin the Indians have procured. Of course there is an end of trade; but previous to their return, the Indians insist upon credit being given on the faith of payment when the trader returns next season. The trader understands this situation, and knowing this credit to be nothing less than the price of his passport, or the privilege of departing in safety to his home, of course narrows down the amount of his credit, by concealing, as far as he can, to avoid the suspicions of the Indians, the remnant of his merchandise. But the amount to be offered must always be such as they have been accustomed to receive; which, in every case, bears a considerable proportion to their whole trade—say the full amount of their summer or redskin hunt. The Indians well know that the traders are in their power, and understand the servile motives which induce them to extend their liberality to themselves, and are therefore the less solicitous to meet their own engagements on the day of payment; to which indifference they are further urged by the traders distributing among them, on these occasions, many articles of the last necessity to the Indians. The consequence is that, when the traders return the ensuing fall, if they obtain only one-half of their credits, they are well satisfied, as this covers their real expenditure.

Again: if it so happened, in the course of the winter's traffic, that the losses of the trader, growing out of the indolence of the Indians and their exorbitant exactions under the appellation of credit, should so reduce his stock in trade that he could not pay the governor the price stipulated for his license and procure a further supply of goods in order to prosecute his trade, the license was immediately granted to some other individual, who, with an ample assortment of merchandise, then visited the place of rendezvous of his predecessor, without the interpolation of a single season. It did not unfrequently happen that the individuals engaged in this commerce, finding one of their number failing from the (*p. 439*) rapacity of some Indian nation with which he had been permitted to trade, were not so anxious to possess themselves of the privilege of trading with that nation; when the governor, of course, rather than lose all advantages, would abate his demands considerably. The new trader, thus relieved of a considerable proportion of the tax borne by his predecessor, and being disposed to make a favorable impression on the minds of the Indians to whom he was about to introduce himself, would, for the first season at least, dispose of his goods to those Indians on more moderate terms than his predecessor had done. The Indians would now find that the aggressions they practiced on their former trader, so far from proving detrimental to them, procured not only their exoneration from the payment of the last credit given them by their former trader, but that the present trader furnished them goods on better terms than they had been accustomed to receive them. Thus encouraged by the effects of their rapacious policy, it is not to be expected that they would alter their plan of operation as respects their new trader, or that they should appreciate the character of the whites in general in any other manner than as expressed in the prevailing sentiment on this subject among several nations on the Missouri, to wit: " *The white men are like dogs ; the more you beat them and plunder them, the more goods they will bring you, and the cheaper they will sell them.*" [2] This sentiment constitutes, at present, the rule of action among the Kansas, Sioux, and others; and if it be not broken down by the adoption of some efficient measures, it needs not the aid of any deep calculation to determine

---

[2] That is a fair and moderate statement—that is the average Indian's honest and sincere conviction. It was so from the start, and will be so to the finish. I was living, less than twenty years ago, among the Yanktons, to whom we issued rations. It never occurred to them that we, having deprived them by force of their means of livelihood, felt under some sort of moral obligation not to let them starve to death—I mean that this was our theoretical view of the situation, though in fact our dealings with the Indians have been a century of national dishonor. The Yanktons used to come for their rations in the spirit I once heard expressed by a haughty fellow : " We cannot kill you, because you are too many for us ; but you are afraid of us, else why do you feed instead of killing us ?"

the sum of advantages which will result to the American people from the trade of the Missouri. These aggressions on the part of the Indians have been encouraged by the pusillanimity of the engagees, who declared that they were not engaged to fight.

The evils which flowed from this system of exclusive trade were sensibly felt by the inhabitants of Louisiana. (*p. 440*) The governor, regardless of the safety of the community, sold to an individual the right of vending among the Indians every species of merchandise; thus bartering, in effect, his only efficient check on the Indians. The trader, allured by the hope of gain, neither shackled with discretion nor consulting the public good, proceeded to supply the Indians, on whom he was dependent, with arms, ammunition, and all other articles they might require. The Indian, thus independent, acknowledging no authority but his own, would proceed, without compunction of conscience or fear of punishment, to wage war on the defenseless inhabitants of the frontier, whose lives and property, in many instances, were thus sacrificed at the shrine of an inordinate thirst for wealth in the governors, who in reality occasioned all these evils.

Although the governors could not have been ignorant that the misfortunes of the people were caused by the independence of the Indians, to which they were accessory, still they were the more unwilling to apply any corrective, because the very system which gave them wealth in the outset, in the course of its progress afforded them many plausible pretexts to put their hands into the treasury of the king, their master. For example: the Indians attack the frontier, kill some of the inhabitants, plunder many others, and agreeably to their custom of warfare retire instantly to their villages with their booty. The governor, informed of this transaction, promptly calls on the inhabitants to aid and assist in repelling the invasion. Accordingly, a party assembles under their officers, some three or four days after the mischief has been done, when the Indians are 100 or 150 miles from them; they pursue them as usual, at no rapid pace, for three or four days, and return without overtaking the enemy, as they might have well known they would do before they set out. On their return the men are dismissed, but ordered to hold themselves in readiness at a moment's warning. When at the end of some two or three months, the governor chooses (*p. 441*) to consider the danger blown over, he causes receipts to be made out for the full pay of two or three months' service, to which the signatures of the individuals are affixed; but as those persons were only absent from their homes ten or twelve days, all that is really paid them does not amount to more than one-fourth or one-fifth of what they receipted for; the balance of course being taken by the governor, as the reward for his faithful guardianship of the lives and property of his majesty's subjects.

The Spaniards, holding the entrance of the Missouri, could regulate as they thought proper the intercourse with the Indians through that channel; but from what has been said, it will be readily perceived that their traders, shackled with the pecuniary impositions of their governors, could never become the successful rivals of the British merchants on the west side of the Mississippi, which, from its proximity to the United States, the latter could enter without the necessity of a Spanish passport, or the fear of being detected by the Spaniards. The consequence was that the trade of the rivers Demoin [Des Moines] and St. Peter's [Minnesota], and of all the country west of the Mississippi nearly to the Missouri, was exclusively enjoyed by British merchants. The Spanish governors, stimulated by their own sordid views, declared that the honor of his majesty was grossly compromitted by the liberty that those adventurers took in trading with the natives within his own territory, without their own permission. They therefore took the liberty of expending his majesty's money by equipping and manning several galleys to cruise in the channels of the Mississippi in order to intercept those traders of the St. Peter's and Demoin rivers, in their passage to and from the entrance of the Ois- consing [Wisconsin] river; but after several unsuccessful cruises, finding the Indians so hostile to them in this quarter that they dared not land, [and could not] remain long in the channel without being attacked, they therefore retired and gave over the project.

The Indians were friendly to the British merchants, and unfriendly to the Spanish, for (*p. 442*) the plain reason that the former sold them goods at a lower rate. The Ayaways, Sacks, Foxes, and Yanktons of the river Demoin, who occasionally visited the Missouri, had it in their power to compare the rates at which the Spanish merchant in that quarter, and the British merchant on the Mississippi, sold their goods. This was always much in favor of the latter; it therefore availed the Spaniards but little when they inculcated the doctrine of their being the only legitimate fathers and friends [of the Indians], and that the British merchants were mere intruders, who had no other object in view but their own aggrandizement. The Indians, deaf to this doctrine, estimated the friendship of both by the rates at which they respectively sold their merchandise; and of course remained the firm friends of the British. In this situation it is not difficult for those to conceive who have felt the force of their machinations, that the British merchants would, in order to extend their own trade, endeavor to break down that of their neighbors on the Missouri. The attachment of the Indians to them afforded a formidable weapon with which to effect their purposes, nor did they suffer it to remain unemployed.

The merchants of the Dog prairie [Prairie du Chien], and of the rivers Demoin and Ayaway, stimulated the nations just mentioned to the commission of acts of rapacity on the merchants of the Missouri; nor were Mr. Cameron[3] and others, merchants of St. Peter's river, less active with respect

---

[3] A trader whose name occurs repeatedly in Pike's and in Long's Expeditions to the upper Mississippi. His demise (?) is noted thus: " Mr. Cameron, a trader, was poisoned by a [Sioux] Indian who administered to him some of the plant used for that purpose [poisoning arrows]." Long's Exped. to the St. Peter's, by Keating, London, 1825, I. p. 432.

to the Cissitons, Yanktons of the plains, Tetons, etc., who occasionally resorted to the Missouri still higher up. War-parties of those nations were consequently found lying in wait on the Missouri to intercept the boats of the merchants of that river at the seasons they were expected to pass, and depredations were frequently committed, particularly by the Ayaways ; who have been known in several instances to cap-ture boats on the Missouri, in their descent to St. Louis, and compelled the crews to load themselves with heavy burdens of their best furs across the country to their towns, where they disposed of them (*p. 443*) to the British merchants. In those cases they always destroyed the periogues, and such of the peltries and furs as they could not carry off. It may be urged that the British merchants, knowing that the United States at present, through mere courtesy, permits them to extend their trade to the west side of the Missis-sippi—or rather, that they are mere tenants at will, whom the United States possesses the means of ejecting at pleas-ure—will under these circumstances be induced to act dif-ferently toward us than they did in relation to the Spanish government ; but what assurance have we that this will be the effect of the mere change of governments without change of measures in relation to them? Suffer me to ask what solid grounds there are to hope that their gratitude for our tolerance and liberality on this subject will induce them to hold a different policy toward us? None, in my opinion, unless we stimulate their gratitude by placing before their eyes the instruments of our power in the form of one or two garrisons on the upper part of the Mississippi.

Even admitting that these people were actuated by the most friendly regard toward the interests of the United States, and at this moment made a common cause with us to induce the Indians to demean themselves in an orderly manner toward our government, and to treat our traders of the Missouri with respect and friendship ; yet, without some efficient check on the Indians, I should not think our citizens or our traders secure ; because the Indians, who have, for ten years and upward, derived advantages from practice in lessons of rapacity taught them by those traders, cannot in a moment be brought back to a state of primitive innocence by the united persuasions of all the British traders. I hold it to be an axiom, incontrovertible, that it is more easy to introduce vice into all states of society than it is to eradicate it; and that this is still more strictly true when applied to man in his savage than in his civilized state. If, therefore, we wish, within some short period, to divest ourselves of the evils which have flowed from the inculca- (*p. 444*) tion of those doctrines of vice, we must employ some more active agent than the influence of the same teachers who first introduced them. Such an agent, in my opinion, is the power of withholding merchandise from them at pleasure; and to accomplish this, we must first provide the means of controlling the merchants. If we permit the British merchants to supply the Indians in Louisiana, as formerly, the influence of our government over those Indians is lost. For the Indian, in possession of his merchandise, feels himself independent of every government, and will proceed to commit the same depredations which he did when rendered independent by the Spanish system.

The traders give themselves but little trouble at any time to inculcate among the Indians a respect for governments; but are usually content with proclaiming their own importance. When the British merchants give themselves the trouble to speak of governments, it is but fair to presume that they will teach the natives to respect the power of their own. And at all events, we know from experience that no regard for the blood of our frontier inhabitants will influence them at any time to withhold arms and ammunition from the Indians, provided they are to profit by furnishing them.

Having now stated, as they occurred to my mind, the several evils which have flowed from the system of intercourse with the Indians pursued by the Spanish government, I shall next endeavor to point out the defects of our own system, and show its incompetency to produce the wished-for reform; then, with some remarks on the Indian character, I will conclude by submitting, for the consideration of our government, the outlines of a plan which has been dictated as well by a sentiment of philanthropy toward the aborigines of America, as by a just regard to the protection of the lives and property of our citizens; and with the further view of securing to the people of the United States, exclusively, (*p. 445*) the advantages which ought of right to accrue to them from the possession of Louisiana.

We now permit the British merchants of Canada, indiscriminately with our own, to enter the Missouri and trade with the nations in that quarter. Although the government of the United States has not yielded the point that, as a matter of right, the British merchants have the privilege of trading in this quarter; yet from what has been said to them, they are now acting under a belief that it will be some time before any prohibitory measures will be taken with respect to them; they are therefore making rapid strides to secure themselves in the affection of the Indians, and to break down, as fast as possible, the American adventurers, by underselling them, and thus monopolize that trade. This they will effect to an absolute certainty in the course of a few years. The old Northwest Company of Canada have, within the last two years, formed a union with the Newyork [New York] Company, who had previously been their only important rivals in the fur trade. This company, with the great accession of capital brought them by the Newyork Company, have, with a view to the particular monopoly of the Missouri, formed a connection with a British house in Newyork and another at New Orleans, and have sent their particular agent, by the name of Jacob Mires, to take his station at St. Louis. It may be readily conceived that the united Northwest and Newyork companies, who had previously extended their trade in opposition to each other, and to the exclusion of all unassociated merchants on the upper portion of the Mississippi, the waters of Lake Winnipec [Winnipeg], and the Athebaskey [Athapasca] country, make the prices of their goods in both quarters similar; and though these may be excessively high, yet, being the same, they will run no risk of disaffecting the Indians by a comparison of the prices at which they receive their goods at those places. If, then, it appears that, the longer we extend the privilege to the Northwest Company of continuing their trade within our territory, the difficulty of excluding them will increase, can we begin the work of exclusion too soon? For my own part I see not the necessity to admit that our own merchants are not at this moment competent to supply the Indians of the Missouri with such (*p. 447*) quantities of goods as will, at least in the acceptation of the Indians themselves, be deemed satisfactory and sufficient for their necessities. All their ideas relative to their necessities are only comparative, and may be tested by a scale of the quantities they have been in the habit of receiving. Such a scale I transmitted to our government from Fort Mandan. From a regard to the happiness of the Indians, it would give me much pleasure to see this scale liberally increased; yet I am clearly of opinion that this effect should be caused by the regular progression of the trade of our own merchants, under the patronage and protection of our own government. This will afford additional security to the tranquillity of our much extended frontier, while it will give wealth to our merchants. We know that the change of government in Louisiana from Spain to the United States has withdrawn no part of the capital formerly employed in the trade of the Missouri; the same persons remain, and continue to prosecute their trade. To these there has been an accession of several enterprising American merchants; several others since my return have signified their intention to embark in that trade within the present year; and the whole of these merchants are now unembarrassed by the exactions of Spanish governors. Under these circumstances, is it fair for us to presume that the Indians are not now supplied by our own merchants with quite as large an amount in merchandise as they were

upper portion of the Missouri until our government shall think proper to dislodge them.

This season there has been sent up the Missouri, for the Indian trade, more than treble the quantity of merchandise that has ever been previously embarked in that trade at any one period. Of this quantity, as far as I could judge from the best information I could collect, two-thirds was the property of British merchants, and directly or indirectly that of the Northwest Company. Not any of this merchandise was destined for a higher point on the Missouri than the mouth of the Vermilion river, or the neighborhood of the Yanktons of the river Demoin. Of course there will be a great excess of goods beyond what the Indians can purchase, unless the goods are sold at one-third their customary price, which the American merchant certainly cannot do without sacrificing his capital.

On my return this fall, I met on the Missouri an American merchant by the name of Robert M'Clellan, formerly a distinguished partisan in the army under General Wayne. (*p. 449*) In conversation with this gentleman I learned that during last winter, in his trade with the Mahas, he had a competitor by the name of Joseph La Croix, believed to be employed by the Northwest Company, but now an avowed British merchant ; that the prices at which La Croix sold his goods compelled M'Clellan to reduce the rates of his own goods so much as to cause him to sink upward of two thousand dollars of his capital in the course of his trade that season ; but that as he had embarked in this trade for two years past, and had formed a favorable acquaintance with the Mahas and others, he should still continue it a few seasons more, even at a loss of his time and capital, in the

in the thirty codices I possess, nor do I even know whether it was first published in this book, or originally printed in another connection.   I imagine that it was a special official report from Captain Lewis to President Jefferson, and that if the original MS. be extant it should be found in the archives of the State Department, in Captain Lewis' handwriting.   It is certainly his literary composition, as we see by the peculiarly involved syntactical form of what is in substance a remarkably clear and cogent presentation of the important subject.

hope that government, seeing the error, would correct it, and that he might then regain his losses, from the circumstance of his general acquaintance with the Indians.

I also met on my way to St. Louis another merchant by the same name, a Captain M'Clellan, formerly of the United States' Corps of Artillerists. This gentleman informed me that he was connected with one of the principal houses in Baltimore—which one I do not now recollect, but can readily ascertain the name and standing of the firm, if it is considered of any importance. He said he had brought with him a small but well-assorted adventure, calculated for the Indian trade, by way of experiment ; that the majority of his goods were of the fine, high-priced kind, calculated for the trade with the Spanish province of New Mexico, which he intended to carry on within the territory of the United States, near the border of that province ; that connected with this object, the house with which he was concerned was ready to embark largely in the fur trade of the Missouri, provided it should appear to him to offer advantages to them ; that since he had arrived in Louisiana, which was last autumn, he had endeavored to inform himself of the state of this trade ; and that from his inquiries he had been so fully impressed with the disadvantages it labored under from the free admission of British merchants, that he (*p. 450*) had written to his house in Baltimore, advising that they should not embark in this trade, unless those merchants were prohibited from entering the river.

I have mentioned these two as cases in point, which have fallen immediately under my own observation: the first shows the disadvantages under which the trade of our own merchants is now actually laboring ; and the second, that no other merchants will probably engage in this trade while the British fur traders are permitted by our government to continue their traffic in Upper Louisiana. With this view of the subject, it is submitted to the government, with which it alone rests to decide whether admission or non-admission of those merchants is at this moment most expedient.

The custom of giving credits to the Indians, which grew out of the Spanish system, still exists; and, agreeably to our present plan of intercourse with these people, is likely to produce more pernicious consequences than it did formerly. The Indians of the Missouri, who have been in the habit of considering these credits rather as presents, or as the price of their permission for the trader to depart in peace, still continue to view it in the same light, and will, therefore, give up their expectations on that point with some reluctance; nor can the merchants well refuse to acquiesce, while they are compelled to be absent from the nations with which they trade five or six months in the year. The Indians are yet too vicious to permit them in safety to leave goods at their trading-houses during their absence, in the care of one or two persons; the merchant, therefore, would rather suffer loss by giving credit than incur the expense of a competent guard or doubling the quantity of his engagees; for it requires as many men to take the peltries and furs to market as it does to bring the goods to the trading-establishment, and the number usually employed are not found at any time to be more than sufficient to give a tolerable security against the Indians.

(*p. 451*) I presume it will not be denied that it is our best policy, and will be our practice, to admit, under the restrictions of our laws on this subject, a fair competition among all our merchants in the Indian trade. This being the case, then it will happen, as it has already happened, that one merchant having trade with any nation, at the usual season gives them credit and departs; a second, knowing that such advance had been made, hurries his outfit and arrives at that nation perhaps a month earlier in the fall than the merchant who had made this advance to the Indians; he immediately assembles the nation and offers his goods in exchange for their redskin hunt; the good faith of the Indians, with respect to the absent merchant, will not bind them to refuse; an exchange, of course, takes place; and when the merchant to whom they are indebted arrives, they have no peltry, either to barter or to pay him for the goods which they have already received. The consequences are that the merchant who has sustained the loss becomes frantic ; he abuses the Indians, bestows on them the epithets of " liar" and " dog," and says a thousand things only calculated to sour their minds and disaffect them to the whites : the rival trader he accuses of having " robbed " him of his credits (for they never give this species of artifice among themselves a milder term), and calls him many opprobrious names; a combat [6] frequently ensues, in which the principals are not the only actors, for their men will, of course, sympathize with their respective employers. The Indians are the spectators of those riotous transactions, which are well calculated to give them a contempt for the character of the whites and to inspire them with a belief of the importance of their peltries and furs. The British traders have even gone farther in the Northwest, and offered bribes to induce the Indians to destroy each other ; nor have I any reason to doubt that the same thing will happen on the Missouri, unless some disinterested person, armed with authority by government, be placed in such a situation (*p. 452*) as will enable him to prevent such controversies.

I look upon this custom of extending credits to the Indians as one of the great causes of all those individual contentions which will most probably arise in the course of this trade, as well between the Indians and whites, as between the whites themselves ; and fear that our agents and officers will be always harassed with settling these disputes, which they never can do in such a manner as to restore a perfect good understanding between the parties. I think it would be best, in the outset, for the government to let it be under-

---

[6] Collisions between rival traders were frequent, and sometimes resulted in bloodshed : see for example the case of Manuel Lisa and one of the M'Clellans named in the present article, as detailed in its main features by Brackenridge, Travels, 1814, p. 243, and at greater length in Irving's Astoria, Chap. xvii *et seq.* This case happened to become notorious because it was so fully written up, and thus passed into history ; but it is only a sample of the fierce hostilities which were engendered by the rivalries and jealousies of the fur-trade.

stood by the merchants that, if they think proper to extend credits to the Indians, it shall be at their own risk, dependent on the good faith of the Indians for voluntary payment; that the failure of the Indians to comply with their contracts shall not be considered any justification for their maltreatment or abusive language ; and that no assistance shall be given them in any shape by the public functionaries to aid them in collecting their credits. If the government interfere in behalf of the traders by any regulation, then it will be the interest of every trader individually to get the Indians indebted to him, and to keep them so in order to secure in future their peltries and furs exclusively to himself. Thus the Indians would be compelled to exchange without choice of either goods or prices, and the government would have pledged itself to make the Indians pay for goods of which they cannot regulate the prices. I presume the government will not undertake to regulate the merchant in this respect by law.

The difficulties which have arisen, and which must arise under existing circumstances, may be readily corrected by establishing a few posts, where there shall be a sufficient guard to protect the property of the merchants in their absence, though it may be left with only a single clerk. To those common marts all traders and Indians should be compelled to resort for the purposes of traffic.

(*p. 453*) The plan proposed guards against all difficulties, and provides for a fair exchange, without the necessity of credit. When the Indian appears with his peltry and fur, competition between the merchants will always insure him his goods on the lowest possible terms ; and the exchange taking place at once, there can be no cause of controversy between the Indian and the merchant, and no fear of loss on the part of the latter, unless he is disposed to make a voluntary sacrifice, through a spirit of competition with others, by selling his goods at an under-valuation.

Some of the stipulations contained in the licenses usually granted our Indian traders are totally incompatible with the local situations and existing customs and habits of almost all the Indian nations in Upper Louisiana. I allude more particularly to that clause in the license which compels them to trade at Indian towns only. It will be seen by reference to my Statistical View of the Indian nations of Upper Louisiana, that the great body of those people are roving bands, who have no villages or stationary residence. The next principal division of them, embracing the Panias, Ottoes, Kansas, etc., have not their villages on the Missouri, and even they pass the greater portion of the year at a distance from their villages, in the same roving manner. The third and only portion of those Indians who can with propriety be considered as possessed of such stationary villages as seems to have been contemplated by this clause of the license, is confined to the Ayaways, Sioux, and Foxes of the Mississippi, and the Ricaras, Mandans, Minnetarees, and Ahwahaways of the Missouri. The consequence is that until some further provision be made, all the traders who have intercourse with any nations except those of the last class, will form their establishments at the several points on the Missouri, where it will be most convenient to meet the several nations with whom they wish to carry on commerce. This is their practice at the present moment, and their houses are scattered on various parts of the Mis- (*p. 454*) souri. In this detached situation, it cannot be expected that they will comply with any of the stipulations of their licenses. The superintendent of St. Louis, distant 800 or 1,000 miles, cannot learn whether they have forfeited the penalty of their licenses or not; they may, therefore, vend ardent spirits, compromit the government, or the character of the whites, in the estimation of the Indians, or practice any other crimes in relation to those people, without the fear of detection or punishment. The government cannot with propriety say to those traders that they shall trade at villages which in reality do not exist; nor can the government for a moment, I presume, think of incurring the expense of sending an Indian agent with each trader, to see that the latter commits no breach of the stipulations of his license. These traders must of course be brought together at some general points, where it will be convenient for several nations to trade with them, and where they can be placed under the eye of an Indian agent, whose duty it should be to see that they comply with the regulations laid down for their government. There are crimes which may be committed without a breach of our present laws, and which make it necessary that some further restrictions than those contained in the present licenses of our traders should either be added under penalties in those licenses, or else be punished by way of a discretionary power lodged in the superintendent, extending to the exclusion of such individuals from the Indian trade. Of these crimes I shall here enumerate three:

First, that of holding conversations with Indians tending to bring our government into disrepute among them, and to alienate their affections from the same.

Second, that of practicing any means to induce Indians to maltreat or plunder other merchants.

Third, that of stimulating or exciting, by bribes or otherwise, any nations or bands of Indians to wage war against other nations or bands; or against the citizens of the United (*p. 455*) States; or against citizens or subjects of any power at peace with the same.

These appear to me to be crimes fraught with more real evil to the community, and to the Indians themselves, than vending ardent spirits or visiting their hunting-camps for the purpose of trade; yet there are no powers vested in the superintendents or agents of the United States to prevent their repeated commission; nor restrictions or fines imposed by our laws to punish such offenses.

It is well known to me that we have several persons engaged in the trade of the Missouri who have within the last three years been adopted as citizens of the United States, and who are now hostile to our government. It is not reasonable to expect that such persons will act with good faith toward us. Hence the necessity of assigning metes and bounds to their transactions among the Indians. On my way to St. Louis last fall I received satisfactory evidence that a Mr. Robideau, an inhabitant of St. Louis, had, the preceding winter, during his intercourse with the Ottoes and Missouris, been guilty of the most flagrant breaches of the first of the misdemeanors above mentioned.' On my arrival at St. Louis I reported the case to Mr. Broom, the acting superintendent, and recommended his prohibiting that person from the trade of the Missouri, unless he would give satisfactory assurance of a disposition to hold a different language toward the Indians. Mr. Broom informed me that the laws and regulations of the United States on this subject gave him no such powers; and Mr. Robideau and sons still prosecute their trade.

The uncontrolled liberty which our citizens take of hunting on Indian lands has always been a source of serious difficulty on every part of our frontier, and is evidently destined to become quite as much so in Upper Louisiana, unless it be restrained and limited within consistent bounds. When the Indians have been taught by commerce duly to appreciate the furs and peltries of their country, they feel (*p. 456*) excessive chagrin at seeing the whites, by their superior skill in hunting, fast diminishing those productions to which they have been accustomed to look as the only means of acquiring merchandise; and nine-tenths of the causes of war are attributable to this practice. The Indians, though well disposed to maintain a peace on any other terms, I am convinced will never yield this point; nor do I consider it as of any importance to us that they should; for with what consistency of precept with practice can we say to the Indians whom we wish to civilize, that agriculture and

---

' That is, the offense of bringing our government into disrepute by misrepresenting it to the Indians and thus making them disloyal : see p. 1235. The Mr. Robideau here in mention is the "Bobidoux" of note [10], p. 1209, *q. v.* I think that the "Mr. Broom" of the present paragraph is Mr. Joseph Browne, who was General and Governor Wilkinson's Territorial Secretary, acting in the Governor's absence.

the arts are more productive of ease, wealth, and comfort than the occupation of hunting, while they see distributed over their forests a number of white men engaged in the very occupation which our doctrine would teach them to abandon. Under such circumstances it cannot be considered irrational in the Indians to conclude that our recommendations to agriculture are interested, and flow from a wish on our part to derive the whole emolument arising from the peltries and furs of their country, by taking them to ourselves.

These observations, however, are intended to apply only to such Indian nations as have had, and still maintain, a commercial intercourse with the whites; such we may say are those inhabiting the western branches of the Mississippi, the eastern branches of the Missouri, and near the main body of the latter, as far up as the Mandans and Minnetarees. Here it is, therefore, that it appears to me expedient we should draw a line and temporarily change our policy. I presume it is not less the wish of our government that the Indians on the extreme branches of the Missouri to the west, and within the Rocky mountains, should obtain supplies of merchandise equally with those more immediately in their vicinity. To effect this, the government must either become the merchants or present no obstacles to its citizens which may prevent their becoming such with those distant nations; but as the former course cannot be adopted, though I really think it would be best for a time, then it (*p. 457*) becomes the more necessary to encourage the latter. Policy further dictates such encouragement being given, in order to contravene the machinations preparing by the Northwest Company for practice in that quarter.

If hunters are not permitted in those distant regions, merchants will not be at the expense of transporting their merchandise thither, when they know that the natives do not possess the art of taking the furs of their country. The use of the trap, by which those furs are taken, is an art which must be learned before it can be practiced to advantage. If the American merchant does not adventure, the field is at once abandoned to the Northwest Company, who will permit the hunter to go, and the merchant will most probably be with him in the outset; for the abundance of rich furs in that country holds out sufficient inducement for them to lose no time in pressing forward their adventures. Thus those distant Indians will soon be supplied with merchandise; while they are taught the art of taking the fur of their country, they will learn its value; and until they have learned its value, we shall run no risk of displeasing them by taking it. When the period shall arrive that the distant nations shall have learned the art of taking their fur, and know how to appreciate its value, then the hunter becomes no longer absolutely necessary to the merchant, and may be withdrawn; but, in the outset, he seems to form a very necessary link in that chain which is to unite these nations and ourselves in a state of commercial intercourse.

The liberty to our merchants of hunting for the purpose of procuring food, in ascending and descending the navigable water-courses, as well as while stationary at their commercial posts, is a privilege which should not be denied them; but as the unlimited extent of such a privilege would produce much evil, it should certainly be looked on as a subject of primary importance. It should, therefore, enter into all those compacts which we may think proper to form with (*p. 458*) the Indians of that country, and be so shaped as to leave them no solid grounds of discontent.

A view of the Indian character, so far as it is necessary it should be known for the purposes of governing them, or of maintaining a friendly commercial intercourse with them, may be comprised within the limits of a few general remarks.

The love of gain is the Indians' ruling passion, and the fear of punishment must form the corrective; to this passion we are to ascribe their inordinate thirst for the possession of merchandise, their unwillingness to accede to any terms, or enter into any stipulations, except such as appear to promise them commercial advantages, and the want of good faith which they always evince by not complying with any regulations which in practice do not produce to them those expected or promised advantages. The native justice of the Indian mind will always give way to his impatience for the possession of the goods of the defenseless merchant; he will plunder him unless prevented by the fear of punishment; nor can punishment assume a more terrific shape to the Indians than that of withholding every description of merchandise from them. This species of punishment, while it is one of the most efficient in governing the Indians, is certainly the most humane, as it enforces a compliance with our will without the necessity of bloodshed. But in order to compass the exercise of this weapon, our government must first provide the means of controlling our traders. No government will be respected by the Indians until they are made to feel the effects of its power, or see it practiced on others; and the surest guarantee of savage fidelity to any government is a thorough conviction in their minds that the government does possess the power of punishing promptly every act of aggression which they may commit on the persons or property of its citizens.

If both traders and Indians throughout Upper Louisiana were compelled to resort to regulated commercial posts, then the trader would be less liable to (*p. 459*) be pillaged, and the Indians would be deterred from practicing aggression; for when the Indians once become convinced that in consequence of having practiced violence upon the persons or property of the traders, they have been cut off from all intercourse with those posts, and cannot resort to any other places to obtain merchandise, then they will make any sacrifice to regain the privilege they previously enjoyed. I am confident that, in order to regain our favor in such cases, they would sacrifice any individual who may be the object of our displeasure, even should he be their favorite chief; for their thirst of merchandise is paramount to every other considera-

tion, and the leading individuals among them, well knowing this trait in the character of their own people, will not
venture to encourage or excite aggressions on the whites,
when they know they are themselves to become the victims
of its consequences.

But if, on the other hand, these commercial establishments
are not general, and we suffer detached and insulated merchants, either British or American, to exercise their own discretion in settling down where they may think proper on the
western branches of the Mississippi, for the purposes of trading with the Indians; then, though these commercial establishments may be so extended as to embrace the Missouri
quite to the Mandans, still they will lose a great part of their
effects; because the roving bands of Tetons and the most
dissolute of the Sioux, being denied permission to trade on
the Missouri at any rate, would resort to those establishments on the Mississippi, and thus become independent of
the trade of the Missouri, as they have hitherto been.   To
correct this, we have three alternatives : First, to establish
two commercial posts in this quarter.   Secondly, to prohibit all intercourse with the Sisitons and other bands of
Sioux, on the St. Peter's and Raven's-wing [8] rivers, informing
those Indians that such prohibition has been the consequence of the malconduct of the Tetons, and thus leaving it
to the former to correct the latter. (*p. 460*) Thirdly, to
make an appeal to arms in order to correct the Tetons
ourselves.

Impressed with a belief, unalloyed with doubt, that the
ardent wish of our government has ever been to conciliate
the esteem and secure the friendship of all the savage nations
within its territory by the exercise of every consistent and
pacific measure in its power, applying those of coertion
[*sic*] only in the last resort, I here proceed, with due defer-

---

[8] Also formerly Crow's-wing or Crow-wing river, now Crow river ; first considerable stream from the west above St. Peter's or the Minnesota river, running
for some distance between Wright and Hennepin counties, Minn., and falling
into the Mississippi at Dayton.   See " Raven Wing R." on Lewis' map of 1806.

ence to better judgment, to develop a scheme which has suggested itself to my mind as the most expedient that I can devise for the successful consummation of our philanthropic views toward those wretched people of America, as well as to secure to the citizens of the United States all those advantages which ought of right exclusively to accrue to them from the possession of Upper Louisiana.[9]

The situation of the Indian trade on the Missouri and its waters, while under the Spanish government.

The exclusive permission to trade with nations.

The giving by those exclusions the right to individuals

---

[9] What follows is evidently mere memoranda, on the basis of which the lamented Lewis intended to develop his Indian policy. These fragments, however, are preserved, as they should be. They represent a sort of index to what has preceded, and may have been the original heads for the foregoing Essay.

I have never seen any manuscript of this article, and know nothing more about it than the reader himself may gather from the printed pages. There is nothing of the sort in all the 3,056 folios of the 30 codices in my hands. As to the date of the composition, this is certainly within a year after September, 1806, for in one place the author speaks of his descending the Missouri "last fall." I suppose the article to have been an official report to the President, or to the government, either by the Captain Lewis whom we now know so well, or by the Governor Lewis of whom we have learned so little. Should the original MS. be extant, it might be found in the archives of the State Department, or other governmental bureau ; I found nothing like it among the documents I was permitted to inspect in the War Department. If ever discovered it will be found in Lewis' handwriting—there is no mistaking the singularly involved syntax and diffuse style, to which I adverted, without animadversion, in note [10], p. 260, *q. v.* I have edited it very nearly as it stands in the Biddle edition, without recasting a single sentence, though not without a touch here and there, in a mere matter of grammar. Aside from any question of its form, however faulty and evidently unfinished, its substance is simply admirable. It is clear in statement of facts, and cogent in the conclusions deduced from those facts. It depicts evils already existent, and foresees abuses that would ensue, unless the corrective were applied. But the lesson was lost, as anyone but an enthusiast might have predicted it would be ; and from the day that Lewis and Clark gave the Indians into the hands of the government, as in some sense the wards of the nation, the policy of the United States has invariably been the most iniquitous that could possibly be carried into effect—and likewise the silliest, because the most expensive, both in blood and money.

to furnish supplies, which rendered the Indians independent of the government.

The times of sending goods to the Indians, and of returning to St. Louis; the necessity of giving credits; therefore the disadvantages of [the same].

The time to which licenses will extend.

The evils which grew out of the method pursued by the Spaniards, as well to themselves as to the Indians.

The independence of individuals of their own government.

The dependence of the Indians on those individuals, and their consequent contempt for the government, and for all other citizens, whom they plundered and murdered at pleasure.

The present rapacity of the Indians, owing to this cause, aided also by the system of giving credits to the Indians, which caused contentions among the traders, which terminated by giving the Indians a contempt for the character of the whites.

(*p. 461*) The permission to persons to hunt on Indian lands productive of many evils, the most frequent causes of war, hostile to the views of civilizing and of governing the Indians.

The first principle of governing the Indians is to govern the whites; the impossibility of doing this without establishments, and some guards at those posts.

The Sisitons may be made a check on the Tetons by withholding their trade on the Mississippi.

Having stated the several evils which flowed from the Spanish system, I now state the Indian character, the evils which still exist, and what they will probably terminate in, if not redressed; the plan recommended to be pursued and the benefits which may be expected to result therefrom; conclude thus: it may be pretty confidently believed that it is not competent to produce the wished-for reform among the Indians.

Hunters permitted in the Indian country pernicious; frequent cause of war between us.

Some of the stipulations of the licenses granted the traders, in application to the state of the Indians on the Missouri, of course not attended to. The incompetency of the Indian agents to see that any of the stipulations are complied with. Whisky or ardent spirits may therefore be introduced, and other corruptions practiced, without our knowledge. There is not at present allowed by law to the superintendent of Indian affairs any discretionary powers, by which he can prohibit our newly acquired citizens of Louisiana, who may be disaffected to our government, from trading with the Indians. The law says that any citizen of the United States who can give sufficient security for the sum of $500 for the faithful compliance with the stipulation of his license shall be permitted to trade. An instance has happened in Mr. Robideau, etc.*

* The preceding observations of Captain Lewis, although left in an unfinished state, are too important to be omitted. The premature death of the author has prevented his filling up the able outline that he has drawn. (Original note.)

APPENDIX II.

ESTIMATE OF THE WESTERN INDIANS.

[By Captains Lewis and Clark.]

[This article requires explanation in several particulars. I am fortunately able to elucidate its scope and aim, both of which, if I may judge by the comments of ethnographers, have not always been clearly understood. 1. In the first place it must be remembered that while Lewis and Clark were wintering at Fort Mandan, in 1804-5, they collected what information they could about the Indians, besides what they had discovered for themselves in ascending the Missouri, and embodied it all in a communication to President Jefferson, dispatched with other papers, etc., by the barge, April 7th, 1805 : see p. 258. Jefferson's Message to Congress of Feb. 19th, 1806, was accompanied by this contribution to ethnology, which, as printed, became the " Statistical View " so often cited in my notes—in fact, embodied in substance in what I have had to say on the subject. The " View " originally appeared as a State Paper, was reprinted in New York next, then in London (in 1807) as an integral part of the genuine Richard Phillips issue, and was later (first in 1809) taken up into those dishonest and bastard books I have stigmatized as the " Apocrypha." (See the Bibliographical Introduction, *anteà*, for particulars of this bookseller's trick.) Now it is a remarkable fact that from the time Lewis and Clark left the Mandans they never saw a single live Indian till Captain Lewis sighted " the lone horseman " in Shoshone Cove, Aug. 11th, 1805 : see p. 477. But from that time until July, 1806, the Expedition was in constant and close relations with the Indians all along their route. These are the " *Western* " Indians of the above caption— that is, the Indians west of the main divide of the Rocky mountains, with whom the Expedition came in contact, or concerning whom Lewis and Clark had any information. Thus it is clear that the present " Estimate of the Western Indians " is a continuation of, or rather a supplement to, the earlier " Statistical View," besides being a sort of census of the tribes treated at greater or less length in foregoing pages. It is to be compared especially with the ethnological matter running pp. 756–762, as to some extent it duplicates that ; and it cannot be said, on the whole, to add much to what we have learned *passim* from foregoing pages of the present work. It is nevertheless a valuable summary, and I observe its convenience for some ethnographers who have never taken the trouble to discover all that L. and C. have to say of the tribes here epitomized. To facilitate matters in this respect, I make the required back-references, and add a few notes. The names will very often be found to differ in spelling, as I adhere scrupulously to my rule of preserving all the varying orthographies of the L. and

C. proper names.   In the Biddle edition the Estimate occupied pp. 471–476, being separated from Lewis' Essay on an Indian Policy by the Summary Statement. I change the sequence of these two pieces to bring the Indian matters together. Also, in the Biddle edition the Estimate was in an awkward semi-tabular form, which I reset in ordinary paragraphs.   The list as " prepared for the press " was in the most dire confusion, which I do not think any editor's or printer's skill could now do away with, unless the whole were run into another form.   The numbering of the tribes was either at random or too occult for comprehension. Item : certain heads and subheads were introduced which by no means divided and subdivided the matter of the Estimate in the manner which the authors in-tended, but had exactly the opposite typographical effect.   In such a slough of despond, I have simply tried my best to bring about an appearance of order, but am prepared to take the consequences of rashly attempting an impossibility. 2. As to the date and authorship of the Estimate : by note [6], p. 1042, it is seen that this article was originally drafted in June, 1806—or more probably an original draft was regarded as then completed, when the Expedition was in camp on Quamash flats, after their month at Camp Chopunnish.   *This* MS. draft, or a copy of it, is now on pp. 147–155 of Codex I, as stated in my article on the codices in Proc. Amer. Philos. Soc. xxxi. Mar. 7th, 1893, p. 25.   But *this* draft, in Captain Clark's hand, was *not* printed.   It was afterward canceled as a whole by Captain, more probably by General, Clark, who notes across p. 150 of it, in red ink : " The estimate of the Nations and tribes West of the Rocky Moun-tains May be Seen More Correctly in a Supplemnt accompanying these [Red] Books WC 80.000 Soles "—whence it is evident that Mr. Biddle went to press with the Estimate from copy later revised by General or Governor Clark, no doubt after Governor Lewis' death in 1809.   This *revised* manuscript I have never seen, and fear that it may not have been preserved.   It probably went the usual way of printer's copy that has been put through the mill.   And here I may remark further, that I have never seen a line of the Biddle copy from which Bradford & Inskeep set this book ; and that assuredly not one of the 3,056 codicean folios ever saw the inside of a printing-office.   Under all the circum-stances, I do not hesitate to ascribe the Estimate to actual joint-authorship, though the form in which we have it is as it finally came from the hands of one of our authors alone.]

(*p. 471*) 1. Shoshonee nation,[1] 60 lodges, 300 persons, reside in spring and summer on the west [read east?] fork of Lewis' river, a branch of the Columbia, and in winter and fall on the Missouri.

[1] That is, one certain tribe of the Shoshone nation, numbering and residing as said.   See several more " Shoshonee (or Snake Indians)," enumerated beyond. Who these Indians were, and where the " west fork of Lewis' river " is, are occult matters.   But probably the Indians here implied are our old friends of the Lemhi and Salmon rivers, as these are nowhere else accounted for in the Estimate.   If so, see pp. 554 *seq.*   See also Nos. 67–70, beyond.

2. Ootlashoot tribe of the Tushshepah nation, 33 lodges, 400 persons, reside in spring and summer in the Rocky mountains on Clark's river, in winter and fall on the Missouri and its waters. [See note ¹⁰, p. 582, and note ¹¹, p. 583.]

3. [A band of the] Chopunnish nation, 33 lodges, 2,000 persons, residing on the Kooskooskee river, below the forks, and on Colter's [Potlatch] creek ; and who sometimes pass over to the Missouri. [See note ¹⁰, p. 988.]

4. Pelloatpallah band of Chopunnish, 33 lodges, 1,600 persons, reside on the Kooskooskee above the forks, and on the small streams which fall into that river, west of the Rocky mountains and Chopunnish river, and sometimes pass over to the Missouri. [See note ¹², p. 1070.]

5. Kimooenim² band of Chopunnish nation, 33 lodges, 800 persons, reside on Lewis' river above the entrance of the Kooskooskee, as high up that river as the forks.

6. Yeletpo band of Chopunnish, 33 lodges, 250 persons, reside under the southwest mountains, on a small river [Asotin creek] which falls into Lewis' river above the entrance of the Kooskooskee, which they call Weaucum. [See note ², p. 1038.]

7. Willewah band of Chopunnish, 33 lodges, 500 persons, reside on a river of the same name³ which discharges into Lewis' river on the S.W. side, below the forks of that river.

8. Soyennom⁴ band of Chopunnish, 33 lodges, 400 per-

---

² A remarkable codex-map, never published, which must be adduced in the present connection, occupies Clark M 1, 2. It is a rude sketch, mainly on Chopunnish Indian information (e. g., p. 996), but has some important points about it. On this map Asotin creek is clearly laid down, unnamed (as in fact it is on Clark's map of 1814) ; the "Kemooenim Nation" is located on Lewis' river just above the mouth of this creek, and the "Wellelatpo Nation," i. e., the Willetpo, Yeletpo, or Waiilatpu, is located about the head of this creek. See next paragraph above (No. 6), and also note ², p. 1038. For "Kimooenim" as a name of Lewis' river itself, see p. 623, and cf. note ⁸, p. 629, and note ¹², p. 635.

³ See "Wil-le-wah R. & Tribe 1000 souls" on Clark's map of 1814, with which codex-map corresponds. This is the Grande Ronde river (see p. 622), the first large branch of the Snake or Lewis' river south of the Blue mountains.

⁴ "Soyennom" is a new name, concerning which I have nothing to offer, except

sons, reside on the N. side of the east fork [Salmon river] of Lewis' river, from its junction to the Rocky mountains, and on Lamaltar creek.

9. Chopunnish of Lewis' river, 40 lodges, 2,300 persons, reside below the entrance of the Kooskooskee, on either side of that river to its junction with the Columbia. [See p. 624.]

10. Sokulk nation, 120 lodges, 2,400 persons, reside on the Columbia above the entrance of Lewis' river, as high up as the entrance of Clark's river. [See pp. 637–639.]

11. Chimnahpum, 42 lodges, 1,860 persons, reside on the N.W. side of the Columbia, both above and below the entrance of Lewis' river, and on the Tapteel river, which falls into the Columbia 15 miles above Lewis' river. [See note [15], p. 537, note [16], p. 641, and note [29], p. 973.]

(*p. 472*) 12. Wollawollah nation, 46 lodges, 1,600 persons, reside on both sides of the Columbia from the entrance of Lewis' river as low as the Muscleshell rapid, and in winter pass over to the Tapteel river. [See note [38], p. 606, p. 645, and p. 967 *seq.*]

13. Pishquitpahs nation, 71 lodges, 2,600 persons, reside on Muscleshell rapid, and on the N. side of the Columbia to the commencement of the high country; this nation winter on the waters of the Tapteel river. [See pp. 966, 967.]

14. Wahowpum nation, 33 lodges, 700 persons, reside on the north branch of the Columbia, in different bands from the Pishquitpahs, as low as the river Lepage; the different bands of this nation winter on the waters of Tapteel and Cataract rivers. [See note [12], p. 964.]

15. Eneshure nation, 41 lodges, 1,200 persons, reside at

that it is So-yen-um on the codex-map, M 2, and that these Indians are there charted on the north side of Salmon river, near its mouth. " Lamaltar " creek is likewise a new name ; it is so on the codex-map ; and it is charted by Clark, 1814, unlettered, as the first tributary of Salmon river, falling in from the north. According to this indication it corresponds to the small stream now known as China creek ; but it might be meant for one of several others, as Waphilla, Mahoney, etc.

the upper part of the Great narrows of the Columbia on either side ; are stationary. [See note [11], p. 672.]

16. Eskeloot nation, 21 lodges, 1,000 persons, reside at the upper part of the Great narrows of the Columbia; on the N. side is the great mart for all the country. [See note [11], p. 672, and note [36], p. 922.]

17. Chilluckittequaw nation, 32 lodges, 1,400 persons, residing next below the narrows, and extending down on the N. side of the Columbia to the river Labiche. [See note [12], p. 673.]

18. Smockshop band of Chilluckittequaws, 24 lodges, 800 persons, reside on the Columbia, on each side of the entrance of the river Labiche, to the neighborhood of the great rapids of that river. [See note [12], p. 673, and note [30], p. 949.]

19. Shahala nation, 62 lodges, 2,800 persons, reside at the grand rapids of the Columbia, and extend down in different villages as low as the Multnomah river ; consist of the following tribes : Yehuh, above the rapids ; Clahclellah, below the rapids ; Wahclellah, below all the rapids ; Neerchokioon, one house, 100 lodges, on the S. side, a few miles above the Multnomah river. [Compare note [9], p. 1251.]

Wappatoo [5] *Indians.*

20. Nechacokee tribe, 1 lodge, 100 persons, reside on the S. side of the Columbia, a few miles below Quicksand river, opposite Diamond island. [See note [36], p. 922.]

21. Shoto tribe, 8 lodges, 460 persons, reside on the N. side of the Columbia, back of a pond nearly opposite the entrance of the Multnomah river. [See note [29], p. 916, and note [3], p. 931.]

22. Multnomah tribe, 6 lodges, 800 persons, reside on

[5] This heading is in the orig. ed., italicized as here. It is " No. 20," and then the tribes following to my No. 32 inclusive have no numbers. This is the only clew the list affords to how many are to be brought under the heading " Wappatoo Indians." According to this I break the list between my Nos. 32 and 33. As has been seen, pp. 931, 932, L. and C. use the names " Wappatoo " and " Multnomah " indifferently for these tribes—a fact which also appears in the present place, where several tribes of " Multnomahs " are so specified in the text.

Wappatoo island in the mouth of the Multnomah; the remains of a large nation.   [See p. 933.]

23. Clannahqueh tribe of Multnomahs, 4 lodges, 130 persons, reside on Wappatoo island, below the Multnomah. [See note [29], p. 916.]

24. Nemalquinner tribe of Multnomahs, 4 lodges, 200 persons, reside on the N.E. side of the Multnomah river, 3 miles above its mouth.   [See notes [39], [40], p. 924.]

(*p. 473*) 25. Cathlacommatups, a tribe of Multnomahs, 3 lodges, 170 persons, reside on the S. side of Wappatoo island on a slur [*sic*—slough or sluice] of the Multnomah. [See note [1], p. 931.]

26. Cathlanaquiahs, a tribe of Multnomahs, 6 lodges, 400 persons, reside on the S.W. side of Wappatoo island.   [See note [3], p. 931.]

27. Clackstar nation, 28 lodges, 1,200 persons, reside on a small [Scappoose] river which discharges on the S.W. side of Wappatoo island.   [See note [25], p. 915, and note [2], p. 931.]

28. Claninnatas,[6] 5 lodges, 200 persons, reside on the S.W. side of Wappatoo island.   [See note below.]

29. Cathlacumups, 6 lodges, 450 persons, reside on the main shore, S.W. of Wappatoo island.   [See note [26], p. 915.]

30. Clannarminnamuns, 12 lodges, 208 persons, reside on the S.W. side of Wappatoo island.   [See note [24], p. 915.]

31. Quathlahpohtle nation, 14 lodges, 900 persons, reside on the S.W. side of the Columbia, above the entrance of Tahwahnahiooks [Lewis'] river, opposite the lower point

But L. and C. discriminate among these one tribe which they specify as Multnomahs most properly so called, agreeably with the indication given on p. 933.

[6] This is a name which I do not think occurs elsewhere in the History. Its absence from among those of the tribes mentioned on p. 931 as inhabiting Wappatoo-island is probably accidental. For I find the "Clah-in-nata" charted by Clark on the codex-map, Lewis K·28, in the position here assigned them in the text, on the S.W. side of the island, immediately on Willamette slough, between the Clannarminnamuns and the Cathlanaquiahs.

of Wappatoo island.   [See note [18], p. 913, and note [22], p. 914.]

32. Cathlamahs,[7] 10 lodges, 200 persons, reside on a [Burris?] creek which falls into the Columbia on the N. side, at the lower part of the Columbian valley.   [See note [2], p. 931.]

———

33. Skilloot nation, 50 lodges, 2,500 persons, reside on the Columbia, on each side in different villages, from the lower part of the Columbia valley as low as Sturgeon island, and on either side of the Coweliskee river.   [See note [9], p. 692; also pp. 694, 695.]

34. Hullooellell, ——, residence on the Coweliskee.   [See note [14], p. 911.]

35. Wahkiacums, 11 lodges, 200 persons, reside on the N. side of the Columbia, opposite the Marshy islands. [See note [18], p. 700.]

36. Cathlamahs, 9 lodges, 300 persons, reside on the S. side of the Columbia, opposite the Seal islands. [See note [22], p. 705.]

37. Chinnooks, 28 lodges, 400 persons, reside on the N. side of the Columbia at the entrance of, and on, Chinnook [now Wallacut] river.   [See note [27], p. 710.]

38. Clatsop nation, 14 lodges, 200 persons, reside on the S. side of the Columbia, and a few miles along the S.E. coast, on both sides of Point Adams.   [See note [40], p. 717.]

39. Killamucks nation, 50 lodges, 1,000 persons, reside from the Clatsops of the coast along the S.E. coast for many miles.   [See note [32], p. 744; and pp. 751, 757.]

[7] This name is clearly a mistake: observe that it duplicates Cathlamahs below (No. 36).   I find " Cal-la-mah's Tribe " in Clark I 155, with the same census, and location, but canceled.   The Indians here meant (No. 32) are doubtless the Cathlahaws of p. 932: see note [3], p. 931.   The "creek on the north," on which they lived, is named Cathlahaws creek in the Summary Statement, where it is given as ten miles below Lewis' river and six above the lower point of Deer island.   The stream nearest to these requirements for position is Burris creek, falling in behind Burke's and Martin's islands.

Indian Information : The following nations speak the Killa-
muck language.[8]

40. Lucktons, 20 persons, reside on the seacoast to the
S.W. of the Killamucks. [See note [13], p. 758.]

41. Kahuncles, 400 persons, reside on the seacoast S.W.
of the Lucktons. [See p. 758.]

42. Lukawis, 800 persons, reside on the seacoast to the
S.S.E.; large town. [See note [14], p. 758.]

43. Youikcones, 700 persons, reside on the seacoast to the
S.S.E.; large houses. [See note [15], p. 758.]

44. Neeketoos, 700 persons, reside on the seacoast to the
S.S.E.; large town. [See note [16], p. 759.]

45. Ulseahs, 150 persons, reside on the seacoast to the
S.S.E.; small town. [See note [17], p. 759.]

46. Youitts, 150 persons, reside on the seacoast to the
S.S.E.; small town. [See note [18], p. 759.]

(*p. 474*) 47. Sheastuckles, 900 persons, reside on the seacoast to the S.E. of the Lucktons; large town. [See note [19],
p. 759.]

48. Killawats, 500 persons, reside on the seacoast to the
S.E. of the Lucktons; large town. [See note [20], p. 759.]

---

49. Cookkoo-oose nation, 1,500 persons, reside on the seacoast to the S. of the Killawats. [See note [22], p. 760.]

50. Shallalah[9] nation, 1,200 persons, reside on the same
course to the S.

[8] This italicized heading is in the orig. ed., but how many tribes it was
intended to cover we are left to find out. For the first tribe under it had a
separate number (No. 27) and then there were no more numbers to the Cookkoo-oose (No. 28), after which there were no more numbers to the next heading.
However, by referring to p. 760, we discover that we are to draw the line between the Killawats and the Cookkoo-oose, which I accordingly do. This heading therefore covers my Nos. 40–48 inclusive. With regard to the statement of
the heading, that these nine tribes speak the Killamuck language : see note [21],
p. 760. The list is substantially a duplicate of that given on pp. 758, 759.

[9] Owing to the similarity of this name, " Shallalah," and " Shahala," No. 19—
both being spelled in several interchangeable ways—the two have become
entirely confounded; and I have been led into error in my note [23], p. 761. The

51. Luckkarso nation, 1,200 persons, reside on the same course to the S. [See note²⁴, p. 761.]

52. Hannakallal nation, 600 persons, reside on the same course to the S. [See note²⁵, p. 761.]

[*Indian information :*] *Indians along the N.W. coast.*¹⁰

53. Killaxthocles tribe, 8 lodges, 100 persons, reside on the seacoast from the Chinnooks to the N.N.W. [See note²⁶, p. 761.]

54. Chiltz nation, 38 lodges, 700 persons, reside from the Killaxthokles along the N.N.W. coast. [See note³⁹, p. 717, and p. 761.]

55. Clamoctomichs, 12 lodges, 260 persons, reside from the Chiltz along the N.N.W. coast. [See note²⁸, p. 761.]

56. Potoashs, 10 lodges, 200 persons, reside on the same coast N.W. of the Clamoctomichs. [See note²⁹, p. 762.]

57. Pailsh tribe, 10 lodges, 200 persons, reside from the Potoash on the N.W. coast. [See note³⁰, p. 762.]

58. Quiniilts, 60 lodges, 1,000 persons, reside from the Pailsh along the N.W. coast. [See note⁸, p. 669, and note³¹, p. 762.]

59. Quieetsos, 18 lodges, 250 persons, reside from the Quiniilts along the N.W. coast. [A Salishan tribe, now known as Quaitso.]

60. Chillates, 8 lodges, 150 persons, reside from the Quieetsos along the N.W. coast. [See note³², p. 762.]

61. Calasthocle, 10 lodges, 200 persons, reside from the Chillate N.W. along the same coast. [See note³³, p. 762.]

Indians there meant by L. and C. are these of No. 50, and not those of No. 19, as I made them out to be. My note is correct in its application to the Shahalas, No. 19, but does not pertain to the Shalalahs of p. 761, or the Shallalahs of No. 50. This explanation, which accentuates the fact of error, may better serve to prevent its recurrence in future, than if I had simply deleted my former note.

¹⁰ This italicized heading can be inferred to extend to my No. 62 inclusive, because in the orig. ed. the first tribe mentioned under it, Killaxthocles, had a number (No. 29), and then there were no more numbers to the Clarkamus nation (No. 30). Accordingly I draw the line between my Nos. 62 and 63. This is also agreeable with pp. 761, 762, of which the present list is substantially a duplicate.

62. Quinnechart nation, 2,000 persons, reside on the sea-coast and creek, N. and N.W. of the Calasthocles. [See note ³⁴, p. 762.]

_____

63. Clarkamus nation, 1,800 persons, reside on a large river of the same name which heads in Mount Jefferson and discharges into the Multnomah, 40 miles up that river on its N.E. side; this nation has several villages on either side. [See note ³⁸, p. 924.]

64. Cushhooks nation, 650 persons, reside on the N.E. bank of the Multnomah, immediately below the falls of that river, about 60 miles above its entrance into the Columbia. [See note ³⁴, p. 921.]

65. Charcowah nation, 200 persons, reside on the S.W. bank of the Multnomah, immediately above the falls; they take salmon in that river. [See note ³, p. 931.]

66. Callahpoewah nation, 2,000 persons, inhabit the country on both sides of the Multnomah, above the Charco-wahs for a great extent. [See note ⁵, p. 932.]

_____

67. Shoshonee ¹¹ (or Snake Indians), 3,000 persons, residing in winter and fall on the Multnomah river, southwardly of the (*p. 475*) southwest mountains, and in spring and summer on the heads of the Towanahiooks [Des Chutes],

¹¹ To the Shoshones here indicated add those noted at No. 1. The present account is mainly upon Indian information of tribes which L. and C. never saw, and hardly furnishes data for useful comment. It does not agree at all with the notice cited from the Statistical View in note ⁹, p. 554, nor in fact with what is charted on Clark's map. Examination of the latter will show " about 10,000 Souls " on upper reaches of the Multnomah ; 2,000 about the headwaters of the Des Chutes ; 4,000 along Snake river and several of its main branches (as indicated at No. 70); also, " Pohah Band of Snake Inds. 1000 Souls " on headwaters of the Snake; " Shoshones 800 Souls " on the Lemhi and Salmon river ; a certain band of 600 souls on headwaters of Madison river ; and " Yeppe Band of Snake Inds. 1000 Souls " about the upper Yellowstone. The " Shobarboobeer " band, No. 69, has been more than once mentioned before, but under different forms of the word, two of which occur on p. 554: see note ³⁷, p. 840. For the modern classification of the Shoshonean family, see note ³, p. 477.

La Page [Lepage], Yaumalolam [Yumatilla], and Wollawollah rivers, and more abundantly at the falls of the
Towanahiooks, for the purpose of fishing.

68. Shoshonees, 6,000 persons, reside on the Multnomah
and its waters; the residence of whom is not well known to
us or to the Indians of the Columbia.

69. Shobarboobeer band of Shoshonees, 1,600 persons,
reside on the S.W. side of the Multnomah river, high up
the said river.

70. Shoshonees, 3,000 persons, reside on the south fork
of Lewis' river, and on the Nemo, Walshlemo, Shallette,
Shushpellanimmo, Shecomshink, Timmoonumlarwas, and
Copcoppakark rivers, branches of the south fork of Lewis'
river.[12]

[12] The seven branches of the main Snake river are easily identified by reference
to Clark's map of 1814. We also have the original sketch, upon Chopunnish
Indian information, on Clark M 2, and the basis of the printed paragraph is on
Clark I 153. On these data I make the following determinations of the seven
branches, taking them up in their reverse order, from above downward on the
Snake, and then adding the lower branches charted by Clark as far down as the
Kooskooskee: 1. Copcoppakark of the text; Copcoppahark, I 153 ; Cop-cop-
hah-ark, M 2 ; Cop-pop-pah-ash of the pub. map. This is Boisé river, on which
is Boise City, Ada Co., Idaho. 2. Timmoonumlarwas of the text; Timmooe-
num-larwas, I 153 ; Tim-moo-e-num, M 2; Tim-mo-a-men of the pub. map.
This is Owyhee river, falling into the Snake opposite Boisé river, in Malheur Co.,
Oregon. 3. Shecomshink of the text ; She-com-shenk, I 153 ; She-cam-skink,
M 2 ; She-com-shenk of the pub. map. This is Malheur river, Oregon,
falling in near Payette river. 4. Shushpellanimmo of the text ; same of
I 153 ; Shurk-pal-ha-nim-mo, M 2 ; Shush-pel-la-mine-mo of the pub. map.
This is the Payette river, Idaho, falling into the Snake in Ada Co. 5. Shallette
of the text ; Shallett, I 153 ; name illegible, M 2 ; no name on the pub. map,
but see "Shalett L." there. This Shalett lake, given as "2 lakes" on the
codex-map, is Payette lake ; and the river flowing from it, i. e., Shallette river
of the text, is therefore the North fork of Payette river, running in Boisé Co.,
Idaho. 6. Walshlemo of the text ; Walshlem, I 153, Walsh-le-mo, M 2 and
pub. map. This is Burnt river, Baker Co., Oregon, although Clark brings it in
above instead of below his Nemo (Weiser) river. 7. Nemo of the text, I 153,
M 2, and pub. map. This is Weiser river, Washington Co., Idaho. 8. Continuing down the Snake, on the Oregon side, M 2 and pub. map have a Flint
river. In assigned position this comes nearest Powder river, but seems too
small. 9. Next, M 2 has Palt-pol-la river, with its branch Ta-nin-pa ; pub.
map has Port-pel-lar with its branch Ta-kin-par. This corresponds in relative

We saw parts of the following tribes at the long narrows.[13]

71. Skaddals nation, 200 persons, reside on Cataract river, 25 miles N. of the Big narrows.

72. Squannaroos, 120 persons, reside on the Cataract river, below the Skaddals.

73. Shallattoos, 100 persons, reside on the Cataract river, above them.

74. Shanwappoms, 400 persons, reside on the heads of Cataract and Tapteel rivers.

———

75. Cutsahnim [14] nation, 60 lodges, 1,200 persons, reside on both sides of the Columbia above the Sokulks, on the northern branches of the Tapteel river, and on the Wahnaachee [Wenatchee] river.

76. Lahanna nation, 120 lodges, 2,000 persons, reside on both sides of the Columbia river, above the entrance of Clark's river.

77. Coospellar nation, 30 lodges, 1,600 persons, reside on a river which falls into the Columbia, to the N. of Clark's river.

position to Pine creek, Union Co., Oregon, but is altogether too large. Nevertheless, I think Nos. 8 and 9 really represent the two streams named, about right in relative position, but reversed in relative size. Passing a small stream, unnamed by Clark, on the Idaho side, we have next : 10. In-na-har, M 2 ; Innahar of the pub. map. This is now Imnaha river, Wallowa Co., Oregon. 11. Then comes Salmon river, L. and C. names of which are North Fork of Lewis' river, Pawnashte, and Tommanamah. The large southern branch of this which Clark charts as Mulpah river is now known as Little Salmon river. 12. Grande Ronde river, the L. and C. name for which is Willewah. 13. Asotin creek, called Weaucum on p. 1246 ; Clark charts it, nameless. 14. The Kooskooskee.

[13] This italicized head covers only the four following tribes, Nos. 71–74. These have been mentioned before : see p. 951. They are charted by Clark on Cataract (Klikitat) river, by the names Ska-ddals, Squanna-roos, Shal-lat-tos, and Chanwappan, but the figures for the census are variant. They are thus brought into relation with the Klikitats, a Shahaptian tribe.

[14] Charted by Clark by this name and located on the " Columbia," just above the entrance of Clark's fork. So the charted location of the Cutsahnim nation is the Okenagan river, not the " Columbia."

78. Wheelpo [15] nation, 130 lodges, 2,500 persons, reside on both sides of Clark's river, from the entrance of the Lastaw to the great falls of Clark's river.

79. Hihighenimmo [16] nation, 45 lodges, 1,300 persons, reside from the entrance of the Lastaw into Clark's river, on both sides of the Lastaw, as high as the forks.

80. Lartielo [17] nation, 30 lodges, 600 persons, reside at the falls of the Lastaw river, below the great Wayton lake, on both sides of the river.

81. Skeetsomish nation, 12 lodges, 2,000 persons, reside on a small river of the same name which discharges into the Lastaw below the falls, around the Wayton lake, and on two islands within the said lake. [See note [12], p. 990.]

82. Micksucksealton [18] tribe of the Tushshepah, 25 lodges, 300 persons, reside on Clark's river, above the great falls of that river, in the Rocky mountains.

(*p. 476*) 83. Hohilpos, [19] a tribe of the Tushshepah, 25 lodges, 300 persons, reside on Clark's river, above the Micksucksealtons, in the Rocky mountains.

84. Tushshepah nation, 35 lodges, 430 persons, reside on a north fork of Clark's river in spring and summer, and in the fall and winter on the Missouri. The Ootlashoots are a band of this nation. [See note [10], p. 582, and note [11], p. 583.]

Whole number of Indians west of the Rocky mountains, 80,000.

[15] Whe-elpo Nation," codex-map M 1, located immediately below the falls of "Clark's river," *i. e.*, of the upper Columbia, apparently Kettle falls, near Kettle river and Fort Colville ; "Whe-el-po T. 3500 Souls" of the 1814 map. The "Lastaw" river of the text, heretofore given as Lautaw river, is the Latah : see notes [12], [13], pp. 990, 991.

[16] " Hi-hi-e-mim-o N.," codex-map M 1; "He-high-e-nim-mo 1500 Souls," on the 1814 map, where located on "Clark's river," *i. e.*, on the Columbia near the entrance of the Latah (meaning the Spokane) river.

[17] So on the codex map ; "Lar-li-e-lo 900 Souls" of the 1814 map, located about Spokane falls.

[18] " Mick-suck-seal-tom," Clark I 152 and map of 1814 ; "Mick-suck-seeal-ton," codex-map M 1, located at the confluence of Great Lake river with Clark's river, and therefore at the entrance of the latter into the Columbia proper.

[19] " Ho-hil-po " and " Ho-yeal-po," codex-map M 1; "Hohilpo 600 Souls," map of 1814, where located on a river of the same name.

APPENDIX III.

SUMMARY STATEMENT.

Summary Statement of the rivers, creeks, and other notable places, their distances from each other and from the Mississippi, up the Missouri, across the Rocky mountains, and down the Columbia to the Pacific, as explored in the years 1804-5-6, by Captains Lewis and Clark.

Names of Remarkable Places.	Side of the Missouri on which situated.	Width of river or creek in yards.	Distance from one place to another in miles.	Distance up the Missouri from the Mississippi in miles.
Village of St. Charles........................	N.E.	....	21	21
Osage-woman's river.........................	N.E.	30	20	41
Charrette's village and creek..................	N.E.	20	27	68
Shepherd's creek.............................	S.W.	....	15	83
Gasconade river..............................	S.W.	157	17	100
[Big] Muddy river............................	N.E.	50	15	115
Grand Osage river............................	S.W.	397	18	133
Murrow [Moreau] creek	S.W.	20	5	138
Cedar island and creek.......................	N.E.	20	7	145
Leadmine hill................................	S.W.	....	9	154
[Little] Manitou creek.......	S.E.	20	8	162
Splitrock creek..............................	N.E.	20	8	170
Saline, or Salt river	S.E.	30	3	173
[Big] Manitou river..........................	N.E.	30	9	182
Goodwoman's river...........................	N.E.	35	9	191
Mine river	S.W.	70	9	200
Arrow prairie................................	S.W.	....	6	206
First Charleton [Charaton] river	N.E.	30	14	220
Second do.	N.E.	70	14	220
Ancient village of the Missouri nation near which place Fort Orleans stood....................	N.E.	....	16	236
Grand river..................................	N.E.	90	4	240
Snake creek	N.E.	18	6	246
Ancient village of the Little Osages...........	S.W.	....	10	256
Tigers' [or Panther] island and creek...........	N.E.	25	20	276
Hubert's [Eau-beau] island and creek	S.W.	....	12	288
Fire-prairie creek............................	S.W.	....	12	300
Fort Point	S.W.	....	6	306
Haycabin creek..............................	S.W.	20	6	312
Coalbank [La Charbonnière]..................	S.W.	....	9	321
Bluewater river....................	S.W.	30	10	331
Kanzas river.................................	S.W.	230	9	340

Names of Remarkable Places.	Side of the Missouri on which situated.	Width of river or creek in yards.	Distance from one place to another in miles.	Distance up the Missouri from the Mississippi in miles.
Little river Platte..........................	N.E.	60	9	349
First old Kanzas village....................	S.W.	....	28	377
Independence creek, a mile below the second old Kanzas village...........................	S.W.	....	28	405
St. Michael's prairie........................	N.E.	....	25	430
Nodawa river...............................	N.E.	70	20	450
Wolf or Loup river.........................	S.W.	60	14	464
Big Nemaha river...........................	S.W.	80	16	480
Tarkio creek................................	N.E.	23	3	483
Neeshnabatona river........................	N.E.	50	25	508
Little Nemaha river.........................	S.W.	48	8	516
Baldpated prairie (the Neeshnabatona within 150 yards of the Missouri).................	N.E.	....	23	539
Weepingwater creek.........................	S.W.	25	29	568
[Great] river Platt or Shoal river............	S.W.	600	32	600
Butterfly or Papillon creek..................	S.W.	18	3	603
Musquetoe creek............................	N.E.	22	7	610
Ancient village of the Ottoes................	S.W.	....	11	621
Ancient village of the Ayaways..............	N.E.	....	6	627
Bowyer's [or Boyer's] river..................	N.E.	25	11	638
Council bluffs (establishment)................	S.W.	....	12	650
Soldier's river..............................	N.E.	40	39	689
Eaneahwaudepon (Little Sioux) river	N.E.	80	44	733
Waucarde or Badspirit creek.................	S.W.	....	55	788
Around a bend of the river to the N.E., the gorge of which is only 974 yards..........	.....	....	21	809
Island 3 miles N.E. of the Maha [Omaha] village........................	.....	....	27	836
Floyd's bluff and river......................	N.E.	35	14	850
Big Sioux river	N.E.	110	3	853
Copperas, cobalt, pyrites, and alum bluffs.....	S.W.	....	27	880
Hot or Burning bluffs .....:................	S.W.	....	30	910
Whitestone river............................	N.E.	30	8	918
Petit-arc, an old Maha village, at the mouth of Littlebow creek............................	S.W.	15	20	938
River Jacques or James' river................	N.E.	90	12	950
Calumet bluff (mineral)	S.W.	....	10	960
Ancient fortification, Goodman's [Bon Homme] island....................................	S.W.	....	16	976
Plum creek..................................	N.E.	12	10	986
Whitepoint [White-paint] creek	S.W.	28	8	994
Quicourre [L'Eau qui Court] river...........	S.W.	152	6	1000
Poncar river and village	S.W.	30	10	1010
Dome, and village of burrowing-squirrels......	S.W.	....	20	1030
Island of cedars............................	.....	....	45	1075
White river	S.W.	300	55	1130
Three rivers of the Sioux pass...............	N.E.	35	22	1152
Lower island, in the Big Bend...............	N.E.	....	20	1172
Upper part of the Big Bend, the gorge of which is 1¼ miles	S.W.	....	30	1202

Names of Remarkable Places.	Side of the Missouri on which situated.	Width of river or creek in yards.	Distance from one place to another in miles.	Distance up the Missouri from the Mississippi in miles.
Tylor's [or Tyler's] river.....................	S.W.	35	6	1208
Loisel's fort on Cedar island.................	S.W.	....	18	1226
Teton river.................................	S.W.	70	37	1263
Upper of five old Ricara villages, reduced by the Sioux and abandoned..................	S.W.	....	42	1305
Chayenne river	S.W.	400	5	1310
Old Ricara village on Lahoocat's island.......	....	....	47	1357
Sarwarkarna river..........................	S.W.	90	40	1397
Wetarhoo river	S.W.	120	25	1422
First Ricaras villages, on an island...........	S.W.	....	4	1426
Second Ricaras three villages................	S.W.	....	4	1430
Stone-idol creek...........................	N.E.	18	18	1448
Warreconne river	N.E.	35	40	1488
Cannonball river...........................	S.W.	140	12	1500
Chesschetar river, near 6 old Mandan villages..	S.W.	38	40	1540
Old Ricara and Mandan villages.............	S.W.	....	40	1580
Fort Mandan (wintering post of 1804)........	N.E.	....	20	1600
Mandan villages on each side................	....	....	4	1604
Knife river (on which the two Minnetaree and Maha villages are situated near the mouth)..	S.W.	80	2	1606
Island......................................	....	....	11	1617
Miry river.................................	N.E.	10	16	1633
Island in the Little basin...................	....	....	28	1661
Little Missouri river.......................	S.W.	134	29	1690
Wild onion creek...........................	N.E.	16	12	1702
Goose-egg lake.............................	N.E.	300	9	1711
Chaboneau's creek..........................	S.W.	20	16	1727
Goatpen creek (Mouse river, waters of lake Winnipec near the Missouri)...................	N.E.	20	16	1743
Hall's strand, lake, and creek................	N.E.	....	47	1790
White-earth river..........................	N.E.	60	50	1840
Rochejaune or Yellowstone river.............	S.W.	858	40	1880
Martha's river.............................	N.E.	50	60	1940
Porcupine river	N.E.	112	50	1990
Littledry creek............................	S.W.	25	40	2030
Bigdry creek...............................	S.W.	100	9	2039
Littledry river.............................	S.W.	200	6	2045
Gulf in the Island bend.....................	....	....	32	2077
Milk river.................................	N.E.	150	13	2090
Bigdry river...............................	S.W.	400	25	2115
Werner's run..............................	N.E.	10	9	2124
Pine creek.................................	N.E.	20	36	2160
Gibson's river..............................	N.E.	35	17	2177
Brownbear-defeated creek...................	S.W.	40	12	2189
Bratton's river.............................	N.E.	100	24	2213
Burntlodge creek...........................	S.W.	50	6	2219
Wiser's creek..............................	N.E.	40	14	2233
Muscleshell river...........................	S.W.	110	37	2270
Grouse creek	N.E.	20	30	2300
North-mountain creek	N.E.	30	36	2336

Names of Remarkable Places.	Side of the Missouri on which situated.	Width of river or creek in yards.	Distance from one place to another in miles.	Distance up the Missouri from the Mississippi in miles.
South-mountain creek......................	S.W.	30	18	2354
Ibex island.................................	.....	....	15	2369
Goodrich's island...........................	.....	....	9	2378
Windsor's creek............................	N.E.	30	7	2385
Elk rapid (swift water)......................	.....	....	15	2400
Thomson's creek...........................	N.E.	28	27½	2427½
Judith's river..............................	S.W.	100	11½	2439
Ash rapid (swift water).....................	.....	....	4	2443
Slaughter river	S.W.	40	11	2454
Stonewall creek, above the natural walls	N.E.	30	26	2480
Maria's river..............................	N.E.	186	41	2521
Snow river	S.W.	50	19	2540
Shields's river	S.W.	35	28	2568
Portage river (five miles below the Great falls).	S.W.	45	7	2575

Leaving the Missouri below the falls, and passing by land to the navigable waters of the Columbia river:

Names of Remarkable Places.	Width of river or creek in yards.	Distance from one place to another in miles.	Distance from the Falls of the Missouri in miles.	Distance from the Mississippi in miles.
Entrance of Medicine river..................	137	18	18	2593
Fort mountain (passing through the plain between Medicine river and the Missouri).............	....	15	33	2608
Rocky mountains, to a gap on the ridge, which divides the waters of the Missouri from those of the Columbia (passing the north part of a mountain and crossing Dearborn's river)	....	35	68	2643
Fork of Cohahlarishkit river from the north (passing four creeks from the north).............	45	40	108	2683
Seaman's creek, from the north...............	20	7	115	2690
Werner's creek, from the north..............	35	10	125	2700
East fork of Clark's river, at the entrance of Cohahlarishkit..........................	120	30	155	2730
Clark's river, below the forks................	150	12	167	2742
Traveller's-rest creek, on the west side of Clark's river, about [above] the forks...............	25	5	172	2747
Forks of Traveller's-rest creek, at a right-hand road..................................	....	18	190	2765
Hot springs on this creek	....	13	203	2778
Quamash glades (passing the head of the creek to a branch of the Kooskooskee).............	....	7	210	2785

Names of Remarkable Places.	Width of river or creek in yards.	Distance from one place to another in miles.	Distance from the Falls of the Missouri in miles.	Distance from the Mississippi in miles.
North branch of the Kooskooskee (a left-hand road leads off at five miles)..................	....	7	217	2792
Junction of the roads on the top of a snowy mountain (the left-hand road passing by a fishery)......................................	....	10	227	2802
Hungry creek from the right (passing on a dividing mountain, covered with deep snow, except on two places, which are open, with a southern exposure, at 8 and 36 miles)...............	....	54	281	2856
Glade on Hungry creek........................	....	6	287	2862
Glade on a small branch of do.................	....	8	295	2870
Glade on Fish creek...........................	10	9	304	2879
Collins' creek...............................	25	13	317	2892
Quamash flats	......	11	328	2903
Kooskooskee or Flathead's river...............	120	12	340	2915

NOTE. In passing from the falls of the Missouri across the Rocky mountains to the navigable waters of the Columbia, you have 200 miles of good road and 140 miles of high, steep, rugged mountains, 60 miles of which is covered from 2 to 8 feet deep with snow in the last of June.

Remarkable Places, descending the [Kooskooskee, Snake, and] Columbia.	Side on which situated.	Width of river or creek in yards.	Distance from one place to another in miles.	Distance descending the Columbia in miles.	Distance from the Mississippi in miles.
Entrance of Rockdam creek	N.	20	8	8	2923
Chopunnish river	N.	120	5	13	2928
Colter's creek.......................	N.	35	37	50	2965
Lewis' river, at the entrance of the Kooskooskee......................	S.	200	23	73	2988
Sweathouse village and run............	S.	....	7	80	2995
Pilot's village.......................	N.	....	11	91	3006
Kemooenim creek.....................	S.	20	48	139	3054
Drewyer's river, below the narrows of Lewis' river	N.	30	5	144	3059
Cave rapid..........................	....	....	28	172	3087
Basin rapid (bad)	....	....	34	206	3121
Discharge rapid (bad)	....	....	14	220	3135
Columbia river, at the mouth of Lewis' river, from the east	S.E.	....	7	227	3142
Wollawollah river (passed 11 large mat lodges of that nation)................	S.E.	40	16	243	3158
Muscleshell rapid (bad). (passed 33 mat lodges of the Wollawollahs).........	....	....	25	268	3183

Remarkable Places, descending the Columbia.	Side on which situated.	Width of river or creek in yards.	Distance from one place to another in miles.	Distance descending the Columbia in miles.	Distance from the Mississippi in miles.
Pelican rapid (passed 48 lodges of the Pishquitpahs)	N.	....	22	290	3205
Twenty-one lodges of the Wahowpums (on 3 islands at the commencement of the high country)	N.	....	18	308	3223
Short rapid (8 lodges of Wahowpums	N.	....	27	335	3250
Rocky rapid (9 lodges of the same nation)	N.	....	13	348	3263
River La Page (bad rapid)	S.	40	9	357	3272
Fishstack rapid (27 lodges of the Eneshure nation)	N.	....	10	367	3282
Towahnahiooks river	S.	180	8	375	3290
Great falls of the Columbia, 57 feet 8 inches (near which are 40 mat lodges of Eneshures)	N.	....	4	379	3294
Short narrows, 45 yards wide	....	....	2	381	3296
Skilloot village (21 large wood houses, at the long narrows, 50 to 100 yards wide)	N.	....	4	385	3300
Chilluckittequaw village (8 large wood houses)	N.	....	14	399	3314
Cataract river (a few miles below a village of 7 houses, and immediately above one of 11 houses, of the Chilluckittequaws)	N.	60	10	409	3324
Sepulchre rock (opposite village of Chilluckittequaws)	N.	....	4	413	3328
River Labiche (opposite 26 houses of the Smackshops, scattered on the north side)	S.	46	9	422	3337
Little Lake [probably Little White Salmon] creek (3 houses of the Smackshops)	N.	28	10	432	3347
Cruzatte's river	N.	60	12	444	3359
Grand rapid (just below the village of the Yehuh tribe of the Shahalas, of 14 wood houses	N.	....	6	450	3365
Clahclellah village of the Shahalas (near foot of the rapids ; 7 houses)	N.	....	6	456	3371
Wahclellah village of the Shahalas (23 houses, just below entrance of Beacon-rock creek)	N.	....	6	462	3377
Tide water.					
Phoca [Seal] rock in the river, 60 feet above water	....	....	11	473	3388
Quicksand river	S.	120	9	482	3397
Seal river	N.	80	3	485	3400
Neechaokee village (opp. Diamond island)	S.	....	4	489	3404
Shahala village (25 temporary houses)	S.	...	12	501	3416
Multnomah river	S.	500	14	515	3430
Multnomah village	S.	....	6	521	3436
Quathlahpotle village	N.	....	8	529	3444
Tahwahnahiooks [Lewis'] river	N.	200	1	530	3445

Remarkable Places, descending the Columbia.	Side on which situated.	Width of river or creek in yards.	Distance from one place to another in miles.	Distance descending the Columbia in miles.	Distance from the Mississippi in miles.
Cathlahaws [Burris?] creek and village..	N.	18	10	540	3455
Lower extremity of Elallah or Deer island	S.	....	6	546	3461
Coweliskee river (about the entrance, and up this river, the Skilloots reside).....	N.	150	13	559	3474
Fanny's island.......................	S.	....	16	575	3490
Sea-otter island......................	....	....	12	587	3502
Upper village of the Wahkiacums.......	N.	....	6	593	3508
Cathlamahs village (9 large wood houses, S. of Seal islands)..................	S.	....	14	607	3522
Point William (opposite Shallow bay)...	S.	....	10	617	3532
Point Meriwether (ab. Meriwether's bay)	S.	....	9	626	3541
Clatsop village (below Meriwether's bay, 7 miles N.W. of Fort Clatsop).	S.	....	8	634	3549
Point Adams, at entrance of the Columbia into the Pacific ocean or Great South Sea, lat. 46° 15′ N., and long. 124° 57′ W. from Greenwich.........	S.	....	6	640	3555

NOTE 1. Fort Clatsop is situated on the west side of Netul river, 3 miles up the river from Meriwether bay, and 7 miles east from the nearest part of the seacoast. At this fort Captains Lewis and Clark passed the winter of 1805–6.

NOTE 2. The route by which we went out, by the way of the Missouri to its head, is 3,096 miles ; thence by land, by way of Lewis' river, over to Clark's river, and down that river to the entrance of Traveller's-rest creek, where all the roads from different routes meet, and thence across the rugged part of the Rocky mountains to the navigable waters of the Columbia, is 398 miles ; thence down the river to the Pacific ocean is 640 miles, making a total distance of 4,134 miles. On our return in 1806, we came from Traveller's-rest creek directly to the falls of the Missouri river, which shortens the distance about 579 miles, and is a much better route, reducing the distance from the Mississippi to the Pacific ocean to 3555 miles. Of this distance, 2575 miles is up the Missouri to the falls of that river ; thence through the plains and across the Rocky mountains to the navigable waters of the Kooskooskee river, a branch of the Columbia, is 340 miles ; 200 miles of which is a good road, 140 miles over a tremendous mountain, steep and broken, 60 miles of which is covered several feet deep with snow, on which we passed the last of June. From the navigable part of the Kooskooskee we descended that rapid river 73 miles to its entrance into Lewis' river ; went down that river 154 miles to the Columbia, and thence 413 miles to its entrance into the Pacific ocean. About 180 miles of this distance is tidewater. We passed several bad rapids and narrows, and one considerable fall, 268 miles above the entrance of this river, of 37 feet 8 inches. The total distance descending the Columbian waters is 640 miles, making a total of 3,555 miles, on the most direct route from the Mississippi, at the mouth of the Missouri, to the Pacific ocean.

APPENDIX IV.

METEOROLOGICAL REGISTER.

Thermometrical observations, showing also the rise and fall of the Mississippi (Missouri) ; appearance of weather, winds, etc., commencing at the mouth of the river Duboes [Du Bois or Wood], in lat. 38° 55′ 19″ 6‴ N., and long. 89° 57′ 45″ W., Jan. 1, 1804. Thermometer on the north side of a tree in the woods.

Explanations of the notations of the weather.

f. means fair weather.

r. means rain.

h. means hail.

l. means lightning.

c. a. s. means cloudy after snow intervening.

c. a. r. s. means cloudy after rain and snow.

c. means cloudy.

s. means snow.

t. means thunder.

a. after, as f. a. r. means fair after rain, which has intervened since the last observation.

Notations of the river.

r. means risen in the last 24 hours, ending at sunrise.

f. means fallen in the last 24 hours, ending at sunrise.

Notations of thermometer.

a. means above naught.

b. means below naught.

Day of the month.	Therm. at sunrise.	Weather.	Wind.	Therm. at four o'clock.	Weather.	Wind.	River. r. and f.	River. Feet.	River. Inches.
1804	Deg.			Deg.					
Jan. 1	....	c.	......	....	c.	......	...	...	...
2	....	c. a. s.	......	....	c.	......	...	...	...
3	....	....	......	2½ a.	f.	N.W.by W.	...	...	...
4	11 a.	f.	W.	....	....	W.	...	...	...
5	....	f.	W.	....	f.	W.	...	...	...
6	....	f.	N.W.W.	30 a.	f.	N.W.W.	...	...	...
7	....	h.	S.W.	....	c. a. r. h.	S.W.	...	...	...
8	....	f.	S.W.	....	f.	S.W.	...	...	...
9	....	f.	S.W.W.	1 b.	c.	N.W.by W.	...	...	...
10	....	f.	......	....	f.	......	...	...	6
11	....	....	......	....	....	......	...	...	...
12	....	....	......	....	....	......	...	...	...

Day of the month.	Therm. at sunrise.	Weather.	Wind.	Therm. at four o'clock.	Weather.	Wind.	River. r. and f.	Feet.	Inches.
1804.	Deg.			Deg.					
Jan. 13	....	c. s.	S.W.	....	r. s.	S.W.	...	..	...
14	....	f. a. s.	......	....	f.	......	...	..	...
15	....	....	......	....	....	......	...	..	...
16	....	....	......	....	....	......	...	..	...
17	8 b.	f.	N.W.	1½ b.	f.	N.W.	f.	..	...
18	1 b.	c.	N.W.W.	1 a.	f. a. s.	N.W.W.	f.	..	...
19	13 a.	c.	N.W.	11 a.	c.	N.W.	f.	..	...
20	5 b.	f.	N.W.	8 a.	c.	N.W.	f.	..	...
21	7 a.	c. s.	N.E.	17 a.	s. h.	N.E.	f.	..	...
22	11 a.	s.	Shifting.	13 a.	s.	N.W.	f.	..	...
23	11 a.	c.	N.E.	17 a.	c.	N.	f.	..	...
24	4 a.	c.	N.W.	11 a.	c.	W.	f.	..	...
25	2 b.	f.	W.N.W.	16 a.	f.	W.	f.	..	...
26	....	c.	S.W.	....	c.	S.W.	f.	..	...
27	....	f.	......	....	f.	......	...	..	...
28	5 a.	c. s.	N.W.	18 a.	c. s.	N.W.	r.	..	...
29	16 a.	f.	W.	23 a.	f.	......	r.	..	...
30	22 a.	c. s.	N.	16 a.	f. a. s.	......	r.	..	...
31	10 a.	f.	S.W. by W.	15 a.	f.	W.	r.	..	...
Feb. 1	10 a.	f.	S.W.	20 a.	f.	S.W.S.	r.	..	1½
2	12 a.	f.	N.W.	10 a.	f.	N.W.	r.	..	1½
3	12 a.	f.	S.W.	19 a.	f.	W.	...	..	...
4	17 a.	f.	S.W.	28 a.	f.	S.	r.	..	½
5	18 a.	f.	S.E.	31 a.	c. a. f.	S.E.S.	r.	2	6½
6	19 a.	f.	N.W.	15 a.	c.	S.	...	..	...
7	29 a.	r. a. c.	S.E.	30 a.	r. c.	S.E.	f.	..	8
8	22 a.	c. a. r.	N.W.	20 a.	c. a. s.	N.	r.	1	...
9	10 a.	f. a. s.	N.N.E.	12 a.	c.	N.E.	r.	2	...
10	3 a.	f.	N.E.	17 a.	f.	S.W.	r.	1	4
11	18 a.	c. a. h.	S.E.	31 a.	s. a. h.	S.E.	r.	1	...
12	15 a.	f.	S.S.E.	25 a.	f.	S.W.	f.	..	2
13	12 a.	f.	N.W.	20 a.	f.	W.	r.	..	1
14	15 a.	f.	S.W.	32 a.	f.	S.W.	...	..	...
15	18 a.	f.	S.W.	32 a.	f.	W.	...	..	...
16	28 a.	c.	S.E.	30 a.	c. a. r.	S.E.	r.	..	2½
17	15 a.	c. a. r.	S.W.	32 a.	f.	W.	r.	..	2
18	10 a.	f.	N.W.	....	....	......	r.	..	7½
19	10 a.	f.	N.W.	....	....	......	...	..	...
20	10 a.	f.	N.W.	28 a.	....	S.W.	f.	..	2½
21	20 a.	f.	N.W.	34 a.	....	N.W.	f.	..	1½
22	14 a.	f.	N.E.	26 a.	....	N.E.	r.	..	1½
23	6 a.	f.	N.W.	24 a.	....	N.W.	r.	..	1
24	6 a.	f.	N.E.	26 a.	....	N.E.	f.	..	2
25	20 a.	f.	N.E.	28 a.	....	S.S.W.	...	..	...
26	16 a.	f.	N.E.	30 a.	....	N.E.	f.	..	½
27	4 a.	c.	N.E.	24 a.	r. s.	N.W.	f.	..	1
28	4 a.	c. s.	N.W.	6 a.	c. a. s.	N.W.	f.	..	2
29	8 a.	h. s.	N.W.	12 a.	c. a. s.	N.W.	f.	..	2½
Mar. 1	20 b.	f.	N.W.	4 b.	....	N.W.	f.	..	9
2	19 b.	f.	N.W.	14 a.	....	E.	f.	..	8

Day of the month.	Therm. at sunrise.	Weather.	Wind.	Therm. at four o'clock.	Weather.	Wind.	River. r. and f.	Feet.	Inches.
1804.	Deg.			Deg.					
Mar. 3	18 b.	f.	E.	10 a.	....	S.W.	f.	...	6¼
4	4 b.	f.	N.E.	12 a.	....	E.	f.	...	5
5	2 a.	f.	N.W.	12 a.	....	N.W.	f.	...	3
6	4 b.	f.	N.W.	2 a.	....	N.W.	f.	...	3
7	16 b.	c. and s.	N.W.	10 a.	c.	N.W.	...	...	...
8	2 b.	c. s.	N.W.	12 a.	s.	N.W.	f.	...	1¼
9	10 a.	c.	N.W.	10 a.	c.	N.W.	r.	...	2
10	6 a.	c.	N.W.	24 a.	f.	N.W.	r.	...	2½
11	12 a.	f.	E.	20 a.	f.	S.W.	f.	...	2½
12	14 a.	f.	N.E.	16 a.	f.	N.E.	r.	...	1½
13	8 a.	f.	N.W.	12 a.	f.	N.W.	f.	...	1½
14	4 a.	f.	N.E.	10 a.	f.	N.E.	f.	...	4½
15	6 b.	c. s.	N.W.	40 a.	r. a. s.	N.E.	r.	...	5
16	2 b.	f.	E.	40 a.	f.	S.S.W.	r.	...	11
17	12 a.	f.	N.E.	38 a.	f.	N.E.	r.	...	7
18	2 a.	f.	E.	44 a.	f.	N.E.	f.	...	3
19	2 a.	f.	N.E.	52 a.	f.	S.S.W.	f.	...	2¼
20	4 a.	f.	E.	60 a.	f.	S.S.W.	f.	...	1½
21	26 a.	f.	S.S.W.	36 a.	f.	N.W.	f.	...	2
22	22 a.	f.	N.W.	40 a.	f.	N.W.	f.	...	2
23	14 a.	f.	N.E.	44 a.	f.	N.E.	r.	...	4
24	6 a.	f.	E.	52 a.	f.	S.S.W.	r.	1	5½
25	16 a.	f.	S.S.W.	46 a.	f.	E.	r.	2	...
26	28 a.	f.	E.	44 a.	f.	E.	r.	...	10
27	34 a.	r. and t.	E.	42 a.	f. a. r.	N.E.	r.	...	7
28	34 a.	c.	N.E.	44 a.	c.	E.	r.	...	5½
29	20 a.	r. a. t.	N.E.	30 a.	h. r.	N.E.	r.	...	1
30	....	c. a. r.	N.W.	....	f.	N.W.	r.	...	2
31	....	f.	N.W.	....	f.	N.W.	r.	...	2
April 1	....	f.	N.E.	....	f.	N.E.	r.	...	2½
2	8 a.	f.	.....	....	f.	N.E.	r.	...	3½
3	42 a.	f.	N.E.	....	r.	N.E.	r.	...	3½
4	44 a.	c. a. r.	N.W.	....	....	......	r.	...	11
5	24 a.	c. a. r.	N.E.	....	t. a. r.	......	r.	...	2
6	18 a.	c. a. r.	N.W.	....	s. a. r.	......	f.	...	4½
7	10 a.	f. a. c.	N.W.	....	c.	......	f.	...	2
8	10 a.	c.	N.E.	....	c. r.	......	f.	...	2½
9	18 a.	f. a. c.	N.E.	....	c.	......	f.	...	2
10	10 a.	f.	N.W.	....	f.	......	f.	...	6½
11	10 a.	f.	N.E.	....	f.	......	f.	...	7½
12	16 a.	c.	N.W.	....	f. a. c.	......	f.	...	7
13	36 a.	c.	N.E.	....	c.	......	f.	...	6½
14	22 a.	f.	S.W.	....	f.	......	f.	...	5
15	22 a.	f.	N.W.	....	....	......	f.	...	6½
16	36 a.	c.	N.W.	....	f. a. c.	......	f.	...	5½
17	26 a.	f. a. c.	N.W.	....	f.	......	f.	...	5
18	16 a.	f. a. c.	N.N.W.	....	c. .	......	f.	...	3
19	34 a.	r.	S.S.E.	....	....	......	f.	...	4
20	34 a.	c. r.	S.E.	37 a.	r.	S.E.	f.	...	3½
21	31 a.	r.	S.W.	42 a.	f. a. r.	W.	r.	1	2

Day of the month.	Therm. at sunrise.	Weather.	Wind.	Therm. at four o'clock.	Weather.	Wind.	River.		
							r. and f.	Feet.	Inches.
1804.	Deg.			Deg.					
April 22	28 a.	c.	N.W.	34 a.	c.	N.W.	r.	1	6
23	22 a.	f.	N.W.	64 a.	f.	W.	f.	...	1
24	36 a.	f.	N.W.	44 a.	f.	N.W.	r.	...	8
25	26 a.	f.	N.W.	38 a.	c.	N.W.	r.	...	2¼
26	16 a.	f.	N.W.	58 a.	f.	N.W.	f.	...	6
27	28 a.	c. and r.	W.	62 a.	f.	S.W.	f.	...	8
28	30 a.	f.	N.W.	64 a.	f.	N.W.	f.	...	7
29	32 a.	f.	N.W.	52 a.	f.	S.E.	f.	...	7
30	18 a.	f.	S.E.	56 a.	f.	N.E.	f.	...	6
May 1	20 a.	f.	S.E.	54 a.	f.	N.E.	f.	...	4½
2	19 a.	f.	S.E.	68 a.	f.	S.S.E.	f.	...	6
3	24 a.	f.	S.S.E.	72 a.	f.	S.S.W.	f.	...	4½
4	40 a.	t. c. r.	S.	56 a.	c. a. r.	S.	r.	...	2
5	42 a.	t. c. r.	W.	58 a.	c. a. r.	W.	r.	...	2¼
6	34 a.	f.	S.W.	70 a.	f.	S.W.	f.	...	2¾
7	38 a.	f.	S.E.	52 a.	f.	S.S.E.	f.	...	4½
8	44 a.	f.	N.E.	62 a.	f.	S.W.	f.	...	4
9	42 a.	f.	E.	76 a.	f.	S.W.	f.	...	2
10	46 a.	c.	N.E.	67 a.	f.	N.W.	f.	...	3¼
11	46 a.	f.	E.	70 a.	f.	S.W.	f.	...	2¼
12	36 a.	f.	E.	72 a.	f.	W.	f.	...	3
13	42 a.	c. a. r.	W.	40 a.	c. a. r.	N.W.	f.	...	2
14 *	34 a.	c.	S.E.	56 a.	f.	N.	...	...	...
Sep. 19	46 a.	f.	S.E.	71 a.	f.	S.E.	...	...	...
20	51 a.	f.	S.E.	70 a.	f.	S.E.	...	...	...
21	58 a.	f.	S.W.	88 a.	f.	S.W.	...	...	...
22	52 a.	f.	E.	82 a.	f.	S.E.	...	...	...
23	50 a.	f.	S.E.	86 a.	f.	S.E.	...	...	...
24	54 a.	f.	E.	82 a.	f.	W.	...	...	...
25	56 a.	f.	S.W.	79 a.	f.	W.	...	...	...
26	54 a.	f.	W.	78 a.	f.	S.W.	...	...	...
27	52 a.	f.	W.	86 a.	f.	S.W.	...	...	...
28	45 a.	f.	S.E.	80 a.	f.	S.E.	...	...	...
29	45 a.	f.	S.E.	67 a.	f.	S.E.	...	...	...
30	42 a.	c. a. r.	S.E.	52 a.	c. a. r.	S.E.	...	...	...
Oct. 1	40 a.	c.	S.E.	46 a.	c.	S.E.	...	...	...
2	39 a.	f.	S.E.	75 a.	c.	N.	...	...	...
3	40 a.	c.	N.W.	45 a.	c. a. r.	N.	...	...	...
4	38 a.	c. a. r.	N.W.	50 a.	c.	N.W.	...	...	...
5	36 a.	f.	N.W.	54 a.	f.	N.W.	...	...	...
6	43 a.	f.	N.W.	60 a.	f.	N.W.	...	...	...
7	45 a.	c.	S.E.	58 a.	f.	S.E.	...	...	...
8	48 a.	f.	N.W.	62 a.	f.	N.W.	...	...	...

* Here is a hiatus in the MS., which it is not in our power to fill up, viz., from the 14th of May to the 19th of Sept. The party were then just beginning the ascent of the Missouri, and it is probable that, among the many other important things which engrossed their attention, this was omitted. (Orig. note.)

Day of the month.	Therm. at sunrise.	Weather.	Wind.	Therm. at four o'clock.	Weather.	Wind.	River.		
							r. and f.	Feet.	Inches.
1804	Deg.			Deg.					
Oct. 9	45 a.	c.	N.E.	50 a.	c. a. r.	N.	...	...	...
10	42 a.	f. a. r.	N.W.	67 a.	f.	N.W.	...	...	...
11	43 a.	f.	N.W.	59 a.	f.	N.W.	...	...	...
12	42 a.	f.	S.	65 a.	f.	S.E.	...	...	...
13	43 a.	f.	S.W.	49 a.	c. a. r.	S.E.	...	...	...
14	42 a.	r.	S.E.	40 a.	r.	S.E.	...	...	...
15	46 a.	r.	N.	57 a.	f. a. r.	N.W.	...	...	...
16	45 a.	c.	N.E.	50 a.	f.	N.E.	...	...	...
17	47 a.	f.	N.W.	54 a.	f.	N.W.	...	...	...
18	30 a.	f.	N.W.	68 a.	f.	N.W.	...	...	...
19	43 a.	f.	S.E.	62 a.	f.	S.	...	...	...
20	44 a.	f.	N.W.	48 a.	f.	N.	...	...	...
21	31 a.	s.	N.W.	34 a.	s.	N.W.	...	...	...
22	35 a.	c. a. s.	N.E.	42 a.	c.	N.E.	...	...	...
23	32 a.	s.	N.W.	45 a.	c.	N.E.	...	...	...
24	33 a.	s. a. f.	N.W.	51 a.	c. a. s.	N.W.	...	...	...
25	31 a.	c.	S.E.	50 a.	c.	S.E.	...	...	...
26	42 a.	f.	S.E.	57 a.	f.	S.E.	...	...	...
27	39 a.	f.	S.W.	58 a.	f.	S.W.	...	...	...
28	34 a.	f.	S.W.	54 a.	f.	S.W.	...	...	...
29	32 a.	f.	S.W.	59 a.	f.	S.W.	...	...	...
30	32 a.	f.	S.W.	52 a.	f.	S.W.	...	...	...
31	33 a.	f.	W.	48 a.	f.	W.	...	...	...
Nov. 1	31 a.	f.	N.W.	47 a.	f.	N.W.	...	...	...
2	32 a.	f.	S.E.	63 a.	f.	S.E.	...	...	...
3	32 a.	f.	N.W.	53 a.	f.	N.W.	...	...	...
4	31 a.	f.	N.W.	43 a.	c.	W.	...	...	...
5	30 a.	c.	N.W.	58 a.	c.	N.W.	...	...	...
6	31 a.	c.	S.W.	43 a.	c.	W.	...	...	...
7	43 a.	c.	S.	62 a.	c.	S.	...	...	...
8	38 a.	c.	S.	39 a.	c.	W.	...	...	...
9	27 a.	f.	N.W.	43 a.	f.	N.W.	...	...	...
10	34 a.	f.	N.W.	36 a.	c.	N.W.	...	...	.
11	28 a.	f.	N.W.	60 a.	f.	N.W.	...	...	...
12	18 a.	f.	N.	31 a.	f.	N.E.	...	...	...
13	18 a.	s.	S.E.	28 a.	c. a. s.	S.E.	f.	...	1⅝
14	24 a.	s.	S.E.	32 a.	c. a. s.	S.E.	r.	...	1
15	22 a.	c.	N.W.	31 a.	c. a. s.	N.W.	r.	...	¼
16	25 a.	c.	N.W.	30 a.	f.	S.E.	r.	...	¼
17	28 a.	f.	S.E.	34 a.	f.	S.E.	r.	...	¼
18	30 a.	f.	S.E.	38 a.	f.	W.	r.	...	¼
19	32 a.	f.	N.W.	48 a.	f.	N.W.	r.	...	1
20	35 a.	f.	N.W.	50 a.	f.	W.	r.	...	1¼
21	33 a.	c.	S.	49 a.	f.	S.E.	r.	...	...
22	37 a.	f.	W.	45 a.	f.	N.W.	r.	...	¼
23	38 a.	f.	W.	45 a.	f.	N.W.	..	...	...
24	36 a.	f.	N.W.	34 a.	f.	N.W.	...	...	...
25	34 a.	f.	W.	32 a.	f.	S.W.	...	...	...
26	15 a.	f.	S.W.	21 a.	f.	W.	...	...	...
27	10 a.	f.	S.E.	19 a.	c.	S.E.	f.	...	3

Day of the month.	Therm. at sunrise.	Weather.	Wind.	Therm. at four o'clock.	Weather.	Wind.	River.		
							r. and f.	Feet.	Inches.
1804.	Deg.			Deg.					
Nov. 28	12 a.	s.	S.E.	15 a.	s.	E.	f.	...	4
29	14 a.	c. a. s.	N.E.	18 a.	f.	W.	f.	...	2½
30	17 a.	f.	W.	23 a.	f.	W.	f.	2	...
Dec. 1	1 b.	f.	E.	6 a.	f.	S.E.	r.	1	...
2	38 a.	f.	N.W.	36 a.	f.	N.W.	r.	...	1
3	26 a.	f.	N.W.	30 a.	f.	N.W.	r.	...	1
4	18 a.	f.	N.	29 a.	f.	N.	r.	...	1
5	14 a.	c.	N.E.	27 a.	s.	N.E.	...	...	...
6	10 a.	s.	N.W.	11 a.	c. a. s.	N.W.	...	...	...
7	0 a.	f.	N.W.	1 b.	c.	N.W.	r.	2	½
8	12 b.	s.	N.W.	5 b.	f. a. s.	N.W.	...	...	...
9	7 a.	f.	E.	10 b.	f.	N.W.	...	...	...
10	10 b.	c.	N.	11 b.	c.	N.	r.	...	⅛
11	21 b.	f.	N.	18 b.	f.	N.	f.	...	½
12	38 b.	f.	N.	16 b.	f.	N.	...	...	...
13	20 b.	f.	S.E.	4 b.	c.	S.E.	...	...	...
14	2 b.	c.	S.E.	2 a.	s.	S.E.	f.	...	1
15	8 b.	c. a. s.	W.	4 b.	c. a. s.	W.	...	...	...
16	22 b.	f.	N.W.	4 b.	f.	N.W.	f.	...	1
17	45 b.	f.	N.	28 b.	f.	N.	r.	...	3
18	32 b.	f.	W.	16 b.	f.	S.W.	r.	...	1
19	2 b.	c.	S.W.	16 a.	f.	S.	r.	...	1
20	24 a.	f.	N.W.	22 a.	c.	W.	r.	...	2
21	22 a.	f.	N.W.	22 a.	c.	N.W.	r.	...	2
22	10 a.	f.	N.W.	23 a.	f.	N.W.	r.	...	2½
23	18 a.	c.	S.W.	27 a.	c.	W.	f.	...	1
24	22 a.	s.	S.W.	31 a.	c. a. s.	W.	f.	...	2½
25	15 a.	s.	N.W.	20 a.	c. a. s.	N.W.	f.	...	1
26	18 a.	c.	N.W.	21 a.	f.	N.W.	...	...	...
27	4 b.	c.	N.W.	14 a.	c.	N.W.	...	...	...
28	12 a.	f.	N.	13 a.	f.	N.W.	r.	...	2½
29	9 b.	f.	N.	3 a.	f.	N.	r.	...	1
30	20 b.	f.	N.	11 b.	f.	N.	r.	...	½
31	10 b.	f.	S.E.	12 a.	c.	S.W.	r.	...	1½
1805.									
Jan. 1	18 a.	s.	S.E.	34 a.	f.	N.W.	r.	...	1
2	4 b.	s.	N.W.	8 b.	f. a. s.	N.	...	...	...
3	14 b.	c.	N.	4 b.	s.	S.E.	...	...	...
4	28 a.	c. a. s.	W.	4 b.	c.	N.W.	r.	...	2⅛
5	20 b.	c.	N.W.	18 b.	s.	N.E.	r.	...	2
6	11 b.	c. a. s.	N.W.	16 b.	f.	N.W.	r.	...	3
7	22 b.	f.	N.W.	14 b.	f.	W.	f.	...	1
8	20 b.	f.	N.W.	10 b.	f.	N.W.	r.	...	1
9	21 b.	f.	W.	18 b.	f. a. c.	N.W.	...	...	...
10	40 b.	f.	N.W.	28 b.	f.	N.W.	...	...	...
11	38 b.	f.	N.W.	14 b.	f.	N.W.	f.	...	½
12	20 b.	f.	N.W.	16 b.	f.	N.W.	r.	...	1
13	34 b.	f.	N.W.	20 b.	f.	N.W.	...	...	...
14	16 b.	s.	S.E.	8 b.	c. a. s.	S.E.	...	...	...
15	10 b.	f.	E.	3 a.	c.	S.W.	r.	...	1

Day of the month.	Therm. at sunrise.	Weather.	Wind.	Therm. at four o'clock.	Weather.	Wind at four o'clock.	River.		
							r. and f.	Feet.	Inches.
1805. Jan. 16	Deg. 36 a.	c.	W.	Deg. 16 a.	f.	S.W.	r.	...	2½
17	2 b.	c.	W.	12 b.	f.	N.W.	...	...	...
18	1 b.	f.	N.E.	7 a.	f. a. c.	N.W.	f.	...	1
19	12 a.	c.	N.E.	6 b.	f.	N.W.	r.	...	1
20	28 a.	f.	N.E.	9 b.	c.	S.E.	r.	...	½
21	2 b.	c.	N.E.	8 a.	f.	S.E.	...	...	...
22	10 a.	f. a. h.	N.W.	19 a.	c.	N.W.	r.	...	1¾
23	20 b.	s.	E.	2 b.	c. a. s.	N.	f.	...	2½
24	12 b.	c.	N.W.	2 b.	f.	N.W.	r.	...	¼
25	26 b.	f.	N.W.	4 b.	f. a. c.	W.	...	...	...
26	12 a.	c.	N.E.	20 a.	f. a. c.	S.E.	...	...	...
27	20 a.	c.	S.E.	16 a.	c.	N.W.	r.	...	2
28	2 b.	f.	N.W.	15 a.	f.	S.W.	...	...	...
29	4 a.	f.	S.W.	16 a.	f.	W.	r.	...	½
30	6 a.	c.	N.W.	14 a.	c.	N.W.	r.	...	1
31	2 b.	c. a. s.	N.W.	8 a.	f. a. c.	N.W.	f.	...	1
Feb. 1	6 a.	c.	N.W.	16 a.	f.	N.W.	r.	...	2½
2	12 b.	f.	N.W.	3 a.	f.	S.	f.	...	1
3	8 b.	f.	S.W.	2 a.	f.	W.	...	...	...
4	18 b.	f.	N.W.	9 b.	f.	W.	...	...	...
5	10 a.	f.	N.W.	20 a.	f.	N.W.	r.	...	1
6	4 b.	f.	N.W.	12 a.	f.	W.	r.	...	½
7	18 a.	f.	S.E.	29 a.	c.	S.	r.	...	½
8	18 a.	f.	N.W.	28 a.	c.	N.E.	f.	...	1
9	10 a.	f.	S.E.	33 a.	c.	S.E.	...	...	...
10	18 a.	c. a. s.	N.W.	12 a.	c.	N.W.	...	...	...
11	8 b.	f.	N.W.	2 b.	f.	N.W.	...	...	...
12	14 b.	f.	S.E.	2 a.	f.	W.	...	...	...
13	2 b.	c.	S.E.	10 a.	c.	N.W.	f.	...	1
14	2 a.	c. a. s.	N.W.	2 b.	f.	N.W.	...	...	...
15	16 b.	f.	S.W.	6 b.	f.	W.	...	...	...
16	2 a.	f.	S.E.	8 a.	f.	W.	f.	...	1
17	4 a.	c.	S.E.	12 a.	f.	N.W.	...	...	...
18	4 a.	s.	N.E.	10 a.	f.	S.	...	...	...
19	4 a.	f.	S.E.	20 a.	f.	S.	...	...	...
20	2 a.	f.	S.	22 a.	f.	S.	...	...	...
21	6 a.	f.	S.	30 a.	f.	S.	...	...	...
22	8 a.	c.	N.	32 a.	c. a. r.		...	...	...
23	18 a.	f.	N.W.	32 a.	f.	W.	r.	...	½
24	8 a.	f.	N.W.	32 a.	f.	W.	...	...	...
25	16 a.	f.	W.	38 a.	f.	N.W.	...	...	...
26	20 a.	f.	N.E.	31 a.	f.	N.	...	...	...
27	26 a.	f.	S.E.	36 a.	f.	E.	f.	...	½
28	24 a.	f.	E.	38 a.	c.	S.E.	...	...	...
Mar. 1	28 a.	c.	W.	38 a.	f.	N.W.	...	...	...
2	28 a.	f.	N.E.	36 a.	f.	N.E.	r.	...	1½
3	28 a.	c.	E.	39 a.	f.	N.W.	...	...	...
4	26 a.	f.	N.W.	36 a.	f.	N.W.	...	...	...
5	22 a.	f.	E.	40 a.	f.	N.W.	...	...	...
6	26 a.	c.	E.	36 a.	f.	E.	r.	...	2

Day of the month.	Therm. at sunrise.	Weather.	Wind at sunrise.	Therm. at four o'clock.	Weather.	Wind at four o'clock.	River. r. and f.	River. Feet.	River. Inches.
1805.	Deg.			Deg.					
Mar. 7	12 a.	f.	E.	26 a.	c.	E.	r.	...	2
8	7 a.	c.	E.	12 a.	f.	E.	r.	...	2½
9	2 a.	c.	N.	18 a.	f.	N.W.	r.	...	2
10	2 b.	f.	N.W.	12 a.	f.	N.W.	r.	...	3½
11	12 a.	c.	S.E.	26 a.	f. a. c.	N.W.	r.	...	4½
12	2 b.	f. a. s.	N.	10 a.	f.	N.W.	r.	...	5
13	1 b.	f.	S.E.	28 a.	f.	S.W.	r.	...	3½
14	18 a.	f.	S.E.	40 a.	f.	W.	...	...	...
15	24 a.	f.	S.E.	38 a.	f.	W.	f.	...	1
16	32 a.	c.	E.	42 a.	c.	W.	f.	...	3
17	30 a.	f.	S.E.	46 a.	f.	S.W.	r.	...	2
18	24 a.	c.	N.	34 a.	c.	N.	f.	...	1
19	20 a.	c. a. s.	N.	31 a.	f.	N.W.	r.	...	1
20	28 a.	c.	N.W.	28 a.	f.	N.W.	r.	...	3
21	16 a.	c.	E.	26 a.	s. and h.	S.	...	...	...
22	22 a.	f. a. s.	S.	36 a.	f.	S.W.	f.	...	4
23	34 a.	f.	W.	38 a.	c. a. r.	N.W.	f.	...	4
24	28 a.	c. a. s.	N.E.	30 a.	c. a. s.	N.	r.	...	1
25	16 a.	f.	E.	32 a.	f.	S.	r.	...	5
26	20 a.	f.	S.E.	46 a.	f.	W.	r.	...	4½
27	28 a.	f.	S.E.	60 a.	f.	S.W.	r.	...	9
28	40 a.	f.	S.E.	64 a.	f.	S.W.	r.	...	1
29	42 a.	f.	N.W.	52 a.	f.	N.W.	f.	...	11
30	28 a.	f.	N.W.	49 a.	f.	N.W.	r.	1	1
31	35 a.	c. a. r.	S.E.	45 a.	c.	S.E.	r.	...	9
Apr. 1	33 a.	c.	N.W.	43 a.	c. a. t.	W.	f.	...	11
2	28 a.	c. a. r.	N.W.	38 a.	f. a. c.	W.	f.	...	5
3	24 a.	f.	N.	44 a.	f.	N.	f.	...	4
4	36 a.	f.	S.	55 a.	f.	N.W.	f.	...	4
5	30 a.	f.	N.W.	39 a.	f.	N.	f.	...	2
6	19 a.	f.	N.	48 a.	c.	N.W.	f.	...	1
7	28 a.	f.	N.	64 a.	f.	S.W.	r.	...	2
8	19 a.	f.	N.W.	56 a.	f.	N.W.	f.	...	2
9	38 a.	f.	S.E.	70 a.	f.	S.W.	f.	...	½
10	42 a.	f.	E.	74 a.	f.	S.W.	r.	...	⅛
11	42 a.	f.	N.W.	76 a.	f.	W.	f.	...	½
12	56 a.	f.	N.W.	74 a.	c. r. t. l.	W.	r.	...	⅛
13	58 a.	f.	S.E.	80 a.	f.	S.E.	f.	...	1
14	52 a.	c.	S.E.	82 a.	f.	S.W.	f.	...	¾
15	51 a.	f.	E.	78 a.	f.	S.W.	f.	...	½
16	54 a.	f.	S.E.	78 a.	f.	S.	f.	...	½
17	56 a.	f.	N.E.	74 a.	c.	N.W.	f.	...	½
18	52 a.	f.	N.E.	64 a.	c.	N.	...	...	...
19	54 a.	c.	N.W.	56 a.	c.	N.W.	...	...	...
20	40 a.	c.	N.W.	42 a.	c. a. s.	N.W.	...	...	...
21	28 a.	f.	N.W.	40 a.	c.	N.W.	f.	...	½
22	34 a.	f. a. c.	W.	40 a.	f.	N.W.	r.	...	2
23	34 a.	f.	W.	52 a.	c.	N.W.	r.	...	2
24	40 a.	f.	N.	56 a.	f.	N.	r.	...	1
25	36 a.	f.	N.	52 a.	f.	N.W.	r.	...	2

Day of the month.	Therm. at sunrise.	Weather.	Wind.	Therm. at four o'clock.	Weather.	Wind at four o'clock.	River. r. and f.	River. Feet.	River. Inches.
1805.	Deg.			Deg.					
Apr. 26	32 a.	f.	S.	63 a.	f.	S.E.	r.	...	3
27	36 a.	f.	S.W.	64 a.	f.	N.W.	f.	...	2
28	44 a.	f.	S.E.	63 a.	f.	S.E.	f.	...	1½
29	42 a.	f.	N.E.	64 a.	f.	E.	f.	...	1½
30	50 a.	f.	N.W.	58 a.	f.	S.E.	f.	...	½
May 1	36 a.	c.	E.	46 a.	c. a. f.	N.E.	f.	...	1½
2	28 a.	s.	N.E.	34 a.	c. a. s.	N.W.	f.	...	1
3	26 a.	f.	W.	46 a.	c.	W.	f.	...	¼
4	38 a.	c.	W.	48 a.	f. a. c.	W.	...	...	..
5	38 a.	f.	N.W.	62 a.	f. a. r.	S.E.	r.	...	1
6	48 a.	f.	E.	61 a.	c. a. r.	S.E.	r.	...	2
7	42 a.	c.	S.	60 a.	f.	N.E.	r.	...	1½
8	41 a.	c.	E.	52 a.	c. a. r.	E.	f.	...	¼
9	38 a.	f.	E.	58 a.	f.	W.	r.	...	¾
10	38 a.	f. a. c.	W.N.W.	62 a.	c. a. r.	N.W.	f.	...	¾
11	44 a.	f.	N.E.	60 a.	c.	S.W.	...	...	...
12	52 a.	f.	S.E.	54 a.	c. a. r.	N.W.	r.	...	2
13	52 a.	c. a. r.	N.W.	54 a.	f. a. c.	N.W.	f.	...	2¼
14	32 a.	f.	S.W.	52 a.	c.	S.W.	f.	...	1¾
15	48 a.	c. a. r.	S.W.	54 a.	c.	N.W.	f.	...	¾
16	48 a.	c.	S.W.	67 a.	f.	S.W.	...	...	...
17	60 a.	f.	N.E.	68 a.	f.	S.W.	...	...	...
18	58 a.	f.	W.	46 a.	c a. r.	N.W.	f.	...	1
19	38 a.	f.	E.	68 a.	f. a. c.	S.W.	...	...	...
20	52 a.	f.	N.E.	76 a.	f.	E.	f.	...	1
21	50 a.	f.	S.W.	76 a.	f.	N.W.	...	...	...
22	46 a.	c.	N.W.	48 a.	c.	N.W.	f.	...	½
23	32 a.	f.	S.W.	54 a.	f.	S.W.	f.	...	½
24	32 a.	f.	N.W.	68 a.	f.	S.E.	r.	...	3½
25	46 a.	f.	S.W.	82 a.	f.	S.W.	r.	...	2
26	58 a.	f.	S.W.	80 a.	f.	S.W.	r.	...	½
27	62 a.	f.	S.W.	82 a.	f.	S.W.	...	...	...
28	62 a.	c.	S.W.	72 a.	c. and r.	S.W.	r.	...	½
29	62 a.	c. a. r.	S.W.	67 a.	r.	S.W.	r.	...	1
30	56 a.	c. a. r.	S.W.	50 a.	r.	S.W.	r.	...	5
31	48 a.	c. a. r.	W.	53 a.	c. a. r.	S.W.	r.	...	1½
June 1	50 a.	c.	S.W.	62 a.	c.	S.E.	r.	...	1½
2	56 a.	c. a. r.	S.W.	68 a.	f.	S.W.	...	...	...
3	46 a.	f.	S.W.	60 a.	f.	S.W.	...	...	...
4	48 a.	f. a. c.	N.E.	61 a.	f.	S.W.	f.	...	¾
5	40 a.	r.	S.W.	42 a.	c. a. r.	N.E.	f.	...	¾
6	35 a.	c. a. r.	N.E.	42 a.	r. a. r.	N.E.	f.	...	1½
7	40 a.	c. a. r.	S.W.	43 a.	r. a. r.	S.W.	f.	...	1½
8	41 a.	r. a. r.	S.W.	48 a.	f. a.	S.W.	f.	...	1¼
9	50 a.	f.	S.W.	52 a.	f.	S.W.	f.	...	1
10	52 a.	f.	S.W.	68 a.	f. a. r.	S.W.	r.	...	2
11	54 a.	f.	S.W.	66 a.	f.	S.W.	...	...	...
12	54 a.	f.	S.W.	64 a.	f. a. r.	S.W.	...	...	..
13	52 a.	f.	S.W.	72 a.	f.	S.W.	r.	...	¾
14	60 a.	f.	S.W.	74 a.	f.	S.W.	f.	...	¾

Day of the month.	Therm. at sunrise.	Weather.	Wind at sunrise.	Therm. at four o'clock.	Weather.	Wind at four o'clock.	River.		
							r. and f.	Feet.	Inches.
1805.	Deg.			Deg.					
June 15	60 a.	f.	S.W.	76 a.	f.	S.W.	f.	...	½
16	64 a.	c. r.	S.W.	58 a.	f.	S.W.	r.	...	½
17	50 a.	c.	S.W.	57 a.	c.	S.W.	f.	...	½
18	48 a.	c.	S.W.	64 a.	f. a. c.	S.W.	f.	...	½
19	52 a.	f.	S.W.	70 a.	f.	S.W.	f.	...	½
20	49 a.	c.	S.W.	74 a.	f. a. r.	S.W.	f.	...	¼
21	49 a.	f.	S.W.	70 a.	c.	S.W.	f.	...	¼
22	45 a.	c.	S.W.	54 a.	f.	S.W.	f.	...	½
23	48 a.	f.	S.E.	65 a.	c.	S.E.	f.	...	¼
24	49 a.	c. a. r.	S.E.	74 a.	f. a. c.	S.W.	f.	...	...
25	47 a.	c. a. r.	S.W.	72 a.	f.	S.W.	...	...	...
26	49 a.	f.	S.W.	78 a.	f.	S.W.	r.	...	½
27	49 a.	f.	S.W.	77 a.	f. a. r. h.	S.W.	r.	...	1¼
28	46 a.	f.	S.W.	75 a.	c. a. f.	S.W.	r.	...	2
29	47 a.	r. t. l.	S.W.	77 a.	f. a. r.	S.W.	r.	...	4½
30	49 a.	f.	S.W.	76 a.	f.	S.W.	r.	...	2¼
July 1	59 a.	f.	S.W.	74 a.	f.	S.W.	r.	...	½
2	60 a.	f. a. r.	S.W.	78 a.	f.	S.W.	...	...	...
3	56 a.	f.	S.W.	74 a.	c.a.f.a.r.	S.W.	...	...	...
4	52 a.	f.	S.W.	76 a.	f. a. r.	S.W.	f.	...	¼
5	49 a.	t. and r.	S.W.	72 a.	f.	S.W.	f.	...	½
6	47 a.	c. a. h.	S.W.	74 a.	f. a. c.	S.W.	f.	...	¼
7	54 a.	c. a. f.	S.W.	77 a.	f. a. c.	S.W.	f.	...	¼
8	60 a.	f.	S.W.	78 a.	f. a. r.	S.W.	f.	...	¼
9	56 a.	f.	S.W.	76 a.	c. a. r.	N.W.	...	...	¼
10	52 a.	f. a. r.	S.W.	66 a.	f.	S.W.	...	...	...
11	46 a.	f.	S.W.	70 a.	f.	S.W.	...	...	...
12	50 a.	f.	S.W.	74 a.	f.	S.W.	f.	...	¼
13	42 a.	f.	S.W.	76 a.	f.	S.W.	f.	...	¼
14	45 a.	f.	S.W.	78 a.	c. a. r.	S.W.	...	...	...
15	60 a.	f. a. r.	S.W.	76 a.	f.	S.W.	f.	...	1½
16	53 a.	f.	S.W.	80 a.	f.	S.W.	f.	...	¾
17	58 a.	f.	S.W.	81 a.	f.	S.W.	f.	...	1½
18	60 a.	f.	S.W.	84 a.	f.	S.W.	f.	...	½
19	62 a.	f.	S.W.	68 a.	c. a. h. r.	S.W.	f.	...	½
20	59 a.	f. a. r.	S.W.	60 a.	f.	N.W.	...	...	...
21	60 a.	f.	N.W.	67 a.	f.	N.W.	f.	...	½
22	52 a.	f.	N.W.	80 a.	f.	N.E.	...	...	...
23	54 a.	f.	S.W.	80 a.	c.	S.W.	f.	...	½
24	60 a.	f.	S.W.	90 a.	f.	S.W.	f.	...	¾
25	60 a.	f.	S.W.	86 a.	f.	S.W.	f.	...	½
26	60 a.	f.	S.W.	82 a.	c. a. r.	S.W.	f.	...	¾
27	52 a.	c.	S.W.	80 a.	c. a. r.	S.W.	f.	...	¾
28	49 a.	f. a. r.	S.W.	90 a.	f.	S.W.	f.	...	½
29	54 a.	f. a. r.	N.	82 a.	f.	N.E.	r.	...	½
30	50 a.	f.	S.E.	80 a.	f.	S.E.	...	...	...
31	48 a.	f.	S.W.	92 a.	f.	S.W.	...	...	...
Aug. 1	54 a.	f.	S.W.	91 a.	f.	S.W.	f.	...	½
2	48 a.	f.	N.W.	81 a.	f.	N.W.	f.	...	½
3	50 a.	f.	N.E.	86 a.	f.	N.E.	f.	...	½

Day of the month.	Therm. at sunrise.	Weather.	Wind at sunrise.	Therm. at four o'clock.	Weather.	Wind at four o'clock.	River. r. and f.	Feet.	Inches.
1805.	Deg.			Deg.					
Aug. 4	48 a.	f.	S.	92 a.	f.	S.	f.	...	¼
5	49 a.	f.	S.E.	79 a.	f.	S.E.	f.	...	¼
6	52 a.	f.	S.W.	71 a.	c.	S.W.	...	...	...
7	54 a.	c. a. r.	S.W.	80 a.	c.	S.W.	...	...	...
8	54 a.	f. a. r.	S.W.	82 a.	c. a. f.	S.W.	...	...	...
9	58 a.	f.	N.E.	78 a.	c.	S.W.	...	...	...
10	60 a.	c. a. r.	S.W.	68 a.	t. l. r.	S.W.	...	...	...
11	58 a.	c. a. r. h.	N.E.	70 a.	f.	S.W.	...	...	...
12	58 a.	f. a. r. h.	W.	72 a.	f.a.r.a.h.	N.W.	...	...	...
13	52 a.	c. a. f.	N.W.	70 a.	f. a. r.	N.W.	...	...	...
14	51 a.	f. a. r.	N.W.	76 a.	f.	N.W.	...	...	...
15	52 a.	f.	S.E.	74 a.	f.	S.W.	...	...	...
16	48 a.	f.	S.W.	70 a.	f.	S.W.	...	...	...
17	42 a.	f.	N.E.	76 a.	f.	S.W.	...	...	...
18	45 a.	c.	S.W.	78 a.	r.	S.W.	...	...	...
19	30 a.	f. a. r.	S.W.	71 a.	f. a. r.	S.W.	...	...	...
20	32 a.	f.	S.W.	74 a.	f.	S.W.	...	...	...
21	19 a.	f.	S.E.	78 a.	f.	E.	...	...	...
22	22 a.	f.	E.	70 a.	f.	E.	...	...	...
23	35 a.	f.	E.	72 a.	f.	S.E.	...	...	...
24	40 a.	f.	S.E.	76 a.	f. a. r.	S.E.	...	...	...
25	32 a.	f. a. r.	S.E.	65 a.	c.	S.E.	...	...	...
26	31 a.	f.	S.E.	45 a.	f.	S.E.	...	...	...
27	32 a.	f.	S.E.	56 a.	f.	S.E.	...	...	...
28	35 a.	f.	S.W.	66 a.	f.	S.W.	...	...	...
29	32 a.	f.	S.W.	68 a.	f.	S.W.	...	...	...
30	34 a.	c.	N.E.	59 a.	c.	N.E.	...	...	...
31	38 a.	c. a. r.	N.E.	58 a.	c. a. r. h.	N.E.	...	...	...
Sep. 1	38 a.	c.	N.W.	67 a.	c.	N.W.	...	...	...
2	36 a.	c. a. r.	N.E.	60 a.	c. a. r. h.	N.E.	...	...	...
3	34 a.	c. a. r.	N.E.	52 a.	c. a. r.	N.E.	...	...	...
4	19 a.	r. a. s.	N.E.	34 a.	c. a. r.	N.E.	...	...	...
5	17 a.	c. a. s.	N.E.	29 a.	c. a. r. s.	N.E.	...	...	...
6	....	c. a. r.	N.E.	....	r.	N.E.	...	...	...
7	....	c. a. r.	N.E.	....	c. a. r.	N.E.	...	...	...
8	....	c.	N.E.	....	c. a. r.	N.E.	...	...	...
9	....	c. a. r.	N.E.	....	f. a. r.	N.E.	...	...	...
10	....	f.	N.W.	...	f.	N.W.	...	...	...
11	....	f.	N.W.	....	f.	N.W.	...	...	...
12	....	f.	N.W.	....	f.	N.E.	...	...	...
13	....	c.	N.E.	....	r.	N.E.	...	...	...
14	....	c. a. r.	S.W.	....	c. a. r.	S.W.	...	...	...
15	....	c. a. s.	S.W.	....	s.	S.W.	...	...	...
16	....	c. a. s.	S.W.	....	f.	S.W.	...	...	...
17	....	f.	S.W.	....	f.	S.W.	...	...	...
18	....	f.	S.W.	....	f.	S.W.	...	...	...
19	....	f.	S.W.	....	f.	S.W.	...	...	...
20	....	f.	S.W.	....	f.	S.W.	...	...	...
21	....	f.	S.E.	....	f.	S.W.	...	...	...
22	....	f.	S.W.	....	f.	S.W.	...	...	...

Day of the month.	Therm. at sunrise.	Weather.	Wind at sunrise.	Therm. at four o'clock.	Weather.	Wind at four o'clock.	River. r. and f.	Feet.	Inches.
1805.	Deg.			Deg.					
Sep. 23	....	f.	S.W.	....	f.	S.W.	...	...	...
24	....	f.	S.E.	....	f.	S.E.	...	...	...
25	....	f.	E.	....	f.	S.W.	...	...	...
26	....	f.	E.	....	f.	S.W.	...	...	...
27	....	f.	E.	....	f.	S.W.	...	...	...
28	....	f.	E.	....	f.	S.W.	...	...	...
29	....	....	E.	....	f.	S.W.	...	...	...
30	....	....	E.	....	f.	S.W.	...	...	...

	October.			November.			December.	
Day of month.	Wind.	Weather.	Day of month.	Wind.	Weather.	Day of month.	Wind.	Weather.
1	E.	f.	1	N.E.	f.	1	E.	c. a. r.
2	N.	f.	2	S.W.	f.	2	S.W.	c. a. r.
3	E.	f.	3	N.E.	f. a. fog.	3	E.	f. a. r.
4	E.	f.	4	W.	c. a. r.	4	S.E.	r.
5	E.	f.	5	S.W.	r. c. r.	5	S.W.	r.
6	E.	f.	6	S.W.	r. a. r.	6	S.W.	r.
7	E.	f.	7	S.W.	r.a.r.fog.	7	N.E.	f. a. r.
8	E.	f.	8	S.W.	f. a. r.	8	N.E.	c.
9	S.W.	c.	9	S.	r.	9	N.E.	c. r.
10	N.W.	f.	10	N.W.	r. a. r.	10	N.E.	r.
11	E. & S.W.	c.	11	S.W.	r.	11	S.W.	r.
12	E. & S.W.	f.	12	S.W.	h. r. t. & l.	12	S.W.	r.
13	S.W.	f. a. r.	13	S.W.	r.	13	S.W.	r.
14	S.W.	f.	14		r.	14	S.W.	r.
15	S.W.	f.	15	S.E.	f. a. r.	15	S.W.	c. a. r.
16	S.W.	f.	16	W.S.W.	f.	16	S.W.	r.
17	S.E.	f.	17	E.	c. a. f.	17	S.W.	f. a. r. & h.
18	S.E.	f.	18	S.E.	f. a. c.	18	S.E.	c. a. r. s. h.
19	S.E.	f.	19	S.E.	c. a. r.	19	S.W.	h. r. & c.
20	S.W.	f.	20	S.E.	f. a. r.	20	S.W.	f. a. r. & h.
21	S.W.	f.	21	S.E.	c. a. r.	21	S.W.	r.
22	S.W.	f.	22	S.S.E.	r.	22	S.W.	r.
23	S.W.	f.	23	S.W.	c. a. r.	23	S.W.	r. h. & t.
24	S.W.	f.	24	W.	f. a. r.	24	S.W.	r.
25	W.	f.	25	E.S.E.	c. a. r.	25	S.W.	c. r.
26	W.	f.	26	E.N.E.	r.	26	S.W.	r. a. t. & l.
27	W.	f.	27	S.W.	r.	27	S.W.	r.
28	N.W.	r. a. f.	28	S.W.W.	r.	28	S.E.	r.
29	W.	f. a. r.	29	S.W.	r.	29	S.E.	c. a. r.
30	S.E.	r. a. r.	30	S.W.	f. a. r. & h.	30	S.E.	f. a. r.
31	S.W.	f. a. r.				31	S.W.	r.

Day of the month.	Weather.	Wind at sunrise.	Weather.	Wind at four o'clock.
1806. Jan. 1	c. a. r.	S.W.	r. a. c.	S.W.
2	c. a. r.	S.W.	r.	S.W.
3	c. a. r. h. t. & l.	S.W.	c. a. r. h. & f.	S.W.
4	c. a. r. & h.	S.W.	r. a. f. & r.	S.E.
5	r.	S.E.	r.	S.E.
6	c. a. r.	S.E.	f.	E.
7	f.	N.E.	c. a. f.	S.E.
8	f.	N.E.	c. a. f.	S.E.
9	f.	S.W.	c. a. f.	S.W.
10	f. a. r.	S.W.	c. a. f.	S.W.
11	c.	S.W.	c. a. r.	S.W.
12	f. a. c.	N.W.	c.	N.W.
13	r.	S.W.	r.	S.W.
14	f. a. r.	N.W.	c. a. f.	S.
15	r. a. c. & r.	S.E.	r. a. r.	S.
16	r. a. r.	S.W.	r. a. r.	S.W.
17	c. a. r.	S.W.	c.	S.W.
18	r. a. r.	S.W.	c. a. r.	S.W.
19	c. a. r.	S.	c. a. r.	S.W.
20	r. a. r.	S.W.	r. a. r.	S.W.
21	c. a. r.	S.W.	c. a. r.	S.W.
22	r. a. r.	S.W.	c. a. r.	S.W.
23	c. a. r. t. & l.	S.W.	c. a. f.	S.W.
24	c. a. r. & s.	S.E.	c. a. r. h. & s.	E.
25	h. a. r. h. s.	N.E.	c. a. r. h. & s.	N.E.
26	c. a. h. & s.	N.E.	c. a. s.	N.E.
27	f. a. s.	N.E.	f.	N.E.
28	f.	N.E.	f.	N.E.
29	f.	N.E.	f.	N.E.
30	s. a. s.	N.	s. a. s.	W.
31	f. a. c.	N.E.	f.	N.E.
Feb. 1	f.	N.E.	f.	N.E.
2	f.	N.E.	c. a. s.	S.W.
3	c. a. s. & r.	N.W.	c. a. f.	N.E.
4	f.	N.E.	f.	N.E.
5	f.	N.E.	f.	N.E.
6	f.	N.E.	c.	S.W.
7	c.	S.W.	c.	S.W.
8	c. a. s. r. h.	S.W.	c. a. f. r. h. & s.	S.W.
9	c. a. r. & h.	S.W.	c. a. r. & h.	S.W.
10	c. a. r. h. s.	N.	c. a. f. & c.	S.W.
11	c. a. f. & c.	S.W.	r. a. f. & r.	S.W.
12	r. a. r. & c.	S.W.	r. a. c. & r.	S.W.
13	c. a. r.	S.W.	c. a. r.	S.W.
14	c. a. f. & s.	S.W.	r. a. r. f. & r.	S.W.
15	c. a. r. & f.	S.	c. a. r. & f.	S.W.
16	r. a. s. & r.	S.W.	r. a. f. & r.	S.W.
17	c. a. r. h. & s.	S.W.	r. a. f. h. s. & r.	S.W.
18	c. a. r. & h.	S.W.	r. a. r. & h.	S.W.
19	r. a. r.	S.W.	r. a. r.	S.W.

Day of the month.	Weather.	Wind at sunrise.	Weather.	Wind at four o'clock.
1806.				
Feb. 20	c. a. r.	S.W.	c. a. r.	S.W.
21	r. a. c. & r.	S.W.	r. a. c. & r.	S.W.
22	f. a. r.	N.E.	c. a. f.	N.E.
23	f.	S.W.	c. a. f.	S.W.
24	c. a. f. & c.	S.W.	r. a. c. & r.	S.
25	r. a. r.	S.	r. a. r.	S.
26	f. a. r.	N.E.	c. a. f. & r.	S.
27	c. a. r.	S.W.	r. a. r.	S.W.
28	r. a. r.	S.W.	c. a. c. & f.	S.W.
March 1	f. a. r. & c.	S.W.	r. a. c. & r.	S.W.
2	r. a. c. & r.	S.	r. a. c. & r.	S.
3	c. a. r.	S.	c. a. r.	S.
4	r. a. c. & r.	S.	r. a. r.	S.
5	c. a. r.	N.E.	c. a. r.	S.
6	f. a. r.	S.E.	c. a. f.	S.E.
7	r. a. r. & h.	S.E.	r. a. f. r. h. c. & f.	S.E.
8	h. & r. a. h. r. & s.	S.	r. a. r. & h.	S.E.
9	s. & h. a. r. s. & h.	S.W.	r. a. h. & r.	S.W.
10	s. & r. a. h. r. & s.	S.W.	f. a. r. h. & s.	S.W.
11	f. a. r. h. & s.	S.E.	f. a. r. & h.	S.E.
12	f. a. c.	N.E.	c. a. f.	N.E.
13	f. a. r.	N.E.	f.	N.E.
14	c. a. f.	N.E.	c.	N.E.
15	c. a. c.	N.E.	f.	N.E.
16	r. a. f. & c.	S.W.	c. a. f. c. r.	S.W.
17	c. a. r.	S.W.	r. a. f. h. s. & r.	S.W.
18	r. a. c. & r.	S.W.	r. a. f. r. & h.	S.W.
19	r. & h. a. c. r. & h.	S.W.	r. a. f. r. & h.	S.W.
20	r. a. r. & h.	S.W.	r.	S.W.
21	r. a. r.	S.W.	c. a. r.	N.E.
22	r. a. r.	S.W.	r. a. c. & r.	S.W. N.E.
23	r. a. r.	S.W.	f. a. c. & r.	S.W.
24	r. a. c. & r.	S.W.	f. a. c.	N.W. S.W.
25	c. a. f.	S.E.	r. a. c. & r.	S.E.
26	c. a. r.	N.W.	c. a. f. & c.	S.E.
27	r. a. c.	S.E.	r. a. c. & r.	S.E.
28	c. a. r.	N.	f. a. f. & r.	S.W.
29	c. a. r. & f.	S.	c. a. r.	S.W.

Day of the month.	Weather.	Wind at sunrise.	Weather.	Wind at four o'clock.	Columbia River.		
					r. and f.	Feet.	Inches.
1806.							
Mar. 30	c.	E.	f. a. c.	S.W.	....	...	....
31	f.	S.E.	......	....	....	...	....
Apr. 1	c. a. f.	S.E.	c. a. f.	S.E.	r.	...	1
2	c.	S.E.	c. a. f.	S.E.	f.	...	½
3	c. a. r.	S.W.	c. a. r.	W.	f.	...	3½
4	c. a. r.	S.W.	c. a. r.	S.W.	f.	...	4½
5	c. a. r.	S.W.	c. a. f. & c.	S.W.	f.	...	2½
6	f. a. c.	S.W.	f.	S.W.	f.	...	1
7	f.	S.W.	f.	S.W.	r.	...	½
8	f.	E.	f.	E.	r.	...	1½
9	f.	W.	f.	W.	....	...	....
10	c. a. r.	W.	c. a. r.	S.W.	r.	...	1
11	r. a. r.	W.	c. a. r.	S.W.	r.	...	2
12	c. a. r.	W.	r. a. c. & r.	W.	r.	...	2
13	r. a. c. & r.	W.	c. a. r. & f.	W.	r.	...	2½
14	f.	W.	f.	W.	r.	...	1
15	f.	W.	f.	W.	....	...	....
16	f. a. c.	S.W.	f.	S.W.	f.	...	2
17	f.	N.E.	c. a. f.	S.W.	f.	...	2
18	f. a. r.	S.W.	f.	S.W.	f.	...	1
19	c. a. r.	S.W.	c.	S.W.	f.	...	3
20	f. a. r.	S.W.	c. a. r.	S.W.	f.	...	2½
21	f.	N.E.	f.	E.	f.	...	2
22	f.	N.W.	f.	W.	f.	...	1
23	f. a. c.	E.	f.	N.E.	f.	...	4
24	f.	N.W.	f.	N.W.	f.	...	2
25	f.	N.E.	f.	N.E.	f.	...	2
26	f. a. c.	N.W.	f.	N.E.	f.	...	2½
27	f. a. r.	S.E.	f.	N.W.	f.	...	1½
28	f. a. t.	S.W.	f.	N.E.	f.	...	2
29	f. a. c.	N.W.	f.	N.W.	f.	...	1
30	c. a. r.	N.W.	f. a. c.	N.W.	f.	...	2
May 1	c. a. r.	S.W.	c.	S.W.	....	...	....
2	f. a. c.	N.E.	f.	S.W.	....	...	....
3	c. a, h. r. s.	S.W.	c. a. r. h. s.	S.W.	....	...	....
4	f. a. h.	S.W.	c. a. r. & h.	S.W.	....	...	....
5	f.	S.W.	f.	S.W.	....	...	....
6	r. a. c. r.	N.E.	f. a. r.	N.E.	....	...	....
7	f. a. c.	N.E.	f.	S.W.	....	...	....
8	f.	S.W.	f.	S.W.	....	...	....
9	f.	S.W.	f. a. c.	W.	....	...	....
10	c. a. r. & s.	S.W.	f. a. s.	S.W.	....	...	....
11	f. a. r.	S.W.	f. a. c.	S.W.	....	...	....
12	f.	E.	f.	S.W.	....	...	....

Day of the month.	Weather.	Wind at sunrise.	Weather.	Wind at four o'clock.	Kooskooskee R.		
					r. and f.	Feet.	Inches.
1806.							
May 13	f.	S.W.	f.	S.W.	....	...	....
14	f.	S.W.	f.	S.W.	....	...	....
15	f.	N.	f. a. c.	N.W.	....	...	....
16	c.	S.E.	c. a. r.	S.E.	r.	...	6
17	r. a. r.	S.E.	c. a. r.	S.E.	r.	...	10¾
18	c. a. r.	S.E.	c.	S.E.	r.	...	2
19	r. a. r.	S.E.	c. a. r.	S.E.	f.	...	4
20	r. a. r.	N.W.	c. a. r.	S.E.	r.	...	2
21	c. a. r.	S.E.	f. a. c.	S.E.	f.	...	1
22	f.	S.E.	f.	S.E.	f.	...	2
23	f.	N.W.	f.	N.W. S.E.	f.	...	1½
24	f.	S.E.	f.	N.W.	f.	...	1
25	c. a. r. & t.	N.W.	f.	N.W.	r.	...	9½
26	f. a. r.	S.E.	f.	N.W.	r.	...	6
27	c.	S.E.	r. a. f. r. t. l.	S.E.	r.	...	6½
28	c. a. r. t. & l.	S.E.	c. a. f. r. t. l.	S.E.	r.	...	11
29	c. a. r. & t.	S.E.	c. a. r.	N.W.	r.	I	5
30	c. a. r.	S.E.	f.	S.E.	f.	...	6
31	c. a. f.	S.E.	f.	S.E.	r.	I	1
June 1	f. a. r. t. & l.	S.E.	f. a. c.	N.W.	....	...	....
2	c. a. c.	N.W.	f. a. c.	S.E.	....	...	....
3	c. a. f. & c.	S.E.	c. a. f.	S.E.	....	...	....
4	c. a. r.	S.E.	f. a. c.	N.W.	....	...	....
5	f.	S.E.	f.	N.W.	....	...	....
6	f.	S.E.	f.	N.W.	....	...	....
7	c. a. r.	N.W.	c. a. f. r. h.	N.W.	....	...	....
8	c.	S.E.	c. a. f.	N.W.	....	...	....
9	c.	S.E.	f. a. c.	N.W.	....	...	....
10	f.	S.E.	f.	N.W.	....	...	....
11	f.	S.E.	f.	N.W.	....	...	....
12	f. a. r. l. & t.	S.E.	f.	N.W.	....	...	....
13	c.	S.E.	c. a. f.	N.W.	....	...	....
14	f.	S.E.	f.	N.W.	....	...	....
15	c.	N.W.	r. a. f. & r.	N.W.	....	...	....
16	f. a. c.	S.E.	c. a. f.	S.E.	....	...	....
17	c. a. r.	E.	c. a. f. & r.	S.E.	....	...	....
18	c. a. r.	E.	c. a. r. & h.	S.W.	....	...	....
19	f. a. c.	S.E.	f.	N.W.	....	...	....
20	f.	S.E.	f.	N.W.	....	...	....
21	f.	S.E.	f.	N.W.	....	...	....
22	f.	N.W.	f.	N.W.	....	...	....
23	f.	N.W.	f.	N.W.	....	...	....
24	f.	N.W.	f.	N.W.	....	...	....
25	c. a. r.	S.E.	c. a. r.	N.W.	....	...	....

Day of the month.	Weather.	Wind at sunrise.	Weather.	Wind at four o'clock.	River.		
					r. and f.	Feet.	Inches.
1806.							
June 26	c. a. r.	S.E.	f.	S.E.	....	...	....
27	f. a. r.	S.E.	f.	S.E.	....	...	....
28	f.	S.E.	f.	S.E.	....	...	....
29	f.	S.E.	f. a. r. h. t.	S.E.	....	...	....
30	f.	S.E.	f.	N.W.	....	...	....
July 1	c. a. f.	N.W.	f.	N.W.	....	...	....
2	f.	S.E.	f.	N.W.	....	...	....
3	f.	S.E.	f.	S.W.	....	...	....
4	f.	S.W.	f.	S.W.	....	...	....
5	f.	N.E.	f.	S.W.	....	...	....
6	f.	S.W.	c. a. r. t. & l.	S.W.	....	...	....
7	c. a. r.	W.	f. a. r.	S.W. by W.	....	...	....
8	f. a. r.	W.	f.	S.W.	....	...	....
9	c.	S.W.	f.	S.W.	....	...	....
10	f.	S.E.	f.	S.W.	....	...	....
11	f.	S.E.	f.	N.N.E.	....	...	....
12	f.	S.E.	f.	N.W.	....	...	....
13	f.	S.S.E.	f.	N.E.	....	...	....
14	f.	N.W.	f.	N.W.	....	...	....
15	f.	S.E. by E.	f.	N.E.	....	...	....
16	c.	N.E.	c.	N.E.	....	...	....
17	f. a. r. h. t. l.	S.E.	f.	S.W.	....	...	....
18	f.	S.W.	f.	S.E.	....	...	....
19	f.	N.W.	f.	S.E.	....	...	....
20	f.	N.E.	f.	N.E.	....	...	....
21	f.	N.E.	c.	N.E.	....	...	....
22	f. a. t. l. & r.	N.E.	c.	N.E.	....	...	....
23	f.	N.E.	c.	S.E.	....	...	....
24	f.	S.W.	r.	S.W.	....	...	....
25	c.	E.	c. a. r.	S.W.	....	...	....
26	c.	S.S.W.	f. a. r.	N.W.	....	...	....
27	f.	N.E.	f.	S.W.	....	...	....
28	c. a. r.	N.E.	f.	N.W.	....	...	....
29	c. a. r. t. & l.	N.E.	f.	N.	....	...	....
30	f. a. r. t. & l.	N.W.	f. a. r.	S.E.	....	...	....
31	f.	N.W.	c. a. r.	N.E.	....	...	....
Aug. 1	c. a. r.	N.W.	r.	N.	r.	5	½
2	c. a. r.	N.	f. a. r.	N.	r.	3	
3	f.	S.W.	f.	S.W.	r.	2	¼
4	f.	N.W.	f.	N.E.	f.	6	¼
5	f.	N.E.	f.	N.E.	f.	7	...
6	c. a. r. t. l.	S.W.	f.	N.E.	f.	2	¼
7	r.	N.E.	c. a. r.	N.	f.	2	½
8	f.	N.	f.	N.W.	f.	...	
9	f.	N.E.	f.	N.E.	f.	1	¼
10	f.	E.	c.	E.	f.	...	¼
11	f.	N.W.	f.	N.W.	f.	2	...
12	f.	S.W.	c.	S.W.	f.	2	¼
13	f. a. r.	S.W.	f.	S.W.	f.	2	½
14	f.	N.E.	f.	S.W.	f.	3	½

Day of the month.	Weather.	Wind at sunrise.	Weather.	Wind at four o'clock.	River. r. and f.	Feet.	Inches.
1806.							
Aug. 15	f.	N.W.	f.	N.W.	f.	2	....
16	f.	N.W.	f.	N.W.	f.	3	¼
17	c.	S.E.	c.	S.E.	....	..	....
18	c. a. r.	S.E.	f.	S.E.	f.	1	½
19	t. l. & r.	S.E.	c.	S.E.	f.	...	½
20	c. a. t. l. & r.	S.W.	f.	N.W.	f.	1	¼
21	f.	S.E.	f.	N.W.	f.	2	⅔
22	c. a. r.	S.W.	f.	S.E.	f.	4	....
23	c.	S.E.	r.	N.W.	f.	1	½
24	f.	N.E.	f.	N.W.	f.	2	....
25	f.	S.W.	f.	N.W.	f.	1	¼
26	f.	S.E.	f.	S.E.	f.	...	¼
27	f.	S.E.	f.	S.E.	f.	1	¼
28	f.	S.E.	f.	N.W.	....	...	....
29	c.	N.W.	f. a. r.	S.E.	f.	...	½
30	c. a. r.	S.E.	f.	S.E.	....	...	....
31	c. a. r. t. l. w.	S.E.	c. a. r.	S.E.	....	...	....

REMARKS AND REFLECTIONS.

[The matter which here follows requires explanation. Captains Lewis and Clark, with the assistance of their non-commissioned officers, kept a Meteorological Register from Jan. 1st, 1804, when they were in winter-quarters in Illinois at the mouth of Du Bois river, and during their whole journey to the Pacific and back (with only one break in the record). The "Remarks and Reflections" which here follow go day by day with the preceding tabular statistics ; and had they been printed where they belong, and where they usually stand in the codices, a folding sheet would have been required. On this account they were separated from the tables by the original editor, and I follow his example in bringing them in thus *en suite*.

The Meteorological Register, including day by day the "Remarks, etc.," will be found in the codices as follows (pagination usually reading backward, as L. and C. began their registrations at the back of a codex and wrote forward on successive folios) : (1) Clark C 246–216, Jan. 14, 1804–Apr. 7th, 1805 (lacking May 15th–Sept. 18th, 1804). As Clark says, C 246, "there is not room in the column [of the codex as ruled off for "Remarks"] for the necessary remarks it is trans-fired by the refference of numbers [*i. e.* of dates] to an adjoining part of this book." (2) Lewis Fe, Apr. 1st–Sept 30th, 1805. The meteorological matter of this codex for Apr., May, and June, really forms Lewis D 152–140, but has been detached, except the last folio, p. 140, which leaves the "Remarks" for June in Codex D. (3) Clark I 14–32, Apr. 1st, 1805–Jan. 31st, 1806. (4) Lewis J 152–145, Jan. 1st, 1806–Mar. 30th, 1806. (5) Lewis K 152–147, Apr. 1st–May

30th, 1806. (6) Lewis L 149-146, June 1st-Aug. 12th, 1806. (7) Clark M 152-146, June 1st-Aug. 31st, 1806. (8). Clark N 152, 151, for the month of Sept., 1806. It will be observed that some of these registers overlap in dates, which doubtless results from the copies in the "red books" being made independently by each captain from a single register kept in the field. As the registration is continued to the end of September, 1806, I do not see why the foregoing Tables break down at Aug. 31st, and the "Remarks" leave off at Aug. 22d, in the Biddle edition.   I shall not complete the tabular matter, as I consider it useless, and in fact have reprinted it only *pro forma*, to justify the statement that nothing in the original edition is omitted from the present. But I will continue the never-published "Remarks" through September.]

Jan. **1**, 1804. Snow one inch deep.

Jan. **2.** Some snow last night.

Jan. **3.** Hard wind.

Jan. **4.** River covered with ice out of the Missouri.

Jan. **5, 6, 7.** River Du Bois rises.

Jan. **8.** River continues to rise, and discharges ice.

Jan. **9.** Some snow last night.

Jan. **10.** The Missouri rises.

Jan. **13.** Snow last night.

Jan. **17, 19.** River covered with ice, some 5½ inches thick.

(*p. 496*) *Jan.* **20.** No ice passing.

Jan. **21.** Ice running out of the Missouri 9 inches thick ; snow 2½ inches deep.

Jan. **22.** Ice running out of the Missouri ; snow 5¾ inches deep.

Jan. **23.** Ice stopped.

Jan. **24.** Trees covered with ice.

Jan. **28.** Ice running, cold, etc.

Feb. **1.** The wind blew hard ; no frost ; snow disappearing fast.

Feb. **2.** Frost this morning ; the snow has disappeared in spots.

Feb. **3.** Frost this morning ; the snow thaws considerably.

Feb. **4.** Frost ; numbers of swan and geese from north and south.

Feb. **5.** Immense quantity of ice running, some of which is 11 inches thick.

Feb. **6.** A quantity of soft ice running ; white frost ; the snow disappeared ; swans passing.

Feb. **7.** A small quantity of floating ice passing ; swans passing.

Feb. **8.** Many swans from the N.W. Creek rose and took off the watermark.

Feb. **9.** The river rose two feet ; large quantity of drift ice from the Missouri.

Feb. **10.** Ice still drifting in considerable quantities ; some geese pass from the south.

Feb. **11.** The sugar-maple runs freely ; swans pass from the north.

Feb. **12.** Pigeons, geese, and ducks of various kinds have returned.

Feb. **13.** First appearance of the blue crains [cranes, *Ardea herodias*].

Feb. **14.** But little drift ice ; the Mississippi not broken up ; sugar-trees run.

Feb. **15.** Immense quantity swans.

Feb. 27.   The river rose three inches and fell immediately.

Feb. 28.   Began to snow, and continued all day.

(*p. 497*) *Feb.* 29.   Snowed all night and until 11 a. m.; then cleared away.

Mar. 7.   Saw the first brant return.

Mar. 8.   Rain, succeeded by snow and hail.

Mar. 9.   Cloudy in the morning.

Mar. 19.   The weather has been generally fair but very cold ; the ice has run for several days in such quantities that it was impossible to pass the river. Visited St. Charles ; saw the first snake, which was the kind usually termed the garter-snake [*Eutænia sirtalis*], saw also a beetle of a black color, with two red stripes on his back, passing each other crosswise from the but [base] of the wing to the extremity of the same.

Mar. 20.   Heard the first frogs on my return from St. Charles.

Mar. 25.   Saw the first white crane [?] return.

Mar. 26.   The weather warm and fair.

Mar. 27.   The buds of the spicewood [*Benzoin odoriferum*] appeared, and the tassels of the mail [male] cottonwood [*Pòpulus moniliferus*] were larger than a large mulberry, with the shape and color of that fruit ; some of them have fallen from the trees.   The grass begins to spring ; the weather has been warm, and no falling weather until this time, though the atmosphere has been very smoky and thick ; a heavy fall of rain commenced, which continued until twelve at night, attended with thunder and lightning.   Saw large insects which resembled mosquitoes, but doubt whether they are really those insects or the fly which produces them [!].   They attempted to bite my horse, but I could not observe that they made any impression with their beaks.

Mar. 31.   Windy.

Apr. 1.   The spicewood is in full bloom ; the dog's-tooth violet [*Erythronium americanum*] and May-apple [*Podophyllum peltatum*] appeared above ground.   A northern light appeared at 10 o'clock p. m., very red.

(*p. 498*) *Apr.* 5.   At St. Louis the buds of the peaches, apples, and cherries appear.

Apr. 6.   A large flock of pelicans [*Pelecanus erythrorhynchus*] appear.

Apr. 7.   The leaves of some of the apple-trees have burst their coverts and put forth ; the leaves of the greenwood bushes have put forth.   Many of the wild plants have sprung up and appear above ground.

Apr. 10.   No appearance of the buds of the Osage apple ; the Osage plum has put forth its leaves and flower buds, though it is not yet completely in blow.

Apr. 13.   The peach-trees are partly in bloom.   The brant, goose, duck, swan, crane, and other aquatic birds have disappeared very much within a few days, and have gone further north, I presume ; the summer-ducks [*Aix sponsa*] raise their young in this neighborhood, and are now here in great numbers.

Apr. 17.   Peach-trees in full bloom ; the weeping-willow [*Salix babylonica*] has put forth its leaves, which are one-fifth of their [full] size ; the violet, dove's-foot, and cowslip are in blow ; the dog's-tooth violet is not yet in bloom. The trees of the forest, particularly the cottonwood, begin to obtain, from the size of their buds, a greenish cast at a distance ; the gooseberry, which is also in this country and black, has put forth its leaves ; frost.

Apr. 26.   The white frost killed much fruit near Kahokia, while that at St. Louis escaped with little injury.

Apr. 30.   White frost, slight ; did but little injury.

May 5.   Thundered and lightened excessively this morning.

May 10.   Distant thunder ; sultry this evening.

May 12.   The wind at four was uncommonly hard.

[*May* 14.   Set out from the river Dubois up the Missouri, Clark C 227.]

May 25.   Strawberries on the prairies ripe and abundant.

May 27.   Service-berries or wild currants ripe and abundant.

May 30.   Mulberries begin to ripen ; abundant in the bottoms of the river.

June 10.   Purple raspberries ripe and abundant.

(*p. 499*) *June* 11.   Many small birds now sitting ; some have young ; the whippoorwill [*Antrostomus vociferus*] sitting.

June 16.   The wood-duck [*Aix sponsa*] now has its young ; these ducks are abundant, and, except one solitary pelican and a few geese, are the only aquatic fowl we have yet seen.

July 1.   Saw some geese [*Bernicla canadensis*] with their young ; caught several ; they are not yet feathered, nor can they fly ; the old geese are in the same situation at this season.

July 4.   A great number of young swans and geese in a lake opposite the mouth of Fourth of July creek ; in the lake there is also an abundance of fish of various species, the pike, perch, carp, catfish, sun-perch, etc.

July 12.   Deer and bear are becoming scarce ; elk begin to appear.

July 23.   Catfish very common, and easily taken in any part of this river ; some are nearly white, particularly above the Platte river.

Sept. 19.   The leaves of some of the cottonwoods begin to fade ; yesterday saw the first brant [*Bernicla brenta*] passing from northwest to southeast.

Sept. 20.   The antelope is now rutting ; the swallow has disappeared twelve days.

Sept. 21.   The elk is now rutting ; the buffalo has nearly ceased [to rut] ; the latter commence the latter end of July or the first of August.

Sept. 22.   A little foggy this morning ; a great number of green-legged plover are passing down the river, also some geese and brant.

Sept. 23.   The air remarkably dry ; plums and grapes fully ripe ; in 36 hours two spoonfuls of water evaporated in a saucer.

Sept. 27.   Saw a large flock of white gulls, with wings tipped with black.

Oct. 1.   The leaves of the ash, poplar, and most of the shrubs begin to turn yellow and decline.

(*p. 500*) *Oct.* 3.   The earth and sand which form the bars of this river are so fully impregnated with salt that it shoots and adheres to the little sticks which appear on the surface ; it is pleasant and seems nitrous.

Oct. 5.   Slight white frost last night ; geese and brant passing south.

Oct. 6.   Frost last night ; saw teel [teal], mallards, and gulls.

Oct. 9.   Wind blew hard this morning; saw some brant and geese passing to the south.

Oct. 14.   Cottonwoods all yellow, and the leaves beginning to fall; abundance of grapes and red berries; the leaves of all the trees, as ash, elm, etc., except the cottonwood, are now fallen.

Oct. 17.   Saw a large flock of white brant with black wings [*Chen hyperboreus*]; antelopes are passing to the Black mountains to winter, as is their custom.

Oct. 18.   Hard frost last night, the clay near the water's edge was frozen, as was the water in the vessels exposed to the air.

Oct. 19.   No mule-deer seen above the Chayenne river.

Oct. 20.   Much more timber than usual; saw the first black haws that we have seen for a long time.

[*Oct.* 27.   Arrived at ½ past 12 o'clock at the point we intended to fix our camp, Clark C 223.]

Oct. 29.   The wind was so hard that it was extremely disagreeable; the sand was blown on us in clouds.

Nov. 3.   Wind blew hard all day.

Nov. 7.   A few drops of rain this evening; saw the aurora borealis at 10 p. m.; it was very brilliant, in perpendicular columns, frequently changing position.

Nov. 8.   Since we have been at our present station [Fort Mandan], the river has fallen nine inches.

Nov. 9.   Very hard frost this morning.

Nov. 10.   Many geese passing to the south; saw a flock of crested cherry-birds [*Ampelis cedrorum*] passing to the south.

Nov. 13.   Large quantity of drift ice running this morning; the river having appearances of closing for this winter.

(*p. 501*) *Nov.* 16.   Hard frost this morning attached to the timber and boughs of the trees.

Nov. 17.   The frost of yesterday remained on the trees until 2 p.m., when it descended like a shower of snow; swans passing from the north.

Nov. 20.   Little soft ice this morning; the boat in much danger from ice.

Nov. 29.   The snow fell eight inches deep; it drifted in heaps in the open ground.

Nov. 30.   The Indians pass the river on the ice.

Dec. 5.   Wind blew excessively hard this night from the northwest.

Dec. 7.   Last night the river blocked up opposite Fort Mandan.

Dec. 8.   The ice one and a half inches thick on the part that had not previously frozen; buffalo appear.

Dec. 14.   Captain Clark set out with a hunting-party on the ice with sleighs.

Dec. 15.   Snow fell half an inch.

Dec. 24.   Snow very inconsiderable.

Dec. 27.   The trees are all white with the frost, which attached itself to their boughs.

Dec. 28.   It blew very hard last night; the frost fell like a shower of snow.

Jan. 3, 1805.   The snow is nine inches deep.

Jan. 6.   At twelve o'clock two luminous spots appeared on each side of the sun, extremely bright.

Jan. 8.   The snow is now ten inches deep, accumulating by frosts.

Jan. 12.   Singular appearance of three distinct halos or luminous rings about the moon appeared this evening at 9.30 p. m., and continued one hour ; the moon formed the center of the middle ring ; the other two, which lay north and south of the moon, had each of them a limb passing through the moon's center and projecting north and south ; a semidiameter beyond (*p. 502*) the middle ring, to which last they were equal in dimensions, each ring appearing to extend [subtend, Clark C 219] an angle of 15° of a great circle.

Jan. 15.   A total eclipse of the moon last night visible here, but partially obscured by the clouds.

Jan. 19.   Ice now three feet thick on the most rapid part of the river.

Jan. 23.   The snow fell about four inches deep last night ; it continues to snow to-day.

It frequently happens that the sun rises fair, and in about 15 or 20 minutes it becomes suddenly turbid, as if the moon had some chemical effect on the atmosphere.

Jan. 31.   The snow fell two inches last night.

Feb. 8.   The black-and-white speckled woodpecker [*Picus villosus*] has returned.

Feb. 14.   The snow fell three inches deep last night.

Mar. 2.   The snow has disappeared in many places ; the river is partially broken up.

Mar. 3.   A flock of ducks passed up the river this morning.

Mar. 12.   Snow but slight ; disappeared to-day.

Mar. 19.   But little snow, not enough to cover the ground.

Collected some roots, herbs, and plants, in order to send by the boat, particularly the root said to cure the bite of a mad dog and rattlesnake.

The Indians raise a kind of artichoke, which they say is common in the prairies ; it is well tasted.

Mar. 21.   Some ducks in the river opposite the fort.

Mar. 24.   But little snow.

Mar. 25.   A flock of swan returned to-day ; the ice in the river has given way in many places, and it is with difficulty it can be passed.

Mar. 26.   The ice gave way in the river about 3 p. m., and came down in immense sheets ; it was very near destroying our new canoes ; some geese passed.

(*p. 503*) *Mar.* 27.   The first insect I have seen was a large black gnat to-day ; the ice is drifting in great quantities.

Mar. 28.   Ice abates in quantity ; wind hard ; river rises 13 inches, and falls 12 inches.

Mar. 29.   A variety of insects make their appearance, as flies, bugs, etc. The ice ceases to run ; it is supposed to have formed an obstruction above.

Mar. 30.   The ice comes down in great quantities ; the Mandans take some floating buffalo.

Mar. 31. Ducks and geese passing ; the ice abates in quantity.

Apr. 1.[1] A fine refreshing shower of rain fell about 2 p. m. This was the first we had witnessed since Sept. 15th, 1804, though rain has several times fallen in small quantities, and was noticed in the diary of the weather; the cloud came from the west and was attended by hard thunder and lightning. I have observed that all thunder-clouds in the western part of the continent proceed from the westerly quarter, as they do in the Atlantic States. The air is remarkably dry and pure in this open country ; there is very little rain or snow, either winter or summer. The atmosphere is more transparent than I ever observed it in any country through which I have passed.

Apr. 4. Observed a flock of brant passing up the river to-day ; the wind blew very hard, as it does frequently in this quarter. There is scarcely any timber to break the winds from the river, the country on both sides being level plains, wholly destitute of timber, the winds blow with astonishing violence in this open country, and form a great obstruction to the navigation of the Missouri, particularly with small vessels, which can neither ascend nor descend should the wind be violent.

Apr. 6. This day a flock of cherry or cedar-birds [*Ampelis cedrorum*] were seen ; one of the men killed several of them. They are (*p. 504*) common in the United States, usually associate in large flocks ; are frequently destructive to the cherry orchards, and in winter, in the lower parts of Maryland and Virginia, feed on the berries of the cedar. It is a small bluish-brown bird, crested with a tuft of dark brown feathers, with a narrow black stripe passing on each side of the head underneath the eye, from the base of the upper beak to the back of the head ; it is distinguished more particularly by some of the shorter feathers of the wings, which are tipped with red spots, which have much the appearance of sealing-wax.

Apr. 8. The killdeer [*Ægialites vociferus*] and large hawk have returned ; the only birds that I observed during the winter at Fort Mandan were the Missouri magpie [*Pica pica hudsonica*], a bird of the genus *Corvus,* the raven [*Corvus carnivorus*] in immense numbers, the small woodpecker [*Picus villosus ?*] or sapsucker, as they are sometimes called, the beautiful eagle [*Aquila chrysaëtos*] or calumet-bird, so called from the circumstance of the natives decorating their pipe-stems with its plumage, and the prairie-hen or grouse [*Pediœcetes columbianus*].

Apr. 9. The crows [*Corvus americanus*] have also returned ; saw the first to-day ; the mosquitoes revisit us ; saw several of them.

Apr. 10. The lark [*Eremophila alpestris* var.], bald eagle [*Haliaëtus leucocephalus*], and the large plover [*Squatarola helvetica*] have returned ; the grass begins to spring up, and the leaf-buds of the willow to appear.

Apr. 11. The lark-woodpecker,[2] with yellow wings and a black spot on the

---

[1] All the foregoing is from Clark C. Observe the change in style with Apr. 1st, when we turn to Lewis Fe. Recall also that after Apr. 7th the Expedition is passing up the Missouri from Fort Mandan.

[2] This is the flicker of the Upper Missouri, of the variety *hybridus* of Baird (Ayres' woodpecker of Audubon), mostly like *Colaptes auratus,* but tending to the characters of *C. mexi-*

breast, common to the United States, has appeared, with sundry small birds. Many plants begin to appear above the ground ; saw a large white gull to-day ; the eagles are now laying their eggs, and the geese have mated. The elm, large-leaved willow, (*p. 505*) and the bush which bears a red berry is in bloom.

Apr. 13. The leaves of the choke-cherry are about half grown ; the cotton-wood is in bloom ; the flower of this tree resembles that of the aspin [aspen] in form, and is of a deep purple color.

Apr. 15. Several flocks of white brant [*Chen hyperboreus*] with black wings pass us to-day, on their flight to the northwest ; the trees now begin to assume a green appearance, though the earth at the depth of about three feet is not yet thawed, which we discover by the banks of the river falling in and disclosing a strata [stratum] of frozen earth.

Apr. 16. Saw the first leather-wing bat ; it appeared about the size of those common to the United States.

Apr. 18. A heavy dew this morning, which is the first and only one we have seen since we passed the Council bluffs last summer ; there is but little dew in this open country. Saw a flock of pelicans [*Pelecanus erythrorhynchus*] pass from southwest to northeast ; they appeared to be on a long flight.

Apr. 19. The trees have now put forth their leaves ; the gooseberries, cur-rant, service-berries, and wild plums are in bloom.

Apr. 21. White frost last night ; the earth frozen along the water's edge.

Apr. 22. Saw the first robin [*Merula migratoria*], also the brown curlew [*Numenius longirostris*].

Apr. 23. Vegetation has progressed but little since the 18th ; in short, the change is scarcely perceptible.

May 2. The wind continued so violent from twelve o'clock yesterday, until five o'clock this evening, that we were unable to proceed ; the snow which fell last night and this morning has not yet disappeared ; it forms a singular contrast with the trees which are now in leaf.

May 3. At 4 p. m. the snow had not yet entirely disappeared ; the new horns of the elk begin to appear.

May 4. The snow has disappeared ; saw the first grasshop- (*p. 506*) pers to-day ; there are great quantities of a small blue beetle feeding on the willows.

May 8. The bald eagle, of which there are great numbers, now have their young ; the turtle-dove [*Zenaidura carolinensis*] appears.

May 9. The choke-cherry is now in bloom.

May 17. The geese have their young ; the elk begin to produce their young ; the antelope and deer as yet have not ; the small species of whippoorwill [*Phalænoptilus nuttalli*] begins to cry ; blackbirds, both large and small [*Scole-cophagus cyanocephalus* and *Molothrus ater*], have appeared. We have had scarcely any thunder and lightning ; the clouds are generally white and accom-panied with wind only.

May 18. Saw the wild rose in bloom. The brown thrush or mocking-bird has appeared ; had a good shower of rain to-day ; it continued about two hours ; this is the first shower that deserves the appellation of *rain*, which we have seen since we left Fort Mandan ; no thunder.

May 22. Saw some particles of snow fall to-day, which did not lie in sufficient quantity on the ground to be perceptible.

May 23. Hard frost last night; ice in the eddy water along the shore, and the water frozen on the oars this morning; strawberries in bloom; saw the first kingfisher [*Ceryle alcyon*].

May 25. Saw the king-bird or bee-martin [*Tyrannus carolinensis*]; the grouse disappear; killed three of the bighorn animals.

May 26. Last night was much the warmest that we have experienced; found the covering of one blanket sufficient; the air is extremely dry and pure.

May 28. A slight thunder-storm; the air was turbid in the forenoon, and appeared to be filled with smoke; we supposed it to proceed from the burning of the plains, which we are informed are frequently set on fire by the Snake Indians to compel the antelopes to resort to the woody and mountainous country which they inhabit; saw a small white and black woodpecker with a red head, (*p. 507*) the same which is common in the Atlantic States [*Melanerpes erythrocephalus*].

May 30. The rain commenced about 4 p. m., and continued moderately through the course of the night; more rain has now fallen than we have experienced since the 15th of Sept.

May 31. The antelopes now bring forth their young; from the size of the young of the bighorn, I suppose they bring forth their young as early at least as the elk.

June 5. Great numbers of sparrows, larks, curlews, and other smaller birds common to prairies are now laying their eggs and sitting; their nests are in great abundance; the large bats or night-hawks [*Chordeiles henryi*] and the common buzzards [*Cathartes aura*] appear; first saw the mountain-cock [*Centrocercus urophasianus*] near the entrance of Maria's river.

June 15. The deer now begin to bring forth their young; the young magpies begin to fly. The brown and grizzly bears begin to copulate.

June 27. At 1 p. m. a black cloud which arose in the southwest came on, accompanied with a high wind and violent thunder and lightning; a great quantity of hail also fell during this storm, which lasted about two hours and a half. The hail, which was generally about the size of pigeons' eggs, and not unlike them in form, covered the ground to one inch and a half. For about 20 minutes during this storm hail fell of an enormous size, with violence almost incredible. When the hailstones struck the ground, they would rebound to the height of 10 or 12 feet, and pass 20 or 30 before they touched again. During this immense storm, Captain Clark was with the greater part of the men on the portage; the men saved themselves, some by getting under a canoe, others by putting sundry articles on (*p. 508*) their heads; two were knocked down, and seven had their legs and thighs much bruised. Captain Lewis weighed one of these hailstones, which weighed 3 ounces and measured 7 inches in circumference; they were generally round and perfectly solid. We are convinced that if one of these had struck a man on his naked head, it would certainly have fractured his skull. Young blackbirds are abundant and beginning to fly.

July 6. A heavy wind from the southwest, attended with rain about the middle of the last night; about day [break] had a violent thunderstorm, attended with hail and rain ; the hail covered the ground, and was near the size of musket-balls ; one blackbird was killed with the hail ; I am astonished that more have not suffered in a similar manner, as they are abundant, and I should suppose the hailstones sufficiently heavy to kill them.

Aug. 7.   The river which we are now ascending is so inconsiderable, and the current so much of [at] a stand, that I relinquished paying further attention to its state.

Aug. 21.[3]   Most astonishing was the difference between the height of the mercury at sunrise and at 4 p. m.   There was the difference of 59 degrees, and this in the space of eight hours ; yet we experience this wonderful transition without feeling it nearly so sensibly as we should have expected.

Nov. 3.   A thick fog continued until twelve o'clock, at which time it cleared off and was fair the remainder of the day.

Nov. 5.   Commenced raining at 2 p. m. and continued at intervals all day ; saw 14 striped snakes.

Nov. 7.   A thick fog this morning, which continued until 11 a. m., at which time it cleared off and con- (*p. 509*) tinued fair about two hours, and then began to rain ; several showers during the evening.

Nov. 12.   Violent wind from the southwest, accompanied with hail, thunder, and lightning ; the thunder excessively loud ; this continued from 3 till 6 a. m., when it cleared off for a short time ; afterward a heavy rain succeeded, which lasted until twelve o'clock, when it cleared off for an hour, and again became cloudy.   Rain has been pretty generally falling since the 7th inst.

Nov. 15.   The after part of this day is fair and calm, for the first time since the 12th inst.; no rain.

Nov. 20.   Rained moderately from 6 a. m. until 1 p. m. on the 21st, after which it became cloudy without rain.

Nov. 22.   The wind violent from the S.S.E., throwing the water of the river over our camp, and rain continued all day.

Nov. 26.   Rained all day ; some hard showers ; wind not so hard as it has been for a few days past ; some rain on the morning of the 23d and night of the 24th inst.

Nov. 27.   Rained moderately all day ; a hard wind from the southwest, which compelled us to lie-by on the isthmus of Point William on the south side.

Nov. 28.   The wind, which was from the southwest, shifted in the after part of the day to the northwest, and blew a storm which was tremendous ; it rained all the last night and to-day without intermission.

Nov. 29.   Rained all last night hard, and to-day moderately.

Nov. 30.   Rained and hailed at intervals throughout last night ; some thunder and lightning.

Dec. 3.   Fair from 12 to 2 p. m.; rained all the last night and this morning ; rained the night of the 1st and the morning of the 2d, and cloudy the remainder

---

[3] We have the remarks belonging to the Weather Diary for the remainder of August and the whole of September and October, but they are very brief, and hardly justify interpolation in the text. At next date, Nov. 3, the Expedition is approaching the mouth of the Columbia.

of the day ; rained at intervals the night of the 2d inst., with constant, hard, and sometimes violent winds.

(*p. 510*) *Dec.* 5. Rained yesterday, last night, and moderately to-day ; all day the wind violent.

Dec. 6. Rained all last night and to-day until six o'clock, at which time it cleared away and became fair ; the wind also ceased to blow violently.

Dec. 7. Rained from 10 to 12 last night ; fair day ; a hard wind from the northwest, and a shower of rain at 2 p. m.

Dec. 10. Rained all day ; the air cool ; I returned from the ocean ; a violent wind last night from the southwest ; rained the greater part of the night of the 8th and all day the 9th inst.

Dec. 15. Rained at short intervals from the 10th inst. until 8 a. m. to-day.

Dec. 16. Rained all the last night ; cold wind violent from the southwest, accompanied with rain.

Dec. 17. Rained all the last night and this morning until 9 o'clock, when we had a shower of hail, which lasted about an hour and then cleared off.

Dec. 18. Rained, snowed, and hailed at intervals all last night ; several showers of hail and snow until meridian [noon].

Dec. 19. Rained last night, and several showers of hail and rain this evening ; the air cool.

Dec. 20. Some hail and rain last night ; rain continued until 10 a. m.

Dec. 23. Rained all last night and moderately all to-day, with several showers of hail, accompanied with hard claps of thunder ; rained 21st and 22d all day and night.

Dec. 25. Rained at intervals last night and to-day. Snake seen.

Dec. 26. Rained and blew hard all last night and to-day ; some hard claps of thunder and sharp lightning.

Dec. 29. Rained moderately without much intermission from the 26th until 7 a. m. this morning ; hard wind from southeast.

Dec. 30. Hard wind and some rain last night ; to-day tolerably fair.

Dec. 31. Rained last night and all this day.

(*p. 511*) *Jan.* 1, 1806. The changes of the weather are exceedingly sudden ; sometimes, though seldom, the sun is visible for a few moments, the next it hails and rains, then ceases and remains cloudy ; the wind blows and it again rains ; the wind blows by squalls generally, and is almost invariably from the south-west ; these vicissitudes of the weather happen two, three, or more times in half a day.

Jan. 3. The thunder and lightning of last evening were violent, a singular occurrence for the time of year. The loss of my thermometer I most sincerely regret. I am confident that the climate here is much warmer than in the same parallel of latitude on the Atlantic ocean, though how many degrees it is now out of my power to determine. Since our arrival in this neighborhood on Nov. 7th, we have experienced one slight white frost only, which happened on the morning of Nov. 16th ; we have seen no ice, and the weather is so warm that we are obliged to cure our meat with smoke and fire to save it ; we lost two parcels by depending on the air to preserve it, though it was cut in very thin slices and sufficiently exposed.

Jan. 10.   Various flies and [other] insects now alive and in motion.

Jan. 12.   The wind from any quarter off the land or along the northwest coast causes the air to become much cooler ; every species of water-fowl common to this country, at any season of the year, continues with us.

Jan. 14.   Weather perfectly temperate ; I never experienced a winter so warm as the present has been.

Jan. 23.   When the sun is said to shine, or the weather to be fair, it is to be understood that the sun barely casts a shadow, and that the atmosphere is hazy, of a milky-white color.

(*p. 512*) *Jan.* 25.   It is now perceptibly colder than it has been this winter.

Jan. 26.   The snow this evening is 4½ inches deep ; the icicles continue suspended from the eaves of the houses during the day ; it now appears something like winter, for the first time this season.

Jan. 27.   The sun shone more brightly this morning than it has done since our arrival at this place ; the snow since 4 p. m. yesterday has increased to the depth of 6 inches, and this morning is perceptibly the coldest that we have had. I suspect the mercury would stand at 20° above zero ; the breath is perceptible in our room by the fire.

Jan. 28.   Last night exposed a vessel of water to the air, with a view to discover the depth to which it would freeze in the course of the night, but unfortunately the vessel was only two inches deep, and it friezed [froze] the whole thickness ; how much more it might have frozen had the vessel been deeper is therefore out of my power to decide ; it is the coldest night we have had, and I suppose the mercury this morning would have stood as low as 15° above zero.

Jan. 31.   Notwithstanding the cold weather, the swan, white brant, geese, and ducks still continue with us ; the sand-hill crane also continues ; the brown or speckled brant are mostly gone, though some few are still to be seen ; the cormorant and a variety of other water-fowls still remain.   The winds from the land bring us cold and clear weather, while those obliquely along either coast or off the ocean brings us warm, damp, cloudy, and rainy weather ; the hardest winds are always from the southwest.   The blue-crested corvus [*Cyanocitta stelleri*] has already begun to build its nest ; the nest is formed of small sticks, usually in a pine-tree.

(*p. 513*) *Feb.* 3.   The rain, which fell in the latter part of the night, froze, and made a slight incrustation on the snow, which fell some days past, and also on the boughs of the trees ; yesterday it continued fair until 11 a. m., when the wind veered about to southwest, and the horizon was immediately overcast with clouds, as uniformly takes place when the wind is from that point.

Feb. 4.   All the water-fowls before enumerated continue with us ; the birds [*Hesperocichla nævia*] which resemble the robin have visited us in small numbers ; saw two of them yesterday about the fort ; they are gentle.

Feb. 8.   The rain of last night has melted down the snow, which has continued to cover the ground since Jan. 24th ; the feeling of the air and other appearances seem to indicate that the rigor of winter has passed ; it is so warm that we are apprehensive our meat will spoil, we therefore cut it in small pieces and hang it separately on sticks. Saw a number of insects flying about. The small brown flycatcher continues with us; this is the smallest of all American birds except the humming-bird.

Feb. 15. The robin has returned and is singing, which reminds us of spring; some other small birds passed on their flight from the south, but were so high that we could not distinguish of what kind they were; the robin had left this place before our arrival in November.

Feb. 16. At 11 a. m. it became fair, and the insects were flying about; at half-past 12 o'clock it clouded up and began to rain.

Feb. 24. Much warmer this morning than usual; aquatic and other birds heretofore enumerated continue with us still; the sturgeon and a small fish like the anchovy begin to run; they are taken (*p. 514*) in the Columbia about 40 miles above us; the anchovy is exquisitely fine.

Feb. 28. Saw a variety of insects in motion this morning, some small bugs as well as flies; a brown fly with long legs, about half the size of the common house-fly, was the most numerous; this is the first insect that has appeared; it is generally about the sinks or filth of any kind; the yellow and brown fly-catcher has returned; it is a very small bird with a tail as long proportionally as a sparrow.

Mar. 1. A great part of this day was so warm that fire was unnecessary, notwithstanding its being cloudy and raining.

Mar. 6. Saw a spider this morning, though the air is perceptibly colder than it has been since the 1st instant. At 9 a. m. it clouded up and continued so the remainder of the day; even the easterly winds, which have heretofore given us the only fair weather which we have enjoyed, seem now to have lost their influence in this respect.

Mar. 7. The elk now begin to shed their horns. A bird of a scarlet color, as large as a common pheasant, and with a long tail, has returned; one of them was seen to-day near the fort by Captain Clark's black man; I could not obtain a view of it.[4]

Mar. 11. It became cloudy at 10 a. m. and rained, attended with some hail; at 6 p. m. it became fair, and the wind changing to northeast, it continued fair during the night; the snow had all disappeared by 4 p. m. this evening.

Mar. 12. It was fair in the morning, but became cloudy at 3 p. m. and continued so during the day.

Mar. 13. Saw a number of insects in motion; among others saw, for the first time this spring and winter, a downy black fly about the size of the common house-fly. The plants begin to appear above the ground; among others the rush, of which the (*p. 515*) natives eat the root, which resembles in flavor the sweet potato.

Mar. 15. The sorrel, with an oval, obtuse, ternate leaf, has now put forth its leaves; some of them have already nearly obtained their growth; the

---

[4] Some mistake here, though the text agrees with the codex, Lewis J 146. No bird of any such description exists in North America. See note [31], p. 159.

birds were singing very agreeably this morning, particularly the common robin.

Mar. 16. The anchovy has ceased to run ; the white salmon-trout have succeeded them ; the weather is so warm that insects of various species are every day in motion.

Mar. 22.[5] The leaves and petals of the flower of the green huckleberry have appeared ; some of the leaves have already obtained one-fourth of their size.

Mar. 24. The brown briery shrub with a broad pinnate leaf has begun to put forth its leaves ; the polecat calwort [kalewort—the skunk cabbage, *Symplocarpus foetidus ?*] is in bloom ; saw the blue-crested fisher [*Ceryle alcyon*] ; birds are singing this morning ; the black alder is in bloom.

Mar. 25. The elder, gooseberry, and honeysuckle are now putting forth their leaves : the nettle and a variety of other plants are springing up ; the flowers of the broad-leaved thorn are nearly blown ; several small plants in bloom.

Mar. 26. The humming-bird has appeared ; killed one of them and found it [to be not] the same with those common to the United States.[6]

Mar. 27. The small or bank martin [*Clivicola riparia*] appeared to-day ; saw one large flock of them ; water-fowl are very scarce ; a few cormorants, geese, and the red-headed fishing-duck [*Mergus serrator*] are all that are to be seen. The red flowering currant is in bloom ; this I take to be the same species I first saw on the Rocky mountains ; the fruit is a deep purple berry, covered with a gummy substance and not agreeably flavored. There is another species, not covered with gum, which I first found on the headwaters of the Columbia, about the 12th of August last.

(*p. 516*) *Mar*. 28. This evening we saw many swan passing to the north as if on a long flight ; vegetation is not by several days as forward here as [it was] at Fort Clatsop when we left that place ; the river is rising fast ; the water is turbid ; the tide only swells the water a little, but does not stop the current ; it is now within two feet of its greatest height.

Mar. 30. The grass is about 16 inches high in the river bottoms ; the frogs are now abundant.

Apr. 1. From the best opinion I could form of the state of the Columbia on the 1st of April, it was about nine feet higher than when we descended it in the beginning of November last.

Apr. 6. The cottonwood has put forth its leaves and begins to assume a green appearance at a distance ; the sweet-willow has not yet burst its buds, while the leaves of the red and the broad-leaved willow are of some size ; it appears to me to be the most backward in vegetating of all the willows ; the narrow-leaved willow is not found below tide water on this river.

Apr. 8. The male flowers of the cottonwood are falling ; the gooseberry has cast the petals of its flowers, and its leaves have obtained their full size ; the elder, which is remarkably large, has begun to bloom ; some of its flowerets

---

[5] Mar. 23d the party started back up the Columbia.

[6] The humming-bird of the " United States " [*Trochilus colubris*] does not occur on the Pacific coast. The species observed was probably *Selasphorus rufus*.

have expanded their corollas; service-berries, choke-berries, the growth which resembles the beech, the small birch and gray willow have put forth their leaves.

Apr. 9.   The vining [twining] honeysuckle has put forth shoots of several inches; the dog-toothed violet is in bloom, as is also both species of mountain-holly, the strawberry, the bear's-claw, the cowslip, the violet, common striped [so Lewis K 151], and the wild cress or tongue-grass.

Apr. 11.   The geese are in large flocks and do not yet appear to have mated ; what I have heretofore termed the broad-leaved ash is now in bloom ; (*p. 517*) the fringe-tree has cast the corolla and its leaves have nearly obtained their full size ; the sacacommis is in bloom.

Apr. 12.   The duckinmallard [*Anas boscas*], which breeds in the neighborhood, is now laying eggs ; vegetation is rapidly progressing in the bottoms, though the snow of yesterday and to-day reaches within a mile of the base of the mountains at the rapids of the Columbia.

Apr. 16.   At Rock-fort camp saw the prairie-lark, a species of the peaweet, the blue-crested fisher [*Ceryle alcyon*], the party-colored corvus [magpie], and the black pheasant ; a species of hyacinth, a native of this place, bloomed to-day ; it was not in bloom yesterday.

Apr. 26.   The last evening was cloudy; it continued to threaten rain all night, but without raining ; the wind blew hard all night ; the air was cold, as it is invariably when it sets from the westerly quarter.

May 1.   Having left the river we could no longer observe its state ; it is now declining, though it has not been as high this season by five feet as it appears to have been the last spring ; the Indians inform us that it will rise higher in this month, which I presume is caused by the snows of the mountains.

May 3.   The mountains on our right seem to have had an increase of snow last evening.

May 10.   It began to rain and hail about sunset, shortly after succeeded by snow, which continued to fall without intermission until 7 a. m., and lay eight inches deep on the plain where we were ; the air was very keen.   A sudden transition this day ; yesterday the face of the country had every appearance of summer ; after 9 a. m. the sun shone, but was frequently obscured by clouds which gave us light showers of snow ; in the after part of the day the snow melted considerably, but there was too great a (*p. 518*) portion to be dissipated by the influence of one day's sun.

May 11.[7]   The crimson haw is not more forward now at this place than it was when we lay at Rock-fort camp in April.

May 20.   A nest of the large blue or sand-hill crane [*Grus canadensis*] was found by one of our hunters ; the young were in the act of leaving the shell ; the young of the party-colored corvus begin to fly.

May 22.   The air is remarkably dry and pure ; it has much the feeling and appearance of the air on the plains of the Missouri ; since our arrival in this neighborhood on the 7th inst. all the rains noted in the diary of the weather were snows on the plain, and in some instances it snowed on the plains when only a small mist was perceptible in the bottoms at our camp.

[7] The station is Camp Chopunnish, May 14th-June 10th.

May 27.   The dove [*Zenaidura carolinensis*] is cooing, which is the signal, as the Indians inform us, of the approach of the salmon.   The snow has disappeared on the high plains, and seems to be diminishing fast on the spurs and lower regions of the Rocky mountains.

May 28.   The river from sunrise yesterday to sunrise this morning rose 22 inches ; drift-wood is running in considerable quantities, and the current is incredibly swift, though smooth.

May 29.   The river rose 6 inches in the course of yesterday, and 17 inches in the course of last night ; it is now as high as there are any marks of its having been in the spring of 1805 ; at 10 a. m. it arrived at its greatest height, having risen 1½ inches from sunrise to that time ; in the balance of the day it fell 7 inches.   The natives inform us that it will take one more rise before it begins to subside for the season, and then the passage of the mountains will be practicable.

May 30.   The river continued to fall until 4 a. m., having fallen 3 inches by that time since sunrise ; (*p. 519*) it was now at a stand until dark ; after which it began again to rise.

June 2.   The river from sunrise until 10 a. m. yesterday rose 1½ inches, from that time until dark fell 4½ inches, and in the course of last night rose again 8 inches ; the Indians inform us that the present rise is the greatest which it annually takes ; that when the water subsides to about the height it was at the time we arrived here the mountains will be passable.   I have no doubt that the melting of the mountain snows in the beginning of June is what causes the annual inundation of the lower portion of the Missouri from the 1st to the middle of July.

June 4.   Yesterday the water was at its greatest height at noon ; between that time and dark it fell 15 inches, and in the course of the night rose 1½ inches ; from Indian information the water will now subside, and may therefore be said to be at its greatest annual height on the 3d inst. at noon.

June 5.   The river fell 3½ inches in the course of the day ; this fluctuating state of the river is no doubt caused by the influence of the sun in the course of the day on the snows on the mountains ; the accession of water thus caused in the day does not reach us until night, when it produces a rise in the river. The river fell 10 inches in the course of this day.   The wild rose is in bloom.

June 6.   In the course of last night the river rose a little, but fell an inch by morning lower than it was last evening ; the seven-bark and yellow vining honeysuckle are just in bloom ; a few of the does have produced their young.

June 7.   The river fell 3 inches last night and 7 yesterday ; the gooseberry is fully grown ; also the service-berry.

(*p. 520*) *June* 10.   The river fell 1 inch last night and 5½ yesterday ; it appears to be falling fast, and in the course of a few days will be as low as it was when we first arrived here ; it is now about six feet lower than it has been.

June 16.   On the top of the hills the dog-toothed violet is just in bloom ; grass is about two inches high ; small huckleberry is just putting forth its leaves.

June 22.   Strawberries are ripe at the Quamash flats ; they are but small and not abundant.

June 29. The quamash and strawberries are just beginning to bloom at the flats on the head of the Kooskooskee river. The sunflower is also just beginning to bloom, two months later than those on the sides of the western mountains near the falls of the Columbia.

July 5.[8] A dew this morning; the nights are cool; the mosquitoes are troublesome until a little after dark, when the air becomes cool, and they disappear.

July 6. I arrived in an open plain in the middle of which a violent wind from the northwest, accompanied with hard rain, lasted from 4 until 5.30 p. m. Quamash in the plains at the head of Wisdom river is just beginning to bloom, and the grass is about six inches high.

July 7. A small shower of rain at 4 a. m. was accompanied with wind from the S.S.W.

July 8. A heavy shower of rain was accompanied with wind from the southwest from 4 to 5 p. m.

July 9. Last night it was very cold and the wind hard from the northeast; the river is twelve inches higher than it was last summer; there is more snow on the adjacent mountains than there was at that time.

July 10. A large white frost last night; the air extremely cold; ice three-quarters of an inch thick on standing water.

(*p. 521*) *July* 11. A slight frost last night; the air cool; the mosquitoes retired a little after dark, and did not return until about an hour after sunrise.

July 17. A heavy shower of rain, accompanied with hail, thunder, and lightning, at 2 a. m., with hard wind from the southwest; after the shower was over it cleared away and became fair.

July 20. The river Rochejhone [*sic*—Roche-jaune] falls about half an inch in 24 hours, and becomes much clearer than above. Grasshoppers [*Caloptenus spretus*] are extremely numerous, and have destroyed every species of grass from 1 to 10 miles above on the river and a great distance back.

July 22. A few drops of rain last night at dark; the cloud appeared to hang to the southwest; wind blew hard from different points from 5 to 8 p. m., at which time it thundered and lightened. The river by 11 a. m. to-day had risen 15 inches, and the water was of a milky-white color.

July 23. The river has fallen within the last 24 hours 7 inches; the wind was violent from the southwest for about 3 hours last night, from 1 to 3 a. m. [so Clark M 147].

July 24. River falling a little; it is six feet lower than the highest appearance of its rise; rained from 3 to 4 p. m. but slightly; the wind violent from the southwest.

July 25. Several showers of rain with hard wind from the south and southwest the fore part of the day. The brooks on each side are high and the water muddy.

July 26. A slight shower this morning with hard wind from the southwest. The river falling but very slowly, 1 inch in 24 hours.

---

[8] The remarks apply to the main party under Captain Clark, from this date till Aug. 12th.

July 28.   A few drops of rain a little before daylight.   River still falling **a** little.

(*p. 522*) *July* 29.   A few drops of rain accompanied with hard peals of thunder and sharp lightning last night ; wind hard from the northeast.

July 30.   A slight shower of rain accompanied with thunder and lightning ; several showers in the course of this day ; it cleared away in the evening and became fair.   River falling a little.   Great quantities of coal in the bluffs on either side.

July 31.   The wind blew hard and it was showery all day, though there was not much rain ; the clouds came up from the west and northwest frequently in the course of the day.

Aug. 22.[9]   The rains which have fallen this month are most commonly from flying clouds which pass in different directions ; these clouds are always accompanied with hard winds, and sometimes with thunder and lightning.   The river has been falling moderately since the 3d of the month ; the rains have made no other impression on the river than causing it to be more muddy, and probably preventing its falling fast.

[9] *Sept.* 1.   A thick fog until 8 A.M. a fiew drops of rain about 1 P.M.

Sept. 2.   Hard wind all day.   Saw the prarie fowl common in the Illinois plains.   Saw Linn [linden] and slipery elm.

Sept. 3.   A stiff breeze from S.E. untill 12 at night when it changed to S.W. and blew hard all night.

Sept. 5.   At 6 P.M. a violent storm of Thunder Lightning and rain untill 10 P.M. when it ceased to rain and blew hard from N.W. untill 3 A.M.

Sept. 6.   Heard the whipperwill common to the UStates at Soldiers river.

Sept. 7.   Saw the whiperwill and heard the common hooting owl Musquetoes very troublesom. killed 3 Elk.

Sept. 8.   Wormest day we have experienced in this year.   Passed River Platt.

Sept. 11.   A fiew drops of rain only a little before day, and some rain at 2 P.M.

Sept. 12.   Heavy dew this morning and fog.   Some rain from 12 to 4 P.M.

Sept. 15.   Day very worm smokey and worm.

Sept. 16.   This day very sultry and much the hottest we have experenced.

Sept. 17.   Day worm, but fiew musquetoes.

Sept. 19.   Saw a green snake as high up as Salt River on the Missouri.   The limestone bluffs commences below Salt river on S. side.

Sept. 21.   A slight shower of rain a little before day light this morning.

Sept. 22.   At St. Charles the raine commenced about 9 P.M. and was moderate untill 4 A.M. when when it increased and rained without intermition untill 10 A.M : Some Thunder and lightning about day light.   it continud cloudy with small showers of rain all day.   We arived at the Mississippi.

Sept. 23.   At St. Louis several light showers in the course of this day.   We arived at St. Louis at 12 oClock.

Sept. 24.   Rained moderately this morning and continud cloudy with moderate rain at intervals all day.

Sept. 26.   Fair and worm.

Sept. 27.   Emencely worm.

Sept. 28.   Do.

Sept. 29.   Do.

Sept. 30.   Do.—Clark N 151, 152.

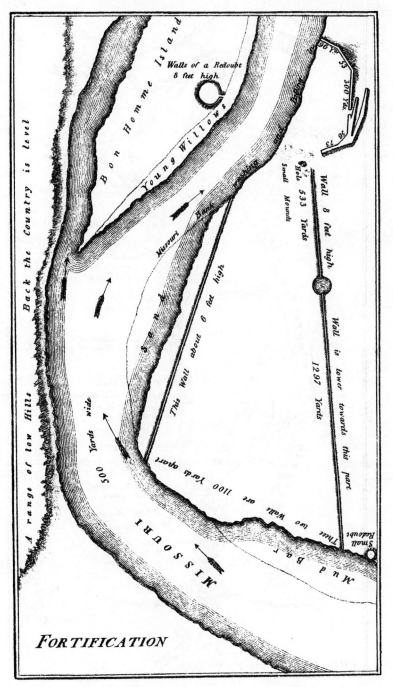

ANCIENT FORTIFICATION ON THE MISSOURI RIVER,
OPPOSITE BONHOMME ISLAND

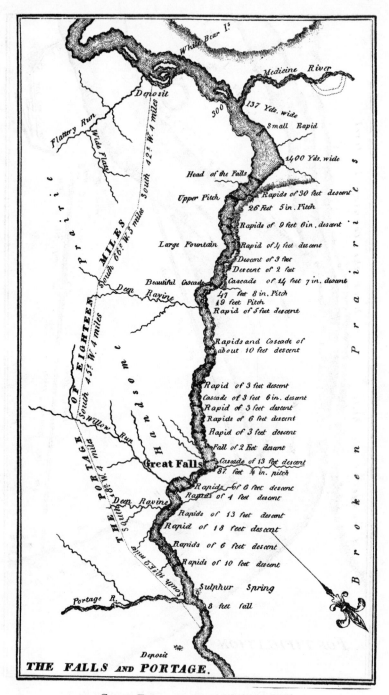

GREAT FALLS OF THE MISSOURI RIVER

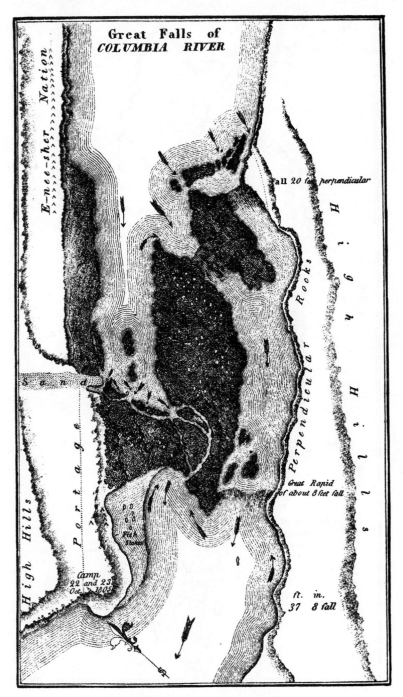

GREAT FALLS OF THE COLUMBIA RIVER

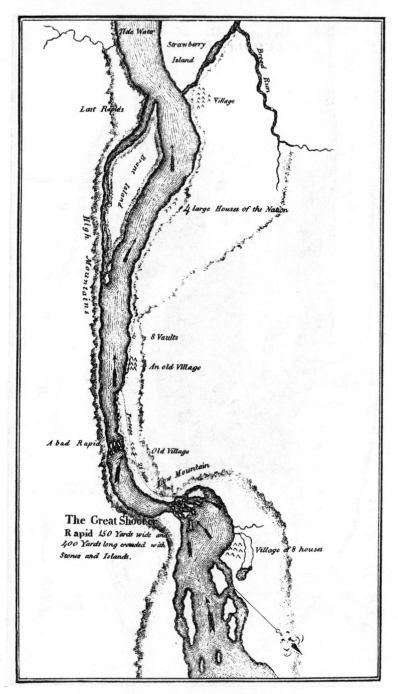

GREAT SHOOT OR RAPIDS OF THE COLUMBIA RIVER

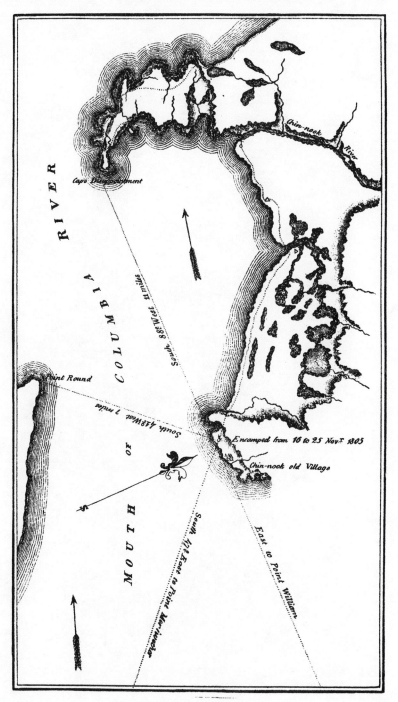

MOUTH OF THE COLUMBIA RIVER

INDEX.

N. B.—This index covers *all* the matter of the three preceding volumes, introductory and appendicial, as well as main text and notes thereto. It is mainly an index of *names*, proper and common, without analysis of what comes under them. All proper names are intended to be indexed, except a few which recur incessantly in the main text and notes, as Lewis, Clark, the Missouri, etc., and a few others of no pointed implication, as Dakota, Montana, Indians, etc., or of mere allusion. Of common names the list is pretty full, though it is exclusive, as a rule, of mere mention, and of incessantly recurring words. Proper names are distinguished from common by capitalization, the same as if they occurred in ordinary sentences. Personal proper names are of course entered by surnames ; as, Smith, John. Names of Indian families and tribes are in the singular number, and not followed by "Inds.," except in distinguishing such from places, etc., of same name. Place-names which are phrases are entered as usually spoken and written ; thus, Camp Chopunnish, Fort Clatsop, but Chopunnish r., Clatsop co., etc. Cross-references are made only in special cases. Variant spellings of proper names are entered, as Arikara, Ricara, both of which require to be looked up to find out all that is given in such cases. The mode of alphabetizing is by taking an entry-word and finishing with phrases under it, when any, before proceeding to its compounds : thus, Cow cr., Cow isl., cowas, cowbane, cow-beetle—not cowas, Cow cr., cowbane, cow-beetle, Cow isl. This introduces a logical element at slight infraction of the alphabet, and the nature of the matter to be indexed seemed to call for such method. Some abbreviations are used ; these are chiefly : br., branch ; co., county ; cr., creek ; fk., fork ; Inds., Indians; isl., island ; ldg., landing ; mt., mts., mountain, mountains ; pra., prairie ; rap., rapid or rapids ; res., (Indian) reservation ; r., river ; spr., spring or springs ; sta., station. Roman numerals all refer to Vol. I.; the unbroken pagination of the rest of the work renders reference by Vol. needless in case of the arabic figures.

A

abalone, 522, 565, 1016
Abbott, Mont., 1093
Abies, 832
    grandis, 749, 831
    nobilis, 829
    subalpina, 425
Abnaki, 148
Absaroka, Absaroke, Absaruque, 198, 1155
acalephs, 898
account current, xci
Acer circinatum, 834
    glabrum, 487
    macrophyllum, 679, 834, 908, 911
Acipenser, 808
    transmontanus, 716, 791, 896

Acorus calamus, 49
Actea spicata arguta, 488
Actitis macularia, 877
Acts of Congress, xxxiv, xxxv, xxxviii, lxxv, cxi
    Tennessee Legislature, lvii, lviii
Ada co., Idaho, 1254
Ada, Mont., 1158
Adams co., Wash., 630
Adams, John Q., lxxv
Adam's needle, 543
adder, 435, 833
Addresses, etc., of Presidents, xx, cviii, and see Messages
Æchmophorus, 888
    occidentalis, 882
Ægialites vociferus, 966, 968, 1287
Æsculus nigra, 38

1299

Garrison Mr. W. P., ix
Garrow, Mr., 245
garter-snake, 437, 697, 898, 899, 912, 915, 1283
Gasconade co., 9
    r., 9, 1211, 1257
Gaskenade, see Gasconade
Gass, Mrs. P., cv
    Sergeant P., xiii, cxvii, 3, 4, 5, 7, 8, 10, 11, etc.; 188, 189, 254, 452, 1064, 1084, 1085, 1107, etc.; his Journal cited throughout ; he lost one eye at battle of Lundy's Lane, which he always thought to be a lucky accident, as it gave him a pension of $8 a month as long as he lived
        Journal, lxxxvi, xciv, cxvii, cxviii, cxix, cxx, cxxi, cxxii
        Life and Times of, cxxiii
        Memoir of, xcix, cviii
Gass' cr., 438
Gate of Hell, 1071
Gates of Rocky mts., 425, 426, 439
Gatlanakoaiq, 931
Gatlapotlh, 914
Gatschet, Mr. A. S., 55, 57, 58, 606, 759, 760, 774
Gaultheria procumbens, 731, 825
    shallon, 731, 739, 791, 798, 825, 1259
Gayarré, 821
Geomys bursarius, 263
    tuza, 263, 994
geese, see goose
Geesem, Mr. R., 1178, see Jess-
gelding horses, 1012
Genesis cited, 986
gensang, 999
George's sound, 713
Georges, one of Thackeray's four, 728
General Assembly of Tennessee, lvii, lviii, lix, lxi
Gens de Canoe, 193
    de Corbeaux, 198
    de Panse, 199
    des Feuilles, 193
    des Serpens, 554
    des Souliers, 183, 198
    des Vaches, 57
    du Grand Diable, 193
    du Lac, 102
Gerald, Mr. David Fitz, ix
German edition of the History, cxxvii
Germantown, Pa., lxiv
Ghent, Treaty of, 728
Ghost cr., 574
giant white pine, 832

Gibbon, Gen. John, x, 1123, 1151
Gibbon's pass, 551, 1123
Gibbonsville, 578, 1123
Gibbs, Mr. Geo., 760, 858, 861, 915
Gibson, Geo., *passim* and 83, 255, 649, 803, 804, 1139, 1141, 1142
Gibson's cr. or r., 309, 1163, 1164, 1259
Gibson's pass, see Gibbon's pass
Gibsonville, see Gibbonsville
Gill, Dr. Theo., ix, 854
ginseng, 1000
Girard, Dr. Chas., 891, 895, 900, see Baird and
girasole, 264
Girdle mts., 439
Gird's cr., 587
Gitlapeleks, 1070
Glade cr., Idaho, 594, 595, 596, 1059, 1063, 1260
    cr., Mont., 1122, 1123, 1124
glade on Fish cr., 1261
    on Hungry cr., 1261
Glasgow, 301
Glasgow, E. A., lxvii
    M. S., lxvii
    Wm., lxvii
glass beads, 245
Glauber's salts, 268
Glendale, 498
Glendive, 1164
    butte, 1164
    cr., 1164, 1165
Glover isl., 641
Glycyrrhiza echinata, 824
    glabra, 739, 824
    lepidota, 302, 711, 739, 824
goat, see antelope
goat, see bighorn
goat, 678, 850, 941, 946, and see Haplocerus
Goat cr., 108
Goat-pen cr., 274, 1117, 1174, 1259
goatsucker, 398
God's Acre, lxii
Goforth, Dr. Wm., xxv
golden eagle, 173, 879, and see eagle
Goldsmith's Animated Nature, 327
golondrina, 239
Goniobasis, 896
gonorrhœa, 780
Good Hope isl., 153
Good Man's isl., 102, 1258
    r., Mo., 7
    r., S. D., 147
    Woman's r., 17, 1257
Goode, Prof. G. Brown, ix
Good-humored isl., 131

THE END.

A CATALOGUE OF SELECTED DOVER
BOOKS IN ALL FIELDS OF INTEREST

RACKHAM'S COLOR ILLUSTRATIONS FOR WAGNER'S RING. Rackham's finest mature work—all 64 full-color watercolors in a faithful and lush interpretation of the *Ring*. Full-sized plates on coated stock of the paintings used by opera companies for authentic staging of Wagner. Captions aid in following complete Ring cycle. Introduction. 64 illustrations plus vignettes. 72pp. 8⅝ x 11¼.   23779-6 Pa. $6.00

CONTEMPORARY POLISH POSTERS IN FULL COLOR, edited by Joseph Czestochowski. 46 full-color examples of brilliant school of Polish graphic design, selected from world's first museum (near Warsaw) dedicated to poster art. Posters on circuses, films, plays, concerts all show cosmopolitan influences, free imagination. Introduction. 48pp. 9⅜ x 12¼.
23780-X Pa. $6.00

GRAPHIC WORKS OF EDVARD MUNCH, Edvard Munch. 90 haunting, evocative prints by first major Expressionist artist and one of the greatest graphic artists of his time: *The Scream, Anxiety, Death Chamber, The Kiss, Madonna,* etc. Introduction by Alfred Werner. 90pp. 9 x 12.
23765-6 Pa. $5.00

THE GOLDEN AGE OF THE POSTER, Hayward and Blanche Cirker. 70 extraordinary posters in full colors, from Maitres de l'Affiche, Mucha, Lautrec, Bradley, Cheret, Beardsley, many others. Total of 78pp. 9⅜ x 12¼.   22753-7 Pa. $5.95

THE NOTEBOOKS OF LEONARDO DA VINCI, edited by J. P. Richter. Extracts from manuscripts reveal great genius; on painting, sculpture, anatomy, sciences, geography, etc. Both Italian and English. 186 ms. pages reproduced, plus 500 additional drawings, including studies for *Last Supper,* Sforza monument, etc. 860pp. 7⅞ x 10¾. (Available in U.S. only)
22572-0, 22573-9 Pa., Two-vol. set $15.90

THE CODEX NUTTALL, as first edited by Zelia Nuttall. Only inexpensive edition, in full color, of a pre-Columbian Mexican (Mixtec) book. 88 color plates show kings, gods, heroes, temples, sacrifices. New explanatory, historical introduction by Arthur G. Miller. 96pp. 11⅜ x 8½. (Available in U.S. only)   23168-2 Pa. $7.95

UNE SEMAINE DE BONTÉ, A SURREALISTIC NOVEL IN COLLAGE, Max Ernst. Masterpiece created out of 19th-century periodical illustrations, explores worlds of terror and surprise. Some consider this Ernst's greatest work. 208pp. 8⅛ x 11.   23252-2 Pa. $6.00

THE AMERICAN SENATOR, Anthony Trollope. Little known, long un-available Trollope novel on a grand scale. Here are humorous comment on American vs. English culture, and stunning portrayal of a heroine/villainess. Superb evocation of Victorian village life. 561pp. 5⅜ x 8½.
23801-6 Pa. $6.00

WAS IT MURDER? James Hilton. The author of Lost Horizon and Good-bye, Mr. Chips wrote one detective novel (under a pen-name) which was quickly forgotten and virtually lost, even at the height of Hilton's fame. This edition brings it back—a finely crafted public school puzzle resplendent with Hilton's stylish atmosphere. A thoroughly English thriller by the creator of Shangri-la. 252pp. 5⅜ x 8. (Available in U.S. only)
23774-5 Pa. $3.00

CENTRAL PARK: A PHOTOGRAPHIC GUIDE, Victor Laredo and Henry Hope Reed. 121 superb photographs show dramatic views of Central Park: Bethesda Fountain, Cleopatra's Needle, Sheep Meadow, the Blockhouse, plus people engaged in many park activities: ice skating, bike riding, etc. Captions by former Curator of Central Park, Henry Hope Reed, provide historical view, changes, etc. Also photos of N.Y. landmarks on park's periphery. 96pp. 8½ x 11.
23750-8 Pa. $4.50

NANTUCKET IN THE NINETEENTH CENTURY, Clay Lancaster. 180 rare photographs, stereographs, maps, drawings and floor plans recreate unique American island society. Authentic scenes of shipwreck, light-houses, streets, homes are arranged in geographic sequence to provide walking-tour guide to old Nantucket existing today. Introduction, captions. 160pp. 8⅞ x 11¾.
23747-8 Pa. $6.95

STONE AND MAN: A PHOTOGRAPHIC EXPLORATION, Andreas Feininger. 106 photographs by Life photographer Feininger portray man's deep passion for stone through the ages. Stonehenge-like megaliths, forti-fied towns, sculpted marble and crumbling tenements show textures, beau-ties, fascination. 128pp. 9¼ x 10¾.
23756-7 Pa. $5.95

CIRCLES, A MATHEMATICAL VIEW, D. Pedoe. Fundamental aspects of college geometry, non-Euclidean geometry, and other branches of mathe-matics: representing circle by point. Poincare model, isoperimetric prop-erty, etc. Stimulating recreational reading. 66 figures. 96pp. 5⅝ x 8¼.
63698-4 Pa. $2.75

THE DISCOVERY OF NEPTUNE, Morton Grosser. Dramatic scientific history of the investigations leading up to the actual discovery of the eighth planet of our solar system. Lucid, well-researched book by well-known historian of science. 172pp. 5⅜ x 8½.
23726-5 Pa. $3.50

THE DEVIL'S DICTIONARY. Ambrose Bierce. Barbed, bitter, brilliant witticisms in the form of a dictionary. Best, most ferocious satire America has produced. 145pp. 5⅜ x 8½.
20487-1 Pa. $2.25

"OSCAR" OF THE WALDORF'S COOKBOOK, Oscar Tschirky. Famous American chef reveals 3455 recipes that made Waldorf great; cream of French, German, American cooking, in all categories. Full instructions, easy home use. 1896 edition. 907pp. 6⅝ x 9⅜.   20790-0 Clothbd. $15.00

COOKING WITH BEER, Carole Fahy. Beer has as superb an effect on food as wine, and at fraction of cost. Over 250 recipes for appetizers, soups, main dishes, desserts, breads, etc. Index. 144pp. 5⅜ x 8½. (Available in U.S. only)
     23661-7 Pa. $2.50

STEWS AND RAGOUTS, Kay Shaw Nelson. This international cookbook offers wide range of 108 recipes perfect for everyday, special occasions, meals-in-themselves, main dishes. Economical, nutritious, easy-to-prepare: goulash, Irish stew, boeuf bourguignon, etc. Index. 134pp. 5⅜ x 8½.
     23662-5 Pa. $2.50

DELICIOUS MAIN COURSE DISHES, Marian Tracy. Main courses are the most important part of any meal. These 200 nutritious, economical recipes from around the world make every meal a delight. "I . . . have found it so useful in my own household,"—N.Y. Times. Index. 219pp. 5⅜ x 8½.
     23664-1 Pa. $3.00

FIVE ACRES AND INDEPENDENCE, Maurice G. Kains. Great back-to-the-land classic explains basics of self-sufficient farming: economics, plants, crops, animals, orchards, soils, land selection, host of other necessary things. Do not confuse with skimpy faddist literature; Kains was one of America's greatest agriculturalists. 95 illustrations. 397pp. 5⅜ x 8½.
     20974-1 Pa. $3.95

A PRACTICAL GUIDE FOR THE BEGINNING FARMER, Herbert Jacobs. Basic, extremely useful first book for anyone thinking about moving to the country and starting a farm. Simpler than Kains, with greater emphasis on country living in general. 246pp. 5⅜ x 8½.
     23675-7 Pa. $3.50

PAPERMAKING, Dard Hunter. Definitive book on the subject by the foremost authority in the field. Chapters dealing with every aspect of history of craft in every part of the world. Over 320 illustrations. 2nd, revised and enlarged (1947) edition. 672pp. 5⅜ x 8½.   23619-6 Pa. $7.95

THE ART DECO STYLE, edited by Theodore Menten. Furniture, jewelry, metalwork, ceramics, fabrics, lighting fixtures, interior decors, exteriors, graphics from pure French sources. Best sampling around. Over 400 photographs. 183pp. 8⅜ x 11¼.   22824-X Pa. $6.00

ACKERMANN'S COSTUME PLATES, Rudolph Ackermann. Selection of 96 plates from the Repository of Arts, best published source of costume for English fashion during the early 19th century. 12 plates also in color. Captions, glossary and introduction by editor Stella Blum. Total of 120pp. 8⅜ x 11¼.
     23690-0 Pa. $4.50

THE CURVES OF LIFE, Theodore A. Cook. Examination of shells, leaves, horns, human body, art, etc., in "*the* classic reference on how the golden ratio applies to spirals and helices in nature . . . . "—Martin Gardner. 426 illustrations. Total of 512pp. 5⅜ x 8½. 23701-X Pa. $5.95

AN ILLUSTRATED FLORA OF THE NORTHERN UNITED STATES AND CANADA, Nathaniel L. Britton, Addison Brown. Encyclopedic work covers 4666 species, ferns on up. Everything. Full botanical information, illustration for each. This earlier edition is preferred by many to more recent revisions. 1913 edition. Over 4000 illustrations, total of 2087pp. 6⅛ x 9¼. 22642-5, 22643-3, 22644-1 Pa., Three-vol. set $25.50

MANUAL OF THE GRASSES OF THE UNITED STATES, A. S. Hitchcock, U.S. Dept. of Agriculture. The basic study of American grasses, both indigenous and escapes, cultivated and wild. Over 1400 species. Full descriptions, information. Over 1100 maps, illustrations. Total of 1051pp. 5⅜ x 8½. 22717-0, 22718-9 Pa., Two-vol. set $15.00

THE CACTACEAE,, Nathaniel L. Britton, John N. Rose. Exhaustive, definitive. Every cactus in the world. Full botanical descriptions. Thorough statement of nomenclatures, habitat, detailed finding keys. The one book needed by every cactus enthusiast. Over 1275 illustrations. Total of 1080pp. 8 x 10¼. 21191-6, 21192-4 Clothbd., Two-vol. set $35.00

AMERICAN MEDICINAL PLANTS, Charles F. Millspaugh. Full descriptions, 180 plants covered: history; physical description; methods of preparation with all chemical constituents extracted; all claimed curative or adverse effects. 180 full-page plates. Classification table. 804pp. 6½ x 9¼. 23034-1 Pa. $12.95

A MODERN HERBAL, Margaret Grieve. Much the fullest, most exact, most useful compilation of herbal material. Gigantic alphabetical encyclopedia, from aconite to zedoary, gives botanical information, medical properties, folklore, economic uses, and much else. Indispensable to serious reader. 161 illustrations. 888pp. 6½ x 9¼. (Available in U.S. only) 22798-7, 22799-5 Pa., Two-vol. set $13.00

THE HERBAL or GENERAL HISTORY OF PLANTS, John Gerard. The 1633 edition revised and enlarged by Thomas Johnson. Containing almost 2850 plant descriptions and 2705 superb illustrations, Gerard's *Herbal* is a monumental work, the book all modern English herbals are derived from, the one herbal every serious enthusiast should have in its entirety. Original editions are worth perhaps $750. 1678pp. 8½ x 12¼. 23147-X Clothbd. $50.00

MANUAL OF THE TREES OF NORTH AMERICA, Charles S. Sargent. The basic survey of every native tree and tree-like shrub, 717 species in all. Extremely full descriptions, information on habitat, growth, locales, economics, etc. Necessary to every serious tree lover. Over 100 finding keys. 783 illustrations. Total of 986pp. 5⅜ x 8½. 20277-1, 20278-X Pa., Two-vol. set $11.00

THE COMPLETE WOODCUTS OF ALBRECHT DURER, edited by Dr. W. Kurth. 346 in all: "Old Testament," "St. Jerome," "Passion," "Life of Virgin," Apocalypse," many others. Introduction by Campbell Dodgson. 285pp. 8½ x 12¼. 21097-9 Pa. $7.50

DRAWINGS OF ALBRECHT DURER, edited by Heinrich Wolfflin. 81 plates show development from youth to full style. Many favorites; many new. Introduction by Alfred Werner. 96pp. 8⅛ x 11. 22352-3 Pa. $5.00

THE HUMAN FIGURE, Albrecht Dürer. Experiments in various techniques—stereometric, progressive proportional, and others. Also life studies that rank among finest ever done. Complete reprinting of *Dresden Sketchbook*. 170 plates. 355pp. 8⅜ x 11¼. 21042-1 Pa. $7.95

OF THE JUST SHAPING OF LETTERS, Albrecht Dürer. Renaissance artist explains design of Roman majuscules by geometry, also Gothic lower and capitals. Grolier Club edition. 43pp. 7⅞ x 10¾ 21306-4 Pa. $3.00

TEN BOOKS ON ARCHITECTURE, Vitruvius. The most important book ever written on architecture. Early Roman aesthetics, technology, classical orders, site selection, all other aspects. Stands behind everything since. Morgan translation. 331pp. 5⅜ x 8½. 20645-9 Pa. $4.50

THE FOUR BOOKS OF ARCHITECTURE, Andrea Palladio. 16th-century classic responsible for Palladian movement and style. Covers classical architectural remains, Renaissance revivals, classical orders, etc. 1738 Ware English edition. Introduction by A. Placzek. 216 plates. 110pp. of text. 9½ x 12¾. 21308-0 Pa. $10.00

HORIZONS, Norman Bel Geddes. Great industrialist stage designer, "father of streamlining," on application of aesthetics to transportation, amusement, architecture, etc. 1932 prophetic account; function, theory, specific projects. 222 illustrations. 312pp. 7⅞ x 10¾. 23514-9 Pa. $6.95

FRANK LLOYD WRIGHT'S FALLINGWATER, Donald Hoffmann. Full, illustrated story of conception and building of Wright's masterwork at Bear Run, Pa. 100 photographs of site, construction, and details of completed structure. 112pp. 9¼ x 10. 23671-4 Pa. $5.50

THE ELEMENTS OF DRAWING, John Ruskin. Timeless classic by great Viltorian; starts with basic ideas, works through more difficult. Many practical exercises. 48 illustrations. Introduction by Lawrence Campbell. 228pp. 5⅜ x 8½. 22730-8 Pa. $3.75

GIST OF ART, John Sloan. Greatest modern American teacher, Art Students League, offers innumerable hints, instructions, guided comments to help you in painting. Not a formal course. 46 illustrations. Introduction by Helen Sloan. 200pp. 5⅜ x 8½. 23435-5 Pa. $4.00

THE ANATOMY OF THE HORSE, George Stubbs. Often considered the great masterpiece of animal anatomy. Full reproduction of 1766 edition, plus prospectus; original text and modernized text. 36 plates. Introduction by Eleanor Garvey. 121pp. 11 x 14¾.
23402-9 Pa. $6.00

BRIDGMAN'S LIFE DRAWING, George B. Bridgman. More than 500 illustrative drawings and text teach you to abstract the body into its major masses, use light and shade, proportion; as well as specific areas of anatomy, of which Bridgman is master. 192pp. 6½ x 9¼. (Available in U.S. only)
22710-3 Pa. $3.50

ART NOUVEAU DESIGNS IN COLOR, Alphonse Mucha, Maurice Verneuil, Georges Auriol. Full-color reproduction of *Combinaisons ornementales* (c. 1900) by Art Nouveau masters. Floral, animal, geometric, interlacings, swashes—borders, frames, spots—all incredibly beautiful. 60 plates, hundreds of designs. 9⅜ x 8-1/16.
22885-1 Pa. $4.00

FULL-COLOR FLORAL DESIGNS IN THE ART NOUVEAU STYLE, E. A. Seguy. 166 motifs, on 40 plates, from *Les fleurs et leurs applications decoratives* (1902): borders, circular designs, repeats, allovers, "spots." All in authentic Art Nouveau colors. 48pp. 9⅜ x 12¼.
23439-8 Pa. $5.00

A DIDEROT PICTORIAL ENCYCLOPEDIA OF TRADES AND INDUSTRY, edited by Charles C. Gillispie. 485 most interesting plates from the great French Encyclopedia of the 18th century show hundreds of working figures, artifacts, process, land and cityscapes; glassmaking, papermaking, metal extraction, construction, weaving, making furniture, clothing, wigs, dozens of other activities. Plates fully explained. 920pp. 9 x 12.
22284-5, 22285-3 Clothbd., Two-vol. set $40.00

HANDBOOK OF EARLY ADVERTISING ART, Clarence P. Hornung. Largest collection of copyright-free early and antique advertising art ever compiled. Over 6,000 illustrations, from Franklin's time to the 1890's for special effects, novelty. Valuable source, almost inexhaustible.
Pictorial Volume. Agriculture, the zodiac, animals, autos, birds, Christmas, fire engines, flowers, trees, musical instruments, ships, games and sports, much more. Arranged by subject matter and use. 237 plates. 288pp. 9 x 12.
20122-8 Clothbd. $14.50

Typographical Volume. Roman and Gothic faces ranging from 10 point to 300 point, "Barnum," German and Old English faces, script, logotypes, scrolls and flourishes, 1115 ornamental initials, 67 complete alphabets, more. 310 plates. 320pp. 9 x 12.
20123-6 Clothbd. $15.00

CALLIGRAPHY (CALLIGRAPHIA LATINA), J. G. Schwandner. High point of 18th-century ornamental calligraphy. Very ornate initials, scrolls, borders, cherubs, birds, lettered examples. 172pp. 9 x 13.
20475-8 Pa. $7.00

CATALOGUE OF DOVER BOOKS

THE SENSE OF BEAUTY, George Santayana. Masterfully written discussion of nature of beauty, materials of beauty, form, expression; art, literature, social sciences all involved. 168pp. 5⅜ x 8½. 20238-0 Pa. $3.00

ON THE IMPROVEMENT OF THE UNDERSTANDING, Benedict Spinoza. Also contains *Ethics, Correspondence,* all in excellent R. Elwes translation. Basic works on entry to philosophy, pantheism, exchange of ideas with great contemporaries. 402pp. 5⅜ x 8½. 20250-X Pa. $4.50

THE TRAGIC SENSE OF LIFE, Miguel de Unamuno. Acknowledged masterpiece of existential literature, one of most important books of 20th century. Introduction by Madariaga. 367pp. 5⅜ x 8½.
20257-7 Pa. $4.50

THE GUIDE FOR THE PERPLEXED, Moses Maimonides. Great classic of medieval Judaism attempts to reconcile revealed religion (Pentateuch, commentaries) with Aristotelian philosophy. Important historically, still relevant in problems. Unabridged Friedlander translation. Total of 473pp. 5⅜ x 8½. 20351-4 Pa. $6.00

THE I CHING (THE BOOK OF CHANGES), translated by James Legge. Complete translation of basic text plus appendices by Confucius, and Chinese commentary of most penetrating divination manual ever prepared. Indispensable to study of early Oriental civilizations, to modern inquiring reader. 448pp. 5⅜ x 8½. 21062-6 Pa. $5.00

THE EGYPTIAN BOOK OF THE DEAD, E. A. Wallis Budge. Complete reproduction of Ani's papyrus, finest ever found. Full hieroglyphic text, interlinear transliteration, word for word translation, smooth translation. Basic work, for Egyptology, for modern study of psychic matters. Total of 533pp. 6½ x 9¼. (Available in U.S. only) 21866-X Pa. $5.95

THE GODS OF THE EGYPTIANS, E. A. Wallis Budge. Never excelled for richness, fullness: all gods, goddesses, demons, mythical figures of Ancient Egypt; their legends, rites, incarnations, variations, powers, etc. Many hieroglyphic texts cited. Over 225 illustrations, plus 6 color plates. Total of 988pp. 6⅛ x 9¼. (Available in U.S. only)
22055-9, 22056-7 Pa., Two-vol. set $16.00

THE STANDARD BOOK OF QUILT MAKING AND COLLECTING, Marguerite Ickis. Full information, full-sized patterns for making 46 traditional quilts, also 150 other patterns. Quilted cloths, lame, satin quilts, etc. 483 illustrations. 273pp. 6⅞ x 9⅝. 20582-7 Pa. $4.95

CORAL GARDENS AND THEIR MAGIC, Bronsilaw Malinowski. Classic study of the methods of tilling the soil and of agricultural rites in the Trobriand Islands of Melanesia. Author is one of the most important figures in the field of modern social anthropology. 143 illustrations. Indexes. Total of 911pp. of text. 5⅝ x 8¼. (Available in U.S. only)
23597-1 Pa. $12.95

HISTORY OF BACTERIOLOGY, William Bulloch. The only comprehensive history of bacteriology from the beginnings through the 19th century. Special emphasis is given to biography-Leeuwenhoek, etc. Brief accounts of 350 bacteriologists form a separate section. No clearer, fuller study, suitable to scientists and general readers, has yet been written. 52 illustrations. 448pp. 5⅝ x 8¼. 23761-3 Pa. $6.50

THE COMPLETE NONSENSE OF EDWARD LEAR, Edward Lear. All nonsense limericks, zany alphabets, Owl and Pussycat, songs, nonsense botany, etc., illustrated by Lear. Total of 321pp. 5⅜ x 8½. (Available in U.S. only) 20167-8 Pa. $3.95

INGENIOUS MATHEMATICAL PROBLEMS AND METHODS, Louis A. Graham. Sophisticated material from Graham Dial, applied and pure; stresses solution methods. Logic, number theory, networks, inversions, etc. 237pp. 5⅜ x 8½. 20545-2 Pa. $4.50

BEST MATHEMATICAL PUZZLES OF SAM LOYD, edited by Martin Gardner. Bizarre, original, whimsical puzzles by America's greatest puzzler. From fabulously rare Cyclopedia, including famous 14-15 puzzles, the Horse of a Different Color, 115 more. Elementary math. 150 illustrations. 167pp. 5⅜ x 8½. 20498-7 Pa. $2.75

THE BASIS OF COMBINATION IN CHESS, J. du Mont. Easy-to-follow, instructive book on elements of combination play, with chapters on each piece and every powerful combination team—two knights, bishop and knight, rook and bishop, etc. 250 diagrams. 218pp. 5⅜ x 8½. (Available in U.S. only) 23644-7 Pa. $3.50

MODERN CHESS STRATEGY, Ludek Pachman. The use of the queen, the active king, exchanges, pawn play, the center, weak squares, etc. Section on rook alone worth price of the book. Stress on the moderns. Often considered the most important book on strategy. 314pp. 5⅜ x 8½. 20290-9 Pa. $4.50

LASKER'S MANUAL OF CHESS, Dr. Emanuel Lasker. Great world champion offers very thorough coverage of all aspects of chess. Combinations, position play, openings, end game, aesthetics of chess, philosophy of struggle, much more. Filled with analyzed games. 390pp. 5⅜ x 8½. 20640-8 Pa. $5.00

500 MASTER GAMES OF CHESS, S. Tartakower, J. du Mont. Vast collection of great chess games from 1798-1938, with much material nowhere else readily available. Fully annotated, arranged by opening for easier study. 664pp. 5⅜ x 8½. 23208-5 Pa. $7.50

A GUIDE TO CHESS ENDINGS, Dr. Max Euwe, David Hooper. One of the finest modern works on chess endings. Thorough analysis of the most frequently encountered endings by former world champion. 331 examples, each with diagram. 248pp. 5⅜ x 8½. 23332-4 Pa. $3.75

THE COMPLETE BOOK OF DOLL MAKING AND COLLECTING, Catherine Christopher. Instructions, patterns for dozens of dolls, from rag doll on up to elaborate, historically accurate figures. Mould faces, sew clothing, make doll houses, etc. Also collecting information. Many illustrations. 288pp. 6 x 9. 22066-4 Pa. $4.50

THE DAGUERREOTYPE IN AMERICA, Beaumont Newhall. Wonderful portraits, 1850's townscapes, landscapes; full text plus 104 photographs. The basic book. Enlarged 1976 edition. 272pp. 8¼ x 11¼. 23322-7 Pa. $7.95

CRAFTSMAN HOMES, Gustav Stickley. 296 architectural drawings, floor plans, and photographs illustrate 40 different kinds of "Mission-style" homes from *The Craftsman* (1901-16), voice of American style of simplicity and organic harmony. Thorough coverage of Craftsman idea in text and picture, now collector's item. 224pp. 8½ x 11. 23791-5 Pa. $6.00

PEWTER-WORKING: INSTRUCTIONS AND PROJECTS, Burl N. Osborn. & Gordon O. Wilber. Introduction to pewter-working for amateur craftsman. History and characteristics of pewter; tools, materials, step-by-step instructions. Photos, line drawings, diagrams. Total of 160pp. 7⅞ x 10¾. 23786-9 Pa. $3.50

THE GREAT CHICAGO FIRE, edited by David Lowe. 10 dramatic, eyewitness accounts of the 1871 disaster, including one of the aftermath and rebuilding, plus 70 contemporary photographs and illustrations of the ruins—courthouse, Palmer House, Great Central Depot, etc. Introduction by David Lowe. 87pp. 8¼ x 11. 23771-0 Pa. $4.00

SILHOUETTES: A PICTORIAL ARCHIVE OF VARIED ILLUSTRATIONS, edited by Carol Belanger Grafton. Over 600 silhouettes from the 18th to 20th centuries include profiles and full figures of men and women, children, birds and animals, groups and scenes, nature, ships, an alphabet. Dozens of uses for commercial artists and craftspeople. 144pp. 8⅜ x 11¼. 23781-8 Pa. $4.50

ANIMALS: 1,419 COPYRIGHT-FREE ILLUSTRATIONS OF MAMMALS, BIRDS, FISH, INSECTS, ETC., edited by Jim Harter. Clear wood engravings present, in extremely lifelike poses, over 1,000 species of animals. One of the most extensive copyright-free pictorial sourcebooks of its kind. Captions. Index. 284pp. 9 x 12. 23766-4 Pa. $8.95

INDIAN DESIGNS FROM ANCIENT ECUADOR, Frederick W. Shaffer. 282 original designs by pre-Columbian Indians of Ecuador (500-1500 A.D.). Designs include people, mammals, birds, reptiles, fish, plants, heads, geometric designs. Use as is or alter for advertising, textiles, leathercraft, etc. Introduction. 95pp. 8¾ x 11¼. 23764-8 Pa. $3.50

SZIGETI ON THE VIOLIN, Joseph Szigeti. Genial, loosely structured tour by premier violinist, featuring a pleasant mixture of reminiscenes, insights into great music and musicians, innumerable tips for practicing violinists. 385 musical passages. 256pp. 5⅝ x 8¼. 23763-X Pa. $4.00

DRAWINGS OF WILLIAM BLAKE, William Blake. 92 plates from Book of Job, *Divine Comedy, Paradise Lost,* visionary heads, mythological figures, Laocoon, etc. Selection, introduction, commentary by Sir Geoffrey Keynes. 178pp. 8⅛ x 11.   22303-5 Pa. $4.00

ENGRAVINGS OF HOGARTH, William Hogarth. 101 of Hogarth's greatest works: *Rake's Progress, Harlot's Progress, Illustrations for Hudibras, Before and After, Beer Street and Gin Lane,* many more. Full commentary. 256pp. 11 x 13¾.   22479-1 Pa. $12.95

DAUMIER: 120 GREAT LITHOGRAPHS, Honore Daumier. Wide-ranging collection of lithographs by the greatest caricaturist of the 19th century. Concentrates on eternally popular series on lawyers, on married life, on liberated women, etc. Selection, introduction, and notes on plates by Charles F. Ramus. Total of 158pp. 9⅜ x 12¼.   23512-2 Pa. $6.00

DRAWINGS OF MUCHA, Alphonse Maria Mucha. Work reveals drafts-man of highest caliber: studies for famous posters and paintings, render-ings for book illustrations and ads, etc. 70 works, 9 in color; including 6 items not drawings. Introduction. List of illustrations. 72pp. 9⅜ x 12¼. (Available in U.S. only)   23672-2 Pa. $4.00

GIOVANNI BATTISTA PIRANESI: DRAWINGS IN THE PIERPONT MORGAN LIBRARY, Giovanni Battista Piranesi. For first time ever all of Morgan Library's collection, world's largest. 167 illustrations of rare Piranesi drawings—archeological, architectural, decorative and visionary. Essay, detailed list of drawings, chronology, captions. Edited by Felice Stampfle. 144pp. 9⅜ x 12¼.   23714-1 Pa. $7.50

NEW YORK ETCHINGS (1905-1949), John Sloan. All of important American artist's N.Y. life etchings. 67 works include some of his best art; also lively historical record—Greenwich Village, tenement scenes. Edited by Sloan's widow. Introduction and captions. 79pp. 8⅜ x 11¼.
                                                    23651-X Pa. $4.00

CHINESE PAINTING AND CALLIGRAPHY: A PICTORIAL SURVEY, Wan-go Weng. 69 fine examples from John M. Crawford's matchless private collection: landscapes, birds, flowers, human figures, etc., plus calligraphy. Every basic form included: hanging scrolls, handscrolls, album leaves, fans, etc. 109 illustrations. Introduction. Captions. 192pp. 8⅞ x 11¾.
                                                    23707-9 Pa. $7.95

DRAWINGS OF REMBRANDT, edited by Seymour Slive. Updated Lipp-mann, Hofstede de Groot edition, with definitive scholarly apparatus. All portraits, biblical sketches, landscapes, nudes, Oriental figures, classical studies, together with selection of work by followers. 550 illustrations. Total of 630pp. 9⅛ x 12¼.   21485-0, 21486-9 Pa., Two-vol. set $15.00

THE DISASTERS OF WAR, Francisco Goya. 83 etchings record horrors of Napoleonic wars in Spain and war in general. Reprint of 1st edition, plus 3 additional plates. Introduction by Philip Hofer. 97pp. 9⅜ x 8¼.
                                                    21872-4 Pa. $4.00

THE EARLY WORK OF AUBREY BEARDSLEY, Aubrey Beardsley. 157 plates, 2 in color: *Manon Lescaut, Madame Bovary, Morte Darthur, Salome,* other. Introduction by H. Marillier. 182pp. 8⅛ x 11. 21816-3 Pa. $4.50

THE LATER WORK OF AUBREY BEARDSLEY, Aubrey Beardsley. Exotic masterpieces of full maturity: *Venus and Tannhauser, Lysistrata, Rape of the Lock, Volpone,* Savoy material, etc. 174 plates, 2 in color. 186pp. 8⅛ x 11. 21817-1 Pa. $5.95

THOMAS NAST'S CHRISTMAS DRAWINGS, Thomas Nast. Almost all Christmas drawings by creator of image of Santa Claus as we know it, and one of America's foremost illustrators and political cartoonists. 66 illustrations. 3 illustrations in color on covers. 96pp. 8⅜ x 11¼. 23660-9 Pa. $3.50

THE DORÉ ILLUSTRATIONS FOR DANTE'S DIVINE COMEDY, Gustave Doré. All 135 plates from Inferno, Purgatory, Paradise; fantastic tortures, infernal landscapes, celestial wonders. Each plate with appropriate (translated) verses. 141pp. 9 x 12. 23231-X Pa. $4.50

DORÉ'S ILLUSTRATIONS FOR RABELAIS, Gustave Doré. 252 striking illustrations of *Gargantua and Pantagruel* books by foremost 19th-century illustrator. Including 60 plates, 192 delightful smaller illustrations. 153pp. 9 x 12. 23656-0 Pa. $5.00

LONDON: A PILGRIMAGE, Gustave Doré, Blanchard Jerrold. Squalor, riches, misery, beauty of mid-Victorian metropolis; 55 wonderful plates, 125 other illustrations, full social, cultural text by Jerrold. 191pp. of text. 9⅜ x 12¼. 22306-X Pa. $7.00

THE RIME OF THE ANCIENT MARINER, Gustave Doré, S. T. Coleridge. Dore's finest work, 34 plates capture moods, subtleties of poem. Full text. Introduction by Millicent Rose. 77pp. 9¼ x 12. 22305-1 Pa. $3.50

THE DORE BIBLE ILLUSTRATIONS, Gustave Doré. All wonderful, detailed plates: Adam and Eve, Flood, Babylon, Life of Jesus, etc. Brief King James text with each plate. Introduction by Millicent Rose. 241 plates. 241pp. 9 x 12. 23004-X Pa. $6.00

THE COMPLETE ENGRAVINGS, ETCHINGS AND DRYPOINTS OF ALBRECHT DURER. "Knight, Death and Devil"; "Melencolia," and more—all Dürer's known works in all three media, including 6 works formerly attributed to him. 120 plates. 235pp. 8⅜ x 11¼. 22851-7 Pa. $6.50

MECHANICK EXERCISES ON THE WHOLE ART OF PRINTING, Joseph Moxon. First complete book (1683-4) ever written about typography, a compendium of everything known about printing at the latter part of 17th century. Reprint of 2nd (1962) Oxford Univ. Press edition. 74 illustrations. Total of 550pp. 6⅛ x 9¼. 23617-X Pa. $7.95

TONE POEMS, SERIES II: TILL EULENSPIEGELS LUSTIGE STREICHE, ALSO SPRACH ZARATHUSTRA, AND EIN HELDEN-LEBEN, Richard Strauss. Three important orchestral works, including very popular *Till Eulenspiegel's Marry Pranks*, reproduced in full score from original editions. Study score. 315pp. 9⅜ x 12¼. (Available in U.S. only)
23755-9 Pa. $8.95

TONE POEMS, SERIES I: DON JUAN, TOD UND VERKLARUNG AND DON QUIXOTE, Richard Strauss. Three of the most often performed and recorded works in entire orchestral repertoire, reproduced in full score from original editions. Study score. 286pp. 9⅜ x 12¼. (Available in U.S. only)
23754-0 Pa. $7.50

11 LATE STRING QUARTETS, Franz Joseph Haydn. The form which Haydn defined and "brought to perfection." *(Grove's)*. 11 string quartets in complete score, his last and his best. The first in a projected series of the complete Haydn string quartets. Reliable modern Eulenberg edition, otherwise difficult to obtain. 320pp. 8⅜ x 11¼. (Available in U.S. only)
23753-2 Pa. $7.50

FOURTH, FIFTH AND SIXTH SYMPHONIES IN FULL SCORE, Peter Ilyitch Tchaikovsky. Complete orchestral scores of Symphony No. 4 in F Minor, Op. 36; Symphony No. 5 in E Minor, Op. 64; Symphony No. 6 in B Minor, "Pathetique," Op. 74. Bretikopf & Hartel eds. Study score. 480pp. 9⅜ x 12¼.
23861-X Pa. $10.95

THE MARRIAGE OF FIGARO: COMPLETE SCORE, Wolfgang A. Mozart. Finest comic opera ever written. Full score, not to be confused with piano renderings. Peters edition. Study score. 448pp. 9⅜ x 12¼. (Available in U.S. only)
23751-6 Pa. $11.95

"IMAGE" ON THE ART AND EVOLUTION OF THE FILM, edited by Marshall Deutelbaum. Pioneering book brings together for first time 38 groundbreaking articles on early silent films from *Image* and 263 illustrations newly shot from rare prints in the collection of the International Museum of Photography. A landmark work. Index. 256pp. 8¼ x 11.
23777-X Pa. $8.95

AROUND-THE-WORLD COOKY BOOK, Lois Lintner Sumption and Marguerite Lintner Ashbrook. 373 cooky and frosting recipes from 28 countries (America, Austria, China, Russia, Italy, etc.) include Viennese kisses, rice wafers, London strips, lady fingers, hony, sugar spice, maple cookies, etc. Clear instructions. All tested. 38 drawings. 182pp. 5⅜ x 8.
23802-4 Pa. $2.50

THE ART NOUVEAU STYLE, edited by Roberta Waddell. 579 rare photographs, not available elsewhere, of works in jewelry, metalwork, glass, ceramics, textiles, architecture and furniture by 175 artists—Mucha, Seguy, Lalique, Tiffany, Gaudin, Hohlwein, Saarinen, and many others. 288pp. 8⅜ x 11¼.
23515-7 Pa. $6.95

YUCATAN BEFORE AND AFTER THE CONQUEST, Diego de Landa. First English translation of basic book in Maya studies, the only significant account of Yucatan written in the early post-Conquest era. Translated by distinguished Maya scholar William Gates. Appendices, introduction, 4 maps and over 120 illustrations added by translator. 162pp. 5⅜ x 8½.
23622-6 Pa. $3.00

THE MALAY ARCHIPELAGO, Alfred R. Wallace. Spirited travel account by one of founders of modern biology. Touches on zoology, botany, ethnography, geography, and geology. 62 illustrations, maps. 515pp. 5⅜ x 8½.
20187-2 Pa. $6.95

THE DISCOVERY OF THE TOMB OF TUTANKHAMEN, Howard Carter, A. C. Mace. Accompany Carter in the thrill of discovery, as ruined passage suddenly reveals unique, untouched, fabulously rich tomb. Fascinating account, with 106 illustrations. New introduction by J. M. White. Total of 382pp. 5⅜ x 8½. (Available in U.S. only)   23500-9 Pa. $4.00

THE WORLD'S GREATEST SPEECHES, edited by Lewis Copeland and Lawrence W. Lamm. Vast collection of 278 speeches from Greeks up to present. Powerful and effective models; unique look at history. Revised to 1970. Indices. 842pp. 5⅜ x 8½.   20468-5 Pa. $8.95

THE 100 GREATEST ADVERTISEMENTS, Julian Watkins. The priceless ingredient; His master's voice; 99 44/100% pure; over 100 others. How they were written, their impact, etc. Remarkable record. 130 illustrations. 233pp. 7⅞ x 10 3/5.   20540-1 Pa. $5.95

CRUICKSHANK PRINTS FOR HAND COLORING, George Cruickshank. 18 illustrations, one side of a page, on fine-quality paper suitable for watercolors. Caricatures of people in society (c. 1820) full of trenchant wit. Very large format. 32pp. 11 x 16.   23684-6 Pa. $5.00

THIRTY-TWO COLOR POSTCARDS OF TWENTIETH-CENTURY AMERICAN ART, Whitney Museum of American Art. Reproduced in full color in postcard form are 31 art works and one shot of the museum. Calder, Hopper, Rauschenberg, others. Detachable. 16pp. 8¼ x 11.
23629-3 Pa. $3.00

MUSIC OF THE SPHERES: THE MATERIAL UNIVERSE FROM ATOM TO QUASAR SIMPLY EXPLAINED, Guy Murchie. Planets, stars, geology, atoms, radiation, relativity, quantum theory, light, antimatter, similar topics. 319 figures. 664pp. 5⅜ x 8½.
21809-0, 21810-4 Pa., Two-vol. set $11.00

EINSTEIN'S THEORY OF RELATIVITY, Max Born. Finest semi-technical account; covers Einstein, Lorentz, Minkowski, and others, with much detail, much explanation of ideas and math not readily available elsewhere on this level. For student, non-specialist. 376pp. 5⅜ x 8½.
60769-0 Pa. $4.50

SECOND PIATIGORSKY CUP, edited by Isaac Kashdan. One of the greatest tournament books ever produced in the English language. All 90 games of the 1966 tournament, annotated by players, most annotated by both players. Features Petrosian, Spassky, Fischer, Larsen, six others. 228pp. 5⅜ x 8½. 23572-6 Pa. $3.50

ENCYCLOPEDIA OF CARD TRICKS, revised and edited by Jean Hugard. How to perform over 600 card tricks, devised by the world's greatest magicians: impromptus, spelling tricks, key cards, using special packs, much, much more. Additional chapter on card technique. 66 illustrations. 402pp. 5⅜ x 8½. (Available in U.S. only) 21252-1 Pa. $4.95

MAGIC: STAGE ILLUSIONS, SPECIAL EFFECTS AND TRICK PHO-TOGRAPHY, Albert A. Hopkins, Henry R. Evans. One of the great classics; fullest, most authorative explanation of vanishing lady, levitations, scores of other great stage effects. Also small magic, automata, stunts. 446 illustrations. 556pp. 5⅜ x 8½. 23344-8 Pa. $6.95

THE SECRETS OF HOUDINI, J. C. Cannell. Classic study of Houdini's incredible magic, exposing closely-kept professional secrets and revealing, in general terms, the whole art of stage magic. 67 illustrations. 279pp. 5⅜ x 8½. 22913-0 Pa. $4.00

HOFFMANN'S MODERN MAGIC, Professor Hoffmann. One of the best, and best-known, magicians' manuals of the past century. Hundreds of tricks from card tricks and simple sleight of hand to elaborate illusions involving construction of complicated machinery. 332 illustrations. 563pp. 5⅜ x 8½. 23623-4 Pa. $6.00

MADAME PRUNIER'S FISH COOKERY BOOK, Mme. S. B. Prunier. More than 1000 recipes from world famous Prunier's of Paris and London, specially adapted here for American kitchen. Grilled tournedos with anchovy butter, Lobster a la Bordelaise, Prunier's prized desserts, more. Glossary. 340pp. 5⅜ x 8½. (Available in U.S. only) 22679-4 Pa. $3.00

FRENCH COUNTRY COOKING FOR AMERICANS, Louis Diat. 500 easy-to-make, authentic provincial recipes compiled by former head chef at New York's Fitz-Carlton Hotel: onion soup, lamb stew, potato pie, more. 309pp. 5⅜ x 8½. 23665-X Pa. $3.95

SAUCES, FRENCH AND FAMOUS, Louis Diat. Complete book gives over 200 specific recipes: bechamel, Bordelaise, hollandaise, Cumberland, apricot, etc. Author was one of this century's finest chefs, originator of vichyssoise and many other dishes. Index. 156pp. 5⅜ x 8. 23663-3 Pa. $2.75

TOLL HOUSE TRIED AND TRUE RECIPES, Ruth Graves Wakefield. Authentic recipes from the famous Mass. restaurant: popovers, veal and ham loaf, Toll House baked beans, chocolate cake crumb pudding, much more. Many helpful hints. Nearly 700 recipes. Index. 376pp. 5⅜ x 8½. 23560-2 Pa. $4.50

AMERICAN BIRD ENGRAVINGS, Alexander Wilson et al. All 76 plates. from Wilson's *American Ornithology* (1808-14), most important ornithological work before Audubon, plus 27 plates from the supplement (1825-33) by Charles Bonaparte. Over 250 birds portrayed. 8 plates also reproduced in full color. 111pp. 9⅜ x 12½.   23195-X Pa. $6.00

CRUICKSHANK'S PHOTOGRAPHS OF BIRDS OF AMERICA, Allan D. Cruickshank. Great ornithologist, photographer presents 177 closeups, groupings, panoramas, flightings, etc., of about 150 different birds. Expanded *Wings in the Wilderness*. Introduction by Helen G. Cruickshank. 191pp. 8¼ x 11.   23497-5 Pa. $6.00

AMERICAN WILDLIFE AND PLANTS, A. C. Martin, et al. Describes food habits of more than 1000 species of mammals, birds, fish. Special treatment of important food plants. Over 300 illustrations. 500pp. 5⅜ x 8½.
20793-5 Pa. $4.95

THE PEOPLE CALLED SHAKERS, Edward D. Andrews. Lifetime of research, definitive study of Shakers: origins, beliefs, practices, dances, social organization, furniture and crafts, impact on 19th-century USA, present heritage. Indispensable to student of American history, collector. 33 illustrations. 351pp. 5⅜ x 8½.   21081-2 Pa. $4.50

OLD NEW YORK IN EARLY PHOTOGRAPHS, Mary Black. New York City as it was in 1853-1901, through 196 wonderful photographs from N.-Y. Historical Society. Great Blizzard, Lincoln's funeral procession, great buildings. 228pp. 9 x 12.   22907-6 Pa. $8.95

MR. LINCOLN'S CAMERA MAN: MATHEW BRADY, Roy Meredith. Over 300 Brady photos reproduced directly from original negatives, photos. Jackson, Webster, Grant, Lee, Carnegie, Barnum; Lincoln; Battle Smoke, Death of Rebel Sniper, Atlanta Just After Capture. Lively commentary. 368pp. 8⅜ x 11¼.   23021-X Pa. $8.95

TRAVELS OF WILLIAM BARTRAM, William Bartram. From 1773-8, Bartram explored Northern Florida, Georgia, Carolinas, and reported on wild life, plants, Indians, early settlers. Basic account for period, entertaining reading. Edited by Mark Van Doren. 13 illustrations. 141pp. 5⅜ x 8½.   20013-2 Pa. $5.00

THE GENTLEMAN AND CABINET MAKER'S DIRECTOR, Thomas Chippendale. Full reprint, 1762 style book, most influential of all time; chairs, tables, sofas, mirrors, cabinets, etc. 200 plates, plus 24 photographs of surviving pieces. 249pp. 9⅞ x 12¾.   21601-2 Pa. $7.95

AMERICAN CARRIAGES, SLEIGHS, SULKIES AND CARTS, edited by Don H. Berkebile. 168 Victorian illustrations from catalogues, trade journals, fully captioned. Useful for artists. Author is Assoc. Curator, Div. of Transportation of Smithsonian Institution. 168pp. 8½ x 9½.

23328-6 Pa. $5.00

GEOMETRY, RELATIVITY AND THE FOURTH DIMENSION, Rudolf Rucker. Exposition of fourth dimension, means of visualization, concepts of relativity as Flatland characters continue adventures. Popular, easily followed yet accurate, profound. 141 illustrations. 133pp. 5⅜ x 8½.
23400-2 Pa. $2.75

THE ORIGIN OF LIFE, A. I. Oparin. Modern classic in biochemistry, the first rigorous examination of possible evolution of life from nitrocarbon compounds. Non-technical, easily followed. Total of 295pp. 5⅜ x 8½.
60213-3 Pa. $4.00

PLANETS, STARS AND GALAXIES, A. E. Fanning. Comprehensive introductory survey: the sun, solar system, stars, galaxies, universe, cosmology; quasars, radio stars, etc. 24pp. of photographs. 189pp. 5⅜ x 8½. (Available in U.S. only)
21680-2 Pa. $3.75

THE THIRTEEN BOOKS OF EUCLID'S ELEMENTS, translated with introduction and commentary by Sir Thomas L. Heath. Definitive edition. Textual and linguistic notes, mathematical analysis, 2500 years of critical commentary. Do not confuse with abridged school editions. Total of 1414pp. 5⅜ x 8½. 60088-2, 60089-0, 60090-4 Pa., Three-vol. set $18.50

Prices subject to change without notice.

Available at your book dealer or write for free catalogue to Dept. GI, Dover Publications, Inc., 180 Varick St., N.Y., N.Y. 10014. Dover publishes more than 175 books each year on science, elementary and advanced mathematics, biology, music, art, literary history, social sciences and other areas.